# Economics of the Employment Relationship

**Robert J. Flanagan**
**Stanford University**

**Lawrence M. Kahn**
**University of Illinois**

**Robert S. Smith**
**Cornell University**

**Ronald G. Ehrenberg**
**Cornell University**

**Scott, Foresman and Company**
**Glenview, Illinois**
**London, England**

The following tables and figures are from *Modern Labor Economics:
Theory and Public Policy* by Ronald G. Ehrenberg and Robert S. Smith.
Copyright © 1985, 1982 Scott, Foresman and Company.
Tables: 2.1, 2.2, 2.3, 2.4, 3.2, 6.1, 7.1, 7.2, 7.3, 7.4, 8.1, 8.2, 8.3
Figures: Example 7.2, 7A.1, 7A.2, 8.1

**Library of Congress Cataloging-in-Publication Data**

Economics of the employment relationship/Robert J. Flanagan . . . [et al.].
    p.  cm.
    Includes bibliographies and index.
    ISBN 0-673-38237-0
    1. Industrial relations.   I. Flanagan, Robert J.
  HD6971.E26   1989                               88-38271
  331—dc19                                     CIP

1 2 3 4 5 6 – RRC – 94 93 92 91 90 89

# PREFACE

*Economics of the Employment Relationship* provides an integrated treatment of economic, legal, and organizational aspects of the employment relationship in both union and nonunion settings. It gives the reader an understanding of modern human resource management, labor unions, and the institutional framework in which collective bargaining takes place. In analyzing hiring, training, and compensation decisions at the company level from an economic perspective, the text summarizes empirical evidence regarding each major theoretical proposition. The intent is to illustrate in extensive detail the usefulness of labor-market analysis in understanding human resource management strategies, labor relations, and how public policies influence the employment relationship. Showing the business and social implications of economic concepts and presenting them in analytic settings through the use of real-life examples increases students' interest and motivation to learn the conceptual material.

*Economics of the Employment Relationship* differs from other textbooks for survey courses in labor economics and labor relations in a number of ways. First and foremost is its extensive emphasis on public and business policy applications and on economic analysis of labor-relations issues. The book integrates institutional features, such as the existence of internal labor markets or the design of company compensation systems, directly into the theoretical models—explaining the institutions within the context of these models rather than discussing them separately. Thus, this text provides more institutional detail about firm-level decisions than do other textbooks in labor economics/labor relations, and it goes well beyond existing textbooks in the personnel/human resource management/compensation areas in its presentation of an economic framework in which to analyze these kinds of decisions. Additionally, the coverage of topics in this book is far more comprehensive, and the discussion of a number of the more common topics is much more thorough than that found in other texts. For example, our chapter on discrimination includes a unique section on the conceptual issues involved in affirmative-action planning, and our discussion of compensation includes an extensive analysis of how pay can be structured over time to elicit self-selectivity among applicants and more effort among workers.

*Economics of the Employment Relationship* is designed for one-term survey courses in labor economics and labor relations, at either the undergraduate or MBA level, for students who do not necessarily have extensive backgrounds in economics or labor relations. The undergraduate courses typically require only principles of economics as a prerequisite, and the graduate courses often have no prerequisites. All the authors have taught such courses over the last decade. It is our experience that an instructor does not have to be highly technical to convey important concepts, and we have found that students with limited backgrounds in economics and labor relations can comprehend a great deal of material in a single course. Accordingly, while this text provides a comprehensive treatment of modern human resource management in union and nonunion settings, it is written in a style that makes the important concepts in the field accessible even to those without much background in economics.

This book draws heavily on its predecessor, *Labor Economics and Labor Relations,* by Flanagan, Smith, and Ehrenberg, and on Ehrenberg and Smith's *Modern Labor Economics,* both published by Scott, Foresman and Company. (The latter is designed for courses in labor economics that do not give heavy emphasis to the institutional framework of collective bargaining.) The response to both books have been overwhelmingly positive, and we have tried to preserve the best features of both. This book differs substantially in the following ways.

* The focus of the applications is shifted to an emphasis on company human resource management.

* New chapters examine company compensation policies (Chapter 9), negotiating labor agreements (Chapter 13), and the future of the employment relationship (Chapter 18).

* An extensive economic analysis of modern compensation systems is detailed.

* Many new examples of business policies illustrate and bring to life the concepts of labor economics.

* A collective bargaining exercise is now included (Appendix 18b).

*Economics of the Employment Relationship* begins by presenting and illustrating basic labor economics concepts of the demand for, and supply of, labor (Chapter 2). The firm's demand for labor is discussed in detail in Chapters 3 and 4, and labor supply issues are closely examined in Chapter 5. Chapter 6 discusses individuals' investments in education and training, as well as the theory of compensating wage differentials, and Chapter 7 analyzes the economics of discrimination. Detailed analyses of employer compensation systems are presented in Chapters 8 and 9, which integrate economic theories about the choice and effects of compensation systems with descriptive material on actual company practices.

Chapters 10–16 make extensive use of economic analysis to examine unions and collective bargaining. Covered material includes American labor history, with a detailed examination of the recent decline of the labor movement; labor law; bargaining structure and tactics; negotiating a labor agreement; disputes and dispute settlement; the content of collective-bargaining contracts; and the economic impact of unions.

As a special supplement to the discussion of collective bargaining, we have added, at the end of the book, a collective-bargaining negotiation exercise that can be conducted in the classroom. This exercise includes a modern collective-bargaining agreement (with provisions establishing two-tier wage structures, profit-sharing, and cost-of-living adjustments), a narrative description of the bargaining relationship between the union and the employer, background economic data, and instructions on how to approach renegotiation of the agreement. This is a fine vehicle for student application of principles learned in this textbook.

Chapter 17 deals with issues of inflation and unemployment. The reasons for unemployment, as well as the impact of government policies, are analyzed. We also examine reasons for a tradeoff between inflation and unemployment and discuss recent proposals for improving this tradeoff.

The final chapter, Chapter 18, discusses the future of the employment relationship. It examines economic and legal pressures on firms, workers, and unions, including international trade and product market deregulation. We discuss innovative responses to such pressures by the union and nonunion sectors. These responses include lobbying for government aid, two-tiered pay systems, flexible compensation systems (including profit-sharing, employee stock acquisition, outright buyouts, and pay for knowledge), and labor-management cooperation (including quality-of-work-life programs). Finally, we use U.S. Department of Labor projections about the labor force in the year 2000 to make forecasts about the future of the employment relationship.

As already noted, *Economics of the Employment Relationship* recognizes that many students have only a limited background in economics and labor relations. All of the necessary analytic tools are carefully developed in the text, and each chapter builds on material that precedes it. We begin the text at a very simple level and explain the derivation of each major concept and tool. We then increase the degree of difficulty in later chapters as the student becomes more familiar with our terminology and methods of analysis. Further, each chapter contains boxed examples that represent applications of that chapter's theory in managerial or cross-cultural settings. Several of these examples contrast collective-bargaining arrangements in the United States with the very different institutional frameworks for labor relations found in other countries. Moreover, each chapter contains review questions, which give students the opportunity to apply what they have learned to specific policy questions, and lists of selected readings that refer students to more advanced sources of study,

## Acknowledgments

Several colleagues have contributed, through their thoughtful evaluations and suggestions, to this text. While we have not always taken their advice, we appreciate the help of the following people: Jack Adams, University of Arkansas at Little Rock; Max H. Bazerman, Northwestern University; Brian Becker, SUNY Buffalo; David Bloom, Harvard University; Peter Capelli, The Wharton School, University of Pennsylvania; John Delaney, Columbia University; Stephen Hills, Ohio State University; Harry Holzer, Michigan State University; Stephen Mangum, Ohio State University; Joshua Schwarz, University of Minnesota.

We also want to thank those who have helped us in other ways. Frank Brechling, George Delehanty, Dale Mortensen, John Pancavel, Orme Phelps, Mel Reder, and Lloyd Ulman were our teachers, and it was they who gave us a foundation and interest in labor economics and labor relations.

# CONTENTS

# Contents

## 13 NEGOTIATING LABOR AGREEMENTS 436

## 14 LABOR DISPUTES AND DISPUTE RESOLUTION 451

## 15 THE COLLECTIVE-BARGAINING AGREEMENT 499

## 16 The Effects of Unions 547

Contents

# PART 1

## Introduction

# CHAPTER 1

## Introduction

This book presents a comprehensive and understandable application of economic analysis to the behavior of, and relationship between, employers and employees. The aggregate compensation received by employees from their employers was $2647.5 billion in 1987, while all *other* forms of personal income that year—from investments, self-employment, pensions, and various government welfare programs—amounted to only $1323 billion. The employment relationship, then, is clearly one of the most fundamental relationships in our lives, and as such it attracts a good deal of legislative attention.

To understand the employment relationship and the huge array of associated social problems and programs, it is essential to master the fundamentals of labor economics, labor union behavior, and the institutional framework in which collective bargaining takes place. As economists who have been actively involved in the analysis of employer and labor union behavior and the evaluation of employment-related programs adopted or considered by various levels of government, we obviously believe labor economics is useful in understanding the effects of these institutions and policies. What is perhaps more important for the nature of this text is that we also believe that analyzing company and public policy is important to the study of the fundamentals of labor economics and labor relations. Each chapter therefore incorporates such analyses for two reasons. First, the relevance and social implications of concepts to be studied makes any subject more interesting to learn. Second, using the concepts of each chapter in an analytical setting serves to reinforce understanding by presenting the concepts "in action."

# The Labor Market

There is a rumor that one recent Secretary of Labor attempted to abolish the term "labor market" from departmental publications. He believed it demeaned workers to implicitly think of labor as being bought and sold like so much grain, oil, or bonds. True, labor is somewhat unique. Labor services can only be rented; workers themselves cannot be bought or sold. Further, because labor services cannot be separated from workers, the conditions under which such services are rented are often as important as the price. Put differently, *nonpecuniary factors*—such as work environment, risk of injury, personalities of managers, and flexibility of work hours—loom larger in employment transactions than they do in markets for commodities. Finally, there are a host of institutions and pieces of legislation influencing the employment relationship that do not exist in other markets.

Nevertheless, the circumstances under which employers rent labor services from employees clearly constitute a "market" for several reasons. First, institutions have developed to facilitate contact between buyers and sellers of labor services. This contact may come through want ads, union hiring halls, employment agencies, placement offices, or at a factory gate.

Second, once contact is arranged, information about price and quality is exchanged. Employment applications, interviews, and even "word-of-mouth" information illustrate this kind of exchange in the labor market.

Third, when an agreement is reached, some kind of *contract* is executed, covering compensation, conditions of work, job security, and even duration of the job. Sometimes the contract is formal, such as with collective-bargaining (union-management) agreements. At other times the agreement is unwritten and informal, with only an implied understanding between the parties that is based on past practices and experience. Nonetheless, it is often useful to think of the employment relationship as governed by a contract.

It is worth noting that labor "contracts" typically call for employers to compensate employees for their *time,* rather than for the product they generate. Only 14 percent of American workers receive piece-rate wages or *commissions,* where compensation is computed directly on the basis of output. The vast majority are paid by the hour, week, or month. They are paid, in short, to show up for work and (within limits) to follow orders. This form of compensation requires that employers give careful attention to worker motivation and dependability in the hiring and promotion processes. It also produces among workers an interest in developing institutions, such as labor unions, that seek to ensure that the orders workers are asked to follow are reasonable and that they are treated fairly by managers.

The end result of employer-employee transactions in the labor market is, of course, the placement of people in jobs at certain rates of pay. This allocation of labor serves not only the personal needs of individuals but the needs of society as well. Through the labor market our most important natural resource, labor, is allocated to firms, industries, occupations, and regions.

## Internal Labor Markets

As we will see in some detail, large organizations set up their own rules for recruiting, motivating, training, allocating, and rewarding labor. Each system of rules characterizes an individual *internal labor market*.[1] Personnel practices such as promotion from within (in which the labor pool for a job opening consists only of current employees), seniority-based pay increases, and protection from layoff are often found in large firms. Further, these companies often make pay decisions based on internal evaluations of job content, a system called *job evaluation*. While companies with internal labor markets often appear to ignore labor market forces at large, we will show that labor market developments outside the firm, such as unemployment or wage inflation, have a strong effect on these internal personnel decisions. In addition, many of the principles guiding labor decisions—such as the comparison of costs and benefits—are used in internal labor markets. For example, seemingly unconnected decisions regarding applicant screening, worker training, and level of pay are related; spending less money on screening applicants or paying workers is likely to raise training costs. A cost-conscious firm must keep track of the influence of one personnel decision on others. However, the long-term relationship between employer and employee that tends to characterize internal labor markets leads, as we will see, to differences between labor markets and the markets for other commodities.

## Labor Relations: Some Basic Concepts

In any country, interaction between employers and employees occurs in an *industrial relations system*. The labor market is one element of this system. A second component is *public policy,* the interventions that create the legal environment surrounding market activities. The nature of employee and employer organizations constitutes a third important aspect.

In virtually all countries, irrespective of ideological orientation or stage of economic development, the most important organizational feature of economic growth has been the appearance of *labor unions*. Early in the twentieth century, Sidney and Beatrice Webb defined a union as "a continuous association of wage earners for the purpose of maintaining or improving the conditions of their working lives." As such, unions present workers with an alternative to public policy for correcting certain market failures and otherwise advancing their interests. The opposite is also true; workers and unions

---

[1] P. Doeringer and M. Piore, *Internal Labor Markets and Manpower Analysis* (Lexington, MA: D.C. Heath and Company, 1971).

may turn to public policy to obtain goals that they are unable to achieve through collective bargaining.

*Collective bargaining* consists of negotiations between one or more unions and one or more employers to establish a formal *labor agreement* that specifies compensation, hours of work, and other conditions of employment that apply to the employers and employees over the term of the agreement. Collective bargaining can be a more effective method of quickly establishing change at the workplace than can the atomistic operation of a competitive market, because negotiations are usually conducted under the threat of collective action (such as a strike or lockout) rather than the smaller threat of individual action (such as quitting). The labor agreement (or collective-bargaining agreement, or labor contract) effectively provides a system of industrial government for workers and their employers for the time that it is in effect. As a result, the rules established in labor agreements can have an important effect on labor-market behavior. By the same token, the labor market has important effects on union behavior. For example, higher unemployment raises the chances that a union will make concessions to management to save union jobs. Economic events outside the labor market can also have a major impact on union behavior. For example, movements in foreign trade can threaten or enhance union members' job security.

In many respects the modern study of the industrial-relations system reveals the interplay (and often tension) between market forces and institutional rules that determine the employment relationship. This interplay is often quite complicated. Institutional rules established in collective bargaining or through public policy may alter the normal outcomes of the labor market. At times, however, institutional rules may simply reflect market outcomes. Consider the announcement of a newly negotiated labor agreement providing for a wage increase of 5 percent over the previous wage level. Are the wages of union members now 5 percent higher than they would have been in the absence of the union, or did employers simply postpone until negotiations a 5-percent wage increase that they would have given anyway? Quite possibly, the result is a combination of both forces, but it should be clear that even though a wage increase is associated with the activity of collective bargaining, it may not be the *result* of collective bargaining. Determining the actual impact of the collective-bargaining agreement is a very complicated task.

This example illustrates that labor-relations outcomes occur in markets that operate under certain principles. To understand the constraints the market imposes on labor relations, we must understand economic behavior. For most of the labor force, moreover, the content of the employment relationship is not established through collective bargaining. It is therefore important to understand the role of economic behavior and legal institutions in shaping the employment arrangements in nonunion organizations. In particular, in addition to the large body of law that governs collective bargaining relationships, the law affects wage setting, layoffs, hiring, promotions, and workplace safety, even in nonunion firms. We will study the economic impact of laws and court decisions that attempt to increase workers' job security, raise their wages, protect workers against discrimination, expand their pension rights, and improve workplace safety.

# Labor Economics: Some Basic Concepts

*Labor economics* is the study of the workings and outcomes of the market for labor. More specifically, labor economics is primarily concerned with the behavior of employers and employees in response to the general incentives of wages, prices, profits, and nonpecuniary aspects (working conditions) of the employment relationship. These incentives serve both to motivate and limit individual choices. The focus in much of economics is on behavior that is impersonal and applies to wide groups of people, as opposed to incentives that are more personal in nature.

In this book we will study the relationship between wages and employment opportunities; the interaction between wages, income, and the decision to work; how general market incentives affect occupational choice; the relationship between wages and undesirable job characteristics; the incentives for, and effects of, educational and training investments; company personnel decisions and the relationship between external and internal labor markets; the incentives for workers to join unions; how bargaining tactics and structures adopted by labor and management influence the outcome of collective bargaining; the interplay between dispute-settlement procedures and the likelihood that strikes will occur; and the effects of unions on wages, productivity, and turnover. In the process, we will analyze the effects of social policies and labor-market institutions such as minimum wages, overtime legislation, pension reform regulations, the Occupational Safety and Health Act, welfare reform, payroll taxes, unemployment insurance, immigration policies, antidiscrimination laws, collective-bargaining legislation, dispute-resolution procedures, and the end of mandatory retirement. We also analyze company pay policies, the trade-off between pay and turnover, the economics of motivating employees, and the impact of laws on company rule making.

Our study of the employment relationship will be conducted on two levels. Most of the time we will be using economic theory to analyze "what is"; that is, we will explain people's behavior, using a mode of analysis called *positive economics*. Less often, we will be using *normative* economic analysis to judge "what should be."

## Positive Economics

*Positive economics* is a theory of behavior in which people are typically assumed to respond favorably to "benefits" and negatively to "costs." In this regard, positive economics closely resembles Skinnerian psychology, which views behavior as shaped by rewards and punishments. The rewards in economic theory are pecuniary and nonpecuniary gains (benefits), while the punishments are forgone opportunities (costs). For example, a person motivated to become a surgeon because of the earnings and status surgeons command must give up the opportunity to be a lawyer and be available for emergency work around the clock. Both the benefits and costs must be considered when making this career choice. Likewise, a firm deciding whether to hire an additional worker must weigh the salary costs against the added revenues or cost savings made possible by expanding its work force; and every union must at some point weigh the benefits and costs of striking for an improved offer rather than accepting what is on the table.

**Scarcity.**   The most all-pervasive assumption underlying economic theory is that of *resource scarcity*. According to this assumption, individuals and society alike do not have the resources to meet all their wants. Hence, any resource devoted to satisfying one set of desires is unavailable to satisfy other wants, which means that there is always a cost to any decision or action. For example, a company's best sales representative may also be the firm's best computer programmer. The real cost of using his or her time to write computer programs is forgone sales. Thus, in popular terms, "There is no such thing as a free lunch," and we must always make choices and live with the rewards and costs these choices bring us. Moreover, we are always constrained in our choices by the resources available to us.

**Rationality.**   The second basic assumption of positive economics is that people are *rational* in the sense that they have an objective and pursue it in a reasonably consistent fashion. When considering *people,* economists assume that the objective being pursued is *utility maximization;* that is, people are assumed to strive toward the goal of making themselves as happy as they can (given their limited resources). Utility, of course, encompasses both pecuniary and nonpecuniary dimensions. When considering the behavior of *firms,* which are inherently nonpersonal entities, economists assume the goal of behavior to be that of *profit maximization.* Profit maximization is really just a special case of utility maximization in which pecuniary gain is emphasized and nonpecuniary factors are ignored. When considering the behavior of *unions,* economists assume that the goal is the maximization of the welfare of the union membership. This, too, is a type of utility maximization, but it is complicated because individual workers often have very different ideas about what their union should do for them. The assumption of rationality implies a *consistency* of response to general economic incentives and an *adaptability* of behavior when those incentives change. These two characteristics of behavior underlie predictions about how workers and firms will respond to various incentives. The existence of rationality cannot be directly established, however, and it has been suggested that even totally habit-bound or unthinkingly impulsive people would be forced to alter their behavior in predictable ways if their resources changed.[2] Thus, while we will maintain the assumption of rationality throughout the textbook, it is clear that this assumption is not

---

[2]  Gary Becker, "Irrational Behavior and Economic Theory," *Journal of Political Economy* 70 (February 1962): 1–13.

absolutely necessary to the derivation of at least *some* of the behavioral predictions contained herein.

## The Models and Predictions of Positive Economics

Behavioral predictions in economics flow more or less directly from the two fundamental assumptions of rationality and scarcity. Workers must continually make choices, such as whether to look for other jobs, accept overtime, seek promotions, move to another area, or acquire more education. Employers must also make choices concerning, for example, the level of output and the mix of machines and labor to use in production. As complex political organizations, unions must choose among alternative combinations of wages, fringe benefits, and working conditions to maximize membership welfare. Economists usually assume that when making these choices, employees, employers, and unions are guided by their desires to maximize utility, profit, or membership benefits, as the case may be, and that they weigh the costs and benefits of various decisions in a reasonably careful way.

One may object that these assumptions are unrealistic and that people are not nearly as calculating, as well informed about alternatives, or as well endowed with a set of choices as economists assume. Economists are likely to reply that if people are not calculating, are totally uninformed, or do not have any choices, then most predictions suggested by economic theory would not be supported by real-world evidence. They thus argue that the theory underlying positive economics should be judged on the basis of its *predictions* and that there may be enough information, calculation, and available options to make the theory useful in explaining or predicting a wide range of behavior.

The reason that we need to make assumptions and create a relatively simple theory of behavior is that the actual workings of the labor market are almost impossibly complex. Millions of workers and employers interact daily, all with their own sets of motivations, preferences, information, and perceptions of self-interest. Collective bargaining has resulted in the existence of close to 150,000 labor agreements in the United States alone. A detailed description of the individual outcomes and the processes that determine them would clearly be of both limited feasibility and limited usefulness. What we need to discover are generalizations or general principles that provide useful insights about the employment relationship. These principles could not be expected to predict or explain behavior with the same accuracy as the laws of physics predict the movement of an object through space, because we are dealing with human beings capable of making choices. Nevertheless, we show in this book that a few forces are so basic to labor market behavior that they alone can predict or explain much of the outcomes and behaviors we observe in the labor market.

Anytime we attempt to explain a complex set of behaviors and outcomes using a few fundamental influences we have created a *model* of such behavior. Models are not intended to capture every complexity of behavior; in fact, they are created for the express purpose of stripping away random and idiosyncratic factors so that we can focus on general principles. An analogy from the physical sciences might make the nature of models and their relationship to actual behavior more clear. Using calculations of velocity and gravitational pull, physicists could predict where a ball would land if it were kicked with a certain force at a given angle to the ground. The actual point of landing might vary from the predicted point due to wind currents and any spin the ball might have—factors that are ignored in basic calculations. If 100 balls were kicked, none might ever land exactly on the predicted spot, although they would tend to cluster around it. The accuracy of the model, while not perfect, may be good enough for a football coach to make a decision about whether to attempt a field goal or not. The point is that we usually need to know just the *average tendencies* of outcomes for policy purposes. To estimate these tendencies we need to know the important forces at work but must confine ourselves to few enough influences so that calculating estimates remains feasible.

## Normative Economics

Any *normative statement* concerns what *ought* to exist and is based on some underlying value. Normative economics rests upon the value premise of *mutual benefit*. A mutually beneficial transaction is one in which there are no losers and, therefore, one that everyone in society could support. A transaction can be unanimously supported when one of the following conditions is met.

1. All parties affected by the transaction gain.
2. Some parties gain and no one else loses.
3. Some gain and some lose from the transaction, but the gainers fully compensate the losers.

When the compensation in case (3) takes place, case (3) is converted to case (2). In practice, economists often judge a transaction by whether the gains of the beneficiaries exceed the costs borne by the losers, thus making it *possible* for there to be no losers. If the losers sustain losses for which the gainers cannot possibly compensate, then the transaction could never be mutually beneficial, and the wisdom of the transaction must be questioned.

To illustrate a mutually beneficial transaction, suppose that people who formerly owned and operated small subsistence farms in West Virginia— earning the equivalent of $6000 per year—take jobs in the growing coal mining industry at $20,000 a year. Assuming the switch in jobs is voluntary, these workers are clearly better off. The income gain of $14,000 per year may be offset to some extent by the unpleasantness of working in a mine, but the fact that they voluntarily choose to become miners tells us that they believe their utility will be enhanced. Mine owners likewise enter into the transaction voluntarily, implying that they obtain at least $20,000 in output from these new workers. The transaction benefits the parties it affects, and as a result it benefits society as a whole. There has been an increase in social output from $6000 to $20,000 per worker, but, more importantly, there has been an increase in the overall utility of workers (the miners are better off and no one else is worse off).

To illustrate a transaction that is not mutually beneficial, suppose that society sought to increase the income of these same subsistence farmers by giving them a cash allowance raised by taxing others. This program would simply transfer money from the pockets of some people to the pockets of others, with no increase in output. There is no possibility for the gainers (farmers) to compensate the losers (those taxed), so unanimous consent about the transaction could not be secured. While economists would not say that this transaction is bad or unwarranted, it cannot be justified on the grounds of mutual benefit. Some other ethical principle—not based on unanimous consent—would have to be invoked to justify the transaction. (One such principle is that the rich should share their wealth with the poor.)

Normative economics, then, is the analysis of actual and potential transactions to see if they conform to the standard of being mutually beneficial. Transactions may fail to meet this standard—or transactions that do meet the standard may fail to occur—for one of several reasons.

**Ignorance.**   First, people may be ignorant of some important facts and thus led to make decisions that are not in their self-interest. For example, a worker who smokes may take a job in an asbestos-processing plant, not knowing that the combination of smoking and inhaling asbestos dust substantially raises the risk of disease. Had the worker known this, he or she would have stopped smoking or changed jobs, but both transactions were "blocked" by ignorance.

**Transaction barriers.**   Second, there may be some barrier to the completion of a transaction that could be mutually beneficial. Often, these barriers are created by government laws. For example, a firm may be willing to offer overtime to production workers at rates no more than 10 percent above their normal wage. Some workers may be willing to accept overtime at the 10-percent premium. However, this transaction, which is desired by both parties, cannot legally be completed in most instances because of a law (the Fair Labor Standards Act) requiring almost all production workers to be paid a 50 percent wage premium for overtime. In this case, overtime will not be worked and both parties will suffer.

Another kind of barrier to mutually beneficial transactions may be the expense of completing the transaction. Unskilled workers facing very limited opportunities in one region may desire to move to take better jobs. Alternatively, they may want to enter job training programs. In either case they may lack the funds to finance the desired transaction.

**Nonexistence of market.**   A third reason why transactions that are mutually beneficial may not occur is that it may be impossible or uncustomary for buyers and sellers of certain resources to transact. As an illustration, assume a woman who does not smoke works temporarily next to a man who does. She would be willing to pay as much as 50 cents per hour to keep her working environment smoke-free, and he could be induced to give up smoking for as little as 25 cents per hour. Thus, the potential exists for her to give him, say,

35 cents per hour and for both to benefit. However, custom or the transience of their relationship may prevent her from offering him money in this situation, and the transaction would not occur.

## Normative Economics and Government Policy

The solution to problems that impede the completion of mutually beneficial transactions frequently involves government intervention. When a government law is creating the barrier to transaction, the "intervention" might be to repeal the relevant law. Laws prohibiting women from working overtime, for example, have been repealed in recent years as their adverse effects on women have been recognized.

In other cases, however, the government may be able to undertake activities to reduce transactions barriers that the private market would not. We will cite three examples, each of which relates to an already-discussed barrier.

**Public goods.**  First take the case of information and its dissemination. Suppose that workers in noisy factories are concerned about the effects of noise on their hearing but that accurately evaluating these effects would require an expensive research program. Suppose further that a union representing sawmill workers considers using members' dues to undertake such research and recouping the expenses by selling its findings to the many other potentially interested unions or workers involved. The workers would then have the information they desire—albeit at some cost—which they could use to make more intelligent decisions concerning their jobs.

The hitch in the preceding scheme is that the union doing the research may not have any customers *even though* others find the results valuable. The reason for the lack of customers is that as soon as the union's findings are published to its own members or its first customers, the results can easily become public knowledge—and thus available *free* from newspapers or by word-of-mouth. Other unions may be understandably reluctant to pay for information they can get free, and the union doing the research ends up getting very little, if any, reimbursement for its expenses. Anticipating this problem, the union will probably decide not to undertake the research.

The information in this example is called a *public good*—a good that can be consumed by any number of people at the same time, including those who do not pay for it. Because nonpayers cannot be excluded from consuming the good, no potential customer will have an incentive to pay. The result is that the good never gets produced by a private organization. Because the government, however, can *compel* payment through its tax system, it becomes natural to look to the government to produce public goods. If information on occupational health hazards is to be produced on a large scale, it is quite possible that the government will have to be involved.

**Capital market imperfections.**  A second example of a situation in which the government might have to step in to overcome a transaction barrier is the case in which loans could conceivably help workers facing a very poor set of choices to have access to better opportunities. Loans such as these are not typically provided by the private sector because they are not secured by anything other than the borrower's promise to pay them back. Banks cannot ordinarily afford to take the risks inherent in making such loans, particularly when the loan recipients are poor, because a number of defaults could put them out of business (or at least lower their profitability). This lack of available loans for financing worthwhile transactions represents a "capital market imperfection."

The government, however, might be willing to make loans in this situation even if it faced the same risk of default, because enabling workers to move to areas of better economic opportunity could improve social welfare and strengthen the economy. In short, because society would reap benefits from encouraging people to enter job training programs or move to areas where their skills could be better utilized, it may be wise for the government to make the loans itself.

**Establishing market substitutes.**   A third type of situation in which government intervention might be necessary to overcome transaction barriers is the case in which the market fails to exist for some reason. In the example, a smoker and nonsmoker were temporarily working next to each other, and their transitory relationship prevented a mutually beneficial transaction from taking place. A solution in this case might be for the government to impose the same result that a market transaction would have generated, and require the employer to designate that area to be a nonsmoking area.

In this case, as in the other examples of government intervention already mentioned, it is important to emphasize that when government intervenes, it must ensure that the transactions it undertakes or imposes on society create more gains for the beneficiaries than they impose costs on others. Since it is costly to produce information, for example, the government should only do it if the gains are more valuable than the resources used in producing it. Likewise, the government would only want to make loans for job training or interregional moves if these activities enhanced social welfare. Finally, imposing nonsmoking areas would be socially desirable only if the gainers gain more than the losers lose. Thus, while normative economics suggests a role for government in helping accomplish mutually beneficial transactions, the role is not unlimited.

## Plan of the Text

With this brief review of basic concepts and principles in mind, we turn now to the specific subject-matter areas of labor economics and labor relations. The study of the employment relationship is mainly a study of the interplay between employers and employees—or between demand and supply—and between market forces and institutional rules. The first part of the book develops the analysis of market forces. Chapter 2 presents a quick overview of demand and supply in the labor market, showing from the outset the interrelationship of the major forces at work shaping labor market behavior. (This chapter contains many concepts that will be familiar to readers who have a good background in microeconomics.) Chapters 3 and 4 are primarily concerned with the demand for labor, while Chapter 5 emphasizes labor supply issues. Chapters 6 through 9 integrate the analysis of demand and supply in studying issues in employee compensation, labor market discrimination, and company personnel decisions.

Unions and collective bargaining are treated in Chapters 10 through 16, in which the economic analysis developed earlier in the book is integrated with legal analysis and principles of collective behavior to examine the nature of relationships and contracts between employers and employees in a union environment. We noted earlier that an industrial-relations system consists of the interaction of employee and employer organizations, the government (which creates a particular legal or public policy environment), and the market. The nature of labor markets and the market behavior of employers, as already indicated, are analyzed in the earlier chapters of the book. Chapters 10 and 11, respectively, examine the nature of union organizations (tracing both the forces determining the growth of unions and factors influencing their internal decision making) and the legal environment of labor-management relations.

Having established the nature of the main actors in an industrial relations system, we then turn to the bargaining process. Collective-bargaining strategy and structure are discussed in Chapters 12 and 13, and the consequences of a breakdown in negotiations—labor disputes and methods of dispute resolution—are covered in Chapter 14. The outcome of a completed set of negotiations is a labor agreement. The nature of labor agreements and their implications for the employment relationship are examined in Chapter 15. The effects of unions on compensation, productivity, and working conditions are reviewed in Chapter 16.

Chapter 17 deals with issues of inflation and unemployment, while the final chapter discusses current trends in the employment relationship. These trends include the continuing decline of unionism, increasing international competition, and changes in the regulatory framework the government imposes on the labor market, as well as the impact of demographic changes in the labor force.

# Review Questions

1. Using the concepts of normative economics, when would the labor market be judged to be at a point of optimality? What imperfections might prevent the market from achieving this point?
2. Are the following statements "positive" or "normative" in nature? Why?
    a. Society should not prohibit women from working more than forty hours per week.
    b. If women are prevented from working overtime, they will not be as valuable to employers as their male counterparts with similar skills.
    c. If the military draft is prohibited, military salaries will increase.

d. The military draft *compels* people to engage in a transaction they would not voluntarily enter into; it should therefore be avoided as a way of recruiting military personnel.

# Selected Readings

Ryan C. Amacher, Robert D. Tollison, and Thomas D. Willet, eds., *The Economic Approach to Public Policy* (Ithaca, NY: Cornell University Press, 1976).

Peter Doeringer and Michael Piore, *Internal Labor Markets and Manpower Analysis* (Lexington, MA: D.C. Heath and Company, 1971).

John Dunlop, *Industrial Relations Systems* (New York: Holt, Rinehart, and Winston, 1958).

Milton Friedman, *Essays in Positive Economics* (Chicago: University of Chicago Press, 1953).

Assar Lindbeck, *The Political Economy of the New Left: An Outsider's View* (New York: Harper & Row, 1971).

# CHAPTER 2

## Overview of the Labor Market

Every society—regardless of its wealth, form of government, or the organization of its economy—must make certain basic decisions. It must decide what to produce, how to produce it, the quantities to be produced, and how the output shall be distributed. Making these decisions requires finding out what consumers want, what forms of production technology are available, what the skills and preferences of workers are, and then coordinating all such decisions so that, for example, the millions of people in New York City and the isolated few in an Alaskan fishing village can each buy the milk, bread, meat, vanilla extract, mosquito repellent, and brown shoe polish they desire at the grocery store. The process of coordination involves creating incentives so that the right amount of labor and capital will be employed at the right place at the required time.

These decisions can, of course, be made by administrators employed by a centralized bureaucracy. The amount of information this bureaucracy must obtain and process to make the literally millions of needed decisions wisely, and the amount of incentives it must create to ensure that these decisions are coordinated are truly mind-boggling. It is even more over-whelming to consider the major alternative to centralized decision making: the decentralized marketplace. Millions of producers striving to make a profit observe prices that millions of consumers are willing to pay for products and the wages millions of workers are willing to accept for work. Combining these pieces of information with data on various technologies, employers decide where to produce, what to produce, whom to hire, and how much to produce. No one employer is in charge, and while there are no doubt imperfections that impede progress toward achieving the best allocation of resources, millions of people find jobs that enable them to purchase thousands of items they desire each year. The production, employment, and consumption decisions are all made and coordinated by price signals arising through the marketplace.

The market that has the job of allocating workers to jobs and coordinating employment decisions is the *labor market*. With roughly 120 million workers and 5 million employers in the United States, thousands of decisions about career choice, hiring, quitting, compensation, and technology must be made and coordinated every day. This chapter will present an overview of what the market does and how it works. For those students who may have already mastered microeconomic theory, this chapter can provide a review of basic concepts.

# The Labor Market: Definitions, Facts, and Trends

Every market has buyers and sellers, and the labor market is no exception; the "buyers" are employers and the "sellers" are workers. Because there are so many buyers and sellers of labor at any given time, the decisions that are made in any particular case are influenced by the behavior and decisions of others. A firm, for example, may decide to increase compensation if other employers are doing so to remain "competitive" in its ability to attract and hold workers. Likewise, an employee may choose to go into personnel work, for example, if he or she discovers that teachers or social workers are having a difficult time finding jobs.

The *labor market* is thus composed of all the buyers and sellers of labor. Some of these participants may not be active at a given moment in the sense that they are not out seeking new jobs or new employees. But on any given day, thousands of firms and workers will be "in the market" trying to transact. If, as in the case of doctors or mechanical engineers, buyers and sellers are searching throughout the entire nation for each other, we would describe the market as a *national labor market*. If buyers and sellers only search locally—as in the case of secretaries or automobile mechanics—the labor market is a *local* one.

Some labor markets, particularly those in which the sellers of labor are represented by a union, operate under a very formal set of rules that partly govern buyer-seller transactions. In the construction and longshoring trades, for example, employers must hire at the union hiring hall from a list of eligible union members. In other cases, the employer has discretion over who gets hired but is constrained by a union-management agreement in matters like the order in which employees may be laid off, procedures regarding employee complaints, the compensation schedule, the workload or pace of work, and promotions. The markets for government jobs and jobs with large nonunion employers also tend to operate under rules that constrain the authority of management and ensure "fair" treatment of employees. When a formal set of rules and procedures guide and constrain the employment relationship *within* a firm, an *internal labor market* is said to exist. We will analyze these rules and procedures in Chapters 8 and 9. In many cases, of course, labor market transactions are not made within the context of written rules or procedures, as is clearly the case in most transactions where the employee is changing employers or newly entering the market. Written rules or procedures generally do not govern internal transactions—such as promotions and layoffs—among smaller, nonunion employers. While jobs in this sector of the labor market can be stable and well paid, many are not. Low-wage, unstable jobs are sometimes considered to be in the *secondary labor market*.[1] We will discuss the concept of secondary labor markets in greater detail in Chapter 7 on discrimination.

When we speak of a particular labor market—for taxi drivers, say—we are using the term *labor market* rather loosely to refer to the companies trying to hire people to drive their cabs and the people seeking employment as cab drivers. The efforts of these buyers and sellers of labor to transact and establish an employment relationship constitute the "market" for cab drivers. However, neither the employers nor the drivers are confined to this market, and in fact both could simultaneously be in other markets as well. An entrepreneur with $100,000 to invest may be thinking of operating either a taxi company or a car wash, depending on the projected revenues and costs of each. A person seeking a cab-driving job may also be trying to find work as an electronics assembler. Thus, all the various "labor markets" that we can define on the basis of industry, occupation, geography, transaction rules, or job character are really interrelated to some degree. We speak of these narrowly defined labor markets for the sake of convenience, and doing so should not suggest that people are necessarily or permanently locked into a market that is somehow independent of other markets.

## The Labor Force and Unemployment

The term *labor force* refers to all the people who are either employed or who would like to be employed for pay at any given time. Those who are not employed for pay but who would like to be are the *unemployed*.[2] People who are not employed and are neither looking for work nor waiting to be recalled from layoff by their employers are not counted as part of the labor force. The total labor force thus consists of the employed and the unemployed.

In 1987 there were 120 million civilians in the labor force, representing 65 percent of the civilian population over 16 years of age. An overall *labor force participation rate* (labor force divided by population) of 65 percent is substantially higher than the rates around 60 percent that prevailed from 1950 to 1970, as shown in Table 2.1. This table also indicates the single most important fact about labor-force trends in this century; namely, *labor force participation rates for men are falling while those for women are increasing dramatically*. These trends and their causes will be discussed in detail in Chapter 5.

The ratio of those unemployed to those in the labor force is the *unemployment rate*. While this rate is crude and has several imperfections, it is the most

---

[1]  P. Doeringer and M. Piore, *Internal Labor Markets and Manpower Analysis* (Lexington, MA: D.C. Heath and Company, 1971).

[2]  The official definition of unemployment for purposes of government statistics includes those who have been laid off by their employers, those who have been fired or have quit and are looking for other work, and those who are just entering or reentering the force but have not yet found a job.

**Table 2.1**   Labor Force Participation Rates by Gender, 1900–1987
(in percent)

| | Total | | Men | | Women | |
|---|---|---|---|---|---|---|
| Year | Of Those Over 14 | Of Those Over 16 | Over 14 | Over 16 | Over 14 | Over 16 |
| 1900 | 54.8 (100) | | 87.3 (100) | | 20.4 (100) | |
| 1910 | 55.7 (102) | | 86.3 ( 99) | | 22.8 (112) | |
| 1920 | 55.6 (102) | | 86.5 ( 99) | | 23.3 (114) | |
| 1930 | 54.6 (100) | | 84.1 ( 96) | | 24.3 (119) | |
| 1940 | 52.2 ( 95) | | 79.0 ( 91) | | 25.4 (125) | |
| 1950 | 53.4 ( 98) | 59.9 | 79.0 ( 91) | 86.8 | 28.6 (140) | 33.9 |
| 1960 | 55.3 (101) | 60.2 | 77.4 ( 89) | 84.0 | 34.5 (169) | 37.8 |
| 1970 | 55.8 (102) | 61.3 | 73.0 ( 84) | 80.6 | 39.9 (196) | 43.4 |
| 1980 | — | 64.3 | — | 78.0 | — | 51.7 |
| 1986 | — | 65.3 | — | 76.3 | — | 55.3 |
| 1987 | — | 65.6 | — | 76.2 | — | 56.0 |

Note: Index numbers, with 1900 = 100, are shown in parentheses. From 1900–1930, the labor force was defined as those "gainfully employed." Gainful workers were those who, whether they were working at the time or not, reported themselves as having an occupation at which they usually worked. In 1940, the present concept of labor force replaced the concept of gainful worker, with the result that inexperienced people looking for their first job were now counted in the labor force. It is the judgment of Clarence D. Long, *The Labor Force Under Changing Income and Employment,* p. 45, that intercensal comparisons remain meaningful despite this change.

Sources for data on ages 14 and older:

1900–1950: Clarence D. Long, *The Labor Force Under Changing Income and Employment* (Princeton, NJ: Princeton University Press, 1958), Table A-2.

1960: U.S. Department of Commerce, Bureau of the Census, *Census of Population, 1960: Employment Status,* Subject Reports, PC(2)-6A, Table 1.

1970: U.S. Department of Commerce, Bureau of the Census, *U.S. Census of Population, 1970: Employment Status and Work Experience,* Subject Reports, PC(2)-6A, Table 1.

Sources for data on ages 16 and older:

U.S. President, *Employment and Training Report of the President* (Washington, DC: U.S. Government Printing Office), transmitted to the Congress 1981, Table A-1.

U.S. Bureau of Labor Statistics, *Employment and Earnings* 35, 1 (January 1988), Tables 1 and 2.

widely cited measure of labor market conditions. When the unemployment rate is in the 3–4 percent range in the United States, the labor market is considered *tight*—indicating that jobs in general are plentiful and hard for employers to fill and that most people who are unemployed will find other work quickly.[3] When the unemployment rate is higher—say, 7 percent or above—the labor market is described as *loose,* meaning that workers are abundant and jobs are relatively easy for employers to fill. To say that the labor market as a whole is loose, however, does not imply that there are no shortages; to say it is tight, of course, can still mean that in some occupations or places those seeking work exceed the number of jobs available at the prevailing wage.

Table 2.2 displays the overall unemployment rate for the first 88 years of this century. The data clearly show the extraordinarily loose labor market

---

[3] Some people are beginning to argue that labor markets are "tight" when unemployment is around 5 percent or even a bit more. This issue will be discussed in Chapter 17.

**Table 2.2**   Unemployment Rates for the Civilian Labor Force over 14 Years Old, 1900–1987

| Year | Rate | Year | Rate | Year | Rate (old series) | Rate (new series) | Year | Rate |
|---|---|---|---|---|---|---|---|---|
| 1900 | 5.0 | 1926 | 1.9 | 1947 | 3.6 | 3.9 | 1958 | 6.8 |
| 1901 | 2.4 | 1927 | 4.1 | 1948 | 3.4 | 3.9 | 1959 | 5.5 |
| 1902 | 2.7 | 1928 | 4.4 | 1949 | 5.5 | 5.9 | 1960 | 5.6 |
| 1903 | 2.6 | 1929 | 3.2 | 1950 | 5.0 | 5.3 | 1961 | 6.7 |
| 1904 | 4.8 | 1930 | 8.9 | 1951 | 3.0 | 3.3 | 1962 | 5.6 |
| 1905 | 3.1 | 1931 | 15.9 | 1952 | 2.7 | 3.1 | 1963 | 5.7 |
| 1906 | 0.8 | 1932 | 23.6 | 1953 | 2.5 | 2.9 | 1964 | 5.2 |
| 1907 | 1.8 | 1933 | 24.9 | 1954 | 5.0 | 5.6 | 1965 | 4.5 |
| 1908 | 8.5 | 1934* | 21.7 | 1955 | 4.0 | 4.4 | 1966 | 3.8 |
| 1909 | 5.2 | 1935* | 20.1 | 1956 | 3.8 | 4.2 | 1967 | 3.8 |
| 1910 | 5.9 | 1936* | 17.0 | 1957 | 4.0 | 4.3 | 1968 | 3.6 |
| 1911 | 6.2 | 1937* | 14.3 | | | | 1969 | 3.5 |
| 1912 | 5.2 | 1938* | 19.0 | | | | 1970 | 4.9 |
| 1913 | 4.4 | 1939* | 17.2 | | | | 1971 | 5.9 |
| 1914 | 8.0 | 1940* | 14.6 | | | | 1972 | 5.6 |
| 1915 | 9.7 | 1941* | 9.9 | | | | 1973 | 4.9 |
| 1916 | 4.8 | 1942 | 4.7 | | | | 1974 | 5.6 |
| 1917 | 4.8 | 1943 | 1.9 | | | | 1975 | 8.5 |
| 1918 | 1.4 | 1944 | 1.2 | | | | 1976 | 7.7 |
| 1919 | 2.3 | 1945 | 1.9 | | | | 1977 | 7.1 |
| 1920 | 4.0 | 1946 | 3.9 | | | | 1978 | 6.1 |
| 1921 | 11.9 | | | | | | 1979 | 5.8 |
| 1922 | 7.6 | | | | | | 1980 | 7.1 |
| 1923 | 3.2 | | | | | | 1981 | 7.6 |
| 1924 | 5.5 | | | | | | 1982 | 9.7 |
| 1925 | 4.0 | | | | | | 1983 | 9.6 |
| | | | | | | | 1984 | 7.5 |
| | | | | | | | 1985 | 7.2 |
| | | | | | | | 1986 | 7.0 |
| | | | | | | | 1987 | 6.2 |

Note:   After 1966, unemployment rates for only those 16 and over are published. The differences between the rates for those over 14 and over 16 in the years in which both were computed are very small. Therefore, a parallel series in this table was not considered necessary. The rates shown from 1967 on relate to those people over 16, and the prior data related to people over 14.

In 1957 the definition of the term *unemployed* was changed to include those who were waiting to be called back to a job from which they had been laid off, were waiting to report to a new wage or salary job scheduled to start within the next 30 days (and were not in school during the survey week), or would have been looking for work except that they were temporarily ill. Prior to 1957, part of those whose layoffs were for definite periods of less than 30 days were classified as employed, as were all those waiting to report to a new job. This new definition was also applied to unemployment data for the years 1947–57.

In the years indicated by an asterisk, workers in some government job-creation programs were counted as unemployed, which raised these published unemployment rates by 4 to 7 percentage points. See Michael R. Darby, "Three-and-a-Half Million U.S. Employees Have Been Mislaid: Or, An Explanation of Unemployment, 1934–1941," *Journal of Political Economy* 84 (February 1976): 1–16.

SOURCES:   1900–1954 (old series): Stanley Lebergott, "Annual Estimates of Unemployment in the United States, 1900–1950," *The Measurement and Behavior of Unemployment* NBER, Special Committee Conference Series no. 8 (Princeton, NJ: 1957), 213–39.

1955–57 (old series): *U.S. Bureau of the Census, Annual Report on the Labor Force,* Current Population Reports, Series P-50 (1955, 1956, 1957).

1947–66 (new series): U.S. Bureau of Labor Statistics, *Employment and Earnings* 13, 7 (January 1967), Table A-1.

1967–87: U.S. Bureau of Labor Statistics, *Employment and Earnings* 35, 1 (January 1988), Table 1.

during the Great Depression of the 1930s and the exceptionally tight labor market during World War II. However, when we look at long stretches of nonwar years, excluding the years of the Great Depression, two interesting patterns emerge. First, the average unemployment rate has clearly risen; it was 4.4 percent in 1900–1914, but in the most recent nonwar periods it was 5.3 percent (1954–65) and 7.2 percent (1973–87). Second, in recent years the unemployment rate has fluctuated less than it did in 1900–1914. In the years from 1900 to 1914, the average yearly change in the unemployment rate was 1.9 percentage points; in contrast, from 1954 to 1965 and from 1973 to 1987, it was 0.8 percentage points. The labor market, then, would appear to be more stable now than it was at the turn of the century, but it operates with proportionately more unemployment. Chapter 17 will present a more detailed analysis of the determinants of the unemployment rate.

## Industries and Occupations: Adapting to Change

As we pointed out earlier, the labor market is the mechanism through which workers and jobs are matched. Over the years in this century, the number of certain kinds of jobs has expanded and the number of others has contracted. Both workers and employers had to adapt to these changes in response to signals provided by the labor market.

An examination of the industrial distribution of employment from 1900 to 1986 reveals the kinds of changes the labor market has had to facilitate. Table 2.3 discloses a major shift; *agricultural employment has declined drastically while employment in service industries has expanded.* From 1900 to 1970, manufacturing jobs increased proportionately to the increase in total employment, so their employment share remained more or less constant. Since 1970, however, the share of manufacturing in employment has fallen. The largest employment increases have been in the service sector. Retail and wholesale trade, which increased from 9.2 percent of employment in 1910 to 23 percent in 1986, showed the largest increases in nongovernment services. However, the largest percentage increase has been in government employment, which quadrupled its share of total employment from 1900 to 1970 and then more or less stabilized. Some describe this shift in employment from agriculture to services as a shift from the *primary* to the *tertiary* sector (manufacturing being labeled the *secondary* sector). Others describe the shift to services as the arrival of the "post-industrial" state. In any case, the shift in employment has been accompanied by large population movements off the farms and to urban areas. These population movements have also been largely coordinated by the labor market.

The combination of shifts in the industrial distribution of jobs and shifts in the production technology within each sector has also necessitated that workers acquire new skills and work in new jos. Table 2.4 on page 22 shows that a large increase in *white-collar,* or nonmanual, jobs has taken place concurrently with a large decline in agricultural jobs. The numbers of manual workers and personal-service workers have shown relatively modest increases since 1900. The largest single gain has come about in clerical jobs,

**Table 2.3**  Employment Distribution by Major Industrial Sector,
1900–1986 (in percent)

| Year | Agriculture[a] | Goods-Producing Industries[b] | Nongovernment Services[c] | Government Services[d] |
|------|------------|-------------------|----------------|--------------|
| 1900 | 38.1 | 37.8 | 20.0 | 4.1 |
| 1910 | 32.1 | 40.9 | 22.3 | 4.7 |
| 1920 | 27.6 | 44.8 | 21.6 | 6.0 |
| 1930 | 22.7 | 42.1 | 28.1 | 7.1 |
| 1940 | 18.5 | 41.6 | 31.1 | 8.8 |
| 1950 | 12.1 | 41.3 | 36.4 | 10.2 |
| 1960 | 6.6 | 41.4 | 38.8 | 13.2 |
| 1970 | 3.8 | 39.8 | 40.5 | 15.9 |
| 1980 | 3.6 | 32.8 | 46.3 | 17.3 |
| 1986 | 3.0 | 29.1 | 52.9 | 15.1 |

Note:  From 1900 to 1930, "employment" refers to "gainful workers." From 1940, "employment" refers to experienced civilian labor force. Where applicable, persons not assigned to an industry were assumed to have the same employment distribution as those who were.

[a] Agriculture includes forestry and fishing.

[b] Included are manufacturing, mining, construction, transportation, communications, and public utilities.

[c] Included are trade; personal, professional, and business services; entertainment; finance; and real estate.

[d] Includes federal, state, and local government workers.

SOURCES:  1900–1940: U.S. Bureau of the Census, *Historical Statistics of the United States, Colonial Times to 1957*, 1960, Table D57–71.

1950: *U.S. Census of Population 1950*, Subject Reports, Vol. IV, Chapter 1D, 1955, Table 15.

1960: *U.S. Census of Population 1960*, Subject Reports, PC(2)-7F, 1967, Table 1.

1970: *U.S. Census of Population 1970*, Subject Reports, PC(2)-7B, 1972, Table 1.

1980: U.S. Bureau of the Census, *Statistical Abstract of the United States*, 103d ed., 1982. Tables 624 and 629.

1986: U.S. Bureau of Labor Statistics, *Employment and Earnings*, 34, 1 (January 1987), Table 24 and U.S. Bureau of Labor Statistics, *Monthly Labor Review*, 110, 6 (June 1987), Tables 6 and 13.

although professional and technical jobs (teachers, engineers, lawyers, and so forth) have also increased disproportionately fast. Since 1970, managerial jobs have had the highest growth rate.

Labor markets must work very effectively if enormous shifts in the industrial and occupational distribution of employment are to be accomplished without long delays or undue hardship. There is disagreement over how effectively and humanely labor markets operate, but there can be no disagreement that the labor market has an incredibly large and important role to perform in society.

## The Earnings of Labor

The actions of buyers and sellers in the labor market serve both to allocate and to set prices for various kinds of labor. From a social perspective, these prices act as signals or incentives in the allocation process, which relies primarily on individual and voluntary decisions. From the worker's point of view, the price of labor is important in determining income and, hence, purchasing power.

**Table 2.4** Occupational Distribution of Experienced Civilian Labor Force, 1900–1987 (in percent)

| | 1900 | 1910 | 1920 | 1930 | 1940 | 1950 | 1960 | 1970 | 1980 | 1987 |
|---|---|---|---|---|---|---|---|---|---|---|
| White-collar workers | 17.6 | 21.0 | 25.0 | 29.4 | 31.1 | 36.6 | 42.2 | 47.5 | 52.2 | 55.9 |
| Professional and technical | 4.3 | 4.6 | 5.4 | 6.8 | 7.5 | 8.6 | 11.3 | 14.6 | 16.1 | 15.8 |
| Managers | 5.9 | 6.5 | 6.6 | 7.4 | 7.3 | 8.7 | 8.5 | 8.1 | 11.2 | 14.6 |
| Clerical | 3.0 | 5.2 | 8.0 | 8.9 | 9.6 | 12.3 | 14.9 | 17.8 | 18.6 | 15.6 |
| Sales | 4.5 | 4.6 | 4.9 | 6.3 | 6.7 | 7.0 | 7.5 | 7.0 | 6.3 | 9.0 |
| Manual workers | 35.8 | 37.5 | 40.2 | 39.6 | 39.8 | 41.1 | 39.7 | 36.6 | 31.7 | 27.6 |
| Craft workers | 10.6 | 11.4 | 13.0 | 12.8 | 12.0 | 14.2 | 14.3 | 13.9 | 12.9 | 12.1 |
| Operatives | 12.8 | 14.4 | 15.6 | 15.8 | 18.4 | 20.4 | 19.9 | 17.9 | 14.2 | 11.3 |
| Laborers (nonfarm) | 12.5 | 11.8 | 11.6 | 11.0 | 9.4 | 6.6 | 5.5 | 4.7 | 4.6 | 4.3 |
| Personal-service workers | 9.1 | 9.4 | 7.9 | 9.8 | 11.8 | 10.5 | 11.7 | 12.9 | 13.3 | 13.4 |
| Domestics | 5.4 | 4.9 | 3.3 | 4.1 | 4.7 | 2.6 | 2.8 | 1.5 | 1.1 | 0.8 |
| Other* | 3.6 | 4.5 | 4.5 | 5.7 | 7.1 | 7.9 | 8.9 | 11.3 | 12.3 | 12.6 |
| Farm workers | 37.5 | 30.4 | 27.0 | 21.2 | 17.4 | 11.8 | 6.3 | 3.1 | 2.8 | 3.1 |
| Farmers and farm managers | 19.9 | 16.3 | 15.3 | 12.4 | 10.4 | 7.4 | 3.9 | 1.8 | 1.5 | 1.2 |
| Farm laborers | 17.7 | 14.2 | 11.7 | 8.8 | 7.0 | 4.4 | 2.4 | 1.3 | 1.3 | 1.9 |

Note: From 1900 to 1930, employment data relate to "gainful workers." From 1940 on, data relate to experienced civilian labor force. 1980 and 1987 data are not strictly comparable because they relate only to the *employed* labor force 16 and over. Data for 1987 are not strictly comparable because of definition changes.

* Included are attendants, barbers, cooks, guards, janitors, police, practical nurses, ushers, waiters, and so forth.

SOURCES: 1900–1950: U.S. Bureau of the Census, *Historical Statistics of the United States, Colonial Times to 1957* (1960). Table D72–122.

1960: U.S. Bureau of the Census, *Census of Population 1960.* Subject Reports, PC(2)-7A, 1967, Table 1.

1970: U.S. Bureau of the Census, *Census of Population 1970.* Subject Reports, PC(2)-7A, 1972, Table 1.

1980: U.S. President, *Employment and Training Report of the President* (Washington, DC: U.S. Government Printing Office, 1981), p. 149.

1987: U.S. Bureau of Labor Statistics, *Employment and Earnings,* 34, 1 (January 1988), Table 20.

The *wage rate* is the price of labor per working hour.[4] The *nominal wage* is what workers get paid per hour in current dollars; nominal wages are most useful in comparing the pay of various workers at a given time. To compare the pay of workers over long periods of time we need to account for changes in the purchasing power of a dollar. Nominal wages divided by some index of

---

[4] In this book, we define the hourly wage in the way most workers would if asked to state their "straight-time" wage. It is the money a worker would lose per hour if he or she has an unauthorized absence. When wages are defined in this way, a paid holiday becomes a "fringe benefit," as we will discuss, because leisure time is granted while pay continues. Thus, a worker paid $100 for 25 hours—20 of which are working hours and 5 of which are time off—will be said to earn a wage of $4.00 per hour and receive time off worth $20.

An alternative is to define the wage in terms of actual hours worked—or as $5.00 per hour in the above example. We prefer our definition, because if the worker seizes an opportunity to work one less hour in a particular week, his or her earnings would fall by $4.00, not $5.00 (as long as the reduction in hours does not affect the hours of paid holiday or vacation time for which the worker is eligible).

prices constitute the definition of *real wages*. Real wages are normally expressed as an *index number,* which provides a rough notion of how the purchasing power of an hour of work compares over time or across cities or countries.[5]

We often apply the term *wages* to the payments received by workers who are paid on a salaried basis (monthly, for example) rather than on an hourly basis. It is important, however, to distinguish among *wages, earnings,* and *income. Wages* refers to the payment for a *unit* of time, while the term *earnings* usually refers to wages multiplied by the number of time units (typically hours) worked. Thus, earnings depend on both wages and the length of time the employee works. *Income*—the total spending power of a person or family during some time period (usually a year)—includes both earnings and *unearned income,* which includes dividends or interest received on investments and transfer payments received from the government in the form of food stamps, welfare payments, unemployment compensation, and the like.

Table 2.5 shows the long-run trends in earnings and wages for American manufacturing production workers. While real weekly earnings in 1987 were over three times their 1914 level, the fall in paid weekly hours from 49 to about 40 represented an additional gain in the general standard of living for workers. Probably the best index of living standards is how much workers receive *per hour,* and Table 2.5 shows that real hourly wages were four times as high in 1987 as in 1914, which implies that an hour of work paid for four times more goods and services in 1987 than in 1914. Table 2.5 shows why it is important to correct for inflation when comparing wages at different times; average real wages have risen much more slowly than average money wages.

The actual increase in living standards attainable by the ordinary worker is perhaps even greater than indicated by the real wage increases shown in Table 2.5. Both wages and earnings are normally defined and measured in terms of direct monetary payments to employees (before taxes for which the employee is liable). *Total compensation,* on the other hand, consists of earnings plus *fringe benefits*—benefits that are either payments-in-kind or deferred. Examples of *payments-in-kind* are employer-provided health care or health insurance, where the employee receives a service or an insurance policy rather than money. Paid vacation time is also in this category, since employees are given days off instead of cash. *Deferred* payments can take the form of employer-financed retirement benefits, including Social Security

---

[5] An index number is expressed as a fraction of some base, where the base is set equal to 100. To understand how index numbers are constructed, please refer to the next-to-last column in Table 2.5, where the index of real hourly wages in 1980 is listed as 403. This means that hourly real wages were four times higher in 1980 than in the base year, which was arbitrarily chosen as 1914. Arriving at an index of *real* hourly wages requires that we calculate an index of nominal wages *and* an index of prices. An index of nominal wages can be constructed for each year with 1914 as a base by dividing the wage in each year by $0.22—the hourly wage in 1914—and multiplying by 100. This fixes the index at 100 in 1914 and yields an index number of 3305 for 1980 [(7.27/0.22) × 100]. The Consumer Price Index, which is based on "pricing out" an unchanging market basket of goods from year to year, is 820 for the year 1980 if 1914 is the base year. Dividing the price index (820) into the index for nominal wages (3305) and multiplying by 100 gives us the figure of 403 noted in the table.

**Table 2.5**  Average Wages and Earnings of Production Workers in Manufacturing, 1914–87

| Year | Weekly Earnings (current dollars) | Average Weekly Hours Paid For | Average Hourly Wage (current dollars) | Consumer Price Index (1914 = 100)[a] | Index of Real Weekly Earnings (1914 = 100) | Index of Real Hourly Wages (1914 = 100) | Annual Percentage Change in Real Hourly Wages over Previous 10 Years |
|---|---|---|---|---|---|---|---|
| 1914 | 10.92 | 49.4 | 0.22 | 100 | 100 | 100 | |
| 1920 | 26.02 | 47.4 | 0.55 | 199 | 120 | 126 | |
| 1925 | 24.11 | 44.5 | 0.54 | 174 | 127 | 141 | 3.1[b] |
| 1930 | 23.00 | 42.1 | 0.55 | 166 | 127 | 151 | |
| 1935 | 19.91 | 36.6 | 0.54 | 137 | 133 | 179 | 2.3 |
| 1940 | 24.96 | 38.1 | 0.66 | 140 | 163 | 214 | |
| 1945 | 44.20 | 43.5 | 1.02 | 179 | 226 | 259 | 3.7 |
| 1950 | 58.32 | 40.5 | 1.44 | 240 | 223 | 273 | |
| 1955 | 75.70 | 40.7 | 1.86 | 266 | 261 | 318 | 2.1 |
| 1960 | 89.72 | 39.7 | 2.26 | 295 | 278 | 348 | |
| 1965 | 107.53 | 41.2 | 2.61 | 314 | 314 | 378 | 1.7 |
| 1970 | 133.73 | 39.8 | 3.36 | 386 | 317 | 396 | |
| 1975 | 189.51 | 39.4 | 4.81 | 536 | 324 | 408 | 0.8 |
| 1980 | 288.62 | 39.7 | 7.27 | 820 | 322 | 403 | |
| 1985 | 385.56 | 40.5 | 9.52 | 1070 | 330 | 404 | |
| 1986 | 396.01 | 40.7 | 9.73 | 1091 | 332 | 405 | −0.1[b] |
| 1987 | 406.31 | 41.0 | 9.91 | 1131 | 329 | 398 | −0.2[c] |

[a] The figures in this column should be interpreted with some caution. They are generated by pricing out a fixed "market basket" of consumer goods each year. Over time, however, new goods have become available and old ones improved in quality, so that comparability of the "baskets" used in making the index diminishes over time.

[b] Change calculated over previous 11 years.

[c] Change calculated over previous 12 years.

SOURCES:  U.S. Bureau of the Census, *Historical Statistics of the United States, Colonial Times to 1970* (Washington, DC: U.S. Government Printing Office, 1975); U.S. Department of Labor, Bureau of Labor Statistics, *Handbook of Labor Statistics 1977,* Bulletin 1966 (Washington, DC: U.S. Government Printing Office, 1977); U.S. President, *Economic Report of the President* (Washington, DC: U.S. Government Printing Office, February 1986); U.S. Bureau of Labor Statistics, *Monthly Labor Review,* vol. 110, no. 6 (June 1987), Tables 14, 15, and 30; U.S. Bureau of Labor Statistics, *Employment and Earnings,* 35, 1, (January 1988) Table 65; U.S. President, *Economic Report of the President* (Washington, DC: U.S. Government Printing Office, February 1988).

taxes, where employers set aside money now that enables their employees to receive pensions later.

In 1976, earnings as conventionally defined constituted only 75 percent of the total compensation of manufacturing production workers. Vacations, pensions, and health care were the largest categories of fringe benefits. Because fringe benefits were virtually nonexistent before 1940, we can assume that total earnings and total compensation were essentially the same in the early 1900s. If earnings in more recent years are adjusted to reflect fringe benefits, we arrive at the conclusion that real compensation per hour around 1980 was more than five times higher than in 1914 for the typical manufacturing worker.

The next section will shift from the foregoing brief description of labor market *outcomes* over time to an analysis of how the market *operates* to generate these outcomes. This analysis of labor market functioning is the central focus of labor economics.

# How the Market Works

The study of the labor market begins and ends with an analysis of the demand for and supply of labor. On the demand side of the labor market, we will study employer behavior regarding the hiring of labor. On the supply side, the behavior of both workers and potential workers will be explored. The interaction of demand and supply is basically what determines working conditions, employment and compensation levels, and the allocation of labor to various occupations, industries, and employers. One can thus think of any labor market outcome as always affected, to one degree or another, by the forces of both demand and supply. To paraphrase economist Alfred Marshall, it takes both demand and supply to determine economic outcomes just as it takes both blades of a pair of scissors to cut cloth.

In this chapter we begin by presenting the basic outlines and broadest implications of the simplest economic model of the labor market. We then discuss some ways in which the more complicated real-world personnel decisions made by businesses and unions modify this model. In later chapters we add further complexities to this basic view of the labor market and explain assumptions and implications more fully. However, the simple model of demand and supply presented here generates some rather profound insights into labor market behavior that can be very useful in forming social, business, and union policy. Every piece of analysis in this text is either an extension or modification of the basic model presented in this chapter.

## The Demand for Labor

Firms are in the business of combining various factors of production—mainly capital and labor—to produce goods or services that are sold in a product market. Their total output and the way in which they combine labor and capital depends on (1) product demand, (2) how much labor and capital they can acquire at given prices, and (3) the choice of technologies available to them. When we study the demand for labor, we are interested in finding out how changes in one or more of these three forces affect the number of workers employed by a firm or set of firms. To simplify the discussion, we will study one change at a time and hold all other forces constant.

**Wage changes.**  Of primary interest for most purposes is the question of how the number of employees (or total labor hours) demanded varies when wages change. Suppose, for example, that we could vary the wages facing a certain industry over a long period of time but keep the technology available, the conditions under which capital is supplied, and the relationship between product price and product demand all unchanged. What will happen to the demand for labor when, say, the wage rate is *increased?*

**Table 2.6**   Labor Demand Schedule for a Hypothetical Industry

| Wage Rate | Desired Employment Level |
|---|---|
| $3.00 | 250 |
| 4.00 | 190 |
| 5.00 | 160 |
| 6.00 | 130 |
| 7.00 | 100 |
| 8.00 | 70 |

Note:  Employment levels can be measured in number of employees *or* number of labor hours demanded. We have chosen here to use number of employees.

First, higher wages imply higher costs and, usually, higher product prices. Because consumers respond to higher prices by buying less, employers would tend to reduce their level of output. Lower output levels, of course, imply lower employment levels (other things being equal). This decline in employment is called a *scale effect*—the effect on desired employment of a smaller scale of production.

Second, as wages increase (assuming the price of capital does not change, at least initially), employers have incentives to cut costs by adopting a technology that relies more on capital and less on labor. Thus, if wages were to rise, desired employment would fall because of a shift toward a more "capital-intensive" mode of production. This second effect might be termed a *substitution effect* because as wages rise, capital is *substituted* for labor in the production process.

The effects of various wages on employment levels might be summarized in a table showing the labor demanded at each wage level. Table 2.6 is an example of such a *demand schedule*. The relationship between wages and employment tabulated in Table 2.6 could be graphed as a *demand curve*. Figure 2.1 shows the demand curve generated by the data in Table 2.6. Note that the curve has a negative slope—indicating that as wages rise, less labor is demanded.

A demand curve for labor tells us how the desired level of employment—measured in either labor hours or number of employees—varies with changes

**Figure 2.1**   Labor Demand Curve

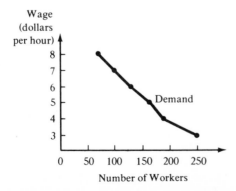

in the price of labor when other forces affecting demand are held constant. These other forces, to repeat, are the product demand schedule, the conditions under which capital can be obtained, and the types of technology available. If wages change and these other factors do not, one can determine the change in labor demanded by moving up or down along the demand curve.

**Changes in other forces affecting demand.**   What happens when one of the other forces affecting labor demand changes?

First, suppose that *demand for the product* of a particular industry were to increase, so that at any output price more of the goods or services in question could be sold. Suppose in this case that technology and the conditions under which capital and labor are made available to the industry do not change. Output levels would clearly rise as firms in the industry sought to maximize profits, and this *scale* (or *output*) *effect* would increase the amount of labor demanded. (As long as the relative prices of capital and labor remain unchanged, there is no *substitution effect.*)

How would this change in the demand for labor be illustrated using a demand curve? Since the technology available and the conditions under which capital and labor are supplied have remained constant, this change in product demand would increase the labor desired at any wage level that might prevail. In other words, the entire labor demand curve *shifts* to the right. This rightward shift, shown as a movement from *D* to *D'* in Figure 2.2, indicates that at every possible wage rate the number of workers demanded has increased.

Second, consider what would happen if the product demand schedule, technology, and labor-supply conditions remain unchanged, but *the supply of capital* changes so that capital prices fall to 50 percent (say) of their prior level. How would this change affect the demand for labor?

Our analysis of this situation is exactly the same as our analysis of a wage change. First, when capital prices decline, the costs of producing tend to decline. Reduced costs stimulate increases in production and these increases will tend to raise the level of desired employment at any given wage. The scale

**Figure 2.2**   Demand for Labor Shifts Due to an Increase in Product Demand

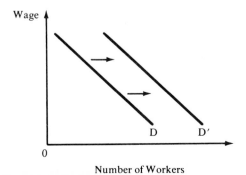

**Figure 2.3** Demand for Labor Shifts Due to "Scale Effect" Resulting from Fall in Capital Prices

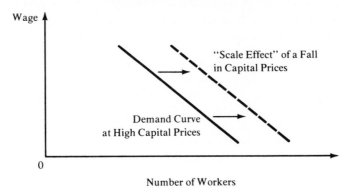

effect of a fall in capital prices thus tends to increase the demand for labor at each wage level, a situation that is represented in Figure 2.3 by a shift to the right of the labor demand curve.

The second effect of a fall in capital prices would be a substitution effect, whereby firms adopt more capital-intensive technologies in response to cheaper capital. Such firms would substitute capital for labor and would use less labor to produce a given amount of output than before. With less labor being desired at each wage rate, the demand-for-labor curve shifts to the left, as shown in Figure 2.4. In some cases this leftward-shifting tendency of the substitution effect would be stronger than the rightward-shifting tendency of the scale effect; in other cases, the scale effect would be stronger.

The hypothesized changes in product demand and capital supply just discussed have tended to *shift* the demand curve for labor. It is important to distinguish between a *shift* in a demand curve and *movement along* a curve. A labor demand curve graphically shows the *labor desired* as a function of the

**Figure 2.4** Demand for Labor Shifts Due to "Substitution Effect" Resulting from Fall in Capital Prices

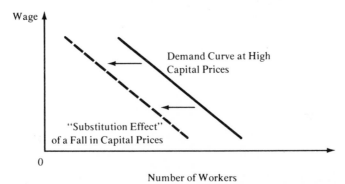

*wage rate* (the wage is on one axis of the graph and the number employed is on the other axis). When the *wage* changes and other forces are held unchanged, one *moves along* the curve. However, when one of the *other forces* changes, the entire labor demand curve will *shift*. Unlike wages, these forces are not directly shown when the demand curve for labor is drawn. Thus, when they change, a different relationship between wages and employment will prevail, and this shows up as a shift of the demand curve. If more labor is desired at any given wage rate, then the curve has shifted to the right. If less labor is demanded at each wage rate that might prevail, then the demand curve has shifted left.

**Market, industry, and firm demand.**  The demand for labor can be analyzed on any one of three different levels.

1.  To analyze the demand for labor *by a particular firm,* we would examine how an increase in the wages of machinists, for example, would affect their employment by a particular aircraft manufacturer.
2.  To analyze the effects of this wage increase on the employment of machinists *in the entire aircraft industry,* we would utilize an industry demand curve.
3.  Finally, to see how the wage increase would affect the *entire labor market* for machinists, in all industries in which they are employed, we would use a market demand curve.

We will see in Chapters 3 and 4 that firm, industry, and market labor demand curves will vary in *shape* to some extent, because scale and substitution effects have different strengths at each of the three levels. However, it is important to know at this point that the scale and substitution effects of a wage change work in the same direction at each level, so that firm, industry, and market demand curves *all slope downward.*

**Long run vs. short run.**  One can also distinguish between *long-run* and *short-run* labor demand curves. Over very short periods of time, employers find it difficult to substitute capital for labor (or vice versa), and customers may not change their product demand very much in response to a price increase. It takes time to fully adjust consumption and production behavior. Over longer periods of time, of course, responses to changes in wages or the other forces affecting the demand for labor will be larger and more complete.

In Chapters 3 and 4 we will draw some important distinctions between short-run and long-run labor demand curves. At this point, we only need to point out again that while these curves will differ, *they both slope downward.* Thus, an increase in the wage rate will reduce the demand for labor—although perhaps by different amounts—in both the short and long run.

## The Supply of Labor

Having looked at a simple model of behavior on the buyer (or demand) side of the labor market, we now turn to the seller (or supply) side of the market. For the purposes of this chapter we will assume that workers have already decided to work and that the questions facing them are what occupations and employers to choose.

**Market supply.**   To first consider the supply of labor to the entire market (as opposed to the supply of a particular firm), let us suppose that the market we are considering is the one for stenographers. How will supply respond to changes in wages stenographers might receive? In other words, what does the supply schedule of stenographers look like?

If the salaries and wages in *other* occupations are *held constant* and the wages of stenographers rise, we would expect to find more people wanting to become stenographers. For example, suppose that each of one hundred people in a high school graduating class has the option of becoming an insurance agent or stenographer. Some of these one hundred people will prefer to be insurance agents even if stenographers are better paid, because they like the challenge and sociability of selling. Some would want to be stenographers even if the pay were comparatively poor, because they hate the pressures of selling. Many, however, could see themselves doing either job; for these people the compensation in each occupation would be a major factor in their decision. If stenographers' pay rose compared to that of insurance agents, more people would want to become stenographers. If the pay of insurance agents rose relative to stenographers' pay, the number of people choosing the insurance occupation would increase and the supply of stenographers would decrease. Of course, at some ridiculously low wage for stenographers, *no one* would want to become one.

Thus, the supply of labor to a particular market is positively related to the wage rate prevailing in that market, holding other wages constant; that is, if the wages of insurance agents are held constant and stenographer wages rise, more people will want to become stenographers because of the relative improvement in compensation (as shown graphically in Figure 2.5).

As with demand curves, each supply curve is drawn holding other prices and wages constant. If one or more of these other prices or wages were to change, it would cause the supply curve to *shift*. As the salaries of insurance agents *rise,* some people will change their minds about becoming stenographers and choose to become insurance agents. Fewer people would want to be stenographers at each level of stenographic wages as salaries of insurance

**Figure 2.5**   Supply Curve for Stenographers

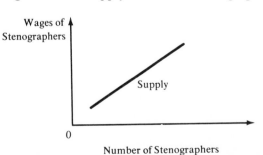

**Figure 2.6**  Labor Supply Curve for Stenographers Shifts as Salaries of Insurance Agents Rise

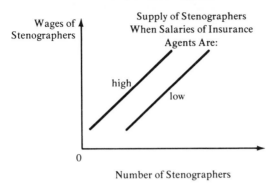

agents rise. In graphical terms (see Figure 2.6), increases in the salaries of insurance agents would cause the supply curve of stenographers to shift to the left.

**Supply to firms.**  Having decided to become a stenographer, the decision then moves to which offer of employment to accept. If all employers were offering stenographic jobs that were more or less alike, the choice would be based on compensation. Any firm unwise enough to attempt paying a wage below what others pay would find it could not attract any employees (or at least it could not attract any of the caliber it wants). Conversely, no firm would be foolish enough to pay more than the going wage, because it would be paying more than was necessary to attract a suitable number and quality of employees. The supply curve to a firm, then, would be horizontal, as can be seen in Figure 2.7. The horizontal supply curve to a firm indicates that at the going wage, a firm can get all the stenographers it needs. If it pays less, however, supply shrinks to zero.

The difference in slope between the market supply curve and the supply curve to a firm is directly related to the type of choice facing workers. In deciding whether to enter the stenographic labor market or not, workers must weigh both the compensation *and* the job requirements of alternative options

**Figure 2.7**  Supply of Stenographers to a Firm

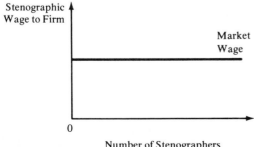

(such as being an insurance agent). If wages of stenographers were to fall, fewer people would want to enter the stenographic market. However, not everyone would withdraw from the market, because the jobs of insurance agent and stenographer are not perfect substitutes. Some people would remain stenographers after a wage decline because they dislike the job requirements of insurance agents.

Once having decided to become a stenographer, the choice of which employer to work for is a choice between alternatives where the job requirements are nearly the *same*. Thus, in our simplified model the choice must be made on the grounds of compensation alone. If a firm were to lower its wage offers below those of other firms, it would lose all its applicants. The horizontal supply curve is, therefore, a reflection of supply decisions made among alternatives that are perfect substitutes for each other.

We have argued that firms wanting to hire stenographers must pay the going wage or lose all applicants. In other words, each firm acts as a wage taker. This may seem unrealistic in light of the emphasis large companies place on setting compensation. At first glance, it seems that such firms' wages have a life of their own, as determined by their personnel offices. However, the insight provided by Figure 2.7 is that a company must be aware of the external labor market in setting its own compensation policy. If, for example, a firm offers jobs *comparable* to those offered by other firms but at a lower level of total compensation, it might be able to attract a few applicants of the quality it desires because a few people will be unaware of compensation elsewhere. Over time, however, knowledge of the firm's poor relative pay would become more widespread, and the firm would find it had to rely on less-qualified people to fill its jobs. It could secure quality employees at below-average pay only if it offered *noncomparable* jobs (more pleasant working conditions, longer paid vacations, and so forth). This factor in labor supply will be discussed in Chapter 6. For now, we assume that neither individual workers nor firms can set a wage much different from the going wage and still hope to transact. (Exceptions to this general proposition will be noted later.)

## The Determination of the Wage

The wage that prevails in a particular labor market is heavily influenced by the forces of demand and supply, whether or not the market involves a labor union. However, because unions are labor-market institutions designed to alter the market outcome, we will first discuss wage determination in the case of nonunionized labor markets.

**The equilibrium wage.** Recall that the market demand curve indicates how many workers employers would want at each wage rate, holding capital prices and consumer incomes constant. The market supply curve indicates how many workers would enter the market at each wage level, holding the wages in other occupations constant. These curves can be overlaid on the same graph to reveal some interesting information, as shown in Figure 2.8.

For example, suppose the market wage were set at $W_1$. At this low wage,

**Figure 2.8** Market Demand and Supply

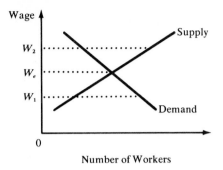

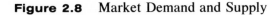

Number of Workers

demand is large but supply is small. More importantly, Figure 2.8 indicates that at $W_1$ demand *exceeds* supply. At this point, employers will be competing for the few workers in the market and a "shortage" of workers would exist. Firms' desires to attract more employees would lead them to increase their wage offers, thus driving up the overall level of wage offers in the market.

As wages rise, two things happen. First, more workers would choose to enter the market and look for jobs (a movement along the supply curve); second, at the same time, increasing wages would induce employers to seek fewer workers (a movement along the demand curve). If wages were to rise to $W_2$, supply would exceed demand. Employers would desire fewer workers than the number available, and not all those desiring employment would be able to find jobs—resulting in a "surplus" of workers. Employers would have long lines of eager applicants for any opening. These employers would soon reason that they could still fill their openings with qualified applicants even if they offered lower wages. Further, if they could pay lower wages they would want to hire more employees. Some employees would be more than happy to accept the lower wages if they could just find a job. Others would leave the market and look for work elsewhere as wages fell. Thus, demand and supply would become more equal as wages fell from the level of $W_2$.

How would such a fall in wages occur at the company level? As we will see, firms often set base pay rates for each job and rarely lower such rates in money terms. However, because of the excess supply of applicants at a wage of $W_2$, companies would be less likely than otherwise to raise their pay scales for this job. Over a period of months, the real wages for the job would fall if prices rose. For example, between 1979 and 1980, money wages for non-agricultural production workers rose by 6.9 percent (from $219.91 per week to $235.10), but their real wages fell by 6.6 percent since prices rose by 13.5 percent.[6] Even if money wages are not reduced, the fall in wages predicted in Figure 2.8 could occur through gradual price inflation. Money wages in an occupation can also fall relative to wages in other occupations. Thus, when

---

[6] U.S. President, *Economic Report of the President* (Washington, DC: U.S. Government Printing Office, January 1987), Tables B-42 and B-57.

we speak of a declining wage rate it can imply a fall *relative to product prices or wages* as well as a decline in the money wage rate itself.

The wage rate at which demand equals supply is the *market-clearing* or *equilibrium* wage. At $W_e$ in Figure 2.8, employers can fill the number of openings they have, and all employees who want jobs in this market can find them. At $W_e$ there is no surplus and no shortage. All parties are satisfied, and no forces exist that would alter the wage. The market is in equilibrium in the sense that the wage will remain at $W_e$.

The equilibrium wage is the wage that eventually prevails in a market. Wages below $W_e$, for example, will not prevail because the shortage of workers leads employers to drive up wage offers. Wages above $W_e$ likewise cannot prevail because the surplus leads to downward pressure on wage rates. The market-clearing wage, $W_e$, thus becomes the *going wage* that individual employers and employees must face. In other words, wage rates are determined by the market and "announced" to individual market participants. Figure 2.9 graphically depicts "market" demand and supply in panel (a) along with the demand and supply curves for a typical firm in that market in panel (b). All firms in the market pay a wage of $W_e$, and total employment of $L$ equals the sum of employment in each firm.

**Disturbing the equilibrium.**  What could happen to change the equilibrium (market) wage once it has been reached? Once equilibrium has been achieved, changes could arise from shifts in either the demand or the supply curve. For example, let us consider what might happen to the wages of stenographers (the majority of whom at present are women) if job opportunities for women in management and other prestigious fields were to improve. The greater availability and improved pay for women in these alternative careers would probably cause some women to leave the stenographer market and seek work in these other fields. Fewer women would

**Figure 2.9**   Demand and Supply at the "Market" and "Firm" Level

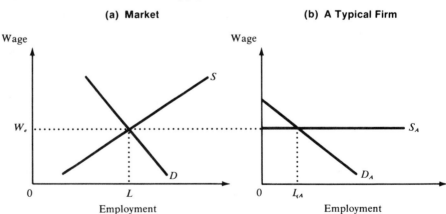

**Figure 2.10**  New Labor Market Equilibrium After Supply Shifts Left

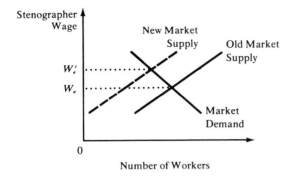

want to become stenographers at the going wage. As Figure 2.10 shows, the market supply curve for stenographers would shift to the left.

As can be seen from Figure 2.10, after the supply curve has shifted, $W_e$ is no longer the market-clearing wage. There is now a shortage of stenographers because demand exceeds supply at $W_e$. As employers scramble to fill stenographic jobs, the wage rate is driven up. The end result of the improved opportunities elsewhere would be to increase the wages of stenographers.

Shifts of the demand curve to the right would also cause wages to rise. Suppose, for example, that the increase in paperwork accompanying greater government regulation of industry causes firms to demand more stenographic help than before. Graphically, as in Figure 2.11, this greater demand would be represented as a rightward shift of the demand curve. This rightward shift depicts a situation in which, for any given wage rate, the number of stenographers desired has risen. The old equilibrium wage ($W_e$) no longer equates demand and supply. If $W_e$ were to persist, there would be a labor shortage in the stenographer market (because demand would exceed supply). This shortage would induce employers to improve their wage offers and eventually drive up the stenographic wage to $W_e^*$.

**Figure 2.11**  New Labor Market Equilibrium After Demand Shifts Right

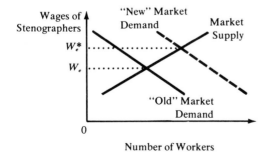

**Figure 2.12**   New Labor Market Equilibrium After Supply Shifts Right

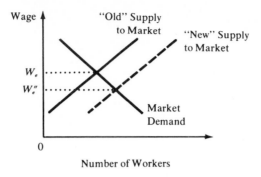

Both the leftward shift of supply and the rightward shift in demand initially created shortages—shortages that led to increases in the market wage rate. The supply-caused shift, however, led to a fall in employment (as compared to the old equilibrium level of employment). Conversely, the demand-caused shift induced an increase in the equilibrium level of employment.

A fall in the equilibrium wage rate will occur if there is increased supply or reduced demand. An increase in supply would be represented by a rightward shift of the supply curve, as more people enter the market at each wage (see Figure 2.12). This rightward shift causes a surplus to exist at the old equilibrium wage ($W_e$) and leads to behavior that reduces the wage to $W_e$ in Figure 2.12. Note that the equilibrium employment level has increased. What could cause this rightward shift of the supply curve? For stenographers, the causes of increased supply at each wage could be (1) a greater desire among people to become stenographers, or (2) reductions in the wages of competing occupations (such as insurance agents in our example).

**Figure 2.13**   New Labor Market Equilibrium After Demand Shifts Left

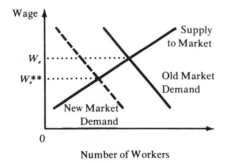

**Figure 2.14**   Elimination of North-South Wage Differentials, 1940–70.

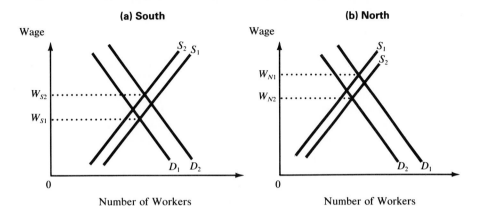

A decrease (leftward shift) in demand would also cause a decrease in the equilibrium wage, although such a shift would be accompanied by a fall in employment, as we can see in Figure 2.13. The leftward demand shift causes a surplus at the original equilibrium wage ($W_e$). When firms find the ratio of applicants to openings is greater than usual and when workers find the jobs are harder to come by, downward pressure on the wage will exist and the market-clearing wage falls to $W_e^{**}$. Money wages may go up, but any increases will be smaller than those received in other occupations. Sadly for the authors, the decline in demand for college professors brought on by a number of financial and demographic pressures offers an excellent example of a "surplus" market. The result was a 17-percent decline in real, after-tax income for college professors over the 1967–78 period.

It is possible, of course, for equilibrium to be disturbed by shifts in both demand and supply at the same time. Figure 2.14 illustrates this outcome for North-South wage differentials. During the 1940–70 period, millions of workers left the southern United States in search of higher-paying jobs in the North. At the same time, businesses began to move from the Northeast and Midwest regions to the South in search of lower-cost labor. Figure 2.14 shows the leftward shift in labor supply in the South (a) and in labor demand in the North (b), while labor demand in the South and labor supply in the North shifted to the right. Our simple model would predict that such movements would tend to reduce the North-South wage differential, an outcome that appears to have happened in real terms by 1970. That is, if we compare workers with similar demographic characteristics, then wages corrected for living costs were about the same in 1970 in the North as in the South.[7]

    [7]   See P. Coelho and M. Ghali, "The End of the North-South Wage Differential," *American Economic Review* 61 (December 1971): 932–37; and D. Bellante, "The North-South Differential and the Migration of Heterogeneous Labor," *American Economic Review* 69 (March 1979): 166–75.

The approximate equality in 1970 of real wages in the North and South does not necessarily mean that money wages were equal: in fact, for similar workers, nominal wages were about 12-percent higher in the North than in the South. However, living costs were also about 12-percent higher in the North than in the South. Historical comparisons of wages across regions are made difficult by the lack of data on regional living cost differences in earlier periods. However, movements in money wages are consistent with the shifts in demand and supply pictured in Figure 2.14; for example, in 1929, money wages were 15–21-percent lower in the South than in the rest of the country.[8]

Since 1970, the older, slow-growing industrial states of New York, Pennsylvania, Ohio, Illinois, and Michigan have been experiencing out-migration, while the faster-growing states in the South and West are experiencing an influx of migrants. During 1980–85, for example, the Northeast and Midwest had a net outflow of 2.1 million people, while the South and West had net inflows of 3.4 million and 2.2 million, respectively.[9]

The net inflow to the South is a complete turnaround from the 1950s, when the region was largely rural and offered relatively few job opportunities. As the South has industrialized, real wages there have risen, so that by the late 1970s the real wages received by urban workers in the South exceeded those typically received by urban workers of comparable skill in each of the other regions.[10] Not surprisingly, then, the South has become the region with the highest net flows of in-migrants.

Note that our theory predicts the elimination of such geographic wage differentials, all else equal: worker and firm and mobility continue until wages equalize as long as both regions are equally attractive to live in, the nonwage job characteristics are the same, and the workers are equally skilled across regions. In Chapter 6 we will analyze the effects on wage differentials of differences in these nonwage factors.

## Applications of the Theory

The preceding section presented a simple model of how a labor market functions. Although this model will be refined and elaborated upon in the following chapters, the model is adequate to explain many important phenomena, including those that follow.

### Accommodation of Baby Boom Workers

During the late 1970s, the overall labor market was forced to accommodate a huge influx of new workers searching for jobs. These new entrants were people born in the late 1950s—during the so-called baby boom. The population of 20-year-olds in 1977 was 44-percent larger than the number in 1962 and

[8]   P. Coelho and M. Ghali, "The End of the North-South Wage Differential."

[9]   U.S. Department of Commerce, *Statistical Abstract of the United States 1987* (Washington, DC: U.S. Government Printing Office, 1986): Table 27.

[10]   Leonard Sahling and Sharon P. Smith, "Regional Wage Differentials: Has the South Risen Again?" *The Review of Economics and Statistics* 65 (February 1983): 131–35

**Figure 2.15**   Labor Market Equilibrium for Teenagers After Population Increase

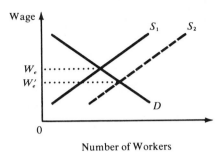

equally large compared to the numbers projected for 1992.[11] Thus, there was a "bulge" in the number of inexperienced workers seeking jobs.

What can we predict would happen as this bulge in supply hit the labor market?

First, new entrants are, by definition, inexperienced workers, and such workers are not very good substitutes for experienced workers. Inexperienced workers tend to be offered *entry-level jobs* while more complicated or responsible jobs higher up on the career ladder are reserved to some extent for experienced workers. Thus, the experienced and the inexperienced are, to a degree, in different labor markets.

What happens when a big bulge of population enters a labor market? The sheer increase in population will shift the supply curve to the right, because there will be more people offering themselves for work at every wage level. Figure 2.15 illustrates this shift from $S_1$ to $S_2$. This shift in supply, if not accompanied by a correspondingly large shift in demand, will reduce wages. (Figure 2.15 shows that the equilibrium wage fell from $W_e$ to $W_e'$.)

Did the baby boom bulge in the late 1970s in fact cause wages of inexperienced workers to fall? To answer this question we must pick a standard against which to measure the fall. Money wages rarely fall, especially during periods when prices are rising. We could, therefore, measure whether *real wages* fell over some time period. Real wages, however, tend to rise due to improvements in technology—a force we would like to filter out if possible so that we can focus only on changes produced by the shift in supply.

The best way to measure the fall in the wages of inexperienced workers is to compare their wages to those of adults in their peak earnings years. These adults will be the beneficiaries, along with inexperienced workers, of technological advances, but they are far enough removed from the baby boomers in experience that the bulge of new labor force entrants will not affect their wages directly. Measured against this group, earnings of new entrants fell dramatically in the late 1970s.

[11]   Data for this section were obtained from Finis Welch, "Effects of Cohort Size on Earnings: The Baby Boom Babies' Financial Bust," *Journal of Political Economy* 87 (October 1979): S65–98.

**Table 2.7**   Economic Position of New Entrants in Labor Force, by Level of Schooling

| Years of School Completed | Percent of Work Force with Less Than 5 Years of Experience in Each Schooling Category | | Weekly Wages of New Entrants Relative to Peak Earners | |
|---|---|---|---|---|
| | 1967–69 | 1973–75 | 1967–69 | 1973–75 |
| 8–11 years | 8.9 | 15.4 | 0.53 | 0.46 |
| 12 years | 15.0 | 20.8 | 0.63 | 0.55 |
| 1–3 years of college | 19.0 | 25.2 | 0.59 | 0.52 |
| 4 or more years of college | 18.7 | 22.9 | 0.63 | 0.54 |

SOURCE:   Finis Welch, "Effects of Cohort Size on Earnings: The Baby Boom Babies' Financial Bust," *Journal of Political Economy* 87, 5 (October 1979): S65–S98.

Table 2.7 tells the story. In every educational category, the proportion of inexperienced workers in the labor force increased during the period from 1967 to 1975—a clear indication that the number of young workers was increasing faster than the number of older workers. This abnormally large rise in employment was accompanied by a 12–15-percent decline in the earnings of new workers relative to adults. Thus, as our model of labor-market behavior suggests, the large increase in employment necessary to accommodate the baby boomers was facilitated by a decline in their wage. The influx of inexperienced workers created a "surplus" at the former wage level, and as new workers competed for jobs, the wage level was driven down. The impact of their large cohort is likely to stay with the baby boomers throughout their working lives. As they gain experience they may find intense competition for a limited number of promotions. Some observers predict that members of this generation will reach career plateaus at an earlier age than those of previous or, by implication, succeeding generations. If this happens, lowered morale and reduced performance may result. Companies may find it increasingly cost-effective to enrich people's jobs by reassigning tasks as traditional lines of promotion get clogged.[12] (In contrast, the cohort of workers entering the labor market in the 1980s and 1990s will benefit from its smaller size.) Again, the labor market will have a major effect on seemingly internal personnel decisions.

## Effects of Unions

Although we will discuss the role and effects of unions on the labor market later in this text, it is important here to briefly establish that the model outlined in this chapter can also apply to unions. This analysis will look only

[12]   C. Dawson, "Will Career Plateauing Become a Bigger Problem?" *Personnel Journal* 62 (January 1983): 78–81.

generally at the effects of unions on wages. Later chapters will analyze union effects on wages in more detail and will also examine their effects on productivity, turnover, and wage differentials across race and gender groups.

Unions represent workers and, as such, primarily affect the *supply* curves to labor markets. They can affect these supply curves in two ways. First, indirectly, most unions operate under labor-management agreements—called *contracts* or *collective-bargaining agreements*—that permit employer discretion in the selection of workers. These contracts cover wages, other forms of compensation, working conditions, procedures for employee complaints, and rules governing promotions and layoffs. The provisions of the contracts are the result of a bargain struck between the management and all workers collectively. In effect, workers band together, agree to a bargaining position, and negotiate as a group. All are bound by the final provisions of the contract—which means that all must receive the agreed-upon wage.

When collective-bargaining agreements are industry-wide in effect, they affect the supply curves in the relevant labor markets by making them horizontal. No one can get paid more or less than the wage agreed upon in the contract (see Figure 2.16).

In Figure 2.16, the supply curve without a union is $S$, and the market-clearing wage is $W_e$. However, the union raises the wage above $W_e$ to $W_u$, the wage specified in the contract, by preventing firms and workers from offering or accepting wages below $W_e$. The result is a wage above equilibrium, employment levels below those that would prevail if the wage were lower, and a surplus of labor (at $W_u$, $L_s$ workers want work in these jobs but only $L_u$ can find work). Because the wage cannot fall, the surplus remains and manifests itself in long lines of workers applying for job openings with union employers.

This graphic analysis is based on the assumption that unions raised the wage above market-clearing levels. This is probably a useful assumption, given that unions certainly intend to do this. Not all unions have the power to affect wages much, for reasons we will discuss in Chapter 3. If these unions agree to wages equal to $W_e$, the market equilibrium wage, then clearly they do not affect wage or employment outcomes in the labor market.

**Figure 2.16**   Effects on Labor-Market Equilibrium of Industrywide Unions

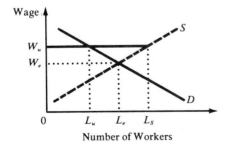

**Figure 2.17**    How Unions That Control Supply of Labor to a Market
Affect Labor Market Equilibrium

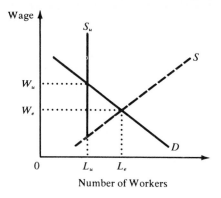

The second way in which some unions affect the supply to markets is by
*directly* limiting supply. Some unions operate under agreements in which
employers hire all labor from the union, and the union controls who and how
many members it lets in. The dual power of being able to restrict its membership and require employers to hire only union members permits the union
to set the level of labor supply to the market (see Figure 2.17).

In Figure 2.17, $S_u$ represents the level of supply determined by union
policy and $W_u$ the resulting wage. $S_u$ is a vertical line because wage increases
or decreases do not affect supply. Supply is set at $L_u$ by union policy. The
wage and employment levels under the union—$W_u$ and $L_u$—can be compared
to the lower wage ($W_e$) and higher employment level ($L_e$) that would prevail in
the absence of a union. The major difference between this case, in which
unions control supply, and the more common situation in which employers
choose workers but make contracts with all workers collectively, is that there
is no surplus of workers standing at the employer's hiring gate. The long line
of disappointed people is at the union's office. Examples of labor unions that
control supply are those representing skilled construction workers, longshoring workers, and theater lighting technicians.[13]

While the examples illustrated in Figures 2.16 and 2.17 show the potential
effects of unions on the labor *supply* curve, some union activities can shift the
*demand* curve for labor. For example, unions in industries subject to international competition (such as autos, steel, or apparel) frequently lobby for
Congressional action to reduce imports through either quotas or tariffs. The
effect of these import restraints is to shift the demand curve for domestically
produced products in these industries. For example, when import restrictions

---

[13] This is not to say that all unions that can control supply are equally prone to do it. Some may fear
the presence of a large number of qualified workers outside the union and figure that it is better to take
them in, collect their dues, and ration jobs among all members than to face stiff nonunion competition. Restricted entry into the union is most likely when employers must hire only union workers.

reduce the availability or increase the cost of foreign substitutes, the quantity of American cars demanded at any given price increases. As we have already seen, an increase in product demand will, other things equal, increase the demand for all inputs, including labor. By shifting the domestic demand for labor in the affected industry to the right, effective import restraints will increase employment and may raise the equilibrium wage rate in the industry.[14] As this example illustrates, unions and management may have a common interest in supporting government policies that shift the demand curve for output and thus labor. As we will discuss in Chapter 18, however, import restrictions, while helping firms and currently employed workers in the protected industries, are likely to adversely affect firms and workers outside these sectors.

The model of labor market behavior presented in this chapter has here been used to explain how unions affect wages. If unions are successful in driving such wages above equilibrium, the model can also be used to analyze the consequences of this wage increase. First, as wages rise above the market-clearing level, employment will be reduced. Second, as union wages rise the number of people wanting union jobs increases. Limited job opportunities, however, will make it difficult for many of these people to find work, and a surplus of labor will develop in the unionized markets. (See Chapters 3 and 16 for an analysis of union effects on wages and employment in nonunion labor markets.) This surplus will exist even if unions have caused the demand for labor to shift, as long as the union wage is above the equilibrium wage.

## Effects of Laws Designed to Help Workers

As is the case with union effects, we will more thoroughly examine in later chapters the effects of protective labor legislation; however, the simple model discussed here yields some initial insights about such laws. In the 1970s and 1980s Congress and our court system have made many decisions that they believed would help workers. For example, in 1970 the Occupational Safety and Health Administration, a federal agency, was set up in order to increase levels of safety on the job. In 1986, Congress passed legislation outlawing mandatory retirement for most workers, an act designed to protect the interests of older workers. In 1974 the Employee Retirement Income Security Act (ERISA), which is intended to protect workers' pension incomes, was passed. In the last 10 to 15 years, state courts have made it increasingly difficult for companies to discharge workers. Under the so-called employment-at-will doctrine, an employer was free to fire workers for any reason that did not violate our laws. However, as of 1986, 23 states held that explicit or implicit promises of job security by firms constituted "implied contracts" and were sufficient to invalidate the employment-at-will principle.

While the protective laws and court decisions apply to different kinds of issues, they have at least one thing in common: they each require employers

---

[14] The industry's equilibrium wage will be raised as long as the labor supply curve to the industry in the absence of unions is upward sloping rather than horizontal.

to increase a particular kind of worker benefit—job safety, pension income, job security, and so forth. Each of these benefit increases costs employers money: raising safety often means buying new equipment; increasing pension income means a direct increase in outlays; limiting firms' abilities to discharge workers may mean reduced flexibility or a requirement to tolerate poor performance. Unless workers accept wage cuts equivalent to these increases in firms' costs, one effect of these government actions will be to increase either the total cost of labor per unit of time hired (in the case of OSHA or ERISA) or the total cost of labor per unit of output produced (in the case of the implied contract exception to employment-at-will). In either case, firms will move leftward along their labor demand curves and workers will end up paying for at least some of the costs imposed by public policy through a decline in employment.

## Job Evaluation and the Links Between Internal and External Labor Markets

Large companies set many of their wage and salary levels internally; for them, the assumption of a horizontal supply curve of labor at the market wage (see Figure 2.7), as noted, may not seem realistic. However, in practice the external labor market has a strong influence on company wage decisions through the process of job evaluation. A job-evaluation program is a systematic plan to determine the relative worth of a company's jobs and is an aid in establishing pay differentials across these jobs. A recent survey showed that about 86 percent of large and medium-sized companies used a formal job-evaluation system. The importance of the external labor market is indicated by the finding that among those companies practicing job evaluation, 99 percent used market wage surveys (their own or bought from others) in setting their internal wage structures.[15]

Job evaluation plans rate jobs according to factors that companies or labor markets value, which are termed *compensable factors*.[16] Such factors may include skill, responsibility, effort, and working conditions. A plan rates each job according to these dimensions, as indicated in Table 2.8.

How do companies use this internal information to set general pay levels for these jobs and for the particular individuals in each job? The crucial decision concerns what weights to place on the compensable factors. For example, how much should an increase of, say, ten points in skill be worth? The answer begins with the grouping of jobs into those filled by workers from the external labor market (often called "key jobs") and those filled by promotion from within the company that are unique in content to the firm ("non-key jobs"). The key jobs usually are common in content across firms. Wage surveys and statistical analyses are then used to find out how the market

---

[15] See T. Mahoney, B. Rosen, and S. Rynes, "Where Do Compensation Specialists Stand on Comparable Worth?" *Compensation Review* 16 (Fourth Quarter 1984): 27–40.

[16] This description of job evaluation is based on D. Schwab, "Job Evaluation and Pay Setting: Concepts and Practices," in E. R. Livernash (ed.), *Comparable Worth: Issues and Alternatives* (Washington, DC: Equal Employment Advisory Council, 1980): 51–77.

**Table 2.8**   A Hypothetical Job-Evaluation System

| Job | Points for Skill | Points for Responsibility | Points for Working Conditions | Points for Effort |
|---|---|---|---|---|
| A | 50 | 60 | 30 | 50 |
| B | 60 | 70 | 25 | 45 |
| C | 70 | 90 | 20 | 60 |
| D | 80 | 80 | 15 | 55 |

weights additional skill points in the key jobs—for example, a company may find that ten more skill points are worth an extra $1000 in the external labor market (we will analyze this situation in more detail in Example 9.1). These weights can then be used to help set pay in the non-key jobs.

The market wage surveys for the key jobs form the link between internal and external labor markets. We should point out that job evaluation is not the only information used in setting pay. For example, within a particular job, companies often use performance evaluation and merit pay to differentiate among individual workers, as we will discuss later in Chapters 8 and 9. However, just as in the case of the horizontal supply curve of labor (see Figure 2.7), in the real world of job evaluation, the firm suffers if its market information is out-of-date. For example, if market wages for a firm's key jobs have increased and if this rise is not reflected in the job evaluation salary weights, the firm will have recruiting and turnover problems. On the other hand, if the firm raises wages in its key jobs as a result of market forces, then a job evaluation system would also imply raises in its non-key jobs. Therefore, even though the labor market for non-key jobs is internal, in the sense that the positions are filled by promotion from within, wages in such jobs are still affected by the external labor market.

## Consequences of Departures from Market Equilibrium Wages

We have shown earlier that when wages are out of equilibrium in competitive labor markets, excess supplies of—or excess demand for—labor tend to push wages back to their equilibrium levels. As noted in the case of unions, however, wages may be held above equilibrium, or employers (by accident or design) may pay wages above market-clearing levels. In either case we would observe long lines of applicants trying for a limited number of positions. In contrast, if wages are held below equilibrium, either unfilled vacancies will result or workers must be *forced* to take jobs, as was the case under the military draft. What are the consequences for society of these situations?

Taking first the case of above-equilibrium wages, which economists define as *overpayment*, employers are paying more than they have to in order to produce. They could cut wages and still find enough qualified workers for their job openings. In fact, if they did cut wages, they could expand output and make their product cheaper and more accessible to consumers. In addition, more workers want jobs than can find them. If wages are reduced a bit, more of these disappointed workers could find work. A wage above equilibrium thus causes consumer prices to be higher and output to be smaller than is possible, and it creates a situation in which not all workers who want the jobs in question can get them.

An interesting—although perhaps extreme—example of above-equilibrium wage rates could be seen in New York City in 1974–75. During this period New York City fire fighters and police officers were receiving salaries roughly 40-percent greater than skilled mechanics and machinists working in the city and some 50-percent greater than area truck drivers. Perhaps the most convincing evidence of "overpayment" and the attendant surplus is that there were enormous numbers of qualified applicants who had passed job-related tests and were waiting for openings. For fire fighters, there were about 12,000 qualified applicants—compared to a total employment of only 10,000—at a time when the city was not even hiring fire fighters. For police officers, there were more than 42,000 qualified applicants on the waiting list, 23,000 current employees, and no hiring to speak of.[17]

An even larger surplus existed for sanitation workers, whose $14,770 yearly salary (in 1974 dollars) was 60-percent higher than the area average for laborers or materials handlers. In that department, there were 36,849 on the waiting list of people who had passed a job-related examination—or 3.4 qualified applicants for each current employee! Again, hiring was almost nil during this period. These numbers clearly point to a "labor surplus"—and thus to "overpayment."

To better understand the social losses attendant to overpayment, let us return to the principles of normative economics. Can it be shown that reducing overpayment will create a situation in which the gainers gain more than the losers lose? Suppose in the case of sanitation workers that only the wages of *newly hired* sanitation workers were lowered—to $10,000, say. Current workers thus do not lose, but many laborers working at $9200 per year (the prevailing wage for them in 1974) will jump at the chance to take a $10,000-a-year job. Taxpayers, knowing that garbage-collection services can now be expanded at lower cost than before will increase their demand for such services, thus creating jobs for these new workers.[18] Thus, some workers gain while no one loses—and social well-being is clearly enhanced.[19]

It should be noted that if the wages of *current* sanitation workers were lowered, city taxpayers could obtain their current level of service for less

---

[17] Sharon P. Smith, *Equal Pay in the Public Sector: Fact or Fantasy?* (Princeton, NJ: Industrial Relations Section, Princeton University, Research Report Series No. 122, 1977): 20.

[18] These new workers, of course, have wanted sanitation jobs with New York City all along, but the high wage prevented job opportunities in that field from expanding.

[19] If the workers who switch jobs are getting paid approximately what they are worth to their former employers, these employers lose $9200 in output but save $9200 in costs; their welfare is thus not affected. The presumption that employees are paid what they are worth to the employer is discussed at length in Chapter 3.

money. Their gains (in tax savings) equal the income losses of sanitation workers, and if we are to arrange the transaction so that no one loses, the gainers would have to compensate the losers by restoring their lost income. For this reason we have assumed that salaries for current sanitation workers are not cut.

A classic example of below-equilibrium wages were those in the U.S. Army. In 1962, for example, when the military draft was in effect, the military paid enlisted personnel salaries and allowances that came to around 80 percent of the earnings of comparably aged civilian workers. Total compensation was so low for the job that an enormous gap between demand and supply existed. As a result a large percentage of all new recruits had to be *drafted* to deal with the shortage. A decade later, when shortages could no longer be met through conscription, salaries and allowances for enlisted personnel had risen to 95 percent of the civilian wage.

How do these definitions of underpayment and overpayment accord with notions of fairness or equity? They square very well with the concept of *horizontal equity*—treating equals equally. If the equilibrium wage were paid to each worker in a particular labor market, no one would be underpaid or overpaid. Equal workers would receive equal pay for essentially the same work. These definitions, however, are ambiguous in relation to the concept of *vertical equity*—treating different groups differently.

How can we justify paying a professor more or less than a sanitation worker? The answer suggested by our definitions is that it is less a matter of justice than it is of getting the job done. We have to pay professors and sanitation workers whatever it takes to get them to provide the level of services we desire. If so few people want to collect garbage that it requires a relatively high wage to attract them, so be it. If we are to have this valuable service performed without resorting to involuntary servitude, there is no choice but to pay the wages necessary to attract the required number and quality of workers.

# REVIEW QUESTIONS

1. The Central Intelligence Agency (CIA) finds out that compensation for coal miners in the Soviet Union is rising much faster than compensation in general in that country. It knows that the Soviet labor market is free in the sense that it relies on incentives (not compulsion) in the allocation process. What can the CIA infer from this sharp rise in mining wages? Can it infer that coal output is increasing? Explain your answers.

2. Analyze the impact of the following changes on wages and employment in a given occupation.
   a. A decrease in the danger of the occupation.
   b. An increase in product demand.
   c. Increased wages in alternative occupations.

3. What would happen to the wages and employment levels of engineers if government expenditures on research and development programs were to fall? Show the effect graphically.

4. Suppose a particular labor market were in equilibrium. What could happen to cause the equilibrium wage to fall? If all money wages rose each year, how would this market adjust?
5. Assume that you have been hired by a company to do a salary survey of its arc welders, who the company suspects are overpaid. Given the company's expressed desire to maximize profits, what definition of "overpaid" would you apply in this situation and how would you identify whether arc welders were, in fact, overpaid?
6. How will a fall in the civilian unemployment rate affect the supply of recruits for the volunteer army? What will be the effect on military wages?
7. Suppose a state government requires all auto mechanics in its jurisdiction to pass competency examinations before they offer their services to the public. What will this licensing requirement do to the wages and employment levels of auto mechanics in the state?

# SELECTED READINGS

John T. Dunlop and Walter Galenson, eds., *Labor in the Twentieth Century* (New York: Academic Press, 1978).

George Milkovich and Jerry Newman, *Compensation, 2nd ed.* (Plano, Texas: Business Publications, Inc., 1987).

Simon Rottenberg, "On Choice in Labor Markets," *Industrial and Labor Relations Review 9* (January 1956): pp. 183–99; Robert J. Lampman, "On Choice in Labor Markets: Comment," *Industrial and Labor Relations Review 9* (July 1956): pp. 629–36; and "On Choice in Labor Markets: Reply," *Industrial and Labor Relations Review 9* (July 1956): 636–41.

# PART 2

## The Demand for, and Supply of, Labor

# CHAPTER 3

## The Demand for Labor

The demand for labor is a derived demand. In most cases, employers hire labor not for the direct satisfaction that such an action brings them, but rather for the contribution they believe labor can make toward producing something for sale. Not surprisingly, then, employers' demand for labor is a function of the characteristics of the product market. Employers' demand is also a function of the characteristics of the production process—more specifically, the ease with which labor can be substituted for capital and other factors of production. Finally, the demand for labor is a function not only of the price of labor, but also of the prices of other factors of production. This chapter and the next will illustrate how knowledge of the characteristics of the demand for labor can be used in various policy and business applications.

For purposes of making or evaluating social policy, the demand for labor has two important features. The first is that it can be shown theoretically—and demonstrated empirically—that labor-demand curves slope downward. The second important feature of the demand for labor is the *degree of responsiveness* of this demand to wage changes. While it is always true (all else equal) that the quantity of labor demanded declines as the wage increases, in some cases this decline is larger than in other cases. For most policy issues, the degree of responsiveness is of critical importance. Thus, we will discuss the forces that determine this responsiveness and suggest ways in which policy makers can estimate the degree of responsiveness in situations for which explicit empirical estimates are not available.

When analyzing the demand for labor, two sets of distinctions are typically made. First, one must specify whether one is concentrating on demand by *firms* or on the demand curves for an entire *market*. As noted in Chapter 2, firm and market-labor demand curves will have different properties, although they will both slope downward. Second, one must specify the *time* period for which the demand curve is drawn: the short run or the long run. The *short run* is defined as a period over which a firm's capital stock is fixed; the only input that is free to be varied is labor. The *long run* is defined as a period over which a firm is free to vary all factors of production, in this case both labor and capital. This distinction between short run and long run is conceptual, and the two concepts do not necessarily correspond closely to any actual period of calendar time. For example, an owner of a steel mill may find that it takes several years to construct a new steel plant, in which case anything less than two years might be considered the short run. In contrast, a small firm that hires people to shovel driveways may find that it can vary its capital stock instantaneously (by buying new shovels). In this case, the firm may never face the short run because it will always be making decisions about both labor and capital. Even though the short run and long run do not correspond neatly to specified calendar periods of time, the distinction does allow us to be more specific about the different forces that influence the demand for labor.

# A Simple Model of Labor Demand

Our analysis of the demand for labor begins with a simple model that yields very basic, but fundamental, behavioral predictions. To simplify the discussion, this model is derived using four assumptions noted below. Later in the chapter, two of the assumptions are dropped to see what differences they make. A third assumption is dropped in Chapter 4.

## The Assumptions

When analyzing employers' demands for labor, we will make four assumptions. First, we will assume that employers seek to maximize *profit* (the difference between the revenue they take in from the sales of their product and their costs of production). This is a standard assumption of positive economics, but it is not absolutely necessary to derive the fundamental conclusion of the chapter—namely, that the demand for labor is a downward sloping function of the wage rate.[1]

Second, we will initially assume that firms employ two homogeneous factors of production—labor and capital—in their production of goods and services. That is, we assume that there is a two-factor *production function* that indicates how various amounts of labor ($L$) and capital ($K$) can be combined to produce output ($Q$):

$$Q = f(L, K) \tag{3.1}$$

In equation (3.1), $f$ stands for "a function of" and is used to represent a *general* mathematical relationship between $Q$ and the factors of production.

---

[1] Totally impulsive or random demand patterns are consistent with downward-sloping demand curves if people or firms have limited resources. This point is made by Gary Becker in "Irrational Behavior and Economic Theory," *Journal of Political Economy* 70 (February 1962): 1–13.

The *specific* relationship between $Q$ and the two factors of production depends on the technology utilized. Later in this chapter we expand this two-factor assumption, noting that there are many different categories of labor. Firms also use other inputs besides *capital* (defined as machinery, equipment, and structures) in their production process, including materials and energy.

Third, we will assume that the hourly wage cost is the only cost of labor. We will initially ignore hiring and training costs as well as those fringe-benefit costs (like holiday pay, vacation pay, and sick leave as well as many forms of social insurance) that do not vary with weekly hours of work. By ignoring these costs here and by assuming that the length of the work week is fixed, we gloss over the distinction between the number of employees that a firm hires and the total number of person-hours of labor that it employs.[2] In Chapter 4 we will drop our simplifying assumption and consider the question of how a firm determines its optimal length of work week—as well as how hiring, training, and nonvariable fringe-benefit costs affect the demand for labor.

Finally, we will initially assume that both a firm's labor market and its product market are competitive. If the firm's labor market is competitive, we can treat the wage rate that it must pay its workers as given; if its product market is competitive, we can treat the product price it faces as given. (Both of these assumptions are relaxed later in the chapter.) The following analyses of labor demand by the firm, in both the long and the short run, are primarily nontechnical.

## Short-Run Demand for Labor by Firms

In the short run, when a firm's capital stock ($K$) and production function are not free to vary, it can be seen from equation (3.1) that the number of units of output that a firm produces can change only if it changes the number of units of labor that it employs. The additional output that can be produced by a firm when it employs one additional unit of labor, with capital held constant, is called the *marginal product of labor* ($MP_L$). For example, if a car dealership can sell 10 cars a month with one salesperson and 21 cars a month with two, the marginal product of hiring one salesperson is 10, and the marginal product of hiring the second is 11 cars per month. If a third equally persuasive salesperson is hired and sales rise to 26 per month, the marginal product of hiring the third salesperson is 5 cars per month. These hypothetical data are summarized in Table 3.1.

Table 3.1 shows that adding an extra salesperson increases output (cars sold) in each case. As long as output *increases* as labor is added, labor's marginal product (the change in output brought about by adding another unit of labor) is *positive*. In our example, however, the marginal product of labor increased at first (from 10 to 11), but then fell (to 5). Why?

The initial rise in marginal product is *not* because the second salesperson is better than the first; we ruled out this possibility by our assumption (already

---

[2] Person-hours, also called labor-hours, are calculated by multiplying the number of employees by the average length of work week per employee.

**Table 3.1**    The Marginal Product of Labor in a Hypothetical Car
Dealership (capital held constant)

| Number of Salespersons | Total Cars Sold | Marginal Product of Labor |
|:----------------------:|:---------------:|:-------------------------:|
| 0 | 0 | |
| 1 | 10 | 10 |
| 2 | 21 | 11 |
| 3 | 26 | 5 |

stated) that labor is homogeneous. Rather, the rise could be the result of the
two salespeople generating promotional ideas or helping each other out in
some way. Eventually, however, as more salespeople are hired, the marginal
product of labor must fall. A fixed building (remember capital is held constant) can contain only so many customers, and thus each additional increment of labor produces progressively smaller increments of output. This law
of *diminishing marginal returns* is an empirical proposition that derives from
the fact that as employment expands, each additional worker has a progressively smaller share of the capital stock to work with.

For expository convenience, we will assume that the marginal product of
labor is always decreasing.[3] Figure 3.1 shows a marginal-product-of-labor
schedule ($MP_L$) for a representative firm. In this figure, the marginal product
of labor is tabulated on the vertical axis and the number of units of labor
employed on the horizontal axis. The negative slope of the schedule indicates
that each additional unit of labor employed produces a progressively smaller
(but still positive) increment in output.

---

[3] We lose nothing by this assumption, because we show later in this section that a competitive firm
will never be operated at a point where its marginal product of labor schedule is increasing.

**Figure 3.1**    Demand for Labor in the Short Run

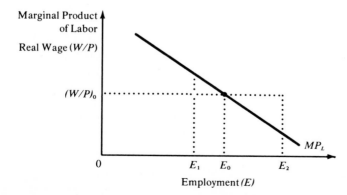

The marginal product of labor is measured as units of added output per unit increase of labor. Suppose we denote the money (nominal) wage rate that the firm pays per unit of labor by $W$ and its product price per unit of output by $P$. These variables have dimensions of dollars per unit of labor and dollars per unit of output, respectively. Thus, the *real wage rate* that the firm pays—its money wage divided by its price level ($W/P$)—also has the dimension *units of output per unit of labor*. For example, if a woman is paid \$10 per hour and the product she makes sells for \$2, she gets paid—from the firm's point of view—five units of output per hour ($10 \div 2$). These five units represent her real wage, and because the real wage and the marginal product of labor are both measured in the same dimension, we can plot both on the vertical axis of Figure 3.1.[4]

In the short run, a firm's demand-for-labor curve coincides with the downward-sloping portion of its marginal-product-of-labor schedule. This result arises from the assumption that firms seek to maximize profit. To accomplish this objective, a firm should employ labor up until the point that the marginal revenue (or additional revenue) it receives from hiring the last employee is just equal to its marginal (or additional) cost of employing that worker. A firm's profit is simply equal to revenues minus costs, so if its marginal revenue exceeds its marginal cost, then overall profits can be increased by expanding employment. Analogously, if its marginal revenue is less than its marginal cost, a firm is losing money on the last unit of labor hired, and it could increase its profit by reducing employment. To maximize profit, therefore, employment should be at the level at which the marginal revenue of hiring the last unit of labor is just equal to its marginal cost.

Given the assumptions that we have made, the marginal cost of an additional unit of labor is simply the money wage rate ($W$) that must be paid. The marginal revenue of hiring an additional unit of labor, or labor's *marginal revenue product, (MRP)*, is equal to the value of the additional output produced. *MRP* equals the marginal product of labor multiplied by the additional revenue that is received per unit of output ($MR$):

$$MRP = (MP_L)(MR). \qquad (3.2)$$

Assuming that a firm sells its output in a competitive market—and hence that product price does not vary with output—the additional revenue per unit of output is simply the firm's product price ($P$). Thus, for firms that operate in competitive output markets, the marginal revenue product obtained from an additional unit of labor equals the product price for the firm's output multiplied by its marginal product of labor:

$$MRP = (P)(MP_L). \qquad (3.3)$$

The marginal revenue of labor is just equal to its marginal cost—and profits

---

[4] For simplicity, here we do not distinguish between the firm's product price and the overall price level. Thus the real wage ($W/P$) represents both the per unit cost of workers (in terms of output) to the firm and the purchasing power of a worker's earnings.

are maximized by the competitive firm—at the point where the marginal revenue product equals the money wage:

$$(P)(MP_L) = W. \tag{3.4}$$

Dividing both sides of equation (3.4) by the firm's product price yields an alternative way of stating the profit-maximizing condition, which is that labor should be hired until its marginal product equals the real wage:

$$MP_L = W/P. \tag{3.5}$$

Given any real wage (by the market), the firm should thus employ labor to the point at which the marginal product of labor just equals the real wage. In other words, *the firm's demand for labor in the short run is equivalent to the downward-sloping segment of its marginal-product-of-labor schedule.*[5] To see that this is true, pick any real wage—for example, the real wage denoted by $(W/P)_0$ in Figure 3.1. We have asserted that the firm's demand for labor will be equal to its marginal-product-of-labor schedule and consequently that the firm would employ $E_0$ employees. Now suppose that a firm initially employed $E_2$ workers as indicated in Figure 3.1, where $E_2$ is any employment level greater than $E_0$. At the employment level $E_2$, the marginal product of labor is less than the real wage rate; the marginal cost of the last unit of labor hired is therefore greater than its marginal revenue product. As a result, profit could be increased by reducing the level of employment. Similarly, suppose instead that a firm initially employed $E_1$ employees, where $E_1$ is *any* employment level less than $E_0$. Given the specified real wage $(W/P)_0$, the marginal product of labor is greater than the real wage rate at $E_1$—and consequently the marginal revenue that an additional unit of labor produces is greater than its marginal cost. As a result, a firm could increase its profit level by expanding its level of employment.

Hence, to maximize profit, given any real wage rate, a firm should stop employing labor at the point where any additional labor would cost more than it would produce. This profit-maximization rule implies two things. First, the firm should employ labor up to the point where its real wage equals the marginal product of labor—but not beyond that point. Second, its profit-maximizing level of employment will lie in the range where its marginal product of labor is *declining*. (If $W/P = MP_L$, but $MP_L$ is *increasing*, then adding another unit of labor will create a situation where marginal product *exceeds* $W/P$. As long as adding labor causes $MP_L$ to exceed $W/P$, the profit-maximizing firm will continue to hire labor. It will only stop hiring when an extra unit of labor would reduce $MP_L$ below $W/P$, which will only happen when $MP_L$ is declining. Thus, the only employment levels that could possibly be consistent with profit maximization are those in the range where $MP_L$ is decreasing.)

---

[5] One should add here, "provided that the firm's revenue exceeds its labor costs." Above some real wage level this may fail to occur, and the firm will go out of business (employment will drop to zero).

The demand curve for labor can therefore be thought of in two equivalent ways. It may be thought of as the *downward-sloping section of the firm's marginal-product-of-labor schedule*—in which case it indicates how many units of labor will be hired at each *real wage*. Alternatively, it can be thought of as the *downward-sloping portion of the firm's marginal-revenue product-of-labor schedule*—which is simply the *marginal product* schedule multiplied by *marginal revenue* (or product price, for a competitive firm). In this second case, the labor demand curve indicates the profit-maximizing level of employment for any given *money* wage. Which version of the demand curve one employs depends solely on analytical convenience, because they are equivalent alternatives. In Example 3.1, which reviews some of the important aspects of the demand for labor in a concrete way, it is more convenient to express the demand curve in terms of marginal revenue product of labor.

It is important to emphasize that the marginal product of any given individual is *not* a function solely of his or her personal characteristics. It should be clear from Figure 3.1 and Example 3.1 that the marginal product of a worker depends upon the number of employees that the firm has already hired. Similarly, an individual's marginal product depends upon the size of the firm's capital stock; increases in the firm's capital stock shift the entire marginal-product-of-labor schedule up. It is therefore incorrect to speak of an individual's productivity as being an immutable factor that is associated only with his or her characteristics, independent of the characteristics of the other inputs that he or she has to work with.

**Objections to the marginal productivity theory of demand.** Two kinds of objections are sometimes raised to the theory of labor demand introduced in this section. Examples of the first kind are that firms do not know what labor's $MP_L$ is, that almost no employer can ever be heard uttering the words "marginal revenue product of labor," and that the theory assumes a degree of sophistication on the part of employers that just is not there. These objections can be answered as follows: whether employers can verbalize the profit-maximization conditions or not, they must instinctively *know* them to survive in a competitive environment. Competition will "weed out" employers who are not good at generating profits, just as competition will weed out pool players who do not understand the intricacies of how speed, angles, and spin affect the motion of bodies through space. Yet one could canvas the pool halls of America and probably not find one player who could verbalize Newton's laws of motion! The point is that firms can *follow* rules without being able to verbalize them. Those who are not good at maximizing profits will not last very long in competitive markets. Conversely, the survivors are those who, whether they can verbalize the general rules or not, *do* know how to maximize profits. As our discussion in Example 3.2 of the Upjohn Company indicates, at least one company is trying to maximize its return.

The second type of objection to the marginal productivity theory of demand is that in many cases it seems that adding labor while holding capital constant would not add to output at all. For example, one secretary and one

EXAMPLE 3.1

## Store Detectives and the Optimal Rate of Shoplifting

At a business conference one day, a department-store executive was boasting that his store had reduced theft to 1 percent of total sales. His colleague shook her head slowly and said, "I think that's too low. I figure it should be about 2 percent of sales."

How can more shoplifting be better than less? The answer is based on the fact that reducing theft is costly in itself! A profit-maximizing firm will not want to take steps to reduce shoplifting if the added costs it must bear in so doing exceed the value of the savings it generates.

The table below shows a hypothetical marginal revenue product (*MRP*) schedule for department-store detectives. Hiring one detective would, in this example, save $50 worth of thefts per hour. Two detectives could save $90 worth of thefts each hour, or $40 more than hiring just one. The *MRP* of hiring a second detective is thus $40. A third detective would add $20 worth more to thefts prevented, and thus adds $20 more to revenues.

| Number of Detectives on Duty During Each Hour Store Is Open | Total Value of Thefts Prevented per Hour | Marginal Value of Thefts Prevented per Hour (MRP) |
|---|---|---|
| 0 | $ 0 | $ — |
| 1 | 50 | 50 |
| 2 | 90 | 40 |
| 3 | 110 | 20 |
| 4 | 115 | 5 |
| 5 | 117 | 2 |

The *MRP* does *not* decline from $40 to $20 because the added detectives are incompetent; in fact, we shall assume that all are equally alert and well trained. *MRP* declines, in part, because surveillance equipment (capital) is fixed; with each added detective, there is less equipment per person. However, the *MRP* also declines because it becomes progressively harder to generate savings. With just a few detectives, the only thieves caught will be the more obvious, less-experienced shoplifters. As more detectives are hired it becomes possible to prevent theft by the more expert shoplifters, but they are harder to detect and fewer in number. Thus, *MRP* falls because theft prevention becomes more difficult once all those who are easy to catch are apprehended.

To draw the demand curve for labor we need to determine how many detectives the store will want to employ at any given wage. For example, at a wage of $50 per hour, how many detectives will the store want? Using the *MRP* = *W* criterion it is easy to see that the answer is "one." At $40 per hour, the store would want to hire two, and at $20 per hour the number demanded would be three. The demand for labor curve that summarizes the store's profit-maximizing employment of detectives is given in the accompanying graph.

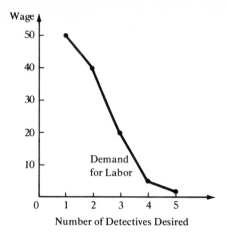

The graph illustrates a fundamental point; the demand-for-labor curve in the short run slopes downward because it *is* the *MRP* curve—and the *MRP* curve slopes downward because of diminishing marginal productivity. The demand curve and the *MRP* curve coincide, as demonstrated by the fact that if one were to graph the *MRP* schedule in the table, one would arrive at exactly the same curve as in our graph. When one person is hired, *MRP* is $50; when two people are hired, *MRP* is $40, and so forth. Since *MRP* always equals *W* for a profit maximizer, the *MRP* and labor-demand curves expressed as functions of the money wage must be the same.

Another point to be made in this example is that there is some level of shoplifting that the store finds more profitable to tolerate than to eliminate. At high wages for store detectives, the store will find it profitable to eliminate less theft than it will at lower wages. To say the theft rate is "too low" thus implies that the marginal costs of crime reduction exceed the marginal savings generated, and the firm is therefore failing to maximize profits.

typewriter can produce output, but it might seem that adding a second secretary (holding the number of typewriters constant) could produce nothing extra, since that secretary would have no machine on which to work. The answer to this objection is that the second secretary could address envelopes by hand—a slower process, but one that would allow the secretary at the typewriter to type more letters per day. The two secretaries could trade off using the typewriter, so that neither becomes fatigued to the extent that mistakes increase and typing slows down. The second secretary could also answer the telephone and in other ways expedite work. Thus, even with technologies that seem to require one machine per person, labor will generally have an *MRP* greater than zero (capital held constant).

**EXAMPLE 3.2**

## Marginal Productivity in Action— The Case of Upjohn

The essense of the theory of the demand for labor presented here is that profit-maximizing companies will hire additional amounts of labor until the marginal revenue product of labor equals its marginal cost. In deciding on its staffing policy, the firm compares the costs and benefits of changes in its employment levels. Such a policy has been in use at The Upjohn Company, which is a major producer of pharmaceutical products and is located in Kalamazoo, Michigan.

Each of the 17 businesses owned by Upjohn submits each year to the company's office of planning and budgeting a five-year plan for investment in capital and human resources. In evaluating these requests, the planning and budgeting office uses the concept of value added to gauge the potential return on these investments:

Value Added = Sales − Purchases of Goods and Services
            = Employee Costs + Capital Costs and Pretax Earnings.

Value added is a measure of the company's contribution to the economy's total output; it equals the total value of the firm's sales minus what it purchased from other companies.

To underscore the importance of the company's ultimate goal of profitability, trends in value added per dollar spent on employees and on capital are computed for each division. Suppose, for example, two divisions have the same value added per dollar spent on capital but one is achieving a higher value added per dollar spent on human resources. Then, other things being the same, the latter division would be a better candidate for an expansion in its human-resources budget. Of course, other factors must be considered in decisions like this—such as what the division wants to do with the increase in its human-resources budget and whether the overall return even in the best division warrants making the investment. Upjohn, however, is clearly implementing the basic principle behind the demand curve for labor. It adds labor only when the marginal revenue attributable to the additional expenditure on labor makes the investment a good one. In addition, the company carefully compares the marginal returns on various possible investments in labor and capital in various divisions. Upjohn is thus also conforming to the principles of the demand for labor in the long run in which profit-maximizing decisions regarding labor and capital are simultaneously made.

SOURCE: Henry L. Dahl, "Measuring the Human ROI," *Management Review* 68 (January 1979): 44–50. The author was, as of 1979, manager for employee development and planning at The Upjohn Company. "ROI" stands for "return on investment."

## Long-Run Demand for Labor by Firms

In the long run, employers are free to vary their capital stock as well as the number of workers that they employ. An increase in the wage rate will affect their desired employment levels for two reasons. First, wages affect employment through a *scale* or *output effect*. A profit-maximizing firm will produce up to the point where the marginal revenue from the last unit of output produced is just equal to its marginal cost of production. Now an increase in the wage rate tends to increase the marginal cost of production without affecting the marginal revenue. As a result, at the firm's previous equilibrium level of output, marginal cost *exceeds* marginal revenue. The firm is losing money on the last units of output that it produces, and it can increase its profits after the wage increase by cutting back on its production level. Reducing output will generally cause the firm to reduce its usage of both capital and labor.

The second reason why an increase in the wage rate affects a firm's desired employment level in the long run is that it induces *factor substitution*. To maximize profit, a firm must be minimizing the cost of producing whatever level of output it produces. This cost minimization is achieved when the last dollar the firm spends on employing capital yields the same increment to output as the last dollar that the firm spends employing labor. To illustrate this point, let us assume that a firm has a given level of output, $Q$, and is considering changing its mix of capital and labor to see if it can reduce cost. Suppose it finds that a dollar's worth of labor adds one unit of output to production, but a dollar's worth of capital adds two units to output. If it decreased its employment of labor by the equivalent of a dollar, and increased its employment of capital by the equivalent of 50 cents, it could produce output level $Q$ at a lower cost! The *current* mix of capital and labor in this example is clearly not profit-maximizing, and extending this reasoning leads to the conclusion that the firm will reach its optimal mix of inputs only when an added dollar spent on (or taken away from) labor and an added dollar spent on (or taken away from) capital lead to equal changes in output.

To better understand factor substitution, let $C$ represent the rental cost per period of a unit of capital equipment. This rental cost depends upon a number of things, including the purchase price of new capital equipment, the interest rate that a firm must pay on borrowed funds, and various provisions that affect the income-tax treatment of firms' investment expenditures (the specific formula for $C$ need not concern us here). Now, to minimize the cost of producing any given level of output, a firm must employ labor and capital up until the point at which the marginal cost of producing the last unit of output is the same regardless of whether capital or labor is employed in generating that last unit. A formal way of stating this requirement is that the wage divided by the marginal product of labor (which is the cost of producing an added unit of output using just labor) must equal the cost of capital ($C$) divided by the marginal product of capital ($MP_K$):

$$(W/MP_L) = (C/MP_K). \qquad (3.6)$$

We can rewrite equation (3.6) as

$$(W/C) = (MP_L/MP_K). \qquad (3.7)$$

Equation (3.7) indicates that to minimize its cost of production, a firm must employ capital and labor up until the point at which their relative marginal costs are just equal to their relative marginal productivities.

Consider what happens when wages increase and capital costs do not. The increase in $W/C$ distorts the equality in equation (3.7), and the left-hand side is now greater than the right-hand side. Since the marginal cost of producing a unit of output is now greater when a firm adds new labor than when it adds new capital, the firm has an incentive to substitute capital for labor—to increase its usage of capital and decrease its usage of labor. The increase in usage of capital leads to a decline in the marginal product of capital, while the decrease in usage of labor leads to an increase in the marginal product of labor. Eventually the equality in equation (3.7) is restored, with fewer workers employed.

## Market Demand Curves

The demand curve (or schedule) for an individual firm indicates how much labor that firm will want to employ at each real wage level. A *market demand curve* (or schedule) is just the *summation* of the labor demanded by all firms in a particular labor market at each level of the real wage.[6] If there are three firms in a certain labor market, and if at $(W/P)_0$ Firm A wants 12 workers, Firm B wants 6, and Firm C wants 20, then the market demand at $(W/P)_0$ is 38 employees. More importantly, because market demand curves are so closely derived from firm demand curves, they too will *slope downward* as a function of the real wage. When the real wage falls, the number of workers that existing firms want to employ increases. In addition, the lower real wage may make it profitable for new firms to enter the market. Conversely, when the real wage increases, the number of workers that existing firms want to employ decreases, and some firms may be forced to cease operations completely.

Figure 3.2 shows a hypothetical market demand-for-labor curve ($D_0$) and a labor supply curve ($S_0$). (Disregard the curve labeled $D_1$ for the moment.) The supply curve is drawn as an upward-sloping function of the real wage, since higher real wages induce more individuals to enter this labor market. In this competitive labor market, the equilibrium real wage ($W_0$) and employment ($E_0$) levels are determined by the intersection of the labor demand and supply curves. If the real wage were lower than $W_0$, then the number of workers that employers would want to hire would exceed the number of individuals who want to work. Employers, facing unfilled positions, would be forced to raise their real wage offers to eliminate the job vacancies. In contrast, if the real wage were above $W_0$, employers would face an excess

---

[6] If firm demand curves are drawn as a function of the money wage, they represent (as we noted) the downward-sloping portion of the firms' marginal revenue product curves. In a competitive industry, the price of the product is "given" to the firm, and thus at the firm level the marginal revenue product of labor has imbedded in it a given product price. When aggregating labor demand to the *market* level, product price can no longer be taken as given, and the aggregation is no longer a simple summation. However, the market demand curves drawn against money wages, like those drawn as the function of real wages, slope downward—which, at this point, is all that is important.

EXAMPLE   3.3

## Wages and the Substitution of Capital for Labor

Many capital investments reduce the amount of labor input needed to produce a given output level. For example, word processing equipment greatly lowers the amount of time spent retyping documents. The following situation shows that wage increases raise firms' incentives to substitute equipment for labor by raising the value of the labor time saved. Suppose a company is considering investing in robotic equipment and that higher expenditures on machinery save additional amounts of labor time:

| Robots Installed | Total Number of Workers Replaced | Marginal Number of Workers Replaced* |
|---|---|---|
| 1 | 5 | 5 |
| 2 | 8 | 3 |
| 3 | 10 | 2 |
| 4 | 11 | 1 |

* This is the change in total number of workers replaced divided by the change in the number of robots installed.

The table indicates that each additional robot saves a smaller increment of labor time. For example, at first robots could replace jobs involving lifting or moving materials, but as the factory became more automated, opportunities for replacing labor diminished. Suppose output is held fixed, and suppose the annual rental capital cost per robot were $120,000, while production labor cost $20 per hour. Assuming a 2000 hour work year (50 weeks of work at 40 hours per week), annual labor costs would be $40,000 per worker. It would clearly pay to install two robots, since a second robot would save an additional three workers or $120,000 per year, an amount equal to its marginal cost. In effect, the marginal revenue product of each robot is its additional savings in labor costs. However, if labor costs go up to $30 per hour, the third robot becomes worth installing because the value of the labor time it replaces has increased.

supply of applicants. The number of individuals willing to work would exceed the number of employees firms want to hire, and employers would eventually realize that they could reduce their real wage offers and still attract the necessary workers.[7]

[7] The reduction in real wages need not occur through a reduction in money wages. Rather, all that is required during a period when prices are rising is that money wages remain constant or rise less rapidly than product prices.

**Figure 3.2** Who Bears the Burden of an Employer-Financed Payroll Tax?

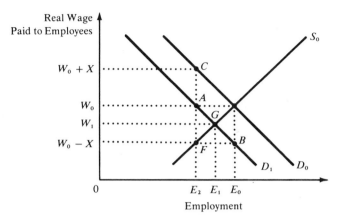

## Policy Application: Who Bears the Burden of the Payroll Tax?

In the United States, several social-insurance programs are financed by payroll taxes. Employers, and in some cases employees, make mandatory contributions of a fraction of the employees' salaries, up to a maximum level (or taxable wage base), to the social-insurance trust funds. For example, the Social Security retirement, disability, and Medicare programs (OASDHI) are financed by a payroll tax paid by both employers and employees, while in most states the unemployment insurance and workers' compensation insurance programs are financed solely by payroll-tax payments made by employers. It is not clear just why payroll taxes on *employers* are so heavily used in the social-insurance area. There seems to be a prevailing notion that such taxes result in employers "footing the bill" for the relevant programs—but this is not necessarily the case.

With our simple labor market model we can show that the party making the social-insurance payment is not necessarily the one that bears the burden of the tax. Suppose for expository convenience that only the employer is required to make payments and that the tax is a fixed dollar amount ($X$) per employee rather than a percentage of payroll. Now consider the demand curve $D_0$ in Figure 3.2—which is drawn in such a way that desired employment is plotted against the real wage *employees receive*. Prior to the imposition of the tax, the wage employees receive is the same as the wage employers pay. Thus, if $D_0$ were the demand curve before the tax was imposed, it would have the conventional interpretation of indicating how much labor a firm is willing to hire at any given wage. However, *after* imposition of the tax, employer wage costs are $X above what employees receive. Thus, if employees receive $W_0$, employers will face costs of $W_0 + X$. They will no longer demand $E_0$ workers; rather, because their costs are $W_0 + X$, they will demand $E_2$ workers. Point $A$ becomes a point on a *new* demand curve, formed when demand shifts down because of the tax (remember, the wage on the vertical axis of Figure 3.2 is the wage *employees receive* and not the wage employers pay). Only if employee wages fell to $W_0 - X$ would the firm want to continue hiring $E_0$ workers—for then *employer* costs would be the same as before the tax. Thus, point $B$ is also on the new, shifted demand curve. Note that with a tax of $X$, the new demand curve ($D_1$) is parallel to the old one and that the vertical distance between the two is $X$.

Now the tax-related shift in the demand curve to $D_1$ implies that there is an excess supply of labor at the previous equilibrium real wage of $W_0$. This surplus of labor creates downward pressure on the real wage, and this downward pressure continues to be exerted until the wage falls to $W_1$, the point at which the quantity of labor supplied just equals the quantity demanded. At this point, employment has also fallen to $E_1$. Thus, *employees* bear part of the burden of the payroll tax in the form of *lower wage rates and lower employment levels*. The lesson is clear; the party legally liable to make the contribution (the employer) is not necessarily the one that bears the full burden of the actual cost.

Figure 3.2, however, does suggest that employers will bear at least *some* of the burden of the tax, because the wages received by employees do not fall by the full amount of the tax ($W_0 - W_1$ is smaller than $X$, which is the vertical distance between the two demand curves). The reason for this is that with an upward-sloping supply curve, employees withdraw labor as their wages fall, and it becomes more difficult for firms to find workers. If wages fell to $W_0 - X$, the withdrawal of workers would create a labor shortage that would serve to drive wages to some point ($W_1$ in our example) between $W_0$ and $W_0 - X$. Only if the labor supply curve were *vertical*—meaning that lower wages have no effect on labor supply—would the *entire amount of the tax* be shifted to workers in the form of a decrease in their wages by the amount of $X$, as shown by supply curve $S_0$ in panel (a) of Figure 3.3.

In general, the extent to which the labor *supply curve* is *vertical* determines the proportion of the employer payroll tax that gets shifted to employees' wages. The more vertical the supply curve—that is, the less responsive labor supply is to changes in wages—the higher the proportion of the tax that gets shifted to workers in the form of a wage decrease. Panel (a) of Figure 3.3 shows that a payroll tax on the employer will depress employee wages more with supply curve $S_0'$ than with supply curve $S_0''$ (the wage corresponding to point $L$ is lower than that corresponding to point $M$). It must also be pointed out, however, that to the degree employee wages do *not* fall, employment levels will; employment losses with supply curve $S_0''$ are larger than with curve $S_0'$. When employee wages do not fall much in the face of an employer payroll tax increase, employer labor costs are increased—and this increase reduces the quantity of labor they demand.

**Figure 3.3**   Conditions That Affect the Shifting of an Employer Payroll Tax

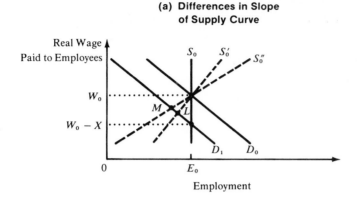

**(a) Differences in Slope of Supply Curve**

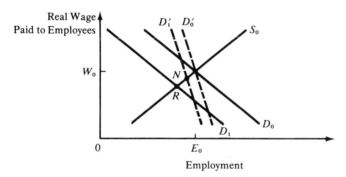

**(b) Differences in Slope of Demand Curve**

The other major influence on the extent to which payroll taxes are shifted to employees is the shape of the demand curve. If the demand curve is relatively horizontal—meaning that employer demand is very sensitive to changes in labor costs—there will be relatively large employment losses and strong downward pressures on employee wages. On the other hand, if employer demand is not very responsive to labor costs—and the demand curve is more vertical—both employment losses and employee wage changes will be smaller. These two conclusions are illustrated by the two sets of demand curves in panel (b) of Figure 3.3. The wage and employment levels for each initial demand curve ($D_0$ and $D_0'$) are assumed to be the same ($W_0$ and $E_0$). When an employer payroll tax of $X$ is imposed, it shifts *both demand curves down by the vertical distance of $X$,* so that the new curves are $D_1$ and $D_1'$.

Point $N$, which lies on the relatively vertical demand curve $D'_1$, is a lot closer to $W_0$ and $E_0$ than is point $R$—the intersection between the supply curve and the relatively horizontal demand curve $D_1$.

A number of empirical studies have sought to ascertain what fraction of employers' payroll tax costs are actually passed on to employees in the form of lower wages or lower wage increases. Although the evidence is by no means unambiguous, two studies concluded that less than half of employers' payroll tax contributions are actually shifted onto labor in the form of real wage decreases.[8]

## Modified Models of Labor Demand

### Monopoly in the Product Market

We have assumed so far that firms take product prices as given. If a firm faces a downward-sloping demand curve for its output—so that as it expands employment and output its product price falls—then the marginal revenue it receives from the last unit of output it produces is not the product price. Rather, the marginal revenue is less than the product price, because the lower price applies to all units it sells, not just the marginal unit. As a result equation (3.4) must be modified in the presence of product market monopoly. In the short run, labor should be employed up until the point at which the wage rate just equals the marginal revenue product of labor ($MRP$)—which, for a firm facing a downward-sloping demand curve in the output market, equals the marginal product of labor multiplied by the marginal revenue ($MR$):

$$(MR)(MP_L) \;=\; W. \tag{3.8}$$

Now one can express the demand for labor in the short run in terms of the real wage by dividing both sides of equation (3.8) by the firm's product price, $P$, to obtain

$$\frac{(MR)(MP_L)}{P} \;=\; \frac{W}{P}. \tag{3.9}$$

Since marginal revenue is always less than a monopoly's product price, the ratio ($MR/P$) in equation (3.9) is less than one. As such, the demand-for-labor curve for a firm that has monopoly power in the output market will lie below and to the left of the demand-for-labor curve for an *otherwise identical* firm that takes product price as given. Put another way, just as output is lower under monopoly than it is under competition, other things equal, so is the level of employment.

[8] Ronald G. Ehrenberg, Robert Hutchens, and Robert S. Smith, *The Distribution of Unemployment Insurance Benefits and Costs*, Technical Analysis Paper No. 58, ASPER, U.S. Department of Labor, October 1978; and Daniel Hamermesh, "New Estimates of the Incidence of the Payroll Tax," *Southern Economic Journal* 45 (February 1979): 1208–19.

**EXAMPLE   3.4**

## The 1986 Immigration Law and the Market for Labor in the Southern California Garment Industry

Prior to November 1986, employers who hired illegal aliens were subject to no legal sanctions, although the workers ran the risk of being caught and deported. But according to the Immigration Reform and Control Act of 1986, firms are not allowed to knowingly hire illegals after November 1986. Further, employers must examine and report on the documentation of new hires' immigration status. In addition, the Act calls for fines against firms in violation of the law and possible jail sentences for repeat-offending employers. The labor market effect of the new immigration law is to increase the costs of employing illegal aliens. The law is having a devastating effect on the garment industry in Southern California, which has thrived on the inexpensive labor of undocumented workers. Since 1980, annual sales of Los Angeles County apparel manufacturers have averaged a 7.1-percent increase, compared with a 3.3-percent nationwide figure for the apparel industry. However, under the new immigration law, garment producers in the Los Angeles area report that they are experiencing labor shortages at the relatively low wages for which illegal immigrants had been willing to work. The shortage (at existing low wage levels) has presumably come about because the new law has reduced the supply of workers who can be hired without penalties. Unfortunately for the local apparel industry, imports continue to provide an effective ceiling on the prices that can be charged. Thus, the higher labor costs that will result from the new law will succeed in driving more of the domestic industry overseas. While the law imposes penalties on employers, it is clear that many undocumented workers are also negatively affected, since jobs in the industry will be lost.

SOURCES:  Pauline Yoshihashi, "Garment Makers Struggle Under the Immigration Laws," *Wall Street Journal,* September 8, 1987, p. 6; Bruce D. May, "Law Puts Immigration Control in Employers' Hands," *Personnel Journal* 66 (March 1987): 106–11; U.S. Department of Commerce, *Statistical Abstract of the United States 1987* (Washington, DC: U.S. Government Printing Office, 1986): 722.

The *wage* rates that monopolies pay, however, are not necessarily different from competitive levels even though *employment* levels are. An employer with a product market monopoly may still be a very small part of the market for a particular kind of employee—and thus be a *price taker* in the labor market even though a *price maker* in the product market.[9] For example, a local utility company may have a product market monopoly, but it will have to compete with all other firms to hire secretaries and thus must pay the going wage.

[9] A *price taker* is someone who is such a small part of a particular market that he or she cannot influence market price. Thus, to such a person, the market price is a given. A *price maker* is someone with enough monopoly power that he or she can influence prices.

There are circumstances, however, where economists suspect that product market monopolies might pay wages that are *higher* than competitive firms would pay.[10] The monopolies that are legally permitted to exist in the United States are regulated by governmental bodies in an effort to prevent them from exploiting their favored status and earning monopoly profits. This regulation of profits, it can be argued, gives monopolies incentives to pay higher wages than they would otherwise pay for one of two reasons. First, regulatory bodies allow monopolies to pass the cost of doing business on to consumers. Thus, while unable to maximize profits, the managers of a monopoly can enhance their *utility* by paying high wages and passing the cost along to consumers in the form of higher prices. The ability to pay high wages makes a manager's life more pleasant by making it possible to hire people who might be more attractive or more personable or who have other characteristics managers find desirable.

Second, monopolies that are as yet unregulated may not want to attract attention to themselves by earning the very high profits usually associated with monopoly. They, too, may therefore be induced to pay high wages in a partial effort to "hide" their profits. The excess profits of monopolies, in other words, may be partly taken in the form of highly preferred workers—paid a relatively high wage—rather than in the usual monetary form.

The evidence on monopoly wages, however, is not very clear as yet. Some studies suggest that monopolies *do* pay higher wages than competitive firms for workers with the same education and experience, while others find no such evidence.[11]

## Monopsony in the Labor Market

When only one firm is the buyer of labor in a particular labor market, such a firm is called a *monopsonist.* Because the firm is the only demander of labor in this market, it can influence the wage rate. Rather than being a *price (wage) taker,* and facing the horizontal labor supply curve that competitive firms are confronted with, monopsonists face an upward-sloping supply curve. The supply curve confronting them, in other words, is the *market* supply curve. To expand its work force, a monopsonist must increase its wage rate. (In contrast, a competitive firm can expand its work force while paying the prevailing market wage as long as that wage is not below market-clearing levels.) Conversely, if a monopsonist lowers wages it will lose some, but not all, of its employees (a competitive firm would lose them all).

[10] For a full statement of this argument, see Armen Alchian and Reuben Kessel, "Competition, Monopoly, and the Pursuit of Money," H. G. Lewis (ed.), *Aspects of Labor Economics* (Princeton, NJ: Princeton University Press, 1962).

[11] James Dalton and E. J. Ford, "Concentration and Labor Earnings in Manufacturing and Utilities," *Industrial and Labor Relations Review* (October 1977): 45–60; Ronald Ehrenberg, *The Regulatory Process and Labor Earnings* (New York: Academic Press, 1979); Leonard W. Weiss, "Concentration and Labor Earnings," *American Economic Review* 56 (March 1966): 96–117; and James Long and Albert Link, "The Impact of Market Structure on Wages, Fringe Benefits and Turnover," *Industrial and Labor Relations Review* 36 (January 1983): 239–50.

**Figure 3.4**   The Effects of Monopsony

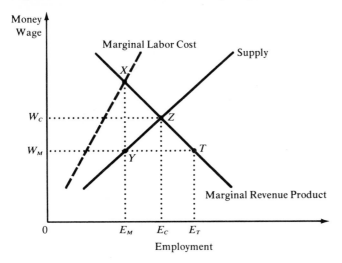

The unusual aspect of a *firm's* being confronted with an upward-sloping labor supply curve is that the *marginal cost of hiring labor exceeds the wage.* If a competitive firm wants to hire 10 workers instead of 9, the hourly cost of the additional worker is equal to the wage rate. If a monopsonist hires 10 instead of 9, it must pay a higher wage to all workers *in addition to* paying the bill for the added worker. For example, suppose that a monopsonist could get 9 workers if it paid $7 per hour but that if it wishes to hire 10 workers it would have to pay a wage of $7.50. The labor cost associated with 9 workers is $63 per hour (9 times $7), but the labor cost associated with 10 workers is $75 per hour (10 times $7.50). Hiring the additional worker cost $12 per hour—which is far higher than the $7.50 wage rate![12]

The fact that the marginal cost of hiring labor is above the wage rate affects the labor market behavior of monopsonists. In maximizing profits, any firm should hire labor until the point where marginal revenue product equals marginal cost. Since the marginal cost of hiring labor for a monopsonist is *above* the wage rate, it will stop hiring labor at some point where marginal revenue product is above the wage rate. In terms of Figure 3.4, the monopsonist hires $E_M$ workers because at that point marginal revenue product equals marginal labor costs (point $X$). However, the wage rate necessary to attract $E_M$ workers to the firm—which can be read off the supply curve—is $W_M$ (see point $Y$). Thus, wages are below marginal revenue product for a monopsonist.

---

[12] We assume here that the monopsonist does not know which workers it can hire for $7 per hour and which workers could only be hired at $7.50. All it knows is that if it wants to hire 10 workers it must pay $7.50, while if it wants to hire 9 it can pay only $7.00. Therefore, all workers get paid the same wage.

If the market depicted in Figure 3.4 were competitive, each firm in the market would hire labor until marginal revenue product equaled the wage. Thus, if the demand curve in that market were the same as the marginal-revenue-product curve shown, the wage rate would be $W_C$ and the employment level would be $E_C$—and the conventional result would be obtained. Note that in a market that is monopsonized, wages and employment levels are *below* $W_C$ and $E_C$. In the real world of personnel decisions, monopsonists wanting to expand may raise existing workers' wages above what the new employees receive. Reasons for the favorable treatment of senior workers will be discussed in Chapters 8 and 9. For our present discussion, if the firm raises the wages of existing workers above the new workers' salary level (as opposed to merely raising them to the new workers' salary), the marginal cost of hiring additional workers becomes even higher.

Examples of pure monopsony in the labor market are difficult to cite; an isolated coal-mining town or a sugar plantation, where the mine or sugar company is literally the only employer, are increasingly rare examples. However, some employers may be large relative to the labor market and may, therefore, find themselves confronted with an upward-sloping supply curve.

Some economists argue that the market for registered nurses—particularly in a small town—is partially monopsonized. Hospitals employ the majority of registered nurses, and in many small towns there is only one hospital. These hospitals, it is argued, behave like monopsonists and pay lower wages than they otherwise would.[13]

If the market for registered nurses is characterized by monopsony, this situation could help explain why a nursing shortage could be perceived to exist even though nursing salaries were not being bid up. At wage $W_M$ in Figure 3.4, the monopsonized employer (the hospital in this case) will hire only $E_M$ workers because that is where marginal revenue and marginal cost are equal. However, *if* it could do all its additional hiring at $W_M$, it would *like* to hire $E_T$. Since at $W_M$ supply falls short of $E_T$, there might appear to be a shortage! In this case, then, hospitals find themselves in the position of wanting to hire more nurses at $E_M$—and being unable to do so—while at the same time being unwilling to raise wage offers necessary to increase employment beyond $E_M$! The "shortage" is thus more apparent than real.

Another market that may be monopsonized is the market for public-school teachers outside of metropolitan areas.[14] However, there is not much evidence that private firms in metropolitan areas have monopsony power.

---

[13] Richard Hurd, "Equilibrium Vacancies in a Labor Market Dominated by Non-Profit Firms: The 'Shortage' of Nurses," *Review of Economics and Statistics* 55 (May 1973): 234–240; and C. R. Link and J. H. Landon, "Monopsony and Union Power in the Market for Nurses," *Southern Economic Journal* 41 (April 1975): 649–59.

[14] Evidence on this point is summarized in Ronald Ehrenberg and Joshua Schwarz, "Public Sector Labor Markets," in *Handbook of Labor Economics*, O. Ashenfelter and R. Layard, eds., (Amsterdam, North-Holland, 1986).

**Figure 3.5**  Effect of an Increase in the Price of One Input ($j$) on the Demand for Another Input ($i$)

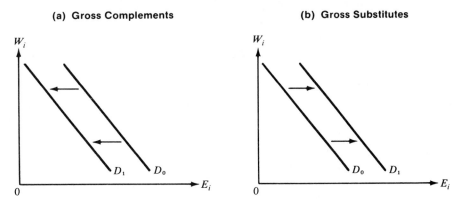

Wages that these firms pay appear to be essentially unaffected by the concentration of employment in the hands of a very few employers.[15]

## More Than Two Inputs

Thus far we have assumed that there are only two inputs in the production process: capital and labor. In fact, labor can be subdivided into many categories (for example, labor can be categorized by age, race, sex, educational level, and occupation). Other inputs besides capital that are used in the production process include materials and energy. If a firm is seeking to maximize profits, in the long run it should employ all inputs up until the point that the additions to output received from spending the last dollar on each input are equal. This generalization of equation (3.6) leads to the somewhat obvious result that the demand for *any* category of labor will be a function not only of its own wage rate, but also of the wage rates for all other categories of labor and of the prices of capital and other inputs. The demand curve for each category of labor will be a downward-sloping function of the wage rate paid to workers in the category, for the reasons discussed earlier. Changes in the prices of the other categories of labor or in the prices of other inputs may shift the entire demand curve for a given category of labor either to the right or to the left. If an increase in the price of one input shifts the demand for another input to the left, as in panel (a) of Figure 3.5, the two inputs are *gross complements;* if a price increase shifts the demand for labor to the right, as in panel (b) of Figure 3.5, the two inputs are *gross substitutes*. Whether two inputs are gross complements or substitutes is a function both of the production process and product demand conditions.

---

[15]  See Robert L. Bunting, *Employer Concentration in Local Labor Markets* (Chapel Hill: University of North Carolina Press, 1962).

EXAMPLE   3.5

## Free Agency, Monopsony, Marginal Productivity, and the Allocation of Baseball Players

Before 1976, Major League baseball players were bound to the team for which they played, unless the team chose to trade or sell their contracts. In effect, each team enjoyed monopsony power since each player could negotiate with only one employer in the "industry." In 1976, a labor-relations ruling was issued (and later followed by a collective bargaining agreement) that allowed certain players the right to become *free agents,* which meant that these players could sell their services to any of several teams. The ruling therefore made the baseball labor market more competitive for these players by reducing each team's monopsony power over them.

Our analysis of monopsony would predict that the institution of free agency would raise players' salaries. Indeed, this appears to have happened; average player salaries moved from $51,501 in 1976 to $76,349 in 1977, the initial year for which the new collective-bargaining agreement applied. Since then, average salaries have grown to $410,732 for the 1987 season. This growth rate of salaries is far greater than that for the overall economy, as shown in Table 2.5. More importantly, recent research shows that since the emergence of the free agency system, baseball players' salaries have risen relative to their contribution to team revenues (relative, that is, to their marginal revenue products).

The gap between pay and marginal revenue product has been eliminated for many players, suggesting the decline of monopsony power. Owners initially objected to the free-agent system. One argument they advanced was that it would harm competitive balance among the teams by enabling the best and richest teams to grab up all the star players. Our observations about marginal productivity and profit maximization can be used to evaluate—and refute—the owners' contention about competitive imbalances.

If team owners are profit maximizers, they will hire a star only if the extra revenue he will generate is greater than his salary; that is, the star's *MRP* must not be lower than his wage. If a team is *already* loaded with stars, an additional good player will not bring very much in terms of added revenues. However, if a team has no star—or very few—the addition of the *same* good player will quite possibly generate a lot in added revenues. Thus, because the *MRP* of a star will probably be lower, *other things equal,* on the best teams, these teams will tend to be the least willing to put up money for the star free agents. Capital stock is one of the "other things" that must be held equal for this prediction to hold, however. For example, if team quality is held constant, one's *MRP* will be higher on teams that have larger stadiums and larger television markets.

These considerations suggest that the teams that will bid most aggressively for the free agents will be those that tend to have poorer records or are located in areas with large potential markets. Although there are instances to the contrary, it is interesting to note that 34 of the first 51 "star-quality" free agents (through 1986) signed with teams that had poorer records than the team they were on—and of the remaining 17, 7 signed with teams located in larger markets.

Thus, free agency appears not to have had harmful effects on the competitive balance of professional baseball teams. Indeed, economic reasoning suggests that free agency would have very little, if any, effect on competitive balance. Before the free-agency era, teams were still free to trade or buy players' contracts from other teams. If, for example, the Red Sox had a player who was worth $100,000 in marginal revenue in Boston but would be worth $200,000 in revenue to the Yankees, New York would presumably make Boston a mutually acceptable offer for the player's contract. The player would thus be moved to the location where his market value was greatest, just as in the free-agency system. The only difference is that the player would now earn closer to the $200,000 than he could before free agency. Thus, whatever competitive imbalances we observe today would likely have been observed without free agency.

SOURCES:  G. Scully, "Pay and Performance in Major League Baseball," *American Economic Review* 64 (December 1974): 915–30; H. Raimondo, "Free Agents' Impact on the Labor Market for Baseball Players," *Journal of Labor Research* 4 (Spring 1983): 183–93; J. Hill and W. Spellman, "Professional Baseball: The Reserve Clause and Salary Structure," *Industrial Relations* 22 (Winter 1983): 1–19; "Baseball Salaries '87," *Sports Illustrated,* April 20, 1987: 54–81. The authors are indebted to Theo Smith and his enormous collection of baseball cards.

Consider a snow-removal firm. Suppose that snow can be removed using either unskilled workers (with shovels) or skilled workers who drive snowplows, and let us focus on the demand for the skilled workers. Other things equal, an increase in the wage of skilled workers will cause the employer to employ fewer of them; their demand curve is a downward-sloping function of their wage. If the wage rate of unskilled workers increases, the employer would want to employ fewer unskilled workers than before—and more of the now relatively cheaper skilled workers—to remove any given amount of snow. To the extent that this substitution effect dominates over the scale effect (the higher unskilled wage leading to reduced output and employment of all inputs), the demand for skilled workers would shift to the right. In this case, skilled and unskilled workers are gross substitutes. In contrast, if the price of snowplows went up, the employer would want to cut back on their usage, which would result in a reduced demand, at each wage, for skilled workers who drive the snowplows. Skilled workers and snowplows are gross complements in this example.

# Policy Application: Minimum-Wage Legislation

## History and Description

The *Fair Labor Standards Act of 1938* was the first major piece of protective labor legislation adopted at the national level in the United States. Among its provisions were a minimum-wage rate, or floor, below which hourly wages could not be reduced, an overtime-pay premium for workers who worked long workweeks, and restrictions on the use of child labor. The minimum-wage provisions were designed to guarantee each worker a reasonable wage for his or her work effort and thus to reduce the incidence of poverty.

When initially adopted, the minimum wage was set at $0.25 an hour and covered roughly 43 percent of all nonsupervisory wage and salary workers—primarily those workers employed in larger firms involved in interstate commerce (manufacturing, mining, and construction). As Table 3.2 indicates, both the basic minimum wage and coverage under the minimum wage have expanded over time. Indeed as of January 1, 1981, the minimum wage was set at $3.35 an hour, and about 80 percent of all nonsupervisory workers were covered by its provisions.

Since 1981, the minimum wage has not changed in nominal terms but, as Table 3.2 indicates, had fallen to 33 percent of the average manufacturing wage as of 1988. As of early 1988, there was a bill pending in Congress that would raise the minimum wage in a series of steps to $4.65 an hour by January 1991, or to about 46 percent of the 1988 average manufacturing wage. Further, the bill would, after 1991, index the minimum wage to equal 50 percent of the

**Table 3.2**    Minimum Wage Legislation in the United States, 1938–88[a]

| Effective Date of Minimum Wage Change | Nominal Minimum Wage | Percent of Nonsupervisory Employees Covered[b] | Minimum Wage Relative to Average Hourly Wage in Manufacturing | |
|---|---|---|---|---|
| | | | Before | After |
| 10/24/38 | $0.25 | 43.4 | — | 0.403 |
| 10/24/39 | 0.30 | 47.1 | 0.398 | 0.478 |
| 10/24/45 | 0.40 | 55.4 | 0.295 | 0.394 |
| 1/25/50 | 0.75 | 53.4 | 0.278 | 0.521 |
| 3/1/56 | 1.00 | 53.1 | 0.385 | 0.512 |
| 9/3/61 | 1.15 | 62.1 | 0.431 | 0.495 |
| 9/3/63 | 1.25 | 62.1 | 0.467 | 0.508 |
| 9/3/64 | 1.25 | 62.6 | | |
| 2/1/67 | 1.40 | 75.3 | 0.441 | 0.494 |
| 2/1/68 | 1.60 | 72.6 | 0.465 | 0.531 |
| 2/1/69 | 1.60 | 78.2 | | |
| 2/1/70 | 1.60 | 78.5 | | |
| 2/1/71 | 1.60 | 78.4 | | |
| 5/1/74 | 2.00 | 83.7 | 0.363 | 0.454 |
| 1/1/75 | 2.10 | 83.3 | 0.423 | 0.445 |
| 1/1/76 | 2.30 | | 0.410 | 0.449 |
| 1/1/78 | 2.65 | | 0.430 | 0.480 |
| 1/1/79 | 2.90 | | 0.402 | 0.440 |
| 1/1/80 | 3.10 | | 0.417 | 0.445 |
| 1/1/81 | 3.35 | | 0.403 | 0.435 |

[a] In mid-1988 the nominal minimum wage was still pegged at $3.35 an hour, although legislation to increase it was being considered. The ratio of the minimum wage to average hourly earnings in manufacturing fell to about 0.33 at the start of 1988.

[b] Excludes executive, administrative, and professional personnel (including teachers in elementary and secondary schools) from the base. Coverage peaked at 87.3 percent of the nonsupervisory work force in September 1977. As of 1978, however, a court decision eliminated most state and local government workers from coverage. As a result, worker coverage fell from 56,100,000 in 1976 to 51,900,000 in 1978.

average manufacturing wage, a high ratio by historical standards (see Table 3.2).[16]

## Economic Effects of the Federal Minimum Wage

Although minimum-wage coverage has grown over time, with somewhere in the range of 87 percent of all nonsupervisory workers in the private sector being covered by the minimum wage, as late as 1965 more than one-third of these private-sector workers were not covered by minimum-wage legislation. The major uncovered sectors then included retail trade, the service industries, and agriculture; today they include primarily employees in these industries who work for small firms. Since coverage is less than complete, it is useful to present a model of minimum-wage effects under incomplete coverage. (A similar model will reappear in Chapter 16 when we discuss the effects of unions on wages.) To simplify the discussion, we will assume the following:

1.  that prices are constant (so that we can talk interchangeably about real and money wages);
2.  that the labor market for unskilled labor is characterized by a vertical supply curve such that the total employment of the unskilled is $E_T$;
3.  that this labor market has a covered and an uncovered sector; and
4.  that unskilled workers move back and forth between sectors seeking jobs where the wages are highest.

These assumptions suggest that without a minimum wage, the wage in each sector will be the same. Referring to Figure 3.6 let us assume that this pre-minimum wage is $W_0$ and that total employment of $E_T$ is broken down into $E_0^C$ in the sector to be covered plus $E_0^U$ in the other sector. If a minimum wage of $W_1$ is imposed on the covered sector, all unskilled workers will prefer to work there. However, the increase in wages there, from $W_0$ to $W_1$, reduces demand—and covered-sector employment will fall from $E_0^C$ to $E_1^C$. Some workers who previously had, or would have found, jobs in the covered sector must now seek work in the uncovered sector. Thus, to the $E_0^U$ workers formerly working in the uncovered sector are added $E_0^C - E_1^C$ other workers seeking jobs there. Thus, all unskilled workers in the market who are not lucky enough to find "covered jobs" at $W_1$ now look for work in the uncovered sector, and the supply curve to that sector becomes $E_1^U$ [$= E_0^U + (E_0^C - E_1^C) = E_T - E_1^C$].[17] The increased supply of workers to that sector drives down the wage there from $W_0$ to $W_2$.

---

[16]  See Hilary Stout, "Propping Up Payments at the Bottom," *New York Times,* January 24, 1988, Section 3, p. 4.

[17]  Under some circumstances it may be rational for these unemployed workers to remain unemployed for a while and to search for jobs in the covered sector. We will discuss this possibility—which is discussed by Jacob Mincer in "Unemployment Effects of Minimum Wages," *Journal of Political Economy* 84 (August 1976): S87–S104—in Chapter 16. At this point we simply note that if it occurs, unemployment will result.

**Figure 3.6** Minimum Wage Effects

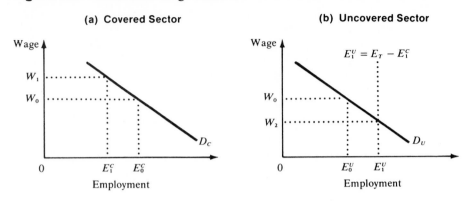

As with most government laws, a partial-coverage minimum wage produces both winners and losers. The winners are those covered-sector workers who keep their jobs after the imposition of the minimum and receive the higher minimum wage. The losers are those low-skilled workers who lose their jobs in the covered sector and now are paid lower wages in the uncovered sector. The losers also include those low-skilled workers in the uncovered sector who kept their jobs but now find their real wages lowered because of the increased supply of labor to the sector. Hence, even in the context of this model, where there are no overall employment effects, it is not obvious that the legislation is desirable on balance. The gains won by some groups must be weighed against the losses suffered by other groups before an unambiguous conclusion can be reached.

## Social Losses

Besides predicting that minimum-wage laws produce both gainers and losers among the poor, this chapter also predicts that such laws will create losses for society as a whole. To understand this point requires a quick review of profit-maximization principles.

A firm will hire labor until labor's marginal revenue product equals the money wage rate. In the partial coverage example above (Figure 3.6), unskilled labor—prior to imposition of the minimum wage—would be hired in both sectors to the point where marginal revenue product equalled $W_0$. Thus, if a worker were transferred from one sector to the other, the value of total output would go down by $W_0$ in the "sending" sector and up by $W_0$ in the "receiving" sector. Overall output would remain unchanged by such a transfer.

After the minimum wage has been imposed on the covered sector, however, employment will be reduced there until labor's marginal revenue product equals $W_1$. Wages in the uncovered sector, in contrast, fall to $W_2$;

employment in that sector will thus increase until labor's marginal revenue product equals $W_2$. The marginal revenue product in the uncovered sector is now *below* that in the covered sector ($W_2$ is less than $W_1$), so that if a worker were transferred from the uncovered to the covered sector output could be increased! (The value of ouput lost in the uncovered sector by this transfer would be $W_2$, while the value of output gained in the covered sector would be $W_1$.)

Since $W_1$ exceeds $W_2$, *the value of output can be increased* by transferring labor from the uncovered to the covered sector. This transfer would occur naturally if there were no minimum wage, because workers seeking the higher-paying jobs in the covered sector would bid down wages there, and employment in that sector would expand. Transfers of labor would stop when the wages in each sector were equalized—and as we have shown above, when wages are equal in both sectors of the unskilled labor market there are no further gains to be made by transfers of labor between the two sectors of that market.

With a minimum wage, however, labor *cannot* transfer out of the sector with the lower wage (and lower marginal revenue product) to the higher-wage sector. Wages in the latter sector cannot legally fall, and therefore employment cannot expand there. A beneficial transfer of resources is blocked, and social losses occur. Put differently, total output could be increased with no change in our total resources merely by transferring labor from one sector to another, and the effective prevention of this transfer by the minimum-wage law implies social losses.

## The Effects of Monopsony

The preceding analysis of the minimum-wage law assumes that firms are sufficiently small that their hiring decisions do not affect the market wage for low-skilled workers; that is, we have assumed there is no monopsony in the low-skilled labor market. While this assumption is probably appropriate for most employers of low-skilled labor, it is theoretically possible that monopsony exists in some communities. To understand the effects of a minimum wage on monopsonized markets, consider a "full coverage" model (with only one employer and no uncovered sector).

You will recall from our earlier discussion of the demand for labor by monopsonists that their marginal labor costs are above the wage rate. In maximizing profits, they choose an employment level ($E_0$ in Figure 3.7) where marginal labor costs equal marginal revenue product (point $A$ in Figure 3.7). The wage corresponding to employment level $E_0$ in Figure 3.7 is $W_0$.

Suppose, now, that a minimum wage of $W_m$ is set in Figure 3.7. This minimum wage prevents the firm from paying a wage less than $W_m$ and effectively creates a horizontal portion in the supply curve facing the firm (which is now *DACS*). The firm's marginal cost of labor curve is now *DACEM,* because up to employment level $E_1$ the marginal costs of labor are

**Figure 3.7**   Minimum Wage Effects Under Monopsony

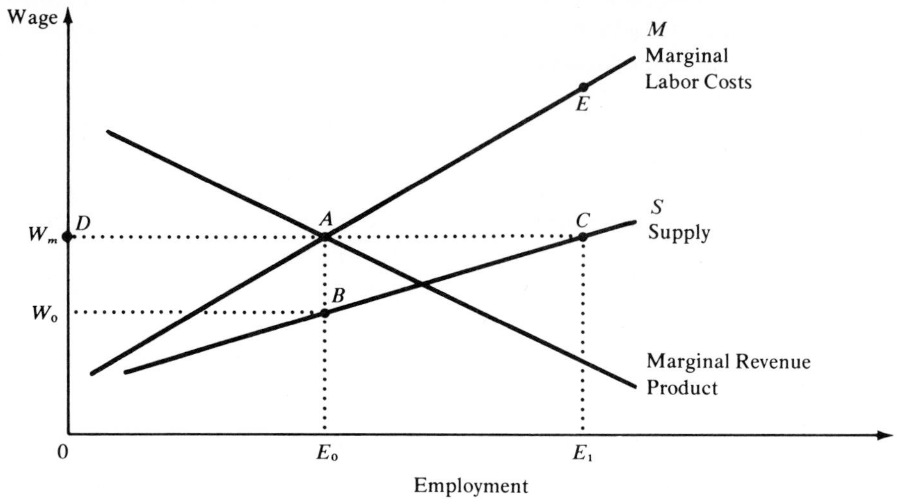

equal to $W_m$. The firm, which maximizes profits by equating marginal revenues with marginal costs (which now occurs at point $A$), will still hire $E_0$ workers—but will pay them $W_m$ instead of $W_0$. Moreover, if the minimum were set at a wage rate *between* $W_0$ and $W_m$, wages *and* employment would increase.

The apparent conclusion that a minimum wage can increase wages without reducing employment in a monopsonized market is subject to two qualifications. First, in the context of Figure 3.7, the minimum wage cannot be set above $W_m$ if employment is to remain at least as large as $E_0$. Above $W_m$ there would be employment losses. The second qualification is that the firm must remain in business for employment not to fall. While an employer may be the only buyer of labor in a particular market, the employing firm may also have many competitors in its product market. If its product market is competitive, its level of profits will be "normal"—which means that if profits were to fall, the firm would find it could earn more profits in another line of business. If, in our initial example (Figure 3.7), wages rose from $W_0$ to $W_m$ and employment remained at $E_0$, firm profits would clearly fall. If the fall were large enough, the firm might go out of business and all $E_0$ workers would lose their jobs.

## Empirical Evidence
Labor economists have devoted much effort to empirically estimating the magnitudes of the effects of minimum-wage legislation on the employment

levels of various age/race/sex groups.[18] Although the precise magnitudes of the relationships have yet to be pinned down, it is now widely agreed that increases in minimum wages do reduce employment opportunities, especially among teenagers. The studies use different data and often ask slightly different questions. Virtually all agree, however, that employment opportunities for teenagers have been reduced by the minimum wage—although the *size* of the reduction is in doubt. One recent study, for example, estimates that the 1970 minimum wage raised the cost of hiring 18- and 19-year-olds by 11 percent and reduced their employment by 15 percent.[19] Another recent study, using different data, estimated that the minimum wage reduced *full-time* job opportunities for teenagers but increased the availability of *part-time* work. This latter study found that overall teenage *employment* was not much affected by the minimum wage but that *hours of work* among teenagers fell as a result of the law.[20] These discrepancies in estimated effects of the minimum wage are not unusual, given the complexity of the world and the need for researchers to effectively control for *other* factors that influence teenage employment opportunities. There is no consensus on the effects of minimum-wage legislation on adults—perhaps because far fewer adults are directly affected by the minimum wage (most have wages in excess of the minimum).

The Fair Labor Standards Act has a certain political sanctity because it was the first piece of protective labor legislation adopted at the federal level; very few people would seriously argue for the repeal of the minimum-wage law today. Instead, given the estimates of the adverse effects of the legislation on youth employment opportunities, many people have recently argued that a youth differential or youth subminimum wage should be instituted. Lower wages for teens, they claim, would help alleviate the teenage unemployment problem. While there appears to be empirical support for this proposition, opponents, including organized labor, point out that reducing the wages of teenagers relative to adults would encourage employers to increase their employment of teenagers at the expense of adult employment. Estimates of the likely magnitude of this substitution are required before intelligent policy decisions can be made with respect to a youth differential; in the language of some opponents, one should not substitute parents' unemployment for that of their children.[21]

---

[18] For a very readable, albeit critical, nontechnical survey of economic research on the minimum wage see Sar Levitan and Richard Belous, *More Than Subsistence: Minimum Wages for the Working Poor* (Baltimore: Johns Hopkins University Press, 1979). For a more sympathetic view, see Finis Welch, *Minimum Wages: Issues and Evidence* (Washington, DC: American Enterprise Institute, 1978). See also C. Brown, C. Gilroy, and A. Kohen, "The Effect of the Minimum Wage on Employment and Unemployment," *Journal of Economic Literature* 20 (June 1982): 487–528.

[19] Welch, *Minimum Wages.*

[20] Edward Gramlich, "Impact of Minimum Wages on Other Wages, Employment, and Family Incomes," *Brookings Papers on Economic Activity* (1976–2): 409–62.

[21] One study found that about one adult job would be lost for every four teenage jobs created by a youth subminimum. See D. Hamermesh, "Minimum Wages and the Demand for Labor," *Economic Inquiry* 20 (July 1982): 365–80.

Two additional reasons may help explain why increases in the minimum wage have not had as dramatic effects on employment or the distribution of income as one might expect. First, there is no reason to suspect that all employers comply with the legislation; only limited resources are expended on enforcement of the legislation, and the penalties for employers found to be not complying (paying covered workers less than the minimum) are quite small. Indeed, certain evidence suggests that only 50 to 70 percent of covered workers who would have earned less than the minimum in the absence of the law are actually paid the minimum. The remainder are paid a wage that is illegally low.[22]

Second, our discussion has ignored the possibility that employers may respond to increases in the minimum wage by lowering other forms of non-wage compensation that are *not* covered by the minimum wage law.[23] As Chapter 8 will discuss, nonwage forms of compensation (including holiday, vacation, and sick leave pay; health insurance; and retirement benefits) now comprise a still-growing share of total compensation. To the extent that employers respond to increases in the minimum wage by lowering the levels (or the rates of growth) of these benefits, increases in the minimum will have smaller effects on total labor costs—and hence smaller employment effects—than might have otherwise been anticipated.

## The Elasticity of Demand for Labor

In this chapter we discussed the effects of government policies on wages and employment and emphasized the downward-sloping demand curve for labor. The size of these employment effects depends on the *shape* of employer demand curves, in particular on the responsiveness of the demand for labor to changes in labor costs. For example, the minimum wage will cause a larger fall in employment the greater is this responsiveness. Economists define the sensitivity of desired employment to changes in wages as the own-wage elasticity of demand for labor. More specifically, the own-wage elasticity of the demand for labor is the percentage change in employment ($E$) caused by a 1-percent increase in the wage rate ($W$):

$$\eta = \frac{\%\Delta E}{\%\Delta W}. \tag{3.10}$$

In equation (3.10), we have used $\eta_{ii}$ to represent elasticity, and the notation $\%\Delta$ to represent "percentage change in." Since labor demand curves slope downward, an increase (decrease) in the wage rate will lead employment to decrease (increase); the own-wage elasticity of demand thus is a negative

---

[22] Orley Ashenfelter and Robert S. Smith, "Compliance with the Minimum Wage Law," *Journal of Political Economy* 87 (April 1979): 335–50.

[23] See Walter Wessels, *Minimum Wages, Fringe Benefits, and Working Conditions* (Washington, DC: American Enterprise Institute, 1981).

number. What is at issue is its magnitude. The larger its *absolute* value, the larger will be the percentage decline in employment associated with any given percentage increase in wages.

Labor economists often focus on whether the absolute value of the elasticity of demand for labor is greater than or less than one. If it is greater than one, a one percent increase in wages will lead to an employment decline of greater than one percent; this situation is referred to as an *elastic* demand curve. In contrast, if the absolute value is less than one, the demand curve is said to be *inelastic;* a one percent increase in wages will lead to a proportionately smaller decline in employment.[24] If the demand curve is elastic, aggregate earnings (defined here as the wage rate times the employment level) of individuals in the category will decline when the wage rate increases, because employment falls at a faster rate than wages rise. Similarly, if the demand curve is inelastic, aggregate earnings will increase when the wage rate is increased.

To see the importance of the magnitude of elasticity, let us return to our analysis of the minimum wage. We saw that an increase in the minimum wage would lead to a decrease in the covered group's employment, if other factors affecting employment were held constant. Does this result imply, from the perspective of low-wage covered workers as a group, that minimum-wage increases are desirable? The answer is ambiguous; it depends upon the extent to which the higher minimum wage for those workers who keep their jobs offsets the loss in employment that occurs. There are obvious equity issues involved here that make such comparisons difficult. However, *if* the demand for covered low-skilled workers is inelastic, an increase in the minimum wage will lead to an increase in aggregate earnings for this group. This increase in aggregate earnings among this group implies that those who keep their jobs could compensate those who lose them and still be better off.[25] (The fact that *low-skill* covered workers, as a *group, might* be made better off by a minimum-wage law does not imply that the gains to *society* as a whole would exceed the losses.)

A second illustration of the importance of the concept of elasticity of demand for labor concerns the determinants of union power. As we will discuss in Chapter 10, since unions are complex organizations it is not always possible to specify what their goals are. Nevertheless, it is clear that in almost all cases unions value both their members' wage and employment opportunities. We would therefore predict that, other things equal, the more elastic the demand for labor, the smaller the wage gain a union will succeed in winning for its members. The reason for this prediction is that the more elastic the demand curve, the greater the percentage employment decline associated

---

[24]   If the elasticity just equals −1, the demand curve is said to be *unitary elastic*.

[25]   Once we include transfer payments, such as unemployment insurance, in the analysis, it becomes possible for the total income of low-skilled workers (including transfer payments) to increase even if the elasticity is greater than one. See Edward Gramlich, "Impact of Minimum Wages on Other Wages, Employment, and Family Incomes."

**Figure 3.8** Relative Demand Elasticities

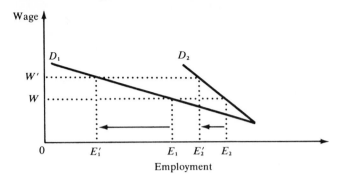

with any given percentage increase in wages. We can expect the following to occur:

1. unions would win larger wage gains for their members in markets with more inelastic demand curves;
2. unions would strive to take actions that reduce the wage elasticity of demand for their members' services; and
3. unions might first seek to organize workers in markets in which demand curves are inelastic (because the potential gains to unionization are higher in these markets).

As we shall see, many of these predictions are borne out by empirical evidence (see Chapters 10–16).

Figure 3.8 shows that the flatter of the two demand curves graphed ($D_1$) has greater elasticity than the steeper ($D_2$). Beginning with any wage ($W$, for example), given wage changes (to $W'$, say) will yield greater responses in employment with demand curve $D_1$ than with $D_2$ (compare $E_1 - E_1'$ with $E_2 - E_2'$).

To speak of a demand curve as having "an" elasticity, however, is technically incorrect. Given demand curves will generally have both elastic and inelastic ranges. We are usually just interested in the elasticity of demand in the range around the current wage rate in any market. Thus, when we speak of "the" elasticity of labor demand in a particular case, it is usually in the context of the responsiveness to small changes from the current wage rate.

# The Hicks-Marshall Laws of Derived Demand

Knowledge of own-wage elasticities of demand is very important for making policy decisions. The factors that influence own-wage elasticity can be summarized by the four "Hicks-Marshall Laws of Derived Demand"—"laws" named after two distinguished British economists, Alfred Marshall and John Hicks, who are closely associated with their development.[26] These laws assert that, other things equal, the own-wage elasticity of demand for a category of labor is high

1.  when the price elasticity of demand for the product being produced is high;
2.  when other factors of production can be easily substituted for the category of labor;
3.  when the supply curves of other factors of production are highly elastic (that is, usage of other factors of production can be increased without substantially increasing their prices); and
4.  when the cost of employing the category of labor is a large share of the total costs of production.

Not only are these laws generally valid as an empirical proposition, but the first three can be shown to always hold. There are conditions, however, under which the final law does not hold.

In seeking to explain why these laws hold, it is useful to pretend that we can divide the process by which an increase in the wage rate affects the demand for labor into two steps. First, an increase in the wage rate increases the relative cost of the category of labor in question and induces employers to use less of it and more of other inputs (the *substitution effect*). Second, when the wage increase causes the marginal cost of production to rise, there are pressures to increase product prices and reduce output—causing a fall in employment (the *scale effect*). The four laws of derived demand each deal with substitution or scale effects.

The greater the price elasticity of demand for the final product, the larger will be the decline in output associated with a given increase in price—and the greater the decrease in output, the greater the loss in employment (other things equal). Thus, *the greater the elasticity of demand for the product, the greater the elasticity of demand for labor will be*. One implication of this result is that, other things equal, the demand for labor at the *firm* level will be more elastic than the demand for labor at the *industry*, or market, level. For example, the product demand curves facing *individual* carpet manufacturing companies are highly elastic, because the carpet of Company X is a very close substitute for the carpet of Company Y. Compared to price increases at the *firm* level, however, price increases at the *industry* level will not have as large an effect on demand because the closest substitutes for carpeting are hardwood, ceramic, or some kind of vinyl floor covering—none of which is a very close substitute for carpeting. The demand for labor is thus much more elastic for an individual carpet manufacturing firm than for the carpet manufacturing industry as a whole. (For the same reasons, the labor demand curve for a monopolist is less elastic than for an individual *firm* in a competitive industry.

[26] John R. Hicks, *The Theory of Wages,* 2nd ed. (New York: St. Martins Press, 1966), 241–47; and Alfred Marshall, *Principles of Economics,* 8th ed. (London: Macmillan, 1923), 518–38.

Monopolists, after all, face *market* demand curves for their product, because they are the only sellers in the particular market.)

Another implication of this first law is that *wage elasticities will be higher in the long run than in the short run*. The reason for this fact is that price elasticities of demand in product markets are higher in the long run. In the short run there may be no good substitutes for a product, or consumers may be locked into their current stock of consumer durables. However, after a period of time, new products that are substitutes may be introduced, and consumers will begin to replace durables that have worn out.

## Substitutability of Other Factors

As the wage rate of a category of labor increases, firms have an incentive to try to substitute other, now relatively cheaper, inputs for the category. Suppose, however, that there were no substitution possibilities; a given number of units of the type of labor *must* be used to produce one unit of output. In this case, the first step in the process described above is not present; there is no reduction in employment due to the substitution effect. In contrast, when substitution possibilities do present themselves, a reduction in employment will occur at this stage. Hence, other things equal, *the easier it is to substitute other factors of production, the higher the wage elasticity of demand will be*.

It is important to note that limitations on substitution possibilities need not be solely technical ones. For example, as we shall see in Chapter 12, unions often try to limit substitution possibilities by including specific work rules in their contracts (for example, minimum crew size for crews in a railroad locomotive). Alternatively, the government may legislate limitations by specifying minimum employment levels for ''safety reasons'' (for example, each public swimming pool in New York State must always have a lifeguard present). Such collectively bargained or legislated restrictions make the demand for labor less elastic. Note, however, that substitution possibilities that are not feasible in the short run may well become feasible over longer periods of time, when employers are free to vary their capital stock. For example, if the wages of railroad workers go up, companies could buy more powerful locomotives and operate with larger trains and fewer locomotives. Likewise, if the wages of lifeguards rose, cities might build larger, but fewer, swimming pools. Both adjustments would occur only in the long run, which is another reason why the demand for labor is more elastic in the long run than in the short run.

## The Supply of Other Factors

Suppose that as the wage rate increased and employers attempted to substitute other factors of production for labor, the prices of these inputs were bid up substantially. This situation might occur, for example, if one were trying to substitute capital equipment for labor. If producers of capital equipment were already operating their plants near capacity—so that taking on new orders would cause them substantial increases in costs because they would have to work their employees overtime and pay them a wage premium—they would only accept new orders if they could charge a higher price for their equipment. Such a price increase would dampen firms' "appetites" for capital and thus limit the substitution of capital for labor.

For another example, suppose an increase in the wages of unskilled workers caused employers to attempt to substitute skilled employees for unskilled employees. If there were only a fixed number of skilled workers in an area, their wages would be bid up by employers. As in the prior example, the incentive to substitute alternative factors would be reduced, and the reduction in employment due to the substitution effect would be smaller. In contrast, if the prices of other inputs did not increase when employers attempted to increase their usage, other things equal, the substitution effect—and thus the wage elasticity of labor demand—would be larger.

Note again that prices of other inputs are less likely to be bid up in the long run than in the short run. In the long run existing producers of capital equipment can expand their capacity and new producers can enter the market. Similarly, in the long run more skilled workers can be trained. This observation is an additional reason why the demand for labor will be more elastic in the long run.

## The Share of Labor in Total Costs

Finally, the share of the category of labor in total costs is crucial to the size of the elasticity of demand. If the category's initial share were 20 percent, a 10 percent increase in the wage rate, other things equal, would raise total costs by 2 percent. In contrast, if its initial share were 80 percent, a 10 percent increase in the wage rate would increase total costs by 8 percent. Since employers would have to increase their product prices by more in the latter case, output—and hence employment—would fall more in that case. *Thus, the greater the category's share in total costs, the higher the wage elasticity of labor demand will tend to be.*[27]

## Empirical Evidence on Wage Elasticities of Demand for Labor

Literally hundreds of studies have been published in recent years that present empirical estimates on the magnitudes of wage elasticities of demand. Some of these studies focus on the aggregate demand for labor in the economy as a whole; others focus on the demand by different industries. Some focus on the demand for different skill classes; still others focus on the demand for different age/race/sex groups. Although our knowledge in a number of these areas is not very precise, it is useful to summarize what we do know.

To be able to draw a particular demand curve with precision requires knowledge of the factors that affect derived demand: the technological possibilities given by the production function (substitutability of capital and labor, labor share in total cost), the supply curve of capital, and the elasticity

---

[27] As we noted earlier, this law does not always hold. More specifically, when it is easy for employers to substitute other factors of production for the category of labor but difficult for consumers to substitute other products for the product being produced (low price elasticity of demand), this law is reversed. For a more formal treatment, see Hicks, *The Theory of Wages.*

**Table 3.3** Representative Estimates of Long-Run Wage Elasticities of Demand, by Industry

| Industry | Long-Run Wage Elasticity |
|---|---|
| Coal mining[a] | |
|   Underground | 0.98 |
|   Surface | 0.86 |
| Manufacturing[b] | 0.09 to 0.62 |
| Retail trade[c] | 0.34 to 1.20 |
| State and local government[d] | |
|   Employees in education sector | 1.06 |
|   Noneducation employees | 0.38 |

   [a] Derived from estimates presented in Morris Goldstein and Robert S. Smith, "The Predicted Impact of the Black Lung Benefits Program on the Coal Industry" in Orley Ashenfelter and James Blum, eds., *Evaluating the Labor-Market Effects of Social Programs* (Princeton, NJ: Princeton University Press, 1976).
   [b] Daniel Hamermesh, "Econometric Studies of Labor Demand and Their Applications to Policy Analysis," *Journal of Human Resources* 11 (Fall 1976): 507–25.
   [c] Philip Cotterill, "The Elasticity of Demand for Low-Wage Labor," *Southern Economic Journal* 41 (January 1975): 520–25.
   [d] Orley Ashenfelter and Ronald G. Ehrenberg, "The Demand for Labor in the Public Sector," in Daniel Hamermesh, ed., *Labor in the Public and Nonprofit Sectors* (Princeton, NJ: Princeton University Press, 1975).

of product demand. In estimating the elasticity of demand for labor, we do not want to hold these factors constant because they are all crucial in determining the *size* of the elasticity of demand. As a practical matter, however, researchers usually have to estimate demand elasticities holding the *price of capital* constant.[28] This is tantamount to assuming that capital usage can be increased or decreased as wages change with no effect on the price at which capital is supplied; that is, capital supply curves are assumed to be horizontal. All elasticity estimates cited below make this assumption.[29]

The *overall,* own-wage elasticity of demand for labor in the economy as a whole is low and probably in the range of $-0.3$.[30] This inelasticity is to be expected, because at the level of the economy *as a whole,* scale effects are likely to be small. Workers losing jobs due to wage increases will become self-employed in some cases. There are federal policies and programs designed to maintain national output and create full employment. Foreign goods and services are often very hard to substitute for domestic goods and services. For all these reasons, the *overall* wage elasticity of demand is small.

The own-wage elasticities of demand at the *industry* level tend to vary widely across industries and in the main are also inelastic. Table 3.3 presents

   [28] *Capital,* even in a given industry, encompasses so many machines, tools, supplies, and buildings that estimating a supply function is really beyond the capability of the data usually available.
   [29] Studies in which the level of *output* or the level of *capital usage* is held constant are ignored here since they assume away either scale or substitution effects.
   [30] Daniel Hamermesh, "Econometric Studies of Labor Demand and Their Application to Policy Analysis," *Journal of Human Resources* 11 (Fall 1976): 507–25.

a representative set of estimates for coal mining, manufacturing, retail trade, and the state and local government sector. That the demand for employees in underground mining (located primarily in the East) is more elastic than the demand for employees in surface or strip mining (located primarily in the West) is not unexpected. Surface mining is much more capital intensive, and labor costs are a smaller share of the total costs of production in that sector. That the estimated elasticities at the industry level tend to be in the inelastic range is also not surprising because scale effects at that level are likely to be relatively small in many cases. The elasticity of product demand *for a firm* is very high, as mentioned earlier, but *at the industry level* it is not likely to be very large.

A third set of empirical findings suggests that the own-wage elasticity of demand is higher for production workers than for nonproduction workers. This difference appears to be the result of the greater substitutability between capital and *production* labor than between capital and nonproduction workers.[31] In general, the more a group of workers is substitutable with capital, the greater will be its elasticity of demand, other things equal.

Research to date suggests that capital and unskilled labor are more easily substituted than capital and skilled labor, but whether this translates into a greater own-wage elasticity of demand depends upon the "other things" affecting elasticity: product demand elasticities, share of labor in total cost, and the supply curve for capital.[32] If these other factors are more or less the same for skilled and unskilled workers, on average, then the own-wage elasticity of demand will tend to be greater for the unskilled.

## Applying the Laws of Derived Demand

Because empirical estimates of demand elasticities that may be required for making decisions are lacking in some cases, it is sometimes necessary to try to guess what these elasticities are likely to be. In making these guesses, we can apply the laws of derived demand to predict these magnitudes for various types of labor. Consider first the demand for unionized New York City garment workers.

Due to foreign competition, the price elasticity of demand for the clothing produced by New York City garment workers is extremely high. Furthermore, employers can easily find other inputs to substitute for these workers; namely, nonunion garment workers in the South (this substitution would require moving the plant to the South, a strategy that many manufacturers have followed). These facts lead one to predict that the demand for New York City unionized garment workers should be very elastic—a prediction that seems to be borne out by union policies in the industry. That is, because the garment workers' union faces a highly elastic demand curve, its wage de-

---

[31] Daniel Hamermesh and James Grant, "Econometric Studies of Labor-Labor Substitution and Their Implications for Policy, *Journal of Human Resources* 14 (Fall 1979): 518–42.

[32] Hamermesh and Grant, "Econometric Studies of Labor-Labor Substitution."

mands historically have been moderate. However, the union has also aggressively sought to reduce the elasticity of product demand by supporting policies that reduce foreign competition, and it has also pushed for higher federal minimum wages in order to reduce employers' incentives to move their plants to the South.

Next, consider the wage elasticity of demand for unionized airplane pilots on commercial scheduled airlines in the United States. The salaries of pilots are only a small share of the costs of operating large airplanes; they are dwarfed by the fuel and capital costs of airlines. Furthermore, substitution possibilities are limited; there is little room to substitute unskilled labor for skilled labor (although airlines can contemplate substituting capital for labor by reducing the number of flights they offer while increasing the size of airplanes). Prior to the deregulation of the airline industry that took place in the late 1970s, many airlines also faced limited competition on many of their routes and/or were prohibited from reducing their prices to compete with other airlines that flew the same routes. These factors all suggest that the demand for airline pilots was quite inelastic. As one might expect, their wages were also quite high because their union could push for large wage increases without fear that such an increase would substantially reduce pilots' employment levels. However, after airline deregulation, competition among airline carriers increased substantially, leading to a more elastic labor demand curve for pilots. As a result, many airlines "requested," and won, reduced wages from their pilots.

Finally, consider the wage elasticity of demand for *domestic* farm workers. This elasticity will depend heavily on the supply of immigrants, either legal or illegal, who are potentially willing to work as farm workers at wages less than the wages paid to domestic workers. The successful unionization of farm workers, coupled with union or government rules that prevent illegal immigrants from accepting such employment, obviously will make the demand curve for domestic farm workers less elastic. Similarly, government regulations that either limit the quantity of foreign farm products that can be imported into the United States (quotas), place tariffs on such products, or limit foreign producers from *dumping* (selling their farm products in the United States at prices less than they charge in their own countries) will all reduce the price elasticity of demand for U.S. farm products (and hence the wage elasticity of demand for domestic farmworkers). This example indicates how government policies can heavily influence wage elasticities in particular labor markets.

# REVIEW QUESTIONS

1. "It is generally agreed that the volunteer army is a dismal failure—the quality of volunteers is down and the number is not sufficient to meet desired force levels. The only alternatives are to raise the pay of volunteers or to reinstitute a draft system. Since the cost to society is clearly higher in the former than in the latter case, from an economist's perspective a draft system would be preferable." Evaluate this position.

2. Suppose the government were to subsidize the wages of all women in the population by paying their *employers* 50 cents (say) for every hour they work. What will be the effect on the wage rate women receive? What will be the effect on the net wage employers pay? (The net wage would be the wage women receive less 50 cents.)

3. The Occupational Safety and Health Administration promulgates safety and health standards. These standards typically apply to machinery—which is required to be equipped with guards, shields, etc. An alternative to these standards is to require the employer to furnish personal protective devices to employees—such as ear plugs, hard hats, safety shoes, and so forth. *Disregarding* the issue of which alternative approach offers greater protection from injury, what aspects of each alternative must be taken into account when analyzing the possible *employment* effects of the two general approaches to the stimulation of safety?

4. In a certain small city with a large university there appears to be a considerable difference in the hourly wage received by people working part time and those of the same skill working full-time.
   a. Using demand and supply curves, and assuming perfect competition, explain the differential in wages.
   b. Suppose university enrollments were to fall. What effect would declining enrollments have on the wage differential?
   c. Suppose full-time and part-time hours were perfect substitutes in production. How would this affect the wage differential?

5. Union A faces a demand curve where a wage of $4 per hour leads to demand for 20,000 person hours and a wage of $5 per hour leads to demand for 10,000 person hours. What is the elasticity of demand for this union's labor? Union B faces a demand curve where a wage of $6 per hour leads to demand for 30,000 person hours while a wage of $5 per hour leads to demand for 33,000 person hours.
   a. Which union faces the *more* elastic demand curve?
   b. Which union will be more successful in increasing the total income (wages times person hours) of its membership?

# SELECTED READINGS

Orley Ashenfelter and Robert Smith, "Compliance with the Minimum Wage Law," *Journal of Political Economy* 87 (April 1979): 335–50.

Charles Brown, Curtis Gilroy, and Andrew Cohen, "The Effect of the Minimum Wage on Employment and Unemployment," *Journal of Economic Literature* 20 (June 1982): 487–528.

Edward Gramlich, "Impact of Minimum Wages on Other Wages, Employment, and Family Incomes," *Brookings Papers on Economic Activity* (1976-2): 409–62.

Daniel Hamermesh, "Econometric Studies of Labor Demand and Their Application to Policy Analysis," *Journal of Human Resources* 11 (Fall 1976): 507–42.

Daniel Hamermesh and James Grant, "Econometric Studies of Labor-Labor Substitution and Their Implications for Policy," *Journal of Human Resources* 14 (Fall 1979): 518–42.

Sar Levitan and Richard Belous, *More Than Subsistence: Minimum Wages for the Working Poor* (Baltimore: Johns Hopkins University Press, 1979).

Jacob Mincer, "Unemployment Effects of Minimum Wages," *Journal of Political Economy* 84 (August 1976): S87–S104.

Finis Welch, *Minimum Wages: Issues and Evidence* (Washington, DC: American Enterprise Institute, 1978).

# CHAPTER 4

## The Hiring and Training of the Work Force

Our analyses of the demand for labor in Chapter 3 basically ignored the substantial *nonwage* labor costs that exist and the *dynamic* nature of firms' employment decisions. These abstractions allowed us to discuss a number of policy issues in the context of a rather simple model. A number of other policy issues can be analyzed only in the context of less restrictive models, however.

This chapter will begin by discussing the magnitudes and growth of various forms of *nonwage* labor costs, including the costs for firms of hiring and training new employees, the costs of legally required social-insurance programs (such as Social Security and unemployment compensation), and the costs of privately negotiated fringe benefits (such as health insurance, vacation and sick-leave pay, and private pensions). These costs typically exceed 20 to 30 percent of employers' payroll costs.

This chapter generalizes our model of employers' demand for labor to incorporate decisions about both the numbers of employees to be hired *and* the average length of the work week for these employees. Because many of the nonwage labor costs do *not* vary at the margin with weekly hours of work, employers may decide to regularly work their employees overtime at legally required premium wage rates rather than increase the level of employment—a phenomenon that has led periodically to the proposal that the legally mandated overtime premium be increased in an effort to discourage employers from authorizing overtime and to encourage them to "spread the work."

Our model of labor demand will also be generalized to explicitly acknowledge the dynamic nature of firms' employment decisions. Employment decisions are often multiperiod in nature. While firms do not always bear the initial costs of employee training, those firms that do must recoup these costs later on. In this chapter we examine models that incorporate employer-borne hiring and training costs and explore the effects of minimum-wage legislation on teenagers' wage growth, why productivity declines during recessions, and the determinants of voluntary and involuntary labor turnover. The rationales for using hiring standards, such as minimum educational requirements, and creating internal labor markets are discussed in the context of hiring and training costs.

# Nonwage Labor Costs

Although simple textbook models of the labor market often refer to the hourly wage rate paid to workers as the cost of labor, there are in fact substantial *nonwage* labor costs that have important implications for labor market behavior. In general, they fall into two categories: hiring or training costs and fringe benefits.

### Hiring and Training Costs

Firms incur substantial costs in hiring and training new employees. *Hiring costs* include all costs involved in advertising positions, screening applicants to evaluate their qualifications, and processing successful applicants who have been offered jobs. One might also include the overhead costs of maintaining employees on the payroll once they have been employed in this category of costs; these costs would include record-keeping costs, the costs of computing and issuing paychecks, and the costs of providing forms to the government (such as W-2 forms to the Internal Revenue Service) about employees' earnings.

New employees typically undergo either formal or informal training and orientation programs. These programs may teach new skills—such as how to use a machine—that directly increase the employees' productive abilities. Alternatively, orientation programs may simply provide newcomers with background information on how the firm is structured—such as whom to call if a machine breaks down or where the rest rooms are.

Such information, while not changing skill levels, does increase productivity by enabling workers to make more efficient use of time. Firms incur at least three types of *training costs*:

1. the *explicit* monetary costs of employing individuals to serve as trainers and the costs of materials used up during the training process;
2. the *implicit* or opportunity costs of the trainee's time (while individuals are undergoing training they are not producing as much output as they could if all of their time were devoted to production activities); and
3. the opportunity costs of using capital equipment and experienced employees to do the training in less formal training situations (for example, if training consists solely of an experienced employee demonstrating how he or she does a job to a new recruit, the demonstrator may work at a slower pace than normal).

**EXAMPLE    4.1**

## Recruiting Strategies

The fact that recruiting and evaluating job applicants is a costly procedure induces employers to carefully select an overall hiring strategy. An employer wanting to hire X employees of a given quality basically has three choices. One is an *intensive-search* strategy, whereby the employer incurs substantial costs in advertising the openings and then interviewing applicants. A second choice is what can be called a *high-wage* strategy. By becoming known as a high-wage employer, an employer can generate large applicant pools very easily—and with so many applicants it can often fill its vacancies with those workers who are *obviously* of high quality (thus saving screening costs). Finally, employers might choose a *training* strategy—where instead of undertaking expensive efforts to ensure a large pool of highly qualified applicants, they accept and train inexperienced applicants. (The two broad kinds of training offered and who pays for each are discussed later in this chapter.)

Whether a given firm decides on intensive search, higher wages, or greater training as its means of recruiting personnel depends on the relative costs of each strategy to that firm. While firms will differ in the strategy, or mix of strategies, they choose, a study of recruiting in Chicago's clerical labor market did find evidence that intensive search, higher wages, and greater training are indeed substitutes. High-wage firms tended to hire only experienced workers and recruited their applicants through very low-cost sources (word-of-mouth, mainly, but there was some use of newspaper ads). Low-wage firms that hired at the lowest level and trained workers for successively more skilled positions—a feasible strategy in large firms where work can be highly specialized—tended to recruit inexperienced applicants very cheaply from local high schools. Low-wage, smaller firms that needed workers who could perform "up-to-speed" from the very beginning spent the most on search; they tended to use employment agencies (whose fees can be very high) to generate and screen a pool of applicants.

Recent research, however, indicates that for the United States in general, the tradeoffs among wages, search intensity, and training are more complicated than those for clerical labor in Chicago. A recent study of a random sample of American firms hiring in a variety of occupations found that high wages, training, and intensive search went together. This finding suggests that companies that train their workers are very concerned about the costs incurred when unqualified employees are hired into positions requiring training. These costs include lost output as well as wasted training. To save such costs, firms hiring into training positions want a high-quality applicant pool and use *both* intensive search and high wages to get it. Thus, while the Chicago study showed that *to get labor of a given quality,* intensive search, high wages, and training were substitutes, the recent national study indicates that high levels of worker quality substitute for lower wages, lower search costs and lower amounts of training as ways to hold down labor costs per unit of output.

SOURCES:   Joseph C. Ullman, "Interfirm Differences in the Cost of Search for Clerical Workers," *Journal of Business* 41 (April 1968): 153, and John Barron, John Bishop, and William Dunkelberg, "Employer Search: The Interviewing and Hiring of New Employees," *The Review of Economics and Statistics* 67 (February 1985): 43–52.

Because a large share of employers' hiring and training costs are implicit in nature, it is not surprising that detailed estimates of the magnitudes of hiring and training costs in the U.S. economy do not exist. Some estimates for individual firms have been made, however, that suggest that the magnitudes are large. For example, a study conducted by the American Management Association in 1960 concluded that the *hiring* and *orientation* costs of new employees varied from around $200 per unskilled laborer to more than $4500 per engineer.[1] This study did not include estimates of training costs, and the costs that were included are not expressed in terms of today's prices. A 1951 International Harvester Company study did include training costs and estimated that its average *hiring* and *training cost* per employee was about $380; in terms of current prices, this figure would be well over $1600.[2] Finally, a survey of 2264 employers conducted in 1982 concluded that, on average, company personnel spent close to 10 hours recruiting, screening, and interviewing applicants to fill one position, and that almost 150 hours were spent during the typical new hire's first three months of employment on informal and formal training. (The latter figure includes the trainee's time.)[3] If we value this time at $10.00 an hour (roughly the average earnings level in the economy in 1988) and ignore fringe benefits (see below), an average hiring and training cost per new hire of roughly $1600 is indicated.

## Fringe Benefits

We have much better data, however, on the other types of *nonwage* labor costs that firms incur. *Fringe benefits* include *legally required* social-insurance contributions and *privately provided* benefits. Examples of legally required benefits are payroll-based payments employers must make to fund programs that compensate workers for unemployment (unemployment insurance), injury (workers' compensation), and retirement (old-age, survivors', disability, and health insurance—or "Social Security"). Examples of privately provided benefits are holiday pay, vacation and sick leave, private pensions, and private health and life insurance.

Tables 4.1 and 4.2 give some idea of the magnitude and growth of these benefits. Department of Commerce data for the nation as a whole, tabulated in Table 4.1, indicate that forms of compensation other than wages and salaries rose from 6.4 percent of total compensation in 1956 to 16.4 percent in 1987. These data understate the importance of nonwage items in total compensation because they include holiday, vacation, and sick pay as wages. A more comprehensive measure, although for a more limited sample, comes from the biennial U.S. Chamber of Commerce survey of large manufacturing establishments. These data, tabulated in Table 4.2, indicate that total fringe

---

[1] See Frederick J. Gaudet, *Labor Turnover: Calculation and Costs* (New York: American Management Association, 1960).

[2] This study is cited in Walter Oi, "Labor as a Quasi-Fixed Factor," *Journal of Political Economy* 70 (December 1962): 538–55.

[3] John Barron and John Bishop, "Extensive Search, Intensive Search and Hiring Costs: New Evidence on Employer Hiring Activity," *Economic Inquiry* 23 (July 1985): 363–82.

**Table 4.1**  Compensation of Employees, 1956–87 (in billions of dollars)

| Year | Total | Wages and Salaries (including vacation and holiday pay) | Supplements | Ratio of Supplements to Total (in percent) |
|------|-------|--------------------------------------------------------|-------------|--------------------------------------------|
| 1956 | $ 244.7 | $ 229.0 | $ 15.7 | 6.4 |
| 1958 | 259.8 | 241.3 | 18.5 | 7.1 |
| 1960 | 296.7 | 272.8 | 23.8 | 8.0 |
| 1962 | 327.4 | 299.3 | 28.1 | 8.6 |
| 1964 | 371.0 | 337.7 | 33.2 | 8.9 |
| 1966 | 443.0 | 400.3 | 42.7 | 9.6 |
| 1968 | 524.7 | 471.9 | 52.8 | 10.1 |
| 1970 | 618.3 | 551.5 | 66.8 | 10.8 |
| 1972 | 726.2 | 638.7 | 87.6 | 12.1 |
| 1974 | 891.3 | 772.2 | 119.1 | 13.4 |
| 1976 | 1057.9 | 899.6 | 158.3 | 15.0 |
| 1978 | 1329.2 | 1119.6 | 209.7 | 15.8 |
| 1980 | 1638.2 | 1372.0 | 266.3 | 16.3 |
| 1982 | 1907.0 | 1586.1 | 320.9 | 16.8 |
| 1984 | 2213.9 | 1838.8 | 375.1 | 16.9 |
| 1986 | 2504.9 | 2089.1 | 415.8 | 16.6 |
| 1987 | 2647.5 | 2212.7 | 434.8 | 16.4 |

Notes: "Compensation of Employees" is the income accruing to employees as remuneration for their work.

"Wages and Salaries" consists of the monetary remuneration of employees, including the compensation of corporate officers; commissions, tips, and bonuses; and of payments in kind.

"Supplements" to wages and salaries consists of employer contributions for social insurance and other labor income. Employer contributions for social insurance comprise employer payments under old-age, survivor's, disability, and hospital insurance, state unemployment insurance, railroad retirement and unemployment insurance, government retirement, and a few other minor social insurance programs. Other labor income includes employer contributions to private pension, health and welfare, unemployment, and workers' compensation funds.

SOURCE: U.S. President, *Economic Report of the President* (Washington, DC: U.S. Government Printing Office, February 1988), Table B-24.

benefits as a percentage of *payroll* (which does not include pension and insurance costs) rose from 20.3 percent to 39.7 percent during the 1957–85 period. Both data sets indicate, then, an approximate doubling of the share of fringes in total compensation over the last 25–30 years. This increase has occurred in both legally required employer payments and privately negotiated benefits. (In Chapter 8 we will discuss *why* fringe benefits have increased as a fraction of total compensation.)

## The Quasi-Fixed Nature of Many Nonwage Costs

The distinction between wage and nonwage costs of employment is important because many nonwage costs are *costs per worker* rather than *costs per hour worked*. That is, many nonwage costs do not vary at the margin with the number of hours an employee works. Economists thus refer to them as *quasi-*

**Table 4.2**   Fringe Benefits as a Percent of Payroll in Manufacturing, 1957–1985

| Year | Legally Required Payments (employer's share) | Pensions, Insurance | Paid Rest | Pay for Time Not Worked | Other Items | Total Fringe Benefits |
|------|------|------|------|------|------|------|
| 1957 | 4.1 | 5.8 | 2.4 | 6.5 | 1.5 | 20.3 |
| 1959 | 4.5 | 6.1 | 2.7 | 6.7 | 1.6 | 21.6 |
| 1961 | 5.5 | 6.8 | 2.8 | 7.2 | 1.3 | 23.6 |
| 1963 | 5.9 | 6.7 | 2.9 | 7.3 | 1.4 | 24.2 |
| 1965 | 5.3 | 6.7 | 2.7 | 7.2 | 1.7 | 23.6 |
| 1967 | 6.4 | 7.0 | 3.0 | 7.3 | 1.9 | 25.6 |
| 1969 | 6.8 | 7.6 | 3.1 | 7.8 | 1.7 | 27.0 |
| 1971 | 6.9 | 9.9 | 3.5 | 8.6 | 1.7 | 30.6 |
| 1973 | 8.3 | 10.2 | 3.5 | 8.5 | 1.5 | 32.0 |
| 1975 | 8.8 | 11.6 | 3.7 | 10.1 | 1.9 | 36.1 |
| 1977 | 9.3 | 12.9 | 3.6 | 9.2 | 2.3 | 37.3 |
| 1979 | 10.1 | 12.1 | 3.6 | 8.8 | 2.6 | 37.2 |
| 1980 | 9.9 | 13.0 | 3.6 | 9.5 | 2.2 | 38.2 |
| 1982 | 10.6 | 13.9 | 3.0 | 9.2 | 2.3 | 39.1 |
| 1984 | 10.9 | 13.8 | 2.1 | 9.2 | 2.8 | 38.8 |
| 1985 | 10.8 | 13.1 | 3.5 | 9.4 | 2.9 | 39.7 |

Notes:   "Payroll" (used as the denominator in calculating the above percentages) includes pay for time not worked, such as vacations and holidays, but does not include pension and insurance costs or payroll taxes. "Other items" includes profit sharing, contributions to thrift plans, bonuses, and employee educational benefits.

SOURCE:   U.S. Chamber of Commerce, *Fringe Benefits and Employee Benefits* (various issues).

*fixed*—in the sense that once an employee is hired the firm is committed to a cost that does not vary with his or her hours of work.[4]

It should be obvious that hiring and training costs are quasi-fixed; they are associated with each new employee, not with the hours he or she works after the training period. Many fringe benefit costs, however, are also quasi-fixed. For example, in most firms holiday and vacation pay are specified as a fixed number of days per year (which may vary with seniority), and overtime hours do not affect these costs. To take another example, an employer's unemployment-insurance payroll-tax liability is specified to be a percentage (the tax rate) of each employee's earnings up to a maximum earnings level (the taxable wage base), which in over half of all states was $7000 in 1986. Since most employees earn more than $7000 per year, having an employee work an additional hour per week will *not* cause any increase in the employer's payroll-tax liability.[5] The quasi-fixed nature of many nonwage labor costs has

---

[4]   See Oi, "Labor as a Quasi-Fixed Factor."

[5]   This is not true for all fringe benefits. For example, the Social Security (OASDHI) payroll-tax liability of employers is also specified as a percentage of earnings up until a maximum taxable wage base; however, this wage base is considerably higher—$45,000 in 1988. Since this level exceeds the annual earnings of most full-time employees, the employer's payroll-tax liability *is* increased when an employer employs a typical employee an additional hour per week.

important effects on employer hiring and overtime decisions. These effects are discussed in the following section.

## The Employment/Hours Trade-Off

The simple model of the demand for labor presented in the preceding chapter spoke of the quantity of labor demanded and made no distinction between the number of individuals employed by a firm and the average length of its employees' work week. Holding all other inputs constant, however, a firm can produce a given level of output with various combinations of the number of employees hired and the number of hours worked per week. Presumably, increases in the number of employees hired will allow for shorter work weeks, while longer work weeks will allow for fewer employees, other things equal. In the short run, with capital and all other inputs fixed, the output ($Q$) a firm can produce is related to both its employment level ($M$) and its average work week per employee ($H$) by the following production function:

$$Q = f(M, H). \tag{4.1}$$

It is reasonable to assume that both inputs in equation (4.1) have positive marginal products ($MP_M > 0$; $MP_H > 0$). That is, increasing the number of employees, holdings hours constant—or increasing the average work week, holding employment constant—will lead to increases in output. While remaining positive, each of these marginal products must surely begin to decline at some point. In the case where the number of employees is increased this decline may be due to the reduced quantity of capital that each employee will have to work with or the fact that the firm may be forced to employ lower-quality workers. In the case where the hours each employee works per week are increased, the decline in marginal product may occur because after some point fatigue sets in.

Given this production function, how does a firm determine its optimal employment/hours combination?[6] Is it ever rational for an employer to work his or her existing employees overtime on a regularly scheduled basis, rather than hiring additional employees?

## Determining the Mix of Workers and Hours

The fact that certain labor costs are *not* hours-related and others are makes it important to examine the marginal cost an employer faces when employing an additional *worker* for whatever length work week other employees are working ($MC_M$). This marginal cost will equal the weekly value of the quasi-fixed labor costs plus the weekly wage and variable (with hours) fringe-benefit costs for the specified length of work week. Similarly, it is important to examine the marginal cost a firm faces when it seeks to increase the *average work week* of its existing work force by one hour ($MC_H$). This marginal cost will equal the

---

[6]  For estimates of such a function, see Martin Feldstein, "Specification of the Labor Input in the Aggregate Production Function," *Review of Economic Studies* 34 (October 1967): 375–86. See also Sherwin Rosen, "Short-Run Employment Variation in Class-I Railroads in the U.S., 1947–67," *Econometrica* 36 (July-October 1968): 511–29.

hourly wage and variable fringe-benefit costs multiplied by the number of employees in the work force. Of course, if the employer is in a situation in which an overtime premium (such as time-and-a-half or double time) must be paid for additional hours, that higher rate is the relevant wage rate to use in the latter calculation.

Viewed in this way, a firm's decision about its optimal employment/hours combination is no different than its decision about the usage of any two factors of production, which was discussed in Chapter 3. Specifically, to minimize the cost of producing any given level of output, a firm should adjust its employment level and its average work-week so that the costs of producing an added unit of output are equal for each:

$$\frac{MP_M}{MC_M} = \frac{MP_H}{MC_H}. \tag{4.2}$$

Put another way, the marginal cost of hiring an additional employee ($MC_M$) relative to the marginal cost of working the existing work force an additional hour ($MC_H$) should be equal to the marginal productivity of an additional employee relative to that of extending the work week by an hour:

$$\frac{MP_M}{MP_H} = \frac{MC_M}{MC_H}. \tag{4.3}$$

The Fair Labor Standards Act (FLSA) requires that all employees covered by the legislation receive an overtime pay premium of at least 50 percent of their regular hourly wage (time-and-a-half).[7] Now while a large proportion of overtime hours are worked because of disequilibrium phenomena—such as rush orders, seasonal demand, mechanical failures, and absenteeism—a substantial amount of overtime appears to be regularly scheduled. Equation (4.3) indicates why this scheduling of overtime may occur. Although overtime hours require premium pay, they also enable an employer to avoid the quasi-fixed employment costs associated with employing an additional worker. This point can be illustrated by considering what would happen if the overtime-wage premium were to be increased.

## Policy Analysis: The Overtime-Pay Premium

Periodically, proposals have been introduced in Congress to raise the overtime premium to double time.[8] The argument made to support such an

---

[7] In 1977, approximately 58 percent of all workers were covered by the overtime pay provisions of the FLSA. *See* U.S. Department of Labor, *Minimum Wage and Maximum Hours Standards Under the Fair Labor Standards Act* (Washington, DC: U.S. Government Printing Office, October 1978). The major categories of noncovered employees include executive, administrative, and professional personnel, outside salespersons, most state and local government employees, and agricultural workers.

[8] One attempt was made by Congressman John Conyers of Michigan in HR 1784, introduced into Congress in February of 1979. To quote a supporter of the proposal, "The AFL–CIO endorses the double-time provision as a means of generating additional jobs. The evidence is persuasive that the overtime-pay requirements of the Fair Labor Standards Act have lost their effectiveness as a deterrent to regularly scheduled overtime work." (*See* the statement by Rudolph Oswald, Director of Research, AFL–CIO, in the minutes of the Hearings before the Subcommittee on Labor Standards on HR 1784, October 23, 1979.)

**Table 4.3**   Hypothetical Effects of Overtime Pay on Costs of
Alternative Methods of Producing the Same Output

|  | Process A | Process B | Process C |
|---|---|---|---|
| Weekly Capital Cost | $10,000,000 | $10,000,000 | $11,000,000 |
| Number of Workers | 10,000 | 12,000 | 9,375 |
| Hours Per Week | 46 | 40 | 40 |
| Weekly Fixed Labor Cost @ $80/Worker | $800,000 | $960,000 | $750,000 |

*Weekly Costs @ $8/hr Straight Time Wage and $12/hr Overtime*

|  | Process A | Process B | Process C |
|---|---|---|---|
| Variable Labor Cost | $3,920,000 | $3,840,000 | $3,000,000 |
| Fixed Labor Cost | 800,000 | 960,000 | 750,000 |
| Total Labor Cost | 4,720,000 | 4,800,000 | 3,750,000 |
| Total Production Cost | $14,720,000 | $14,800,000 | $14,750,000 |

*Weekly Costs @ $8/hr Straight Time Wage and $16/hr Overtime*

|  | Process A | Process B | Process C |
|---|---|---|---|
| Variable Labor Cost | $4,160,000 | $3,840,000 | $3,000,000 |
| Fixed Labor Cost | 800,000 | 960,000 | 750,000 |
| Total Labor Cost | 4,960,000 | 4,800,000 | 3,750,000 |
| Total Production Cost | $14,960,000 | $14,800,000 | $14,750,000 |

increase is that even though unemployment remains a pressing national problem, the use of overtime hours has not diminished. Moreover, the argument continues, the deterrent effect of the overtime premium on the use of overtime has been weakened since the FLSA was enacted because of the growing share of hiring and training costs, fringe benefits, and government-mandated insurance premiums in total compensation (see Tables 4.1 and 4.2). As already noted, many of these costs are *quasi-fixed*—or employee-related rather than hours-related—and thus do not vary with overtime hours of work. An increase in them increases employers' marginal costs of hiring new employees relative to the costs of working their existing work forces overtime.

It is claimed, therefore, that the growth of these quasi-fixed costs has been at least partially responsible for increased use of overtime hours and that an increase in the overtime premium is required to better "spread the work."[9] Such an increase, by raising the marginal cost of overtime hours relative to the marginal cost of hiring new workers, should induce employers to substitute new employees for the overtime hours employers might otherwise schedule.

Table 4.3 illustrates the hypothetical effects on a firm of raising the overtime premium to double-time from time-and-a-half. The table compares the costs of different production processes that all lead to the same output. Suppose for a moment that only Processes A and B were available. A and B

---

[9] Weekly overtime hours of work in manufacturing averaged 2.56 hours per employee between 1956 and 1963. However, over the 1964–77 period, the average rose to 3.34 hours per employee, an increase of more than 30 percent.

## EXAMPLE   4.2

## Growth of Part-Time Employment

Just as the use of overtime hours has increased, part-time employment has grown as a share of total employment in most European countries and the United States in recent years. For example, between 1955 and 1984 the percentage of employees in U.S. nonagricultural industries who were employed part-time (defined as less than 35 hours per week) rose from 10.5 to 18.8. Explanations for this growth have focused in the main on the supply side of the labor market and on the changing industrial composition of employment. The growing shares of married women with children in the labor force (see Chapter 5), of older workers phasing into retirement, and of students who need to work to finance their educations are all thought to have increased the fraction of workers willing to work part-time. On the other side of the market, growth in the share of service sector employment (see Table 2.3) has increased the fraction of jobs in which part-time workers can be easily employed.

Recently, however, attention has shifted to the role that relative costs play in the growth of part-time employment. Assuming that part-time and full-time workers are substitutes in production, if the hourly labor costs (wages and hour-related fringes) or the quasi-fixed costs (nonhour-related fringes and hiring/training costs) of part-time workers fall relative to those of full-time workers, part-time employment should expand relative to full-time employment.

While it is well known that part-time workers' wages and fringe benefits are often lower than those of full-time workers, and that part-time workers in some European countries are often not eligible for social insurance programs financed by payroll taxes on employers, little is known about whether the part-time/full-time hourly labor cost and quasi-fixed cost ratios have *fallen* over time. One study did show, however, that employment of part-time workers in Great Britain expanded most rapidly during periods when they were covered by relatively few social insurance programs and protective legislation. Specifically, Britain's passage of the *Employment Protection Act of 1975,* which increased the eligibility of part-time employees for (among other things) job separation payments and maternity benefits, seemed to be associated with a slowdown in its part-time employment growth. Two other studies that used American data have also documented that across industries in the United States, the part-time/full-time employment ratio *does* appear to be negatively related to the part-time/full-time wage ratio; that is, in industries in which part-time workers' wages are lowest relative to full-time workers' wages, usage of part-time employees is highest relative to full-time employees.

SOURCES:  Ronald G. Ehrenberg, Pamela Rosenberg, and Jeanne Li, "Part-Time Employment in the United States" (NY State School of Industrial and Labor Relations, Cornell University, April 1986); R. Disney and E. M. Szyszczak, "Protective Labor Legislation and Part-Time Employment in Great Britain," *British Journal of Industrial Relations* 22 (March 1984): pp. 78–100; John Owen, *Working Hours* (Lexington, MA: D. C. Heath, 1979).

both use the same capital equipment but A uses fewer employees for a longer work week. Because B uses more workers, who must be recruited and perhaps trained, it would require the firm to undertake more quasi-fixed costs than would A; however, by avoiding payment of the overtime premium, process B has lower hourly (variable) costs of labor. With time-and-a-half overtime, Process A has lower costs than B. But if overtime wages are raised to twice the straight hourly wage, then B saves $160,000 per week compared to A. The firm might well be induced to add workers and cut the work week from 46 to 40 hours.

Adding workers and reducing the use of overtime is the outcome that advocates of a higher overtime premium expect to happen in many firms. Suppose now, however, that the more capital-intensive Process C is available. At time-and-a-half for overtime, A is still the least-cost method. But at double time for overtime, C is the cost-minimizing technique. We would expect the firm to adapt C and lay off workers in response to the higher overtime premium.

Table 4.3 illustrates that the overtime premium can cause a substitution of capital for labor as well as a substitution of people for hours. In addition, the table assumes that output is constant. Since an increase in the overtime premium raises overall production costs, there will also be a scale effect leading to the use of less labor and capital. Thus the number of jobs created by a higher overtime premium is likely to be less than its advocates might believe.[10]

## Hiring and Training Costs and the Demand for Labor

The models of the demand for labor given in Chapter 3 were *static,* in the sense that they considered only *current* marginal productivities and *current* labor costs. If all of a firm's labor costs are variable each year, then clearly it will employ labor in *each period* to the point where labor's marginal product equals the real wage. Once we begin to consider hiring and training costs, however, the analysis changes somewhat.[11] Hiring and training costs are usually heavily concentrated in the initial periods of employment and then do not recur. Later on, however, these early "investments" in hiring and training raise the productivity of employees. Once having made the investment, it is cheaper for the firm to *continue* employing its previous workers than to hire, at the same wage rate, new ones (who would have to be trained). Likewise, with an investment required for all *new* workers, employers will have to consider not only *current* marginal productivity and labor costs but also *future* marginal productivity and labor costs in deciding whether (and

[10] Ronald G. Ehrenberg, "The Impact of the Overtime Premium on Employment and Hours in U.S. Industry," *Western Economic Journal* 19 (June 1971): 199–207; Joyce Nussbaum and Donald Wise, "The Employment Impact of the Overtime Provisions of the FLSA" (Final Report submitted to the U.S. Department of Labor, 1977); Loren Solnick and Gene Swimmer, "Overtime and Fringe Benefits—A Simultaneous Equations Approach" (mimeograph, 1978); and Ronald G. Ehrenberg and Paul Schumann, *Longer Hours or More Jobs? An Investigation of Amending Hours Legislation to Create Employment* (Ithaca, NY: New York State School of Industrial and Labor Relations, Cornell University, 1982).

[11] This section draws heavily on Gary Becker's pioneering work, *Human Capital,* 2nd ed. (New York: National Bureau of Economic Research, 1975); and on Oi, "Labor as a Quasi-Fixed Factor." In what follows, all of the wage and hiring and training cost variables are measured in *real* terms.

**EXAMPLE   4.3**

## Fixed Labor Costs and the Erosion of the Employment-at-Will Doctrine

Until the 1970s, private sector employers were essentially free to hire or fire at will, unless prevented by a contract (union or individual) or specific law (for example, antidiscrimination laws). Increasingly, however, state courts have recognized exceptions to this doctrine, in effect giving current employees more protection against discharge. State courts have recognized three kinds of exception to employment-at-will: (1) Public Policy—28 states protect workers against firing if that action contravenes public policy such as being fired for missing work due to jury duty or for filing a workers' compensation claim; (2) Implied Contract—23 states treat implicit or explicit promises of job security, including oral statements or material in employment application forms or employee handbooks, as enforceable in court; and (3) Good Faith and Fair Dealing—3 states recognize that, even if the Public Policy or Implied Contract exceptions are not applicable, that an employer may not fire at will if such firing is a result of unfair treatment or bad faith by the employer.

The direct costs to employers of these exceptions to employment-at-will involve the possibility of lawsuits brought by terminated employees. Since many of these suits are torts, workers can claim punitive damages as well as compensatory damages for lost pay. For example, in California from January 1982 to February 1986, jury awards for general damages in employment-at-will cases (mostly brought by executives) averaged about $344,000, while punitive damages averaged $557,000, and the plaintiff prevailed in 75 percent of the verdicts.

The possibility of such lawsuits is leading some employers to change their personnel policies. For example, one way to reduce the likelihood of wrongful discharge suits is to spend more resources screening and recruiting potential employees. In addition, firms are being advised to promise less in their advertising and employee handbooks regarding job security. While reducing the implied offer of job security can diminish a firm's potential liability in lawsuits, it may also make it more difficult to recruit employees who value job security. Again, more resources may have to be devoted to recruiting.

Whether firms take the risk of being sued or alter their recruiting policies, erosion of employment-at-will raises the costs associated with each new hire. If this form of employee protection continues to increase, we would predict further incentives for employers to substitute capital for labor and hours for people.

SOURCES:  Robert J. Flanagan, "Labor Market Behavior and European Economic Growth," in Robert Z. Lawrence and Charles L. Schultze, eds., *Barriers to European Growth: A Transatlantic View* (Washington, DC: The Brookings Institution, 1987): 175–211; William H. Holley, Jr. and Roger S. Wolters, "An Employment-at-Will Vulnerability Audit," *Personnel Journal* 66 (April 1987): 130–38; Alan F. Westin, "Firing at Will on the Maginot Line," *Across the Board* 20 (December 1983): 56–58; David L. Nye, "Firing at Will—Careful, Now, Careful," *Across the Board* 19 (November 1982): 37–40; and Ronald Ehrenberg, "Workers' Rights: Rethinking Protective Labor Legislation," *Research in Labor Economics* vol. 8, Part B, ed. R. Ehrenberg (Greenwich, CT: JAI Press, 1986).

**EXAMPLE   4.4**

## Compulsory Health Insurance and the Demand for Labor

In 1987, a bill was introduced in Congress to amend the Fair Labor Standards Act to require minimum health care coverage. The bill would cover all people working at least 17.5 hours per week and their dependents. The bill would limit the worker's share of premium costs and the health-care deductible payable by the employee. While firms with generous health insurance plans would already be in compliance with the bill, many firms would find dramatic cost increases in their benefits packages. For example, one study found that major retailers could be forced to double their health care insurance expenses.

For those companies whose health care insurance costs would rise under the proposed bill, this law would raise the fixed costs of employing workers for at least 17.5 hours per week. Firms would thus have the following incentives. First, some companies would be induced to reduce work hours for part-time workers to below 17.5 per week, to escape the required health care coverage. Second, the added fixed costs for employees working at least 17.5 hours would induce a substitution of hours for people; that is, for the firms offering full-time work (the vast majority), the bill would likely cause an increase in the work week and a reduction in the number of jobs. Companies facing increased demand might now find it cheaper to pay their current workers overtime rather than add new workers and incur the associated health insurance costs. Likewise, firms facing reduced demand might now find it cheaper to reduce their workforces rather than cut the hours per worker.

Third, if product markets are competitive, firms for which health care costs have increased would hold the line on future wage increases, and wages would fall below the level that would have prevailed had it not been for the health care bill. Even if wages fell by the full amount of the increase in health care costs, the net effect of the first two changes would be to reduce the number of *full-time* jobs in the economy.

SOURCES: "Kennedy's Mandate For Minimum Health Benefits," *Employee Benefit Plan Review* 42 (August 1987): 56–61 and "Labor Letter," *Wall Street Journal,* September 1, 1987, p. 1.

how many) to hire. In short, the presence of investment costs—hiring and training expenses—means that hiring decisions must take into account past, present, and future factors.

To illustrate the hiring decision in the face of labor-investment costs, let us consider a firm that is seeking to determine its employment level over a two-period horizon. Suppose the firm incurs hiring and training costs only in the first period (period 0) and that these *direct outlays* amount to $H per worker. Suppose also that during the initial period, when workers are undergoing training, their actual marginal product schedule is lowered from $MP^*$ to $MP_0$ (as shown in Figure 4.1)—in other words, $MP^* - MP_0$ represents the *implicit* costs of training. In the period after training (period 1), the marginal

**Figure 4.1** Multiperiod Demand for Labor

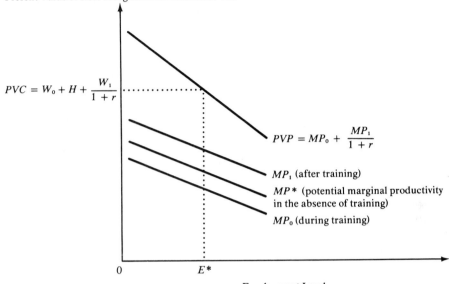

Marginal Product of Labor *(MP)*
Present Value of Marginal Product of Labor *(PVP)*
Present Value of Real Marginal Cost of Labor *(PVC)*

$PVC = W_0 + H + \dfrac{W_1}{1 + r}$

$PVP = MP_0 + \dfrac{MP_1}{1 + r}$

$MP_1$ (after training)
$MP*$ (potential marginal productivity in the absence of training)
$MP_0$ (during training)

0

$E*$

Employment Level

productivity of trained employees is higher ($MP_1$). Finally, suppose that the wage a firm must pay each employee is $W_0$ and $W_1$ in periods 0 and 1, respectively; for now, we take these wages as given by the market, although we will shortly examine how they are determined.

## The Concept of Present Value

In determining its optimal employment level over the two periods, the firm clearly must consider the costs of employing workers in both periods and their marginal products in both periods. A *naive* approach would be to simply add up the costs ($W_0 + W_1 + H$), add up the marginal products ($MP_0 + MP_1$), and then stop hiring when the sum of the marginal products that the last worker produces over the two periods is just equal to the sum of his or her wages and hiring and training costs. This approach is naive because it ignores the fact that benefits accruing in the future are worth less to the firm than an equal level of benefits that accrue now. Similarly, costs that occur in the future are less burdensome to the firm than equal dollar costs that occur in the present.

Why should this be the case? The answer hinges on the role of interest rates. A dollar of revenue earned by a firm today can be invested at some market rate of interest so that by the second period it will be worth more than a dollar. Hence, faced with a choice of employing a worker whose marginal product is 5 in period 0 and 2 in period 1, or a worker whose marginal product is 2 in period 0 and 5 in period 1, the firm would prefer the former (if wages for the two workers were equal in each period). The sooner the product is produced and sold, the quicker the firm can gain access to the funds, invest them, and earn interest.[12]

Similarly, faced with the option of paying a $100 wage bill today or $100 next period, the firm should prefer the second option. It could earn interest on the $100 in the first period, make the payment in the next period, and have the interest left over. If the firm had made the payment in the initial period, it would not have had the opportunity to earn interest income.

These examples illustrate that firms prefer benefit streams in which the benefits occur as early as possible and prefer cost streams in which the costs occur as late as possible. But how do we compare different benefit and cost streams when benefits and costs occur in more than one period? Economists rely on the concept of *present value*, which we define to be the value *now* of an entire stream of benefits or costs.

Suppose a firm receives the sum of $\$B_0$ in the current period and will receive nothing in the next period. How much money could it have in the second period if it invested $\$B_0$ at a rate of interest that equals $r$? It would have its original sum, $B_0$, plus the interest it earned, $rB_0$:

$$B_1 = B_0 (1 + r). \tag{4.4}$$

Since assets of $B_1$ can be automatically acquired by investing $B_0$ at the market rate of interest, $B_0$ *now and* $B_1$ *next period are equivalent values*. That is, a person who is offered $B_0$ now or $B_1$ in one year would regard the offers as exactly the same as long as $B_1 = B_0 (1 + r)$. Following this line of reasoning, suppose that the firm knows it will receive $B_1$ in the second period. What is the sum that if received in the first period would be equivalent to receiving $B_1$ a year later? The firm would need to have sum $X$ in the first period in order to invest this sum and wind up with principal plus interest equal to $B_1$ in period 2:

$$X (1 + r) = B_1. \tag{4.5}$$

Dividing both sides by $(1 + r)$,

$$X = \frac{B_1}{(1 + r)}. \tag{4.6}$$

The quantity $X$ in equation (4.6) is called the *discounted value* of $B_1$ earned one period in the future. The *present value* of a firm's earnings over two periods is equal to its earnings in the first period plus the discounted value of its earnings in the second period.[13] Returning to our two-period hiring decision example given at the start of this section, the *present value* of marginal

---

[12]   We are assuming here, of course, that the real price the firm receives for its product is constant and that the real rate of interest is positive.

[13]   Earnings in the first period are not discounted because they are received *now*, not in the future.

productivity (*PVP*) can now be seen as

$$PVP = MP_0 + \frac{MP_1}{1 + r}. \tag{4.7}$$

That is, the value of a worker's marginal productivity *now* to the firm is the marginal productivity in the current period ($MP_0$) plus the marginal productivity in the second period *discounted* by $(1 + r)$. Likewise, the present value of the real marginal *cost* of labor (*PVC*) is equal to

$$PVC = W_0 + H + \frac{W_1}{1 + r} \tag{4.8}$$

where $r$ is the market rate of interest. $W_0$ and $H$ are not discounted because they are incurred in the current period. However, $W_1$ is discounted by $(1 + r)$ because it is incurred one year into the future.

The present value calculation reduces a stream of benefits or costs to a single number that summarizes a firm's entire stream of revenues or liabilities over different time periods. For example, the *PVC* can be thought of as the answer to the question, "Given that a firm incurs costs of $(W_0 + H)$ this period and $W_1$ next period per worker, how much does it have to set aside today to be able to cover both periods' costs?" The *PVC* is *less* than $W_0 + H + W_1$, because $W_1$ is not owed until the second period, and any funds set aside to cover $W_1$ can be invested now. If it sets aside $W_1/(1 + r)$ to cover its labor cost in the next period, and invests this amount earning a rate of return $r$, the interest $r[W_1/(1 + r)]$, plus principal, $W_1/(1 + r)$, available in the next period will just equal $W_1$. Similarly, the *PVP* can be thought of as the answer to the question, "Given that a worker's marginal product will be $MP_0$ in this period and $MP_1$ next period, what is the value of that output stream to the employer today?" The *PVP* is less than $MP_0 + MP_1$ because if the firm were to attempt to borrow against the employee's future marginal product, it could borrow at most $MP_1/(1 + r)$ today and still afford to repay the principal plus interest, $r[MP_1/(1 + r)]$, out of earnings in the second period.[14]

## The Multiperiod Demand for Labor

The concept of present value can help clarify what determines the demand-for-labor function in our two-period model. Rather than focusing on the marginal product of labor in each period, an employee's productivity must be

---

[14] More generally, if the firm expects to receive benefits of $B_0, B_1, B_2, \ldots, B_n$ dollars over the current and next $n$ periods, and if it faces the same interest rate, $r$, in each period, its present value of benefits (*PVB*) is given by

$$PVB = B_0 + \frac{B_1}{1 + r} + \frac{B_2}{(1 + r)^2} + \frac{B_3}{(1 + r)^3} + \cdots + \frac{B_n}{(1 + r)^n}.$$

An analogous expression exists for the present value of costs. The reader should make sure that he or she understands why the denominator of $B_2$ is $(1 + r)^2$, the denominator of $B_3$ is $(1 + r)^3$, and so forth. If one thinks in terms of a series of one-period loans or investments, it should become obvious. For example, $X_0$ invested for one period yields $X_0 (1 + r)$ at the end of the period. Let us call $X_0 (1 + r) = X_1$. $X_0$ invested for two periods is equal to its value after one period ($X_1$) times $(1 + r)$, or $X_2 = X_1 (1 + r)$. But $X_1 = X_0 (1 + r)$, so $X_2 = X_0 (1 + r)^2$. To find the present value of $X_2$ we divide by $(1 + r)^2$, so that $X_0 = X_2 / (1 + r)^2$.

summarized by the *present value* of the marginal-product schedule, which is drawn as the curve *PVP* in Figure 4.1. Similarly, rather than focusing on the hiring and training costs and the wage rates in each period separately, an employer must consider the *present value* of the marginal cost of labor (*PVC*). To maximize its present value of profits, a firm should employ labor up until the point that adding an *additional* employee yields as much as it costs (when both yields and costs are stated as present values):

$$PVP = PVC, \text{ or } MP_0 + \frac{MP_1}{1 + r} = W_0 + H + \frac{W_1}{1 + r}. \tag{4.9}$$

Given the particular values of $W_0$, $W_1$, $H$, and $r$ that are specified in Figure 4.1, this proves to be the employment level $E^*$. More generally, the employer's demand-for-labor schedule coincides with the present value of the marginal-product-of-labor schedule. Now equation (4.9) merely states the familiar profit-maximizing condition—that marginal returns should equal marginal costs—in a multiperiod context. If $H$ were zero, for example, equation (4.9) implies that profits could be maximized when labor is hired so that $MP_0 = W_0$ and $MP_1/(1 + r) = W_1/(1 + r)$—or, since $(1 + r)$ is the denominator on both sides of the equation, $MP_1 = W_1$. Thus, when $H$ is zero and there are no hiring or training costs, the conditions demonstrated in Chapter 3 are sufficient to guarantee profit maximization in the multiperiod context. However, when $H$ is positive—which means that firms make initial investments in their workers—the conditions for maximizing profits change. To understand the change in profit-maximizing conditions suggested by equation (4.9), suppose that in the first period the wage the worker receives ($W_0$) plus the firm's direct outlays ($H$) exceed the extra worker's output ($MP_0$). We can call this difference the *net cost* to the firm of hiring an additional worker in the first period ($NC_0$):

$$NC_0 = W_0 + H - MP_0 > 0. \tag{4.10}$$

For the firm to maximize the present value of its profit stream, it must thus get a net *surplus* in the second period—see equation (4.9). If it does not, the firm will not have any incentives to hire the additional worker. The discounted value of the second period's surplus ($G$) is defined as:

$$G = \frac{MP_1}{1 + r} - \frac{W_1}{1 + r} = \frac{MP_1 - W_1}{1 + r}. \tag{4.11}$$

From equations (4.9), (4.10), and (4.11), we see that the discounted value of the second-period surplus must equal the net cost ($NC_0$) in the first period if the firm is to maximize profits:

$$W_0 + H - MP_0 = \frac{MP_1 - W_1}{1 + r}. \tag{4.12}$$

A second-period surplus can *only* exist if wages in that period ($W_1$) lie *below* marginal product ($MP_1$). This surplus makes up for the fact that the employer's labor costs in the first period ($W_0 + H$) were above the worker's marginal product ($MP_0$).

To this point we have established two things. First, equation (4.9) has shown that in a multiperiod model of labor demand, the firm's demand curve is the same thing as the curve representing the *present value* of labor's marginal product over the periods of hire. Thus, the firm maximizes profits when the present value of its marginal labor costs equals the present value of labor's marginal product. Second, we demonstrated in equation (4.12), that maximizing profits when the firm's labor costs in the first period exceed the worker's first-period marginal product requires wages in the second period to be below marginal productivity in the second period (so that a surplus is generated). The only situations in which a second-period surplus is not necessary to induce the hiring of an additional employee are (1) where investment costs ($H$) are zero in the first period, or (2) where investment costs of $H$ exist, but the first-period wage is decreased to such an extent that it equals $MP_0 - H$. In this latter case, employees pay for their own training by accepting a wage in the first period that is decreased by the direct costs of training. Understanding how $W_0$ and $W_1$ are determined, then, is central to the task of analyzing the demand for labor in the presence of investment costs. To understand the level and time profile of wages, however, we must first examine the nature of job training.

## General and Specific Training

The relevance of our conceptual model of training is indicated by the fact that about 85 percent of companies have on-site training programs for their workers. Among those companies with programs, 92 percent of blue-collar workers are taught particular job skills, while 65–84 percent of white-collar workers are taught job-related skills.[15]

Following Gary Becker, it is useful to conceptually distinguish between two types of training: (1) *general training* that increases an individual's productivity *to many employers* equally, and (2) *specific training* that increases an individual's productivity *only at the firm* in which he or she is currently employed.[16] Pure general training might include teaching an applicant basic reading skills or teaching a would-be secretary how to type. Pure specific training might include teaching a worker how to use a machine that is unique to a single employer—or showing him or her the organization of the production process in the plant. The distinction is primarily a conceptual one, because most training contains aspects of both types; however, the distinction does yield some interesting insights. Suppose (continuing our two-period model) that a firm offers *general* training to its employees and incurs a first-period net cost equal to $NC_0$ of equation (4.10). This training increases employee marginal productivity to $MP_1$ in the second period, and the firm scales its wages ($W_1$) in the second period so that there is a surplus in that period whose present value ($G$) equals $NC_0$. What will happen?

The trained employee is worth $MP_1$ to several other firms, but is getting paid less than $MP_1$ by the firm doing the training (so that it can obtain the

[15]   Harriet Gorlin, *Personnel Practices I: Recruitment, Placement, Training, Communication,* Conference Board Information Bulletin 89 (New York: The Conference Board, 1981), Table 34.
[16]   Becker, *Human Capital.*

required surplus). The employee can thus get *more* from some other employer—who did not incur training costs and thus will not demand a surplus—than he or she can from the employer offering the training. This situation will induce the employee to quit after training and seek work elsewhere. Assuming all other conditions of employment are the same, the firm would have to pay its employees $MP_1$ after training to keep them from quitting. If firms must pay a wage equal to $MP_1$ after training, they will not be willing to pay for general training of their employees. They either will not offer training or will force the trainees to bear the full cost of their own training by paying wages that are less than marginal product in the period of training by an amount equal to the direct training costs; that is, for them to offer training $NC_0$ must equal zero. Exceptions to this conclusion can be found in cases where the employee is bound to the firm in some way.

For example, the federal government requires employees it has sent to college (in Master of Business Administration programs, for example) to remain in the federal service for a specified number of years or to repay the costs of the training. Similarly, firms may offer to pay for the general training of long-term employees bound to the firm by pension rights or unique promotion opportunities (see Chapter 8 for further discussion).

In contrast, consider an individual who receives *specific training* that increases marginal productivity with the *current* employer to $MP_1$ in the second period. Since the training is firm-specific, the trainee's marginal product in *other* firms remains at its pretraining level of $MP^*$. Now the firm that trains the worker *will* have an incentive to offer (and at least partially pay for) the job training, because it can pay a wage above $MP^*$ but below $MP_1$ in the second period. Why will it pay above $MP^*$ in the second period? It will do so because if it makes a first-period investment in the worker it does not want the worker to quit. If it pays $MP^*$, the worker will not have much of an incentive to stay with the firm, since he or she can get $MP^*$ elsewhere too. The higher $W_1$ is compared to $MP^*$, the less likely the worker is to quit. Why will the firm pay less than $MP_1$? As noted earlier, the firm must obtain a surplus in the second period to recoup its first-period investment costs. Thus, the firm prefers *a second-period* wage that is above $MP^*$ and below $MP_1$:

$$MP^* < W_1 < MP_1. \tag{4.13}$$

This second-period wage is also preferred by employees. If, for example, they were promised a wage equal to $MP_1$ in the second period, the lack of employer surplus would mean two things. First, employees would be required to pay the *full* cost of training in the first period, and, second, they would live in fear of being laid off. Since their second-period wage would be equal to their marginal productivity, a firm would not lose much if it laid them off—and *the workers* would lose all of the investment costs they incurred in the first period. However, if the workers generate a surplus for the employer, layoff is less likely in the post-training period. The wage scheme in equation (4.13) thus suggests that both employer and employee should be willing to share in the costs of specific training. If employees bear *all* of the costs of training, then

**EXAMPLE   4.5**

# Paternalism in Japan: Is It Rooted in Feudalism or Economics?

In Japan there are many large firms in which employer and employee are mutually committed to a virtual lifetime relationship. These firms almost never lay off workers, and all of their new hires have recently left school. Employees, on the other hand, are given incentives to remain with the firm for their entire careers. Wages are strongly linked to seniority, pensions and paid vacations are formulated to encourage a long job tenure, and company loyalty is encouraged through the provision of "paternalistic services," such as company housing, health care, and recreational facilities. According to James Abegglen, the following are consequences of these employment policies:

> At whatever level of organization in the Japanese factory, the worker commits himself on entrance to the company for the remainder of his working career. The company will not discharge him even temporarily except in the most extreme circumstances. He will not quit the company for industrial employment elsewhere. He is a member of the company in a way resembling that in which persons are members of families.

While the paternalistic employment relationship just described really pertains to less than half of all Japanese workers—full-time, year-round, predominantly male workers in large firms—the mere existence of such a seemingly permanent employer-employee attachment for so many workers in Japan has drawn much comment. Abegglen views this lifelong relationship as a natural outgrowth of Japan's feudal system prior to industrial development, with its emphasis on the reciprocal loyalty of lord and vassal:

> The loyalty of the worker to the industrial organization, the paternal methods of motivating and rewarding the worker, the close involvement of the company in all manner[s] of what seem to western eyes to be personal and private affairs of the worker—all have parallels with Japan's preindustrial social organization.

Adherents of this explanation seem to conclude that the Japanese system of industrial relations represents a continuation of an ancient, elitist paternalism rather than a system that was consciously chosen for economic reasons by rational industrialists.

An alternative view is that the Japanese system just described finds its roots in profit-maximization calculus. Those who espouse this view argue that Japan's rapid industrialization beginning around 1900 was accompanied by severe shortages of skilled factory workers. Firms competed against each other for skilled labor, and by the end of World War I this fierce competition for workers had led to annual turnover rates of 100 percent for many factories. By 1917 firms were using bribes, cash bonuses, and even physical threats to secure and retain a work force. A government report in 1919 lamented, "The virtue of long and diligent service has been supplanted by a propensity to change jobs."

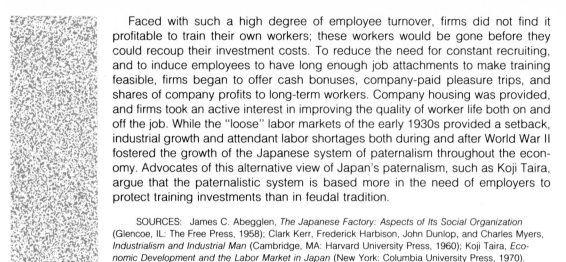

Faced with such a high degree of employee turnover, firms did not find it profitable to train their own workers; these workers would be gone before they could recoup their investment costs. To reduce the need for constant recruiting, and to induce employees to have long enough job attachments to make training feasible, firms began to offer cash bonuses, company-paid pleasure trips, and shares of company profits to long-term workers. Company housing was provided, and firms took an active interest in improving the quality of worker life both on and off the job. While the "loose" labor markets of the early 1930s provided a setback, industrial growth and attendant labor shortages both during and after World War II fostered the growth of the Japanese system of paternalism throughout the economy. Advocates of this alternative view of Japan's paternalism, such as Koji Taira, argue that the paternalistic system is based more in the need of employers to protect training investments than in feudal tradition.

SOURCES:  James C. Abegglen, *The Japanese Factory: Aspects of Its Social Organization* (Glencoe, IL: The Free Press, 1958); Clark Kerr, Frederick Harbison, John Dunlop, and Charles Myers, *Industrialism and Industrial Man* (Cambridge, MA: Harvard University Press, 1960); Koji Taira, *Economic Development and the Labor Market in Japan* (New York: Columbia University Press, 1970).

there will be no second-period surplus to protect them from layoff. If employers bear *all* of the costs, they may not be able to pay their employees enough in the second period to guard against their quitting. It is in their *mutual* interest to foster a long-term employment relationship, which can best be done by sharing the investment costs of the first period.

## Implications of the Theory

**Layoffs.**  One major implication of the presence of specific training is the above-menioned reluctance of firms to lay off workers in whom they have invested. We have seen that in the post-training period, wages must be less than marginal productivity if the firm is to have any incentives at all to bear some of the initial training costs. This gap between $MP_1$ and $W_1$ provides protection against employee layoffs—even in a recession.

Suppose a recession were to occur and cause product demand to fall. The marginal productivity associated with each employment level would fall (from $MP'$ to $MP''$ in Figure 4.2). For workers whose wage was equal to marginal productivity before the recession, this fall would reduce their marginal productivity to *below* their wage—and profit-maximizing employers would reduce employment, as shown in panel (a) of Figure 4.2, to maximize profits under the changed market conditions. In terms of Figure 4.2 (a), employment would fall from E' to E".

For a worker whose wage was *less* than marginal productivity—owing to past specific training—the decline in marginal productivity might *still* leave such productivity *above* the wage. Firms would not be making enough surplus in the second period to earn back their net labor costs incurred during the

**Figure 4.2**   The Effect of a Decline in Demand on Employment with General and Specific Training

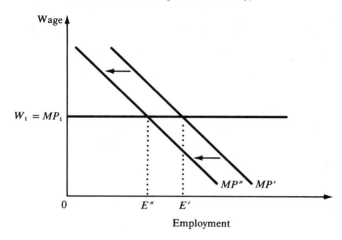

**(a) General Training**
(a decline in *MP* will reduce employment
for those whose wage = $MP_1$ initially)

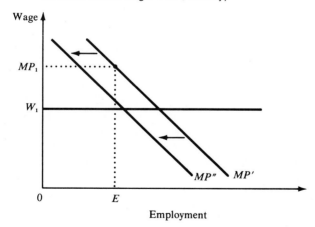

**(b) Specific Training**
(a decline in *MP* will not necessarily reduce employment
for those whose wage $<$ $MP_1$ initially)

training period. However, these costs have already been spent and they cannot get them back. They will not hire and train *new* workers, but neither will they fire the ones they have trained. After all, these trained workers are still generating more than the company is paying them, and to lay them off would only reduce profits further! Thus, as panel (b) of Figure 4.2 shows, workers in whom their employers have invested are shielded to some extent from being laid off in business downturns. Of course, if marginal productivity fell to the point where it was below the wage, even trained workers might be laid off.[17]

Thus, this model suggests that during an economic downswing firms will have an incentive to lay off workers with either no training or with general training but to retain workers who have specific training. Although it is difficult to estimate the extent to which workers have specific training "imbedded" in them, there is some evidence that layoffs are lower for workers with higher skill levels, holding all other things (including their *wage rates*) constant.[18] Since the divergence between skill (productivity) and wages during the post-training period can be taken as a measure of the extent of specific training, this finding provides some support for the theory.

**Labor productivity.**   A second phenomenon our revised theory of demand can help explain is the fall in average productivity—output per labor hour—that occurs in the early stages of a recession.[19] As demand and output start to fall, firms that have invested in specific training respond by maintaining their specifically trained workers on their payrolls. Such *labor hoarding* causes measured productivity to fall. Of course, the converse of this result is that when demand picks up, firms can increase their output levels without proportionately increasing their employment levels because they, in effect, maintained an "inventory" of skilled labor. Labor hoarding due to specific investments in human capital thus causes average productivity to increase in the early stages of a cyclical expansion and to decrease in the early stages of a recession.

**Minimum wage effects again.**   A third implication of our theory has to do with "training" effects of the minimum wage. We have seen that firms will offer *general* training only if the employee fully pays for it. For this to be the case, the employee must receive a first-period wage that is below actual marginal productivity by an amount equal to the direct costs of training. If the minimum wage is set so that receiving such a low wage is precluded, then employers will not offer them training. They may be willing to *hire* workers— if the minimum wage is not above their marginal productivity—but any training would have to take place off the job.

---

[17]   If the downturn is expected to be short, and if marginal productivity is not too much below the wage, firms might not lay off workers and chance losing them. Why any adjustment would come in the form of layoffs rather than by workers temporarily reducing their wages is discussed in Chapter 17.

[18]   For a summary of the evidence, see Donald O. Parsons, "Models of Labor Market Turnover: A Theoretical and Empirical Survey" in Ronald G. Ehrenberg (ed.), *Research in Labor Economics,* 1 (Greenwich, CT: JAI Press, 1977). Parsons also provides evidence on the existence of a negative relationship between quit rates and specific training; as noted earlier, this is another implication of the theory.

[19]   See the 1977 *Employment and Training Report of the President* (Washington, DC: U.S. Government Printing Office, 1977), pp. 23–25.

This same analysis would also hold for *specific* training. If the minimum wage prevented the *first* period wage from going low enough, firms offering specific training might *not* be able to offer *second* period wages that are higher than workers' alternative offers. If this is the case, trained workers will always be on the verge of quitting in the second period—which places the firm's first period investment at risk. Under these conditions, firms will have little incentive to offer specific training. Minimum-wage legislation may thus reduce the number of jobs offering training options that are available to low-skilled youths and lower their rates of wage growth. In fact, there is some preliminary evidence that this has occurred.[20]

# Credentials or Screening Devices and the Internal Labor Market

The addition of hiring and training costs and other quasi-fixed costs of labor into models of labor demand has been shown in this chapter to lead to numerous insights about firms' employment/hours decisions and about the demand for labor in a multiperiod setting. This final section will sketch several additional extensions of these multiperiod models, including the use of credentials or other screening devices and the internal labor market.

## Credentials or Screening Devices

Because firms often bear the costs of hiring and training workers, it is in their interests to make these costs as low as possible. Other things equal, firms should prefer to obtain a given quality work force at the least possible cost. Similarly, they should prefer to hire workers who learn quickly because such workers could be trained at less cost. Unfortunately, it may prove expensive for firms to extensively investigate the backgrounds of every possible individual who applies for a job to ascertain his or her skill level and ability to undertake training.

One way to reduce these costs is to rely on *credentials*, or *signals*, in the hiring process rather than intensively investigating the qualities of individual applicants.[21] For example, if *on average* college graduates are more productive than high-school graduates, an employer might specify that a college degree is a requirement for the job. Rather than interviewing and testing all applicants to try to ascertain the productivity of each, the firm may simply select its new employees from the pool of applicants who meet this educational standard. Similarly, if employers believe that married men are less

[20]  Linda Leighton and Jacob Mincer, "Effects of Minimum Wages on Human Capital Formation," in Simon Rottenberg ed. *The Economics of Legal Minimum Wages* (Washington, DC: American Enterprise Institute, 1981).

[21]  See Michael Spence, "Job Market Signaling," *Quarterly Journal of Economics* 87 (August 1973): 355–74.

**EXAMPLE    4.6**

## Training at the Company Level: The Xerox Corporation

During the 1980s the Xerox Corporation, a major office equipment company, has faced many industry problems. The office equipment industry has become increasingly competitive; technology in this field has been advancing rapidly; and pressures have increased to develop new products. These economic forces have led Xerox to an increased emphasis on the continuing training of its engineering workforce.

In addition to paying full tuition for any employee who completes a bachelor's or advanced degree, Xerox offers an extensive set of over 150 training programs for its technical personnel. Employees serve as "faculty" for these courses, and instructor workshops are provided on a regular basis. The instructors are paid from funds provided by a tuition of $15 per employee per course. As an alternative to classroom training, Xerox also operates two "learning centers" in which employees choose from 80 self-instructional courses in subjects such as computer programming, electrical engineering, business, mathematics, and quality control. In 1985, about 30 percent of Xerox's salaried employees enrolled in at least one technical course (either in the classroom or at a learning center).

Employees are given an incentive to enroll in such training courses through the performance-appraisal process. Each year, supervisors grade each of their employees on his or her performance, and each worker's level of skills is explicitly discussed. The performance review makes it clear that employees' career progression at Xerox can be enhanced through the company's training programs. Because of the rapid technological changes in this industry, many employees enroll in training to reduce the risk that their skills will become obsolete.

While it is difficult to determine whether the employees "pay" for such training in the form of reduced wages (recall our discussion of general and specific training), Xerox's executives note that their engineering employees are a very stable group with low turnover rates. In such a setting, the company may well be able to recoup investments in skills that are of potential value to other companies as well.

SOURCE:  Richard A. Morano and Norman Deets, "Keeping Technologists on the Road to the Future," *Training and Development Journal* 40 (December 1986): 38–41.

---

likely to quit their jobs than single men, or that 25-year-olds are less likely to quit than teenagers, they may give preferential treatment to married men and 25-year-olds over single men and teenagers in their hiring decisions.

Such forms of *statistical discrimination*—judging individuals by *group* characteristics—have obvious costs. On the one hand, for example, there may be some high-school graduates who are fully qualified to work for a firm that insists on college graduates. The exclusion of them from the pool of potential applicants imposes costs on them (they do not get the job); however, it also imposes costs on the employer *if* other qualified applicants cannot be

**EXAMPLE   4.7**

## Coping with Fluctuations in Product Demand: The Use of Product Inventories, Temporary-Help Services, and Reserve Workers

The demand for a firm's product is never constant over a given period. It fluctuates from day to day, week to week, and month to month. If a firm finds it feasible to hold inventories of its finished goods, these fluctuations in demand can be absorbed by *product inventories*—thus permitting the firm to keep its employment and production levels constant during the period. That is, in periods when product demand does not absorb what is produced, the firm stores its unsold output; in periods when demand exceeds output, these stores are drawn down. Many firms, however, find that the costs of maintaining inventories are very high. Some products are perishable, and they either spoil or become obsolete very quickly. Other products are expensive to make or bulky to store, and keeping inventories of them ties up funds and building space, requires large insurance coverage, and imposes added property taxes on the firm. Still other firms produce services, which by their very nature are impossible to produce ahead of demand. How can firms with high inventory costs cope with fluctuating demand?

One way to cope is to hire workers on a temporary basis when product demand is unusually high. As indicated in the text, however, the one-time costs of advertising an opening, screening candidates, and processing the paperwork necessary to put workers on the payroll can be quite high. If the tenure of the job is relatively short, the firm may have insufficient time to recoup these costs. In this case, the firm might consider "renting" workers from a temporary-help service. Temporary-help services specialize in screening and hiring workers who are then put to work in client companies that need temporary workers. These temporary workers are technically employees of, and receive their paychecks from, the temporary-help service; however, they work under the direction and supervision of the client. The temporary-help service bills its clients for the time its workers spend under their direction. The hourly charges to its clients are generally *above* the wage the client would pay if it hired directly—a premium the client is willing to pay because it is spared the investment costs associated with hiring. Because obtaining temporary jobs through the temporary-help service also saves employees repeated investment costs associated with searching and applying for the available temporary openings, the employees are willing to take a wage *less* than what they otherwise would receive. The difference between what its clients are charged and what its employees are paid, of course, permits the successful temporary-help service to cover the investment costs necessary in obtaining a match of employer and employee, and to earn a profit.

The temporary-help service industry has been growing rapidly of late. For example, in 1977 the industry employed about 293,000 workers, but by 1985 it had 735,000 employees. In addition, businesses appear to be contracting out services (for example, data processing) that they used to do themselves. One reason for such changes is believed to be the increased vulnerability of the economy to foreign competition and the resulting increased value firms put on flexibility. Contracting out allows firms to change the number of employees—as well as the skills used—without requiring layoffs or retraining.

Hiring of temporary workers is clearly not feasible if a significant amount of specific training must be undertaken before the job can be adequately performed. When job tenure is expected to be short, neither employer nor employee has a long enough time to recoup training costs. (For this reason, temporary help services deal mainly with jobs requiring general training: typing, drafting, simple clerical skills, and so forth.) Where specific training is important, the firm might use *overtime* as a means of meeting fluctuations in product demand. This option, discussed at length in the text, involves paying a substantial wage premium, in some cases leads to problems associated with fatigue, and could cause problems of coordinating production in some industries.

The final option for meeting fluctuations in demand is to hire *reserve workers*—workers who are hired on a full-time basis but who are idle or partially idle some of the time. Some very large plants with easily predicted absentee rates hire and train workers for the specific purpose of filling in for absentees. What may be more common, however, is to keep everyone partially idle during "normal" periods by running production lines at less than maximum speed. During periods of increased demand, production rates can be increased without having to hire more labor or resort to overtime. The cost of reserve workers, of course, is associated with the fact that they are paid even when essentially idle.

Which strategy a firm will choose to cope with product-demand fluctuations depends on the relative costs of each. One study, for example, found greater evidence of the use of reserve workers in industries in which product inventory costs are relatively high. If the firm finds that all strategies to meet product-demand fluctuations are too costly, it can exercise its final option and let orders go unfilled—which runs the risk of losing both current and future customers.

SOURCES: Roger LeRoy Miller, "The Reserve Labour Hypothesis: Some Tests of Its Implications," *Economic Journal* 81 (March 1971): 17–35; Robert S. Smith, "Analysis of Labor Market Adjustments in the Clerical Temporary Help Market: 1953–60" (unpublished doctoral dissertation, Stanford University), 1971; Robert H. Topel, "Inventories, Layoffs, and the Short-Run Demand for Labor," *American Economic Review* 72 (September 1982): 769–87; and Jeffrey Pfeffer and James Baron, "Taking the Workers Back Out: Recent Trends in the Structuring of Employment," forthcoming in B. Staw and L. Cummings, eds., *Research in Organizational Behavior,* vol. 10 (Greenwich, CT: JAI Press).

readily found. On the other hand, there may be some "lemons" among the group of college graduates, and if the employer hires them he or she may well suffer losses while they are employed. However, if the reduction in hiring costs that arises when *signals* (such as educational credentials, marital status, or age) are used is large, it may prove profitable for an employer to use them even if an occasional lemon sneaks through. Put another way, the total costs of hiring, training, and employing workers may well be lower for some firms when hiring standards are used than when such firms rely upon more intensive investigations of applicant characteristics. (In Chapter 7 we will return to the issue of statistical discrimination.)

Screening is a widespread phenomenon, especially for white-collar workers. About 88 percent of firms check employment references for their blue-collar workers, with about a 93-percent figure for white-collar workers. In addition, formal employee testing is done by 21 percent of companies for blue-collar workers and 37 percent for white-collar workers. Among these companies using tests, about one-half to three-quarters conduct preemployment screening tests.[22]

## Internal Labor Markets

The issues of screening and credentials arise because companies do not have full information about workers' capabilities. This problem continues even after one is hired; companies continue the information-gathering process over a period of years on their incumbent employees.

The information-collection process continues after employees are hired. Ninety percent of these companies maintain a probationary period, usually around three months, for newly hired blue-collar workers, with 67–75 percent reporting a probationary period for white-collar workers. If an employee is "on probation," company rules often make it easier to discharge the person for poor performance.[23] Further, performance appraisals are used by 75 percent of firms for their blue-collar workers and by about 93 percent of firms for their white-collar workers. In addition to providing information about worker productivity, such appraisals can provide incentives for good performance (see Example 4.6 and Chapter 9).

All of these information-gathering methods presumably provide more accurate information than simple screening on the basis of education or marital status. However, reference checks, testing, and performance appraisal may be relatively expensive to carry out, and companies must weigh these costs against the benefits. Most firms have found that using a combination of information sources, some pertaining to an applicant's "group" and some pertaining to the applicant's own qualities, is the cost-effective way to learn about their workers. Personal attributes, such as dependability, motivation, honesty, and flexibility, are difficult to observe using credentials. This difficulty with screening has induced some firms to adopt a policy of hiring workers at low-level jobs, observing their behavior, and filling all upper-level jobs from within the firm (that is, filling all upper-level vacancies with people whose characteristics have been carefully observed in other jobs the firm has given them to do).

This second approach to the problem of minimizing hiring costs while maximizing the productivity of employees creates an *internal labor market,* because most jobs in the firm are filled from within the ranks of current

---

[22] The figures on company screening, testing, probationary periods, and performance appraisal discussed in this section are taken from Harriet Gorlin, *Personnel Practices I: Recruitment, Placement, Training, Communication,* Tables 8, 14, 19, and 20.

[23] See Fred Foulkes, *Personnel Practices in Large Nonunion Companies* (Englewood Cliffs, NJ: Prentice-Hall, 1980): 73.

employees.[24] The hiring done from outside the firm tends to be heavily concentrated at certain low-level "ports of entry." These jobs—such as "general laborer," "machine cleaner," and "packer" for blue-collar applicants or "management trainee" for white-collar applicants—are of sufficiently low responsibility levels that an unqualified employee cannot do too much damage to the firm or its equipment. However, these jobs do give the firm a chance to observe *actual* productive characteristics of the employees hired, and this information is then used to determine who stays with the firm and how fast and how high employees are promoted.

The *benefit* of using an internal labor market to fill vacancies is that the firm knows a lot about the people working for it. Hiring decisions for upper-level jobs in either the blue-collar or white-collar work forces will thus offer few surprises to the firm. The *costs* of using the internal labor market are associated with the restriction of competition for the upper-level jobs to those in the firm. Those in the firm may not be the best employees available, but they are the only ones the firm considers for these jobs. Firms most likely to decide that the benefits of using an internal labor market outweigh the costs are those whose upper-level workers must have a lot of firm-specific knowledge and training that can best be obtained by on-the-job learning over the years. For those firms, the number of qualified *outside* applicants for upper-level jobs is relatively small. Firms in the steel, petroleum, and chemical industries tend to rely on internal labor markets to fill vacancies, while those in the garment and shoe industries do not.[25] The former group of industries has highly automated, complicated, and interdependent production technologies that can only be mastered through years on the job. The garment- and shoe-manufacturing industries employ workers who perform certain discrete crafts—skills that are not specific to one firm.

As noted earlier, firms engaged in *specific training* will want to ensure that they obtain a stable, long-term work force that can learn quickly and perform well later on. For these firms, the internal labor market offers two attractions. First, it allows the firm to observe workers on the job, where it can see firsthand who learns quickly, who is easily motivated, who is dependable, and so forth, and thus make better decisions about which workers will be the recipients of later, perhaps very expensive, training. Second, the internal labor market tends to foster an attachment to the firm by its employees. They know that outsiders will not be considered for upper-level vacan-

[24] For a detailed discussion of internal labor markets, *see* Peter Doeringer and Michael Piore, *Internal Labor Markets and Manpower Analysis* (Lexington, MA: D. C. Heath and Company, 1971). The same general concept has been identified by others as "industrial feudalism," "Balkanization of labor markets," and "property rights" in a job. See Arthur Ross, "Do We Have a New Industrial Feudalism?" *American Economic Review* 48 (December 1958): 914; Clark Kerr, "The Balkanization of Labor Markets," in E. Wight Bakke, et al., *Labor Mobility and Economic Opportunity* (Cambridge, MA: MIT Press, 1954); and Frederick Meyers, *Ownership of Jobs: A Comparative Study,* Institute of Industrial Relations Monograph Series (Los Angeles, University of California Press, 1964). Other reasons for the existence of internal labor markets are found more recently in Oliver Williamson, et al., "Understanding the Employment Relation: The Analysis of Idiosyncratic Exchange," *Bell Journal of Economics* 16 (Spring 1975): 250–80.

[25] Doeringer and Piore, *Internal Labor Markets and Manpower Analysis*, p. 43.

cies and that they, therefore, have an inside track on job vacancies. If they quit the firm, they would lose this privileged position. They are thus motivated to become long-term employees of the firm. The full implications of internal labor markets for wage policies within the firm will be discussed in the chapters on compensation (Chapters 8 and 9).

The mechanism most companies use to implement their policies of promotion from within is job posting. This practice involves using a company bulletin board to announce job vacancies at various levels. A 1979 survey of companies showed that at least 61 percent of firms use job posting for white-collar openings and 75 percent post blue-collar openings. Among those companies posting jobs, 75–80 percent do it whenever an opening occurs, while 10–20 percent post jobs only if no one in the relevant work group is qualified for the opening, a very strong form of promotion from within.[26] Job posting helps companies utilize the talent from their internal labor markets. For example, in large companies there may be employees who are well qualified for higher-level jobs who might otherwise get overlooked. In addition, many companies allow lateral moves through their job-posting systems. These moves do not involve a promotion but offer opportunities that the employee may desire for other reasons, such as location or scheduling. While allowing lateral moves may increase the number of internal bids the personnel department must process, it may reduce turnover by providing a better match between workers and jobs.[27]

# REVIEW QUESTIONS

1. Both low-skilled workers and high-paid professors have high rates of voluntary quits. What do they have in common that leads to a high quit rate?
2. Wages in the U.S. Postal Service have been attacked for being higher than wages elsewhere for people of the same age and education. The Postal Service answers that it *must* pay higher wages than workers could get elsewhere in order to keep their quit rate below the quit rate in other jobs. Are there circumstances under which this argument has any merit?
3. Suppose the government wants to reduce recidivism of ex-convicts by improving their employment prospects and job stability. Suppose further that the government is considering subsidizing half of employer costs incurred in training ex-convicts for jobs in their plants. How will this subsidy affect the job prospects and stability of ex-convicts, assuming ex-convicts are the only group subsidized?
4. Unemployment insurance is financed through a payroll tax levied on the employer. Assume that taxes paid = tax rate × the first $7000 of each worker's yearly pay. Generally speaking, the tax rate increases when a firm lays off workers. Assuming the firm is unable to shift the tax, what effect will abolition of this tax have on the firm's decision to:
   a. lay off workers?
   b. hire workers?
   c. schedule overtime work?

[26] Harriet Gorlin, *Personnel Practices I: Recruitment, Placement, Training, Communication,* Table 15.

[27] Fred Foulkes, *Personnel Policies in Large Nonunion Companies,* Chapter 7.

5. In its presentation to the Democratic and Republican national platform committees, the AFL–CIO proposed the following changes to the Fair Labor Standards Act in 1976:
   a. Raise the federal minimum wage to $3.00 per hour (the minimum was then less than $3.00);
   b. Increase overtime pay to double the standard wage (it was then 1½ times the standard);
   c. Reduce the standard work week to 35 hours (down from 40), so that overtime pay would be owed to a worker after 35 hours per week.
   Analyze the employment effects of these proposals.

# SELECTED READINGS

Gary Becker, *Human Capital,* 2nd ed. (New York: National Bureau of Economic Research, 1975).

Peter Doeringer and Michael Piore, *Internal Labor Markets and Manpower Analysis* (Lexington, MA: D. C. Heath, 1971).

Ronald G. Ehrenberg and Paul L. Schumann, *Longer Hours or More Jobs? An Investigation of Amending Hours Legislation to Create Employment* (Ithaca, NY: New York State School of Industrial and Labor Relations, Cornell University, 1982).

Walter Oi, "Labor as a Quasi-Fixed Factor," *Journal of Political Economy* 70 (December 1962): 538–55.

Michael Spence, "Job Market Signaling," *Quarterly Journal of Economics* 87 (August 1973): 355–74.

Oliver Williamson et al. "Understanding the Employment Relation: The Analysis of Idiosyncratic Exchange," *Bell Journal of Economics* 16 (Spring 1975): 250–80.

# CHAPTER 5

## Supply of Labor to the Economy: The Decision to Work

In this chapter and the next we will focus on issues of *worker* behavior; that is, in Chapters 5 and 6 we will discuss and analyze various aspects of *labor-supply* behavior. Labor-supply decisions can be roughly divided into two categories. The first category, which is addressed in this chapter, includes decisions about whether to work at all, and if so, how long to work. Questions that must be answered include whether to participate in the labor force, whether to seek part-time or full-time work, and the length of one's working life. The second category of decisions, which is addressed in Chapter 6, deals with the questions that must be faced by a person who has decided to seek work: the occupation or general class of occupations in which to seek offers. This chapter begins with some basic facts concerning labor-force participation rates and hours of work and then moves on to an analysis of the decision to work for pay. This analytical framework is useful in the context of formulating business compensation policies and income-maintenance programs.

## Trends in Labor-Force Participation and Hours of Work

When a person actively seeks work, he or she is, by definition, in the *labor force*. As pointed out in Chapter 2, the *labor-force participation rate* is the percentage of a given population that either has a job or is looking for one. Thus, one clear-cut statistic that is important in measuring people's willingness to work outside the home is the labor-force participation rate.

Perhaps the most revolutionary change taking place in the labor market today is the tremendous increase in the proportion of women—particularly

**Table 5.1**  Labor Force Participation Rates of Females over 16 Years of Age, by Marital Status, 1900–1986 (percent)

| Year | All Females | Single | Widowed, Divorced | Married |
|------|-------------|--------|-------------------|---------|
| 1900 | 20.6 (100) | 45.9 (100) | 32.5 (100) | 5.6 (100) |
| 1910 | 25.5 (124) | 54.0 (118) | 34.1 (105) | 10.7 (191) |
| 1920 | 24.0 (117) | | | 9.0 (161) |
| 1930 | 25.3 (123) | 55.2 (120) | 34.4 (106) | 11.7 (209) |
| 1940 | 26.7 (130) | 53.1 (116) | 33.7 (104) | 13.8 (246) |
| 1950 | 29.7 (144) | 53.6 (117) | 35.5 (109) | 21.6 (386) |
| 1960 | 35.7 (173) | 42.9 ( 94) | 38.7 (119) | 30.6 (546) |
| 1970 | 41.6 (202) | 50.9 (111) | 39.5 (122) | 39.5 (705) |
| 1980 | 51.7 (250) | 61.2 (133) | 44.1 (136) | 50.2 (896) |
| 1986 | 54.7 (266) | 65.3 (142) | 43.1 (133) | 55.0 (982) |

Note:  Index numbers, with 1900 = 100, are shown in parentheses.
SOURCES:  1900–1950: Clarence D. Long, *The Labor Force Under Changing Income and Employment* (Princeton: Princeton University Press), 1958, Table A–6.
1960: U.S. Department of Commerce, Bureau of the Census, *Census of Population, 1960: Employment Status* (Subject Reports PC(2)–6A), Table 4.
1970: U.S. Department of Commerce, Bureau of the Census, *Census of Population, 1970: Employment Status and Work Experience* (Subject Reports PC(2)–6A), Table 3.
1980: U.S. President, *Employment and Training Report of the President, 1980* (Washington, DC: U.S. Government Printing Office, 1981), Tables A2, B1.
1986: U.S. Department of Commerce, *Statistical Abstract of the United States 1987* (Washington, DC: U.S. Government Printing Office, 1986), Table 653. (The data for 1980 and 1986 are not strictly comparable to that from earlier years because they are derived from a monthly survey, not the decennial census.)

married women—working outside the home. Table 5.1 shows the extraordinary dimensions of this change. As late as 1950, only 21.6 percent of married women were in the labor force. By 1960 this percentage had risen to 30.6 percent, and by 1980 it had increased to 50.2 percent—almost two and a half times what it had been in 1950. Married women's labor-force participation continued to increase in the 1980s to its 1986 level of 55 percent.

We need not dwell here on the social changes that have been associated with this increasing tendency for women to seek work outside the home. Changes in family income, child-rearing practices, and the family relationship itself are obvious. Less obvious are the effects on the demand for education by females and on the unemployment rate, which will be discussed in Chapters 6 and 17. The longer life span of females is another factor that will affect labor supply and will become an important issue, for example, in funding pension plans (see Chapter 8). Of paramount concern in this chapter are the factors that have influenced this fundamental increase in the propensity of women to seek work outside the home.

A second major trend in labor-force participation is the decrease in the length of careers for males—as can be seen in Table 5.2. The overall labor-force participation rate of men has been falling, as was noted in Chapter 2, but the really substantial decreases have been among the very young and the very

**Table 5.2**    Labor Force Participation Rates for Males, by Age,
1900–1987 (percent)

| Year | \|Age Groups| | | | | |
| | 14–19 | 16–19 | 20–24 | 25–44 | 45–64 | Over 65 |
|---|---|---|---|---|---|---|
| 1900 | 61.1 | — | 91.7 | 96.3 | 93.3 | 68.3 |
| 1910 | 56.2 | — | 91.1 | 96.6 | 93.6 | 58.1 |
| 1920 | 52.6 | — | 90.9 | 97.1 | 93.8 | 60.1 |
| 1930 | 41.1 | — | 89.9 | 97.5 | 94.1 | 58.3 |
| 1940 | 34.4 | — | 88.0 | 95.0 | 88.7 | 41.5 |
| 1950 | 39.9 | 63.2 | 82.8 | 92.8 | 87.9 | 41.6 |
| 1960 | 38.1 | 56.1 | 86.1 | 95.2 | 89.0 | 30.6 |
| 1970 | 35.8 | 56.1 | 80.9 | 94.4 | 87.3 | 25.0 |
| 1980 | — | 60.5 | 85.9 | 95.4 | 82.2 | 19.1 |
| 1986 | — | 56.4 | 85.8 | 94.7 | 79.5 | 16.0 |
| 1987 | — | 56.1 | 85.2 | 94.6 | 79.7 | 16.3 |

SOURCES: 1900–1950: Clarence D. Long, *The Labor Force Under Changing Income and Employment* (Princeton: Princeton University Press), 1958, Table A–2.

1960: U.S. Department of Commerce, Bureau of the Census, *Census of Population, 1960: Employment Status,* Subject Reports PC(2)-6A, Table 1.

1970: U.S. Department of Commerce, Bureau of the Census, *Census of Population, 1970: Employment Status and Work Experience,* Subject Reports PC(2)-6A Table 1.

1980: U.S. President, *Employment and Training Report of the President, 1981* (Washington, DC: U.S. Government Printing Office, 1980), Table A2, and U.S. Bureau of Labor Statistics, *Handbook of Labor Statistics,* December 1983 (Washington, DC: U.S. Government Printing Office, 1983), Table 4 (this source was used for the rates for 16–19-year olds for 1950–80).

1986: U.S. Bureau of Labor Statistics, *Employment and Earnings* 34 (January 1987), Table 3.

1987: U.S. Bureau of Labor Statistics, *Employment and Earnings* 35 (January 1988), Table 3.

(The data for 1980, 1986, and 1987 are not strictly comparable to that for earlier years because they are derived from a monthly survey, not the decennial census.)

old. The labor-force participation rate of teenagers fell from 61.1 percent in 1900 to 35.8 percent in 1970—a 41–percent decline—although the growth of the student labor force since World War II has slowed the decrease somewhat. The decrease for men over 65 has been even more dramatic—from 68.3 percent in 1900 to 25 percent in 1970 and down to 16.3 percent by 1987. Participation rates for men of "prime age" have declined only slightly. Clearly, men are starting their careers later and ending them earlier than they were at the beginning of this century.

Other measures reflecting the decisions people make about work are the weekly hours of work, the fraction of people who work *part-time*, and the proportion of people who hold more than one job ("moonlighting"). It is not common for people to think of the *hours* of work as being a *supply* variable that is subject to *employee* choice. After all, don't employers—in responding to the factors discussed in Chapter 4—establish the hours of work? They do, of course, but this does not mean that employees have no choice of, or influence on, their working hours. The *weekly* hours of work offered by employers vary to some extent, so that in choosing employers a worker can also choose hours of work. The range of choice may be limited—70 percent of

**Table 5.3**  Average Weekly Hours Actually Worked by Manufacturing
Production Workers During the Peak Employment Years
in Each Business Cycle, 1900–1973 (excluding 1940–45)

| | *Average Hours Worked* | *Average per Decade Decline in Hours Worked* |
|---|---|---|
| 1901 | 54.3 | |
| 1906 | 55.0 | |
| 1913 | 50.9 | |
| 1919 | 46.1 | 2.2 |
| 1923 | 48.9 | |
| 1926 | 47.8 | |
| 1929 | 48.0 | 4.6 |
| 1948 | 38.8 | |
| 1953 | 38.6 | |
| 1956 | 38.2 | 0.3 |
| 1969 | 38.3 | |
| 1973 | 38.0 | |

SOURCE:  The data for 1900–1957 were taken from Ethel Jones, "New Estimates of Hours of Work
Per Week and Hourly Earnings, 1900–1957," *The Review of Economics and Statistics*, 45C (November
1963): 374–85. Data for 1969 and 1973 were calculated from the *Annual Survey of Manufactures*, which
contain worker hours actually worked (exclusive of vacations, sick leave, and holidays).

all full-time plant workers normally worked a 40-hour week in 1973, for
example, and most of the rest were within 5 hours of that—but choice does
exist. Among full-time, nonsupervisory office workers in 1973, only 59 percent worked 40 hours a week, while 17 percent worked 37½ hours, and 13
percent worked 35-hour weeks.[1] Moreover, firms with the same 40-hour
standard work week will offer different *yearly* hours of work because of
different vacation and holiday policies. Finally, *occupational* choice has a
working-hours dimension. The weekly or yearly hours of work are different if
one chooses to become a teacher rather than an accountant, a retail clerk
rather than a traveling sales representative, or a Wall Street lawyer rather
than a small-town one.

Thus employees can, in effect, exercise some choice over their hours of
work in the short run by choosing their employment. In the long run, a similar
mechanism gives employees some influence on working hours. If employees
receiving an hourly wage of $X for 40 hours per week really wanted to work
only 30 hours at $X per hour, some enterprising employer would seize on their
dissatisfaction and offer jobs with 30-hour weeks—ending up with a more
satisfied work force in the process. As noted in Table 5.3 and in the next
paragraph, large declines in the average hours worked per week took place in
this century well before the advent of unions and federal legislation concerning hours of work.

[1]  U.S. Department of Labor Employment Standards Administration, *1973 Survey of Establishment
Characteristics and Practices* (Washington, DC: U.S. Government Printing Office, 1979), Table 15.

**Table 5.4**   Percentages of Nonagricultural Employee Groups
in Voluntary Part-Time Status, Selected Years

|  | All Workers | Male Workers, Age 20+ | Female Workers, Age 20+ | Both Sexes, Age 16–19 |
|---|---|---|---|---|
| 1955 | 7.1% | — | — | — |
| 1960 | 9.0 | — | — | — |
| 1965 | 10.6 | — | — | — |
| 1970 | 13.3 | 4.1 | 20.8 | 47.3 |
| 1975 | 13.8 | 4.4 | 20.7 | 46.7 |
| 1980 | 13.9 | 4.7 | 19.7 | 47.6 |
| 1984 | 13.1 | 4.7 | 18.6 | 50.3 |
| 1986 | 13.4 | 4.8 | 18.5 | 53.1 |
| 1987 | 13.5 | 4.8 | 18.4 | 54.2 |

Note:   A part-time worker is one who works between 1 and 34 hours per week. Voluntary part-timers are those who work part-time because of family or school responsibilities.

SOURCES:   Ronald G. Ehrenberg, Pamela Rosenberg, and Jeanne Li, "Part-Time Employment in the United States," N.Y. State School of Industrial and Labor Relations, Cornell University, April 1986 and U.S. Bureau of Labor Statistics, *Employment and Earnings* 34 (January 1987), Table 33, and U.S. Bureau of Labor Statistics, *Employment and Earnings* 35 (January 1988), Table 33.

Table 5.3 displays the historical change in *actual* weekly hours of work in this century after correcting for the fact that these hours tend to rise in prosperity and fall in recessions.[2] What the table shows is that weekly hours fell steadily until the 1940s but since then have more or less stabilized. Overall, the typical manufacturing worker has 16 more hours of leisure each week than he or she had in 1901—virtually an entire waking day! Yet perhaps equally worth emphasizing is that almost all of this change came in the first 45 years of this century—much of it in the first 30 years, when unions and federal legislation could not have exerted much influence. An explanation for this must include an analysis of factors influencing both the demand for, and supply of, weekly hours per worker. The supply factors are considered in this chapter, while the demand-side influences were treated in Chapter 4.

Table 5.4 contains data indicating that the fraction of employed workers who voluntarily work part-time (less than 35 hours per week) has risen from 7.1 percent in 1955 to 13.5 percent in 1987. This rise has partly occurred because the fastest-growing groups in the labor force were teenagers and women—groups for which part-time employment is relatively common. Trends in the propensity to choose part-time work are consistent with movements in labor-force participation noted earlier; namely, adult women are choosing part-time work less often, while men and teenagers are choosing part-time work more often.

In contrast to trends in part-time employment, there appears to be no trend in the percentage of workers holding two or more jobs. Since 1956, the

[2]  Chapter 2 noted, when defining wages and fringe benefits, that hours of *actual* work and the hours for which an employee is *paid* are two different things. Since World War II, the *paid* hours of work are greater than the *actual* hours of work because of the growing prevalence of paid holidays and paid vacations.

proportion of employed workers holding two or more jobs has fluctuated around 5 percent—achieving lows of 4.5 percent in 1959 and 1974 and a high of 5.7 percent in 1963. In 1977 exactly 5 percent of employed workers were "moonlighters."

Because labor is the most abundant factor of production, it is fair to say that this country's well-being is heavily dependent on the willingness of its people to work. As we will demonstrate, leisure and other ways of spending time that do not involve work for pay are also important in generating well-being; however, our economy relies heavily on goods and services produced for market transactions. Therefore, it is important to understand the *work-incentive* effects of higher wages and incomes, different kinds of taxes, and various forms of income maintenance programs.

Work incentives, for example, will become critically important as our population—through longer life spans and a declining birth rate—gradually becomes older. When this happens, there will be a period when relatively few people (of working age) will have to support a large number of retirees. Their ability to do this and still maintain current standards of living obviously depends on the age at which older people retire and the fraction of the working-age population in the labor force.

Individual companies, as well as government policy makers, are acutely aware of the issue of work incentives. As we will see, problems of absenteeism and early retirement are work-incentives issues. Companies that design their personnel policies with incentives in mind will be in a better position to compete than firms that ignore the incentives issue.

## A Theory of the Decision of Work

The decision to work is ultimately a decision about how to spend time. One way to use one's available time is to spend it in pleasurable leisure activities. The other major way in which people use time is to work.[3] One can work around the home, performing such *household production* as raising children, sewing, building, or even growing food. Alternatively, one can work for pay and use one's earnings to purchase food, shelter, clothing, and child care.

Because working for pay and engaging in household production are two ways of getting the same jobs done, we will ignore the distinction between them and treat work activities as working for pay. We will therefore be characterizing the decision to work as a choice between leisure and working for pay. Most of the crucial factors affecting work incentives can be understood in this context.

If we regard the time spent eating, sleeping, and otherwise maintaining ourselves as more or less fixed by natural laws, then the discretionary time we have (16 hours a day, say) can be allocated to either work or leisure. Since the

---

[3] Another category of activity is to spend time acquiring skills or doing other things that enhance one's future earnings capacity. These activities will be discussed in Chapter 6.

amount of discretionary time spent on leisure is time not spent on working, and vice versa, the *demand for leisure* can be considered the reverse side of the coin labeled *supply of labor*. It is actually more convenient to analyze work incentives in the context of the demand for leisure—because one can apply the standard analysis of the demand for any good to the demand for leisure—and then simply subtract leisure hours from total discretionary hours available to obtain the *labor-supply* effects.

## A Verbal Analysis of the Labor/Leisure Choice

Since we have chosen to analyze work incentives in the context of the demand for leisure, it is instructive to briefly consider the factors that affect the demand for any good. Basically, the demand for a good is a function of three factors:

1.  the *opportunity cost* of the good (which is often but not always equal to *market price*),
2.  one's level of *wealth*, and
3.  one's set of *preferences*.

For example, heating oil consumption will vary with the *cost* of such oil; as that cost rises, consumption will tend to fall unless one of the other two factors intervene. As *wealth* rises people generally want larger and warmer houses that obviously require more oil to heat.[4] Even if the price of energy and the level of personal wealth were to remain constant, the demand for energy could rise if a falling birth rate and lengthened life span resulted in a higher proportion of the population being aged and probably wanting warmer houses. This change in the composition of the population amounts to a shift in the overall *preferences* for warmer houses and thus leads to a change in the demand for heating oil.

To summarize, the demand ($D$) for any good can be characterized as a function of opportunity costs ($C$) and wealth ($V$):

$$D = f(\overset{-}{C}, \overset{+}{V}), \tag{5.1}$$

where $f$—the particular relationship between demand and the variables $C$ and $V$ for an individual—depends on preferences. The notation above $C$ and $V$ indicates the direction in which the demand for a good is expected to go when the variable in question *increases*—*holding the other one constant*. The demand would move in the opposite direction if the variable were to decrease.

Note: Economists usually assume that preferences are given and not subject to immediate change. For policy purposes, the changes in $C$ and $V$— not changes in the function $f$—are of paramount interest to us in explaining changes in demand, because $C$ and $V$ are most susceptible to change by

---

[4] When the demand for a good rises with wealth, economists say the good is a *normal good*. If demand falls as wealth rises, the good is said to be an *inferior good* (traveling or commuting by bus is sometimes cited as an example of an inferior good).

government policy. For the most part, we will assume preferences are *given* and *fixed* at any time.[5]

To apply this general analysis of demand to the demand for leisure, we must first ask, "What is the opportunity cost of leisure?" The cost of spending an hour watching television is basically what one could earn if one had spent that hour working. Thus, the opportunity cost of an hour of leisure is very closely related to one's *wage rate*—so closely related, in fact, that to simplify the analysis we will say that leisure's opportunity cost *is* the wage rate.[6]

Next, we must understand and be able to measure wealth. Naturally, wealth includes a family's holdings of bank accounts, financial investments, and physical property. Workers' skills can also be considered assets, since these skills can be, in effect, rented out to employers for a price. The more one can get in wages, the larger is the value of one's human assets. Unfortunately, it is not usually possible to directly measure people's wealth. It is much easier to measure the *returns* from that wealth, because data on total *income* are readily available from government surveys. Economists thus often use total income as an indicator of total wealth, since the two are conceptually so closely related.[7]

If we replace the general demand function in equation (5.1) with the *demand for leisure function*, it would become equation (5.2):

$$D_L = f(\overset{-}{W}, \overset{+}{Y}), \qquad (5.2)$$

where $D_L$ is the demand for leisure hours, $W$ is the wage rate, $Y$ is total income, and $f$ (as before) depends on preferences people have for leisure independent of $W$ and $Y$. The signs over $W$ and $Y$ indicate what happens to the demand for leisure if the variable in question increases, holding the other variable constant.

If income increases, holding wages (and $f$) constant, equation (5.2) asserts that the demand for leisure goes up. Put differently, *if income increases (decreases), holding wages constant, hours of work will go down (up)*. Economists call this predicted response the *income effect*. The income effect is based on the simple notion that as incomes rise, holding leisure's opportunity

---

[5] On occasion the government attempts to influence consumption patterns of people by changing preferences rather than prices. For example, rather than raising cigarette taxes to discourage cigarette consumption, the federal government in the 1970s prohibited cigarette manufacturers from advertising on television, and it even sponsored radio and television campaigns against smoking. The effectiveness of these attempts to change preferences is difficult to assess.

[6] This statement assumes that individuals can work as many hours as they want at a fixed wage rate. While this assumption may seem overly simplistic, it will not lead to wrong conclusions with respect to the issues analyzed in this chapter. More rigorously, it should be said that leisure's *marginal* opportunity cost is the marginal wage rate (the wage one could receive for an extra hour of work).

[7] The best indicator of wealth is one's *permanent*, or long-run, potential *income*. One's current income may differ from one's permanent income for a variety of reasons (unemployment, illness, being a student, and so on). For our purposes, however, the distinction between current and permanent income is not too important.

cost constant, people will want to consume more leisure (which means working less).

Using algebraic notion, the income effect is defined as the change in the hours of work ($\Delta H$) produced by a change in income ($\Delta Y$), holding wages constant ($\overline{W}$):

$$\text{Income Effect} = \frac{\Delta H}{\Delta Y}\Big|\,\overline{W} < 0. \tag{5.3}$$

We say the income effect is *negative* because the *sign* of the *fraction* in equation (5.3) is *negative*. If income goes up (wages held constant), hours of work fall. If income goes down, hours of work increase. The numerator ($\Delta H$) and denominator ($\Delta Y$) in equation (5.3) move in opposite directions, giving a negative sign to the income effect.

Equation (5.2) also suggests that *if income is held constant, an increase (decrease) in the wage rate will reduce (increase) the demand for leisure—thereby increasing (decreasing) work incentives.* This *substitution effect* occurs because as the opportunity costs of leisure rise (income held constant), working hours are substituted for leisure hours.

In contrast to the income effect, the substitution effect is *positive*. Because this effect is the change in hours of work ($\Delta H$) induced by a change in the wage ($\Delta W$), holding income constant ($\overline{Y}$), the substitution effect can be written as:

$$\text{Substitution Effect} = \frac{\Delta H}{\Delta W}\Big|\,\overline{Y} > 0. \tag{5.4}$$

Because the numerator ($\Delta H$) and denominator ($\Delta W$) always move in the same direction—at least in theory—the substitution effect has a positive sign.

At times, it is possible to observe situations or programs that create "pure" income or substitution effects. Usually, however, both effects are simultaneously present—often working against each other.

**A "pure" income effect.**   Winning a state lottery is an example of the income effect by itself. The winnings enhance one's wealth (income) *independent* of the hours of work. Thus, income is increased *without* a change in the compensation received from an hour of work. In this case, the income effect induces the person to consume more leisure, thereby reducing the willingness to work. (If the change in nonlabor income were *negative*, on the other hand, the income effect suggests that people would work *more*.)

**A "pure" substitution effect.**   In the 1980 presidential campaign, one of the candidates—John Anderson—proposed a program aimed at conserving gasoline. His plan consisted of raising the gasoline tax but offsetting this increase by a reduced Social Security tax payable by individuals on their earnings. The idea was to raise the price of gasoline without reducing people's overall spendable income.

EXAMPLE   5.1

## Labor Supply and Early-Retirement Incentives

Many companies, especially during recessions, express a desire for a mechanism to make it easier to reduce the employment of senior workers. This desire may result from a perceived need to improve promotion opportunities for junior workers. Alternatively, as we will see in Chapters 8 and 9, companies often base their pay in part on seniority. Thus, senior workers are likely to be more expensive relative to comparable junior workers, and during a reduction-in-force companies may be tempted to reduce their employment of these senior workers.

The 1978 amendments to the Age Discrimination in Employment Act (ADEA) prohibited firms, in most cases, from having policies of mandatory retirement for workers below the age of 70. In 1986, Congress outlawed mandatory retirement in most instances altogether. These changes in law mean that firms wanting to reduce their employment of older workers may have to change their personnel policies. In particular, as a result of the ADEA, companies may not coerce senior workers into leaving; instead, they must rely on voluntary mechanisms. One such voluntary mechanism is the "open-window" offer of a financial incentive for early retirement that is extended for a limited amount of time. For example, from 1970 to 1983, 36 percent of U.S. companies made open-window offers, with a particularly heavy concentration in the recession years of 1982 and 1983. Eighty-six percent of the companies making such offers paid to qualifying retirees a cash bonus that supplemented ordinary pension benefits to which they were entitled; the other 14 percent merely liberalized their retirement packages. The cash bonuses sometimes took the form of a lump sum, while in other cases the bonus was paid out over a particular time period. For most companies, the open window lasted from two to six months and was only available to older workers and/or those with long company service.

From the standpoint of labor supply theory, these open-window offers have income and substitution effects that both lead to less labor supply (that is, to earlier retirement). First, the open window bonus raises one's retirement income. There may well be some currently employed workers for whom the regular pension benefits are insufficient to induce retirement; however, the open-window bonus may, on top of the pension, lead to a high enough income level to cause one to consume more leisure by retiring. For example, a bonus available for retirement any time in 1988 may cause one to retire in January rather than December.

Second, the open window lowers the price of leisure taken after the expiration of the firm's offer. For example, suppose one's salary is $30,000 per year and that one is eligible for regular retirement benefits of $20,000 per year. An open window bonus paid out in the form of an extra $2,000 per year in post-retirement income lowers the price of retiring during the offer period from $10,000 to $8000 per year in forgone income. A lump sum open-window bonus also gives workers an incentive to retire earlier. The lump sum has an income effect leading one to consume more leisure. Moreover, since the lump sum disappears if one does not retire during the specified time period, this bonus plan reduces the gain to working through the expiration date of the open window.

While companies using open-window offers clearly want to reduce the employment of older workers, these policies do not represent increases in coercion of older workers. Compared to regular pension rules, open-window offers expand the options of older workers.

SOURCE:  Shirley H. Rhine, *Managing Older Workers: Company Policies and Attitudes* (New York: The Conference Board, Inc., 1984).

For our purposes, this plan is interesting because it creates a pure substitution effect on labor supply. Social Security revenues are collected by a tax on earnings, so reductions in the tax are, in effect, an increase in the wage rate.[8] However, for the average person, the increased wealth associated with this wage increase is exactly offset by increases in the gasoline tax.[9] Hence, wages are increased while income is held more or less constant. This program would thus create a substitution effect that induces people to work more hours.

**Both effects occur when wages rise.**   While the preceding examples illustrate situations in which the income or substitution effects are present by themselves, normally both effects are present—often working in opposite directions. The presence of both effects creates ambiguity in predicting the overall labor supply response in many cases. Consider the case of a person who receives a wage increase.

The labor-supply response to a simple wage change will involve *both* an income and a substitution effect. The *income effect* is the result of the worker's enhanced wealth (or potential income) after the increase. For a given level of work effort, he or she now has a greater command over resources than before (because more income is received for any given number of hours of work). The *substitution effect* results from the fact that the wage increase raises the opportunity costs of leisure. Because the actual labor supply response is the *sum* of the income and substitution effects, we cannot predict the response in advance; theory simply does not tell us which effect is stronger.

If the *income* effect is dominant, the person will respond to a wage increase by decreasing his or her labor supply. This decrease will be *smaller* than if the same change in wealth were due to an increase in *nonlabor* wealth,

---

[8]  Social Security taxes are levied on yearly earnings up to some maximum—$45,000 in 1988. Once that maximum level is reached within a year, no more Social Security taxes are paid. People whose yearly earnings exceed the base experience no change in the marginal opportunity cost of leisure, because an additional hour of work per year is not subject to Social Security taxes anyway. However, the marginal opportunity cost of leisure would be increased for many—if not most—workers.

[9]  An increase in the price of gasoline will reduce the income people have left for expenditures on nongasoline consumption only if the demand for gasoline is inelastic. In this case, the percentage reduction in gasoline consumption is smaller than the percentage increase in price; total expenditures on gasoline would thus rise. Our analysis assumes this to be the case.

**Figure 5.1**   An Individual Supply-of-Labor Curve Can Bend Backwards

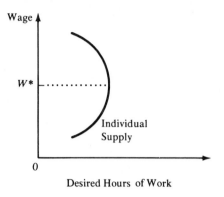

because the substitution effect is present and acts as a moderating influence. However, in the case where the *income* effect dominates, the substitution effect is not large enough to prevent labor supply from *declining*. It is entirely plausible, of course, that the *substitution* effect will dominate. If so, the actual response to the wage increase will be to *increase* labor supply.

Should the substitution effect dominate, the person's labor-supply curve—relating, say, desired hours of work to wages—will be *positively sloped;* that is, labor supply will increase with the wage rate. If, on the other hand, the income effect dominates, the labor-supply curve will be *negatively sloped*. Economic theory cannot say which effect will dominate, and in fact individual labor supply curves could be positively sloped in some ranges of the wage and negatively sloped in others. In Figure 5.1, for example, the person's desired hours of work increase (substitution effect dominates) as wages go up, as long as wages are low (below $W^*$). At higher wages, however, further increases result in reduced hours of work (the income effect dominates); economists refer to such a curve as "backward-bending."

While economic theory is unable to predict whether the income or substitution effect will dominate in an individual's labor-supply curve, it can bring some useful insights to bear on important policy issues. The work-incentive effect of the personal income tax is an important case in point.

**Tax-rate cuts and "supply-side" economics.**   The election of Ronald Reagan as President in 1980 brought to power an administration convinced that high rates of inflation (that is, rising prices) and lagging labor productivity could be at least partially overcome by cutting taxes in such a way that investment and work effort would be stimulated.[10] The notion that tax-rate cuts and

[10]   We are indebted to Sharon Smith of AT&T for suggesting this policy application to us.

tax-related investment incentives could be used to stimulate output is central to what came to be called "supply-side" economics. An important element of the supply-side strategy proposed by President Reagan was the Kemp-Roth plan to cut personal income-tax rates across the board by 30 percent over a three-year period.[11] It was believed that cuts in personal income-tax rates would, among other things, increase the incentives of people to work:

> According to supply-siders, large tax-rate cuts would cause an increase in investment and work effort that would reduce fundamental inflationary pressures.[12]

Is the belief by supply-siders that income-tax rate cuts will increase work effort theoretically sound? Suppose, first, that Congress were to lower the income-tax rates of (say) lower-income workers but not cut the level of government services provided for this group. A decrease in their income-tax rates is equivalent to an increase in wages, because the workers would take home more income for each hour of work. This wage increase would generate an income and substitution effect, and theoretical reasoning alone cannot predict which effect will dominate. If the substitution effect dominated, labor supply would increase; if the income effect were dominant, the tax cuts would be accompanied by a *fall* in labor supply! The issue is ultimately an empirical question.[13]

The supply-siders who claim that reducing income-tax rates would increase work incentives have a valid point, however, when one considers *general* income-tax-rate reductions. Let us examine, for example, how a general 10-percent reduction in income-tax rates might be handled. While a cut in tax rates would, of course, increase workers' wage rates, it would have the *initial* effect of reducing by 10 percent the revenues available to the government. Unless the government were trying to combat a recession and accompanying unemployment, it might respond to reduced revenues by cutting back on various services it formerly provided: mail delivery on Saturday, educational subsidies, and road-construction funds, for example. Thus, while *wages* would be increased, real income would be held more or less constant by the cut in government services.[14] Workers would have more take-home income but fewer government-provided services.[15] There would be a substitu-

---

[11] The plan is named for its Congressional sponsors, Representative Jack Kemp and Senator William Roth. In the summer of 1981, Congress voted to cut taxes 25 percent over three years and to adjust tax brackets for inflation thereafter.

[12] "Reagan's Top Problem: Braking Inflationary Expectations," *Business Week,* December 1, 1980, p. 110.

[13] Later, this chapter will show that the income effect may dominate for men but not for married women.

[14] Some people would be more affected by the governmental spending cuts than others, but the overall change in real wealth would be zero.

[15] The alternative to cutting services, at least initially, is to borrow money. However, borrowing increases the money supply if it is done, as is most often the case, from banks—and this would tend to be inflationary. A rise in *prices* would lower the real wage and mitigate any substitution effects (if before-tax money wages remained constant).

**Figure 5.2** The Aggregate Supply-of-Labor Curve Must Always Slope Upward

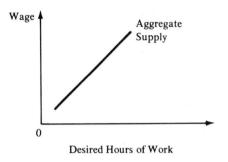

tion effect but no overall income effect, and the aggregate labor-supply curve would slope upward, as shown in Figure 5.2.

In 1986 Congress passed further tax legislation that served to lower tax rates on individuals while eliminating certain deductions and raising corporate taxes enough to maintain the same tax revenue (hence holding workers' real incomes constant). For most individuals, the maximum tax rate fell from 50 percent in 1986 to 28 percent in 1988. Thus, the 1986 tax law has a substitution effect, tending to raise after-tax wages, but no income effect. Overall, it should call forth greater labor supply.

## Empirical Findings on the Labor/Leisure Choice

This chapter has argued that the income effect on labor supply is negative and that the substitution effect is positive. While these predictions are often useful for policy purposes—as we saw in the discussions of the work-incentive effect of the income tax—it is also important to know *how large* the two effects are. It is the *relative size* of each effect that determines the ultimate *observed* effect. Evidence on the absolute and relative sizes of income and substitution effects can be obtained in two different ways:

1. the *time-series study* can be used to look at *trends* in labor-force participation rates and hours of work over time.
2. the *cross-section study* can be used to analyze the patterns of labor supply across individuals at a given time.

**Time-series studies.** Chapter 2 pointed out that real hourly wages rose fourfold from 1914 to 1987. Associated with that rise was a rather sharp decline in the labor-force participation rate of older males, clearly reflecting a trend toward earlier retirement. One can also observe substantial declines in the hours of work. One is therefore tempted to conclude from these trends that the income effect dominates the substitution effect—meaning that when wages rise the propensity to work will fall.

There are three potential objections to, or problems with, the conclusion that the income effect is larger than the substitution effect. First, the earlier retirement of males can be seen as a function of greater availability of pensions. Pensions pay older people for not working, thereby creating incentives not to work at an elderly age (see Example 5.1). Interestingly, however, a large part of the decline in labor-force participation rates for elderly males came *before* 1940, during an era in which pensions were virtually nonexistent.

A second disturbing fact that raises questions about the relative strength of the income and substitution effects is the much smaller decline in hours of work after World War II. Has the income effect grown weaker relative to the substitution effect? Not necessarily. Hours of work are *jointly* determined by employers and employees, and while rising real wages may be inducing employees to want to work less, a number of developments have led employers to offer incentives for workers to work longer hours (these forces were discussed in Chapter 4). It is important to remember that countervailing forces may well be coming from the *demand* side of the market in determining hours of work.

Third, while we cannot rule out the possibility that the income effect dominates the substitution effect for males, how do we interpret the dramatic rise in participation rates among females? One possible explanation is that preferences among women have changed, particularly since their heavy involvement in the labor market during World War II. For example, the stigma against working wives or mothers has weakened. This change in preferences may explain some of the rising propensity of women to work, but it does not explain the *cause* of the changing preferences. Since women's attitudes may be most strongly influenced by the sheer increase in the number of working women, it is critical to understand what originally started the increase.

Because wives have tended to work in the home more than men and unmarried women, there are reasons to believe that general wage increases have created an income effect for them that is smaller, and a substitution effect that is larger, than for men and single women. The plausibility of a smaller income effect rests on the observation that at any point in time, many married women are out of the labor force and many others are working less than full time. Thus, a given wage increase will generate a smaller income effect than it would if virtually all were working (for pay) full time.

A larger substitution effect is plausible for married women because household and market (paid) work are close substitutes, whereas market work and leisure are not. Suppose that women and men have roughly the same preferences regarding leisure and work. These two alternative ways to spend time are substitutes, but they are not close substitutes. Thus, a change in the opportunity cost of leisure may not elicit a large change in the supply of working hours for either sex; leisure and work are simply too different for a large responsiveness to changes in opportunity costs to be observed. However, there are two different types of *work* activity—market work (for pay) and household work—and there is a high degree of substitutability between *these* alternatives. If market work is performed, household chores are hired out to specialists (baby-sitters, cleaning services) or done by machines (frost-free refrigerators). If household work is substituted for market work, these costs of hiring out tasks are saved. Thus, doing household work oneself or working for pay and hiring out these chores represent two ways of getting the same job done. They are very close substitutes, so that when the incentives to pursue one alternative change, a large response in time spent doing the other can be expected. Because married women have traditionally performed household work to a greater extent than have men and unmarried women, we would expect this second influence on the overall substitution effect (the substitution between work activities) to be relatively stronger for married women.

Another theory for the growing population of working women is based on the observation that under the traditional division of labor in the family, women really have a tripartite choice of how to spend time: leisure, market work, and nonmarket (household) work. The invention and increased availability of automatic washers and dryers, frost-free refrigerators, microwave ovens, and prepared foods—to name a few—have reduced the time required to perform given household tasks in recent years. Being able to perform these tasks faster has reduced the savings from staying home instead of working for pay. Thus, yet another force has affected the incentives of women to work for pay.

It is clear that looking at *trends* in the labor-force participation rates and hours of work for evidence on the relative strength of income or substitution effects is not completely satisfactory. So many other factors affect these variables over time that isolating income and substitution effects is impossible. Indeed, the growth of pensions, changes in employer desires concerning hours of work, time-saving household inventions, and changed attitudes toward working women all cloud our analysis of trends.

**Cross-section studies.** Numerous studies of labor-supply behavior have relied on cross-sectional data.[16] These studies basically analyze labor-force participation or annual hours of work as they are affected by wage rates and unearned income. The most reliable and informative studies are those done on large samples of males, primarily because the labor supply behavior of women is complicated by child-rearing and household-work arrangements for which data are sketchy at best. The findings discussed here are of *nonexperimental studies*—studies in which variations in wages and incomes are *observed,* rather than *generated by,* the researchers (findings from experimental studies are summarized later in this chapter in the discussion of income-maintenance programs). Just about all studies of male labor-supply behavior indicate that the income effect dominates the substitution effect—and thus that males have (individual) negatively sloped supply curves.

---

[16] The studies and conclusions reported here are for *individual* wage changes and *individual* supply-of-labor curves. They do *not* pertain to *aggregate* labor supply responses to a general wage change (where, as noted earlier, there can be no overall income effect).

## EXAMPLE   5.2

# "Discouraged" vs. "Additional" Workers

Changes in one spouse's productivity, either at home or in market work, can alter the family's basic labor-supply decision. Consider, for example, a family in which market work is performed by the husband and in which the wife is employed full-time in the home. What will happen if a recession causes the husband to become unemployed?

The husband's market productivity declines, at least temporarily. He may be a highly specialized worker and unable to find similar work at the moment. The drop in his market productivity relative to his household productivity (which is unaffected by the recession) makes it more likely that the family will find it beneficial for him to engage in household production. If the wage his wife can earn in paid work is not affected, the family *may* decide that, to try to maintain the family's prior level of utility (which might be affected by both consumption and *savings* levels), *she* should seek market work and *he* should stay home for as long as the recession lasts. He may remain a member of the labor force as an unemployed worker awaiting recall, and as she begins to look for work she becomes an "added" member of the labor force. Thus, in the face of falling family income, the number of family members seeking market work may increase—a phenomenon akin to the *income effect.*

At the same time, however, we must consider the *wage rate* someone without a job can *expect* to receive if he or she looks for work. This expected wage, denoted by $E(W)$, can actually be written as a precise statistical concept:

$$E(W) = \pi W,$$

where $W$ is the wage rate of people who have a job and $\pi$ is the probability of obtaining the job. For someone without a job, the price of an hour at home—the opportunity cost of staying home—is $E(W)$. The reduced availability of jobs that occurs when the unemployment rate rises causes the expected wage of those without jobs to fall sharply, for two reasons. First, an excess of labor supply over demand tends to push down real wages (for those with jobs) during recessionary periods. Second, the chances of getting a job fall in a recession. Thus, both $W$ and $\pi$ fall in a recession, causing $E(W)$ to decline.

Noting the *substitution effect* that accompanies a falling expected wage, some have argued that people who would otherwise have entered the labor force become "discouraged" in a recession and tend to remain out of the labor market. Looking for work has such a low expected payoff for them that such people decide that spending time at home is more productive than spending time in job search. The reduction of the labor force associated with discouraged workers in a recession is a force working opposite to the "added-worker" effect—just as the substitution effect works against the income effect. While we have evidence that both the additional and discouraged worker effects exist, studies have shown that the discouraged worker dominates: *the labor force shrinks during recessions and grows during expansions.* The dominance of the discouraged-worker effect creates what some call the "hidden unemployed": people who would like to work but who believe that jobs are so scarce that looking for work is of little or no use. Because they are not looking for jobs, they are not counted as unemployed. There were 1.026 million such people in 1987, and counting them as unemployed would have raised the yearly unemployment rate from 6.2 percent to 7.0 percent.*

* To say that including "discouraged workers" in unemployment statistics would change the published unemployment rate does not imply that it *should* be done. For a summary of the arguments for and against counting discouraged workers as unemployed, see the final report of the National Commission on Employment and Unemployment Statistics, *Counting the Labor Force* (Washington, DC, 1979): 44–49.

SOURCES:  U.S. Bureau of Labor Statistics, *Employment and Earnings,* 35 (January 1988), Tables 1 and 35; Jacob Mincer, "Labor Force Participation of Married Women," in *Aspects of Labor Economics:* A Conference of the Universities—National Bureau Committee on Economic Research (Princeton, NJ: Princeton University Press, 1962).

There is as yet no universal consensus about the *size* of the labor-supply response. However, one careful review study claims that once various statistical and definitional problems are accounted for, the effect of raising a man's wage by 10 percent would be a 1–2 percent reduction in his labor supply.[17] This observed effect is the result of something like a 2.5-percent reduction resulting from the income effect and roughly a 1-percent increase associated with the substitution effect.

The estimates for women are less well defined, perhaps for the reasons already cited. Nevertheless, the results of cross-sectional studies usually indicate that the *substitution* effect dominates, yielding a positively sloped labor-supply curve for females.[18] Studies comparable to those for males have generally found similar income effects among females, but the estimated substitution effects for women are much larger.[19]

It is interesting—and somewhat heartening—that the results of nonexperimental, statistically sophisticated cross-section studies generally support the observations based on trends over time. Namely, the income effect appears to dominate for males, and the substitution effect appears dominant for females. As noted earlier, the relatively larger substitution effect among women probably reflects the traditional household role of married women rather than gender-related differences in work/leisure preferences. However, as women become more permanently attached to the labor force, and if the

[17] George Borjas and James Heckman, "Labor Supply Estimates for Public Policy Evaluation," *Proceedings of the Industrial Relations Research Association* (1978): 320–31.

[18] See Jacob Mincer, "Labor Force Participation of Married Women," in *Aspects of Labor Economics* (Princeton, NJ: Princeton University Press, 1962); Glen G. Cain, *Married Women in the Labor Force* (Chicago: University of Chicago Press, 1966); and William G. Bowen and T. Aldrich Finegan, *The Economics of Labor Force Participation* (Princeton, NJ: Princeton University Press, 1969).

[19] See Glen G. Cain and Harold W. Watts, "Toward a Summary and Synthesis of the Evidence," *Income Maintenance and Labor Supply: Econometric Studies* (Chicago: Markham, 1973); and James Smith and Michael Ward, "Time-Series Growth in the Female Labor Force," *Journal of Labor Economics* 3 (January 1985): S59–S90.

traditional family division of labor weakens, we would expect a decline in the dominance of the substitution effect for women.

# Business and Government Policy Applications

Virtually all government income-maintenance programs—from welfare payments to unemployment compensation—have work incentive effects, and the direction and size of these effects are often critical issues in constructing such programs. Business compensation policies also have work incentive effects that companies cannot afford to ignore when designing such policies. This final section will discuss the labor supply implications of several of these government and business policies.

## Incentives and Absenteeism

The problem of employee absenteeism is significant and growing. A 1947 study of absences in manufacturing industries suggested a daily absentee rate of about 4.3 percent, while more recent manufacturing data indicate that absentee rates are currently around 7 percent.[20] Are workers becoming more sickly? Are they less motivated? Is the workplace more alienating? Is management more inept? These are some of the many questions that arise concerning this problem. The concepts introduced in this chapter suggest yet another question: is absenteeism caused to some extent by the structure of compensation? As documented in Chapter 4 (and again discussed in Chapter 8), fringe benefits form a large and increasing proportion of total compensation. What has happened over time is that employees have received an ever-larger proportion of their pay increases in the form of fringe benefits rather than wages. In some cases, these fringe-benefit packages have included paid sick leave provisions, which serve as an obvious inducement for a certain amount of absenteeism. Because workers can call in sick for a specified number of days per year without losing any pay, it is not surprising that a study of public school teachers found that absenteeism was greater in districts with more generous paid sick leave provisions.[21]

However, the growth of fringe benefits frequently offers incentives for greater absenteeism independent of paid sick leave. It is often the case that an absence causes a worker to lose his or her daily wage, but the value of many fringe benefits is invariant with respect to an absence. (For example, the value of a worker's medical insurance policy or future pension benefits is not affected by absence from work in most cases.) Thus, when increased compensation comes in the form of fringe benefits rather than wages, an *income effect*

---

[20] Max Kossoris, "Illness Absenteeism in Manufacturing Plants in 1947," *Monthly Labor Review* 66 (March 1948): 265–67; and Janice N. Hedges, "Absence from Work—Measuring the Hours Lost," *Monthly Labor Review* 100 (October 1977): 16–23.

[21] Donald Winkler, "The Effects of Sick-Leave Policy on Teacher Absenteeism," *Industrial and Labor Relations Review* 33 (January 1980): 232–40.

on the demand for leisure is created *without a corresponding substitution effect!*

The increased use of fringe benefits as a form of compensation has had a possibly profound effect on the incentives to come to work on days when one is feeling slightly ill, in need of a "break," or has a personal problem. The increased compensation that has accompanied economic growth tends to induce greater consumption of all normal goods, including leisure; however, to the extent *wages* are not increased, the price of leisure is not raised. Thus, the changing structure of compensation suggests that relatively stronger income effects, and correspondingly weaker substitution effects, on the demand for leisure have been accompanying economic growth in recent years.

Because absenteeism is one way that leisure is consumed, it may well be that rising absenteeism is at least partially caused by the increased use of fringe benefits in pay packages. Indeed, absenteeism appears to be higher when fringe benefits are more extensively used; for example, rates are higher in manufacturing than retail trade, and higher in large manufacturing plants than small ones. Moreover, a careful intra-industry statistical study has uncovered evidence suggesting that a compensation package weighted toward fringe benefits rather than wages will be accompanied by greater absenteeism.[22]

While the growth of fringe benefits has increased workers' incentives for absenteeism, companies are currently building in incentives to reduce the problem. For example, in the early 1980s New York Life Insurance Company experienced chronic absenteeism. To combat the problem, in January 1985 the company instituted a lottery in which, for each quarter, all employees with perfect attendance records are eligible. The prizes range from $200 bonds to a paid day off. In addition, the company holds an annual lottery for those with no absences during the year and awards prizes of $1000 bonds and five paid days off. The plan appears to have had substantial effects, as New York Life reported a 21-percent decline in absenteeism compared to the year preceding the plan's adoption.[23]

The lottery provides a clear substitution effect by raising the cost of taking time off. However, there may be an income effect in the future for those who win prizes—a $1000 prize might allow some to afford greater absenteeism in the next year. Of course, continuation of the program would still provide a substitution effect, tending toward less absenteeism.

## Income-Replacement Programs

Unemployment insurance and workers' compensation are what might be called *income-replacement programs*. Unemployment insurance benefits are

---

[22] Steven G. Allen, "Compensation, Safety and Absenteeism: Evidence from the Paper Industry," *Industrial and Labor Relations Review* 34 (January 1981): 207–18.

[23] See Allan Halcrow, "Incentive! How Three Companies Cut Costs," *Personnel Journal* 65 (February 1986): 12–13.

**EXAMPLE    5.3**

## Freedom of Labor Supply Scheduling: Flexitime

The theory of labor supply introduced in this chapter assumed that workers get utility from both leisure and income; however, no assumption was made about the timing of leisure. In reality, taking time off from work is more or less desirable depending on when it occurs. For example, some workers may be "morning people" and work especially well early in the day. Alternatively, taking time off may be especially important if one's children are sick or need rides to after-school activities. The issue of work time flexibility is becoming more important as more of the labor force consists of dual career couples, as indicated by the increase in married women's labor force participation rates (see Table 5.1). For example, in the United States flexible working hours (known as "flexitime") policies were virtually nonexistent before 1973; by 1985, however, 12.3 percent of full-time and 18.6 percent of part-time wage and salary workers had flexitime.

Flexitime is a labor supply issue in that a given wage rate with flexible scheduling may lead some workers to supply more labor than the same wage rate with a rigid work schedule. For example, suppose a working parent places a very high value on time away from work during the hours of 3–5 P.M., needing to take care of children after school. Assume that the parent's employer offers a rigid 9 A.M. to 5 P.M. full-time schedule or a 9 A.M. to 1 P.M. part-time work schedule, each at $10/hour pay. The worker may well choose the part-time job to be free from work from 3 to 5 P.M. However, a flexitime arrangement, where one could work from say 8 A.M. to 3 P.M. and 5–6 P.M. might well induce him or her to take a full-time job at the same pay.

Whether flexitime is used by a firm depends on the size of both benefits and costs. On the one hand, a company is likely to put more time and effort into scheduling if its workers are on flexitime. On the other hand, there may be benefits of reduced turnover or of providing a cost-saving method of increasing the total labor supply of its workers. In the above example, an alternative method of getting the parent to accept full-time work on a rigid 9 A.M.–5 P.M. schedule would be to raise the pay of full-time workers. Flexitime can eliminate the need for paying this extra price to induce employees to work full-time on rigid schedules. One company found, for example, that its unions were willing to make concessions to management in return for the company's granting a flexible work time plan to its workers. The unions in effect were saying that their members were willing to work for less pay if hours could be more flexibly scheduled.

SOURCES:  See John D. Owen, "Flexitime: Some Problems and Solutions," *Industrial and Labor Relations Review* 30 (January 1977): 152–60; Earl Mellor, "Shift Work and Flexitime: How Prevalent Are They?" *Monthly Labor Review* 109 (November 1986): 14–21; and Wallace Martin, "Taking Control of Time Off," *Personnel Administrator* 32 (June 1987): 195–200.

paid to workers who have been laid off, permanently or temporarily, by their employers. Workers' compensation is paid to employees who have been injured on the job. Both programs are intended to compensate workers for earnings lost while out of work.[24]

**Complete replacement?**   Given that both the unemployment-insurance and workers'-compensation programs are intended to replace lost earnings, it may seem a bit odd—if not callous—that both programs typically replace roughly just *half* of before-tax lost earnings.[25] It is true that as of 1987, workers' compensation benefits were not taxed (although unemployment-insurance benefits were), so that the fraction of *after-tax* earnings replaced can be higher than 50 percent. However, it is also true that lost fringe benefits are not replaced, so that lost compensation is far from completely replaced. Why?

The reason for incomplete earnings replacement has to do with work incentives. Both injured and unemployed workers have some discretion over how long they will remain out of work. A man with a lacerated arm might be able to carry out his normal duties with some discomfort after a few days of recuperation, or he might choose to wait until his wound is completely healed before returning to work. An unemployed woman might accept the first offer of work she obtains, or she may prefer to wait a while and see if she can generate a better offer. In both cases the worker has the legal latitude to decide (within some limits) when to return to work. These decisions will obviously be affected by work incentives inherent in the income-replacement programs affecting them. Replacing *all* of lost income could result in *overcompensation*—by generating a higher level of utility than before the loss of income—and would motivate the recipients of benefits to remain out of work as long as possible.[26]

Suppose, for example, that before one's employment ceased, a person earned $120/day for eight hours' work. If, when employment ceases, the worker receives benefits equal to $120 per day, he or she will have the same income as before but eight extra hours per day of leisure. The recipient would be better off not working, and full earnings replacement would thus inhibit program beneficiaries from returning to work at the earliest possible time.

**Actual income loss vs. "scheduled" benefits.**   A second issue in income-replacement programs is how to structure workers' compensation for permanent disabilities. Should workers who are either totally or partially

---

[24]   For a complete description of these programs, see George E. Rejda, *Social Insurance and Economic Security* (Englewood Cliffs, NJ: Prentice-Hall, 1976). We will return to the unemployment insurance and workers' compensation programs in the chapters on unemployment (Chapter 17) and compensating differentials (Chapter 6).

[25]   Both programs are run at the state level and thus vary in their characteristics across states. Benefits in both programs are bounded by minimums and maximums.

[26]   We are assuming here that the psychic costs of injury or layoff are small. It could be argued that complete income replacement is justified on the grounds that it compensates for large psychic losses, but our analysis of work-incentive effects would be unchanged.

disabled receive benefits that replace their *actual* lost earnings, or should they receive benefits according to some impersonal schedule appropriate for people with their disability? One might initially think that replacing actual losses is more fair, but such a program would create an enormous disincentive to work. Suppose a worker has become partially disabled because of an injury on the job and must now seek jobs that pay less than he or she earned before. If the worker earned, say, $600 per week before the injury and workers' compensation replaced all earnings loss up to $600 per week, then the worker takes home no extra money by accepting a job. In effect the workers' compensation program "taxes" away all wages (on jobs paying up to $600 per week) in the form of a dollar-for-dollar reduction in benefits. The price of leisure becomes zero, and when people cannot increase their income by working, there is usually no incentive to work.

One way to avoid the disincentives inherent in replacing *actual* lost earnings for disabled workers is to grant benefits according to some schedule drawn up with reference to the disability but without regard to the individual's actual earnings loss. For example, in the state of New York, a worker losing the first three fingers of one hand receives two thirds of the before-injury weekly wage for a period of 101 weeks irrespective of actual earnings during or after this 101-week period.[27] After that, he or she receives no further workers' compensation for that injury. Other states compensate permanent, partial disabilities in a similar manner.

Using an impersonal schedule of disability benefits preserves at least some incentive to work, because benefits are not reduced if earnings increase. The benefits received become a grant of nonwage income (so that increasing them has an income effect), but they do not alter the recipient's wage rate (price of leisure). Suppose, in the preceding example, that the injured worker receives $600 in workers' compensation regardless of subsequent earnings. In this case there will still be an income effect (as in the "actual earnings loss" case), but the price of leisure is not reduced. The injured worker will be more likely to work when the $600 benefit is not reduced than when it is reduced by the amount of earnings up to $600/week.

The conclusion that scheduled payments offer stronger work incentives than benefits based on actual losses would become even stronger if the scheduled benefits were smaller. For if scheduled benefits were lower, the income effect falls, while the price of leisure remains unchanged; in this case, lower benefits reduce one's ability to consume leisure. Maximum work incentives are retained when there is no income-transfer program—a situation in obvious conflict with the overall *goal* of helping workers who find themselves economically disadvantaged.[28]

---

[27] New York State, *Workmen's Compensation Law* (Hempstead, NY: Workmen's Compensation Board, 1970): 65.

[28] Chapter 6 will show that workers who are injured may be compensated *in advance* of injury by having higher wages (due to the risk inherent in their job) than they would otherwise have. These *compensating wage differentials* must also be taken into account when establishing programs on post-injury compensation.

## Income-Maintenance Programs

*Income-maintenance programs*—more commonly known as "welfare" or "relief" programs—have the goal of *raising* the income of the poor to some minimum acceptable level. They thus differ from income-replacement programs, which were aimed at *restoring* lost income. Because poverty is generally an income-related concept, the benefits paid out under income-maintenance programs generally are affected by the level of the beneficiary's actual income. As we shall see, income-conditioned benefits inevitably reduce work incentives below what such incentives would be with no income-support system for the poor. They simultaneously increase income while reducing the price of leisure (the wage rate), both of which should cause the demand for leisure to increase and the supply of labor to fall. This fact is the root of much of the controversy welfare programs have generated over the years.

While the rules of our welfare system have been changed several times over the last 20 years, it has always had the same basic form. The system would guarantee an eligible family or individual a minimum level of income and reduce government-paid benefits when market income was received. The rate at which these benefits decline with increases in market income is an implicit "tax rate." For example, as of 1981, for the first four months of work, a welfare recipient's earnings above $30 are "taxed" at the rate of 67 percent (that is, for every $100 earned, welfare benefits are reduced by $67). Beyond four months' employment, the tax rate becomes 100 percent because welfare benefits are reduced one dollar for each dollar of earnings. Thus the current welfare system, by increasing the incomes of poor people, creates an income effect inducing them to work less. A strong substitution effect also inducing less work is created by reducing the price of leisure to nearly zero after four months of work. The system is qualitatively similar to the previous example of workers' compensation in which benefits were adjusted to provide complete earnings-loss replacement.

**Welfare dilemmas.** While it may seem that the obvious solution to this work-incentive problem is to reduce the implicit tax rate, this remedy is not costless. Suppose the implicit tax for the first four months is reduced from its 67-percent level to 25 percent, thus allowing the welfare recipient to keep three out of every four dollars earned. If $16 is the daily benefit when there are no earnings, with a 67-percent tax rate workers can earn at most $24 per day and still receive benefits. However, with a 25-percent tax rate, workers can earn up to $64 per day and still receive some welfare benefits.[29] Clearly, a low implicit tax rate and a reasonably generous guarantee level are inconsistent with confining welfare benefits to only the needy! This dilemma pervades just about all disputes over welfare policy; that is, reducing implicit tax rates

---

[29] This example ignores the relatively small $30/month one is allowed to keep "tax-free."

to increase work incentives leads to an increase in the number of people eligible for benefits.[30]

**Empirical Studies of Welfare and Work Incentives.** Although making welfare benefits available to people who were not previously eligible for them will clearly decrease their work incentives, the relevant policy question is: By how much will their work incentives be decreased? Some studies use estimates of income and substitution effects obtained from nonexperimental data in the late 1960s to answer this question. These studies imply that, for males, a guaranteed (zero earnings) benefit of about 75 percent of the poverty level (which was $3300 per year in 1967) and a 50-percent implicit tax rate would cause male labor supply to decrease by 8–15 percent.[31]

Experimental data, however, can also be used to estimate the size of income and substitution effects. Four large social experiments were conducted in New Jersey, Seattle-Denver, Gary (Indiana), and rural North Carolina in the late 1960s and early 1970s for the purpose of measuring labor supply responses to various income maintenance policies. They were conceived and funded because researchers and policymakers did not want to rely solely on estimates derived from the nonexperimental studies cited above.

While the details in each experiment varied, the welfare programs in the experiments had benefit guarantee levels (benefits with zero earnings) ranging from 50–125 percent of the poverty level.[32] The implicit tax rates on earnings in each experiment ranged from 30–80 percent. The typical response for males to these benefit levels and "tax" rates was to reduce labor supply by 3–5 percent.[33] The somewhat smaller response than the nonexperimental prediction above is perhaps due to the known and limited duration of each experiment; responses might have been larger if recipients knew the program would be available to them indefinitely.

In examining the labor supply response of females in these experiments, it is useful to recall two facts from the nonexperimental studies. First, the estimates of income and substitution effects for women are much less precise

---

[30] It is also worth noting here that, because the welfare subsidy is conditioned on income, and because income is to some extent under the control of an individual, it is possible that some people previously above the welfare-cutoff level of income will reduce their labor supply enough to qualify for the subsidy.

[31] Borjas and Heckman, "Labor Supply Estimates for Public Policy Evaluation," p. 331.

[32] Poverty-level incomes are those below which the federal government considers a family to be living in poverty. These income thresholds are defined for farm and nonfarm families separately and are also calculated by family size and the age/gender of the household head. The threshold in each case is based on the 1963 cost of an inexpensive, but nutritionally sound, food plan designed by the Department of Agriculture. This cost was multiplied by 3, reflecting an assumption that families of three or more persons spend one third of their income on food, and has been adjusted upward each year since 1963 by changes in the Consumer Price Index. For a nonfarm family of four, the 1976 poverty threshold was $5815, up from $3128 in 1963; by 1986 changes in the Consumer Price Index implied a poverty level of around $11,000 per year. (See U.S. Bureau of the Census, Current Population Reports, *Consumer Income,* Series P-60, no. 115, issued July 1978, for a more detailed explanation of poverty thresholds.)

[33] Philip K. Robins, "A Comparison of the Labor Supply Findings from the Four Negative Income Tax Experiments," *Journal of Human Resources* 20 (Fall 1985): 567–82.

than for men; second, the substitution effect for market work appears to be larger. Since the substitution effect of income maintenance programs induces a withdrawal of labor supply, it is not surprising that the labor supply responses of women in the experiments tended to be larger than for men. For wives, the typical response was for labor supply to decline by a bit over 20 percent, while for single women who headed households the labor supply reduction was typically in the 13–16 percent range. The responses of youth were similar to those of married women.[34] Thus, the labor supply effects of expanded welfare coverage are not likely to be innocuous. At some point, society will have to decide whether the improvements in social equity that result from more generous welfare programs are counterbalanced by the social losses attendant on reduced labor supply.[35] In making this decision, of course, society may feel quite differently about reductions in market work by some groups (say, mothers of small children) from the way it feels about labor supply reductions of other groups.

# REVIEW QUESTIONS

1. Indicate whether the following statement is true, false, or uncertain: ``Leisure must be an inferior good for an individual's labor supply curve to be backward-bending.'' Explain your answer.

2. The way the Workers' Compensation system works now is that employees permanently injured on the job receive a payment of $X each year whether they work or not. Suppose the government were to implement a new program where those who do not work at all get $0.5X but where those who do work get $0.5X plus Workers' Compensation of 50 cents *for every hour worked*. What would be the change in work incentives associated with this change in the way Workers' Compensation payments are calculated?

3. Suppose our welfare system were structured *initially* as follows: all people earning below income $X would be given a cash grant to bring their income up to $X. Next, suppose we change the welfare system to incorporate a *work test*. This means that persons who work *fewer* than Y hours get no welfare payment at all. Above Y hours of work, the people receive a welfare payment sufficient to bring up their income to $X. Now answer the question: *Which system has stronger work incentives? Why?*

4. The Secretary of Labor has received the following memo from a member of the President's staff:

> The growth of interest in worker-owned enterprises raises some important questions relating to profit sharing. If workers with no previous investment income begin to receive a portion of profits, the effects on labor supply could be large. Would you please have your staff prepare an analysis of the labor-supply implications of widespread workers' participation in profits?

---

[34] Ibid. For other reviews of these experimental findings, see Michael C. Keeley, *Labor Supply and Public Policy: A Critical Review* (New York: Academic Press, 1981); Robert Moffitt and Kenneth Kehrer, ``The Effect of Tax and Transfer Programs on Labor Supply: The Evidence from the Income-Maintenance Experiments,'' in *Research in Labor Economics,* ed. R. Ehrenberg (Greenwich, CT: JAI Press, 1981); John Pencavel, ``Labor Supply of Men: A Survey,'' in *Handbook of Labor Economics,* O. Ashenfelter and R. Layard eds. (Amsterdam: North-Holland, 1986); and Mark Killingsworth, *Labor Supply* (Cambridge: Cambridge University Press, 1983).

[35] The general issue of equity vs. output considerations is treated in a readable manner by Arthur Okun, *Equality and Efficiency: The Big Trade-Off* (Washington, DC: The Brookings Institution, 1975).

The paper should cover the direction of the labor-supply effects as indicated by theory and the likely ways in which these labor-supply effects could be manifested. In particular, however, I am interested in a comparison of the labor-supply effects of alternative bases upon which profits can be shared among workers. Which basis or bases have the smallest labor-supply effects?

Write the paper avoiding the use of undefined jargon words. In other words, explain the concepts and hypotheses fully.

5. Suppose you are working in the personnel department of a large company with an absenteeism problem. What alternatives are there for dealing with the problem? What does the Vice-President for Personnel need to know in order to decide which alternative (if any) to implement?

# SUGGESTED READINGS

William G. Bowen and T. Aldrich Finegan, *The Economics of Labor Force Participation* (Princeton, NJ: Princeton University Press, 1969).

Glen G. Cain, *Married Women in the Labor Force* (Chicago: University of Chicago Press, 1966).

Glen G. Cain and Harold W. Watts, eds. *Income Maintenance and Labor Supply* (Chicago: Markham, 1973).

H. G. Lewis, "Hours of Work and Hours of Leisure," *Proceedings of the Industrial Relations Research Association* (1957): 196–206.

Robert Moffitt and Ken Kehrer, "The Effect of Tax and Transfer Programs on Labor Supply: The Evidence from the Income Maintenance Experiments," in Ronald G. Ehrenberg, ed., *Research in Labor Economics,* 4 (Greenwich, CT: JAI Press, 1981): 103–50.

J. A. Pechman and P. M. Timpane, eds., *Work Incentives and Income Guarantees: The New Jersey Income Tax Experiment* (Washington, DC: The Brookings Institution, 1975).

# APPENDIX 5A

## A Graphical Analysis of the Labor/Leisure Choice: The Fundamentals

Graphical analysis requires a level of rigor that is more convincing than verbal analysis and incorporates visual aids that make the analysis easier to understand. The graphical analysis, however, is simply a more rigorous, visible repetition of our verbal analysis; hence, none of the conclusions or definitions reached in this chapter will be changed in any way.

**Preferences.**   Let us assume that there are two major categories of goods that make people happy—leisure and money income (which can, of course, be used to buy other goods). Collapsing all goods into two allows our graphs to be drawn in two-dimensional space.

Since both leisure and money can be used to generate satisfaction (or *utility*), these two goods are to some extent substitutes for each other. If one were forced to give up some money income—by cutting back one's hours of work, for example—there would be some increase in leisure time that could be substituted for this lost income to keep the person as happy as before. A very thoughtful consumer/worker, in fact, could reveal a whole *variety* of combinations of money and leisure hours that would yield him or her this same level of satisfaction.

To understand how preferences can be graphed, suppose a thoughtful consumer/worker is asked to decide how happy he or she would be with a daily income of $64 combined with eight hours of leisure (point *a* in Figure 5A.1). This level of happiness could be called "utility level *A*." Our consumer/worker could name *other combinations* of money income and leisure hours that would *also* yield utility level *A*. Assume that our respondent names five other such combinations. All six combinations of money and leisure that

**Figure 5A.1**   Two Indifference Curves for the Same Person

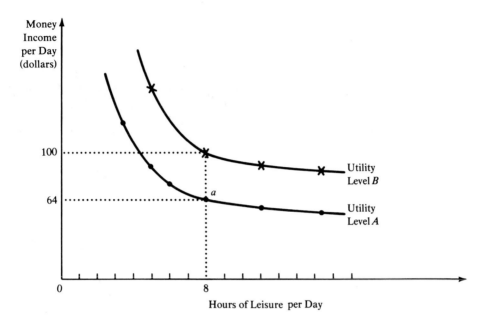

yield utility level *A* are represented by heavy dots in Figure 5A.1. The curve connecting these dots is called an *indifference curve*—a curve connecting the various combinations of money and leisure that yield equal utility. (The term *indifference curve* got its name from the fact that, since each point on the curve yields equal utility, a person is truly indifferent about where on the curve he or she will be.)

   Our worker/consumer could no doubt achieve a higher level of happiness if he or she could combine the eight hours of leisure with an income of $100 per day instead of just $64 a day. This higher satisfaction level could be called "utility level *B*." The consumer could name other combinations of money income and leisure that would also yield *this* higher level of utility. These combinations are denoted by the *X*s in Figure 5A.1 that are connected by a new indifference curve.

   Indifference curves have certain specific characteristics that are reflected by the way they are drawn:

1.   Utility level *B* represents more happiness than level *A*. Every level of leisure consumption is combined with a higher income on *B* than on curve *A*. Hence our respondent prefers all points on indifference curve *B* to any point on curve *A*. A whole *set* of indifference curves

**Figure 5A.2**   An Indifference Curve

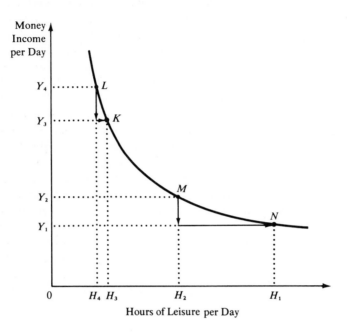

could be drawn for this one person, each representing a different utility level. Any such curve that lies to the northeast of another one is preferred to any curve to the southwest, because the northeastern curve represents a higher level of utility.

2.  Indifference curves *do not intersect*. If they did, the point of intersection would represent *one* combination of money and leisure that yields *two* different levels of satisfaction. We assume our worker/consumer is *not* so inconsistent in stating his or her preferences that this could happen.

3.  Indifference curves are *negatively sloped,* because if either money or leisure hours is increased, the other is reduced to preserve the same level of utility. If the slope is steep—as at segment *LK* in Figure 5A.2—a given loss of income need not be accompanied by a large increase in leisure hours in order to keep utility constant.[1]

---

[1]  Economists call the change in money income needed to hold utility constant when leisure hours are changed by one unit the *marginal rate of substitution* between leisure and money income. This marginal rate of substitution can be graphically understood as the slope of the indifference curve at any point. At point *L*, for example, the slope is relatively steep so economists would say that the marginal rate of substitution at point *L* is relatively high.

When the curve is relatively flat—as at segment $MN$ in Figure 5A.2—a given decrease in income must be accompanied by a large increase in the consumption of leisure to hold utility constant. Thus, where indifference curves are relatively steep, people do not value money income as highly as when such curves are relatively flat—for when they are flat, a loss of income can only be compensated by a large increase in leisure if utility is to be kept constant.

4.  Indifference curves are *convex*—steeper at the left than at the right. This shape reflects the assumption that when money income is relatively high and leisure hours are relatively few, leisure is more highly valued than when leisure is abundant and money relatively scarce. At segment $LK$ in Figure 5A.2, a great loss of income (from $Y_4$ to $Y_3$, for example) can be compensated for by just a little increase in leisure, whereas a little loss of leisure time (from $H_3$ to $H_4$, for example) would require a relatively large increase in income to maintain equal utility. Conversely, when income is low and leisure is abundant (segment $MN$ in Figure 5A.2), income is more highly valued. Losing income (by moving from $Y_2$ to $Y_1$, for example) requires a huge increase in leisure for utility to remain constant. What is scarce is assumed to be highly valued.

5.  Finally, different people will have different sets of indifference curves. The curves drawn in Figures 5A.1 and 5A.2 were for *one person only*. Another person would have a completely different set of curves. People who value leisure more highly, for example, would have indifference curves that are generally steeper (see Figure 5A.3). People who do not value leisure highly will have relatively flat curves.[2] Thus, individual preferences can be portrayed graphically.

**Income and wage constraints.**   Now everyone would like to maximize his or her utility, which could be best done by consuming every available hour of leisure combined with the highest conceivable income. Unfortunately, the resources anyone can command are limited. Thus, all that is possible is to do the best one can, given limited resources. To see these resource limitations graphically requires superimposing constraints over one's set of indifference curves to see which combinations of income and leisure are available and which are not.

Suppose the person whose indifference curves are graphed in Figure 5A.1 has no source of income other than labor earnings. Suppose, further, that he or she can earn \$8 per hour. Figure 5A.4 contains the two indifference curves drawn in Figure 5A.1 but also contains a straight line ($DE$) connecting combinations of leisure and income that are possible for a person with an \$8 wage

---

[2]  The two curves shown in Figure 5A.3 should be compared in *slope* only. Levels of utility for two different people cannot be compared because happiness is not objectively measurable. Figure 5A.3 simply shows that people with different preferences will have indifference curves with different *shapes*. The fact that the two curves in Figure 5A.3 intersect is thus not important, since the curves are for different people.

**Figure 5A.3**   Indifference Curves for Two Different People

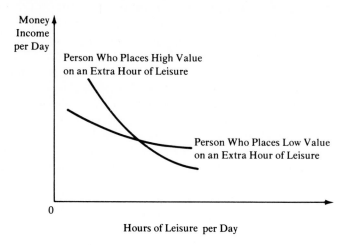

**Figure 5A.4**   Indifference Curves and Budget Constraint

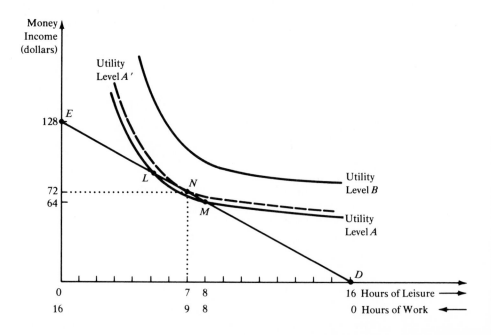

and no outside income. If 16 hours per day are available for work and leisure, and if this person consumes all 16 in leisure, then money income will be zero (point $D$ in Figure 5A.4). If 8 hours a day are devoted to work, income will be $64 per day (point $M$), and if 16 hours a day are worked income would be $128 per day (point $E$). Other points on this line—the point of 15 hours of leisure (1 hour of work) and $8 of income, for example—are also possible. This line, which reflects the combinations of leisure and income that are possible for the individual, is called the *budget constraint*. Any combination to the right of the budget constraint is not achievable; the person's command over resources simply is not sufficient to attain these combinations of leisure and money income.

The *slope* of the budget constraint is a graphical representation of the wage rate. One's wage rate is properly defined as the increment in income ($\Delta Y$) derived from an increment in the hours of work ($\Delta H$):

$$\text{Wage Rate} = \frac{\Delta Y}{\Delta H}.$$

Now $\Delta Y/\Delta H$ is exactly the slope of the budget constraint (in absolute value).[3] Figure 5A.4 shows how the constraint rises $8 for every one-hour increase in work: if the person works zero hours, income per day is zero; if the person works one hour, $8 in income is possible; if he or she works 8 hours, $64 in income can be achieved. The reason the constraint rises $8 for every unit increase in hours of work is because the wage rate the person commands is $8 per hour. If the person could earn $16 per hour, the constraint would rise twice as fast and be twice as steep.

It is clear from Figure 5A.4 that our consumer/worker cannot achieve utility level $B$. He or she can achieve *some* points on the indifference curve representing utility level $A$; specifically, those points between $L$ and $M$ in Figure 5A.4. However, if our consumer/worker is a utility maximizer, he or she will realize that a utility level *above* $A$ is possible. Remembering that there are an infinite number of indifference curves that can be drawn between curves $A$ and $B$ in Figure 5A.4—one representing each possible level of satisfaction between $A$ and $B$—we can draw a curve ($A'$) that is northeast of curve $A$ and is just *tangent* to the budget constraint. Any movement along the budget constraint *away* from the tangency point places the person on an indifference curve lying *below* $A'$.

An indifference curve that is just tangent to the constraint represents the highest level of utility that the person can obtain given his or her constraint. It is the most northeast curve with an achievable point on it, and no curve superior to it can be reached. If this highest possible curve is denoted as utility level $A'$ in Figure 5A.4, then point $N$ represents the utility-maximizing combination of leisure and income.

---

[3] The vertical change for a one-unit change in horizontal distance is the definition for *slope*. *Absolute value* refers to the size of the slope, disregarding whether it is positive or negative.

Thus, our consumer/worker is best off—given his or her preferences and constraints—working nine hours a day, consuming seven hours of leisure, and having a daily income of $72. All other possible combinations, such as eight hours of work and $64 of income, yield lower utility.

## The Decision Not to Work

In the example just discussed—and illustrated in Figure 5A.4—a point of tangency (*N*) existed between the individual's indifference curve and the budget constraint. That point of tangency indicated the utility-maximizing labor/leisure combination. What happens if there is no point of tangency? What happens, for example, if the person's indifference curves are at every point more steeply sloped than the budget constraint (see Figure 5A.5)? If the person places a very high value on extra hours of leisure, then indifference curves that represent an individual's preferences are very steeply sloped (see Figure 5A.3). A very high hourly wage would be required to compensate the person for an hour of lost leisure (that is, an hour of work). If the increase in money income required to compensate the worker for an hour of work (to keep utility constant) is greater than the wage rate of every feasible number of

**Figure 5A.5**   The Decision Not to Work Is a "Corner Solution"

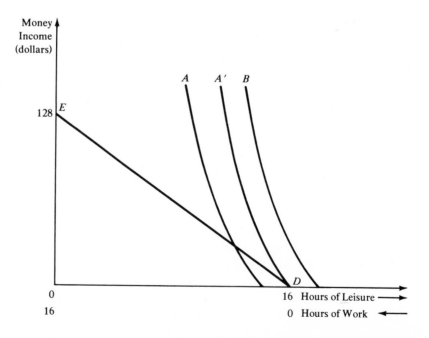

leisure hours, then the person simply will choose not to work. Figure 5A.5 indicates that utility is maximized at point *D*—a point of zero hours of work. Point *D* is *not* a tangency point; there can be no tangency if the indifference curve has no points at which the slope equals the slope of the budget constraint. Thus, utility in Figure 5A.5 is maximized at a corner—a point at the extreme end of the budget constraint—and at this point (*D*) the person does not choose to be in the labor force.

## Income and Substitution Effects

**The income effect.**   Suppose now that the person depicted in Figure 5A.4 is lucky and falls into a source of income independent of work. Suppose, further, that this *nonlabor* income amounts to about $36 per day. Thus, even if this person worked zero hours per day, his or her daily income would be equal to $36. Naturally, if the person worked more than zero hours, his or her daily income would be equal to $36 plus earnings (the wage multiplied by the hours of work).

The source of nonlabor income has clearly increased our person's command over resources, as can be shown by drawing a new budget constraint to reflect the nonlabor income. As shown by the broken line in Figure 5A.6, the end points of the new constraint are (1) zero hours of work and $36 of money income (point *d*), and (2) at point *e,* 16 hours of work, and $164 of income ($36 in nonlabor income plus $128 in earnings). Note that the new constraint is *parallel* to the old one. Parallel lines have the same slope; since the slope of each constraint reflects the wage rate, we can infer that the increase in nonlabor income has not changed the person's wage rate.

We have just described a situation in which a pure *income effect* should be observed. Income (wealth) has been increased, but the wage rate has remained unchanged. In this chapter, we noted that if wealth increased and the opportunity cost of leisure remained constant, the person would consume more leisure and work less. We thus concluded that the income effect was *negative;* as income goes up (down), holding wages constant, hours of work go down (up). This negative relationship is illustrated graphically in Figure 5A.6. When the old (solid) budget constraint was in effect, the person's highest level of utility was reached at point *N,* where he or she worked nine hours a day. With the new (dashed) constraint, the optimum hours of work are eight per day. The new source of income, but not altering the wage, has caused an income effect that results in one less hour of work per day.

**Income and substitution effects with a wage increase.**   Suppose that, instead of increasing one's command over resources by receiving a source of nonlabor income, the wage rate for another person were to be increased from $8.00 to $12.00 per hour. This increase, as noted earlier, will cause *both* an income and a substitution effect; the person is both wealthier *and* faces a higher opportunity cost of leisure. Both effects can be illustrated

**Figure 5A.6**   Indifference Curves and Budget Constraint (with an increase in nonlabor income)

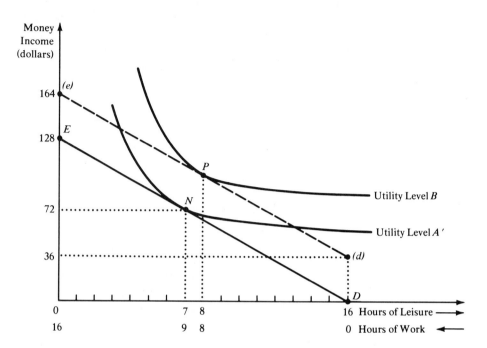

graphically; see Figures 5A.7 and 5A.8 on pages 158 and 159. Figures 5A.7 and 5A.8 illustrate the *observed effects* of the wage change as well as the two (hidden) *components* of the observed change: the income and substitution effects. Figure 5A.7 illustrates the case where the observed response is to increase the hours of work; in this case, the substitution effect is stronger than the income effect. Figure 5A.8 illustrates the case where the income effect is stronger, and the response to a wage increase is to reduce the hours of work. Both cases are plausible. Theory tells us in what direction the income and substitution effects should go, but theory does not tell us which effect will be stronger. The difference between the two cases lies *solely* in the shape of the indifference curves (preferences); the budget constraints, which reflect wealth and the wage rate, are exactly the same.

Figures 5A.7 and 5A.8 show a new budget constraint. We are assuming that no source of nonlabor income exists for the person depicted, so that both the old and new constraints in each diagram are anchored at the same place—zero income for zero hours worked. However, the new constraint rises 50-percent faster than the old constraint, reflecting the 50-percent increase in the wage rate (from $8 to $12 per hour). The left endpoint of the new constraint is now at $192 (16 hours of work times $12 per hour) rather than at $128 (16 hours times $8). In Figure 5A.7, the new constraint implies that utility level

$U_2$ is the highest that can be reached, and the tangency at point $N_2$ suggests that 11 hours of work per day is the optimum. When the old constraint was in effect, the utility-maximizing hours of work were 8 per day. Thus, the wage increase has caused the person's hours of work to increase by three per day.

This observed effect, however, masks the underlying forces at work. These underlying forces are, of course, the income and substitution effects. These forces are not directly observable, but they are there (and working against each other) nonetheless. A physical analogy can be used to explain how these forces work.

Suppose a riderless boat is set adrift in the Mississippi River on a day in which the wind is blowing *across* the river. The river's current carries the boat downstream, but the crosswind also exerts a force that blows the boat east (for example). We observe where the boat is when it passes under a certain bridge. While we *observe* where the boat crosses under the bridge, we cannot directly see the two independent forces that together dictate where the boat ends up. There is the influence of the current and of the wind, and for some purposes it may be useful to measure these effects separately. How would we do it?

We would measure the influence of the current by asking ourselves, "Where would the boat have passed under the same bridge if there had been no wind?" This hypothetical question holds two elements constant: the wind (zero velocity) and the bridge under which the boat passes. The answer to the question is thus designed to identify the "pure" effect of the current. The influence of the wind could be measured by comparing where the boat actually crossed under the bridge with where it *would have crossed* had there been no wind.

Turning now to Figure 5A.7, we will identify the income effect (as we did the "current effect") by asking, "What would have been the change in the hours worked if the person had reached indifference curve $U_2$ (the bridge) by a change in *nonlabor* income with *no* change in the wage rate (no wind)?' We answer this question by moving the old constraint to the northeast, maintaining its original slope (reflecting the old wage of $8.00), which holds the wage constant. By definition, we must hold the wage constant when dealing with the income effect. However, moving the old constraint hypothetically "allows" nonlabor income to increase so that the person arrives at the new level of utility. The dashed constraint in Figure 5A.7 depicts this hypothetical constraint, which is tangent to indifference curve $U_2$ at $N_3$. This tangency suggests that had the person received nonlabor income, with no change in the wage, sufficient to reach the new level of utility, he or she would have *reduced* work hours from eight ($N_1$) to seven ($N_3$) per day. This shift is a graphical "proof" that the income effect is negative, assuming that leisure is a normal good.

The substitution effect can be measured once the pure effect of the wage change is known. We measure the substitution effect as the difference between where the person ends up and where he or she *would* have ended up

**Figure 5A.7**    Wage Change with Substitution Effect Dominating

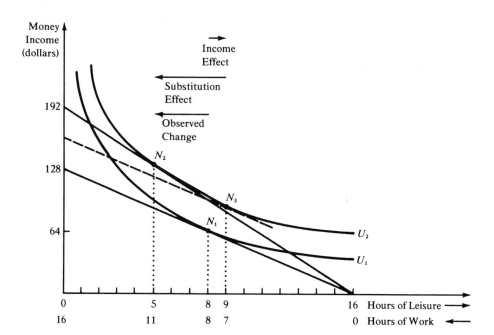

without a wage change. *With* the wage change, the person represented in Figure 5A.7 ended up at point $N_2$, working 11 hours a day. *Without* the wage change, the person would have arrived at point $N_3$, working 7 hours a day. The wage change *by itself* (holding utility, or real wealth, constant) caused work hours to increase by 4 per day. This increase demonstrates that the substitution effect is positive.

To summarize, the observed effect of raising wages from $8 to $12 per hour increased the hours of work in Figure 5A.7 from 8 to 11 per day. This observed effect, however, is the *sum* of two component effects. The income effect—which operates because an increased wage increases one's real wealth—tended to *reduce* the hours of work from 8 to 7 per day. The substitution effect—which captures the pure effect of the change in leisure's opportunity cost—tended to push the person toward 4 more hours of work per day. The end result was an increase of 3 in hours worked each day.

Figure 5A.8 can be analyzed in the same way. Here, the *observed* effect of the increased wage is a *reduction* in hours of work from 8 to 6 per day (points $N_1$ to $N_2$). This change is the result of an income effect, which by itself tended to *decrease* by three hours the hours of work per day, and a substitution effect, which tended to *increase* working hours by one per day. The net result of these forces is, of course, a reduction in hours of work by 2 per day.

The differences in the observed effects of a wage increase between Figures 5A.7 and 5A.8 are due to differences in the shapes of the indifference

**Figure 5A.8**   Wage Change with Income Effect Dominating

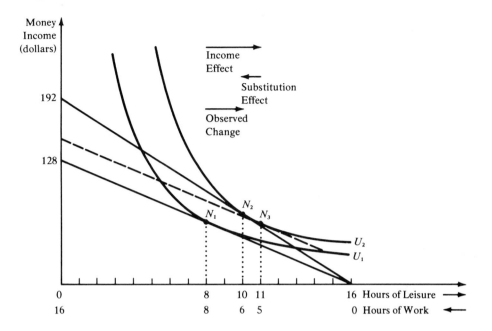

curves—or, in other words, to different preferences. The substitution and income effects worked in their predicted directions in both cases, but their relative strengths are a function of preferences (which are reflected in the shape and placement of indifference curves). Although theory cannot predict whether the income or substitution effect will dominate, it can be readily understood that the income effect of any given wage change is *larger* for individuals who are *working many hours* for pay than for those who are working few hours. Changes in income represent changes in one's command over resources, and it is clear that a wage increase (for example) fosters greater increases in wealth the more hours one works. (In terms of our graphical analysis, it can be seen from Figures 5A.7 and 5A.8 that the budget constraint representing a wage of $12 per hour lies further to the northeast of the one representing an $8 wage in its upper portion—where more hours are worked.)

# PART 3

## Wage Differentials in
## Labor Markets

# CHAPTER 6

## Compensating Wage Differentials and Human Capital

In Chapter 5 we studied workers' decisions about *whether to seek employment* and *how long to work*. In this chapter we will analyze workers' decisions about the industry, occupation, or firm in which they choose to work, emphasizing the influences on job choice of such employment characteristics as work environment or risk of injury. We also analyze the effects of required educational *investments* on occupational choice. A major result of the economic analysis of occupational choice is that people who start out with equal talents may, even in competitive labor markets, earn different wages.

We begin this chapter by studying the importance of both *current* wages and nonpecuniary job characteristics in allocating labor. However, many labor supply choices require a substantial initial investment by the worker—investments that economists refer to as enchancing *human capital* (a worker's skills can be thought of as a stock of capital that can be "rented" out to employers). Recall that investments, by definition, entail an initial cost that is then recouped (hopefully) over some period of time. Because of this investment behavior, we broaden the initial framework of this chapter by analyzing workers' choices about investment in themselves. We then show how firms take into account nonwage job characteristics and workers' investments in themselves when determining their pay policies.

## An Analysis of Occupational Choice

If all jobs were exactly alike and located in the same place, an individual's decision about where to seek work would be relatively simple. He or she would attempt to obtain a job where the expected compensation was highest. Any differences in compensation would cause workers to seek work with the highest-paying employers and avoid applying for work with the low-paying ones. The high-paying employers, having an abundance of applicants, might decide they are paying more than necessary to staff their vacancies. The low-paying employers would have to raise wage offers to compete for workers. Ultimately, if the market works without hindrance, wages of all employers would equalize. All jobs are not the same, however. Some jobs require much more education or training than others. Some jobs are in clean, modern offices, and others are in noisy, dusty, or dangerous factories. Some permit the employee some discretion over the pace of work at various points throughout the day, while some involve highly rigid assembly-line work. Some are challenging and call for decision making by the employee; others are monotonous. While the influence of educational and training requirements will be discussed later in this chapter, we will discuss here how the variations in job characteristics influence individual choice and the observable market outcomes of that choice.

## Individual Choice and Its Outcomes

Suppose several unskilled workers have received offers from two employers. Employer X pays $5.00 per hour and offers clean, safe working conditions. Employer Y also pays $5.00 per hour, but offers employment in a dirty, noisy factory. Which employer would the workers choose? Most would undoubtedly choose Employer X, because the pay is the same while the job is performed under less disagreeable conditions.

Clearly, then, $5.00 is not an equilibrium wage in both firms.[1] Because Firm X finds it very easy to attract applicants at $5.00, it will "hold the line" on any future wage increases. Firm Y, however, must either clean up the plant, pay higher wages, or do both if it wants to fill its vacancies. Assuming it decides not to alter working conditions, it must clearly pay a wage *above* $5.00 to be competitive in the labor market. The extra wage it must pay to attract workers is called a *compensating wage differential,* because the higher wage is paid to compensate workers for the undesirable working conditions. If such a differential did not exist, Firm Y could not attract the unskilled workers that Firm X can obtain.

Suppose that Firm Y raises its wage offer to $5.50 while the offer from X remains at $5.00. Will this 50-cent-per-hour differential—an extra $1000 per year—serve to attract *all* the workers in our group to Firm Y? If it did attract them all, Firm X would have an incentive to raise its wage and Firm Y might want to lower its offers a bit; the 50-cent differential in this case would *not* be an equilibrium differential. More than likely, however, the 10-percent-higher wage in Firm Y would attract only *some* of the group to Firm Y. Some people are not bothered by dirt and noise a much as others are, and these people may

---

[1] There may be a few people who really do not care about noise and dirt in the workplace. We assume here that these people are so rare—or Firm Y's demand for workers so large—that Y cannot fill all its vacancies with just those who are totally insensitive to dirt and noise.

decide to take the extra pay and put up with the poorer working conditions.[2] Others, however, may be very sensitive to noise or allergic to dust, and they will decide that they would rather get paid less than expose themselves to working conditions that are very unpleasant. If firm Y cannot obtain the quantity and quality of workers it seeks with a 50-cent differential, it would have to offer an even higher wage rate. If both firms can obtain the quantity and quality of workers they want with the 50-cent differential, it *would* be an equilibrium differential—in the sense that there would be no forces causing the differential to change.

The desire of workers to avoid unpleasantness or risk, then, should force employers offering unpleasant or risky jobs to pay higher wages than they would otherwise have to pay. Put another way, to attract a work force, these employers will have to pay higher wages to their workers than firms that offer pleasant, safe jobs to comparable workers.

This wage differential serves two related, socially desirable ends. First, it serves a *social* need by giving people an incentive to do—voluntarily—dirty, dangerous, or unpleasant work. Likewise the existence of a compensating wage differential also imposes a financial penalty on employers who have unfavorable working conditions. Second, at an *individual* level, it serves as a reward to workers who accept unpleasant jobs by paying them more than comparable workers in more pleasant jobs.

**The allocation of labor.**   Society has a number of jobs that are either un-avoidably nasty or would be very costly to make safe and pleasant (coal mining, deep-sea diving, and coke-oven cleaning are examples). There are essentially two ways to recruit the labor necessary for such jobs. One is to compel people to do these jobs, the military draft being the most obvious American example of forced labor. The second way is to induce people to do the jobs voluntarily. Most modern societies rely mainly on incentives—compensating wage differentials—to recruit labor to unpleasant jobs volun-tarily. Workers will mine coal, collect garbage, and bolt steel beams together 50 stories off the ground, because, compared to alternative jobs for which they would qualify, these jobs pay well. The 1500 commercial deep-sea divers in the United States, for example, who are exposed to the dangers of drowning, the rigors of construction work with cumbersome gear, a lonely and hostile work environment, and several physiological disorders as a result of compression and decompression, made $20,000 to $45,000 per year in the mid-1970s, or about 20–130 percent more than the average high-school graduate.

As another example, the *failure* to pay sufficiently high wages to U.S. military personnel has occasionally created difficulties in recruiting and re-taining such people. While the pay for military recruits with less than two

---

2  The assertion that people are affected differently by noise is documented in *Community Reaction to Airport Noise,* vol. I (report to the National Aeronautics and Space Administration prepared by Tracor, Inc. of Austin, Texas), July 1971. This study showed, for example, that around 10 percent of people are "highly susceptible" to noise annoyance, while around half are "highly adaptable" to airport noises.

**EXAMPLE   6.1**

## Compensating Wage Differentials for the Evening and Night Shifts

Roughly 25 percent of production workers living in metropolitan areas work on the evening or night shifts. This percentage has been stable for two decades, but it varies by industry. Over 50 percent of the workers in the cotton and synthetic textiles, cigarette, and glass-container industries work in the evening or at night. Because evening and night work requires sleeping and leisure patterns that differ from the norm, one might expect that firms scheduling such work would have to pay a wage premium to attract workers. Indeed, a 1984 study found that 90 percent of evening and night workers received higher pay than their daytime co-workers; evening workers earned 23 cents per hour more and night workers 30 cents per hour more in manufacturing industries. Given an average manufacturing wage of $9.18 in 1984, shift workers received wages that were about 3 percent higher than they would have received if they had worked during the day.

SOURCE:  Sandra L. King and Harry B. Williams, "Shift Work Pay Differentials and Practices in Manufacturing," *Monthly Labor Review* 108 (December 1985): 26–33.

years of service was 14-percent above the pay for civilian youth right after the draft was eliminated in 1973, the relative pay advantage had fallen to 2 percent by 1979. This fall in relative pay for recruits was accompanied by a rather severe shortage in the quantity and ability levels of enlistees, despite the decline in civilian job opportunities that accompanied a large rise in the unemployment rate over that six-year period. By 1982, both the quality and quantity aspects of the military shortage had ended, due partly to a very high civilian unemployment rate, but probably mostly to military pay raises that increased the pay for recruits to 18 percent above that of civilian youth. If the government wants to maintain armed services without resorting to the draft, it is clear that military pay must rise to a level sufficient to overcome the hazards and inconveniences of military life.[3]

**Compensation for workers.**   Compensating wage differentials also serve as *individual* rewards by paying those who accept bad or arduous working conditions more than they would otherwise receive. In a parallel fashion, those who opt for more pleasant conditions have to "buy" them by accepting lower pay. For example, if a person takes the $5.00-per-hour job with Firm X,

---

[3]  See "The Retention Problem," *The Wall Street Journal* (March 19, 1980), 24, and an unpublished table provided to us by Robert Lockman, Center for Naval Analyses. What is pleasant or unpleasant is determined in the market at the *margin*. For example, even if most people dislike night work, there might be enough who do not to fill night-shift jobs without a compensating wage differential. See Example 6.2 for a discussion of this issue.

he or she is giving up the $5.50-per-hour job with less pleasant conditions in Firm Y. The better conditions are being bought, in a very real sense, for 50 cents per hour. Thus, compensating wage differentials become the price at which good working conditions can be purchased by—or bad ones sold to—workers.

Contrary to what is commonly asserted, a monetary value *can* often be attached to events or conditions of which the effects are primarily psychological in nature. Compensating wage differentials provide the key to the valuation of these nonpecuniary aspects of employment.

In the area of occupational-health-and-safety policy, there is continuous debate about whether to make machines safer or to simply protect the worker from machine hazards with personal protective devices.[4] For example, high noise levels can eventually damage the hearing of workers. The Department of Labor has favored reducing noise levels through engineering changes, such as putting mufflers on—or baffles around—noisy machines. Employer representatives have consistently claimed that such engineering changes are inordinately expensive and that compelling workers to wear earplugs would preserve workers' hearing at much less cost. Because resources are scarce, our society would like to achieve hearing protection at minimum cost, but we must be sure to count *all* the costs. One of the costs of wearing earplugs is the *psychic* cost: they are very uncomfortable for most people to wear. The cost of this discomfort *must* be counted along with the purchase price of earplugs in arriving at the total cost of wearing earplugs.

How could we put a dollar value on earplug discomfort? A straightforward way to determine this dollar value would be to find a set of employers who *require* the use of earplugs as a condition of employment and to compare the wages they pay to those of *comparable* firms that allow, but *do not require,* the wearing of earplugs. If workers do in fact find earplugs more uncomfortable than the noise, wages in the firm that requires their use should be higher—and this wage differential is the estimate of what value workers place on this discomfort.

Suppose, for example, that the research showed that companies requiring earplugs pay 10 cents an hour—or $200 per year—more than *otherwise similar* firms pay for *comparable* labor.[5] Workers accepting jobs there are indicating by their behavior that they are willing to take $200 per year as compensation for the discomfort they must bear; that is, the cost of the discomfort to them is equal to, or less than, $200 per year. Those refusing to work at the plant place a value higher than that on their discomfort costs, because $200 is insufficient to compensate them. Thus, the cost of discomfort at the margin is $200 per year (that is, to induce one more worker to wear earplugs would require added compensation of about $200 per year).

---

[4] The debate about whether the government should be involved at all in the occupational safety and health area is discussed later in this chapter.

[5] Firms may be willing to do this if they believe requiring earplugs will reduce workers' compensation claims for hearing loss in the future.

**EXAMPLE   6.2**

## Compensating Differentials and Company Relocation Policy

An increasingly difficult personnel problem of the 1980s is the issue of relocating employees. Large companies with offices all over the country often find that their best internal candidates for managerial openings at a particular location currently work and live in another area that may be hundreds of miles away. There are significant monetary and psychic costs associated with moving to a new area. For example, in addition to direct moving expenses, and the psychic costs of relocation, new mortgages may be very expensive to obtain, and taxes or living costs may be higher in the new area. Also, families increasingly take into account both husbands' and wives' careers in deciding whether to move; an attractive move for one family member may be turned down if another must leave a very good job.

Companies recognize these costs and offer compensating differentials to workers who relocate. For example, as of 1981, 63 percent of major American corporations offered relocating workers a mortgage interest differential allowance. This benefit gave the worker an allowance equivalent to the additional mortgage interest and housing costs associated with the move. Further, many companies offer a cost-of-living salary supplement to make up for increases in living costs when one moves into a higher-cost area. Finally, firms must often offer new hires a "signing bonus" to induce them to relocate.

While the data on relocation policies indicate that many companies must pay a compensating differential to employees who relocate, firms can reduce such costs by seeking out those who are most willing to move. This can be done through employee-attitude surveys. In addition, a cost-of-living supplement can be avoided by moving people from one high cost-of-living area to another. In effect, companies look for those workers for whom a compensating differential for relocation is either unnecessary or is smaller than it is for other workers. Of course, firms must weigh the productivities of various workers as well as the costs of relocating them.

SOURCES:  Margaret Magnus and John Dodd, "Relocation: Changing Attitudes and Company Policies," *Personnel Journal* 60 (July 1981): 538–45; Gaylord F. Milbrandt, "Relocation Strategies: Part II," *Personnel Journal* 60 (August 1981): 644–46; Gaylord F. Milbrandt, "Can Relocation Costs be Managed?" *Personnel Journal* 62 (August 1983): 657–59.

Before concluding that the psychic costs of wearing earplugs are $200 per year, we must remember that our hypothetical findings are for the marginal worker. People differ in the amount of discomfort they feel and in the value they place on what they feel. Those most likely to take the extra pay in return for having to wear earplugs are those who are least sensitive to discomfort or most willing to trade discomfort for money. If we were to compel *all* workers in noisy factories to wear earplugs, we would be forcing earplugs on some for whom the costs of discomfort are in excess of $200.

As this example illustrates, compensating wage differentials are the price at which various *qualitative* job characteristics are bought and sold. As such, they offer a way of placing a value on things that most people think of as "noneconomic." This illustration, of course, does not prove that compensating wage differentials exist or that such differentials are equilibrium prices— issues that will be discussed later in the chapter.

## Assumptions and Predictions

We have seen how a simple theory of job choice by individuals leads to the *prediction* that compensating wage differentials will be associated with various job characteristics. Positive differentials (higher wages) will accompany "bad" characteristics, while negative differentials (lower wages) will be associated with "good" ones. However, it is very important to understand that this prediction can *only* be made *holding other things equal*.

Our prediction about the existence of compensating wage differentials grows out of the reasonable assumption that if a worker has a choice between a job with "good" working conditions and a job of equal pay with a "bad" set of working conditions, he or she will choose the "good" job. If the employee is an unskilled laborer he or she may be choosing between an unpleasant job spreading hot asphalt or a more comfortable job in an air-conditioned warehouse. In either case, he or she is going to receive something close to the wage rate unskilled workers typically receive. However, our theory would predict that this worker would receive *more* from the asphalt-spreading job than from the warehouse job.

Thus the predicted outcome of our theory of job choice is *not* that employees working under "bad" conditions receive more than those working in "good" conditions. The prediction is that, *holding worker characteristics constant,* employees in bad jobs receive higher wages than those working under more pleasant conditions. The characteristics that must be held constant include all the other things that influence wages: skill level, age, race, gender, union status, region of the country, and so forth. Because there are many influences on wages *other* than working conditions, our theory leads us to expect employers offering "bad" jobs to pay higher wages than employers offering "good" jobs to *comparable* workers. This theory is based on three assumptions about workers and one concerning employers.

**Assumption 1: Utility maximization.**  Our first assumption is that workers seek to maximize their *utility,* not their income. If workers sought to maximize income, they would always choose the highest-paying job available to them and this behavior would eventually cause wages to be equalized across the jobs open to any set of workers. In contrast, compensating wage differentials will only arise if some people do *not* choose the highest-paying job offered—preferring instead a lower-paying (but more pleasant) job. This behavior allows the employers offering the lower-paying, pleasant jobs to be competitive for labor. Wages do not equalize in this case. Rather, the *net* *advantages*—the overall utility from the pay and the psychic aspects of the job—tend to equalize for the marginal worker.

**Assumption 2: Worker information.**   The second assumption implicit in our analysis is that workers are aware of the job characteristics of potential importance to them. Whether they know about them before they take the job or find out soon after taking it is not too important. In either case, a company offering a ''bad'' job with no compensating wage differential would have trouble recruiting or retaining workers—trouble that would eventually force it to raise its wage.

It is quite likely, of course, that workers will quickly learn of dust, dirt, noise, rigid work discipline, and other obvious bad working conditions. It is equally likely that they will *not* know the *precise* probability of being laid off, say, or being injured on the job. However, even with respect to these probabilities, their own direct observation or word-of-mouth reports from other employees can give them enough information to evaluate the situation with some accuracy. For example, the proportion of employees considering their work ''dangerous'' has been shown to be rather closely related to the actual injury rates published by the government for the industry in which they work.[6] This finding illustrates that, while workers are probably not able to state the precise probability of being injured, they do form accurate subjective judgments about the relative risk among several jobs.

Where our predictions may disappoint us, however, is with respect to *very* obscure characteristics. For example, while we now know that asbestos dust is highly damaging to worker health, this fact was not widely known 40 years ago. One reason information on asbestos dangers in plants was so long in being generated is that it takes more than 20 years for asbestos-related disease to develop. Cause and effect were thus obscured from workers and researchers alike—creating a situation in which worker job choices were made in ignorance of this risk. Compensating wage differentials for this danger thus could not possibly arise at that time. Our predictions about compensating wage differentials, then, hold only for job characteristics that workers know about.

**Assumption 3: Worker mobility.**   The third assumption implicit in our theory is that workers have a range of job offers from which to choose. Without a range of offers, workers would not be able to select the combination of job characteristics they desire or avoid the ones to which they do not wish exposure. A compensating wage differential for risk of injury, for example, simply could not arise if workers were able to obtain only dangerous jobs. It is the act of choosing safe jobs over dangerous ones that forces employers offering dangerous work to raise wages.

One manner in which this choice can occur is for each job applicant to receive several job offers from which to choose. However, another way in

---

[6]  Kip Viscusi, ''Labor Market Valuations of Life and Limb: Empirical Evidence and Policy Implications,'' *Public Policy* 26 (Summer 1978): 359–86.

which choice could be exercised is for workers to be (at least potentially) highly mobile. In other words, workers with few concurrent offers could take a job and continue their search for work if they thought an improvement could be made. Thus, even with few offers at any *one* time, a worker could conceivably have many choices over a *period* of time—which would eventually allow them to select the job that maximizes their utility.

While there are no general data on the number of concurrent offers a typical job applicant receives, it does seem to be true that job mobility among American workers is relatively high. The reported quit rate in manufacturing is normally between 1–2 percent per month—or about 12–24 percent per year. With job openings from quits and from general business expansion, manufacturing businesses newly hire 3 percent of their employees each month. Turnover is so great, in fact, that the median length of job tenure is 3.6 years—meaning that half of all workers have been on their current job less than three and one-half years.[7]

Another way to understand the amount of choice workers have in the job market is to look at job mobility over time. Consider male, blue-collar operatives (semiskilled workers)—a group of males many believe face severe restrictions on job choice. Among those operatives who were over age 25 in 1965, 18 percent were working in *completely different* occupations by 1970 (almost 9 percent had moved to skilled jobs, 3.5 percent had entered managerial or professional/technical occupations, and 3 percent were in unskilled jobs). The main point is that almost one worker in five had had a major occupational change in that five-year period.[8] Many more, of course, changed their jobs or their place of employment while still retaining semiskilled work. It is thus difficult to conclude that workers are typically lacking in job choice.

**Assumption 4: Employer profit maximization.** As emphasized throughout this text, wages are determined by the interaction of supply and demand. Workers may want higher wages, but employers must be willing to pay them. Why would an employer offering a dangerous job be willing to pay a higher wage than some other firm that offers safer employment? The assumption here is that the disagreeable aspects of jobs are costly for the employer to eliminate. An employer with a dangerous workplace, for example, can make it safer only by incurring the costs of installing safety devices, training employees, or issuing protective equipment to its workers. In attempting to maximize profits, the firm will try to attract its desired work force in the least costly manner. The firm compares the higher wage costs associated with offering dangerous jobs to the net costs required to make these jobs safer. (''Net'' costs are the expenditures on safety less such nonwage savings as reduced machine damage and less worker time lost.) If the wage savings

[7]    Robert E. Hall, ''The Importance of Lifetime Jobs in the U.S. Economy,'' *American Economic Review* 72 (September 1982): 716–24.

[8]    U.S. Bureau of the Census, *Characteristics of the Population, 1970: U.S. Summary,* Vol. I, Sec. 2 (Washington, DC: U.S. Government Printing Office, 1973), Table 230. These data do not indicate what fraction of those who changed occupation also changed employers.

from offering safer jobs exceed the net costs of reducing risk, the firm will decide to offer safer, lower-paying jobs. However, if the net costs of providing more safety are greater than the extra wage costs required to recruit employees for dangerous work, the profit-maximizing employer will choose not to offer safer jobs; instead, higher wages will be offered to attract the desired employees. Thus, the firms that are willing to pay higher wages do so because they are able to attract workers without having to undertake an expensive safety program. The higher wages, in other words, allow them to cut costs elsewhere. The firms that pay lower wages to comparable workers are those that find the provision of safety a cheaper option for attracting labor. In a real sense, these latter firms *must* pay lower wages to remain competitive in the product market, because they have incurred greater safety-related expenses than the firms offering dangerous, higher-paying jobs.

### Empirical Tests of the Theory of Compensating Wage Differentials

The prediction that there are compensating wage differentials for undesirable job characteristics is over 200 years old. Adam Smith, in his *Wealth of Nations,* published in 1776, proposed five "principal circumstances which . . . make up for a small pecuniary gain in some employments, and counterbalance a great one in others." One of these, the difficulty of learning the job, is discussed later in this chapter. Another two will be discussed in other chapters: the constancy of employment (Chapter 17) and the probability of success (Chapters 8 and 9). Our discussion in this section, while it could draw upon any of Smith's "principal circumstances" to illustrate the concept of compensating wage differentials, will focus on his assertion that "the wages of labour vary with the ease or hardship, the cleanliness or dirtiness, the honourableness or dishonourableness of the employment."[9]

One would think that 200 years is a sufficient period of time over which to have accumulated substantial evidence concerning an important prediction. Unfortunately, the prediction has only been seriously tested in the last fifteen years, and then in only a limited way. The reasons for this lack of evidence are twofold.

First, the prediction is that, *other things equal,* wages will be higher in unpleasant or dangerous jobs. The prediction can only be tested validly if the researcher is able to control for the effects of age, education, gender, region, race, union status, and all the other factors that typically influence wages. Only when the effects of these factors on wages are known can the researcher

---

[9] See Adam Smith, *Wealth of Nations* (New York: Modern Library, 1937), Book I, Chapter 10. The fifth "principal circumstance" is "the small or great trust which be reposed in the workmen." This job characteristic has not been widely studied in the context of compensating wage differentials, but positive compensating wage differentials have been found for supervisory jobs. See, for example, Martha S. Hill, "Authority—A Job Quality with Greater Benefits for Men Than Women," Working Paper Series, Survey Research Center, University of Michigan, 1983.

filter out the *separate* influence on wages of (for example) injury risk.[10] Statistical procedures can control for these other factors, but these procedures require large data samples and the use of computers, and only in the last fifteen years or so have the necessary data and computers been widely available to researchers.

The second problem that has hindered the empirical testing for compensating wage differentials is the problem of specifying, in advance of these tests, job characteristics that are generally regarded as disagreeable. For example, while some people dislike outdoor work and would have to be paid a premium in order to accept it, others prefer such work and dislike desk jobs. Similar observations can be made about such job characteristics as repetitiveness, chances to make decisions, and amount of physical exertion.

Compensating wage differentials for a job characteristic that many find unpleasant will not arise if the positions can be adequately staffed by workers who are not bothered by this characteristic. Only when the number of people bothered is large relative to demand will firms need to pay compensating differentials, for only then will they need to attract workers who find the job characteristic in question unpleasant. (Economists call these latter workers "marginal," because even with the higher wage rate, they are often close to being dissatisfied enough to quit; their attachment to the job in question is therefore "marginal.") If a job characteristic is universally regarded as disagreeable—or is regarded as such by firms' marginal workers—compensating wage differentials should arise. However, if the number of people who do not find the characteristic unpleasant is relatively large, differentials will not be created. Tests of the theory require selecting job characteristics on which there is widespread agreement about what is "good" or "bad" at the margin.

For this reason, many of the most credible and convincing tests of the theory have dealt with the level of *danger* on the job. While people may respond with different intensities to danger, it is difficult to believe that anyone prefers injury to safety; danger is an unambiguous "bad." The risk of injury is also objectively measured from injury rates published, most commonly, by industry.

The strongest evidence of compensating wage differentials for on-the-job danger relates to the risk of *fatal* injury. Several studies using different sets of

---

[10] It is especially important to control for these other influences because safety is probably a normal good (meaning that higher-income workers desire more of it). A *simple* correlation of risk levels and earnings is thus negative—not positive as predicted by theory. However, the simple correlation fails to account for all the *other* factors that influence earnings. Only if the influence of these factors can be accounted for would we expect to obtain the predicted positive relationship between earnings and risk.

The adequacy of studies in which the wage/risk relationship is inferred from a cross section of workers has been challenged by several authors on the grounds that there are many unmeasured characteristics whose omission from the data set could bias the results. These authors propose the use of longitudinal data in which two or more observations on each worker are recorded, permitting unmeasured, person-specific characteristics to be controlled for. See, for example, Charles Brown, "Equalizing Differences in the Labor Market," *Quarterly Journal of Economics* 94 (February 1980): 113–34; and Greg Duncan and Bertil Holmlund, "Was Adam Smith Right After All? Another Test of the Theory of Compensating Wage Differentials," *Journal of Labor Economics* 1 (October 1983): 366–79.

data from the United States, Great Britain, Sweden, and Korea have found that wages are positively associated with the risk of being killed on the job, other things equal. The results vary in magnitude and are rather sensitive to changes in the sample of workers used for estimation; however, they suggest that workers receive between $20 and $300 more per year for every one-in-ten-thousand increase in the risk of being killed on the job.[11] (One death for every 10,000 workers is roughly the yearly average for steel mills, while a rate of 10 deaths per 10,000 workers is the average for logging camps.) While these estimates seem small, they do imply that a plant with 1000 employees could save between $20,000 and $300,000 in wage costs *per year* if it undertook a safety program that would save one life every ten years.

When testing for compensating differentials associated with *nonfatal* injuries, one must take into account that injured workers are at least partially compensated through the workers' compensation system.[12] Holding the generosity of workers' compensation benefits constant, increases in risk of nonfatal injury should be associated with increased wages; however, holding risk constant, increasing the generosity of such insurance payments should serve to reduce wages because injury-related losses are now smaller. Thus, tests of the theory in the context of nonfatal injuries must include data on both risk and workers' compensation. Such tests have generally offered some support for the theory, but the results are not consistently strong.[13] It may be that the losses that can be expected each year by the typical worker are too small to

---

[11] Eight studies are reviewed in Robert S. Smith, "Compensating Wage Differentials and Public Policy: A Review," *Industrial and Labor Relations Review* 32 (April 1979): 339–52. See also Alan Marin and George Psacharopoulos, "The Reward for Risk in the Labor Market: Evidence from the U.K. and a Reconciliation with Other Studies," *Journal of Political Economy* 90 (August 1982): 827–53; Stuart Dorsey, "Employment Hazards and Fringe Benefits: Further Tests for Compensating Differentials," in *Safety and the Work Force*, ed. John D. Worrall (Ithaca, NY: ILR Press, 1983); Duncan and Holmlund, "Was Adam Smith Right After All?"; and Sung-Joong Kim, "Compensating Wage Differentials for Job Hazards in Korea," unpublished master's thesis, New York State School of Industrial and Labor Relations, Cornell University, 1985. For an example of the sensitivity of the estimates to the sample employed, compare William Dickens, "Differences Between Risk Premiums in Union and Nonunion Wages and the Case for Occupational Safety Regulations," *Papers and Proceedings: American Economic Review* 74 (May 1984): 320–23; and Alan Dillingham and Robert Smith, "Union Effects on the Valuation of Fatal Risk," *Proceedings of the Industrial Relations Research Association, Thirty-Sixth Annual Meeting* (1984): 270–77. See also Alan Dillingham, "The Influence of Risk Variable Definition on Value-of-Life Estimates," *Economic Inquiry* 23 (April 1985): 277–94.

[12] Workers' compensation payments are also made in cases involving death, but obviously they cannot compensate the victims themselves.

[13] On this subject see Stuart Dorsey and Norman Walzer, "Workers' Compensation, Job Hazards, and Wages," *Industrial and Labor Relations Review* 36 (July 1983): 642–54; Richard J. Arnould and Len Nichols, "Wage-Risk Premiums and Workers' Compensation: A Refinement of Estimates of Compensating Wage Differentials," *Journal of Political Economy* 91 (1983): 332–40; W. Kip Viscusi and Michael Moore, "Workers' Compensation: Wage Effects, Benefit Inadequacies, and the Value of Health Losses," *The Review of Economics and Statistics,* 69 (May 1987): 249–61; and John Ruser, "Workers' Compensation Benefits and Compensating Wage Differentials," U.S. Bureau of Labor Statistics Working Paper no. 153, 1985. For a recent paper that also distinguishes between the *probability* of injury and the duration of the recovery period see Daniel S. Hamermesh and John R. Wolfe, "Compensating Wage Differentials and the Duration of Wage Loss," Working Paper no. 1887, National Bureau of Economic Research, 1986.

statistically distinguish their effects from those of the other forces that influ-ence wages.[14]

## Policy Applications

The insights of the theory of compensating differentials can be applied to some very critical business and social issues: the economics of job satisfaction, job redesign, and the federal occupational safety and health program.

**Job Satisfaction: An Economic View.**   In the last decade or so, managers and researchers have expressed much interest in job satisfaction—and most are inclined to view dissatisfaction as a result of *employer* policies concerning job tasks, working conditions, or compensation. Economists, however, view the phenomenon of job satisfaction somewhat differently. Workers are viewed as making choices of jobs and employers from among competing alternatives; if they are unhappy in a particular occupation or with a particular employer, they will be motivated to seek other employment. Moreover, as noted in this chapter, pecuniary and nonpecuniary aspects of jobs are viewed as substitutes for each other; higher wages, for example, might compensate for poor working conditions and lead to overall satisfaction with one's job. Thus, economists tend to view job satisfaction as an outcome of the employer-worker *matching* process and not solely as the result of employer policies. If the matching process is impeded by factors inhibiting mobility, workers may be "stuck" in jobs they dislike. If workers are aware of alternatives and are able to leave jobs they view as unsatisfactory, they should eventually find something close to their best option.

A survey of job satisfaction around 1970 found that 47 percent of all workers were "very satisfied" with their jobs, roughly 38 percent were "somewhat satisfied," while only 15 percent were either "not too satisfied" or "not at all satisfied." A more sophisticated statistical analysis of job-satisfaction responses in this survey found that workers were more likely to indicate a feeling of satisfaction as they became older and as their *actual* earnings exceeded an estimate of their *alternative* earnings.[15] A recent study of airline employees in the 1980s also found increased job satisfaction as one's current earnings grew relative to one's alternative wage prospects.[16]

---

[14]   The statistical problem is one of distinguishing the influence of injuries from all the other influ-ences, including random ones, on wages. It is a little bit like trying to locate the position of Pluto in the sky from one's backyard. When Pluto is close to earth, the moon is merely a crescent, there is no haze, and the city is dark, it can be done. If the moon is full, Pluto is far from the earth, and ground light and haze are present, Pluto's weak light signal cannot be seen or "filtered" out from that of all the other stars or planets.

[15]   See Daniel S. Hamermesh, "The Economics of Job Satisfaction," Technical Analysis Paper No. 22, Office of the Assistant Secretary for Policy, Evaluation and Research, U.S. Department of Labor (May 1974), Appendix. A revised version of this paper, without the appendix, was published with the same title in Orley Ashenfelter and Wallace Oates, eds., *Essays in Labor Market Analysis* (New York: John Wiley and Sons, 1978).

[16]   Peter Cappelli and Peter Sherer, "Satisfaction, Market Wages, and Labor Relations: An Airline Study," *Industrial Relations* 27 (January 1988): 56–73.

Taken together, these results offer some evidence on worker mobility, a characteristic critical to the functioning of the labor market. The small number of people who report themselves to be even mildly dissatisfied, coupled with the finding that dissatisfaction falls with age, suggests that job mobility may be an antidote for dissatisfaction. It appears that, on the one hand, employees "try out" occupations and employers, and that they are able to leave situations they dislike. On the other hand, if they realize that the job they have is, on the whole, better-paying than their alternatives, they express greater satisfaction and are presumably less likely to leave it. Thus, a "trial-and-error" process, fueled by information about one's alternatives, may well be at work, producing generally satisfactory matches between workers and jobs in the long run.

**Job Redesign.** Paying compensating wage differentials and finding workers with the most tolerance for unpleasant aspects of work are both strategies firms use when nonwage conditions of employment might otherwise cause turnover, loss of morale, or difficulty in recruiting. A third strategy, which may under some circumstances be profitable, is to redesign jobs to improve working conditions as seen by workers. For example, in the late 1960s and early 1970s Volvo automobile factories in Sweden experienced high levels of turnover and absenteeism, and they had to employ foreign-born workers because of difficulties in recruiting Swedish workers.[17] Part of the problem, as diagnosed by Volvo management, was the monotonous nature of assembly line production. On the assembly line, each worker did the same job repeatedly, with little variance of the pace of work. Workers had no influence over their work environment, did not identify with the product, and could not communicate with each other. In 1972, Volvo decided to build a new factory at Kalmar, Sweden, with a radically different work design. The new plant, opened in 1974, organized production in 25 different work teams. On each team, the workers had a variety of operations to carry out and could make decisions about the best way to rotate jobs.

Employees who had worked both at the Kalmar plant and at traditional auto plants said they liked working conditions better at the new plant. Management reported lower turnover and absenteeism at Kalmar than at similar Volvo plants organized on an assembly line basis. In addition, supervision costs were lower at Kalmar because the work teams performed many of the functions done by supervisors at other plants. For example, the team integrated new workers into the process and handled reports on the volume and quality of their work. While job redesign may not always reduce costs, the Volvo experience reminds us that, ultimately, firms must offer their employ-

---

[17] This example is taken from Peter Dundelach and Nils Mortensen, "Denmark, Norway and Sweden," in International Labor Office (ILO), ed., *New Forms of Work Organisation* 1 (Geneva: ILO, 1979), 9–43.

ees a compensation and work-environment "package" that is at least comparable to what they could obtain elsewhere.[18]

**Occupational Safety and Health.**   Do workers benefit by the reduction of risk? In 1970, Congress passed the Occupational Safety and Health Act, which directed the U.S. Department of Labor to issue and enforce safety and health standards for all private employers. The stated goal of the act was to ensure the "highest degree of health and safety protection for the employee."[19] Despite the *ideal* that employees should face the minimum possible risk in the workplace, the discussion below suggests that implementing this ideal as social *policy* may not necessarily be in the best interests of workers.

Suppose a labor market is functioning like our textbook model, in that workers are well informed about dangers inherent in any job and are mobile enough to avoid risks they do not wish to take. In these circumstances, wages will be positively related to risk (other things equal), and workers will sort themselves into jobs according to their preferences. A worker (Person B) who does not worry much about being injured, may decide to accept a more dangerous job because of the higher wage ($W_B$) being offered. Another (Person A) may find that the higher wage is not enough to compensate him or her for the higher risk; this kind of worker will take a safer job at lower pay ($W_A$).

Now suppose the Occupational Safety and Health Administration (OSHA)—the Department of Labor agency that is responsible for implementing the federal safety and health program—promulgates a standard that, in effect, says that any risk level above that faced by Person A ($R_A$) is illegal. The effects, although unintended and perhaps not immediately obvious, would be detrimental to employees like B. Reducing risk is costly, and the best wage offer a worker can obtain at risk $R_A$ is $W_A$. For Person B, however, wage $W_A$ and risk $R_A$ generate *less utility* than did B's higher-wage and higher-risk job! This conclusion can be inferred from B's behavior *if,* as we assumed above, the labor market is characterized by both information and choice. After all, B *could* have worked at the lower risk and wage level before OSHA's standard was promulgated; the fact that B rejected that option and chose instead a higher-wage, higher-risk job suggests that the latter job yielded greater utility, all things considered.

When the government mandates the reduction of risk in a market in which workers are compensated for the risks they take, it penalizes workers like B, who are not terribly sensitive to risk and appreciate the higher wages associated with higher risk. The critical issue, of course, is whether workers have the knowledge and choice necessary to generate compensating wage differentials. Many people believe that because workers are ignorant, unable to

---

[18]   More limited experiments in team auto production have been carried out in the 1970s at General Motors in the United States, but the results of these experiments for efficiency are less clear-cut than the effects of Volvo's program. See Harry Katz, *Shifting Gears* (Cambridge, MA: The MIT Press, 1985).

[19]   Section 6(b)(5) of the Occupational Safety and Health Act.

comprehend different risk levels, or immobile, most do not choose risky jobs voluntarily. If this belief were true, government regulation *could* make workers better off—and, indeed, such conditions almost undoubtedly prevail in some markets. However, the arguments already presented concerning information and mobility, and the evidence of the positive relationship between wages and risk of death, should challenge the assumption that, in general, the labor market fails to generate compensating differentials.

An additional role for OSHA is in the area of research on hazardous substances. Many workplace chemicals produce diseases that are observed only 20 to 30 years after exposure to them, a problem that inhibits the acquisition of knowledge about the dangers these substances pose to workers. It is clear from our discussion earlier about the prerequisites (worker information and mobility) for the existence of compensating wage differentials that generating information on workplace health hazards is vital to the smooth functioning of the labor market. Will private firms or labor unions, operating in an unregulated market, produce an adequate amount of information on such substances?

To make a profit in doing health-hazard research, a privately financed research firm would have to prevent customers from selling the firm's findings to other potential customers at low cost. Research findings, as argued in Chapter 1, are a "public good," the consumption of which cannot easily be confined to those who pay for it. Traditionally, we have a system of patents that protects a company's right to exclusive marketing of any products it may develop or processes it may invent. However, to allow a patent over research findings about hazardous substances would not only be socially unacceptable practice, it may also be difficult to enforce. In any case, we may have severe doubts about whether enough information about hazardous substances would be produced by the private sector. Thus, even in competitive markets, OSHA may play a positive role in this area, whether it conducts the research itself or subsidizes private-sector research. Further, if society cannot be sure that workers have full information about hazardous substances, then minimum safety standards may be an appropriate policy for OSHA to enforce.

## Investments in Human Capital

A basic message of the theory of compensating differentials is that competitive labor markets may establish different wages for similar workers. An additional source of wage differences across individuals is different levels of investments that workers make in themselves. Workers undertake three major kinds of investments: (1) education and training, (2) migration, and (3) search for new jobs. All three investments involve an initial cost, and all three are made in the hope and expectation that the investment will pay off well into the future. To emphasize the essential similarity of these investments to other kinds of investments, economists refer to them as investments in *human capital*—a term that conceptualizes workers as embodying a set of skills that can be "rented" out to employers. The knowledge and skills a worker

**EXAMPLE   6.3**

## Mandatory Risk Reduction in Coal Mining

The caution with which government should proceed with *mandatory* risk-reduction programs is underscored by events in coal mining. The Federal Coal Mine Health and Safety Act of 1969 directs that miners be offered chest X-rays to detect black-lung disease. (This disease is technically known as *coal workers' pneumoconiosis*—a condition in which the inhalation of coal dust eventually reduces the functional capacity of the lungs. It is progressive, disabling, and sometimes fatal.) When it appears miners have the disease, their employers must, under the law, offer them jobs in less dusty areas of the mine. These jobs are lower-paid and less prestigious than the dusty jobs at the "face" of the mine. Consequently, only 10 percent of the miners offered such jobs in the 1970s accepted them. The behavior of most miners thus tells us that they were willing to undertake a known risk because the compensation (monetary and psychic) of the dangerous job was great enough to offset this risk. A law *compelling* them to leave the dusty jobs would clearly reduce their welfare, at least as they see it.

develops through education and training, including the training that experience yields, generate a certain *stock* of productive capital. However, the *value* of this amount of productive capital is derived from how much these skills can earn in the labor market. Job search and migration are activities that increase the value of one's human capital by increasing the price (wage) received for a given stock of skills.

Society's total wealth should therefore be thought of as a combination of both human and nonhuman capital. Human capital includes accumulated investments in such activities as education, job training, and migration, whereas nonhuman wealth includes society's stock of land, buildings, and machinery. Total wealth in the United States was estimated at $15.6 trillion in 1973, or about $75,000 for every man, woman, and child. Of this, 52 percent—or $39,000 per capita—took the form of *human* wealth.[20] Thus, investments in human capital are enormously important in our society.

The expected *returns* on human-capital investments are, as noted, a higher level of earnings, greater job satisfaction over one's lifetime, and a greater appreciation of nonmarket activities and interests. Generally speaking, the investment *expenditures* can be divided into the following three categories.

1.  *Out-of-pocket* or *direct* expenses include tuition and books (education), moving expenses (migration), and gasoline (job search).

---

[20]  U.S. Congress, Joint Economic Committee, *Economic Growth and Total Capital Formation* (Washington, DC: U.S. Government Printing Office, February 18, 1976).

2. *Forgone earnings* are another source of cost because during the investment period it is usually impossible to work, at least full-time.

3. *Psychic losses* are a third kind of cost incurred because education is difficult and often boring, because job search is tedious and nerve-wracking, and because migration means saying good-bye to old friends.

In this section we will analyze educational investments and their labor-market implications. Because most such investments are closely related to the supply of labor to occupations, this aspect of human-capital theory adds more depth to the analysis of occupational choice presented earlier in this chapter. As for the other forms of human-capital investments, Chapter 2 briefly touched on migration, and aspects of job search are treated in Chapter 17.

# Demand for Education by Workers

There are many ways in which workers—or potential workers—can enhance their earning capacity through education. They can attend high school, junior college, or a university. They can go to a trade school or technical institute. They can enter an apprenticeship program, or they can acquire skills on the job. The analysis of the demand for any of these types of education or training is essentially the same. Therefore, this section will analyze the demand for a college education as an illustration and application of human-capital theory.

People will want to attend college when they believe they will be better off by so doing. For some, the benefits may be short-term, because they like the courses or the lifestyle of a student. Students attending for these reasons regard college as a *consumption good;* that is, they are going to college primarily for the satisfaction it provides during the period of attendance. Others, however, are attending college because of the *long-term* benefits it provides. These benefits are partly in the form of higher earnings, partly in the form of gaining access to more interesting, challenging, or pleasant jobs, and partly in the form of prestige or enhanced enjoyment of nonmarket activities. Attendance for the long-term benefits—or *investment behavior*—is the behavior we will study in this section.

## An Overview of the Benefits and Costs of an Educational Investment

Calculating the benefits of an investment over time requires the progressive discounting of benefits lying farther into the future (see Chapter 4). Benefits that are received in the future are worth less to us now than an equal amount of benefits to be received today, for two reasons. First, if people plan to consume their benefits, they will prefer to consume earlier than later. (One is relatively sure of being able to enjoy such consumption now, but the uncertainties of life make future enjoyment problematic.) Second, if people plan to invest the monetary benefits rather than use them for consumption, they can earn interest on the investment and enlarge their funds in the future. Thus, no matter how people intend to use their benefits they will discount future receipts to some extent.

As Chapter 4 explained, the present value of a stream of yearly benefits (*B*) over a time horizon (*T*) can be calculated as follows:

$$\text{Present Value} = \frac{B_1}{1 + r} + \frac{B_2}{(1 + r)^2} + \frac{B_3}{(1 + r)^3} + \dots + \frac{B_T}{(1 + r)^T}, \quad (6.1)$$

where the interest rate (or discount rate) is *r*. As long as *r* is positive, benefits into the future will be progressively discounted. For example, if $r = 0.06$, benefits payable in 30 years would receive a weight that is only 17 percent of the weight placed on benefits payable immediately $((1/1.06)^{30} = 1/5.74 = 0.17)$

The costs of going to college are normally incurred over a relatively short period of time. These costs include (1) the direct costs of tuition, fees, and books; (2) the forgone earnings attendant to being a full-time student; and (3) the psychic costs of studying and being examined. The total costs of going to college are thus very high, with the monetary costs alone (direct costs plus forgone earnings) well over $12,000 per year in 1988.

A person considering college has, in some broad sense, a choice between two streams of income over his or her lifetime. Stream *A* begins immediately but does not rise very high; it is the earnings stream of a high-school graduate. Stream *B* (the college graduate) has a negative income for the first four years

**Figure 6.1**  Alternative Income Streams

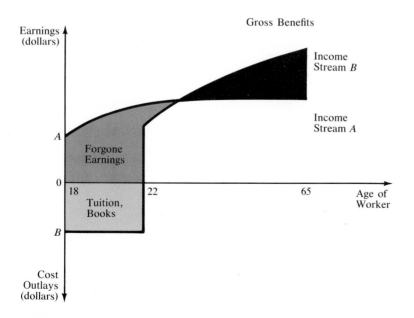

(due to college tuition costs), followed by a period when the salary may be less than what a high-school graduate is making, but then it takes off and rises above stream *A*. Both streams are illustrated in Figure 6.1. (Why these streams are *curved* will be discussed later in this chapter.) The streams shown in the figure are stylized so that we can emphasize some basic points. Actual earnings streams are shown in Figure 6.2 on page 186.

Obviously, the earnings of the college graduate would have to rise above those of the high-school graduate in order to induce someone to invest in a college education (unless, of course, the psychic or consumption-related returns are large). The gross benefits—the difference in earnings between the two streams—must total much more than the costs because such returns are in the future and are therefore discounted. For example, if it costs $12,000 per year to obtain a four-year college education, and if the interest rate is 6 percent, the after-tax returns (if they are the same each year) must be $3200 for 40 years to justify the investment on purely monetary grounds. These returns must be so high because $48,000 invested at a 6 percent interest rate can provide a payment (of interest and principal) totaling $3200 a year for 40 years.[21]

## A Formal Model of Choice and Its Implications

The preceding discussion emphasized that investing in a college education is worthwhile if the present value of the benefits (monetary and psychic) are at least as large as the costs. In mathematical terms this criterion can be expressed as:

$$\frac{B_1}{1 + r} + \frac{B_2}{(1 + r)^2} + \ldots + \frac{B_T}{(1 + r)^T} \geq C, \qquad (6.2)$$

where $C$ equals the total costs of a college education and $B_t$ equals the differences in earnings between college and high-school graduates in year $t$.

There are two ways one can measure whether the criterion in equation (6.2) is met. Using the *present-value method,* one can specify a value for the discount rate, $r$, and determine if the present value of benefits is greater than or equal to costs. Alternatively, one can adopt the *internal-rate-of-return-method,* which asks, "How large could the discount rate be and still render college profitable?" Clearly, if the benefits are so large that even a very high discount rate would render college profitable, then the project is worthwhile. In practice, one calculates this internal rate of return by setting the present value of benefits equal to costs and solving for $r$. The internal rate of return is then compared to the rate of return on other investments. If the internal rate

---

[21]　This calculation is made using the *annuity formula:*

$$Y = X\frac{1 - [1 / (1 + r)^n]}{r},$$

where $Y$ equals the total investment ($48,000 in our example), $X$ = the yearly payment ($3200), $r$ = the rate of interest (0.06), and $n$ = the number of years (40). In this example, we treat the costs of a college education as being incurred all in one year rather than being spread out over four—a simplification that does not alter the magnitude of required returns much at all.

of return exceeds the alternative rate of return, the investment project is considered profitable.[22]

In deciding whether to attend college, no doubt few students make the very precise calculations suggested in equation (6.2). Nevertheless, if they make less formal estimates that take into account the same factors, four predictions concerning the demand for college education can be made:

1.  Present-oriented people are less likely to go to college than forward-thinking people (other things equal).
2.  Most college students will be young.
3.  College attendance will increase if the costs of college fall (other things equal).
4.  College attendance will increase if the gap between the earnings of college graduates and high-school graduates widens (again, other things equal).

**Present-orientedness.** Psychologists use the term *present-oriented* to refer to people who do not weight future events or outcomes very heavily. While all people discount the future with respect to the present, those who discount it more than average—or, at the extreme, ignore the future altogether—could be considered present-oriented. In terms of equations (6.1) and (6.2), a present-oriented person is one with a very high discount rate ($r$).

Suppose one were to calculate investment returns using the *present-value method*. If $r$ is large, the present value of benefits associated with college will be lower than if the discount rate being used is smaller. Thus, a present-oriented person would impute smaller benefits to college attendance than one who is less present-oriented, and those who are present-oriented would be less likely to attend college. Using the *internal-rate-of-return method* for evaluating the soundness of a college education, one would arrive at the same result. If a college education earns an 8-percent rate of return, but the individuals in question are so present-oriented that they would insist on a 25-percent rate of return before investing, they would likewise decide not to attend.

**Age.** Given similar *yearly* benefits of going to college, young people have a larger present value of *total* benefits than older workers simply because they have a longer remaining work life ahead of them. In terms of equation (6.2), $T$ for younger people is greater than for older ones. We would therefore expect younger people to have a greater propensity than older people to obtain a college education or engage in other forms of training activity. This prediction is parallel to the predictions in Chapter 4 about whether employers will make hiring or specific training investments.

---

[22] For our purposes here, the present-value and internal-rate-of-return methods may be considered interchangeable in evaluating investment alternatives. In *some* circumstances, however, the two methods would not provide identical rankings of investment opportunities. See J. Hirshleifer, "On the Theory of Optimal Investment Decision," *Journal of Political Economy* 66 (August 1958): 329–52.

**Costs.** A third prediction of our model is that human-capital investments are more likely when costs are lower. The major monetary costs of college attendance are forgone earnings and the direct costs of tuition, books, and fees. (Food and lodging are not always opportunity costs of going to college, because much of these costs would have to be incurred in any event.) Thus, if forgone earnings or tuition costs fall, other things equal, we would expect an increase in college enrollments. The costs of college attendance offer an additional reason why we observe older people attending less often than younger people. As workers age, they acquire levels of experience and maturity that employers are willing to reward with higher wages. Because older workers thus command higher wages (on average), their opportunity costs of college attendance are higher than those for younger students. Older people are thus doubly discouraged from attending college: their forgone earnings are relatively high, and the period over which they can capture benefits is comparatively short.

The psychic costs of going to college cannot be ignored. While these costs cannot be easily observed, they are likely to be related to ability. People who learn easily and who do well in school settings have an easier and more pleasant time in college than people who do not. Given that loans to attend college often are not readily available, the financial resources of the investor are an important factor in the decision to invest. Students from wealthy families are able to obtain funds from their families, often at very low cost, while in the absence of government-subsidized loans, students from less wealthy families must borrow at market interest rates (if their loan applications are accepted at all). Thus, the common observation that people from high-income families are more likely to attend college than those from low-income families may be a result of the lower cost of funds faced by the wealthy.[23]

**Earnings Differentials.** The fourth prediction of human capital theory is that the demand for education is positively related to the *returns,* that is, to the increases in lifetime earnings or psychic benefits that a college education allows. In practice, this prediction can be tested only with reference to money returns, since psychic returns are unobservable; however, this prediction has been used to explain the sharp fall in college enrollments that occurred in the early 1970s.[24]

Beginning around 1970, the labor market for college graduates began to exhibit signs of a surplus. Jobs in the professional fields, in which college graduates typically found employment, began to dwindle relative to the sup-

---

[23] See Gary S. Becker, *Human Capital,* 2nd ed. (Chicago: University of Chicago Press, 1975): 79.

[24] There is evidence, although it is somewhat weak, that better-educated workers are more likely to describe themselves as satisfied with their jobs. See Daniel Hamermesh, "Economic Aspects of Job Satisfaction," pp. 53–72. *Quantifying* job or nonjob psychic benefits, however, is still not possible. The analysis in the succeeding paragraphs relies heavily on Richard Freeman, "Overinvestment in College Training?" *Journal of Human Resources* 10 (Summer 1975): 287–311.

ply, and more and more college graduates had to take jobs as sales, clerical, or blue-collar workers. For example, in 1958 only 10.5 percent of recent female college graduates and 13.8 percent of recent male college graduates were employed in nonprofessional, nonmanagerial jobs such as sales, clerical, or blue-collar work. For 1970–71 college graduates, these percentages had more than doubled to 24.4 percent for women and 30.5 percent for men. The deterioration in employment prospects for college graduates was also manifest in the starting salaries for graduates with bachelor's degrees. Table 6.1 tells the story for men, for whom comparative data over time are more available and reliable than the data for women. From 1961 to 1969, starting salaries for male college graduates increased faster than wages and prices in general, indicative of a pre-existing shortage of college graduates (see Chapter

**Table 6.1**   Compound Annual Changes in the Starting Salaries of Male Bachelor's Graduates, 1961–69 and 1969–74

|  | 1961–69 Period of Relative Market Boom | | 1969–74 Period of Relative Market Bust | |
|---|---|---|---|---|
|  | Annual Percent Change in Salaries | Annual Percent Change Minus Change in CPI[a] | Annual Percent Change in Salaries | Annual Percent Change Minus Change in CPI |
| Accountant | 6.0 | 3.4 | 4.0 | −2.2 |
| Business-general | 5.7 | 3.1 | 2.4 | −3.8 |
| Humanities and social science | 5.3 | 2.7 | 1.1 | −5.1 |
| Aeronautic engineering | 4.8 | 2.2 | 3.1 | −3.1 |
| Chemical engineering | 5.8 | 3.2 | 3.8 | −2.4 |
| Civil engineering | 5.7 | 3.1 | 3.9 | −2.5 |
| Electrical engineering | 5.1 | 2.5 | 3.2 | −3.0 |
| Mechanical engineering | 5.3 | 2.7 | 3.5 | −2.7 |
| Industrial engineering | 4.7 | 2.1 | 3.3 | −2.9 |
| Physical sciences, mathematics | 4.8 | 2.2 | 2.1 | −4.1 |
| Changes in annual earnings of year-round full-time workers | 4.7 | 2.1 | 6.6[b] | +0.4 |

[a] CPI = Consumer Price Index.

[b] 1974 estimated by percentage change in average hourly earnings of all private industry production workers from March 1973 to March 1974.

SOURCE:  From "Overinvestment in College Training?" by Richard Freeman, *Journal of Human Resources* 10, 3 (Summer 1975), Table 1. Copyright © 1975 by the Board of Regents of the University of Wisconsin System. Reprinted by permission of The University of Wisconsin Press.

2 for a review of the concepts of *shortage* and *surplus*). From 1969 to 1974, starting salaries for male bachelor's graduates increased more slowly than both average wages and the price level, which is what one would expect in sectors in which labor surpluses exist.

In analyzing the potential effects of this surplus of college graduates on college enrollments, however, one must not ignore the fact that our model stresses the discounted stream of benefits *over a lifetime,* while the data just presented refer mainly to employment prospects *immediately after gradua-tion.* Nevertheless, there are two reasons to believe that immediate post-college prospects are of crucial importance in the decision to go to college. First, being closer to the present, earnings immediately after graduation are less heavily discounted than earnings later on. Second, in the absence of any better information, people may use current employment trends for college graduates as estimates of what prospects in the more distant future will be like. If there is a surplus now, people may assume it will last long enough to render college a poor investment.

Associated with the surplus of college graduates was a decline in the proportion of young men going to college. Among males, for whom labor market conditions appeared to change most in the early 1970s, the percentage of high-school graduates going to college fell from 58 percent (1969) to 50 percent (1973). Further, the proportion of 18- to 24-year-old males going to college, after rising almost steadily since 1950, fell from 35 percent (1969) to 27 percent (1973).

Among females, rather than a decline, the enrollment response was an abrupt cessation of growth in the proportion of young women enrolled in college. Nevertheless, this response did represent a significant departure from the trend in growing college attendance during the 1960s. (The failure of enrollments to fall can possibly be explained, at least in part, by the tremen-dous increase in the propensity of women to seek work outside the home that has occurred in recent years. The longer one expects to work outside the home, the greater are the benefits of college attendance.) One might also argue that the differential response of men and women in terms of college attendance was due to changes during the early 1970s in the draft laws, which effectively removed the incentives for men to attend college to avoid the draft. While the draft law changes did have an effect, the timing of the decline in enrollments makes it clear that such changes can explain only part of the decline in demand for college education among men. Declining returns to a college education were clearly a major stimulus for the changed patterns of college attendance in the early 1970s.

Interestingly, in the years since 1979 there has been a sharp rise in the ratio of earnings of recent college graduates to those of recent high-school graduates: the ratio for males in the 25- to 29-year-old age group went from 1.17 in 1979 to 1.32 in 1983. The response was an increase in the percentage of 18- to 24-year-olds going to college! This percentage for men rose from 25.8 to 27.3 in that four-year period, while the percentage for women rose from 24.2 to 25.1. Thus, despite the fact that the population of 18- to 24-year-olds actually fell from 1979 to 1983, college enrollments—probably stimulated by the rising returns to higher education—continued to rise.[25]

## The Education/Wage Relationship

The theory outlined in this chapter so far indicates that workers generally need the expectation of higher earnings to induce them to undertake costly educational investments. Put differently, because educational programs can be very costly, people will invest in them only if they can reasonably expect to receive a return on this investment. While a level of earnings higher than they would otherwise receive is not the only benefit of an educational investment, it is certainly an important one for many workers. Thus, to induce workers to invest in human capital, higher earnings generally will have to be received by those who do invest.

Higher earnings for better-educated workers, however, will be received only if employers are willing to pay them. Theory suggests that firms would be willing to pay greater wages to workers with more schooling *if* these workers were in fact more productive. After all, if workers were of different productivities yet received the *same* wage, the more productive ones would be preferred by all employers, and their wages would naturally rise above those paid to the less productive workers. While some economists assert that schooling *causes* workers to become more productive, and others contend that schooling is a screening device that just *certifies* who is already more productive, the ultimate effect on the firm is the same; more highly schooled people *are* likely to be more productive.[26]

The relationship between education and earnings is well documented and can be observed graphically in Figure 6.2. This figure presents (for males) *age/earnings profiles*—or lifetime earnings patterns—for five different levels of schooling. The following two conclusions are immediately obvious.

1.  Better-educated males have higher earnings than less-educated males at each post-schooling age level, as predicted by our theory. Note, however, from the (dashed) earnings profile of men with education beyond the bachelor's degree, that earnings while in school are lower than they would otherwise be (a graphical representation of the concept of forgone earnings).

---

[25] Dave M. O'Neill and Peter Sepielli, *Education in the United States,* Special Demographic Analysis CDS–85–1, U.S. Bureau of the Census (Washington, DC: U.S. Government Printing Office, 1985): 41, 42, 52–53.

[26] Recent papers on this topic come to varying conclusions. Kevin Lang and David Kropp, "Human Capital Versus Sorting: The Effects of Compulsory Attendance Laws," *Quarterly Journal of Economics* 101 (August 1986): 609–24, and Andrew Weiss, "High School Graduation, Performance, and Earnings," NBER Working Paper no. 1595, April 1985, argue that their evidence supports the screening hypothesis; M. Boissiere, J. Knight, and R. Sabot, "Earnings, Schooling, Ability, and Cognitive Skills," *American Economic Review* 75 (December 1985): 1016–31, find support for the human-capital hypothesis, that is, that schooling causes higher productivity. If schooling in fact does not cause higher productivity, then the social return to schooling may be less than the private return. See Michael Spence, *Market Signaling* (Cambridge, MA: Harvard University Press, 1973).

**Figure 6.2**  Total Money Earnings (mean), All Males, 1984

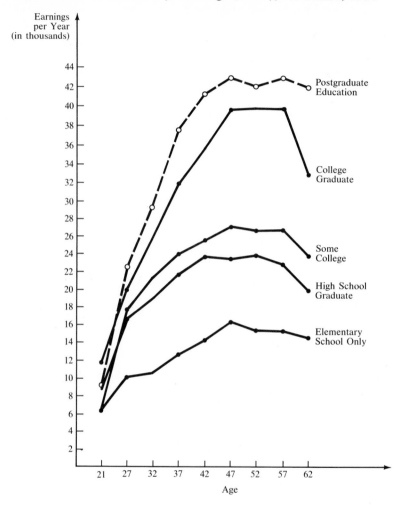

SOURCE:  U.S. Bureau of the Census, *Money Income of Households, Families, and Persons in the United States: 1984*, Current Population Reports, Series P-60 no. 151 (1986), Table 34.

2.  The age/earnings profiles for workers with more education are steeper than the profiles of workers with less education; that is, the differences in earnings associated with education tend to widen as workers grow older. In the early years the earnings gap is small. Workers who have gone to college have not had a chance to acquire the work experience of their colleagues who have been working rather than attending college. Later, after they have had a chance to gain experience, their earnings rise much more sharply. (A more detailed discussion of *why* age/earnings profiles are steeper for more educated workers will be presented later in this chapter.)

While it is well-established that workers with more education tend to earn higher wages, it is natural to ask whether the earnings of college graduates are *enough* higher to render profitable an investment in college. An individual deciding whether to go to college would naturally ask, "Will I increase my monetary and psychic income enough to justify the costs of going to college?" The next subsection deals with the issue of individual returns from educational investments.

## Is Education a Good Investment for Individuals?

Individuals about to make an investment in a college education are committing themselves to costs of at least $12,000 per year. Is there evidence that this investment pays off for the typical student? Several studies have tried to answer this question by calculating the internal rates of return to educational investments. While the methods and data used vary, these studies normally estimate benefits by calculating earnings differentials at each age from age/earnings profiles such as those in Figure 6.2 (*earnings* are usually used to measure benefits because higher wages and more stable jobs are payoffs to more education). The *rate of return* is that discount rate that equates the present value of benefits to the cost of acquiring the level of education in question. It should be stressed that all such studies have analyzed only the monetary—and not the psychic—costs and returns to educational investments.

The rates of return typically estimated in these studies generally fall in the range of 5–15 percent (after adjusting for inflation). These findings are interesting, because many other investments generate returns in the same range. Thus, it appears—at least at first glance—that an investment in education is about as good as an investment in stocks, bonds, or real estate. This conclusion must be qualified, however, by recognizing that there are systematic biases in the estimated rates of return to education. These biases—which are of unknown size—work in opposite directions.

**The upward bias.**  The typical estimates of the rate of return to further schooling overstate the gain an individual student could obtain by investing in education because they are unable to separate the contribution *ability* makes to higher earnings from the contribution made by *schooling*. The problem is that (1) people who are smarter, harder-working, and more dynamic are more likely to obtain more schooling, and (2) such people may be more productive, and hence earn higher-than-average wages even if they did not complete more years of schooling than others. When measures of ability are not observed or accounted for, the studies attribute *all* of the earnings differential associated with college to college itself. None of the earnings differential is attributed to ability—even though *some* of the added earnings college graduates typically receive would probably be received by an equally able high-school graduate who did not attend college.

Most studies attempting to identify the separate effects of ability and schooling have concluded that the effects of ability are relatively small—

accounting for, at most, one-fifth of observed earnings differentials.[27] However, these studies have used aptitude-test scores—such as IQ or mathematical reasoning—as measures of ability, and these measures are primarily designed to predict success in school, not in the workplace. Success in the world of work is also affected by interpersonal skills, work habits, motivation, and resourcefulness—attributes that are not easily measured by a test.

One interesting attempt to control for all the unmeasured aspects of ability used data on twins.[28] When the researcher first calculated rates of return to an added year of education ignoring any controls for ability, the estimated return was 8 percent. When he looked only at earnings differences between identical twins—people with a common *genetic and environmental* background—with different levels of schooling, he found that the rate of return to schooling dropped to 3 percent. While no one study is conclusive, the results do suggest that part—and perhaps a large part—of earnings differentials associated with higher levels of schooling are due to inherently abler persons obtaining more schooling.

**The downward bias.**   By focusing only on the earnings differentials associated with an educational investment, the studies of returns to educational investments ignore other aspects of the returns to schooling. First, some benefits of college attendance are not necessarily reflected in higher productivity, but rather in an increased ability to understand and appreciate the behavioral, historic, and philosophical foundations of human existence. While these benefits may be difficult to measure, they exist nonetheless. Second, most rate-of-return studies fail to include fringe benefits; they measure money earnings, not total compensation. Because fringe benefits as a fraction of total compensation tend to rise as money earnings rise, ignoring fringe benefits tends to create a downward bias in the estimation of rates of return to education. The size of this bias is largely unknown at present.[29]

Third, some of the job-related rewards of college are captured in the form of psychic or nonmonetary benefits. Jobs in executive or professional occupations are probably more interesting and pleasant than the more routine jobs typically available to people with less education. While executive and professional jobs do pay more than others, the total benefits of these jobs are probably understated when just earnings differences are analyzed.

An interesting example of the role nonmonetary costs and benefits play in schooling decisions can be seen in that there is near-universal agreement that conventionally calculated rates of return fall as the educational level rises; that is, the rate of return to a high-school education is higher than for a college education, and higher yet than the average returns from going to graduate

[27]   See, for example, Gary Becker, *Human Capital*; Zvi Griliches and William M. Mason, "Education, Income, and Ability," and John C. Hause, "Earnings Profile: Ability and Schooling," both in *Journal of Political Economy* 80 (May/June 1972).

[28]   Paul Taubman, "Earnings, Education, Genetics, and Environment," *Journal of Human Resources* 11 (Fall 1976): 447–61.

[29]   Greg J. Duncan, "Earnings Functions and Nonpecuniary Benefits," *Journal of Human Resources* 11 (Fall 1976): 462–83.

school. This fact can be understood when psychic benefits and costs are accounted for, because students who acquire the most education are, on average, the ones who dislike school the least. They may also be the ones who, because of their higher learning abilities, derive the most psychic benefits from college. They thus require a smaller monetary incentive to attend college than do their less-able colleagues.

It is difficult to summarize the findings on the question of whether education is a sensible investment for an individual. Considering only monetary costs and benefits, rates of return to educational investments are modest (once ability is accounted for)—but not out of line with the "real" returns on many other types of investments. Moreover, if benefits other than money earnings were measured, the estimated returns to education would probably be higher.

## Post-Schooling Investments and Age/ Earnings Profiles

Schooling is a largely a full-time, formally organized activity. There are less formal kinds of human-capital investments that are more difficult to observe. These investments take the form of training that normally occurs in the workplace. Some of this "training" is *learning-by-doing* (as one hammers nails month after month, one's skills naturally improve), but much of it takes place on the job, under close supervision, or consists of a formal program in the workplace. All forms of training are costly in the sense that the productivity of learners is low, and all represent a conscious *choice* on the part of the employer to accept lower current productivity in exchange for higher output later. It has been estimated that the average worker acquires the equivalent of at least two years of college in on-the-job training and that the annual cost of such training amounts to 3 percent of gross national product.[30]

Who bears the cost of on-the-job training? You will recall that Chapter 4 argued that the cost of *specific training*—training of use *only* to one's employer—would be shared by the worker and firm. The employee might be paid a wage greater than marginal product (*MP*) during the training period, but after training the employee's wage is below *MP* (but above what the employee could get elsewhere). In the case of general training, in which employees acquire skills they can use elsewhere, it is they alone who pay for the training costs.

How do employees pay the costs of general training provided by their employer? They work for a wage lower than they would get if they were not receiving training. Their wage is less than their *MP* (which is decreased during the training period when trainees make mistakes or require time off the job to engage in classroom learning) by an amount equal to the supervisory or instructional costs to the firm associated with training. Why do employees accept this lower wage? They accept it for the same reason that some decide

---

[30] Jacob Mincer, "On-the-Job Training: Costs, Returns, and Some Implications," *Journal of Political Economy* 70 (Supplement 1962): 50–79.

to obtain schooling: in the expectation of improving the present value of their lifetime earnings. In other words, employees incur current investment costs (lower wages) to obtain increased earnings later.

**The timing of post-schooling investments.** In this chapter we have argued that if people are going to invest in themselves they will tend to undertake most of the investment at younger ages for two reasons.

1. Investments made at younger ages have a longer period over which to capture returns and thus will tend to have higher total benefits.
2. One big cost of investing in education and training is forgone earnings—and this cost rises as one gets older and earnings become higher (if, for no other reason, because of learning-by-doing).

Consequently, putting off human-capital investments will lower the returns to such investments. It is not surprising to find, then, that schooling—largely a full-time activity—is followed by on-the-job training, which is normally a part-time activity. Further, we should also find that job training declines with age, being most heavily concentrated in one's early years on the job when opportunity costs are lower. However, in the case of job training, for which scholarships and loans are not available and the training is part-time, investment will not take place all at once. Too much current consumption would have to be forgone by the ordinary worker if one's entire lifetime amount of job training were acquired completely in the first two years (say) of one's career. Thus, employees will tend to parcel out their job training over a number of years, but they will gradually reduce such training as time goes by.

**The timing of investment and age/earnings profiles.** The preceding theory of post-schooling investments helps to explain why age/earnings profiles are concave: rising more rapidly at first, then flattening out, and ultimately falling (see Figure 6.3). Earnings, low at first because of training investments, rise quickly as new skills are acquired. However, as workers grow older, the pace of training investment slows and so does the rate at which productivity increases.

**Figure 6.3** Age/Earnings Profile

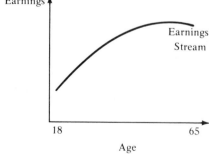

Earnings Stream

Toward the end of one's working life skills may have depreciated—due to lack of continued investment and the aging process—to the extent that retirement, semiretirement, or a change in jobs is necessary for many workers. This depreciation contributes to the downturn in *average* earnings near retirement age.

**The fanning out of age/earnings profiles by education.** As noted earlier in this chapter, the differences in average earnings between people of the same age, but with different educational levels, increase over time (see Figure 6.2). This phenomenon is also consistent with what human-capital theory would predict. The answer to the question, "Who will invest most in post-school training?" should be familiar by now. Those who expect the highest benefits and workers who learn most quickly will do the most investing in job training. The fact that they learn rapidly shortens the training period, which both reduces investment costs and increases the duration of benefits. But who are these fast learners? They are most likely the people who, because of their abilities, were best able to reap benefits from formal schooling. Thus, human-capital theory leads us to expect workers who invested more in schooling to also invest more in post-schooling job training.

The tendency of the better-educated workers to invest more in job training explains why their age/earnings profiles start low, rise quickly, and keep rising after the profiles of their less-educated counterparts have leveled off. Their earnings rise more quickly because they are investing more heavily in job training, and they rise for a longer time for the same reason. In other words, people with the ability to learn quickly select the ultimately high-paying jobs for which much learning is required and thus put their abilities to greatest advantage.

# Compensating Differentials, Human Capital, and Company Wage-Setting Practices

In this chapter we have argued that competitive market forces lead firms to pay compensating wage differentials for unpleasant job characteristics and higher wages for more highly educated and trained workers. At the company level, these forces are often felt through the job-evaluation procedure. Recall from Chapter 2 that a job-evaluation system rates jobs on factors that companies believe are important in contributing to productivity or to the quality of the job for the worker. A company then will often perform a market wage survey to determine how the market rewards these factors and use this information in setting wages or salaries for its jobs.

As we noted in Chapter 2, about 86 percent of large- and medium-sized American companies have formal job-evaluation plans. In addition, the traditional job-evaluation criteria of skill, effort, and responsibility are viewed by the vast majority of personnel managers as important determinants of wages.[31] A look at several specific job-evaluation systems shows that education (or training), experience, and working conditions are always present as factors upon which compensation is based.[32] Thus, human capital and non-pecuniary conditions of employment are both important components of job-evaluation systems in the vast majority of large- and medium-sized firms in the United States.

How, then, do job-evaluation systems translate wage changes in the market into the determination of wages within firms' internal labor markets? Consider the 1969–74 period of surplus of college graduates (discussed earlier in this chapter). Companies hiring for entry-level positions requiring a college degree found rising supplies of qualified applicants at existing salary levels. Firms did not need to increase salaries for these jobs by as much as otherwise to attract or retain workers. These market forces eventually were reflected in salary surveys conducted by many companies. The new surveys showed a smaller wage advantage for entry-level jobs requiring a college education over jobs that did not.

For many jobs above the entry level, there may not exist well-defined market survey data. In such cases, firms often compare the job-evaluation point scores of these jobs with the "key," or entry-level, jobs (recall Chapter 2). A certain relationship between pay and point-score levels is established. Thus, when firms in this example use the new surveys of entry-level jobs (reflecting the lower premium for a college degree), the higher-level jobs requiring a college degree would also receive lower pay relative to lower-level jobs. In this way, a market surplus of college graduates affects jobs internal to many firms.

A process similar to the case of college graduates would be set into motion by, say, a decrease in workers' willingness to tolerate regimented working conditions, as presumably happened at Volvo in the 1970s (see the discussion earlier in this chapter). The wage premium associated with adverse-working-conditions point scores would rise as market wages increased (to attract employees), reflecting the increased compensating wage differential established in the market for key jobs. These changes in the internal wage structures of firms induced by outside market forces would be widespread, as indicated by the high percentages of firms using formal job evaluation and using skill and effort as important compensable factors in their job-evaluation systems.

## REVIEW QUESTIONS

1. Is the following true, false, or uncertain: "Certain occupations, such as coal mining, are inherently dangerous to workers' health and safety. Therefore, unambiguously, the most appropriate government policy is the establishment and enforcement of rigid safety and health standards." Explain your answer.

---

[31]   See Thomas Mahoney, Benson Rosen, and Sara Rynes, "Where Do Compensation Specialists Stand on Comparable Worth?" *Compensation Review* 16 (Fourth Quarter 1984): 36.

[32]   See David Belcher and Thomas Atchison, *Compensation Administration*, 2nd ed. (Englewood Cliffs, NJ: Prentice-Hall, 1987): 204.

2. Statement 1: "Business executives are greedy profit maximizers, caring only for themselves." Statement 2: "It has been established that workers doing filthy, dangerous work receive higher wages, other things equal." Can both of these statements be generally true? Why?
3. How would college enrollments be affected if
   a. income-tax rates were substantially cut for higher-income workers but only modestly reduced for lower-income employees?
   b. the real rate of interest increased?
   c. government subsidies for college students were reduced?
   d. young people became more present-oriented?
   e. the *work* life of employees became longer (that is, if people retired at a later age)?
4. Many crimes against property (burglary, for example) can be thought of as acts that have immediate gains but entail long-run costs (sooner or later the criminal may be caught and imprisoned). If imprisoned, the criminal loses income from both criminal and noncriminal activities. Using the framework for occupational choice in the long run, analyze what kinds of people are most likely to engage in criminal activities. What can society do to reduce crime?
5. Why do those who argue that more education "signals" greater ability believe that the most able people will obtain the most education?

# SELECTED READINGS

Gary Becker, *Human Capital* 2nd ed. (New York: National Bureau of Economic Research, 1975).

Mark Blaug, "Human Capital Theory: A Slightly Jaundiced Survey." *Journal of Economic Literature* 14 (September 1976): 827–55.

Milton Friedman, *Price Theory: A Provisional Text* (Chicago: Aldine Publishing Co., 1962). See the chapter entitled, "The Supply of Factors of Production."

Richard B. Freeman, *The Overeducated American* (New York: Academic Press, 1976).

Jacob Mincer, "On-the-Job Training: Costs, Returns, and Some Implications." *Journal of Political Economy* 70 (Supplement 1962): 50–79.

Jacob Mincer, *Schooling, Experience and Earnings* (New York: National Bureau of Economic Research, 1974).

Jacob Mincer, "The Distribution of Labor Incomes: A Survey with Special Reference to the Human Capital Approach," *Journal of Economic Literature* 8 (March 1970): 1–26.

Theodore Schultz, *The Economic Value of Education* (New York: Columbia University Press, 1963).

Adam Smith, *Wealth of Nations* (New York: Modern Library, 1937), Book I, Chapter 10.

Robert S. Smith, "Compensating Wage Differentials and Public Policy: A Review," *Industrial and Labor Relations Review* 32 (April 1979): 339–52.

Robert S. Smith, *The Occupational Safety and Health Act: Its Goals and Its Achievements* (Washington, DC: The American Enterprise Institute for Public Policy Research, 1976).

W. Kip Viscusi, *Employment Hazards: An Investigation of Market Performance* (Cambridge, MA: Harvard University Press, 1979).

# CHAPTER 7

## The Economics of Discrimination

We have learned that wages differ across individuals or jobs for numerous reasons. They vary with the amount of general or specific training, with job and location characteristics, and with age. Many of these sources of wage differentials may be regarded either as necessary in the allocation of labor or as socially legitimate on other grounds. There are, however, sizable wage differentials that appear to be associated solely with race and gender, and these differentials are often thought to be synonymous with widespread discrimination against minority groups—especially blacks and Hispanics—and against women. This chapter discusses the evidence and theories of discrimination and concludes with an analysis of government policy in this area.

## What Is Discrimination?

The term *discrimination* is often used imprecisely because the relationship between *prejudice* and discrimination often is unclear. One might assert, for example, that a firm with two racially segregated branch offices is discriminating by failing to integrate both offices, even if workers in both branches are paid the same wages and have the same opportunities for advancement. This assertion raises the question of whether discrimination is always present when there is prejudice, or just when some harm comes from this prejudice. Conversely, some people allege that discrimination exists in cases in which prejudice may not. For example, a firm offering specific training may prefer to hire younger workers who will stay with the firm long enough for it to recoup training costs. Is this age discrimination or good business?

Another confusing issue is whether discrimination can be identified by inequality of *achievement* or inequality of *opportunity*. Is an accounting firm located in a small, mostly white town guilty of discrimination if it has no black auditors on its staff? Would the answer change if the firm could show it had advertised job openings widely and had made the same offers to blacks as to whites, but that the offers to blacks had been rejected?

Discrimination can occur in many forms and places. If it occurs in the labor market, workers with equal preparation and productivity receive different wages. If it occurs among educational institutions, students of equal ability are treated differently and emerge from formal schooling with unequal educations. If it occurs in childhood, young children with equal potential are raised with quite different aspirations and attitudes. Discrimination can also occur in a variety of other settings: the housing market, various product markets, and treatment under the law.

The kind of discrimination this chapter will analyze most deeply is discrimination in the labor market. This emphasis should not imply that other forms of discrimination are unimportant or unrelated to labor-market discrimination. Indeed, *past* labor-market discrimination may have been instrumental in causing the poverty or attitudes that are *now* manifest in child-rearing practices, academic-achievement levels, and career or gender role aspirations. However, since the focus of our analysis is on *current labor-market discrimination,* we shall lump all *other* forms of discrimination into a more general category we shall call *premarket differences.*

An operational definition of *current labor-market discrimination* is "the valuation in the labor market of personal characteristics of the worker that are unrelated to productivity."[1] This definition recognizes that one's value in the labor market depends on all the demand *and* supply factors affecting marginal productivity. When factors that are *unrelated* to productivity acquire a positive or negative value in the labor market, discrimination can be said to occur. Race and gender are currently the most prominent of these factors alleged to be unrelated to productivity, but physical handicaps, religion, age, sexual preferences, and ethnic heritage are also on the list.

Three points should be noted about the preceding definition. First, the emphasis in identifying discrimination is on measurable market outcomes, such as earnings, wages, occupational attainment, or employment levels. While prejudicial attitudes may be felt by members of one group toward those of another, these feelings must be accompanied by some *action* that results in a different market outcome for us to assert that discrimination is present.

Second, we are not concerned with the routine random differences in outcomes that are matters of luck. Rather, the concept of discrimination encompasses only those differences that are so systematic that they do not cancel each other out within large groups.

---

[1] Kenneth J. Arrow, "The Theory of Discrimination," *Discrimination in Labor Markets,* eds. Orley Ashenfelter and Albert Rees (Princeton, NJ: Princeton University Press, 1973): 3.

Finally, our definition of labor-market discrimination suggests an operational way to distinguish between *labor-market* and *premarket* factors that cause earnings differentials. Differentials that derive from differences in average *productivity* levels across race or sex groups, for example, can be categorized as *premarket* in nature. Differentials that are attributed to race or gender, *holding productivity constant,* may be evidence of labor-market discrimination.

It is very important for policy purposes to measure the relative size of labor-market and premarket factors that lead to systematic earnings differences among various population groups. Any attempts to combat discrimination must be grounded in accurate information concerning the *source* of that discrimination; otherwise, effective antidiscrimination programs can not be formulated. If the evidence points to a significant amount of labor-market discrimination, programs aimed at employers and the hiring/promotion process may be effective. If, however, most of any systematic earnings differences related to race or gender appear to be rooted in premarket factors, then programs aimed at education, training, and the process of socializing children will be required.

# Earnings Disparities by Race, Ethnicity, and Gender

There have been, and continue to be, strikingly large income disparities between whites and most minorities and between men and women. These differences cause widespread social concern about discrimination, its sources, and possible remedies. In this chapter we will analyze various theories and their consequences for antidiscrimination policies after first describing the race and gender differences in earnings that actually exist. (We focus on *earnings* differences for the practical reason that data on *total compensation,* which would be preferable because of the inclusion of fringe benefits, are not generally available by race and gender.)

## Racial and Ethnic Differences

**Blacks.** In 1985 the earnings of the typical male, full-time, year-round, black worker were 70 percent of his white counterpart's. While this disparity in incomes is large and has varied considerably in the recession-plagued years after 1975, there is a gradual trend toward greater equality in the ratio of black to white incomes. As indicated in Table 7.1, the 1985 ratio was 4–6 percentage points higher than in the 1960s and 2–3 points higher than in the early 1970s. At no point since 1974 has the ratio fallen below what it was before 1974.[2]

Similar patterns for black women can be observed from the data in Table 7.1, although much greater equality has been achieved among women. Black

---

[2] The earnings ratios in Table 7.1 are for full-time, year-round workers. As we will see in Chapter 17, blacks have substantially higher unemployment rates than whites. Thus, the earnings differentials in Table 7.1 are likely to understate the differences in labor incomes for white and black workers.

**Table 7.1**   Black/White Ratio of Median Income for Full-Time, Year-Round Workers

| | Black/White Income Ratio | |
| --- | --- | --- |
| Year | Males | Females |
| 1959 | 0.61 | 0.66 |
| 1961 | 0.66 | 0.67 |
| 1963 | 0.66 | 0.64 |
| 1965 | 0.64 | 0.71 |
| 1967 | 0.64 | 0.74 |
| 1969 | 0.66 | 0.80 |
| 1971 | 0.68 | 0.88 |
| 1973 | 0.67 | 0.85 |
| 1974 | 0.70 | 0.91 |
| 1976 | 0.72 | 0.93 |
| 1977 | 0.69 | 0.93 |
| 1978 | 0.77 | 0.93 |
| 1980 | 0.70 | 0.93 |
| 1981 | 0.71 | 0.90 |
| 1982 | 0.75 | 0.91 |
| 1983 | 0.76 | 0.91 |
| 1984 | 0.74 | 0.93 |
| 1985 | 0.70 | 0.89 |

SOURCES:   U.S. Bureau of the Census, *Money Income of Households, Families, and Persons in the United States: 1984*, Consumer Income Series P–60, no. 151 (April 1986), Table 28, and U.S. Bureau of the Census, *Money Income of Households, Families, and Persons in the United States: 1985*, Consumer Income Series P–60, no. 156 (August 1987), Table 34. Data before 1980 refer to persons age 14 or older; data for 1980 on refer to age 15 or older.

and white women who worked full time at year-round jobs had virtually the same income ratios as did men in the early 1960s (around 0.65). However, in the mid-1960s the ratio for women began to rise until by 1985, black women who worked full time earned, on average, 89 percent as much as full-time white female workers.

While these ratios and their trends are very interesting and important, they do not help us identify the immediate *source* of the disparities. Are the differences primarily due to current labor-market discrimination, or are they the result of premarket factors? Blacks in the labor market, for example, tend to be younger and less educated, on average, than whites. Further, it may well be that the average *quality* of schooling received by blacks is lower than the average for whites.[3] We know that earnings rise with both education and experience, so *some* of the black/white earnings differences are surely attributable to these characteristics. How much of the overall differential in

---

[3]   As noted in Chapter 6, one's choice of education is influenced by expected labor-market earnings over the life cycle. Hence, ensuring that market discrimination against blacks is reduced or eliminated should serve as an incentive for blacks to stay in school longer. See Finis Welch, "Education and Racial Discrimination," in *Discrimination in Labor Markets*, eds. Orley Ashenfelter and Albert Rees, pp. 43–81.

average earnings is due to differences in the characteristics that affect productivity and how much is due to labor-market discrimination?

To measure the extent of market discrimination, one must answer the following question: "What would be the black/white earnings ratio if blacks and whites had the same productive characteristics?" In other words, if blacks (on average) had the same education, training, experience, turnover rate, health and marital status, and region of residence as whites, what would be the ratio of their earnings to those of whites? The answers to this question vary with the data sample and method employed, but they do establish a range within which the true ratio probably lies.

Two studies using data from the late 1960s estimated that 60–75 percent of the overall black/white disparity in wage rates for males was attributable to premarket differences—implying that, in the absence of measurable differences in productive characteristics, black males would have earned between 85 and 90 percent of what white males earned.[4] A study using data from the mid-1970s implied that, in the absence of premarket differences, black males would have earned wages that were 88 percent of those earned by white males.[5] Finally, research using 1980 data indicated that black male high-school graduates earned from 83 to 94 percent as much as comparable white males (the percentages varied with age, but not systematically).[6] Interestingly, the latter study found that for male college graduates under 30 years of age in 1980, blacks earned from 10 to 18 percent *more* than their white counterparts.

The finding that from 50 to 80 percent of the difference in average earnings can be explained by differences in productive characteristics implies that current labor-market discrimination *may* account for 20–50 percent of the overall differential, suggesting a rather significant role for antidiscrimination programs or policies in the labor market. However, the figures of 20–50 percent may be biased estimates of the extent of labor-market discrimination because researchers simply do not have complete data on the productive characteristics of individuals or groups. Researchers can measure age, education, and, in many cases, experience, but they rarely have data on school quality, work habits, aspirations, degree of alienation, and other intangibles that clearly affect one's productivity. These intangibles, moreover, *may* vary across race (or gender) owing to such premarket factors as social treatment, socioeconomic status of one's parents, and cultural background. If the unmeasured characteristics tend to depress the productivity of minorities or women relative to white males, attributing all of the unexplained difference in average earnings to current labor-market discrimination will clearly overstate

[4] Robert J. Flanagan, "Labor Force Experience, Job Turnover, and Racial Wage Differentials," *The Review of Economics and Statistics* 56 (November 1974): 521–29, and A. S. Blinder, "Wage Discrimination—Reduced Form and Structural Estimates," *Journal of Human Resources* 8 (Fall 1973): 436–55.

[5] Mary Corcoran and Greg Duncan, "Work History, Labor Force Attachment, and Earnings Differences Between the Races and Sexes," *Journal of Human Resources* 14, 1 (Winter 1979): 3–20.

[6] Saul Hoffman and Charles Link, "Selectivity Bias in Male Wage Equations: Black and White Comparisons," *The Review of Economics and Statistics* 66 (May 1984): 320–24.

the extent of that discrimination. *Some* of the unexplained 20–50 percent may be the result of unmeasured productive characteristics and thus may be more appropriately labeled *premarket* in nature. (Of course, if the unmeasured characteristics tend to raise the productivity of minorities or women relative to white men, attributing all the unexplained differences in earnings to current labor-market discrimination will understate the extent of that discrimination.)

As we noted in Chapter 6, people's investments in human capital depend on expected wage returns. Labor-market discrimination against blacks may thus reduce their incentives to acquire human capital. If this is true, then controlling for such personal characteristics as education or experience may understate the total effects of current labor-market discrimination.

After estimating the portion of the *average* race/gender earnings differential that is explained by differences in average productivity characteristics, one is left with a residual, or unexplained, portion. One part of the residual may be the result of current labor-market discrimination, but the effects of any unmeasurable (or at least unmeasured) differences in average productive characteristics show up in the residual also. Because of this methodological defect, which is mainly the result of the difficulties of measuring all characteristics that affect productivity, accurate measures of the extent of labor-market discrimination do not exist. Assuming that *all* the unexplained residual is due to labor-market discrimination, we can estimate the effects discrimination *might* have; however, we are unable to say if actual labor-market discrimination is below or above these estimates.

**Hispanics.**   In 1984, male Hispanics who worked full time, year-round had incomes averaging only 69 percent those of white, non-Hispanic males. Moreover, this percentage appears to be dropping; it was 74 in 1976, 73 in 1978, and 71 in 1980.[7] To estimate what fractions of these wage differences are due to differences in productivity characteristics, we need to control for human-capital characteristics, including proficiency in English as well as time in the United States. Studies controlling for these factors have recently been done, and they suggest that language proficiency may be the biggest influence on Hispanic/non-Hispanic wage differentials[8]; one study, indeed, found that

---

[7]   U.S. Bureau of the Census, *Money Income in 1976 of Families and Persons in the United States,* Consumer Income Series P–60, no. 114 (July 1978), Table 55; *Money Income of Families and Persons in the United States: 1978,* Series P–60, no. 123 (June 1980), Table 62; *Money Income of Households, Families and Persons in the United States: 1980,* Series P–60, no. 132 (July 1982), Table 58; and *Money Income of Households, Families and Persons in the United States: 1984,* Series P–60, no. 151 (April 1986), Table 26.

[8]   Cordelia W. Reimers, "Labor Market Discrimination Against Hispanic and Black Men," *The Review of Economics and Statistics* 65 (November 1983): 570–79. The findings are generally corroborated by an earlier study by James D. Gwartney and James E. Long, "The Relative Earnings of Blacks and Other Minorities," *Industrial and Labor Relations Review* 31 (April 1978): 336–46. See also Geoffrey Carliner, "Returns to Education for Blacks, Anglos, and Five Spanish Groups," *Journal of Human Resources* 11 (Spring 1976): 172–84; George J. Borjas, "The Earnings of Male Hispanic Immigrants in the United States," *Industrial and Labor Relations Review* 35 (April 1982): 343–53; and Gilles Grenier, "The Effects of Language Characteristics on the Wages of Hispanic-American Males," *Journal of Human Resources* 19 (Winter 1984): 35–52.

language proficiency explained virtually all the Hispanic/non-Hispanic wage differences.[9]

**Asians.**   The issue of discrimination against Asians in the United States has not attracted much attention, probably because of their small numbers and generally high incomes. For example, the earnings among males of Asian ancestry were equal, on average, to those of white males in 1980 (Asian women made 13 percent more than white women). These data do not rule out current labor-market discrimination against males of Asian ancestry because they do not control for productive characteristics. Once these differences are accounted for, however, there appears to be no difference between the weekly earnings of whites and those of Chinese ancestry and only a 4-percent differential (in favor of whites) for males of Japanese ancestry. Filipinos, however, earn about 15 percent less per week than comparable white males.[10]

## Gender Differences

Differences in earnings between female and male workers are large. The average white, female, full-time worker earns just slightly more than 60 percent of what her male counterpart earns. As one can see from Table 7.2, this ratio has followed a U-shaped pattern since the mid-1950s, remaining below 0.6 throughout the 1960s and 1970s and only recently approaching its pre-1960 level. However, movements in the ratio have been relatively small, and explaining the sizable disparity that remains between the average earnings of men and women is of considerable interest.[11]

There are several factors other than labor-market discrimination that could cause this large disparity. First, because the market work-life of a woman historically has been shorter than that of a man, women have had fewer incentives to invest in schooling and post-schooling training that is specifically oriented to the labor market.[12] (They, in essence, prepare for two

[9]   Walter McManus, William Gould, and Finis R. Welch, "Earnings of Hispanic Men: The Role of English Language Proficiency," *Journal of Labor Economics* 1 (April 1983): 101–30. Indeed, in a later article, McManus estimated that the present value of lost earnings to Hispanic men caused by a lack of English fluency ranged from $19,000 to $36,000 per man. The failure of these workers to make the investments in language necessary to reap the benefits of fluency McManus attributes to limited horizons (for older immigrants), borrowing constraints, or very high discount rates (for illegal immigrants—who also may have relatively short time horizons). See Walter McManus, "Labor Market Costs of Language Disparity: An Interpretation of Hispanic Earnings Differences," *American Economic Review* 75 (September 1985): 818–27.

[10]   Barry Chiswick, "An Analysis of the Earnings and Employment of Asian-American Men," *Journal of Labor Economics* 1 (April 1983): 197–214.

[11]   Recent articles analyzing the trend in female/male earnings are June O'Neill, "The Trend in the Male-Female Wage Gap in the United States," *Journal of Labor Economics* 3, part 2 (January 1985):S91–S116, Victor R. Fuchs, "His and Hers: Gender Differences in Work and Income: 1959–79," *Journal of Labor Economics* 4, part 2 (July 1986):S245–S272, and Francine D. Blau and Andrea H. Beller, "Trends in Earnings Differentials by Gender, 1971–1981," *Industrial and Labor Relations Review*, 41 (July 1988): 513–29.

[12]   In 1970, the expected work life of women at age 20 was 21.3 years, but by 1980 this had risen to 27.2 years. In contrast, for men aged 20 the expected work-life fell from 37.3 years in 1970 to 36.8 in 1980. Thus, while women still had a shorter work-life than men, the gap was narrowing in part due to women's increasing attachment to the labor force. See Shirley Smith, "Revised Work-life Tables Reflect 1979–80 Experience," *Monthly Labor Review* 108 (August 1985): 23–30.

**Table 7.2** Ratio of Female/Male Wage and Salary Income for Year-Round, Full-Time White Workers

| Year | Ratio of Female/Male Income |
| --- | --- |
| 1955 | 0.65 |
| 1964 | 0.59 |
| 1967 | 0.58 |
| 1970 | 0.59 |
| 1973 | 0.56 |
| 1977 | 0.58 |
| 1980 | 0.59 |
| 1981 | 0.60 |
| 1982 | 0.62 |
| 1983 | 0.64 |
| 1984 | 0.63 |
| 1985 | 0.65 |
| 1986 | 0.64 |

SOURCES: U.S. Bureau of the Census, *Money Income of Households, Families, and Persons in the United States: 1984,* Consumer Income Series P–60, no. 151 (April 1986), Table 38, and U.S. Bureau of the Census, *Money Income and Poverty Status of Families and Persons in the United States: 1986,* Consumer Income Series P–60, no. 157 (July 1987), Table 7.

careers—one at home and one in the labor market—and are thus typically less specialized than men.)

Second, because of traditional home responsibilities, women are less likely than men to work overtime or to choose occupations that offer jobs with high pay but long hours. As a result, the weekly hours worked by women who work full time throughout the year are 8–10 percent lower than those worked by comparable men.[13] Home responsibilities also mean that women usually work closer to home than do men, a fact that implies lower wages, to the extent that women may turn down jobs that require a relatively long commute.[14]

Finally, wives have historically tended to "follow" husbands when the husbands chose the geographic location of their jobs. Husbands, in effect, have been relatively free to choose their best offer, while wives have usually done the best they could *given* their geographical location. This sort of family decision-making behavior has also tended to reduce women's earnings.[15]

[13] June O'Neill, "The Trend in the Male-Female Wage Gap in the United States." "Protective" labor legislation at the state level until recently often limited the maximum hours per week a woman could work, thus closing women out of overtime opportunities available to men.

[14] See Michelle White, "Sex Differences in Urban Commuting Patterns," *American Economic Review Papers and Proceedings* 76 (May 1986):368–72, for a more extensive discussion.

[15] Evidence that geographic migration usually causes husbands' earnings to rise but wives' earnings to fall is based on S. Polachek and K. Horvath, "A Life Cycle Approach to Migration," in *Research in Labor Economics,* vol. 1, ed. Ronald Ehrenberg (Greenwich, CT: JAI Press, 1977). Other articles on the same topic are Robert H. Frank, "Why Women Earn Less: The Theory and Estimation of Differential Overqualification," *American Economic Review* 68 (June 1978):360–73, and Jacob Mincer and Solomon Polachek, "Family Investments in Human Capital: Earnings of Women," *Journal of Political Economy* 82 (March/April 1974):S76–S108. Of course, increased female labor-market attachment suggests that such patterns will not necessarily persist in the future.

While the preceding *premarket* differences are not immediately generated by labor-market discrimination, they will be *affected* by the presence of such discrimination. As in the case of racial differences in pay, labor-market discrimination against women may well affect the qualifications women bring to the labor market. If current discrimination exists, the resulting lower wage for women strengthens incentives for them to be the ones who engage in *household production*. The expectation that women will be the ones to stay home with children, for example, is probably the major reason behind each of the three premarket forces just presented. Anything that reduces the disproportionate share of women in household production will tend to increase their incentives to acquire human capital, work longer hours for pay, and select their jobs from a wider area. Thus, even though premarket differences are clearly important and deeply rooted in factors other than current labor-market discrimination, measuring the extent of labor-market discrimination and taking steps to end it are of obvious importance.

The best way to estimate the effects of market discrimination on the basis of gender is to perform the same kind of analysis reported earlier for black and white males. Thus we must ask, "What would the female/male earnings ratio be, on average, if women had the same education, training, experience, hours of work, commuting distance, turnover rate, and other productive characteristics as their male counterparts?" Studies that have attempted to answer this question have generally concluded that differences in education, training, turnover, and experience—but primarily experience—account for one third to two thirds of the earnings differences between men and women.[16] Thus, it appears that labor-market discrimination can account for no more than two thirds of the earnings gap between men and women.

One aspect of purported labor-market discrimination against women is *occupational segregation*—the reservation of some jobs for men and others (mostly lower-paying ones) for women. Some dimensions of this segregation and its effects can be seen in Table 7.3, which presents the share of women in a variety of high-paying and low-paying occupations for 1970 and 1981. Two things are especially notable in Table 7.3. First, very few of the high-paying occupations employed women to an extent even close to their overall proportion among all employed workers (43 percent in 1981). On the contrary, women were heavily *over*represented in the low-paying occupations. Second, in the 11 years from 1970 to 1981, the proportion of women in most of the high-paying jobs rose much faster than their overall proportion among the employed, while their proportions in the lower-paying jobs fell.

How much of the market discrimination against women takes the form of occupational segregation and how much takes the form of different wages *within* given occupations? A crude answer to this question can be obtained by

---

[16] Corcoran and Duncan, "Work History, Labor Force Attachment, and Earnings Differences Between the Races and Sexes"; Mincer and Polachek, "Family Investments in Human Capital: Earnings of Women"; Sharon P. Smith, *Equal Pay in the Public Sector: Fact or Fantasy* (Princeton, NJ: Industrial Relations Section, Princeton University, 1977); and Blau and Beller, "Trends in Earnings Differentials by Gender, 1971–81."

**Table 7.3**   Representation of Women in Ten High-Paying and Ten Low-Paying Occupations, 1970 and 1981

| | *Percent Female* | |
| --- | --- | --- |
| *Occupation* | *1970* | *1981* |
| High-paying | | |
| Stock and bond sales agents | 8.6 | 17.1 |
| Managers and administrators, n.e.c.[a] | 11.6 | 19.6 |
| Bank officials and financial managers | 17.4 | 36.5 |
| Sales representatives, manufacturing | 8.5 | 16.0 |
| Designers | 23.5 | 23.9 |
| Personnel and labor relations workers | 31.2 | 48.7 |
| Sales representatives, wholesale | 6.4 | 10.7 |
| Computer programmers | 22.7 | 28.4 |
| Low-paying | | |
| Practical nurses | 96.3 | 97.3 |
| Hairdressers and cosmetologists | 90.4 | 85.3 |
| Cooks, except private household | 62.8 | 50.9 |
| Health aides, except nursing | 83.9 | 82.7 |
| Nurses' aides | 84.6 | 84.3 |
| Sewers and stitchers | 93.8 | 96.7 |
| Farm laborers | 13.2 | 12.3 |
| Child-care workers, except private household | 93.2 | 86.7 |
| All occupations | 37.7 | 43.0 |

[a] The initials n.e.c. mean "not elsewhere classified."

SOURCES:   Sharon Smith, "Men's Jobs, Women's Jobs and Differential Wage Treatment," *Job Evaluation and EEO: The Emerging Issues,* papers presented at the Industrial Relations Counselors Colloquium, September 14–15, 1978, Atlanta, Georgia (New York: Industrial Relations Counselors, 1979), pp. 67–84; Nancy R. Rytina, "Earnings of Men and Women: A Look at Specific Occupations," *Monthly Labor Review* 105 (April 1982):25–31.

estimating the wage women would make if they had productive characteristics similar to those of the average male. Comparing this estimated wage to the average male wage may yield an upper-bound estimate of overall labor-market discrimination. If we then estimate the wage women would receive if they had the same productive characteristics *and* the same *occupational* distribution as men, we can calculate the wage disparities caused solely by occupational differences. The most widely quoted study of the effects of occupational segregation suggests that equalizing the occupational distribution of men and women with the same education and years of experience would reduce the earnings gap by 9 percentage points.[17]

[17]   Ronald Oaxaca, "Male-Female Wage Differentials in Urban Labor Markets," *International Economic Review* 14 (October 1973): 693–709. For other studies related to occupational segregation and its effects, see Julianne M. Malveaux, "Moving Forward, Standing Still: Women in White-Collar Jobs," in *Women in the Workplace,* ed. Phyllis A. Wallace (Boston: Auburn House Publishing Co., 1982): 101–34, Andrea H. Beller, "Occupational Segregation by Sex: Determinants and Changes," *Journal of Human Resources* 17 (Summer 1982): 371–92, and Barbara Reskin, et. al., *Women's Work, Men's Work: Sex Segregation on the Job* (Washington, DC: National Academy Press, 1986).

It would appear, then, that perhaps half of the overall 40-percent differential between the earnings of men and women is due to premarket factors. Of the remaining 20 percentage points, which could be due to current market discrimination, roughly half again (9 percentage points) appears to be the consequence of occupational segregation. The effect of occupational segregation *could* be larger than this, however, because the "occupations" referred to in the study are very general categories, such as professional-technical worker, manager, clerical worker, skilled craft worker, and so forth. Not captured in the analysis, then, are the effects of segregation *within* these broad groupings. For example, an insurance company that was later the object of a sex-discrimination lawsuit had, between 1964 and 1970, hired men and women with college degrees to be "claims adjustors" and "claims representatives." The educational requirements for each job were the same, but only men were hired as "adjustors," and almost all "representatives" were women. Claims adjustors received $2500 more in yearly salary to begin with, and only adjustors could be promoted to higher-level supervisory positions. Both positions are in the same general occupational class, but pay and future opportunities were much better for the male workers.[18]

A study of 1981 data from firms of 100 or more employees found that within narrowly defined occupations the ratio of female-to-male earnings was relatively high; however, women were less likely to be found in the higher-paying grades.[19] The data in Table 7.4 suggest, for example, that in the first four "accountant" pay grades women earned from 95 to 99 percent of what comparable males earned, while in the highest pay grade the earnings ratio was 90 percent. However, 59 percent of all female accountants were in the lowest two pay grades, as compared to 21 percent for males, and it can be seen from the table that women are progressively underrepresented as pay and responsibility rise. Thus, because accountants in the highest pay grades earned so much more, and because women were so underrepresented in those top grades, the *overall* ratio of female to male earnings was only 0.83! Whether this underrepresentation represents employer hiring practices, as suggested in the preceding paragraph, or the labor-supply behavior of women (who tend to have lower levels of tenure with their employers) cannot be determined from the table. However, Table 7.4 does suggest the important role that disparities in the occupational distribution continue to play in understanding gender-related pay differentials.

Note, however, that not all occupational segregation is the result of current employer practices that exclude qualified women from higher-paying jobs. Premarket forces, beginning early in childhood, instill beliefs in women and men alike that some occupations are "women's work" and some are "men's work." These beliefs keep women out of many low-paying laborer

[18] Barbara Bergmann, "Reducing the Pervasiveness of Discrimination," in *Jobs for Americans*, ed. Eli Ginzburg (Englewood Cliffs, NJ: Prentice-Hall, 1976).

[19] Mark Sieling, "Staffing Patterns Prominent in Female-Male Earnings Gap," *Monthly Labor Review* 107 (June 1984): 29–33.

**Table 7.4** Female/Male Earnings Ratios in Medium-Sized and Large Firms,[a] Selected Occupations, 1981

| Occupation | Earnings Ratio | Average Monthly Earnings | % Female in Occupation |
|---|---|---|---|
| Accountant  I | .99 | $1,377 | 46 |
| II | .98 | 1,679 | 34 |
| III | .96 | 1,962 | 19 |
| IV | .95 | 2,402 | 11 |
| V | .90 | 2,928 | 5 |
| All accountants | .83 | [b] | 23 |
| Attorney  I | 1.03 | $1,873 | 28 |
| II | .97 | 2,338 | 24 |
| III | .95 | 3,031 | 13 |
| IV | .94 | 3,738 | 9 |
| All attorneys | .78 | [b] | 15 |
| Accounting clerk  I | .94 | 798 | 95 |
| II | .89 | 953 | 94 |
| III | .89 | 1,121 | 91 |
| IV | .84 | 1,407 | 82 |
| All accounting clerks | .82 | [b] | 92 |

[a] For most industries, firms had to have at least 100 employees to be included in the sample.
[b] Not reported.
SOURCE:  Mark Sieling, "Staffing Patterns Prominent in Female-Male Earnings Gap," *Monthly Labor Review* 107 (June 1984):29–33.

jobs while also excluding them from high-paying jobs. These notions will probably change over time as alternative role models become available, but not *all* these feelings can be attributed to *current* employer practices.

Whether occupational segregation is caused by employer exclusion *or* by women's career choices, it results in a larger supply of labor to "women's" jobs and a smaller supply of labor to "men's" jobs than if there were no segregation. According to the "overcrowding hypothesis," these effects on labor supply serve to further lower the relative wages in women's jobs.[20] An implication of this hypothesis is that as women enter traditionally male fields, relative wages in the women's jobs will rise.

# Theories of Market Discrimination

As argued in the previous section, one cannot rule out the presence of substantial discrimination against women and minorities in the labor market. Before one can design policies to end discrimination, one must understand the *sources* and *mechanisms* causing it. The goal of this section is to lay out and evaluate the different theories of discrimination proposed by economists.

---

[20] See Janice Fanning Madden, *The Economics of Sex Discrimination* (Lexington, MA: D.C. Heath and Co., 1973):30–36, and Barbara Bergmann, "The Effect on White Incomes of Discrimination in Employment," *Journal of Political Economy* 79 (March-April 1971): 294–313.

Three general sources of labor-market discrimination have been hypothesized, and each source suggests an associated model of how discrimination is implemented and what its consequences are.[21] The first source of discrimination is *personal prejudice,* wherein employers, fellow employees, or customers dislike associating with workers of a given race or sex.[22] The second general source is *statistical prejudgment,* whereby employers project onto *individuals* certain perceived *group* characteristics. Finally, there are models according to which the desire for, and use of, *monopoly power* is the source of discrimination. While all the models generate useful, suggestive insights, none has been convincingly established as superior.

## Personal Prejudice

**Employer Discrimination.**  Suppose that white male *employers* are prejudiced against women and minorities but that (for simplicity's sake) customers and fellow employees are not prejudiced. This prejudice may take the form of aversion to associating with women and minorities; it may be manifested as a desire to help fellow white males whenever possible; or it may be motivated by status considerations and take the form of occupational segregation. In whatever form, this prejudice is assumed to result in the discriminatory treatment of women and minorities. Further, we assume for the purposes of this model that the women and minorities in question have the same productive characteristics as white males. (This assumption directs our focus to market discrimination by putting aside premarket factors.)

If employers have a decided preference for hiring white males in high-paying jobs despite the availability of equally qualified women and minorities, they will act *as if* the latter were less productive than the former. By virtue of our assumption that the women and minorities involved are equally productive in every way, the devaluing of their productivity by employers is purely subjective and is a manifestation of personal prejudice. The more prejudiced an employer is, the more actual productivity will be discounted.

It is immediately clear that discriminating employers are not maximizing their profits. For example, suppose that employer prejudice results in a male-female pay gap of $3 per hour for equally productive men and women. Profit-maximizing firms will hire women and have a cost advantage over the discriminating firms that hire men at the $3-per-hour premium. This practice should raise the question of how companies that discriminate survive. Firms in competitive product markets *must* maximize profits just to make a normal rate of return on invested capital. Those who do not make this return will find they can earn a better return by investing some other way—a way, perhaps, that does not involve hiring workers. Conversely, since profit-maximizing

---

[21] Two of the three general models were labeled by Kenneth Boulding, "Toward a Theory of Discrimination," in *Equal Opportunity and the AT&T Case,* ed. Phyllis Wallace (Cambridge, MA: The MIT Press, 1976).

[22] The models of personal prejudice are based on Gary S. Becker, *The Economics of Discrimination,* 2d ed. (Chicago: University of Chicago Press, 1971).

(nondiscriminatory) firms would normally make more money from a given set of assets than would discriminators, we should observe nondiscriminatory firms buying out others and gradually taking over the market. In short, if competitive forces were at work in the product market, employers who discriminate would be punished and discrimination could not persist.[23]

**Customer Discrimination.** A second personal-prejudice model stresses *customer* prejudice as a source of discrimination. Customers may prefer to be served by white males in some situations and by minorities or women in others. If their preferences for white males extend to jobs requiring major responsibility—such as physician, stockbroker, or airline pilot—and their preferences for women and minorities are confined to less-skilled jobs—nurse or flight attendant, say—then occupational segregation that works to the disadvantage of women and minorities will occur. Further, if women or minorities are to find employment in the jobs for which customers prefer white males, they must either accept *lower wages* or be *more qualified* than the average white male. The reason for this is that their value to the firm is lower than that of *equally qualified* white males because of customers' preferences for white males.

The theory of customer discrimination predicts that women or minorities in responsible jobs with customer contact would face the largest discriminatory pay differentials. While they might hope to escape discrimination by working in sectors with no customer contact, there may be a crowding effect lowering wages even in these sectors.[24]

**Employee Discrimination.** A third source of discrimination based on personal prejudice might be found on the supply side of the market, where white male workers may avoid situations in which they will have to work with minorities or women in contexts they consider inappropriate. For example, they may resist taking orders from a woman, sharing responsibility with a minority member, or working where women or minorities are not confined to low-status jobs. If white male workers have these discriminatory preferences, they will tend to quit (or avoid) employers who employ women or minorities on a nondiscriminatory basis. Employers who want to hire or retain white males will have to pay them more than they would if they confined women and minorities to their "traditional," lower-status jobs.

[23] For evidence on competition and employer discrimination, see Becker, *The Economics of Discrimination,* p. 48; Ray Marshall, "The Economics of Racial Discrimination: A Survey," *Journal of Economic Literature* 12 (September 1974): 864; David P. Taylor, "Discrimination and Occupational Wage Differences in the Market for Unskilled Labor," *Industrial and Labor Relations Review* 21 (April 1968): 375–90; and Orley Ashenfelter and Timothy Hannan, "Sex Discrimination and Product Market Competition: The Case of the Banking Industry," *Quarterly Journal of Economics* 101 (February 1986): 149–73.

[24] For discussion and evidence on customer discrimination, see Lawrence M. Kahn, "Customer Discrimination in a General Equilibrium Framework," mimeo, University of Illinois, May 1987; Lawrence M. Kahn and Peter D. Sherer, "Racial Differences in Professional Basketball Players' Compensation," *Journal of Labor Economics* 6 (January 1988): 40–61; and George J. Borjas, "The Politics of Racial Discrimination in the Federal Government," *Journal of Law and Economics* 25 (October 1982): 271–99.

In some cases employers may be able to avoid the higher costs of employing white males by running plants segregated by race or gender. Segregated plants, however, are not always legally or economically feasible. Thus, the costs to employers of hiring women or minorities in certain jobs may be elevated by employee discrimination, serving to reduce demand and lower wages for women and minorities in those jobs.[25]

## Statistical Discrimination

Another source of discrimination might be the kind and quality of information used in making hiring decisions.[26] Employers must try to *guess* the potential productivity of applicants, but rarely will they know what actual productivity will be. The only information available to them at the time of hire is information that is thought to be *correlated* with productivity: education, experience, age, test scores, and so forth. These correlates are imperfect predictors of actual productivity, however, and employers realize this. To some extent, then, they supplement information on these correlates with a subjective element in making hiring decisions, and this subjective element could *look* like discrimination even though it might not be rooted in personal prejudice.

Statistical discrimination can be viewed as a part of the *screening problem,* which arises when observable personal characteristics that are correlated with productivity are not perfect predictors.

Suppose that, *on average,* minorities with high school educations are discovered to be less productive than white males with high school educations owing to differences in schooling quality. Or suppose that, because of shortened career lives, women with a given education level are, *on average,* less valuable to firms than men of equal education. Employers might use this group information to modify individual data when making hiring decisions. The result would be that white males with given measured characteristics would be systematically preferred over women or minorities with the same characteristics, a condition that would be empirically identified as labor-market discrimination.

One unfortunate side effect of using group data to supplement individual data is that, while it could lead employers to the correct hiring decisions on average, it assigns a group characteristic to people who may not be typical of the group. There are women who will have long, uninterrupted careers, just as there will also be minority high school graduates of substantial ability who

---

[25] For some limited evidence supporting this model, see Barry R. Chiswick, "Racial Discrimination in the Labor Market: A Test of Alternative Hypotheses," *Journal of Political Economy* 81 (November 1973): 330–52.

[26] The considerations developed in this section are more formally and completely treated in Dennis J. Aigner and Glen G. Cain, "Statistical Theories of Discrimination in Labor Markets," *Industrial and Labor Relations Review* 30 (January 1977): 175–87. A similar theory is developed in M. A. Spence, "Job Market Signaling," *Quarterly Journal of Economics* 87 (August 1973): 355–74. Shelly J. Lundberg and Richard Startz, "Private Discrimination and Social Intervention in Competitive Labor Markets," *American Economic Review* 73 (June 1983): 340–47, consider the social gains that can be theoretically obtained from regulating a labor market characterized by statistical discrimination.

would have gone to college had not family poverty intervened. These particular group members are stigmatized by the use of group data. They may have actual productivity equal to that of those who are hired, but because of the group association they do not get the job.

Thus, *statistical discrimination* could lead to a systematic preference for white males over others with the same *measured* characteristics, and it could also create a situation in which minorities or women who are the equals of white males in *actual* productivity are paid less because of the already-mentioned group stigma. Both problems are caused by the use of group data in making hiring decisions, but this use need not be motivated by prejudice. The results, however, have the same appearance and effects as if prejudice were present.

An important implication of this model of statistical discrimination is that the use of group data will become a more costly screening device as members of each group become more dissimilar. For example, as greater proportions of women desire to work in full-time, year-round careers and do not intend to drop out of the labor force to raise children, employers using gender as a handy index of labor-force attachment will find themselves making costly mistakes. They will reject many female applicants who have a permanent labor-force attachment (in whom an investment in specific training would be very worthwhile), and they may accept male applicants who are less productive. In either case, firms using incorrect screening devices will have lower profits than those that adopt appropriate screens.[27] Thus, as *premarket* differences between the races or genders narrow, the use of race or gender *group* data should lessen and statistical discrimination should gradually disappear.

## Monopoly Power Models

The persistence of large race/gender earnings disparities has led some labor economists to wonder whether the above models are really appropriate. These economists are dissenters from the orthodox view that labor markets are essentially competitive; instead, they advance *monopoly power theories* of discrimination. Inherent in these more radical views of the labor market is the assertion that discrimination exists and persists because it is *profitable* for the discriminators.

---

[27]   For example, firms might deny training to women on the grounds that they are more likely than men to quit their jobs, leading to the loss of the firm's training investment. However, several studies have found that, all else equal (including pay and experience), women are no more likely to quit their jobs than are men. Companies that reject female applicants on the basis of their supposed higher quit propensities may be accepting lower-quality male applicants and losing compared to other companies. See Francine D. Blau and Lawrence M. Kahn, "Race and Sex Differences in Quits by Young Workers," *Industrial and Labor Relations Review* 34 (July 1981): 563–77, and W. Kip Viscusi, "Sex Differences in Worker Quitting," *The Review of Economics and Statistics* 62 (August 1980): 388–98. Indeed, one study of a single firm found that women were *less* likely to quit than comparable, equally paid males in the same jobs. See Andrew Weiss, "Determinants of Quit Behavior," *Journal of Labor Economics* 2 (July 1984): 371–87. Blau and Kahn as well as Weiss argue that if there is market discrimination, then in a given firm paying men and women the same, the males will have better outside opportunities than the females. These opportunities could then lead such men to have higher quit rates than similarly situated women.

While monopoly power theories of discrimination vary from each other in emphasis, they tend to share the feature that race or gender is collectively used to divide the labor force into *noncompeting* groups, creating or perpetuating a kind of worker caste system. These theories clearly suggest that competitive forces fail to operate in the labor market.[28] Two versions of these models are outlined below.

**Dual Labor Markets.**  A variant of the monopoly hypothesis is the view, held by some economists, that there is a *dual labor market*. Dualists see the overall labor market as divided into two noncompeting sectors: a *primary* and a *secondary* sector.[29] Jobs in the primary sector offer relatively high wages, stable employment, good working conditions, and opportunities for advancement. Secondary-sector jobs, however, tend to be low-wage, unstable, dead-end jobs with poor working conditions, and the returns to education and experience are thought to be close to zero in this sector. Of key importance to the dualists' approach is that mobility between sectors is thought to be limited. Workers relegated to the secondary sector are tagged as unstable, undesirable workers and are thought to have little hope of acquiring primary-sector jobs. Historically, dualists continue, a large proportion of minorities and women have been employed in the secondary sector, and this leads to perpetuation of discrimination against them. Minorities and women, it is argued, are discriminated against because they tend (as a group) to have unstable work histories, but these histories are themselves a result of being unable to break into the primary labor market.

The dual-labor-market description of discrimination does not really explain what initially caused women and minorities to be confined to do secondary jobs. Some Marxist economists view the existence of noncompeting sectors as at least partially due to attempts by capitalists to divide labor and thus to diffuse organized opposition to the capitalist system; this theory of discrimination is discussed later in the section on collusive action.[30] Some economists operating within more neoclassical frameworks view the existence of two sectors, and the assignment of workers to the two sectors, as arising because of differences in monitoring costs between categories of workers.[31] As will be discussed in Chapter 8, firms may use high wages or steeply sloped age/earnings profiles (characteristics of the primary sector) as compensation strategies to motivate workers and discourage shirking. These strategies deliberately encourage—and are predicated upon—a long-term relationship between workers and the firm. For workers with relatively short

---

[28]  For a summary of these views, see Glen G. Cain, "The Challenge of Segmented Labor Market Theories to Orthodox Theory: A Survey," *Journal of Economic Literature* 14 (December 1976): 1215–57.

[29]  Michael J. Piore "Jobs and Training: Manpower Policy," in *The State and the Poor*, eds. S. Beer and R. Barringer (Cambridge, MA: Winthrop Press, 1970).

[30]  See, for example, David Gordon, Richard Edwards, and Michael Reich, *Segmented Work, Divided Workers* (Cambridge: Cambridge University Press, 1982), who assert, "The segmentation of labor forged and reproduced materially based divisions among U.S. workers that inhibited the growth of a unified working class movement" (p. 3).

[31]  See, for example, Jeremy Bulow and Lawrence Summers, "A Theory of Dual Labor Markets with Application to Industrial Policy, Discrimination and Keynesian Unemployment," *Journal of Labor Economics* 4 (July 1986): 376–414.

expected tenure, direct monitoring of work effort is required; there are no incentives for firms to adopt high-wage or delayed-compensation strategies. That females have historically entered and left the labor force frequently (because of marriage and/or childbearing) explains why they might initially have been assigned to the secondary sector.[32] Why minorities were initially confined to the secondary sector is less obvious in the neoclassical framework. Recent empirical evidence does suggest, however, that there are two distinct sectors of the labor market—one in which education and experience are associated with higher wages and one in which they are not—and that nonwhites are more likely to be in the latter sector.[33]

Such evidence in favor of the dual-labor-market hypothesis helps to explain why discrimination persists. It calls into question the levels of competition and mobility that exist and suggests that the initial existence of noncompeting race/sex groups will be self-perpetuating. In short, the dual-labor-market hypothesis is consistent with any of the models of discrimination analyzed previously; what it does suggest is that if some of these theories *are* applicable, we cannot count on natural market forces to eliminate the discrimination that results.

**Collusive Action.** Other nonorthodox theories claim that white employers collude and become monopsonists with respect to the hiring of minority labor. Minorities are subjugated and held immobile while monopsonistic wages are forced on them.[34] One of the more cogent and complete *power theories* of discrimination argues that prejudice and the conflicts it creates are inherent in a capitalist society because they serve the interests of owners.[35] Even if the owners of capital did not conspire to *create* prejudice, they nevertheless find that if it continues they can enhance their profits. Workers divided by race or gender are harder to organize and, if they *are* unionized, they are less cohesive in their demands. Further, antagonisms on the shop floor deflect attention from grievances related to working conditions. Hence, it is argued that owners of capital gain, while *all* workers—but particularly minorities and women—lose from discrimination.

The monopoly power theories can muster only weak empirical support. They also share with the orthodox theories problems of logical consistency or completeness. If discrimination is created or at least perpetuated by capitalists, how does one account for its existence in precapitalist or socialist societies? It may be true that if all white employers conspire to keep women and minorities in low-wage, low-status jobs, they can all reap monopoly profits. However, if Employers A through Y adhere to the agreement, Em-

---

[32] See Claudia Goldin, "Monitoring Costs and Occupational Segregation by Sex: A Historical Analysis," *Journal of Labor Economics* 4 (January 1986): 1–27.

[33] William Dickens and Kevin Lang, "A Test of Dual Labor Market Theory," *American Economic Review* 75 (September 1985): 792–805; and William Dickens and Kevin Lang, "Testing Dual Labor Market Theory: A Reconsideration of the Evidence," National Bureau of Economic Research, Working Paper no. 1670, July 1985.

[34] Lester Thurow, *The Economics of Poverty and Discrimination* (Washington, DC: The Brookings Institution, 1969).

[35] Michael Reich, "The Economics of Racism," in *Problems in Political Economy: An Urban Perspective,* ed. David M. Gordon (Lexington, MA: D. C. Heath and Co., 1971): 107–13.

ployer Z will always have incentives to *break* the agreement! Z can hire women or minorities cheaply because of the agreement among *other* employers not to hire them, and Z can enhance profits by hiring these otherwise equally productive workers to fill jobs that A through Y are staffing with high-priced white males. Since every other employer has the same incentives as Z, the conspiracy will tend to break down unless cheaters can be disciplined in some way. The dual-labor-market and power theorists do not tell us how the conspiracy is maintained and coordinated among the millions of American employers. Thus their theories, like the orthodox ones, are less than completely satisfactory.

## Evaluation of Discrimination Theories

Our analysis of the different theories of discrimination suggests that if discrimination persists, it is the result of forces that hinder *competition* or labor market *adjustments* to competitive forces. Some theories—the "power" models—postulate the existence of noncompetitive or monopoly elements at the outset. The "orthodox" theories do not, but they have trouble explaining why discrimination *would* persist. The market should punish employers who discriminate or who fail to change their screening methods as the average characteristics of minorities or women change. A competitive market should drive employers to adopt *segregated* workplaces if employee discrimination exists; if customer discrimination exists, customers who discriminate will be punished by having to pay the higher prices associated with being served only by white males.

It would thus appear that all models of discrimination agree on one thing: any persistence of labor-market discrimination would be the result of forces or motivations that are blatantly noncompetitive or very slow to adjust to competitive forces. While no one model can be demonstrated to be superior to the others in explaining the facts, the various theories and the facts they seek to explain suggest that government intervention could be useful in eliminating the noncompetitive (or sluggish) influences.

# State Fair-Employment-Practice Legislation

Since the 1930s, about 30 states have enacted *fair-employment-practice laws* prohibiting discrimination in employment on the basis of race, creed, color, or national origin. (Unlike the federal legislation discussed later, the state laws did not address employment discrimination by gender.) These state laws normally established enforcement commissions and provided for fines and/or imprisonment for violators of the law.

Under state fair-employment-practice legislation, it is normally illegal for an organization to do at least one of the following: refuse employment or discharge employees because of race, or discriminate in compensation or other terms of employment by race. As summarized next, an analysis of market discrimination earlier in the chapter suggests that if a law contains only one of these provisions, it is likely to be ineffective in reducing labor-market discrimination.

That analysis predicted that even prejudiced employers would hire minority workers if they could be "compensated" by paying minorities less. On the one hand, therefore, a state law that does not address discrimination in compensation permits prejudiced employers to comply with the law by hiring minorities but paying them less than other workers of comparable quality. On the other hand, an equal-pay-for-equal-work law that only forbids wage discrimination is likely to reduce the relative employment of minorities (and either increase their relative unemployment or reduce their rate of labor-force participation) unless it is accompanied by a requirement forbidding employment discrimination, since prejudiced employers will be less willing to hire minorities if they are unable to practice wage discrimination.

With sufficient enforcement, laws that forbid *both* employment and wage discrimination may reduce discrimination in the labor market by raising the cost of such actions to violators. How effective have state fair-employment-practice laws been in reducing discrimination? Some studies have found that, after accounting for differences in human capital between whites and nonwhites, the relative wages and occupational positions of nonwhites are higher in states with fair-employment-practice laws than in states that have not passed such laws. Such findings, however, raise a basic question of causality when they do not consider the way legislation is established. Fair-employment-practice laws are passed by the vote of legislators, who must represent the preferences of their constituencies to remain in office. When we find that the relative earnings of minorities are higher in states with fair-employment-practice laws, does that represent the effect of the law or a tendency of such laws to be passed in states where prejudice is relatively low (reflected in part by the higher relative wages received by minorities)? There is some evidence that it represents the latter. Indeed, the existence of state fair-employment-practice legislation appears to have little or no effect on racial earnings differentials, once independent measures of prejudice and the extent of unionization in a state are controlled for. (A measure of prejudice independent of earnings differentials is clearly needed to sort out the issue of causation; one measure used is electoral support for political candidates who are known to oppose civil-rights or equal-opportunity legislation.) Unions have been shown to increase the relative earnings of minorities, and because fair-employment laws tend to be found in states with above-average levels of unionization, studies attempting to find the separate effects of fair-employment-practice laws must filter out the effects of unions on earnings differentials.[36]

# Federal Programs to End Discrimination

The federal government has enforced two sets of rules in an attempt to eliminate market discrimination. One is a *nondiscrimination* requirement imposed on almost all employers. The other is a requirement that federal

---

[36] See William M. Landes, "The Economics of Fair Employment Laws," *Journal of Political Economy* 76 (August 1968): 507–52.

contractors engage in *affirmative action*—that is, actively seeking out minorities and women to staff their vacancies.

In addition to passing legislation designed to protect women and minorities, Congress has outlawed discrimination against older workers (aged 40–70). We will discuss age discrimination in the next chapter, when we examine seniority arrangements and long-term employment relationships.

## Equal Pay Act of 1963

Over the years prior to the 1960s, sex discrimination was officially sanctioned by so-called *protective labor laws,* which limited women's total hours of work and prohibited them from working at night, lifting heavy objects, and working during pregnancy. Not all states placed all these restrictions on women, but the effect of these laws was to limit the access of women to many jobs. These laws were overturned by the Equal Pay Act of 1963, which also outlawed separate pay scales for men and women using similar skills and performing work under the same conditions.

The act was seriously deficient as an antidiscrimination tool, however, because it said nothing about equal opportunity in hiring and promotions. As noted earlier, if there is prejudice against women from any source, employers will treat female employees as if they were less productive or more costly to hire than equally productive males, and the market response will be for female wages to fall below male wages. The Equal Pay Act took a step toward the elimination of wage differentials, but by so doing it tended to suppress a market mechanism that helped women obtain greater access to jobs.[37] The act failed to acknowledge the principle that if labor-market discrimination is to be eliminated, legislation must require *both* equal pay *and* equal opportunities in hiring and promotions for people of comparable productivity.

## Title VII of the Civil Rights Act

Some defects in the Equal Pay Act of 1963 were corrected the next year. Title VII of the Civil Rights Act of 1964 made it unlawful for any employer ''to refuse to hire or to discharge any individual, or otherwise to discriminate against any individual with respect to his compensation, terms, conditions, or privileges of employment, because of such individual's race, color, religion, sex, or national origin.''

Union practices were also addressed by the new legislation. Historically, it had been very difficult for racial minorities to obtain admission into certain craft unions representing workers in the skilled trades—an exclusion that denied minorities access to both the skills training provided through union apprenticeship programs and the employment opportunities dispensed through union hiring halls. Unions representing workers in large industries were generally more integrated, although in a few unions the quality of

---

[37] Some critics of the Equal Pay Act of 1963 argued that its motivation was to help men compete with lower-paid women. See Nancy Barrett, ''Women in the Job Market: Occupations, Earnings, and Career Opportunities,'' in *The Subtle Revolution,* ed. Ralph E. Smith (Washington, DC: The Urban Institute, 1979): 55.

representation in collective bargaining and in the administration of the labor agreement varied by race. Title VII made it unlawful for any labor organization to exclude individuals from membership, to segregate membership, to refuse to refer for employment, or to discriminate in admission to apprenticeship programs on the basis of race, color, religion, sex, or national origin.

This broad statement of a national policy favoring nondiscriminatory employment practices was qualified in certain repsects, however. First, Title VII was not retroactive; it was written to apply to acts of discrimination occurring after its effective date of July 1, 1965. Second, the law permits exceptions to its general requirement of nondiscrimination "where religion, sex, or national origin is a bona fide occupational qualification reasonably necessary to the normal operation of a business." In practice, this applies to a limited number of situations (for example, certain jobs in religious organizations, or nursing homes in which patients are of a predominant gender).

Third, Title VII permits an employer to differentiate wages and other employment conditions "pursuant to a bona fide seniority system . . . provided that such differences are not the result of an intention to discriminate." Finally, no party subject to the statute is required to grant preferential treatment to any group because of existing imbalances in the work force. As will become clear, these last two qualifications have raised difficult issues in applying the law to certain situations.

Title VII applies to all employers in interstate commerce with at least 25 employees and is enforced by the Equal Employment Opportunity Commission (EEOC), which has the authority to mediate complaints, encourage lawsuits by private parties or the U.S. Attorney General, or (since 1972) bring suits itself against employers who have violated the law. To enhance the effect of the law, the courts permitted individual plaintiffs to expand their suits into "class actions" in which the potential discriminatory impact of an organization's employment practices on an entire group of workers is assessed by the courts.

Over the years, the federal courts have fashioned two standards of discrimination that may be applied when discriminatory employment practices are alleged—*disparate treatment* and *disparate impact*.

Disparate treatment occurs under Title VII if individuals are treated differently (for example, paid different wages or benefits) because of their race, sex, color, religion, or national origin, and if it can be shown that there is an intent to discriminate. While this is probably the more obvious approach to defining discrimination, it is not the definition that the courts have relied on most frequently. The difficulty raised by this standard is that personnel policies that appear to be neutral in the sense that they ignore race, gender, and so forth, may nevertheless often perpetuate the effects of past discrimination. For example, word-of-mouth recruiting (a seemingly neutral policy) in a plant with a largely white work force would be suspect under Title VII even if the selection of new employees from among the applicants was done on a nondiscriminatory basis, since the racial composition of the applicants is likely to be influenced by the racial composition of the current workforce.

The concern with addressing the present effects of past discrimination led to the "disparate impact" standard. Under this approach it is the result, not the motivation, that matters. Personnel policies that appear to be neutral, but lead to different impacts by race or gender, are prohibited under Title VII unless they can be related to job performance.[38] For example, employers may use tests and educational standards to screen applicants, but these tests must be validated against job performance. In the words of the Supreme Court, "Tests must measure the person for the job; not the person in the abstract." Job-application forms may ask about *convictions* but not *arrests* (arrest rates among minorities tend to be higher, but the courts reason that it is conviction that is important to the employer). Marital status cannot be used as a screening device unless it is applied uniformly to both sexes and is clearly a job-related requirement. In interpreting Title VII, the federal courts have generally taken the position that neutral (for example, colorblind or sexblind) personnel practices that carry forward the effects of past discrimination constitute present discrimination. As a result, plaintiffs, employers, and the courts have become interested in how closely the race or gender composition of groups selected for employment, promotion, training, or termination accords with the race or gender composition of the pool of workers available for selection.

The adoption of the disparate impact standard by the courts as a standard of discrimination has mounted a significant challenge to employer personnel-screening devices. As noted in Chapter 4, when it is extremely costly to ascertain the qualifications of individual applicants, employers have an incentive to rely on screening devices that sort job applicants on the basis of the "average" characteristics of a group, rather than according to individual merit. While the use of screening devices often results in lower costs of personnel administration, it also gives rise to the statistical discrimination discussed earlier in this chapter. In taking the position that workers must be judged on the basis of their individual abilities, rather than average group characteristics, the courts have launched a strong assault against mechanisms of statistical discrimination, and one consequence of this assault has been higher costs to employers of human-resource management.[39]

In certain instances, the application of the disparate-impact standard and other efforts to combat labor-market discrimination have been limited (see Example 7.1). In recent years, two particularly difficult issues have arisen in the application of the law: the treatment of seniority arrangements perpetuating the effects of past discrimination and the adoption of a "comparable

---

[38] *Willie S. Griggs* v. *Duke Power Company* 401 U.S. 424 (1971).

[39] One must be careful to distinguish here between the costs to employers (*private* costs) and the costs to society (*social* costs) of statistical discrimination. Although employers' private costs for human-resource management may be low because of statistical discrimination, the costs to society may be high if qualified applicants are rejected simply because of the group to which they belong. While prohibiting statistical discrimination may increase the private costs of human-resource management, it may decrease the social costs.

**EXAMPLE  7.1**

## Discrimination Law, Promotion, and Performance Appraisal

As we have noted, equal-employment-opportunity law has reduced the use of statistical discrimination in personnel selection through the use of the disparate-impact standard. This standard is also used in evaluating employer promotion decisions. Just as in the case of hiring, firms must justify the particular performance-appraisal techniques used if they produce a disparate result. In fact, in some court cases, the judge bypassed the question of disparate impact and looked directly at the performance-appraisal system. Thus, appraisal methods have come under careful scrutiny in federal courts.

What kinds of evidence have employers presented that cause courts to decide that their promotion policies were not discriminatory? One method is to validate their performance-appraisal systems. This can be done by showing that there is a clear relationship between performance ratings and success on the job to which one is being promoted. For example, in one case, the employer won because the factors upon which workers' performance was rated were related to the job being applied for rather than to the current job. This kind of validation is similar to what companies have to use to avoid charges of hiring discrimination—that is, any test given to job applicants must be shown to be job-related if it has an adverse impact on women or minority applicants. However, judges generally appear to be more reluctant to examine the validity of *performance appraisal* systems than of *job-applicant testing* programs. In particular, in many promotion-discrimination cases, judges have been more concerned with whether the appraisals intentionally discriminated against women or minorities than with whether the criteria used in performance appraisals were actually job-related. Put differently, in promotion-discrimination cases, judges are more likely to apply the "disparate-treatment" than the "disparate-impact" standard.

In assessing whether there is intentional discrimination, judges have often favored the use of "objective" criteria such as production or attendance records, while finding against employers who used "subjective" criteria such as maturity or "drive". Often, judges have found that ratings by workers' immediate supervisors can be tainted by prejudiced attitudes and therefore not a legitimate defense against a charge of discrimination. These findings illustrate the tension between business efficiency and enforcement of equal-employment-opportunity laws. First-line supervisors are in the best position to give accurate performance ratings, but they are also in the best position to perpetuate prejudiced stereotypes. Taking authority away from them may lead to less accurate appraisals as well as to reduced discrimination against women and minorities.

Companies using subjective performance-rating systems have successfully defended themselves against discrimination charges through careful design of these systems. For example, in one case, company policy stated that supervisors' continued employment depended on their willingness to enforce fair treatment of minorities. The judge ruled that raters had an incentive to avoid prejudicial ratings. Another successful technique is for a company to provide a system of checks and balances. For example, ratings may be reviewed at higher levels, and employees

may have the opportunity to file a grievance against ratings they believe to be unfair. Each of these employer defenses involves devoting more resources to personnel administration. While they involve increased employer costs of doing business, there may be significant social benefits of using procedures that are perceived to be fair.

SOURCES:  Lawrence S. Kleiman and Richard L. Durham, "Performance Appraisal, Promotion and the Courts: A Critical Review," *Personnel Psychology* 34 (May 1981): 103–21; *Cintron* v. *Adams* 18 FEP 1542, 1978; *Baxter* v. *Savannah Sugar Corp.* 350 F. Supp. 139, 1972; *Crawford* v. *Western Electric Co.* 14 EPD 7696, 1977; *Thompson* v. *McDonnell Douglas Corp.* 416 F. Supp. 972, 1976; and *U.S.* v. *City of Chicago* 385 F. Supp. 543, 1974.

worth" standard by which to judge pay equality when occupations are segregated.

**Seniority.**   Most unionized firms and many nonunion firms use seniority as a consideration in allocating promotion opportunities. Moreover, employees are frequently laid off in order of reverse seniority, the least senior first, in a recession. It was partially in recognition of the historically important role of seniority in American personnel arrangements that Congress appeared to exempt seniority systems from challenge under Title VII. Yet seniority systems have the strong potential for perpetuating the effects of past discrimination. We have seen how occupational segregation—the tendency of women or minorities to be restricted to relatively low-wage jobs despite qualifications for higher positions—has been one historical mechanism of discrimination in the labor market.

In many instances, particularly in the South, job segregation was accompanied by departmental seniority arrangements. That is, seniority was computed as time employed in a department, not as time employed in the plant or company. When companies sought to break down historical patterns of job segregation to comply with Title VII, two types of adjustment occurred: women and minorities were moved within a company from low-wage jobs to higher-wage jobs in other departments, and women and minorities were hired by companies into some jobs for the first time. Under either mechanism, women and minorities ended up with relatively low seniority under departmental seniority systems.

Many of these adjustments occurred during the late 1960s, when the general demand for labor was high. With the less-favorable economic circumstances of the 1970s, however, firms began to lay off workers, and under departmental seniority arrangements a disproportionate number of those laid off were minorities and women. In many of these cases, individuals with very little departmental seniority had more *plant* seniority than workers who retained their jobs in the high-wage departments, and they might have been able to retain their jobs if they had the seniority that they had accrued in their former departments. Departmental seniority arrangements resulted in a disparate impact on women and minorities and perpetuated the effects of past discrimination. The resulting Title VII litigation presented the courts with a quandary. Under the disparate impact standard, the seniority systems were discriminatory, but the language of Title VII explicitly permitted "bona fide seniority systems." The lower courts tended to resolve the quandary by taking the position that a seniority system was not "bona fide" if it discriminated, and that under the prevailing definition of discrimination, only plant-wide seniority systems were "bona fide." When the Supreme Court considered the issue, however, it reversed the appellate courts and held that the language in Title VII permitted even departmental seniority systems that perpetuated the effects of discrimination.[40]

Minorities and women who were hired for the first time following passage of Title VII were susceptible to layoff under either plant or departmental seniority. Some were individuals who had been victims of hiring discrimination prior to the passage of the law or who did not apply for employment because the company had a reputation for discriminating. In litigation arising out of these cases, plaintiffs often argued that the appropriate remedy was an award of seniority retroactive to the date when the individual would have been hired if the company had not practiced discrimination. (This is sometimes referred to as "fictional seniority.") On this issue the Supreme Court has ruled that fictional seniority is an appropriate remedy for individuals who can demonstrate that they were victims of unlawful discrimination. However, the Supreme Court has argued that it is not appropriate to dismiss current employees as part of the remedy for past discrimination.[41] It has also ruled that laying off more-senior white employees instead of more-recently hired minorities just to preserve racial balance is unconstitutional.[42]

**Comparable Worth.**   We noted earlier in this chapter that women are disproportionately employed in certain occupations in which wages are relatively low. Some have argued that the wages in these jobs are low because they are filled to a large extent by women, who are the victims of market discrimination. To the extent that the labor market is biased against women, it is argued further that discrimination is perpetuated by using the market as a basis for paying, say, clerical workers (a job historically filled largely by women) less than, say, maintenance workers (a job historically filled largely by men).

Two remedies have been proposed for the kind of discrimination that some believe results in occupational segregation. First, if male-dominated fields were opened up to women and if the principle of equal pay for equal work were enforced, then discrimination would be eliminated. In fact, such a solution would reverse the over-crowding mechanism discussed earlier in this chapter: as more women entered traditionally male jobs, the relative wages of the female-dominated jobs would rise. Unfortunately, this mechanism for eliminating discrimination would probably take a very long time, because the opportunities for women would exist mainly in entry-level positions. Many

[40]   *International Brotherhood of Teamsters* v. *United States* 431 U.S. 324, 14 FEP 1514 (1977).

[41]   *Franks* v. *Bowman Transportation* 424 U.S. 747, 12 FEP Cases 549 (1976), and *Fire Fighters Local 1784* v. *Stotts*, U.S. Sup Ct, no. 82–206, June 12, 1984.

[42]   *Wygant* v. *Jackson Board of Education*, U.S. Sup Ct, no. 84–1340, May 19, 1986.

older women in clerical positions, say, might not find it worthwhile to acquire the training necessary to enter male fields that may have previously been closed to women (recall from Chapter 6 the impact of age on the training investments by workers).

The long time period necessary for the strategy of integration of occupations to work leads some to propose the second method for dealing with occupational segregation. This strategy is to pay women (or minorities) their "comparable worth"—that is, to pay them for the intrinsic value of their jobs. The intrinsic value of a job would be established by a comparison of its importance to some other (presumably more highly paid) job predominantly held by males, rather than by reference to market wages. (See the appendix to this chapter for more details on procedures for making these comparisons.)

The comparable worth idea has proved difficult to define precisely. How much of the wage difference between two jobs can be attributed to the fact that one is largely staffed by women and the other by men? The evidence reviewed earlier in this chapter indicates that a significant portion of the wage difference between men and women reflects differences in human-capital investments and other qualifications. The amount of the difference that might be attributed to discrimination is likely to vary from one set of job comparisons to another. An additional influence on wage differences between jobs was discussed in Chapter 6—nonpecuniary conditions of work. To the extent that working conditions vary substantially between a job held predominantly by men and one held predominantly by women, one would expect the wages to differ as well. All these factors must be considered in estimating how much of the wage differential between "male" jobs and "female" jobs is the result of market discrimination.

Comparable-worth advocates propose to use job-evaluation techniques in order to implement their strategy. For example, by 1987, 28 states had begun or completed job-evaluation studies for their government employees with comparable-worth considerations in mind. Twenty of these states had set aside money to eliminate salary discrepancies believed to be based on gender or race.[43] At first glance, job evaluation appears to be a natural way to implement comparable worth. After all, it is a technique designed to compare the requirements of different jobs, including different working conditions (see Chapter 6). While market wages are used in the job-evaluation process, all wage comparisons in comparable-worth-adjustment situations are done internally (within the firm).

While it is tempting to use job evaluation, it may not be possible to evaluate the intrinsic worth of different job requirements. Even in a non-discriminatory labor market, both supply and demand forces influence wages as well as employer demand. For example, if workers' tastes change so that

---

[43] See Michel McQueen, "States Set Pace on Innovative Laws for Child Care, Parental Leaves, Women's Pay-Equity Standards," *Wall Street Journal,* October 1, 1987, p. 60, and Ronald G. Ehrenberg and Robert S. Smith, "Comparable Worth in the Public Sector," in *Public Compensation,* ed. David Wise (Chicago: University of Chicago Press, 1987).

more people want to work in service jobs, then a bias-free labor market would eventually reward these jobs less than before, even though their job requirements might not have changed. The "worth" of these jobs (as defined by what they would pay if there were no discrimination) cannot be defined independently of the supply of labor.

Some job-evaluation systems would be able to take into account such changes in supply. In particular, in assigning wages to given jobs, any job-evaluation system must decide how much weight to put on the various compensable factors, such as skill, experience, effort, and responsibility. In such a process, wage surveys, in which a company estimates how much the *market* rewards these factors (see Chapters 2 and 6), are utilized. If, for example, more workers seek positions of responsibility, then relative market wages for these positions would fall, and this fall would be reflected in job-evaluation weights for this factor. However, in using market wages, the job-evaluation system may well reproduce any discrimination that exists in the market in general. Thus, the dilemma facing those who want to use job evaluation for implementing the comparable-worth principle is whether to use market wages in weighing the compensable factors. If market wages are not used, then the system will not be able to take into account differences in supply to different occupations. If they are used, then the system may reproduce existing discrimination.[44]

In addition to the operational difficulties with comparable worth, the concept raises several fundamental policy questions. For example, is it likely to be more effective to use the law to break down occupational barriers caused by discriminatory job segregation or to develop a compensation scheme (via comparable worth) that may leave job segregation unchanged? Will raising the wage rates of traditional "female" occupations reduce women's incentives to seek occupational advancement? Will raising women's wages have an adverse effect on female employment levels?[45] Answers to these questions will be important components of any complete evaluation of comparable worth.

---

[44] See Donald P. Schwab, "Job Evaluation and Pay Setting: Concepts and Practices," in E. Robert Livernash, ed., *Comparable Worth: Issues and Alternatives* (Washington, DC: Equal Employment Advisory Council, 1980): 49–77; Donald J. Treiman and Heidi L. Hartmann, eds., *Women, Work and Wages: Equal Pay for Jobs of Equal Value* (Washington, DC: National Academy Press, 1981); and Heidi L. Hartmann, ed., *New Directions for Research on Comparable Worth* (Washington, DC: National Academy Press, 1984).

[45] In general, increasing the wage rate for a group should lead to a decline in the group's employment. The one exception to this rule is if employers behave as monopsonists; we showed in the context of our discussion of the minimum wage (Chapter 3) that in this situation one could set a minimum wage above the current wage (within a certain range) without suffering any employment losses. A number of studies cited in Chapter 3 also suggest that registered nurses and public-school teachers, both traditionally female occupations, have their wages depressed because their employers have some monopsony power. For these groups, at least, comparable worth wage adjustments might not lead to employment losses. Empirical evidence that the effects on female employment of comparable-worth wage adjustments in the state and local government sector are likely to be small are presented in Ronald G. Ehrenberg and Robert S. Smith, "Comparable Worth Wage Adjustments and Female Employment in the State and Local Sector," *Journal of Labor Economics* 5 (January 1987): 43–62.

## EXAMPLE    7.2

# Comparable Worth and the University

Some of the difficulties involved with the concept of *comparable worth* are illustrated by an example in which gender does not even enter. Consider the labor market for university professors in the fields of computer science and English, and suppose that initially the demand and supply curves for both are given by $D_{0c}$ and $S_{0c}$ and $D_{0e}$ and $S_{0e}$, respectively. As the figure indicates, in this circumstance the same wage, $W_0$, will prevail in both markets, and $E_{0c}$ computer-science professors and $E_{0e}$ English professors will be hired. Suppose also that in some objective sense the quality of the two groups of professors is equal.

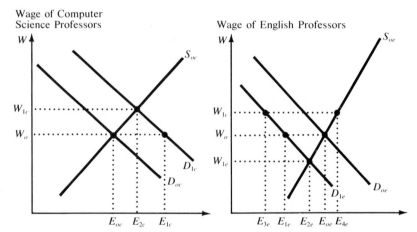

Wage of Computer Science Professors

Wage of English Professors

Number of Computer Science Professors    Number of English Professors

Presumably, this is a situation that advocates of comparable worth would applaud. Both types of professors require the same amount of training, represented by a Ph.D., and both are required to engage in the same activities, teaching and research. Unless one is willing to assign different values to the teaching and research produced in different academic fields, one must conclude that the jobs are truly comparable. Hence, if the two groups are equal in quality, equal wages would be justified according to the concept of comparable worth.

Suppose now, however, that the demand for computer-science professors rises to $D_{1c}$ as a result of the increasing numbers of students who want to take computer-science courses. Suppose at the same time the demand for English professors falls to $D_{1e}$ because fewer students want to take elective courses in English. At the old equilibrium wage rate there is an excess demand for computer-science professors of $E_{1c} - E_{0c}$ and an excess supply of English professors of $E_{0e} - E_{1e}$.

How can universities respond? One possibility is to let the market work; the wage of computer-science professors will rise to $W_{1c}$ and that of English professors will fall to $W_{1e}$. Employment of the former will rise to $E_{2c}$ while employment of the latter will become $E_{2e}$.

Another possibility is to keep the wages of the two groups of professors equal at the old wage rate of $W_0$. Universities could respond to the excess demand for computer scientists and the excess supply of English professors by reducing hiring standards for the former and raising them for the latter. Since the average quality of English professors would then exceed the average quality of computer scientists, the wage paid per "quality-unit" would now be higher for the computer scientists. Hence, true comparable worth—equal pay for *equal-quality* workers performing comparable jobs—would not be achieved. Moreover, employment and course offerings in this situation would not change to meet changing student demands.

Alternatively, some advocates of comparable worth might argue that universities should respond by raising the wages of *all* professors to $W_{1c}$. While this would eliminate the shortage of computer-science professors, it would exacerbate the excess supply of English professors, raising it to $E_{4e} - E_{3e}$. Universities would respond by drastically reducing the employment of English professors even further to $E_{3e}$ (and reducing course offerings). Moreover, the excess supply again would permit universities to raise hiring standards for English professors, so again average quality would rise. As a result, once more the wage per quality-unit of English professors would be less than that of computer-science professors, and again true comparable worth would not be achieved.

The message one takes away from this example is that it is difficult to "trick the market." In the face of changing relative-demand conditions, either wage differentials for the two types of professors must be allowed to arise or quality differentials will arise. In neither case, however, can comparable worth be achieved. Put another way, the value of a job cannot be determined independently of market conditions.

How have universities actually responded to the changing relative demand conditions for faculty in the fields portrayed in this example? Some evidence can be found from data on faculty salaries, categorized by academic field, obtained each year from a survey of public universities and colleges conducted by Oklahoma State University. In the academic year 1976–77, respondents reported average salaries for new assistant professors of $15,526 in computer science and $13,321 in English and literature. By 1983–84, average starting salaries of the former had risen by 84.3 percent to $28,266, while those for the latter had risen only 49.7 percent to $19,936. As a result, while the typical new assistant professor in English and literature earned 85.8 percent (13,321/15,526) of what the average new assistant professor in computer science earned in 1976–77, he or she earned only 70.5 percent (19,936/28,266) by 1983–84. Relative starting salaries for assistant professors in academia did adjust quite rapidly, then, to changing relative demand conditions.

SOURCE: Data are from W. Lee Hansen, "Changing Faculty Salaries," in *American Professors*, eds. H. Bowen and J. Schuster (New York: Oxford University Press, 1986), Table 6.10.

## The Federal Contract Compliance Program

In 1965, the Office of Federal Contract Compliance Programs (OFCCP) was established to monitor the hiring and promotion practices of federal contractors (firms supplying goods or services to the federal government). OFCCP requires contractors above a certain size to analyze the extent of their underutilization of women and minorities and to propose a plan to remedy any such underutilization. Such a plan is called an *affirmative-action plan*. Contractors submitting unacceptable plans or failing to meet their goals are threatened with cancellation of their contracts and their eligibility for future contracts, although these drastic steps are rarely taken.

Affirmative-action planning is intended to commit firms to a schedule for rapidly overcoming unequal career opportunities afforded women and minorities. Such planning affects both *hiring* and *promotion* practices, but it also raises numerous philosophical and practical questions that tend to make the planning process highly controversial.

Suppose an insurance company is attempting to construct an affirmative-action plan with regard to secretaries. Its first step in setting hiring goals is to decide what number of minorities are "available" and what fraction they constitute of all available workers. If blacks constitute, say, 9 percent of the labor supply available to the firm, then it might seem to be a simple matter of setting a goal of 9 percent. However, the planner must resolve some serious questions. First, should the pool of black secretaries be estimated based on the firm's *actual applicant* pool? The answer is probably no, since any discriminatory practices in the past will discourage black applicants currently. Further, affirmative-action planning is intended to force companies to *change* their hiring practices. On the other hand, a firm's location within a city can attract more or fewer black applicants, depending on how far from the firm blacks live and the level of compensation offered. Moreover, the mix of *fringe benefits* in the total compensation package can alter the attractiveness of an employer to women, the young, and the poor.[46] Thus, to some extent the potential pool of *interested* applicants is a legitimate consideration. Should the potential pool be estimated from the fraction of all *trained secretaries* in the area who are black? If we are interested in eradicating *market* discrimination, this may be the logical measure, since it would force firms to hire black secretaries in the same proportion as they are found in the labor market. However, years of discrimination may have induced blacks to avoid training for this occupation, with the result that blacks may be substantially underrepresented in the secretarial labor market. Should firms, then, be compelled to hire black secretaries in proportion to their numbers in the adult *population* of the city at large? This goal implicitly sets out to eliminate all discrimination,

[46] For a review of the economic factors affecting "availability," see Ronald Ehrenberg and Robert Smith, "Economic and Statistical Analysis of Discrimination in Hiring," *Proceedings of the Thirty-Fifth Annual Meeting of the Industrial Relations Research Association* (Madison, WI: Industrial Relations Research Association, 1984).

both market and premarket, but if blacks are underrepresented in the occupation, the attainment of this goal is impractical in the short run. Firms attempting to hire more black secretaries than are available would have two choices. They could hire black high school graduates and train them in secretarial skills. Remember, however, that such training is *general* in nature, so the firms would not offer it unless the workers involved paid for it in some way. Without training as an option, firms would simply try to bid against each other for the services of existing black secretaries, which would drive up their wages. The higher wage rates would induce more blacks to seek secretarial training, and their underrepresentation in the occupation would disappear in the long run.

While population-based goals would appear to fight both kinds of discrimination, they might in fact fight neither. It stands to reason that if hiring goals are set beyond the immediate reach of firms, each will individually fail to meet them. Can the government reasonably punish firms for failing to hire beyond the numbers currently available? If it cannot, then failure to meet goals will not result in punishment, which seems to remove the incentive for firms to take energetic steps to integrate their work forces.

A final issue in hiring has to do with how the goals are applied. If black secretaries, to continue our example, are 9 percent of the available pool, does that mean that 9 percent of all *newly hired* secretaries should be black? This goal might seem reasonable from a firm's point of view, but if labor turnover is low it would take a very long time for the 9 percent of *new hires* to accumulate to the point where blacks were 9 percent of the firm's total secretarial work force. Since the Civil Rights Act of 1964 prohibits workers of one race from being fired to make room for those of another, getting rid of employment imbalances must occur through new hiring. However, only if aggrieved groups are *favored* in hiring can the effects of past discrimination be eradicated quickly.

Favoritism in hiring not only raises the issue of *reverse discrimination,* wherein whites or males can assert that they are being discriminated against because of race or sex, but also raises the issue of how firms, as a whole, can hire women or blacks in proportions greater than their current availability. The courts have yet to resolve the considerable tension between Title VII's standard of nondiscrimination, which protects all groups from disparate treatment, and the OFCCP's standard of affirmative action. (See Example 7.3.)

It is testimony to the difficulty of these questions about affirmative-action planning that the government's requirements for calculating "availability" are rather vague. The OFCCP has proposed that, for purposes of affirmative-action planning, federal contractors compute availability of minorities and women using either of two methods: the "civilian labor force" method or the "four-factor" method.[47] Under the former alternative, availability is esti-

---

[47] Bureau of National Affairs, Labor Relations Reporter, *Fair Employment Practices Manual* 401:5005.OFCCP's proposal is a revision of its 1974 guidelines for federal contractors, under which eight factors were considered. As of this writing the revised guidelines have not yet been implemented.

mated from the percentages of women and minorities in the *metropolitan area's* civilian labor force. The "four-factor" alternative would require the contractor to devise estimates by taking into account the following considerations:

1. The percentage of minorities and women in the civilian labor force in the *immediate labor area* (defined as the geographic area from which employees and applicants may reasonably commute to the establishment);

2. The percentage of minorities and women with requisite skills in the *immediate labor area;*

3. The percentage of minorities and women with requisite skills in the *relevant recruitment area* (defined as the geographic area from which the contractor may reasonably recruit its employees, including areas not contiguous to the immediate labor area); and

4. The percentage of minorities and women among those promotable or transferable within the contractor's organization.

## Affirmative Action, Goals, and Quotas

Title VII of the Civil Rights Act and the Supreme Court's decision to enforce a standard based on discriminatory impact as well as discriminatory intent produced a revolution in personnel administration. Individual employees who claimed to be the victims of discrimination could also bring *class actions*—legal suits alleging that the discriminatory treatment that they had experienced was typical of an entire class of "similarly situated" workers in a company or union. A class could be very large—for example, all female workers in a company or all black applicants for particular jobs—and backpay awards and other monetary damages from successful class actions could be enormous. Courts also began to approve or even order specific remedial actions, such as goals or quotas for the hiring of minorities or women, either when discrimination was proved or as part of a settlement (or consent decree) to avoid litigation.

Faced with these developments, many companies and unions began to alter their personnel practices in an effort to avoid liability. In some instances, nondiscriminatory procedures were implemented. In others, organizations concluded that simply prohibiting discriminatory practices was not enough to remedy the effects of past practices and instituted *affirmative-action plans*. An affirmative-action plan goes beyond nondiscrimination—it gives preference to individuals based on their race or sex in an effort to overcome the present effects of past discrimination. While these plans were started voluntarily, it is no doubt true that some companies and unions started the plans in an effort to avoid lawsuits alleging employment discrimination.

Affirmative-action efforts raise the potential for conflict with Title VII, which sets a general nondiscrimination standard. Indeed, Section 703(j) explicitly states that the statute does not " . . . require any employer, employment agency, labor organization, or joint labor-management committee . . . to grant preferential treatment to any individual or to any group because of employment imbalances.'' By the mid-1970s, the Supreme Court held that whites, males, and other ''majority'' groups are protected from race or sex discrimination by Title VII.[48] But does this mean that affirmative-action plans are generally prohibited under Title VII?

In an early case, the Supreme Court rejected a plan designed to admit more minorities into the University of California at Davis Medical School because of its rigid quotas, but left the door open for plans with more flexible methods for increasing minority representation.[49] The court reached a major turning point on affirmative action in the *Weber* case, in which a white worker who was employed by the Kaiser Aluminum and Chemical Corporation alleged that he had been discriminated against because of his race.[50] Prior to 1974, Kaiser hired only workers with previous craft experience to fill the craft positions in the plant. This practice virtually restricted the craft positions to white workers, since blacks had historically been excluded from the craft unions, which were the sources of training through apprenticeship programs. In 1974, Kaiser signed a collective-bargaining agreement with the United Steelworkers of America that included an affirmative-action plan designed to eliminate racial imbalances. As a part of the plan, Kaiser agreed to train its production workers to fill craft positions. Selection for the training program was on the basis of seniority, subject to the provision that at least half of the trainees would be black until the percentage of black craft workers in the plant was similar to the percentage in the outside labor force. Some of the white workers whose applications for the program were rejected had more seniority than some of the black workers who were selected, and one of these workers filed the lawsuit.

In a controversial decision, the Supreme Court held that while Title VII does not *require* preferential treatment, it *permits* such treatment when arrived at *voluntarily*. While the court refused to ''define the line of demarcation between permissible and impermissible affirmative-action plans,'' it nonetheless provided several clues. It noted that in the Kaiser case, the purpose of the affirmative-action plan was to break down historical patterns of occupational segregation by race—clearly an objective of Title VII—and the plan did not ''trammel the interests of white employees,'' since none was discharged. Moreover, the plan did not create ''an absolute bar to the advancement of white employees,'' because some were admitted to the training program.

Since 1979, the court has considered the legality of several other affirmative-action plans in the light of the principles stated in the Weber case. While not all of the issues are settled, the following appear to be the most important considerations determining the legality of voluntary affirmative-action plans. First, when are employment preferences based on race or sex justified? What kinds of problems justify this remedy? On the one hand, the court has looked

---

[48] *McDonald v. Santa Fe Trail Transportation Co.*, 427 US 273 (1976).
[49] *University of California Regents v. Bakke*, 438 US 265 (1978).
[50] *United Steelworkers v. Weber*, 443 US 193 (1979).

for evidence of an imbalance between the employment and availability of minorities or women in "traditionally segregated job classifications." On the other hand, a majority of the justices have not required that an employer provide explicit evidence of past discrimination as a justification for initiating affirmative action.

Second, when affirmative action is justified, what kinds of race or sex preferences are permissible? The court is opposed to quotas—the reservation of explicit numbers of positions for minorities. However, flexible affirmative-action plans in which race or sex is one of several factors governing an employment decision are likely to be approved. The court also appears to favor plans that are transitional rather than of indefinite duration. Courts are opposed to the development of a permanent system of job classifications more or less reserved for a particular race or sex.

Finally, there is the question of the treatment of innocent third parties. Public policy seeks to eliminate the present effects of past discrimination. But this may mean that the costs of eliminating discriminatory effects falls on parties who bear no responsibility for the discrimination. The preferential hiring of minorities could result in the layoffs of white employees, for example. This conflict of interest is inherent in any system of preferential treatment. In practice, the courts have made judgments about the degree of harm to third parties from alternative forms of affirmative action. They have not permitted plans that required the layoffs of third parties in order to fill hiring goals.[51] However, they have supported preferential hiring plans that do not require layoffs, even though the preference forecloses some opportunities to individuals who are not responsible for past discrimination (see Example 7.3).

## Effectiveness of Federal Antidiscrimination Programs

A question of obvious interest is just how effective the two federal anti-discrimination programs have been in increasing the relative earnings of minorities and women. The question is not easy to answer, however, because we must make some guesses as to what earnings differentials *would have been* in the absence of these programs. As we have seen, the ratio of black to white incomes has risen since 1960 (see Table 7.1), especially in the mid-1970s. Has this rise in the ratio been a result of government efforts, or have other forces been working to accomplish this result? Three other forces are commonly cited. First, an improvement in the *educational attainment* of black workers relative to whites during this period is thought to have played an important role in raising the ratio of black to white incomes.[52] Second, the evidence that

---

[51] *Wygant* v. *Jackson Board of Education,* U.S. (1986)

[52] Orley Ashenfelter, "Changes in Labor Market Discrimination Over Time," *Journal of Human Resources* 5 (Fall 1970): 403–30; Richard Freeman, "Black Economic Progress After 1964: Who Has Gained and Why?" in *Studies in Labor Markets,* ed. Sherwin Rosen (Chicago: University of Chicago Press, 1981); and Barry R. Chiswick and June A. O'Neill (eds.), *Human Resources and Income Distribution: Issues and Policies* (New York: W. W. Norton, 1977): 20–21.

**EXAMPLE**   **7.3**

## Is Affirmative Action Consistent with Equal Employment Opportunity?

In December 1978, the County Transit District of Santa Clara County, California adopted an affirmative-action plan in which the agency was authorized to consider the gender of a qualified applicant as one factor in making promotions to job classifications in which women had been traditionally underrepresented. At that time, none of the 238 skilled craft positions in the Transit District was held by a woman. The long-term goal of the plan was to attain a work-force composition representative of the area labor force, but there was no specific timetable for attaining the goal, and the plan did *not* establish a specific number (quota) of positions for minorities or women.

A year later, the Transit District announced a vacancy for road dispatcher, and twelve county employees applied for the position. Nine were found to be qualified. Seven of the qualified applicants became eligible by scoring above 70 in an interview. A man by the name of Johnson was tied for second with a score of 75, while a woman named Joyce ranked third with a score of 73. After a second interview, three Transit District supervisors recommended Johnson for the promotion, but the agency's affirmative-action officer noted the absence of women in the craft positions. The Director of the Transit District, who was authorized to choose any of the seven eligible applicants, selected Joyce for the promotion. Johnson filed a suit alleging that the Transit District had violated Title VII by denying him a promotion because of his gender. In a 6–3 ruling, the Supreme Court upheld the selection of Joyce and the validity of the Transit District's affirmative-action plan. The decision is of interest because it clarifies some of the factors determining the legality of affirmative-action plans. The first question raised by the court is whether there is a need for remedial action. In this case it concluded that "consideration of the sex of applicants was justified by the existence of a 'manifest imbalance' that reflected underrepresentation of women in 'traditionally segregated job categories'."

Second, the court stressed the flexibility of the plan and the fact that the goals could not be construed as rigid "quotas." The court indicated that the plan would have been suspect if it authorized "blind hiring" on the basis of work-force imbalances and failed to take distinctions in qualifications into account. The fact that gender was one of several criteria rather than the only criterion for promotion was important to the court.

Third, the court noted that the plan did not create an absolute barrier to the advancement of male employees of the Transit District. The majority of the court stressed the fact that the plan did not reserve any positions for women; opportunity was preserved for both sexes.

The Supreme Court, as well as public opinion, remains sharply divided over the issue of affirmative action. One signal of the division is the claim by the minority dissent that this decision "completes the process of converting [Title VII] from a guarantee that race or sex will *not* be the basis for employment determinations, to a guarantee that it often *will*."

SOURCE:   *Johnson v. Transportation Agency, Santa Clara County,* (1987)

the *quality* of schooling received by blacks improved from 1960 to 1970 more than it did for whites lends further impetus to the increase in relative earnings.[53] Finally, blacks have historically experienced relative gains in periods of low unemployment and suffered disproportionately in periods of economic distress. The late 1960s were a period of very full employment, which could have helped increase the black/white earnings ratio from 1960 to 1970. However, general business conditions in the 1970s and 1980s were not as good as in the late 1960s, so recent improvements are unlikely to be solely the result of overall business conditions.[54] Two types of studies have attempted to distinguish the effects of the government programs from the other factors that affect relative earnings: time-series studies and analyses of federal contractors.

**Time-Series Studies.** There seems to have been a significant upturn in the black/white earnings ratio after the EEOC was created in 1964—an upturn that was independent of both the effects of *educational* gains by blacks and changes in the *unemployment rate*.[55] It also appears, however, that the labor-force participation rate of blacks fell relative to whites after 1964, a year in which many income-maintenance programs began to become more generous.[56] If, as seems likely, the blacks with the lowest wages were the ones who left the labor market, their exit would increase the average wage paid to blacks and give the *appearance* of improvement. Some—probably less than half—of the post-1964 improvement is due to this latter factor.[57] Thus, there seems to be at least *some* evidence that post-1964 government efforts to lessen discrimination helped blacks.

**Analysis of Federal Contractors.** If the contract-compliance program administered by OFCCP is effective, we should observe that the economic status of blacks improves faster among federal contractors than noncontractors. Several studies have tested this hypothesis, and some have even distinguished whether or not the contractors involved have been subjected to a compliance review by the government (the government does not have the

[53] Finis Welch, ''Black-White Differences in Returns to Schooling,'' *American Economic Review* 63 (December 1973): 893–907.

[54] For a recent analysis, see James P. Smith and Finis R. Welch, *Closing the Gap: Forty Years of Economic Progress for Blacks* (Santa Monica, CA: Rand Corporation, 1986).

[55] See R. Freeman, ''Changes in the Labor Market for Black Americans,'' *Brookings Papers on Economic Activity* (1973–1): 67–132, and (a study which updates Freeman) Richard Butler and James Heckman, ''The Goverment's Impact on the Labor Market Status of Black Americans: A Critical Review,'' *Equal Rights and Industrial Relations* (Madision, WI: Industrial Relations Research Association, 1977): 235–80.

[56] Butler and Heckman, ''The Government's Impact on the Labor Market Status of Black Americans.''

[57] Charles Brown, ''The Federal Attack on Labor Market Discrimination: The Mouse That Roared?'' in *Research in Labor Economics,* vol. 5, ed. Ronald G. Ehrenberg (Greenwich, CT: JAI Press, 1982): 32–68. Evidence that Title VII lawsuits have played a significant role in increasing black employment is found in Jonathan S. Leonard, ''Antidiscrimination or Reverse Discrimination: The Impact of Changing Demographics, Title VII, and Affirmative Action on Productivity,'' *Journal of Human Resources* 19 (Spring 1984): 145–74.

resources to inspect the affirmative-action plans of *all* its contractors). The results suggest that blacks and other minorities have made faster gains in contractor firms.[58]

One problem in assessing the *overall* effects of OFCCP, however, is that because the contract-compliance program relates only to *some* employers (contractors), the gains in (say) black employment among these firms may come at the expense of losses among noncontractors. Eligible blacks may just be bid away from noncontractors, although it should be pointed out that anyone successfully bid away from a former employer must have experienced an expected gain in utility. Perhaps more serious is the problem that becoming or remaining a federal contractor is a voluntary decision. Firms that perceive the costs of affirmative action to be high may simply choose not to be contractors. The contract-compliance program may end up concentrating its efforts on the firms within which discrimination is a relatively small problem.

A final reason to temper optimism about the government's efforts to end discrimination is that it appears that the gains of white women have not matched those of blacks among contractors.[59] The growth of white female employment relative to total employment was slower among federal contractors than among noncontractors in the early 1970s, before women were a focus of the contract-compliance program; but between 1974 and 1980, the growth of white female employment among contractors was significantly greater (although smaller than the gains for blacks). Why the gains among white women are smaller has not yet been convincingly explained; however, there is other evidence that women have been helped by the contract-compliance program. One study, for example, looked at *quit rates,* rather than wages or employment ratios, as an index of perceived well-being. What it found (for 1978–79) was that, in industries in which federal contracts comprised a larger fraction of total sales and the OFCCP had initiated more compliance reviews, women had lower quit rates than would be expected, given their wages and other factors affecting quits.[60] The inference is that women in these industries perceived themselves to be better off than women elsewhere.

In summary, it appears that some of the gains registered by blacks since 1964 may be due to efforts by the EEOC and OFCCP, but the efforts of these programs on women appear mixed. Effects on other minorities have not been extensively studied.

---

[58] For a comprehensive review of these studies, see Jonathan Leonard, "The Effectiveness of Equal Employment Law and Affirmative Action Regulation," in *Research in Labor Economics,* vol. 8, part B, ed. Ronald G. Ehrenberg (Greenwich, CT.: JAI Press, 1986).

[59] Leonard, "The Effectiveness of Equal Employment Law and Affirmative Action Regulation."

[60] Paul Osterman, "Affirmative Action and Opportunity: A Study of Female Quit Rates," *The Review of Economics and Statistics* 64 (November 1982): 604–12. Corroborating evidence is found in Andrea Beller, "The Impact of Equal Opportunity Policy on Sex Differentials In Earnings and Occupations," *American Economic Review Papers and Proceedings* 72 (May 1982):171–75.

# REVIEW QUESTIONS

1. Assume that women live longer than men, on the average. Suppose an employer hires men and women, pays them the same wage for the same job, and contributes an equal amount per person toward a pension. However, the promised monthly pension after retirement is smaller for women than for men because the pension funds for them have to last longer. According to the *Manhart* decision by the Supreme Court, the above employer would be guilty of discrimination because of the unequal monthly pension benefits after retirement.

   a. Comment on the Court's implicit definition of discrimination. Is it consistent with the definition normally used by economists? Why or why not?

   b. Analyze the economic effects of this decision on men and women.

2. Assume there is a central city school district in which the student population is predominantly black. Surrounding the central city are predominantly white suburban school districts. Together, the central city and suburban school districts can be thought of as a local labor market for teachers. Other things being equal, black teachers in this labor market are equally willing to work in central city and suburban schools, but white teachers prefer suburban schools and are reluctant to accept jobs in the central city. There are too few black teachers to completely staff central city schools, and teachers generally have choices in the jobs they can accept. If federal law requires equal salaries for teachers of all races *within* a given school district but allows salaries to vary across school districts, will black teachers earn more, less, or the same salary as they would if white teachers were not prejudiced against black students? (Note: The prejudice of white teachers extends only to students, not to black teachers as coworkers. Note also: The chain of reasoning required in this answer should be made explicit in your answer.)

3. Suppose government antidiscrimination laws require employers to disregard marital status and sex in screening and hiring workers.

   a. Disregarding the employers who are engaged in discrimination, which employers will be most affected by this ruling?

   b. What alternatives do these employers have in coping with the problems created by this decision?

   c. What are the likely consequences of each alternative on employment levels and job stability among these employers?

4. Suppose the government has two methods of awarding contracts to firms. One is competitive, with the award going to the lowest bidder (who cannot then charge more than his or her bid). The other is noncompetitive, with the award going to a selected contractor who is reimbursed for actual costs incurred plus a certain percentage for profits. Suppose, too, that government contractors must hire a certain quota of minorities, many of whom require general training to be fully productive. Suppose also that federal legislation prevents the employer from shifting the costs of this general training to the minority employees. If you were an already-trained minority worker, which method of contract award would you prefer? Why?

5. The Defense Department (DOD) is expanding its purchases of equipment from the private sector, and of course the firms with which it contracts must adhere to a policy of affirmative action (the hiring of minorities and women in increased proportions in the better jobs, and equal pay for equal work). The current administration is convinced that minorities and women in the firms with which DOD will now contract are subject to discrimination, but it is not sure whether the *source* of the discrimination is fellow *employees* or *customers*. It is interested in knowing how the enforcement of affirmative-action regulations will affect the *unit-labor costs* (the labor costs per unit of output) of the firms with which it deals. Will the *source* of discrimination make a difference to the administration's estimates of what happens to costs? (Answer this question assuming the only possible sources of discrimination are *employees* or *customers*. Also assume in answering the question that white males earn more than

others of comparable quality, that discrimination may take place by confining women and minorities to low-wage jobs, and that prior efforts to eradicate discrimination in the industries with which DOD is dealing were entirely unsuccessful. Finally, assume that DOD will become the sole customer of the firms with which it contracts.) Analyze the effects and consequences of the two types of discrimination, and then analyze what will happen to unit labor costs when DOD steps into the picture.

6. You are involved in an investigation of charges that a large university in a small town is discriminating against female employees. You find that the salaries for professors in the nearly all-female School of Social Work are 20 percent below average salaries paid to those of comparable rank elsewhere in the university. Is this university exhibiting behavior associated with *employer* discrimination?

# SELECTED READINGS

Dennis J. Aigner and Glen G. Cain, "Statistical Theories of Discrimination in Labor Markets," *Industrial and Labor Relations Review* 30 (January 1977): 175-87.

Gary Becker, *The Economics of Discrimination.* 2d ed. (Chicago: University of Chicago Press, 1971).

George Borjas and Marta Tienda (eds.), *Hispanics in the U.S. Economy* (New York: Academic Press, 1985).

Charles Brown, "The Federal Attack on Labor Market Discrimination: The Mouse That Roared?" in *Research in Labor Economics,* vol. 5, ed. Ronald Ehrenberg (Greenwich, CT: JAI Press, 1982): 33-68.

Glen G. Cain, "The Challenge of Segmented Labor Market Theories to Orthodox Theory: A Survey," *Journal of Economic Literature* 14 (December 1976): 1215-57.

Glen G. Cain, "The Economic Analysis of Labor Market Discrimination: A Survey," in eds. O. Ashenfelter and R. Layard *Handbook of Labor Economics,* vol. 1.

Ronald Ehrenberg and Robert Smith, "Economic and Statistical Analysis of Discrimination in Hiring," *Proceedings of the Thirty-Sixth Annual Meeting of the Industrial Relations Research Association* (Madison, WI: Industrial Relations Research Association, 1984).

Richard Freeman, "Black Economic Progress After 1964: Who Has Gained and Why?" in *Studies in Labor Markets,* ed. Sherwin Rosen (Chicago: University of Chicago Press, 1981): 247-94.

Jonathan Leonard, "The Effectiveness of Equal Employment Law and Affirmative Action Regulation." In *Research in Labor Economics,* vol. 8, part B, ed. Ronald Ehrenberg (Greenwich, CT: JAI Press, 1986).

Janice F. Madden, *The Economics of Sex Discrimination* (Lexington, MA: Lexington Books, 1973).

Ray Marshall, "The Economics of Racial Discrimination: A Survey," *Journal of Economic Literature* 12 (September 1974): 849-71.

Michael Reich, "The Economics of Racism," in *Problems in Political Economy: An Urban Perspective,* ed. David M. Gordon (Lexington, MA: D. C. Heath and Co., 1971): 107-13.

# APPENDIX 7A

## Estimating "Comparable Worth" Earnings Gaps: An Application of Regression Analysis

Although many economists have difficulty with the notion that the "worth" of a job can be established independently of market factors, formal job-evaluation methods have existed for a long time. The state of Minnesota is one that has begun to implement "comparable worth" pay adjustments for its employees based on such an evaluation method. The purpose of this appendix is to give the reader an intuitive feel for how one might use data from job evaluations to estimate whether discriminatory wage differentials exist.[1]

Minnesota, in conjunction with Hay Associates, a prominent national compensation consulting company, began an evaluation of state government jobs in 1979. Initially evaluated were 188 positions in which at least 10 workers were employed and which could be classified as either *male* (at least 70-percent male incumbents) or *female* (at least 70-percent female incumbents) positions. Each position was evaluated by trained job evaluators and awarded a specified number of *Hay Points* for each of four job characteristics or factors: required know-how, problem solving, accountability, and working conditions. The scores for each factor were then added to obtain a total Hay Point, or job-evaluation, score for each job. These scores varied across the 188 job titles, from below 100 to over 800 points.

Given these objective job-evaluation scores, the next step is to ask what the relationship is between the salary ($S_i$) each male job pays and its total

---

[1] For a more complete discussion of the Minnesota job-evaluation and comparable-worth study, see *Pay Equality and Public Employment* (St. Paul, MN: Council on the Economic Status of Women, March 1982).

**Figure 7A.1**   Estimated Male "Comparable Worth" Salary Equation

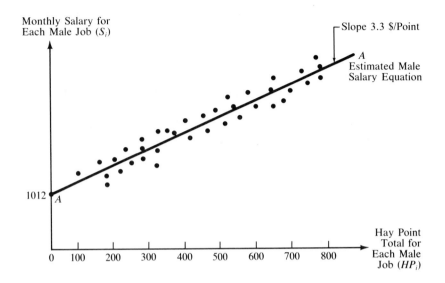

Hay Point ($HP_i$) score. Each dot in Figure 7A.1 represents a male job, and this figure plots the monthly salary for each job against its total Hay Point score. On average, it is clear that jobs with higher scores receive higher pay.

Although these points obviously do not all lie on a single straight line, it is natural to ask what straight line fits the data best. An infinite number of lines can be drawn through these points, and some precise criterion must be used to decide which line fits best. The procedure typically used by statisticians and economists is to choose that line for which the sum (across data points) of the squared vertical distances between the line and the individual data points is minimized. The line estimated from the data using this method—the *method of least squares*—has a number of desirable statistical properties.[2]

Application of this method to data for the *male* occupations contained in the Minnesota data yielded the following estimated line[3]:

² These include that, on average, you get the correct answer; the estimates are the most precise possible among a certain class of estimators; and the sum of the positive and negative vertical deviations of the data points from the estimated line will be zero (that is, on average, you get the correct prediction). For a more formal treatment of the method of least squares, see any statistics or econometrics text. A good introduction for the reader with no statistical background is David Sjoquist, Larry Schroeder, and Paula Stephan, *Interpreting Linear Regression Analysis: A Heuristic Approach* (Morristown, NJ: General Learning Press, 1974).

³ These estimates are obtained in Ronald G. Ehrenberg and Robert S. Smith, "Comparable Worth in the Public Sector," in *Public Compensation,* ed. David Wise (Chicago: University of Chicago Press, 1987).

$$S_i = 1012 + 3.3\, HP_i \tag{7A.1}$$

So, for example, if male job $i$ were rated at 200 Hay Points, we would predict that the monthly salary associated with job $i$ would be $1012 + (3.3)(200)$, or $1672. This estimated male salary equation is drawn in Figure 7A.1 as line $AA$.

   Now, if the value of a job could be determined solely by reference to its job evaluation score, one would expect that, in the absence of wage discrimination against women, male and female jobs rated equal in terms of total Hay Point scores would pay equal salaries (at least on the average). Put another way, the same salary equation used to predict salaries of male jobs could be used to provide predictions of salaries for female jobs, and any inaccuracies in the prediction would be completely random. Hence, a test of whether female jobs are discriminated against is to see if the salaries they pay are systematically less than the salaries one would predict they would pay, given their Hay Point scores and the salary equation for male jobs.

   Figure 7A.2 illustrates how this is done. Here each dot represents a salary/Hay Point combination for a female job. Superimposed on this scatter of points is the estimated male job salary equation, $AA$, from Figure 7A.1. The vast majority of the data points in Figure 7A.2 lie below the male salary line, suggesting that female jobs tend to be underpaid relative to male jobs with the same number of Hay Points. For example, the female job that is rated at 300 Hay Points (point $a$) is paid a salary of $S_{300}^F$. However, according to the estimated male salary line, if that job were a male job it would pay $S_{300}^M$. The

**Figure 7A.2**   Using the Estimated Male "Comparable Worth" Salary Equations to Estimate the Extent of Underpayment of Female Jobs

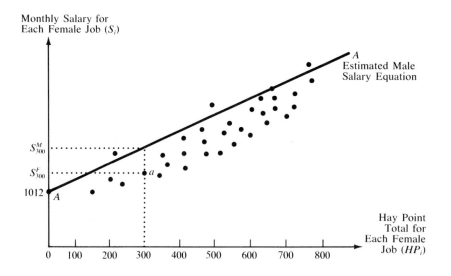

difference in percentage terms between $S_{300}^M$ and $S_{300}^F$ is an estimate of the "comparable worth" earnings gap—the extent of underpayment—for the female job. Indeed, calculations suggest that the average (across all the female occupations) "comparable worth" earnings gap in the Minnesota data was over 16 percent.[4]

This brief presentation has glossed over a number of complications that must be addressed before such estimates can be considered estimates of wage discrimination against female jobs.[5] These include issues relating to the reliability and/or potential sex bias in the evaluation methods, whether salaries and Hay Point scores may be related in a nonlinear fashion, whether the *composition* of any given total Hay Point score (across the four sets of job characteristics) affects salaries, and whether variables other than the job evaluation scores can legitimately affect salaries. Nonetheless, it should give the reader a sense of how "comparable-worth wage gap" estimates are computed.

---

[4] See Ehrenberg and Smith, "Comparable Worth in the Public Sector." Analogous estimates for four other states are presented there and in Elaine Sorensen, "Implementing Comparable Worth: A Survey of Recent Job Evaluation Studies," *American Economic Review Papers and Proceedings* 76 (May 1986): 364–67.

[5] For a more complete discussion of these issues, see Ehrenberg and Smith, "Comparable Worth in the Public Sector," and Mark Killingsworth, "Economic Analysis of Comparable Worth and Its Consequences," *Proceedings of the Thirty-Seventh Annual Meeting of the Industrial Relations Research Association* (Madison, WI: IRRA, 1985): 183–89.

# PART 4

## Firm Compensation Policy

**8** Economic Issues in Compensation

**9** Company Compensation Policies

# CHAPTER 8

## Economic Issues in Compensation

In Chapter 5 we examined factors influencing the decision to work for pay and the desired hours of work. Chapter 6 analyzed the day-to-day and human capital aspects of occupational choice. We now turn to a discussion of yet another set of factors influencing job choice and work effort decisions: employer compensation policies both at one point in time and over several periods of time. This chapter analyzes the goals companies hope to achieve with their compensation systems, while the next chapter presents detailed information on important aspects of compensation policies as they are carried out today.

What ultimately matters to workers in making labor supply decisions is the total compensation they receive per unit of time worked. This total compensation paid to employees consists of far more than hourly, weekly, or monthly pay for time worked. There are numerous *fringe benefits,* offered in varying combinations by employers, that have value to employees but are not paid to them as cash. Employers can also offer, explicitly or implicitly, different bases for computing or timing pay over one's career. These various forms of compensation affect employee behavior and labor market outcomes in interesting ways.

We begin this chapter by describing and analyzing the consequences of fringe benefits. One particular policy application is then discussed in some detail: namely, the issue of pension fund regulation by the federal government. In this chapter we also discuss various methods of compensation that provide strong incentives for employees to maximize their productivity and remain attached to a firm for long periods of time. These methods include paying above market-clearing compensation levels, offering compensation profiles that increase with experience more rapidly than does workers' productivity, and relating compensation directly to some measure of individual or group output rather than solely to time worked. As we shall see, several of these methods may arise as a natural consequence of internal labor markets. Moreover, one of these methods used to stimulate worker productivity— profit or revenue sharing—has some fascinating and potentially important implications for stabilizing the demand for labor over a business cycle; these implications are analyzed in Chapter 17.

## The Economics of Fringe Benefits

As noted in Chapter 4, the proportion of total compensation coming in the form of cash payments to workers has fallen over time as the use of fringe benefits has risen. According to the data presented in Table 8.1, the most common fringe benefits are paid vacations, medical insurance, unpaid maternity leaves, pensions, life insurance, and paid sick leave. Less common, but still available to large numbers of workers, are company-paid education or training; discounted meals, merchandise, or work clothing; dental care, eye care, or legal benefits; stock options or savings plans; and paid maternity leave. In addition to these private fringes, there are also publicly mandated

**Table 8.1**  Fringe Benefits Available to Workers

| Fringe Benefits | Percentage of Workers Reporting the Availability of the Benefit in 1977* |
|---|---|
| Paid vacation | 80.8 |
| Medical, surgical, or hospital insurance that covers any illness or injury that might occur *off* the job | 78.1 |
| Maternity leave with full re-employment rights | 74.5 |
| Retirement program | 67.4 |
| Life insurance that would cover a death occurring for reasons *not* connected with job | 64.1 |
| Sick leave and full pay | 62.8 |
| Training (or education) program to improve skills | 49.0 |
| Thrift or savings plan | 39.8 |
| Free or discounted merchandise | 34.3 |
| Dental benefits | 29.4 |
| Maternity leave with pay | 29.4 |
| Eyeglass or eye-care benefits | 21.8 |
| Profit sharing | 19.8 |
| Stock options | 17.6 |
| Work-clothing allowance | 16.8 |
| Free or discounted meals | 16.3 |
| Legal aid or services | 10.3 |
| Day-care facilities | 2.2 |

* Includes only wage and salaried workers.

SOURCE: From *The 1977 Quality of Employment Survey* by Robert P. Quinn and Graham L. Staines. Copyright © 1979 by The University of Michigan. Reprinted by permission of the Institute for Social Research of The University of Michigan.

**Table 8.2**    Employee Compensation for Private, Nonagricultural
Workers, 1977 (percent)

| | Percentage of Employer's Total Compensation Expenditures | |
|---|---|---|
| | Office Workers | Nonoffice Workers |
| Pay for working time | 75.8 | 77.5 |
| Pay for leave time (vacations, holidays, sick leave, personal days) | 7.9 | 6.2 |
| Private pension plans | 4.8 | 3.5 |
| Life, accident, and health insurance | 3.6 | 4.3 |
| Government-required contributions to Social Security, workers' compensation, and unemployment insurance | 5.6 | 7.9 |
| Other | 2.3 | 0.6 |
| Total compensation | 100.0 | 100.0 |

Note:  The data are for workers in plants with 20 or more employees.
SOURCE:  U.S. Department of Labor, Bureau of Labor Statistics, *Handbook of Labor Statistics 1980,* Bulletin 2070 (Washington, DC: U.S. Government Printing Office, 1980). These data are no longer collected by the BLS.

benefits that employers must fund, at least in part: Social Security, workers' compensation, and unemployment insurance.

Table 8.2, which compares office and nonoffice employees of all but the smallest firms in the private sector, illustrates another interesting fact: fringe benefits as a percentage of compensation are slightly, but not markedly, higher for office than nonoffice workers. Further, government-required fringes and pay for nonworking time comprise the two largest components of the fringe package in both cases. What accounts for the growth and size of fringe benefits? What are the consequences of this growth and size? To answer these questions, we must examine both the employee and employer sides of the market.

## Employee Preferences

The distinguishing feature of all fringe benefits is that they compensate workers in a form *other* than currently spendable cash. In general, there are two broad categories of such benefits. First and largest are *payments in kind,* that is, compensation in the form of some commodity. As we have seen, it is very common for employers to partly or completely pay for insurance policies of one kind or another on behalf of their employees. Slightly less obvious as payments in kind are paid vacations and holidays. A woman earning $15,000 per year for 2000 hours of work can have her hourly wage increased from $7.50 to $8.00 by either a straightforward increase in current money payments or a reduction in her working hours to 1875 with no reduction in yearly earnings. If her raise comes in the form of an increase in money payments, she will receive $1000 (before taxes) more in yearly income that she can use to buy a variety of things (she could even buy time off by giving money back to her employer in exchange for days off). If she receives her raise in the form of paid vacation time, however, she is in fact being paid in the form of a commodity: leisure time. The second general type of fringe benefit is *deferred compensation,* compensation that is earned now but will be paid in the form of money later on. Pension benefits make up the largest proportion of these fringes.

**Payments in Kind.**  It is a well-established tenet of economic theory that, *other things equal,* people would rather receive $X in cash than a commodity that costs $X. The reason is simple. With $X in cash the person can choose to buy the particular commodity or choose instead to buy a variety of other things. Cash is thus the form of payment that gives the recipient the most discretion and options in maximizing utility. In-kind payments are inherently more restrictive, and while they generate utility, they do not ordinarily generate as much as cash payments of equal monetary value. As might be suspected, however, "other things" are not equal. Specifically, in-kind payments offer employees a sizable tax advantage because, for the most part, they are not taxable under current income-tax regulations. The failure to tax important in-kind payments is a factor that tends to offset their restrictive nature in affecting employee demands for in-kind payments. A worker may prefer $1000 in cash to $1000 in some in-kind payment; but if his or her income- and payroll-tax rates total 25 percent, the comparison is really between, for example, $750 in cash and $1000 in the in-kind benefit.[1]

**Deferred Compensation.**  Like payments in kind, deferred-compensation schemes enjoy a tax advantage over current cash payments. With deferred payments the tax advantage is that the compensation is not taxed until it is received by the worker. In the case of pensions, for example, employers contribute currently to a pension fund, but employees do not obtain access to this fund until they retire. Neither the pension fund *contributions* made on behalf of employees by employers nor the *interest* that compounds when these funds are invested is subject to the personal income tax. Only when the retirement benefits are received does the ex-worker pay taxes, but because of lower income and special tax advantages given the elderly, the tax rates actually paid are relatively low. Because of the above-noted tax advantages accorded to pension fund contributions, employees who want to save for retirement have incentives to do so through a pension fund, rather than receiving cash payments and saving from that (although workers whose employers do not offer a pension plan can obtain the same tax advantages by establishing their own Individual Retirement Accounts). Saving through a

---

[1]  This tax advantage has recently declined as Congress has lowered marginal tax rates on individuals. For example, the maximum federal tax bracket in 1986 was 50 percent, while for most taxpayers the maximum rate was 28 percent in 1988. On the other hand, tax reform left fringe benefits untaxed, so this incentive to substitute benefits in kind for cash, while weaker, still exists. See Charles E. McClure and George R. Zodrow, "Treasury I and the Tax Reform Act of 1986: The Economics and Politics of Tax Reform," *Journal of Economic Perspectives* 1 (Summer 1987): 37–58.

pension fund defers the taxation of part of one's compensation (the pension fund contributions) until old age and permits funds for retirement to accumulate on a tax-free basis. What one *loses* with saving through a pension fund is the ability to currently control one's assets: by putting money into a pension fund, one is forgoing the ability to use that money now for routine or emergency needs.

Again, then, two opposing forces are at work on the demand for fringe benefits by employees. With both kinds of benefits there is a loss of discretion in spending one's total compensation, which tends to render fringes inferior to cash payments in generating utility. However, the special tax advantages accorded to both kinds of benefits as compared with cash payments tend to increase the demand for fringes.[2]

Before turning to a discussion of employer preferences regarding fringe benefits, it is interesting to note that the presence of labor unions appears to increase the share of total compensation devoted to fringe benefits.[3] As we mention when discussing this issue in Chapter 16, one possible reason for this effect is that unions may be more effective than employers at identifying the desire for a given fringe benefit among workers. It may also be that by raising wages, unions place their members in higher tax brackets and make it more likely that they will become permanently attached to the firm; both of these factors should increase the desirability of fringe benefits. Moreover, if union leaders are politically more responsive to the preferences of older, longer-term members than younger, more mobile workers, the preferences of the former group will tend to dominate in the negotiating process.[4] Thus, while tax advantages may be the driving force behind the relatively recently growth of fringe benefits, unions also appear to have facilitated this growth.

## Employer Preferences

Suppose employers are totally indifferent about whether to spend $X on wages or $X on fringes. Both expenditures are of equal sums of money and are equally deductible as a business expense. If so, the composition of total compensation does not matter to them; only the *level* of compensation is of concern. If employees want an insurance policy costing $300, employers will provide it and reduce wages by $300. There are some reasons to expect that firms might offer fringe benefits to their employees on something other than the dollar-for-dollar basis assumed above, however. For one, by increasing compensation in the form of fringes rather than wages, employers can often

---

[2]  Stephen Woodbury, "Substitution Between Wage and Nonwage Benefits," *American Economic Review* 73(March 1983): 166–82, shows that wages and fringe benefits (especially pensions) are viewed by workers as very good substitutes, and that tax rate increases play a large role in explaining the growth of fringe benefits.

[3]  Richard B. Freeman, "The Effect of Unionism on Fringe Benefits," *Industrial and Labor Relations Review* 34(July 1981): 489–509.

[4]  For evidence on this issue, see Stanley M. Nealey, "Pay and Benefit Preference," *Industrial Relations* 3(October 1963): 17–28. Other evidence that the preferences of younger and older workers diverge can be found in Jonathan Eaton and Harvey Rosen, "Agency, Delayed Compensation and the Structure of Executive Remuneration," *Journal of Finance* 38(December 1983): 1489–1505.

avoid taxes and required insurance payments that are levied as a fraction of payroll. Social Security taxes and workers' compensation premiums are examples of costs that generally increase with salaries and wages but not with fringe benefits, thus making it more costly for an employer to increase compensation by increasing salaries than by increasing benefits.[5]

There are also more subtle factors that might cause firms to offer fringes to their employees on something other than a dollar-for-dollar basis. Some fringe benefits allow firms to attract a certain kind of worker in situations in which the use of wage rates would be of questionable legal validity. For example, suppose a firm prefers to hire mature adults, preferably those with children, in the hopes of acquiring a stable, dependable work force. An employer attempting to attract these people by offering them higher wages than single, younger, or much older adults would risk charges of discrimination. Instead, the firm can accomplish the same effect by offering its employees fringe benefits that are of much more value to workers with families than to others. For example, offering *family* coverage under a health insurance plan has the effect of compensating those with families more than others, because single or childless people cannot really take advantage of the full benefit. Offering dental insurance covering orthodontia or tuition assistance for children who attend college accomplishes similar purposes. Thus, at times fringe benefits allow the firm to give preferential treatment to a group it wants to attract without running afoul of discrimination laws.

The preferential treatment given to some groups of workers, however, has become of increasing concern to employees as fringes have grown in importance. Many families, for example, have dual earners and have no need of two family medical insurance policies. In a move to take into account employee dissatisfaction with biases in fringe benefits, some 22 percent of the nation's largest firms have adopted *cafeteria plans* that allow workers to elect their own fringe benefits up to some dollar limit.[6] Instead of receiving a redundant medical insurance policy, for example, a worker already covered by a spouse's insurance policy could elect to receive a longer paid vacation. One firm implementing such a plan found that only 10 percent of its employees elected to receive the same benefits offered by its old program.[7]

Another subtle reason why a firm may prefer to put an extra dollar of compensation into fringe benefits rather than wages is found whenever the government regulates profits or controls wages. Regulated monopolies or governmental bodies, for example, fearing that the granting of large wage increases would call forth an investigation or outrage public opinon, could

---

[5]  The argument that the presence of Social Security taxes levied on the employer increases the costs of granting salary increases holds only for workers who earn less than the maximum taxable earnings base, which in 1988 was 45,000. Earnings beyond 45,000 in 1988 were not subject to the Social Security tax.

[6]  William C. Banks, "The Way We'll Work: Shorter Hours, Bigger Bonuses," *Money* 14 (November 1985): 158.

[7]  "Making Job Benefits Flexible," *The New York Times*, March 13, 1981, pp. D1, D3, and Hay/Huggins *Bulletin* (June 1984).

hide an increase in compensation by granting increases in fringe benefits that are difficult to estimate the cost of: a nicer work environment, shortened days in the summer, time off for religious observances, top-quality food in the workplace cafeteria for bargain prices, low-cost loans to employees for buying a home, and so forth.[8] Similar behavior will occur among firms that are having trouble recruiting employees during a period when the government is attempting to control wages to fight inflation. Wages are easy to observe and measure. Many fringe benefits are very difficult to observe and quantify, and can thus be used to increase compensation without violating wage controls.[9] Examples of fringes that are difficult for wage control boards to monitor are increased rest times on the job, larger crew sizes in dangerous activities, and better recreational facilities for employees.

As noted earlier in Chapter 5, however, some fringe benefits could conceivably increase absenteeism, thus reducing the firm's profitability. Life insurance, health insurance, and pensions, for example, are all awarded to current employees regardless of their actual hours of work during the year (assuming they work enough to keep their jobs). If an increase in compensation comes in the form of increasing one of these benefits, workers' *incomes* are increased in the sense that they need to save less for ''rainy days'' and are thus freer to spend their cash income. However, this increase in income is accomplished without an increase in the price of leisure, because the hourly wage has not risen. Recall from Chapter 5 that an increase in income with no change in the price of leisure causes people to want to work less. In this case workers will not quit their jobs, but they may be absent from work more often. (The connection between absenteeism and a fringe benefit is even more obvious in the case of paid sick leave.[10]) Aside from the possibility of contributing to absenteeism, some fringe benefits compress the differentials in compensation between skilled and unskilled workers, thereby reducing the incentives of employees to obtain training for skilled positions.[11] Fringes such as medical insurance and free or discounted merchandise are of equal value to all workers with families of similar size, no matter how much they earn. Because the value of these benefits represents a larger percentage of a low-

---

[8] For further arguments along this line, see Armen Alchian and Reuben Kessel, ''Competition, Monopoly, and the Pursuit of Money,'' *Aspects of Labor Economics,* H. G. Lewis (ed.) (Princeton, NJ: Princeton University Press, 1962).

[9] For a brief discussion of the difficulties inherent in controlling fringe benefits, see John Dunlop, ''Wage and Price Controls As Seen by a Controller,'' *Proceedings of the Industrial Relations Research Association* (Madison, WI: Industrial Relations Research Association, 1975): 457–63.

[10] Although there has not been much empirical work on this issue, a study of absenteeism in the paper and box industry found that it was positively related to pensions and negatively related to wage rates. See Steven G. Allen, ''Compensation, Safety, and Absenteeism: Evidence from the Paper Industry,'' *Industrial and Labor Relations Review* 34(January 1981): 207–18. See also his ''An Empirical Model of Work Attendance,'' *The Review of Economics and Statistics* 63(February 1981): 77–87. For evidence on teacher absenteeism, see Donald R. Winkler, ''The Effects of Sick-Leave Policy on Teacher Absenteeism,'' *Industrial and Labor Relations Review* 33 (January 1980): 232–40.

[11] See Chapter 6 for the complete argument on how wage differentials affect the incentives of workers to acquire human capital.

wage worker's compensation, such benefits tend to compress earnings differentials between skilled and unskilled workers.

To summarize, employees may find that a dollar spent on fringes has the same effect on profits as a dollar spent on wages; or, they may find that a dollar spent on fringes costs either more or less than a dollar nominally spent on wages.[12]

## The Joint Determination of Wages and Fringes

If product markets are competitive, companies will be able to earn a "normal" (competitive) profit on their operations in the long run. If, for example, profits in one industry were higher as a percent of invested capital than in other industries, then capital would move to the high-profit industry. The supply of the industry's product would increase, which would serve to reduce both prices and the rate of return on new capital investment. The reverse applies to an industry with a below-normal profit rate.

To survive, companies must operate successfully in both the product and labor markets. Because of product market competition, the employers hiring from a given labor market can be assumed to be earning normal profits, and there will be a level of total compensation (wages plus fringes) that corresponds to this level of profits. Companies paying above this level will not be making normal profits and will go out of business, while companies paying below this level will not be able to attract labor (workers will take jobs with their competitors, who are pressured to pay at prevailing levels). We therefore predict that employers, in effect, will offer workers a trade-off between wages and fringe benefits, just as there is a trade-off between pay and job safety (see Chapter 6). Economic theory thus implies that workers pay for their fringe benefits through lower wages than they would otherwise receive. Employees who attach relatively great importance to the availability of current spendable cash will choose to accept offers in which total compensation comes largely in the form of wages. Employees who may be less worried about current cash income but more interested in the tax advantages of fringe benefits will accept offers in which fringe benefits form a higher proportion of total compensation. Thus, as noted above, employers can tailor their compensation packages to suit the preferences of the workers they are trying to attract. If the employees they prefer tend to be young, poor, or present-oriented, for example, their compensation packages may be heavily weighted toward wages and include relatively little in the way of pensions and insurance. Alternatively, if they are trying to attract people in an area where family incomes are high and hence fringe benefits offer relatively large tax savings, firms may offer packages in which fringe benefits constitute a large proportion of the total compensation.

---

[12] Many fringe benefits, like pensions and paid vacations, become more generous as the worker's tenure with the firm increases. These policies are clearly designed to reduce costly turnover, but they are more a matter of the *timing* of compensation than anything else.

**EXAMPLE    8.1**

## The Wage/Fringe Trade-off in the Collective-Bargaining Process

Although management and unions are usually reluctant to explicitly acknowledge that workers might be paying for their own fringe benefits, the wage/fringe trade-off sometimes can be directly observed in the collective bargaining process. In 1950, for example, the United Automobile Workers (the UAW) called a strike against Chrysler over the issue of pensions. Chrysler had promised a pension benefit to its workers for the first time, but it had not promised to put aside current funds to guarantee retirees that they would obtain benefits in the future. Fearing that Chrysler could become bankrupt, the UAW wanted this pension promise to be backed up with current funding, and it called a strike. (In the early 1980s Chrysler did teeter on the edge of bankruptcy, although by 1983 the company was again solvent.) The union's last offer to Chrysler before the strike is an excellent illustration of a wage/fringe trade-off; it asked Chrysler either to pay 6 cents per hour (per worker) to a pension fund and 4 cents to buy medical insurance, or to give workers a 10-cents-per-hour raise in cash wages.

SOURCE: *The Daily Labor Report,* January 17, 1960, p. A–17

Actually observing the trade-off between wages and fringe benefits is not easy. Because firms that pay high wages usually also offer very good fringe benefits, it often appears to the casual observer that wages and fringes are *positively* related. Casual observation in this case is misleading, however, because it does not allow for the influences of *other* factors, such as the demands of the job and the quality of workers involved, that influence total compensation. The other factors are most conveniently controlled for statistically, and the few statistical studies on this subject tend to support the prediction of a negative relationship between wages and fringe benefits.[13] The policy consequences of this predicted trade-off between wages and fringe

[13] Empirical studies of the trade-offs between wages and pensions are as yet few in number. Many of the studies that do exist indicate that workers pay, perhaps dollar for dollar, for their pensions in the form of lower wages. For a review of these studies, see Ronald Ehrenberg and Robert Smith, "A Framework for Evaluating State and Local Government Pension Reform," in *Public Sector Labor Markets,* Peter Mieszkowski and George E. Peterson (eds.) (Washington, DC: The Urban Institute, 1981). However, not all studies done in this area have found the predicted trade-offs, perhaps because of data problems. For a discussion of data requirements for estimating these trade-offs, see Robert Smith and Ronald Ehrenberg, "Estimating Wage-Fringe Trade-Offs: Some Data Problems," in *The Measurement of Labor Cost,* Jack E. Triplett (ed.), National Bureau of Economic Research, Conference on Research in Income and Wealth, Studies in Income and Wealth, vol. 48 (Chicago: University of Chicago Press, 1983).

One study found that in effect, union workers with cost of living escalator clauses pay for them in the form of lower wages than they would have been able to negotiate if they had not had escalators. See Wallace E. Hendricks and Lawrence M. Kahn, "Wage Indexation and Compensating Wage Differentials," *The Review of Economics and Statistics* 68 (August 1986): 484–92.

benefits are enormously important, because government legislation designed to improve fringe benefits might well be paid for by workers in the form of lower future wage increases. We discuss these consequences below.

**Policy application: Pension-reform legislation.** Pension plans provided by employers are of two general types: *defined contribution* plans and *defined benefit* plans. The less common are *defined contribution* plans, in which the employer merely promises to contribute a certain amount each year to a fund to which the employee has access upon retirement. The fund is increased each year by employer, and perhaps also employee, contributions and by returns from investments made by the fund's managers. One's retirement benefits depend solely on the size of the fund at the age of retirement.

More common are *defined benefit* pension plans, in which the employer promises employees a certain benefit upon retirement. This benefit may be a fixed sum per month or a fixed fraction of one's earnings prior to retirement. In either case employers guarantee the size of the pension benefit, and it is up to them to make sure that the funds are there when the promised benefits need to be paid.

The *vesting* provisions of any pension plan are the rules about who becomes eligible to receive a pension. If a plan is unvested, any worker who quits the company before retirement age loses all rights to a pension benefit. Once workers are vested, they can receive a pension from Company X even if they quit X before retirement age and work elsewhere. How much they receive from X at retirement, of course, depends on their length of service with X and their preretirement earnings; however, the point is that they receive *something* from X upon retirement if they are vested.

In 1974 Congress passed the Employee Retirement Income Security Act (ERISA), which, among other things, required private-sector employers to adopt liberalized vesting rules. The Tax Reform Act of 1986 required even more liberalized (earlier) vesting beginning in 1989. The intent of these mandated changes was to help employees by making it more likely that they would receive pension benefits in their old age. However, as we have seen with other programs designed to help workers, good intentions can sometimes be undone by unintended side effects. What are the side effects of liberalized vesting provisions? From the employees' perspective, rules that entitle them to become vested, or vested sooner, enhance their welfare if nothing else in the compensation package is changed. They are not penalized as much for voluntarily leaving an employer, nor are they as economically vulnerable to being fired. However, the value different workers attach to liberalized vesting may vary widely. The Tax Reform Act of 1986, for example, requires full vesting after 5 years of service, as compared to the 10-year vesting required under ERISA.[14] Employees who plan on working for a given employer less

---

[14] The vesting referred to here is known as "cliff vesting," in which a worker suddenly goes from being unvested to being fully vested. Both ERISA and the Tax Reform Act allowed for *partial* vesting plans, under which a fractional right to a pension upon retirement is granted earlier than 10 or 5 years, respectively, but full vesting occurs somewhat later.

than 5 years do not benefit at all from the liberalized vesting; neither do workers who have more than 10 years of service with the company. However, workers who might want to change employers after 5 to 10 years of service, or who might be fired during that period, stand to gain from liberalized vesting.

From the employers' perspective, the new vesting rules impose costs because they make it possible for more workers to qualify for pensions. Will firms simply absorb these costs, or will they force workers to pay for their more liberal pension benefits in the form of lower wages? Our theory suggests that employers probably will not—and in a competitive product market cannot—absorb the added pension costs. Those firms for which pension costs are increased will have to hold the line on future wage increases to remain competitive in the product market, and over time the wages they pay will fall below what they would have paid had it not been for the pension reform legislation.[15] Alternatively, firms whose expected pension costs rise because of liberalized vesting may choose to offset this rise with a reduction in promised pension benefits. In either case, theory suggests that it is the workers who bear the cost of the mandated change in vesting rules.

# Implicit Contracts, Explicit Contracts, and Asymmetric Information

Agreements between employers and employees concerning job duties and compensation can be considered contracts, whether or not they are formally written. An *explicit contract,* such as a formal written agreement between a union and a firm, specifies what transactions or events will occur when some contingency arises. Thus, such contracts may spell out how the firm is to respond if layoffs are necessary or what is to be done when a job vacancy occurs. Nonunion employees, however, typically do not work under explicit contracts. These employees, who constitute a majority of American workers, have relationships with their employers that are governed by *implicit contracts.* An implicit contract is a set of shared, informal understandings about how firms and workers will respond to contingencies.[16]

The major difference between explicit and implicit contracts is that provisions of the former are legally enforceable, whereas those of the latter may or may not be.[17] This distinction, however, may not be quite as significant as it first appears, because the *market* could provide a means for enforcing implicit contracts. More specifically, if either employer or employee acquires a reputation for breaking the promises inherent in implicit agreements, others will be

---

[15]   The two studies that have looked at the effects of vesting on wages have both found that nonvesting (public) employers pay higher wages, other things equal, than ones who vest. See Ehrenberg and Smith, "A Framework for Evaluating State and Local Government Pension Reform," for more details.

[16]   For a more detailed analysis of implicit contracts, see Robert Flanagan, "Implicit Contracts, Explicit Contracts and Wages," *American Economic Review, Papers and Proceedings* 74(May 1984): 345–49, or Sherwin Rosen, "Implicit Contracts," *Journal of Economic Literature* 23(September 1985): 1144–75.

[17]   Recall our discussion of the employment-at-will doctrine (Chapter 4), in which we reported that 23 states recognize an implied contract on this issue.

less willing to do business with them in the future.[18] Thus, differences between the two contracts in enforceability are mostly a matter of degree. Moreover, since drawing up an explicit list of all foreseeable contingencies and specifying rules for responding to them would be very costly to both parties, even employment relationships governed largely by explicit contracts remain implicit to some extent.

Over the years, but especially lately, labor economists have been interested in the forces that shape some fundamental characteristics common to explicit and implicit contracts in the labor market. For example, economic theory has been used to explain the following compensation phenomena:

1. wages are typically tied to hours of work, rather than to units of output produced;
2. nominal wages are rarely reduced, even in the nonunion sector, so when the demand-for-labor curve shifts left during a recession, the labor market typically adjusts through layoffs;
3. workers typically receive higher wages as they become older, but are then required—or offered a large "bribe" (a pension)—to fully retire from their companies at a specified age; and
4. firms—especially large ones—frequently offer their workers a compensation package that appears to have a value above market-clearing levels.

Analyses of these phenomena tend to stress three themes: there are costs associated with agreeing upon or adjusting contract provisions; the two parties may have different attitudes toward fluctuations in income; and there are costs associated with enforcing contractual promises. The implications of enforcement costs have received much attention in recent years, and we shall briefly outline this theme here before moving on to analyses of the above phenomena.

Each party to a contract is interested in holding the other to its promises; thus, it is very important to know when a contingency covered by the contract has really occurred. A contract may specify, for example, that employees who steal or shirk their duties can be fired, but a given firm might find it very difficult to prove that an individual has violated rules on stealing or shirking, or to what extent. Likewise, a contract may permit the wage rate to be reduced during times of economic distress, but workers, lacking access to the company's records, may find it difficult to ascertain just how much distress their employer is really facing.

Put differently, one of the problems facing each party in enforcing a contract is that the other party may have greater information about a particular contingency. In this respect, access to information is *asymmetric*. Moreover, the party with the greater information may have incentives to mislead the other: a firm that is actually prospering during a recession may claim it is

---

[18] See H. Lorne Carmichael, "Reputation in the Labor Market," *American Economic Review* 74 (September 1984): 713–25, for an interesting analysis of the role reputation plays.

being hurt so that it can reduce wages, just as a shirking worker will attempt concealment. Because this asymmetry of information makes cheating possible, and because monitoring by the other party is often very difficult or costly, ways must be found to make contracts *self-enforcing*. That is, incentives must be built in to labor contracts that induce both parties to refrain from cheating the other when each has the opportunity to do so.

In the remainder of this chapter we shall examine economic analyses of phenomena 1, 3, and 4 above; that is, we shall consider why labor contracts typically pay workers for their time instead of their output; why workers at age 64 (say) who are highly paid, apparently highly valued members of a production team, are suddenly strongly urged to retire at age 65; and why workers often appear to be paid above market-clearing wage levels. We shall defer our consideration of phenomenon 2—nominal wage inflexibility over a business cycle—until Chapter 17. In analyzing each of these compensation phenomena, we shall bring one or more of the three analytical themes mentioned above to bear.

# The Basis of Pay

The agreements between employers and employees concerning job duties and compensation can be considered *contracts,* whether or not they are formally written. As mentioned briefly in Chapter 1, there are two basic types of pay provisions in labor contracts. One rewards employees for the *time* they work, and the other rewards them for some *result* of their work.[19] Some contracts, however, contain a hybrid system of rewards.

The most common reward structure is payment for time worked, with about 86 percent of U.S. employees paid either by the hour or by the month. When employees are paid for time at work, it becomes management's challenge to motivate them not to shirk during that time. An alternative that would appear to alleviate the problem of shirking is payment by results, or incentive pay. *Piece-rate pay,* under which workers earn a certain amount for each item produced, is the most common form of individually based incentive pay for production workers.[20] Another system linking earnings to individuals' output is payment by *commission,* under which workers (usually salespeople) receive a fraction of the value of the items they sell. *Profit-sharing* plans attempt to relate workers' pay to the profits of their firm or subdivision; this form of pay rewards work groups rather than individuals. Under all these systems, workers are paid at least somewhat proportionately to their output or to the degree their employer prospers. Because a payments-by-results

---

[19]   This distinction concerning labor contracts is analyzed in Herbert A. Simon, "A Formal Theory of the Employment Relationship," *Econometrica* 19 (July 1951): 293–305, and more recently in Joseph E. Stiglitz, "Incentives, Risk, and Information: Notes Toward a Theory of Hierarchy," *Bell Journal of Economics* 6(Autumn 1975): 552–79.

[20]   A variant of piece-rate pay is the allowance of a *standard time* to complete a given task. A worker who finishes the task more *quickly* is paid for the full standard time regardless of how little time was actually spent; if the worker takes *longer* to complete the task, pay reverts to an *hourly* basis.

policy contains such an obvious incentive to work industriously, one is led to wonder why time-based pay systems are so dominant.[21]

Selecting the basis for pay, however, is ultimately a matter of satisfying the interests of *both* employer and employee. We turn now to an analysis of some factors affecting the choice of a pay system.

## Employee Preferences

If employees were told that their average earnings over the years under a time payment system would be equal to their earnings under an individual incentive-pay scheme, they would probably choose to be paid on a *time* basis. Why? Earnings under a piece-rate or commission system depend on the thought and energy one is able to bring to the job. There are days and even weeks in any person's life when he or she is depressed, preoccupied, tired, or otherwise distracted from maximum work effort. There are other periods when one is exceptionally productive. If employees are paid on a piece-rate basis, their earnings could be more *variable* over time because of the somewhat uncontrollable swings in productivity. This variability in income could cause them anxiety that several low-productivity months could be strung together, making it difficult to meet mortgage payments and other obligations. Because of this anxiety about less-productive periods of time, employees might prefer the certainty of time-based pay to the uncertainty of piece-rate pay *if* both schemes paid the same average wage over time. Thus, to induce employees to accept piece-rate pay, employers would have to pay higher average wages over time; that is, a compensating differential would have to exist to compensate workers for the anxiety associated with variations in their earnings. Conversely, to obtain more certainty in their stream of earnings, employees would probably be willing to accept a somewhat lower average wage.

## Employer Considerations

The willingness of employers to pay a wage premium to induce employees to accept piece rates depends on the costs and benefits to employers of incentive-pay schemes. If workers are paid with piece rates or commissions they bear the consequences of low productivity, as noted above; thus, employers can afford to spend less time screening and supervising workers and monitoring the amount of output per worker (see Example 8.2). If workers are paid on a *time* basis, the *employer* accepts the risk of variations in their productivity. When they are exceptionally productive, profits increase; when they are less productive, profits decline.

---

[21] While the focus here is on the work-*incentive* aspects of various pay schemes, another important subject of analysis is how they affect the demand for labor. A theoretical analysis of the choice between piece rates and time-based pay can be found in Edward P. Lazear, "Salaries and Piece Rates," *Journal of Business* 59 (July 1986): 405–31.

**EXAMPLE   8.2**

## Piece Rates and Supervisory Effort in California Agriculture

We have emphasized that piece-rate pay schemes allow employers to operate with relatively little supervisory effort. In some cases workers are paid under pure piece rates work, essentially as subcontractors, out of their homes; these workers are not directly supervised at all. Others paid pure piece rates work in factories, but supervision may be relatively loose. For example, a contemporary account of work in a California cannery in the 1920s described worker behavior that, on the one hand, seems like a major absence of industrial discipline, but on the other can be looked upon as an early example of *flexible time* (in which firms allow workers, within limits, to set their own work schedules):

> One cannery checker . . . complained that the piece-rate system instilled a sense that each woman was "in business for herself," and, as a consequence, piece workers often came late and left the cannery early. Preparation workers were likely to leave if incoming produce slacked off or was of less-workable quality.

Pure piece-rate pay schemes at times also allow firms to hire workers whose capabilities or work habits render their productivity so low or so variable that they would not ordinarily be hired by a firm paying time-base wages. Consider this description of "hiring standards" in California's harvest labor market around 1950:

> Differences in skill, age, and sex become matters of relative indifference, provided only that the elementary distinction between a ripe grape or a ripe peach and a green one can be communicated. Thus California agriculture is able to provide productive employment for men, women, and children, for the experienced and inexperienced, for alcoholic derelicts from the "slave" markets and for the skilled Filipino, at a labor cost per unit of output which does not vary widely.

SOURCES:  Martin Brown and Peter Philips, "The Decline of Piece Rates in California Canneries: 1890–1960," *Industrial Relations* 25 (Winter 1986): 81–91, and Lloyd H. Fisher, *The Harvest Labor Market in California* (Cambridge, MA: Harvard University Press, 1953): 8–11

Employers, however, may be less anxious about these *variations* than employees are. They typically have more assets and can thus weather the lean periods more comfortably than can individual workers. More important, perhaps, employers usually have several employees, and the chances are that not all will suffer the same swings in productivity at the same time (unless there is a morale problem in the firm). Thus, employers may not be as willing to pay for income certainty as are workers.

Employers must also consider that incentive-pay schemes are likely to increase worker productivity in two ways. First, because workers bear (or

**Table 8.3**   The Percentage of Production Workers Paid at Least Partially Under Piece-Rate Schemes, Selected Manufacturing Industries, 1972–76

| Industry | Percentage of Workers |
|---|---|
| *Highest* | |
| Work clothing | 80 % |
| Footwear | 73 |
| Men's and boys' shirts | 72 |
| Men's and boys' suits and coats | 71 |
| Children's hosiery | 65 |
| Women's hosiery | 62 |
| Men's hosiery | 57 |
| Cigars | 45 |
| *Lowest* | |
| Paints | 0 % |
| Synthetic fibers | 1 |
| Glass containers | 1 |
| Fabricated structural steel | 3 |
| Prepared meat | 3 |
| Misc. plastic | 3 |
| Paperboard containers | 3.5 |
| Meat packing | 4 |

SOURCE:  Eric Seiler, "Piece Rate vs. Time Rate: The Effect of Incentives on Earnings," *The Review of Economics and Statistics* 66, (August 1984), Table 1.

share) the risk of low productivity, incentive-pay schemes are likely to attract the most productive workers within each occupation. Put differently, schemes that reward high productivity implicitly punish low productivity; thus, firms offering such pay schemes will tend to attract those who anticipate the highest rewards. Second, because workers (whatever their quality) directly benefit from their own diligence in a piece-rate scheme, they have incentives to work harder than if paid only for their time. A full analysis, however, of these productivity-related incentives and the costs of implementing them must take into account differences between *individual* and *group* incentive-pay plans.

## Individual Rewards: Piece Rates and Commissions

The use of piece rates varies considerably by industry. Data on their usage are difficult to obtain, but as Table 8.3 indicates for the 1970s, they seem most prevalent in clothing manufacturing. Other data from the 1970s found that nearly half of the production workers in U.S. auto-repair shops were paid incentive rates: roughly one quarter received some fraction of the labor costs charged to the customer (they were paid by *commission,* in essence), and the other quarter were paid a flat rate (*piece rate*) for each kind of repair performed.[22] The big advantage of these compensation schemes from the employer's perspective is that they induce employees to adopt a set of work

[22]  Sandra King, "Incentive and Time Pay in Auto Dealer Repair Shops," *Monthly Labor Review* 98 (September 1975): 45–48.

goals that are consistent with those of their employer. Employees paid a piece rate are motivated to work quickly, while those paid by commission are induced to very thoroughly evaluate the servicing needs of the firm's customers. Moreover, these inducements exist without the need for, or expense of, close monitoring by the firm's supervisors.

Auto-repair shops, however, provide a specific example of several general disadvantages to individually based incentive-pay schemes—disadvantages that help to explain why individual incentive-pay schemes are not more widely used. These general problems include maintaining quality standards, misusing equipment, setting the rate, and measuring output.

**Maintaining Quality Standards.** Workers paid according to the number of completed projects are motivated to work quickly, but they are also motivated to have minimal regard for quality. Repair workers paid by commission, for example, are motivated to be so thorough in ferreting out servicing needs that they may fix things that are not broken. Both bases for compensation thus create a need for close supervisory attention to the quality of work performed, a need and an expense that in many cases will offset the supervisory savings associated with incentive pay.

**Equipment Misuse.** Allied to the problem of work quality is the problem of equipment misuse. Workers receiving incentive pay are motivated to work so quickly that machines or tools are often damaged or otherwise misused. It is often asserted, for example, that piece-rate workers disengage safety devices on machinery in their desire to maximize output. This problem is mitigated to the extent that equipment damage causes *downtime* that results in lost employee earnings. Many firms using piece rates require workers to provide their own machines or tools.

**Setting the Rate.** A third problem, probably more often associated with piece rates than with commissions, is setting the rate. For example, it may be standard practice in the auto-repair industry to assume that an engine tune-up will require two hours of work and to translate this time requirement into a "per job" piece rate. Suppose, however, that some new tool or electronic device is adopted that reduces the time required for a tune-up. A new piece rate will have to be adopted, but how do the shop's owners determine the standard time requirement for tune-ups now? The best way may be to observe mechanics using the new devices, but if these workers know they are being observed for purposes of setting a new rate, they may deliberately work slowly so that the time requirement is overestimated, to drive up the piece rate. The problem is compounded in industries facing frequent changes in products or technology. In the women's apparel industry around the turn of the century, for example, it was common to have seasonal strikes over piece rates coinciding with seasonal changes in fashions.[23]

---

[23] Louis Levine, *The Women's Garment Workers* (New York: B. W. Huebsch, 1924): 42. The observation that a stable technology is important for the success of an incentive-pay system is also made by Sumner H. Slichter, James J. Healy, and E. Robert Livernash, *The Impact of Collective Bargaining on Management* (Washington, DC: The Brookings Institution, 1960): 519.

**Measuring Output.** A fourth reason why individual incentive-pay schemes are not more widely used is the problem of measuring and motivating individuals in the context of *team* production. The output of an auto mechanic, salesperson, or a dressmaker is relatively easy to measure in terms of quantity, but what about that of an office manager or auto assembly-line worker? The manager has a number of duties and deals with a multitude of problems; combining them into a single index of output would be next to impossible. Assembly-line workers, on the other hand, may have an easily counted output, but it is not individually controlled. In both cases, *individual* incentive pay would be arbitrary or useless; however, *group* incentives might be attractive in these situations.

## Group Incentive Pay

When individual output is hard to monitor or control, group incentive-pay schemes are sometimes adopted to bring the interests of workers in line with those of the employer.[24] The forms these pay schemes take are analogous to the schemes discussed above. In some cases work groups are paid by the piece for output produced *by the group*. In other cases employees share in the profits of the firm each year—a close analogue to the commission basis for individual pay. In still other cases workers might *own* the firm and split the profits among themselves, or more commonly, be partially compensated in shares of company stock.[25]

One drawback to group incentives is that groups are composed of individuals, and it is at the individual level that decisions about work effort are ultimately made. A person who works very hard to increase group output or the firm's profits winds up splitting the fruits of his or her labor with all the others, who may not have put out extra effort. Group incentives, then, are sometimes no incentive at all. People come to realize that they can reap the rewards of someone else's hard work without doing any extra work of their own, and that if they do put out extra work, the rewards mainly go to others. Such schemes thus give workers incentives to cheat on their fellow employees by shirking.

In very small groups, however, cheating may be easy to detect, and group punishments, such as ostracism, can be effectively used to eliminate it. In these cases, group incentive-pay systems can accomplish their aims (subject, of course, to all the drawbacks of individual incentive-pay systems noted above). However, if the group of workers receiving incentive pay is large, cheating (shirking) probably cannot be effectively handled. Group incentive-pay schemes thus become less effective as group size increases.

---

[24] Pay based on company profits also represents a way firms have of controlling their real wage costs. When the product price of a given firm goes up with prices in general, firms may seek to adopt a policy of tying their wage increases to some aggregate measure of prices (such as the consumer price index). However, when an industry's product prices are declining relative to prices in the aggregate, firms in the industry may find profit-sharing plans advantageous. Under these plans the compensation of their workers is closely tied to the firm's profitability, and increases are granted only if the firm is profitable.

[25] For a detailed treatment of worker-owned enterprise, the most widespread example of which is in Yugoslavia, see Jaroslav Vanek, *The General Theory of Labor-Managed Market Economies* (Ithaca, NY: Cornell University Press, 1970).

The *basis* upon which incentive payments are made can be very important in determining the overall profitability of the firm. For example, consider a firm wanting to maximize profits over the *long run* and trying to decide how to compensate its executives in such a way that this long-term goal will be achieved. If it adopts a yearly profit-sharing plan in which a fraction of year-end profits is given to each executive, its executives may be induced to pursue strategies designed to maximize profits in the current period. These short-run strategies may not be consistent with long-run profit maximization, but the executives involved may use their short-run performances to obtain positions with other firms before the long-run consequences of their strategies are fully observed. Perhaps for these reasons, 40 percent of the 200 largest industrial companies in the United States give their executives rights to future payments that are directly tied to company performance over a *multiyear* period.[26] Ninety-five percent of all these long-term "performance attainment" plans base their awards on some measure of company prosperity over a period of three-to-five years—apparently in the belief that a period of less than three years is too short to measure long-term performance, while one more than five years would represent so long a delay in receiving rewards that motivational effects would be weakened.

A number of recent studies have gone beyond the formal pay practices for executives in the largest corporations to look at executive pay generally. In particular, these studies are concerned with whether executive earnings are tied, implicitly or explicitly, to the economic performance of firms.[27] Some studies define performance in terms of reported profits, while others use the *total return* (dividends plus capital gains) on the firms' stocks. Virtually all studies find that executive pay is dependent, at least to some extent, on firm performance. Moreover, there is evidence that tying executive pay to firm performance enhances that performance. One study showed that firms whose executives' compensation was at least implicitly tied to firm performance outperformed other firms during a 20-year period.[28] Other studies show that the adoption of executive performance attainment plans leads to improved short-run stock market performance of these firms. Apparently the stock market believes that performance attainment plans will increase profits.[29]

[26] Lawrence C. Bickford, "Long-Term Incentives for Management, Part 6: Performance Attainment Plans," *Compensation Review* (Third Quarter, 1981): 14–29.

[27] See, for example, T. Coughlin and R. Schmidt, "Executive Compensation, Management Turn-over, and Firm Performance: An Empirical Investigation," *Journal of Accounting and Economics* 7(April 1985): 43–66, and Kevin Murphy, "Corporate Performance and Managerial Remuneration: An Empirical Analysis," *Journal of Accounting and Economics* 7(April 1985): 11–42.

[28] Robert Masson, "Executive Motivations, Earnings, and Consequent Equity Performance," *Journal of Political Economy* 79(November 1971): 1278–92.

[29] See, for example, J. Brickley, S. Bhagat, and R. Lease, "The Impact of Long-Run Managerial Compensation Plans on Shareholder Wealth," *Journal of Accounting and Economics* 7(April 1985): 115–29. An alternative explanation for these findings, however, is that executives may push for the adoption of these plans only when they believe firm performance is likely to be good. If this occurs, adoption may *signal* to the stock market that the firm expects "good times" ahead. The resulting observed improvement in stock market performance may reflect only this signal, not any anticipated incentive effects.

## Earnings Under Piece and Time Rates

Two observations lead to the prediction that workers on incentive pay earn more per hour than comparable workers paid on a time basis. First, if workers have a preference for being paid on a time basis, employers will have to pay a premium, a compensating wage differential, to induce them to accept an incentive-pay scheme. This earnings differential would compensate workers for accepting the risks associated with incentive pay. Second, the workers most likely to accept a job with incentive pay are those most likely to be successful at it: the fastest, most-intense workers within each occupational group.

Although there are few studies of this issue, the prediction that incentive-pay workers earn more appears to hold up. A 1960s study of punch-press operators in Chicago found that piece-rate workers earned about 9-percent more per hour of work than did those paid an hourly wage.[30] Research by the Bureau of Labor Statistics found that auto-repair workers paid on an incentive basis earned 20–50 percent more per hour than those paid on a time basis.[31] Finally, a recent study estimated that piece-rate workers in the footwear and men's and boys' suit and coat industries earned 14–16 percent more than comparable workers receiving time-based pay. Only a small part of this differential could be attributed to a compensating wage differential; most of the differential was associated with greater productivity.[32]

## Merit Pay

While most companies do not use piece rates or commissions, most do consider individual performance when setting pay. A merit pay system is one in which a worker's performance is evaluated and some part of pay is contingent on the performance evaluation. (Piece-rate systems are an extreme example of merit pay in that one's entire wage is based on measured performance.) Use of the merit pay concept is widespread in American industry. For example, a survey of 500 companies found that 95 percent of them gave pay increases based at least in part on a worker's performance.[33] While the next chapter describes in more detail the workings of systems that base pay on performance, we note here that a considerable amount of research has been done on the effects of such systems. Forty-four studies of the adoption of pay-for-performance systems showed that, in almost all cases, a substantial improvement in performance was realized. In fact, merit-based financial incentives were found to be more effective at improving performance than job

---

[30]  John Pencavel, "Work Effort, On-the-Job Screening, and Alternative Methods of Remuneration," in *Research in Labor Economics,* vol. 1, ed. Ronald Ehrenberg (Greenwich, CT: JAI Press, 1977): 225–58.

[31]  King, "Incentive and Time Pay in Auto Dealer Repair Shops," p. 46.

[32]  Eric Seiler, "Piece Rate vs. Time Rate: The Effect of Incentives on Earnings," *The Review of Economics and Statistics* 66 (August 1984): 363–76.

[33]  See CompFlash, "Companies Praise Pay-for-Performance Programs," *AMA Compflash* 84 (1984): 6.

enrichment or increased worker participation in decision-making.[34] While these studies do not compare the dollar costs and benefits of various personnel decisions, they do support the idea that worker performance responds to incentives.

Although the bulk of research on this question supports a connection between merit pay and subsequent performance, merit pay systems are not universally successful. For example, the Civil Service Reform Act of 1978 required that, for managers in Federal agencies, half of one's pay increase was to be automatic, and half was to be based on performance. A study of the implementation of this system showed no improvement in managers' performance. The authors attributed this lack of effect to the mistrust of the merit pay system (it was perceived to have been politically motivated).[35]

# Internal Labor Markets and the Level and Time Pattern of Compensation

To the extent that there are difficulties and disadvantages of implementing the common forms of individual or group incentive pay, firms might consider methods of motivating workers using a time-based pay system. One approach to motivating workers within the context of time-based pay involves close supervision. If close supervision is impossible or very costly, two other approaches might be considered. Workers can be paid wages that exceed what they could get elsewhere, thereby creating an incentive for them to work hard enough to maintain their jobs and continue to qualify for the above-market wage. Alternatively, workers can be offered delayed rewards—promotions, large pay increases, or generous pensions—only *after* years of diligent effort.

Approaches that combine time-based wages and relatively low supervisory efforts suggest the existence of a *long-term relationship* between employer and employee. Many workers, after a period of "job shopping," establish this long-term relationship. It has been estimated, for example, that over half of all working men and one-fourth of all working women find employers for whom they will work at least 20 years. Moreover, 8 percent of men in the 45–59-year-old age group have worked for only one employer over

---

[34] See E. A. Locke, D. B. Feren, V. M. McCaleb, K. N. Shaw, and A. T. Denny, "The Relative Effectiveness of Four Methods of Motivating Employee Performance," in K. D. Duncan, M. M. Gruneberg; and D. Wallis (eds.), *Changes in Working Life* (New York: John Wiley & Sons, 1980): 363–88. For further discussion of merit pay, see George T. Milkovich and Jerry M. Newman, *Compensation, 2d ed.* (Plano, Texas: Business Publications, Inc., 1987), Chapters 8–10.

[35] See Jone L. Pearce, William B. Stevenson, and James L. Perry, "Managerial Compensation Based on Organizational Performance: A Time Series Analysis of the Effects of Merit Pay," *Academy of Management Journal* 28 (June 1985): 261–78.

their entire work history.[36] Most of the long-term employment that characterizes much of the American labor market is found in large firms with *internal labor markets,* wherein higher-level jobs are exclusively or primarily filled from within the organization.

## Internal Labor Markets and Employee Pay

Recall from Chapter 4 that firms sometimes create an *internal labor market,* wherein hiring is done only at certain *entry-level* jobs and all other jobs are filled from within the firm. This hiring and promotion system serves in part as a substitute for the difficult task of screening job applicants with respect to crucial personal characteristics. Workers are hired at low levels of responsibility and then observed over time to determine their actual productive characteristics. Once the firm has discovered who the productive, dependable workers are, it wants to retain them. Internal labor markets can be useful in constructing compensation systems designed to motivate workers when close daily supervision is costly. These systems require worker efforts to be monitored over long periods of time, so that even if shirking in any one year is not likely to be detected, it will be observed eventually if it exists.

If employees are hired with the expectation that they will spend an entire career with a firm—an expectation that is certainly encouraged by a policy of promoting only from within—then the critical element in their choice of an employer is the *present value of their career earnings;* that is, they will be concerned about their likely earnings over their entire *career,* not just the pay on the job for which they are initially hired. A firm with an internal labor market must therefore offer a *stream* of earnings over time whose overall present value is at least equivalent to that offered by other firms competing in the same labor market.

To say that the present value of an earnings stream must be at least equivalent to that paid elsewhere does *not* imply that the wages offered for each job or at each stage in one's career must be at least equal to those paid by other firms. Firms that pay low wages initially but offer high earnings later on may be very competitive with firms offering initially higher wages but not raising them much over time. For example, suppose a firm offered a 10-year job sequence in which the workers were paid $15,000 in each of the first five years and $18,000 for the next five years. Using a discount rate of 2 percent, an income stream with the same present value could be achieved by a labor market competitor who offered $10,000 for each of the first five years and paid $23,500 per year for the last five!

---

[36] Robert E. Hall, "The Importance of Lifetime Jobs in the U.S. Economy," *American Economic Review* 72(September 1982): 716–24. See also George Akerlof and B. G. M. Main, "An Experience Weighted Measure of Employment and Unemployment Durations," *American Economic Review* 71(December 1981): 1003–11; and Walter Oi, "The Durability of Worker-Firm Attachments," a report prepared for the U.S. Department of Labor, Office of the Assistant Secretary for Policy, Evaluation, and Research, March 25, 1983, p. 16.

Besides having to offer workers a stream of earnings that is sufficient to attract their services, the firm with an internal labor market must also keep its pay within a zone that allows it to compete successfully with its product market competitors. It can pay higher than market wages and compete in the product market only if its workers are more productive, less likely to quit, or cheaper to supervise. Thus, it should be clear that firms offering workers *careers,* and not just jobs, have some latitude in setting the level and sequencing of compensation within the general context of having to remain competitive in both labor and product markets. We now turn to more detailed analyses of the major compensation-based approaches to worker motivation when times wages are paid.

## Efficiency Wages

In situations where the potential for long-term attachment between workers and firms exists, it may prove profitable for employers to pay workers wages *above* what the workers can earn elsewhere. One rationale for this was discussed in Chapter 4 when hiring and training investments were analyzed; there, the payment of higher wages was seen to be profitable for employers if it led to reduced turnover and consequent greater savings in hiring and training costs. It has also been emphasized in various chapters that the payment of high wages allows a firm to assemble a high-quality work force (high wages generate so many applicants that hiring only the best is a feasible strategy). Still another rationale relates to the difficulties employers face in monitoring employee work effort under time-based compensation arrangements. As discussed above, employees working under a time-based compensation scheme do not face the same direct incentives to work hard that employees under a piece-rate or commission system face. In some situations, it may prove very costly for employers to supervise and monitor the effort levels of workers receiving time-based pay. Moreover, if the employer is paying hourly wages equal to what employees could earn elsewhere, they face no particularly strong incentive not to shirk; if at great cost the employer succeeded in repeatedly observing shirking and discharged the offending workers, the workers could obtain comparable employment elsewhere. Put another way, the cost to workers of shirking is relatively low when they are paid only what they could earn elsewhere.

Suppose instead that the firm were to pay its workers wages that exceeded what they could earn elsewhere. This obviously would increase the firm's labor costs, but such a scheme offers the firm at least two types of benefits. First, workers now would face an incentive not to shirk, for if they were caught and discharged they would lose (in present-value terms) the difference between the higher earnings at the firm and their potential earnings elsewhere, over the entire period they had expected to remain with the firm. To the extent that the employees responded by working harder, the firm's revenues would increase. Second, since the firm would now know that its workers would be shirking less, it could save money by devoting fewer resources to supervising and monitoring their behavior.[37]

Raising the wage above the level that workers can earn elsewhere obviously has both benefits *and* costs to the employer. While initial increases in the wage may well serve to increase the profits of the firm, after a point the costs to the employer of further increases may well exceed the benefits. The wage level at which the marginal benefits to the employer of a further increase just equal the marginal costs is the wage level that will maximize profits. This has become known recently as the *efficiency wage*.[38]

Note that the payment of wages above what workers could earn elsewhere makes sense here only because workers expect to have long-term employment relationships with firms. If workers switched jobs every period they would face no incentive to reduce shirking when a firm paid above-market wages, because firing someone who is going to quit anyway is not an effective penalty; as a result firms would have no incentive to pursue an efficiency-wage policy. Thus, high-wage policies of the type described here are likely to arise only in situations where structured internal labor markets exist. Moreover, other things equal, the longer workers' expected tenure with the firm, the greater is the financial loss if a shirking worker is fired and hence the more likely it is that such schemes will have their intended effects.[39]

## Pay in Large Firms

The theoretical association between internal labor markets and efficiency wages may help to explain the very strong empirical relationship between wage levels and firm size. It appears, for example, that workers in manufacturing firms with 100–500 workers receive wages that are 6 percent higher than those of workers in smaller firms who have the same measurable human capital characteristics; workers in firms of over 500 workers earn about 12 percent more.[40]

---

[37] The argument actually is a bit more complicated, since the willingness of workers to shirk depends not only on the "penalty" (loss of high wages) they will face if caught but also on the probability they will get caught. Reduced employer monitoring presumably will reduce this probability. For simplicity, we ignore this complication in the text; introducing it into more formal models does not change any of the conclusions that follow.

[38] Besides inducing lower turnover, the acquisition and retention of higher-quality employees, and more employee effort with less supervisory input, it has also been argued that the "gift" of high wages by an employer encourages a reciprocal "gift" of high effort by employees. For further discussions of efficiency wages, see George A. Akerlof, "Gift Exchange and Efficiency Wages: Four Views," *American Economic Review* 74(May 1984): 78–83; Janet Yellen, "Efficiency Wage Models of Unemployment," *American Economic Review* 74(May 1984): 200–208; Jeremy Bulow and Lawrence Summers, "A Theory of Dual Labor Markets with Applications to Industrial Policy, Discrimination and Keynesian Unemployment," *Journal of Labor Economics* 4(July 1986): 376–414; Lawrence Katz, "Efficiency Wage Theories: A Partial Evaluation," National Bureau of Economic Research Working Paper no. 1906, April 1986; and Joseph E. Stiglitz, "The Causes and Consequences of the Dependence of Quality on Price," *Journal of Economic Literature* 25 (March 1987): 1–48.

[39] The payment of above market-clearing, efficiency wages by some firms can also be shown to lead to unemployment in the economy. See Janet Yellen, "Efficiency Wage Models of Unemployment."

[40] Wesley Mellow, "Employer Size and Wages," *The Review of Economics and Statistics* 64 (August 1982): 495–501.

A variety of hypotheses have been advanced to explain this positive relationship between wage levels and employer size, but at the moment none seems entirely satisfactory.[41] It has been argued that large firms have more rigid, impersonal work environments, and that they must therefore pay a compensating wage differential to their workers; however, the size-related differential persists even when measurable working conditions have been held constant. It has been argued that large firms need workers who have intrinsic qualities that are hard to measure (motivation and dependability, for example), but the size-related wage differential also survives after controlling for these unmeasurables.[42] Likewise, the arguments that large firms ''hide'' monopoly profits by paying above-market wages (refer to Chapter 3) and that they pay high wages just to keep out labor unions seem unable to completely explain the differential. Thus, while our understanding of the wage differences associated with employer size is incomplete, the greater possibilities for the existence of efficiency wages among larger firms may have something to do with it.[43]

## Employment Contracts and the Sequencing of Pay

Employers with internal labor markets also have options for *sequencing* workers' pay while still offering jobs with at least the same *present value* of career compensation as paid by the market generally.[44] It may be beneficial to both employer and employee to arrange workers' pay over time so that employees are ''underpaid'' early in their careers and ''overpaid'' later.

This sequencing of pay will increase worker productivity (for reasons discussed below) and enable firms to pay *higher* present values of compensation than otherwise, for two reasons. An understanding of these reasons takes us back to the problem of creating self-enforcing contracts in the presence of asymmetric information.

First, employment contracts that underpay workers in the early years of their careers and overpay them later will appeal most to workers who intend

[41] The discussion in this paragraph is based on Charles Brown and James Medoff, ''The Employer Size Wage Effect'' (unpublished paper, Department of Economics, University of Michigan, November 1985).

[42] Controlling for worker characteristics that are impossible to measure is done by tracking the wage *changes* of workers who have moved between small and large firms. Clearly, workers' intrinsic qualities do not change over short periods of time, so that the observed wage changes cannot be attributable to these qualities; rather, it is reasonable to infer that they are associated with changes in the size of one's employer. As longitudinal data—data on the same workers in different years—have become available, analyses of person-specific wage changes over time have been used to control for worker characteristics that affect productivity but are unobservable to the researcher.

[43] Another empirical regularity for which our understanding is incomplete concerns wage differences *across industries*. As with the size-related patterns, the differences in wages across industries persist even after controlling for measurable and unmeasurable employee characteristics, working conditions, and unionization. Moreover, industry-related differentials appear to be fairly consistent over time and across countries. Theories of efficiency wages are again being challenged to explain these facts. For a review of the issue, see William T. Dickens and Lawrence Katz, ''Inter-Industry Wage Differentials and Theories of Wage Determination'' (unpublished paper, National Bureau of Economic Research, July 1986).

[44] Our discussion here draws on Edward Lazear, ''Why Is There Mandatory Retirement?'' *Journal of Political Economy* 87 (December 1979): 1261–84.

to establish long-term relationships with their employers and work diligently enough to avoid being fired before their deferred rewards can be collected. Thus, in the absence of knowledge by employers of which applicants are diligent and not likely to quit, a pay scheme featuring deferred compensation appears to be a clever mechanism to force employees to reveal information about themselves that employers otherwise could not obtain.[45] Second, a company that pays poorly to begin with but well later on increases the incentives of its employees to work industriously. Once in the job, an employee has incentives to work diligently in order to qualify for the later overpayment. The employer need not devote as many resources to supervision each year as would otherwise be the case, because the firm has several years in which to identify shirkers and withhold from them the reward. Workers are less likely to take chances and shirk their responsibilities, because the penalties for being caught and fired are forfeiture of a large reward. Because all employees work harder than they otherwise would, their total compensation tends to be higher also. One feasible compensation-sequencing scheme would pay workers *less* than their marginal product early in their careers and *more* than their marginal product later on. This scheme, however, must satisfy two conditions. First, the present value of the earnings streams offered to employees must be at least equal to alternative streams offered to similar workers in the labor market; if not, the firm cannot attract the workers it wants. Since pay that is deferred into the future is discounted, deferred sums must be larger the higher is the discount rate, or *present-orientedness,* of workers (see Chapter 6). Second, the scheme must also satisfy the equilibrium conditions that firms maximize profits and do not earn supernormal profits. If profits are not maximized, the firm's existence is threatened; if firms make supernormal profits, new firms will be induced to enter the market. Thus, in neither case would equilibrium exist.

These two conditions will be met if hiring is done until the present value of one's career-long marginal product equals the present value of one's career earnings stream. (This career-long condition is the multiyear analogue of the single-year profit conditions discussed in Chapter 3 and the two-year profit-maximization criterion discussed in Chapter 4.) Thus, for firms choosing the "underpayment now, overpayment later" compensation scheme to be competitive in both the labor and the product markets, the present value of the yearly amounts by which marginal product ($MP$) exceeds compensation early on must equal the present value of the later amounts by which $MP$ *falls short* of pay.

The preceding compensation plan is diagrammed in Figure 8.1. We assume that $MP$ rises slightly over one's career, but that during the first $t^*$ years of employment, compensation remains below $MP$. At some point in one's career with the firm—year $t^*$ in the diagram—compensation begins to exceed $MP$. From $t^*$ onward are the years in which employees are rewarded by receiving compensation in excess of what they could receive elsewhere

[45] Walter Oi, "The Durability of Worker-Firm Attachments," pp. 41–45.

**Figure 8.1**   A Compensation Scheme Designed to Increase
Worker Motivation

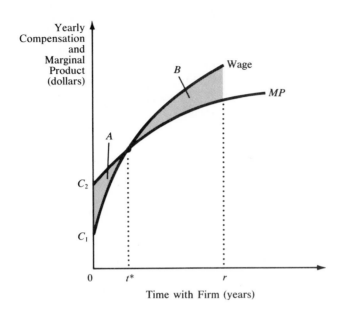

(namely, their *MP*). For the firm to be competitive in both the labor and the
product markets, the *present value* of area *A* in the diagram must equal the
*present value* of area *B*. (Area *B* is larger than area *A* in Figure 8.1 because
sums received farther in the future are subjected to heavier discounting when
present values are calculated.)

   To be sure, there are risks to both parties in making this kind of agreement. Employees agreeing to this compensation scheme take a chance that
they may be fired without cause or that their employer may go bankrupt
before they have collected their reward in the years beyond *t**. It is easy to
see that employers will have some incentives to renege, since older workers
are being paid a wage that exceeds their immediate value (at the margin) to the
firm. However, employers who do not want to fire people face the risk that
older, "overpaid" employees will stay on the job longer than is necessary to
collect their reward; that is, they may stay on longer than time *r* in Figure 8.1.
Knowing that their current wage is greater than the wage they can get
elsewhere, since it reflects payment for more than current output, older
employees will have incentives to keep working longer than is profitable for
the firm.

   A partial solution to these problems of risk is to agree on a formal
employment contract that has two elements. One element protects older
employees from arbitrary discharge by stipulating the grounds under which
employees can be discharged and guaranteeing "seniority rights" for older

workers. According to these seniority provisions, workers with the shortest durations of employment with the firm are usually laid off first when the firm cuts back its work force. Without these seniority rights, firms might be tempted to lay off older workers, whose wages are greater than *MP*, and keep the younger ones, who are paid less than *MP* at this point in their careers.

The second element of a formal employment contract designed to reduce the risk inherent in this compensation plan is some form of retirement clause. Unless firms can induce workers to retire before the present value of area *B* in Figure 8.1 exceeds that of *A*, or unless they can force older employees to accept wage cuts so that after year *r* their wages equal *MP*, employers will not agree to the compensation-sequencing plan under discussion.

In some instances, formal employment contracts have included a mandatory retirement age, which prior to 1978 was normally set at age 65. Under these agreements employees had to retire at age 65, whether they wanted to or not. In other cases there may be inducements offered for voluntary early retirement. For example, the 1965 contract between the automakers and the United Automobile Workers permitted workers to retire as early as age 55 if they had 30 years of service. Moreover, the monthly pension benefit before age 65 was much larger than after 65, yielding an average present value of early retirement benefits equal to $18,365, compared to a present value of $9,700 associated with retirement at age 65.[46] (A study of pension plans in 190 of the largest companies in the United States found that it is common for the present value of pension benefits to decline as retirement is postponed.)[47]

In making an early retirement decision, one must compare the utility generated by one's income and leisure streams if retirement occurs at 65 (say) with that generated by early retirement and its associated streams of leisure and pension income. When the stream of pension income associated with early retirement is increased in some way, the utility associated with early retirement is enhanced. Inducing early retirement by essentially bribing people to retire makes economic sense when older employees are paid more than they are currently worth (recall Example 5.1).

Formal, explicit agreements cannot remove risks altogether, however. There is, on the employee side, no assurance that the firm will be in business during the employee's older years. Even large, once-profitable firms go bankrupt, close down plants, or are bought out by other firms—all of which can have the effect of reducing jobs or wage opportunities for older workers in the firm. While most *pension* promises are backed up by a separate fund that remains even if the employer goes bankrupt, there is really nothing to back up a promise of future pay increases. On the employer side, mandatory retirement agreements can be, and have been, voided by federal legislation. Amendments made to the Age Discrimination in Employment Act in 1978 and

[46]   See Richard Burkhauser, "The Pension Acceptance Decision of Older Workers," *Journal of Human Resources* 14(Winter 1979): 63–75.

[47]   Edward Lazear, "Pensions as Severance Pay," in *Financial Aspects of the United States Pension System*, Zvi Bodie and John Shoven (eds.), (Chicago: University of Chicago Press, 1983).

1986, for example, have now effectively precluded mandatory retirement for most workers.

Thus, *explicit* contracts safeguarding the deferral of earnings to late in one's career are not risk-free. Even more risky are *implicit contracts,* which are understood to exist but are not formally written and signed by both parties. In these contracts the employee is protected from arbitrary dismissal mainly by the need for the employer to recruit *other* workers. If a certain employer gains a reputation for firing older workers despite an implicit agreement not to do so, that employer will have trouble recruiting new employees (as noted earlier), which is one incentive to adhere to the implicit contract. However, if the company is in permanent decline, if it faces an unusually adverse market, or if information on company employment policies is not easily or accurately available to applicants, the incentives to renege on implicit contracts are probably very strong.

## Pensions as Deferred Payments

One way to ensure that employees receive their delayed reward is to provide a pension. According to statistics published by the Bureau of Labor Statistics, those retiring at age 65 in 1984, after 20 years of service with their employer and with yearly earnings of $15,000, received an average yearly benefit of $3156.[48] While this sum is not overwhelmingly large, a yearly payment of this size beginning at age 65 and lasting 15 years (the average life expectancy of a 65-year-old) requires a fund of $40,500 to finance it at a 2-percent rate of interest. Thus, giving pensioners $3156 per year from age 65 until death is equivalent to giving the average retiree a lump-sum payment of $40,500. If the pension benefits were more generous, the lump-sum equivalent would increase proportionately. For example, the typical worker earning $15,000 per year and retiring in 1984 with 30 years of service receives $4620 per year in retirement benefits, with a lump-sum equivalent of $59,360 (at a 2-percent interest rate). It is obvious, then, that pensions represent the equivalent of a deferred payment to workers at the end of their careers. Under ERISA, the money to finance this payment must be set aside each year by the employer in a separate fund so that employees have some assurance of receiving their reward even if the firm goes bankrupt. As discussed in this chapter, firms offering their employees pensions must pay lower wages, other things equal, to remain competitive. Thus, pensions offer a mechanism whereby spendable pay is reduced during one's working years but a reward is received later on.

The strongest incentives for diligence under a pension scheme would exist if the pension were not vested. Nonvested employees can be threatened with loss of a pension up to the day before retirement. Vesting, however, modifies the incentive effects of this compensation scheme somewhat. After 1989, most private sector employees with pensions will become vested after five years, so that the threat of losing all rights to their pension is, strictly

[48]   Donald G. Schmitt, ''Today's Pension Plans: How Much Do They Pay?'' *Monthly Labor Review* 108 (December 1985): 19–25.

speaking, only there for the first five years. This in itself may be a long enough time to motivate and observe reliable work habits, but even being fired after becoming vested entails loss. A vested worker fired by Firm X may be able to obtain a pension from X at retirement, but this pension will be smaller to the extent that one's tenure with X is shorter. To receive a *full* pension benefit would require the worker to qualify for a pension with *another* firm—a process that will normally take five more years. Thus, while vesting softens the threat of being fired for cause after five years, it does not remove all the incentive to work honestly and diligently throughout one's career.

## Promotion Lotteries

Another form of worker motivation within the context of internal labor markets might best be called a *promotion lottery*. Suppose a group of entering management trainees were hired with the expectation that *one* of them would become a high-ranking corporate officer and make an extraordinary sum of money each year. The employees who did not make it to the top would be guaranteed a spot in the firm somewhere, but they would not achieve such high earnings.

Now, if everyone knew in advance who would be promoted, this scheme would not be incentive-producing nor would it have aspects of a lottery. However, if no one knew in advance who would "win," but all were told that winning the top job depended on hard work, all would be attracted by the large salary (or prestige) and work hard to get it. Here, as in the previous schemes, the prospect of obtaining large sums toward the end of one's career offers incentives for diligent work throughout earlier years.

In this scheme, however, not all diligent workers get the prize at career's end; only the winner does. Further, once the prize has been awarded and the losers are known, they no longer have the same strong incentives to work hard. Moreover, the employer, knowing the losers have reduced incentives, has every reason to want to get rid of them. Put differently, dangling a lucrative job in front of everyone increases the incentives of all, even the eventual losers, to work hard; however, once the prize has been awarded, the losers are of substantially less value to the firm. The problem for the employer is that employees may not be willing to enter this lottery unless even the losers are treated relatively well. A firm known for firing older mid-level managers may not be able to attract a large enough group of young management trainees from which to produce an excellent corporate officer in the future. For this reason, a firm may be tempted to agree to essentially guarantee the losers desirable jobs somewhere in the organization.

Since workers whose wages are less than or equal to their marginal product do not need any guarantee of job security, it is most likely true that the losers of promotion lotteries have wages or salaries that *exceed* marginal product. If this is the case, the employer will obviously want to offer strong incentives for these employees to retire at a certain point. Again, then, a mandatory retirement clause or inducements to retire voluntarily may be an essential ingredient in the running of a promotion lottery. Hypothesizing that promotion lotteries exist helps explain three phenomena that are widely observed in the labor market. First, it helps explain why, after a number of candidates are carefully considered for a top executive job, one is selected and paid perhaps three times what the others receive. Is it because he or she is three times as productive as the others? If so, the others would not have been serious contenders for the job. The huge pay differential most likely exists to serve as an incentive for younger employees to work hard so they can win the next lottery.[49] Second, the existence of promotion lotteries helps explain why corporations sometimes tolerate *deadwood,* older employees who obviously are not going to be promoted and who clearly are not as productive as they used to be. Such deadwood is the unfortunate cost to the firm of running a successful lottery. Third, because deadwood can be tolerated for a while but not indefinitely, there have arisen mandatory retirement rules or other inducements for employees to retire before they might otherwise decide to do so.

## Policy Issue: Age Discrimination and Implicit Contracts

At several points in this text, we have made reference to Federal legislation concerning age discrimination. In 1967, Congress passed the Age Discrimination in Employment Act, which outlawed employment discrimination against workers aged 40–65 years. In 1978, the Act was amended to protect workers up until age 70 and, as we noted, to outlaw mandatory retirement until age 70. Finally, in 1986, a further amendment was passed that effectively outlawed mandatory retirement for almost all workers.

Age discrimination is a rapidly growing area of employment litigation. For example, the number of age discrimination cases rose by nearly 200 percent from 1980 to 1984, and by another 66 percent in 1985. During the 1980s, about 67 percent of age discrimination cases have dealt with allegedly discriminatory termination of employment.[50] The implicit contract model discussed in this chapter, in which "underpaying" employees in the early stages of their careers and "overpaying" them later serves as an incentive for employees to work well, can at least partially explain this rise in age discrimination cases. In particular, the early 1980s were characterized by severe recessionary conditions in several of our basic industries, such as autos and steel. In this period, many companies went bankrupt and/or lost money for a considerable period of time.[51] According to the implicit contract theory, the older workers

---

[49] This argument is advanced by Edward Lazear and Sherwin Rosen, "Rank-Order Tournaments as Optimum Labor Contracts," *Journal of Political Economy* 89(October 1981): 841–64; and Sherwin Rosen, "Prizes and Incentives in Elimination Tournaments," *American Economic Review* 76(September 1986): 701–15.

[50] See Michael R. Carrell and Frank E. Kuzmits, "Amended ADEA's Effects on HR Strategies Remain Dubious," *Personnel Journal* 66 (May 1987): 111–19; and Michael Schuster and Christopher S. Miller, "An Empirical Assessment of the Age Discrimination in Employment Act," *Industrial and Labor Relations Review* 38 (October 1984): 64–74.

[51] In Chapters 10 and 18, we will discuss the effects of this recession on collective bargaining in these industries. Since 69 percent of age discrimination cases are instituted by professional, managerial, or clerical workers, unions are unlikely to be directly involved in them. See Michael Schuster and Christopher S. Miller, "An Empirical Assessment of the Age Discrimination in Employment Act."

terminated were probably being paid more than they were currently worth. Thus, terminating their employment would be a tempting source of cost savings. In normal times, a firm's concern for its reputation might prevent it from terminating the older workers; however with bankruptcy or large losses looming on the horizon, companies were probably less concerned with their long-run reputations as good employers than they might otherwise have been. Older workers who were terminated might well have felt cheated, having put in their time as relatively underpaid junior employees but being denied the chance to fully recover the earnings sacrificed earlier.

Age-discrimination legislation is leading to changes in personnel practices by many firms. First, companies are being advised to develop objective performance measures that are job-related. Such evidence is typically necessary for a firm to win an age discrimination case.[52]

Second, the 1986 amendment to the Age Discrimination in Employment Act requires firms to continue coverage of their older workers in any company health insurance plan. This provision could greatly increase health insurance costs for firms, and continued coverage of older employees might also serve to delay workers' retirement. Third, we would expect greater efforts on the part of firms to provide voluntary retirement incentives such as the "open window" policies discussed in Example 5.1. While companies could, in principle, reduce older workers' wages to the level of their marginal revenue products, such a move itself would undoubtedly lead to age discrimination charges.

This discussion of changes in personnel practices caused by the legislated ending of mandatory retirement raises the question of who gains and who loses from such legislation. It is clear that employers lose, as the costs of the long-term employment relationship have risen. It is equally clear that people who are currently near retirement gain. Their gain, however, lies in the fact that governmental authority has been used to break a key element of a contract from which they benefited in the past. The fact that firms can no longer enforce a critical element of their old contracts removes from them the incentive to agree to future contracts of the same type. Thus, younger employees may be harmed by the forced elimination of mandatory retirement. In fact, the gains to older employees occur only *once*—to the group that is allowed to break its contract. Future generations of older workers do not gain, since their employment contracts and compensation schemes will be made under the new rules of the game.[53]

## Why Do Earnings Increase with Experience?

Several explanations for the tendency of earnings to increase with a worker's tenure with a firm have been offered in Chapter 5 and this chapter. The first

---

[52]  See Michael R. Carrell and Frank E. Kuzmits, "Amended ADEA's Effects on HR Strategies Remain Dubious."

[53]  For further analysis of the winners and the losers, see Ronald G. Ehrenberg, "Retirement Policy, Employment, and Unemployment," *American Economic Review*, 69 (May 1979): 131–36.

**EXAMPLE  8.3**

# Pay and Seniority in Japan:
# The Nenko System

Large Japanese companies offer essentially lifetime employment (until mandatory retirement) and seniority-based wage increases. Roughly 85 percent of workers in large firms have such benefits, and they comprise about 25 percent of the Japanese labor force. *Nenko* is the practice of basing pay on age and seniority.

While lifetime employment and seniority-based pay are similar to the workings of U.S. internal labor markets we have described in this chapter, the Japanese system also differs from the American system in many interesting ways. For example, large companies in Japan do not respond to economic downturns by laying off their permanent employees even temporarily, as often happens in the U.S. In addition, unlike U.S. workers, Japanese workers receive a large portion of their compensation in the form of semi-annual bonuses. For example, in 1980, among large firms in Japan (those with at least 1000 workers), annual bonuses for males were 35 percent of base annual earnings. In the U.S., only top corporate executives have bonuses that approach this level of relative importance. This bonus system makes Japanese wages somewhat more flexible than those in the U.S. A bad year for a Japanese company lowers the firm's bonus payments, while a good year results in higher bonuses. This flexible form of compensation makes it easier for firms to retain their employees during economic downturns than would a system of rigid compensation.

A second important feature of the Nenko system is that Japanese workers receive continual retraining and are paid by seniority rather than according to the particular job they do. This practice enables firms to reassign workers to different jobs when needed. Moreover, there is evidence that workers in the Japanese system have longer tenure and more steeply sloped seniority-earnings profiles than in the United States. Some believe that these features of the Japanese labor market mean that there is more firm-specific training in Japan. The fact that workers in Japan receive continual retraining and frequently change jobs within their firms supports this idea.

Some aspects of the Japanese system suggest that the incentive issues we have raised in this chapter may also be relevant in several ways. First, high pay, a large bonus component, and a steeply-sloped tenure-earnings profile are all especially pronounced at large Japanese firms and are present to a lesser extent at smaller firms. Larger firms are thus able to be highly selective among applicants and are presumably able to choose workers for whom lifetime employment will be a good match. Second, a high reliance on bonuses in the Japanese case is an example of group incentives, since the bonus payments do not vary by individual performance. The bonus system thus serves as a motivator, subject to the difficulties of a group incentive system we have discussed earlier in this chapter. Third, even though the Japanese system is characterized by lifetime employment, this benefit is not an absolute guarantee. Dismissals occur in the event of "anti-social" behavior, for example. While this probability of dismissal may be small, Japan's extreme reliance on seniority implies that the losses a worker suffers when dismissed will be especially large. As in the efficiency wage and implicit contract

models, these losses, when combined with even a small (but positive) likelihood of dismissal, may motivate workers to perform well. Further, Japanese workers appear to have more contact with management, as supervisors regularly work beside production workers. This practice is said to build up company loyalty. Evidently one is less likely to shirk with a manager working nearby than if one were unsupervised.

SOURCES: Masanori Hashimoto and John Raisian, "Employment Tenure and Earnings Profiles in Japan and the United States," *American Economic Review* 75 (September 1985): 721–35; Nan Weiner, "The Japanese Wage System," *Compensation Review* 14 (First Quarter 1982): pp. 46–56; Nanshi Matsuura, "Japanese Management and Labor Relations in the U.S. Subsidiaries," *Industrial Relations Journal* 15 (Winter 1984): 38–46; and Koji Taira, *Economic Development and the Labor Market in Japan* (New York: Columbia University Press, 1970).

explanation is that increased earnings are a reward for workers' investments in implicit and explicit training during the early years of their careers. The second is that the use of earnings profiles that increase with experience serves to motivate workers and reduce shirking. To these a third can be offered, namely that workers with long job tenures tend to be workers who have made good "job matches" and thus are more productive, on average, than otherwise identical workers with shorter job tenures.[54] Is it possible to ascertain which of these three explanations is most correct?

In fact, a number of recent econometric studies provide support for *each* of these explanations. One study found that earnings increase most rapidly with seniority for workers during the stages of their careers in which they are undergoing formal or informal training.[55] Two other studies found that a share of the apparent return to experience is due to the more-experienced workers having made better job matches.[56] Finally, a fourth study has provided evidence in favor of the incentive compensation argument.[57]

These findings illustrate that the various theories of the relationship between earnings and experience are not mutually exclusive. To say that one explanation appears to have support does *not* imply that the others are unimportant. Rather, it appears that *each* of the theories provides a partial explanation for the increase of earnings with job tenure.

## REVIEW QUESTIONS

1. There is a law that compensation of federal government employees must be comparable to that of private sector employees of similar skills who perform similar duties. Suppose that pay in the two sectors were compared by measuring salaries or wages of a "typical" worker in each sector (one, say, with 10 years of experience). In what respects would this approach be deficient?

[54] Boyan Jovanovic, "Job Matching and the Theory of Turnover," *Journal of Political Economy* 87 (October 1979): 972–90.

[55] James Brown, "Are Those Paid More Really No More Productive?" Princeton University Industrial Relations Section Working Paper no. 169, October 1983.

[56] Joseph Altonji and Robert Shakotko, "Do Wages Rise with Job Seniority?" *Review of Economic Studies* 54 (July 1987): 437–59; and Katharine Abraham and Henry Farber, "Job Duration, Seniority and Earnings," *American Economic Review* 77(June 1987): 278–97.

[57] Robert Hutchens, "A Test of Lazear's Theory of Delayed Payment Contracts," *Journal of Labor Economics* 5 (October 1987, Part 2): S153–S170.

2. In 1981 the President's Commission on Pension Policy proposed that every employee in the country be covered by a Minimum Universal Pension (MUP). This pension would vest immediately and would be fully *portable*. (That is, all workers would qualify for a pension no matter how many employers they worked for in their lifetime or how long they worked for each. Currently, employees are not eligible to receive any private pension benefits at age 65 unless they have worked for an employer 5 years.) What impact would a MUP have on labor costs and productivity?

3. Suppose that when mandatory retirement was abolished, firms undertook various strategies to induce *voluntary* retirements at age 65. Some of these possible strategies are listed below. The firm's objectives are to unambiguously increase the incentives for people over 65 to retire, but to do so in a way that offers the strongest incentives to the *least productive* of the older workers to retire. (For our purposes, the least productive will be defined as the workers no other firm would want at anything close to their current wage. Assume that productive workers, even though elderly, could get jobs elsewhere at close to their current wage.) Evaluate each of the following strategies to determine whether it will accomplish the firm's objectives.
   a. Cut the wages of all workers after the age of 65
   b. Provide a large lump-sum payment to anyone who quits his or her employment *at the firm* at age 65
   c. Increase the monthly pension benefit of anyone who *retires* (and does not work elsewhere) at age 65

4. In 1982 the State of New York paid its employees for only 50 of the 52 weeks they worked. This 4 percent pay cut was accomplished by increasing pay periods from 14 to 15 days apart for 14 pay periods (the other 11 pay periods were the normal 14 days). The two weeks of pay not given to employees was placed in a fund to be paid (with interest) when employees quit or retired. While the purpose of this scheme may have been to "force" employees to lend money to their state employer, the *effects* of schemes like this on quits and retirements may not be neutral. Explain.

5. Many states, particularly in the Snowbelt, have experienced the problem of "runaway" firms (firms that close down operations within their borders and move to another state, usually in the Sunbelt). Some states have adopted policies to discourage firms from closing operations and leaving the state. One such policy is to require firms closing down to provide *severance pay* to their workers; that is, if a firm permanently closes down operations within the state's borders, it is required to make a lump-sum payment to its former employees. What are the labor market effects of requiring firms in this situation to give severance pay to employees?

# SELECTED READINGS

Jeremy Bulow and Lawrence Summers, "A Theory of Dual Labor Markets with Applications to Industrial Policy, Discrimination and Keynesian Unemployment," *Journal of Labor Economics* 4(July 1986): 376–414.

Peter Doeringer and Michael Piore, *Internal Labor Markets and Manpower Analysis* (Lexington, MA: D. C. Heath and Co., 1971).

Ronald Ehrenberg and Robert Smith, "A Framework for Evaluating State and Local Government Pension Reform," *Public Sector Labor Markets*, Peter Mieszkowski and George E. Peterson (eds.) (Washington, DC: The Urban Institute, 1981).

Robert Flanagan, "Implicit Contracts, Explicit Contracts and Wages," *American Economic Review Papers and Proceedings* 74(May 1984): 345–49.

Edward Lazear, "Why Is There Mandatory Retirement?" *Journal of Political Economy* 87(December 1979): 1261–84.

John Pencavel, "Work Effort, On-the-Job Screening, and Alternative Methods of Remuneration," *Research in Labor Economics*, vol. 1, ed. Ronald Ehrenberg (Greenwich, CT: JAI Press, 1977): 225–58.

Sherwin Rosen, "Implicit Contracts," *Journal of Economic Literature* 23(September 1985): 1144–75.

# CHAPTER 9

## Company Compensation Policies

In the previous chapter we discussed the goals firms want to achieve using their systems of compensation: recruitment, retention, and motivation of their employees. In this chapter, we will take a closer look at the specific compensation policies used by employers. We will pay particular attention to job-evaluation systems, pay for performance, and bonus payments. In addition, we will examine recent trends and innovations in compensation policy. The focus will be on the nonunion sector, which covers over 80 percent of American workers. In Chapter 18 we will discuss innovations in compensation policy for union workers. Our emphasis will always be on the costs and benefits of following various policies.

## Job Evaluation and Internal Labor Markets

A major feature of internal labor markets that we have discussed earlier in several places is the insulation from external market forces provided to both workers and firms. For example, recall our Chapter 4 discussion of firm-specific training. After training, firms have incentives to pay workers more than they could get elsewhere but less than their marginal revenue products. Workers' alternative wages could therefore rise to some extent and they would not quit; likewise, their marginal revenue products could fall by some amount and they would not quit or be laid off by the firm. Thus, to a degree, both firms and workers are cushioned from market forces.

Further, from our discussion of implicit contracts in the previous chapter, recall that in the delayed-payments compensation scheme senior workers are paid more than their alternative compensation levels; firms' concerns for their reputations prevent discharges. Junior workers are paid less than their marginal revenue products, and the prospects of higher future earnings keep them from quitting. Again, a long-term employment relationship is the outcome, and outside market events may not immediately affect the behavior of workers or management.[1]

For any company with an internal labor market, two related kinds of issues must receive considerable attention: (1) the relationship of its compensation structure to the external labor market; and (2) the incentive effects and perceptions of the fairness of its internal wage structure. To some degree these issues pose conflicts for company policy. For example, external competitiveness may require that some jobs be paid more than others, an outcome that some workers may perceive as inequitable. Nonetheless, companies must be aware of both kinds of issues.

**External Competitiveness.**   In Chapters 2 and 6 we discussed problems that might occur if a company paid insufficient attention to the external labor market. If, for example, a firm does not adjust its starting salaries in entry-level jobs ("key jobs") as wages for these jobs rise elsewhere, then it will have difficulty attracting or retaining workers of the appropriate quality. Conversely, a company whose entry wages rise well above those elsewhere may find that it is paying more than is necessary to attract or retain workers. In this case, its costs may be higher than those of its competitors, and its product market share could thus decline.

**Internal Pay Structure.**   A firm's choice of an internal pay structure—that is, the relationships among pay levels in different jobs and among workers in the same job—has several important consequences for the company's success. First, psychological research has established that workers perceive some pay structures as more equitable than others, depending on how rates of pay compare to the qualifications required, the type of working conditions, and the value of the work performed.[2] Furthermore, these perceptions evidently have consequences; as the compensation literature has argued, if workers perceive a pay structure as unfair, they will be more likely to quit or to resist change and less likely to perform well than otherwise.[3] In addition, there is evidence that a nonunion firm's internal pay structure affects its workers' support of trade unions. Apparently, a potential cost of a pay structure perceived to be unfair is an increased likelihood of union organization.[4] Additional evidence indicates that union policies indirectly lower pay

---

[1] Recall from Chapter 8 that in the efficiency wage model, the worker is paid more than his or her best alternative (reducing the likelihood of quitting), but is merely paid according to the marginal revenue product. Thus, dismissals are a real possibility and in fact are a motivating force in this model. Of course, there may be elements of efficiency wages as well as specific training and implicit contracts associated with internal labor markets. This combination may well occur in Japan, as discussed in Example 8.3.

[2] For a summary of this research, see George T. Milkovich and Jerry M. Newman, *Compensation,* 2d ed. (Plano, TX: Business Publications, Inc., 1987), Chapter 2.

[3] This notion has been termed *equity theory.* See J. S. Adams, "Injustices in Social Exchange," in *Advances in Experimental Social Psychology,* Vol. 2, ed. L. Berkowitz (New York: Academic Press, 1965): 267–99; and George Milkovich and Jerry Newman, *Compensation,* p. 44.

[4] See Henry S. Farber and Daniel H. Saks, "Why Workers Want Unions: The Role of Relative Wages and Job Characteristics," *Journal of Political Economy* 88 (April 1980): 349–67. In Chapter 11 we will analyze the individual worker's decision to join a union.

differentials among nonunion workers in the same industry, further suggesting that nonunion companies perceive that their pay policies affect the likelihood of being unionized.[5]

Second, different internal pay structures have different incentive effects. Wage differentials among jobs are often necessary to motivate workers to accept training, increased responsibilities, unpleasant working conditions, or inconvenient hours of work.[6] For example, Example 6.1 showed that workers on the night and evening shifts earned about 3-percent more than they would have received if they worked during the day.[7]

## Job Evaluation Procedures

Job evaluation attempts to accomplish both objectives of meeting external competitiveness as well as demonstrating internal fairness. Recall from Chapter 2 that about 86 percent of large and medium-sized companies use some form of job evaluation when setting pay. Further, a recent study showed that coverage by job-evaluation plans was uniform across several industries: in 1982, at least 89 percent of large manufacturing companies, 88 percent of banks, 88 percent of insurance companies, and 73 percent of diversified finance firms had job-evaluation systems.[8] Table 9.1 illustrates some of the characteristics of job-evaluation plans for a sample of large- and medium-sized companies. It reveals several interesting patterns.

First, within this sample of companies, the largest ones are more likely than the smaller ones to have job-evaluation plans; the table indicates that 89 percent of larger-than-average firms have formal job-evaluation systems, as compared to 77 percent for smaller-than-average firms. This difference points to one reason for having such a plan: a systematic method for keeping track of all of a company's different jobs is needed, and this need is especially acute for a large company.

Second, 56 percent of companies with job evaluation plans use outside help in developing their plans. Again, larger firms are more likely to use consultants than smaller firms, and larger firms are more likely than smaller firms to use commercially available job-evaluation plans. Evidently, the greater complexity of large firms provides a better justification for spending

---

[5] See Lawrence M. Kahn and Michael Curme, "Unions and Nonunion Wage Dispersion," *The Review of Economics and Statistics* 69 (November 1987): 600–607. While this narrowing of nonunion pay differentials may reflect a perceived fairness of more equal pay, it may also reflect the idea that the lowest paid workers simply gain more from a union. See our discussion in Chapter 16 of unions and wage inequality.

[6] See Edward P. Lazear, "Severance Pay, Pensions, and Efficient Mobility," Working Paper No. 854, National Bureau of Economic Research, Cambridge, MA, February 1982.

[7] See Sandra L. King and Harry B. Williams, "Shift Work Pay Differentials and Practices in Manufacturing," *Monthly Labor Review* 108 (December 1985): 26–33.

[8] See Charles Peck, *Pay & Performance: The Interaction of Compensation & Performance Appraisal,* Conference Board Research Bulletin 155 (New York: The Conference Board, 1984), pp. 4 and 7. We use the term "at least" because about 1 percent of the sample did not respond to the question about job evaluation, but the author did not break down this non-response by industry. The figures given here are the number of companies with job-evaluation plans as a percentage of the total sample including those not answering the question. Since the response rate was about 99%, the figures are accurate enough.

**Table 9.1**  Characteristics of Job-Evaluation Plans

| Compensation Policy or Practice | Above Average[a] for Industry | Average for Industry | Small for Industry | Total |
|---|---|---|---|---|
| Existence of formal job evaluation | 89.0% | 86.0% | 76.9% | 86.4% |
| Development of current job evaluation system[b] | | | | |
| By outside consultant | 58.0% | 55.0% | 47.5% | 55.5% |
| By personnel or compensation specialist | 44.6 | 42.8 | 40.0 | 43.3 |
| By committee with employee representation | 11.9 | 4.2 | 7.8 | 7.5 |
| Through collective bargaining | 5.2 | 3.4 | 0.0 | 3.8 |
| Administration and application of job-evaluation system | | | | |
| By personnel department | 91.0% | 80.0% | 80.0% | 85.0% |
| By management-employee committee | 10.1 | 6.2 | 5.0 | 7.9 |
| By outside consultants | 1.9 | 4.2 | 5.1 | 3.2 |
| Percent of jobs covered by job evaluation | 87.1% | 87.0% | 84.2% | 86.8% |
| Use of a single job-evaluation plan across all jobs | 37.8% | 40.6% | 52.9% | 40.6% |
| Use of jobs grouped into clusters (for example, clerical, managerial) for job evaluation | 61.5% | 59.4% | 47.1% | 59.1% |
| Use of commercially available job-evaluation plans (for example, Hay system) | 50.3% | 42.5% | 33.3% | 45.2% |
| Use of weighting of compensable factors on a statistical basis | 35.5% | 43.2% | 38.7% | 39.1% |
| Use of weighting of compensable factors on a judgmental basis | 62.9% | 54.9% | 61.3% | 59.4% |
| Wage survey practices | | | | |
| Conduct own wage survey | 3.2% | 6.3% | 5.1% | 4.7% |
| Purchase wage survey | 9.6 | 13.3 | 10.5 | 11.2 |
| Both | 86.5 | 79.0 | 84.6 | 83.1 |

[a]  Size categories refer to a company's size relative to its industry. The study did not provide specific quantitative criteria for classifying firms by size. Therefore, the size categories should be viewed as qualitative.

[b]  Figures from here on refer to percentages of those companies with job evaluation plans.

SOURCE:  From *Compensation Review,* "Where Do Compensation Specialists Stand on Comparable Worth?" by Thomas Mahoney, Sara Rynes, and Benson Rosen. Copyright © 1984 by American Management Association. All rights reserved. Reprinted by permission.

money on outside consultant services than does the simpler organization of smaller companies. The use of job-evaluation plans may be an example of economies of scale in which the larger the firm is, the less expensive the system becomes per worker hired.[9]

---

[9]  See Robert S. Smith, "Comparable Worth: Limited Coverage and the Exacerbation of Inequality," *Industrial and Labor Relations Review* 41 (January 1988): 227–39.

Third, most companies use different plans for different types of "job clusters" (such as clerical, sales, or production and maintenance), and this practice is especially pronounced for large firms. Companies use more than one system because different types of job clusters have different attributes that the company wants to reward. For example, a set of production and maintenance jobs may require mechanical skills, while decision-making skills are likely to be important in a job-evaluation plan for managers. Having separate plans for different groups of jobs allows greater flexibility in their design and greater accuracy in capturing the differences in jobs than does relying on one plan for everyone. From the data in Table 9.1 it is evident that larger, more complex firms are more likely to benefit from using separate plans for different departments. Finally, the near-universal usage of wage surveys indicates an awareness of external labor market conditions.

To design and use a job-evaluation system, a company must make several basic policy decisions.[10] First, the factors the firm wants to measure must be chosen (the "compensable factors"). These factors are items such as knowledge, skill, working conditions, and responsibility. Second, the relative weights attached to the different factors must be chosen. For example, how much should an extra 10 points on a scale measuring knowledge be worth (in setting a score for the job) compared to an extra 10 points on a scale measuring responsibility? Finally, how should differences in job-evaluation scores be translated into pay differences? Should all jobs with the same job-evaluation score receive the same base pay? Should all workers in the same job receive the same base pay? What factors besides job-evaluation scores should a company take into account when setting pay levels? This is the point at which outside salary surveys usually affect internal wage decisions.

**Choosing compensable factors.** Finding the compensable factors starts with an accurate description of the responsibilities and duties associated with each job title. A job description is developed through a job-analysis procedure that includes both tours of the work site by a job analyst and interviews with employees and supervisors.[11] While there are many possible different compensable factors, a small number of them occur over and over again in different plans. As we have noted, these factors are skill, effort, responsibility, and working conditions. Such factors are very close to the job characteristics that Adam Smith believed two hundred years ago would lead to compensating wage differentials (recall Chapter 6).[12] Thus, most job-

---

[10] For further discussion of issues of design and implementation of job evaluation plans, see George T. Milkovich and Jerry M. Newman, *Compensation*, Chapters 3–5; Donald P. Schwab, "Job Evaluation and Pay Setting: Concepts and Practices," in E. Robert Livernash, ed., *Comparable Worth: Issues and Alternatives* (Washington, D.C.: Equal Employment Advisory Council, 1980), pp. 49–77; and David W. Belcher and Thomas J. Atchison, *Compensation Administration*, 2nd ed. (Englewood Cliffs, N.J.: Prentice-Hall, Inc., 1987), Chapters 9–11.

[11] See George T. Milkovich and Jerry M. Newman, *Compensation*, p. 68. Such documentation may well be necessary should there be any challenge under the discrimination laws of a company's wage decisions. Recall from Chapter 7 that for a hiring discrepancy to be considered nondiscriminatory, it must be shown to be job-related.

[12] See Donald P. Schwab, "Job Evaluation and Pay Setting: Concepts and Practices," p. 64.

**Table 9.2**   Factors and Weights for Selected Salaried
Job-Evaluation Plans

| Factors | NEMA* | Employers Assn. | Consultant | Trade Assn. | Appliance Mfgr. |
|---|---|---|---|---|---|
| Education | 17.5 | 10.6 | 15.0 | 12.3 | |
| Experience | 29.0 | 16.0 | 9.0 | 19.0 | 10.1 |
| Training | | | 9.0 | | 10.1 |
| Complexity | 14.5 | 10.6 | | 12.3 | |
| Mental Skill | | | 27.0 | 3.3 | 48.2 |
| Responsibility for: | | | | | |
|   Function | | 10.6 | 22.0 | | |
|   Procedures | | 6.3 | | | |
|   Confidential data | | 4.2 | | 3.3 | |
|   Assets | | 8.0 | | | |
|   Errors | | | | 11.0 | 11.6 |
| Monetary responsibility | 8.8 | | | | |
| Contacts | 8.8 | 8.0 | 7.0 | 11.0 | 10.8 |
| Working conditions | 3.8 | 3.7 | 5.0 | 3.3 | 9.2 |
| Hazards | | 7.0 | | | |
| Types of supervision | 8.8 | 7.5 | 3.0 | 11.0 | |
| Extent of supervision | 8.8 | 7.5 | 3.0 | 13.5 | |
| Total | 100.0 | 100.0 | 100.0 | 100.0 | 100.0 |

*"NEMA" stands for "National Electrical Manufacturers Association."
SOURCE:   From *Compensation Administration* 2d ed. by David W. Belcher and Thomas J. Atchinson, p. 204. Copyright © 1987 by Prentice-Hall, Inc. Reprinted by permission.

evaluation procedures reward the same things that the theory we discussed in Chapter 6 predicted would be rewarded in competitive labor markets.

**Weighting the Compensable Factors.**   Table 9.2 illustrates factor weights for several widely used job-evaluation plans for salaried positions. While similar factors are rewarded, they receive different weights. For example, workers under the National Electrical Manufacturers Association (NEMA) plan receive a greater relative reward for additional experience required on the job than under the other plans. Greater use of firm-specific training, on-the-job learning, or delayed-payments contracts for firms in the NEMA could explain the larger weight experience gets in their plan as compared to other plans.

On what basis are such factor weights selected? Table 9.1 shows that about 60 percent of companies with job-evaluation plans choose weights on a judgmental basis, while 39 percent use some form of statistical analysis to construct weights. Companies using statistical analysis generally relate the various factors to market forces. Companies using their judgment may or may not take into account the external labor market in setting weights. For example, about 33 percent of companies with job-evaluation systems use a plan developed by Hay Associates, a management consulting company.[13] This is

---

[13]   Charles Peck, *Pay & Performance: The Interaction of Compensation & Performance Appraisal* Conference Board Research Bulletin 155 (New York: The Conference Board, 1984). p. 11.

an internal plan that forms point values independent of the market.[14] As mentioned several times, however, even though companies using such plans will generate job-evaluation scores that do not directly reflect the market, they will take market forces into account at the final stage at which one moves from job-evaluation scores to wage rates.

While the Hay System uses administratively determined factor weights, other plans use market wages to help form factor weights. As described in Example 9.1, such a process in effect gives each compensable factor a weight equal to the relative pay premium that the market places on it for key jobs (that is, jobs filled by external hires). Changes in the market for workers in key jobs will therefore directly affect job evaluation factor weights and hence the total job point scores for non-key jobs.

**Using Weighted Factor Scores to Determine Salaries.**  Once a company has decided upon its list of compensable factors and the relative weights placed on them, the firm must then decide how to use these weighted factor scores to determine salaries. There are at least two steps involved in such a process. First, the company must decide on its overall pay level relative to the market. Should it be a high-wage employer, for example? Second, it must combine the job-evaluation results with other information to determine pay differentials within the firm.

Regarding the overall pay level, we mentioned in earlier chapters that companies may derive benefits from paying high wages. These benefits include a larger supply of applicants, lower turnover, and better morale and higher performance levels of its workers. For firms with product market monopoly power, we mentioned in Chapter 3 that high wages may be a convenient way of hiding a high rate of return that might otherwise provoke government regulation. A further benefit of high pay for a nonunion company is a reduced likelihood of being unionized. These benefits must be weighed against the direct costs of paying higher compensation.

Having decided on an overall pay level, companies exercise considerable discretion in translating their job evaluation results into salaries. In the first instance this is done by relating the job-evaluation scores in "key" jobs—those filled from the external labor market—to market pay (either above, at, or below the average paid for these jobs in the market). After the appropriate relationship between job scores and pay is determined for "key" jobs, that same relationship is applied to "non-key" jobs.

The company's choice of what jobs to call "key" is clearly crucial to the workings of the job-evaluation system. Some middle- or high-level jobs are filled mostly from the inside, so a job score/pay relationship set of factor weights derived only from lower-level jobs may be inappropriate if applied to these upper-level jobs. However, as indicated in Table 9.3, many higher-level jobs are filled both externally and internally; this is especially true of computer jobs, but applies to sales and clerical jobs as well. Clearly, then, some

---

[14]  See A. D. Bellak, "The Hay Guide Chart-Profile Method of Job Evaluation," in M. Rock, ed. *Handbook of Wage and Salary Administration*, 2d ed. (New York, McGraw-Hill, 1983), pp. 384–412.

EXAMPLE     9.1

# Market Wages and Job-Evaluation Factor Weights

As discussed earlier, about 40 percent of job-evaluation systems use statistical analysis to form weights for their compensable factors. It is very common among such plans to use market wages as an aid in constructing weights. This example illustrates how this analysis is done. First, a company must locate its key jobs—the externally filled jobs for which a well-developed external labor market exists. A market-wage survey is then either taken or bought by the company. In this survey, average external compensation levels for the firm's key jobs are tabulated. Next, the firm must measure its compensable factors for the key jobs. Suppose these factors are skill ($X_1$), responsibility ($X_2$), effort ($X_3$), and working conditions ($X_4$), four of the most common items.

The firm then conducts a *regression analysis* (see Appendix 7A) to compute the effect on wages in key jobs of one more point in each category, holding points in all the other categories constant. Put differently, regression analysis is used to estimate the market value of an added point in *each* category. In such an analysis, it is posited that for the key jobs,

$$C = a + b_1X_1 + b_2X_2 + b_3X_3 + b_4X_4 + u,$$

where $C$ is a job's market compensation level, $b_1$, $b_2$, $b_3$, and $b_4$ are factor weights to be estimated using regression analysis, $a$ is a constant (also to be estimated by regression analysis), and $u$ summarizes all other influences on compensation that we are not able to measure. If, for example, a job has factor scores $X_1$, $X_2$, $X_3$, and $X_4$, then its predicted compensation is $a + b_1X_1 + b_2X_2 + b_3X_3$, and $b_4X_4$.

Once the factor weights ($b_1$ through $b_4$) and constant ($a$) are estimated using key jobs, the predicted compensation for each non-key job can be computed by applying the weights and constant to the factor scores in each category. (This process requires a lot of key jobs in order to establish a meaningful statistical relationship.) This predicted compensation can then be used in setting base pay for the non-key jobs. Even though the non-key jobs may not have well-developed external labor markets (because they are filled by promotion from within), their pay rates will respond directly to changes in the external labor market for key jobs. For instance, an increasing abundance of educated workers in the market will lower pay for highly educated employees relative to less-educated workers. When a new wage survey is taken and new factor weights are computed through regression analysis, the new factor weight for skill will be smaller than the old one, reflecting the reduced premium for highly educated workers.

Note:   The plan described here differs from the one in Appendix 7A in that the weights for that plan were not chosen using a statistical process. Rather, the factor weights were chosen administratively, and regression analysis was then used to estimate the relationship between salary and the total job-evaluation score. The plan described in this example relates pay to points for *each* category, not simply to the total.

SOURCES:   David D. Robinson, Owen W. Wahlstrom, and Robert C. Mecham, "Comparison of Job Evaluation Methods: A "Policy-Capturing" Approach Using the Position Analysis Questionnaire," *Journal of Applied Psychology* 59 (October 1974): 633–37; Donald J. Treiman, *Job Evaluation: An Analytic Review*, Interim Report to the Equal Employment Opportunity Commission (Washington, DC: National Academy of Sciences, 1979); and Donald P. Schwab, "Job Evaluation and Pay Setting: Concepts and Practices," in E. R. Livernash, ed., *Comparable Worth: Issues and Alternatives* (Washington, DC: Equal Employment Advisory Council, 1980): 65–67.

**Table 9.3**   External versus Internal Hiring in Twelve Large Boston-Area White-Collar Companies

| Job Category | Percentage of Firms for Which External Hiring Is Reported as Common or Very Common | |
|---|---|---|
| | High-level Position | Mid-Level Position |
| Sales | 28% | 16% |
| Managerial | 10 | 0 |
| Computer | 40 | 50 |
| Clerical | 25 | 70 |

SOURCE:  Paul Osterman, "White-Collar Internal Labor Markets," in *Internal Labor Markets*, Paul Osterman (ed.), (Cambridge, MA: The MIT Press, 1984), p. 172.

"judgment calls" must be made concerning whether a job is to be considered "key" (filled externally) or "non-key."[15]

Many companies that use job evaluation implement a *range-of-rates* system in which there is a range of pay rates for each job. For example, a company may have decided on the basis of a job evaluation that the junior accountant position is worth $30,000. However, the firm may set a range of $24,000 to $36,000 for actual salaries of workers in this job. Where a particular worker may fall in such a range will usually depend on personal characteristics such as merit, experience, or seniority.

Table 9.4 reports the results of a 1984 U.S. Bureau of Labor Statistics study of the pay practices of 3100 firms employing white-collar workers.[16] The table shows that about 80 percent of white-collar employees are covered by formal salary plans in which pay rates and/or ranges are systematically mapped out for each job. In virtually all cases in which there is a formal salary plan, there is a range of rates; this is true for over 99.5 percent of professional and administrative employees and for 97.5 percent of technical and clerical employees. Further, the data in Table 9.4 imply that among workers covered by formal salary plans, there are merit reviews for 84 percent of professional and administrative workers and 67 percent of technical and clerical employ-

---

[15] Note that Table 9.3 shows that 28 percent of top-level sales jobs are filled from outside, while only 16 percent of middle-level sales positions are entered from outside the company. Further, top-level managerial jobs are also more likely to be filled from the outside than middle-level jobs. Compared to other types of jobs, productivity of top-level sales people or managers in other companies may be especially visible. For example each sales representative is likely to have a "portfolio" of customers that may be common knowledge in the industry. Thus the information problems that lead to promotion from within (see Chapter 4) are likely to be less severe for sales representatives than for other types of workers. Similar reasoning applies to top level managers; outsiders can observe the overall performance of a top executive's company or division and give credit or blame for the unit's performance to the executive.

[16] See Martin E. Personick, "White-Collar Pay Determination Under Range-of-Rate Systems," *Monthly Labor Review* 107 (December 1984): 25–30.

**Table 9.4** Percent of White-Collar Employees, by Method of Wage Payment and Rate Range Characteristics, March 1984

| Method of Salary Payment and Rate Range Characteristics | Professional and Administrative Employees | Technical and Clerical Employees |
|---|---|---|
| *Method of salary payment* | | |
| All employees | 100% | 100% |
| Formal plans | 81 | 79 |
| Range of rates | 81 | 77 |
| Merit review | 68 | 53 |
| Length of service | 1 | 11 |
| Combination | 11 | 14 |
| Single rate | (*) | 2 |
| Individual determination | 18 | 20 |
| Other type of plan | 1 | (*) |
| *Selected characteristics* | | |
| Employees under rate ranges | 100% | 100% |
| Minimum and maximum rate specified | 98 | 95 |
| Minimum is specified, no set maximum | 2 | 4 |
| Maximum is specified, no set minimum | 1 | (*) |
| Rate range is typically adjusted: | | |
| More than once a year | 3 | 5 |
| Once a year | 81 | 78 |
| Less than once a year | 5 | 5 |
| No formal provision | 11 | 11 |
| Information not available | 1 | (*) |
| Normal hiring rate within rate range at: | | |
| Minimum of range | 25 | 42 |
| Lower fourth of range | 25 | 21 |
| Lower half of range | 21 | 14 |
| Other part of range | 9 | 6 |
| No formal provision | 19 | 16 |
| Information not available | 1 | 1 |
| Location of job's market value: | | |
| Midpoint of range | 62 | 59 |
| Maximum of range | 2 | 5 |
| Minimum to midpoint of range | 4 | 5 |
| Midpoint to maximum of range | 13 | 9 |
| No established concept | 17 | 20 |
| Information not available | 1 | 2 |

\* Less than 0.5 percent.

Note: Because of rounding, sums of individual items may not equal 100.

SOURCE: Martin E. Personick, "White-Collar Pay Determination Under Range-of-Rate Systems," *Monthly Labor Review* 107 (December 1984): 27.

ees. If we presume that some kind of merit review is involved for those workers in the "individual determination" category, the study indicates that merit reviews affect virtually all white-collar workers' salaries. The next section takes a closer look at the operation of such merit reviews.

According to Table 9.4, length of service (seniority) either by itself or in combination with merit directly enters into the formal salary plans for only 15–32 percent of white-collar workers covered by these plans. However, it is possible that merit reviews themselves take seniority into account. (Example 9.2 is a case in which seniority does affect the merit review process, and it may be typical of many merit plans.) To the extent that merit reviews are influenced by seniority, then seniority may affect salaries indirectly as well as directly. A 1980 case study of two large firms showed that within a job grade level, workers with more seniority were paid higher salaries, even after controlling for precompany experience, performance rating, and educational background.[17] While it may not be valid to generalize from this case study, it does suggest that seniority can have its own effect on salaries even in companies using merit reviews to set salaries within the range for a particular job. Such evidence would support the delayed-payments, implicit-contract model discussed in Chapter 8.

The characteristics of rate-range systems are illustrated in Tables 9.4 and 9.5. Several aspects of these systems emerge in the tables. First, almost all plans have both maximum and minimum rates for each job. Second, the scale of pay is adjusted at least once a year in over 80 percent of the cases, implying that these systems can respond to changes in labor market conditions. Third, almost all new hiring is done in the lower half of the rate range, a practice consistent with the existence of a seniority premium. Fourth, in about 60 percent of the plans, the midpoint of the range equals the job's "market value," defined in Table 9.4 to be the value to the firm of the job when it is competently performed. This correspondence suggests a close connection between average pay levels for a job and marginal revenue product (recall the Upjohn case discussed in Example 3.2).[18]

Finally, the average widths of rate ranges for various job classes are shown in Table 9.5. The table indicates a considerable variation in rates within particular jobs, with maximums exceeding minimums by over 50 percent in higher-level jobs and by 37–49 percent for lower-level white-collar jobs. The more compressed ranges for lower-level jobs invite at least two kinds of explanation. On the one hand, the higher-level jobs are more complex, and there may be more room for differences in performance levels for

---

[17] See James L. Medoff and Katherine Abraham, "Experience, Performance, and Earnings," *Quarterly Journal of Economics* 95 (December 1980): 703–36. See also our discussion in Chapter 8 on why earnings increase with experience.

[18] The finding that the midpoint of the range equals the marginal revenue product suggests that in those cases where seniority is a factor determining where one is paid in the range, junior workers may be "underpaid," while senior workers may be "overpaid." These outcomes are consistent with the model of delayed-payments implicit contracts discussed in Chapter 8.

**Table 9.5**   Width of Range Rates for Workers Covered
by Rate-Range Systems, March 1983

| | *Mean Width of Establishment Rate Range (percent by which the maximum rate exceeds the minimum rate)* |
|---|---|
| *Professional-Administrative* | |
| Accountants | 51–54% |
| Auditors | 52–53 |
| Attorneys | 53–57 |
| Buyers | 51–54 |
| Programmer/analysts | 50–53 |
| Job analysts | 53–56 |
| Directors of Personnel | 51–56 |
| Chemists | 51–54 |
| Engineers | 52–56 |
| *Technical-Clerical* | |
| Computer operators | 46–49% |
| Drafters | 41–44 |
| Engineering technicians | 42–47 |
| Photographers | 48–52 |
| Accounting clerks | 43–45 |
| File clerks | 42–47 |
| Key entry operators | 44 |
| Messengers | 44 |
| Secretaries | 45–49 |
| Stenographers | 37–48 |
| Typists | 45–47 |
| Personnel clerks | 44–48 |
| Purchasing assistants | 41–44 |

SOURCE:  Martin E. Personick, "White-Collar Pay Determination Under Range-of-Rate Systems," *Monthly Labor Review* 107 (December 1984): 28–29.

workers in these jobs. On the other hand, workers are less likely to be promoted out of high-level jobs, suggesting the possibility of higher accumulated seniority in them. This higher seniority could widen the rate ranges for these jobs.

What is the actual, as compared to the potential, range of pay rates for jobs? There appears to be less clustering of employees at the low end of pay ranges in upper-level jobs. For example, in the U.S. Bureau of Labor Statistics study from which Tables 9.4 and 9.5 are taken, 46 percent of Accountant I workers were paid within 10 percent of their minimums, while only 26 percent of the Accountant III workers were within 10 percent of their minimum pay levels. Similar differences in clustering were found between Drafter I and III (44 percent vs. 27 percent) and Accounting Clerk I and III (38 percent vs. 21

**Table 9.6**    Types of Private-Sector Pay Increases Given in the
United States, 1974–75

| | *Type of Increase* | | | |
| | *(Percentage of Firms Employing a Given Type* *of Worker Providing a Given Type of Increase)* | | | |
| *Employee Class* | *General* | *Merit* | *COLA[a]* | *Longevity* |
|---|---|---|---|---|
| Union hourly | 87% | 10% | 39% | 27% |
| Nonunion hourly | 69 | 49 | 10 | 17 |
| Nonexempt salaried | 49 | 88 | 11 | 7 |
| Exempt salaried[b] | 41 | 87 | 9 | 3 |
| Officers | 25 | 91 | 4 | 1 |

[a] "COLA" increases are cost-of-living-based raises that may be automatic or discretionary but are given across the board.

[b] "Exempt" employees are those not covered by the overtime provisions of the Fair Labor Standards Act. They are generally in professional, managerial, or administrative positions.

SOURCE:   From "Compensating Employees: Lessons of the 1970s," by David Weeks, *Conference Board Report* no. 707. Copyright © 1976 The Conference Board, Inc. Reprinted by permission.

percent).[19] Again, since workers are less likely to be promoted out of the higher-level jobs, it is not surprising to see less clustering near the minimum salary level in these jobs.

# Pay for Performance: Merit Pay and Bonus Systems

In designing their pay systems, companies must balance the competing goals of external competitiveness, internal fairness, and individual work incentives. Job evaluation, as we have seen, can be tailored to maintain external competitiveness and can be viewed by employees as a fair means of rewarding good work. As the discussion of rate ranges indicates, however, companies usually have pay differentials for workers in the same jobs. In Chapter 8 we discussed some of the incentive effects of such differentials, which are frequently based on seniority and merit. This section takes a closer look at merit pay and bonus systems, as they appear to be the most common forms of incentive pay.[20]

Table 9.6 gives information from the 1970s on the frequency of various types of pay increases that workers in different occupations received. The table shows clearly that salaried workers' compensation increases were more tied to individual performance than those of hourly workers. In fact, merit pay is relatively rare among union workers, for reasons we will explore in Chapter

[19]   See Martin E. Personick, "White-Collar Pay Determination Under Range-of-Rate Systems," p. 29.

[20]   Recall from Chapter 8 that piece-rate systems, in which a person's physical output (or sales volume) is actually measured and rewarded according to a fixed formula, are relatively rare, for reasons discussed in that chapter.

**EXAMPLE   9.2**

# Merit Pay at an Insurance Company

The following table describes a merit-pay guideline plan for the professional, managerial, and administrative employees of a particular insurance company. This plan's guidelines vary not only according to an employee's performance rating; they also vary according to one's position in the salary hierarchy and the time since one's last merit increase. For most positions in the salary range, the guidelines call for a substantial premium for the top performers. For example, for those at the midpoint of their salary range, the merit raise for people who "meet most of their accountabilities" is 5 percent, while the raise for one who "well exceeds" his or her accountabilities is 12–15 percent and is awarded three months sooner than the 5-percent raises. While we do not know how differently people are rated, the possibility for substantial salary variation over a period of years is contained in this plan.

Multivariable Merit-Increase Guideline: An Insurance Company

| Performance | Position in Range in Relation to Midpoint | | | | |
|---|---|---|---|---|---|
| | Below 0.80 (Below Minimum) | 0.81–0.95 | 0.96–1.05 | 1.06–1.20 | Above 1.20 (Above Maximum) |
| Well exceeds accountabilities | 12%–15% 9 months[a] | 12%–15% 12 months | 12%–15% 12 months | 11%–14% 15 months | 7% * 18 months |
| Exceeds accountabilities | 9%–11% 9 months | 9%–11% 12 months | 9%–11% 12 months | 8%–10% 15 months | 6% 18 months |
| Meets accountabilities | 6%–8% 9 months | 6%–8% 12 months | 6%–8% 12 months | 5%–7% 15 months | 5% * 18 months |
| Meets most accountabilities | 5% 9 months | 5% 12 months | 5% 15 months | 5% 18 months | No Increase |
| Meets few accountabilities | No Increase | No Increase | No Increase | No Increase | No Increase |

[a] In all cases, months since last increase.

\* Requires special approval

SOURCE: From "Pay & Performance: The Interaction of Compensation & Performance Appraisal," by Charles Peck, *Conference Board Research Bulletin* 155. Copyright © 1984 The Conference Board, Inc. Reprinted by permission.

In addition to providing a clear reward for excellent performance, this plan tilts its merit increases toward those at or below the midpoint of the salary range. For workers at a given performance level (for example, "exceeds accountabilities"), the merit increase is more generous in percentage terms for those at or below the median of their range than for those above the median. For those over 20 percent above the median, the room for further merit increases is very limited (they are relatively small and must receive special approval), and the differentiation between adequate performers and outstanding ones is very small.

The timing of merit reviews also favors the lower-paid workers; the lowest paid get a review every 9 months, while the highest paid must wait 18 months. Since the merit raises for each adjustment are greater for the lower-paid employees, lower-paid employees can expect percentage raises that are two-to-four times as large as those of more highly paid workers of comparable performance levels. Among workers in the middle performance level, for example, in each 18-month period the lowest paid would receive 12–16 percent in merit raises, while the highest paid would receive 5 percent.

What implications does this insurance company's merit system have for our discussion of seniority and merit? While merit plays a strong role in this plan, so does seniority. For companies in general, most employees are hired into a position at or below the median of the pay range. One can reach the higher end of the range by getting large merit raises and/or being employed long enough to receive a large number of smaller merit raises. This plan in effect gives senior workers a lower percentage raise than junior workers with the same performance level. While this feature appears to be seniority "in reverse," it actually serves to limit the pure-seniority pay effect within a job grade; that is, for two equally performing employees in the same job, there will be a positive seniority effect on salary levels that will narrow as the employees remain in the job.

In addition, the plan's low reward for highly paid employees *within a job grade* may serve as a financial incentive for people to try for promotions into a higher grade. While the plan also eventually provides low raises for continued excellent performance for those who do not get promoted, these are precisely the employees who are most likely to get promoted. According to the Conference Board, this plan is typical of many merit plans, in that it takes into account both position in the salary range and time since the last merit increase.

SOURCES: Charles Peck, *Pay & Performance: The Interaction of Compensation & Performance Appraisal,* Conference Board Research Bulletin 155 (New York: Conference Board, 1984), pp. 13–15 and Martin E. Personick, "White-Collar Pay Determination Under Range-of-Rate Systems," *Monthly Labor Review* 107 (December 1984): 25–30.

16. Roughly the same percentages (about 90 percent) of firms use merit-pay salary increases for their lower- and higher-level salaried employees; moreover, the upper-level salaried employees, especially corporate officers, are much less likely to receive across-the-board increases (general, COLA, or longevity) than are other employees. (Also note the sharply declining incidence of seniority increases as we move out of the union sector. In Chapter 16 we will discuss the union emphasis on seniority.) Finally, Table 9.6 suggests that delayed-payments, implicit-contracts policies are more widely used in blue-collar than white-collar jobs—at least judging from the explicit reliance on longevity pay. However, as discussed above and in Example 9.2, seniority considerations can still affect pay even in companies using only merit systems for awarding pay increases.

**Table 9.7**   Comparison of 1982 Merit-Increase Medians, by Industry Category (as percents of salary at time of increase)

| Industry Category | Low Merit Increase vs. Median Merit Increase | | | High Merit Increase vs. Median Merit Increase | | |
|---|---|---|---|---|---|---|
| | Low Merit Increase | Median Merit Increase | Difference | High Merit Increase | Median Merit Increase | Difference |
| Manufacturing | 5.0% | 8.7% | 3.7 | 14.0% | 8.7% | 5.3 |
| Banking | 4.0 | 8.7 | 4.7 | 15.0 | 8.7 | 6.3 |
| Insurance | 5.0 | 9.0 | 4.0 | 14.0 | 9.0 | 5.0 |
| Diversified finance | 5.0 | 9.0 | 4.0 | 15.5 | 9.0 | 6.5 |
| Total | 5.0 | 8.8 | 3.8 | 14.3 | 8.8 | 5.5 |

SOURCE:   From "Pay and Performance: The Interaction of Compensation & Performance Appraisal," by Charles Peck, *Conference Board Research Bulletin* 155. Copyright © 1984 The Conference Board, Inc. Reprinted by permission.

## Characteristics of Merit Pay Systems

Companies with merit pay plans must decide not only on a total budget to allocate to merit increases; they must also make decisions about the ranges of rewards they give to high and low performers. Regarding the overall size of the merit-increase budget, a survey of over 500 companies' merit-pay systems for higher-level salaried employees found that external pay relationships were the most important factor in this decision.[21] This result illustrates a recurring theme in our discussion of internal pay policies; they are significantly affected by the external labor market.

Table 9.7 illustrates typical spreads from the lowest to the highest merit increases for individual firms, tabulated by industry. The table shows a spread of about 10 percentage points from the minimum to the maximum merit raise in 1982. The table also shows that, relative to the median, low performers are punished less than high performers are rewarded. A minimum merit raise of 5 percent, in a year with about 4-percent inflation, shows a reluctance on the part of many companies to be too hard on the lowest performers.[22]

How does a company fairly and accurately measure a worker's performance? If employees do not trust the system or feel that they are not being evaluated in a fair way, then the supposedly positive incentive effects of merit-pay systems may not be realized. While Chapter 8 surveyed evidence on the effect of merit systems that was largely positive, about 16 percent of companies with merit systems admit that their plans are not successful.

---

[21]   See Charles Peck, *Pay & Performance: The Interaction of Compensation & Performance Appraisal,* p. 13. Other factors affecting the size of merit-increase budgets, in descending order of importance, were company financial results and prospects, internal pay relationships, cost-of-living changes, and ability to hire.

[22]   From December 1981 to December 1982, the Consumer Price Index rose by 3.9 percent. See U.S. Bureau of Labor Statistics, *Monthly Labor Review,* various issues.

The two major reasons given for an unsuccessful merit plan are a lack of consistency in ratings among different managers and overuse of the middle categories.[23] A survey of large nonunion companies found considerable distrust of merit systems for nonmanagerial employees, while it found that managers were wary of accusations of favoritism that could potentially lead to reduced morale or to an organizing drive by a union.[24] These reported difficulties with merit-pay systems illustrate the conflict between companies' desires to motivate their employees and workers' aversion to risk. If workers do not trust the performance-evaluation process, and if merit pay is a large component of compensation and is viewed as unpredictable or out of a worker's control, then it increases uncertainty among workers. However, a performance-appraisal system in which workers know how their work will be rated can reduce some of their uncertainty about future pay increases.

## Compensation Beyond Salaries and Benefits: Bonuses and Stock Option Plans

Tables 9.8 and 9.9 illustrate the frequency of various nonsalary compensation plans (excluding stock option plans) primarily for professional, managerial, and administrative workers (who are exempt from the overtime provisions of the Fair Labor Standards Act). Table 9.8 shows that 58-percent of companies have bonuses for top management. The next most frequently used nonsalary compensation method is the long-term incentive, a technique mentioned in Chapter 8 that rewards executives according to the long-run performance (often over a three-to-five-year period) of the company. Finally, various forms of group incentives are offered by about 22 percent of firms.

Table 9.9 depicts the importance of nonsalary compensation relative to base salary for different levels of job. These variable forms of nonsalary compensation assume greater importance for higher-level employees. For example, the table shows that in manufacturing, bonuses and incentives make up about 38-percent of base salary for top executives, while they comprise only 10-percent of base salary for lower management. When we consider that stock options typically apply only to top-level executives, their compensation becomes even more variable relative to that of lower-level managers.

**Stock option plans.**  Stock option plans are systems, usually reserved only for top-level executives, that allow one to buy company stock at favorable or guaranteed prices.[25] For example, an *incentive stock option* is the granting of special rights to management to buy up to $100,000 of stock (a limit imposed by tax law) at a price no less than the market value on the date of the

---

[23]  See Charles Peck, *Pay & Performance: The Interaction of Compensation & Performance Appraisal*, pp. 7 and 23.

[24]  See Fred Foulkes, *Personnel Policies in Large Nonunion Companies* (Englewood Cliffs, NJ: Prentice-Hall, 1980), Chapter 9.

[25]  This discussion of stock option plans draws from David W. Belcher and Thomas J. Atchison, *Compensation Administration*, 2d ed. (Englewood Cliffs, NJ: Prentice-Hall, Inc., 1987): 384–85.

**Table 9.8**  Nonsalary Compensation Plans Including Exempt Employees, by Industry Category (1982)*

| | Industry Category | | | | | | | | | |
| | Manufacturing (N = 302) | | Banking (N = 145) | | Insurance (N = 95) | | Diversified Finance (N = 15) | | Total (N = 557) | |
| Type of Plan | Number | Percent of Companies | Number | Percent of Companies | Number | Percent of Companies | Number | Percent of Companies | Number | Percent of Companies |
|---|---|---|---|---|---|---|---|---|---|---|
| Top executive bonus | 219 | 73% | 68 | 47% | 32 | 34% | 3 | 20% | 322 | 58% |
| Long-term incentive | 91 | 30 | 7 | 5 | 3 | 3 | — | — | 101 | 18 |
| All employee bonus | 28 | 9 | 8 | 6 | 5 | 5 | 4 | 27 | 45 | 8 |
| Current profit sharing | 24 | 8 | 28 | 19 | 7 | 7 | 2 | 13 | 61 | 11 |
| Group productivity incentive | 7 | 2 | 6 | 4 | 3 | 3 | 1 | 7 | 17 | 3 |
| Group cost control incentive | 2 | 1 | — | — | — | — | 1 | 7 | 3 | — |

* Figures do not include stock option plans.

N = number of firms

SOURCE: From "Pay and Performance: The Interaction of Compensation & Performance Appraisal," by Charles Peck, *Conference Board Research Bulletin* 155. Copyright © 1984 The Conference Board, Inc. Reprinted by permission.

**Table 9.9**  1982 Total Awards to Exempt Employees from Nonsalary Compensation Plans, by Industry Category (as percent of salary at time of award)*

| | Manufacturing | | | Banking | | | Insurance | | | Total | | |
| | | Middle 50-Percent Range | | | Middle 50-Percent Range | | | Middle 50-Percent Range | | | Middle 50-Percent Range | |
| Level of Employee | Median | Low | High | Median | Low | High | Median | Low | High | Median | Low | High |
|---|---|---|---|---|---|---|---|---|---|---|---|---|
| Top executive | 38% | 24% | 52% | 20% | 11% | 30% | 15% | 10% | 23% | 30% | 16% | 47% |
| Middle management | 20 | 12 | 27 | 13 | 9 | 18 | 10 | 5 | 13 | 18 | 10 | 25 |
| Lower management | 10 | 6 | 15 | 10 | 6 | 15 | 5 | 2 | 6 | 10 | 5 | 15 |
| Other exempt | 6 | 3 | 10 | 9 | 6 | 11 | 5 | 2 | 6 | 7 | 4 | 10 |

* Figures do not include stock option plans.

SOURCE: From "Pay and Performance: The Interaction of Compensation & Performance Appraisal," by Charles Peck, *Conference Board Research Bulletin* 155. Copyright © 1984 The Conference Board, Inc. Reprinted by permission.

grant. By law, the right must be exercised within 10 years. The value of such a plan is that the stock's price may appreciate while the executive may buy it at the guaranteed price. Another stock option plan is *stock appreciation rights,* in which the executive doesn't have to actually buy stock but will be awarded a bonus equal to the appreciation in the value of a certain amount of stock. Finally, a *restricted stock plan* is one in which the company gives the executive a certain amount of stock but requires him or her to keep it for a specified period of time.

Tables 9.10 and 9.11 illustrate the popularity and generosity of stock option plans. Table 9.10 shows that these plans are especially prevalent in manufacturing, services, and retail trades. Further, there has been an increase in the use of stock option plans from 1982 to 1986. While some of this increase may have been due to the improvement in the stock market during these years, we will show that other forms of contingent executive compensation have been increasing as well.[26] Table 9.11 shows the net capital gain on stock options exercised in 1985—that is, the difference between the market value of stock bought and the price paid under stock option plans. In each industry, an average of about three executives per company exercised such options. Since this was a time of stock price appreciation, we might infer that most executives who had stock option rights then would have exercised them. If this were true, it would suggest that a relatively small number of executives had stock option rights. Table 9.11 further shows that the median capital gain in exercising such options ranged from $102,000 to $172,000, which was equiv-

---

[26] For example, in 1982, the Dow Jones Industrial stock price index averaged 884.4 but grew to 1328.4 in 1985. In early October 1987, it stood at 2355, signaling a period of large capital gains in a small number of years. Even after the "crash" of October 1987, the index was high relative to historical standards. See U.S. Department of Commerce, *Statistical Abstract of the United States 1987* (Washington, DC: U.S. Department of Commerce, 1986), Table 834 and *Wall Street Journal,* October 16, 1987, p. 1 and February 1, 1988, p. 1.

**Table 9.10**    Incidence of Stock Option Plans for Top Executives

| Type of Business | Total Companies | May 1986 With Stock Option Plan | | May 1982 Percent with Stock Option Plan |
|---|---|---|---|---|
| | | Number | Percent | |
| Diversified service | 23 | 23 | 100% | No Data |
| Manufacturing | 404 | 330 | 82 | 81% |
| Retail trade | 52 | 38 | 73 | 65 |
| Commercial banking | 153 | 94 | 61 | 43 |
| Construction: traded | 16 | 9 | 56 | 57 |
| Insurance: stock | 62 | 28 | 45 | 39 |
| Gas and electric utilities | 86 | 21 | 24 | 20 |

SOURCE:   From "Top Executive Compensation, 1987 Edition," by Charles Peck, *Conference Board Report,* no. 889. Copyright © 1986 The Conference Board, Inc. Reprinted by permission.

**Table 9.11**  Net Gain on Stock Options Exercised in 1985

| | | | Gain at Exercise | | | |
|---|---|---|---|---|---|---|
| | | | Dollars | | Percent of Salary | |
| Type of Business | Number of Companies | Number of Executives | Median | Middle 50 Percent Range | Median | Middle 50 Percent Range |
| Manufacturing | 162 | 484 | $102,000 | $44,000 to $269,000 | 39% | 17% to 97% |
| Retail trade | 14 | 43 | 172,000 | 39,000 to 367,000 | 45 | 18 to 106 |
| Commercial banking | 40 | 124 | 108,000 | 55,000 to 240,000 | 58 | 30 to 123 |
| Insurance: stock | 11 | 29 | 104,000 | 46,000 to 182,000 | 41 | 27 to 87 |

SOURCE:  From "Top Executive Compensation, 1987 Edition," by Charles Peck, *Conference Board Report*, no. 889. Copyright © 1986 The Conference Board, Inc. Reprinted by permission.

alent to 39–58 percent of base salary. Thus, for those who have stock option rights, the financial incentives are very great.

Why do companies provide stock option plans for their executives? One reason is the tax system. Until 1988, capital gains were taxed at a lower rate than ordinary income, such as wages, salaries, or cash bonuses. Stock options give executives income partly in the form of capital gains, and the tax advantage to capital gains relative to ordinary income was greatest for those in the highest tax brackets, such as top executives. Starting in 1988, capital gains were taxed at the same rate as ordinary income, reducing the tax advantage of stock options; however, one can defer taxes on capital gains by not selling one's shares of stock.[27] For example, if one bought stock in 1988 for $100,000 and this stock rose in value to $200,000 by 1992, one pays no tax on this gain until the stock is sold. By deferring this tax, one is in effect given an interest-free loan by the government equal to the deferred tax payments! Thus, stock options will continue to carry some tax advantages.

A second reason for using stock options is similar to other forms of pay for performance. To the extent that a manager's compensation depends on the financial performance of the company, as the value of the stock option clearly does, the executive is given an incentive to make decisions that raise the market value of the company.

**Executive Compensation and Risk.** Tables 9.8, 9.9, and 9.11 suggest that the compensation of higher-level executives is more dependent on company performance than is that of lower-level managers. Making compensation contingent on the firm's performance serves as a clear motivating mechanism for top management; however, it should be recognized that to some extent such performance is a function of forces outside the control of management. For example, a company can be very profitable in a given year either because of good decisions made by its chief executive officer or because the economy is strong and demand for the firm's products is high. Further, the performance of all lower-level employees, which is not completely controllable by the chief executive officer, also contributes to the success of the company.

Recall from Chapter 8 that there is some evidence that company performance is positively affected by use of incentive-pay mechanisms for top management. However, to the extent that company performance is affected by events beyond the chief executive's control, top management is being asked, in effect, to bear the largest share of the risk of an uncertain business environment. Of course, chief executives are well paid: in 1985, average total compensation for chief executives in 404 large manufacturing companies was $436,000, with an average base salary of $318,000.[28] While some of this high pay probably serves to compensate for the riskiness of the compensation package, it is also likely that any variability associated with the large nonsal-

---

[27] See Richard A. Musgrave, "Short of Euphoria," *Journal of Economic Perspectives* 1 (Summer 1987): 59–71.

[28] See Charles Peck, *Top Executive Compensation: 1987 Edition, Conference Board Report*, no. 889 (New York: Conference Board, 1986), pp. 10–11.

**Table 9.12**  Use of Bonus Plans for Top Executives

| | May 1986 | | May 1982 |
| --- | --- | --- | --- |
| Type of Business | Total Companies | Percent with Bonus Plan | Percent with Bonus Plan |
| Diversified service | 23 | 91% | No Data |
| Manufacturing | 404 | 91 | 94% |
| Retail trade | 52 | 86 | 76 |
| Construction | 51 | 84 | 90 |
| Commercial banking | 153 | 82 | 67 |
| Insurance | 114 | 68 | 66 |
| Gas and electric utilities | 86 | 48 | 22 |

SOURCE: From "Top Executive Compensation, 1987 Edition," by Charles Peck, *Conference Board Report*, no. 889. Copyright © 1986 The Conference Board, Inc. Reprinted by permission.

ary component of their pay attracts individuals who are less averse to risk than most people.[29] It is therefore possible that companies structure the compensation of their top executives to attract risk takers as well as to provide performance incentives for them.

# Recent Trends in Compensation Practices

Companies in the 1980s appear to be moving to more flexible forms of compensation, including increased use of incentives and other contingent compensation for lower-level workers as well as for top executives. Table 9.10 showed an increase in the use of stock options for top executives from 1982 to 1986. Tables 9.12 and 9.13 also indicate increases in the use of bonuses and long-term incentive plans for top executives. As discussed in Chapter 8, these long-term incentives often are bonuses tied to a three-to-five-year average growth rate in after-tax profits per share of stock.[30] However, the recent growth in incentive pay has not been confined to top-level management.

A technique known as *gainsharing* is growing in popularity. A gainsharing plan is a group incentive plan in which a portion of the gains in productivity, reductions in cost, increases in product quality, or other measures of group success are shared among the work group.[31] A recent survey of 1598 companies found that as of 1987, 13 percent of firms had some form of gainsharing

[29] As an illustration of the potential risk in executive compensation, several executives in effect lost millions of dollars of stock appreciation as the value of their stock options plunged on October 19, 1987. See Amanda Bennett, "Executives See Stock Options Drop in Value," *Wall Street Journal*, October 21, 1987, p. 31.

[30] See Charles Peck, *Top Executive Compensation: 1987 Edition*, p. 3 and Lawrence C. Bickford, "Long-Term Incentives for Management Part 6: Performance Attainment Plans," *Compensation Review* 13 (Third Quarter 1981): 14–29.

[31] Edward E. Lawler, "Gainsharing," David B. Balkin and Luis R. Gomez-Mejia (eds.), *New Perspectives on Compensation* (Englewood Cliffs, NJ: Prentice-Hall, 1987): 225–29.

**EXAMPLE** **9.3**

## Gainsharing

As we mentioned in the last chapter, group incentive plans must overcome the potential difficulty that individuals may be tempted to shirk, since they may perceive that the *group's* output will not be much affected (this is known in economics as the "free rider" problem). This observation helps explain why *individual* incentives, such as merit pay, are much more prevalent than group incentives. However, as we have discussed in this chapter, group incentives are on the rise; the experience of one apparently successful group incentive plan illustrates several of the principles we have discussed in this and the previous chapter.

In the early 1980s the Dana Spicer Heavy Axle Division opened a truck-axle plant in which a gainsharing plan was implemented shortly after the plant began operations. According to the plan, workers receive a bonus if in any month the ratio of labor costs to sales is less than the targeted ratio. Labor costs include both direct (production and maintenance) labor as well as overhead labor (warehousing, for example). To promote product quality, the plan doubles the costs of any defective product returned by the customer and subtracts this amount from any earned group bonus.

Since adopting the plan, the company has shown both gains in labor efficiency (that is, decreases in labor costs per dollar of sales) and in product quality. For example, since the beginning of the plan, quality improved enough to allow the company to issue a 500,000-mile warranty on axles, an unusually long warranty in this industry. Employee suggestions led to the clearing of floor space and an increase in production and hiring. Monthly bonuses as a percentage of workers' wages averaged 12 percent in 1984, 16 percent in 1985, and 20 percent in 1986. Thus the plan has meant significant financial incentives for production workers.

While the company has reported gains under the plan, it is possible that such gains would have occurred without the gainsharing system. The plan was implemented as the new factory was starting up, and productivity improvements probably would have been observed anyway as the plant began to reach peak efficiency through the learning process. However, several other aspects of the Dana gainsharing plan suggest that it was adopted under ideal conditions.

First, it was established in a new plant, so that there was no existing set of expectations among the workers about the appropriate way to run things. In particular, the target labor-cost-to-sales ratio was periodically adjusted as a moving base. This procedure was evidently not viewed as unfair by employees, since there was no stable, historically determined labor-cost ratio. Many gainsharing plans run into difficulty if workers believe that management is manipulating the standard against which performance is measured. However, at Dana, management had monthly meetings and shared financial information with the employees in explaining the reasons for changing the target labor cost ratio. Thus, the potential problem of asymmetric information, discussed in Chapter 8, did not appear to be severe at Dana.

Second, in recruiting an initial labor force for the plant, the company carefully screened applicants and chose those who would best fit into a team-oriented situation. Because the firm's compensation package was in the top 10 percent for

manufacturing companies in the area, management was able to be selective about those hired. Thus, the hiring process was done with the potential free-rider problem in mind.

Third, under the Dana gainsharing plan, each worker serves as his or her own inspector. When work is poorly done, the production worker responsible is identifiable; the double-costing approach to returned work and the relatively high bonus levels can provide a significant group penalty for shoddy work. Shirking by an individual worker not only reduces the total bonus pool available; it also reduces the likelihood that any bonus will be paid, since the penalty can sharply raise the labor-cost-to-sales ratio. Thus, it is likely that strong group pressures are at work here, leading workers to keep product quality and labor efficiency high.

SOURCE:   Larry Hatcher, Timothy L. Ross and Ruth Ann Ross, "Gainsharing: Living Up to Its Name," *Personnel Administrator* 32 (June 1987): 153–64.

**Table 9.13**   Use of Long-Term Incentives for Top Executives

| | May 1986 | | May 1982 |
| --- | --- | --- | --- |
| *Type of Business* | *Total Companies* | *Percent with Performance Plan* | *Percent with Performance Plan* |
| Diversified service | 23 | 52% | No Data |
| Manufacturing | 404 | 38 | 32% |
| Retail trade | 52 | 19 | 16 |
| Insurance | 114 | 19 | 17 |
| Gas and electric utilities | 86 | 19 | 3 |
| Commercial banking | 153 | 18 | 15 |
| Construction | 51 | 8 | 5 |

SOURCE:   From "Top Executive Compensation, 1987 Edition," by Charles Peck, *Conference Board Report*, no. 889. Copyright © 1986 The Conference Board, Inc. Reprinted by permission.

and that 73 percent of all existing gainsharing systems had been started since 1980, illustrating the newness of such programs.[32]

In addition to the increased use of gainsharing, companies in this survey also reported increases in the use of profit-sharing and lump-sum bonuses. Additionally, a recent survey of 550 companies by a management consultant found that firms planned to increase the share of their 1988 compensation increases contingent upon individual, group, or company performance.[33]

These recent data indicate that the compensation of both executives and other employees is being restructured to some extent, with an emphasis on rewarding performance. One reason appears to be an increase in competition within the economy. A recent survey found that 48 percent of all goods-producing firms reported an increase in foreign and domestic competition, but

[32]  See Carla O'Dell and Jerry McAdams, "The Revolution in Employee Rewards," *Management Review* 76 (March 1987): 31.

[33]  "Linking Pay to Profits," *The New York Times*, October 18, 1987, Section 3, p. 1.

over 90 percent of these firms that had adopted more performance-contingent reward systems reported an increase in competition.[34] Evidently, an increase in competition is perceived by firms to require increased flexibility in rewarding workers.

Another reason why performance-related pay is growing is that, as we will see in the next chapter, union representation has sharply fallen in the 1980s. Thus the value to nonunion companies of imitating traditional union pay schemes (with fixed pay levels or with heavy emphasis on seniority) has probably diminished.[35]

# Review Questions

1. Some observers criticize merit-pay systems as unfair, since they place control of the employee's pay in the hands of the supervisor. What are the merits, as it were, of this kind of argument? Suppose that workers at a particular company believed this to be true. What options would a firm have?
2. Proponents of comparable worth believe that this policy could easily be implemented by using existing job-evaluation plans. Can comparable worth be achieved in this way?
3. Top executives' compensation appears to be much more tied to performance than is the pay of other workers. What explanations are there for this difference?
4. Internal labor markets give workers some protection against the forces of the external labor market. Surveying current personnel practices, evaluate the extent to which this protection is prevalent.

# Selected Readings

David B. Balkin and Luis R. Gomez-Mejia, *New Perspectives on Compensation* (Englewood Cliffs, NJ: Prentice-Hall), 1987.

David W. Belcher and Thomas J. Atchison, *Compensation Administration* 2d ed. (Englewood Cliffs, NJ: Prentice-Hall), 1987.

Fred K. Foulkes, *Personnel Policies in Large Nonunion Companies* (Englewood Cliffs, NJ: Prentice-Hall), 1980.

E. Robert Livernash, ed. *Comparable Worth: Issues and Alternatives* (Washington, DC: Equal Employment Advisory Council), 1980.

George T. Milkovich and Jerry M. Newman, *Compensation* 2d ed. (Plano, Texas: Business Publications, Inc.), 1987.

Charles Peck, Pay & Performance: *The Interaction of Compensation & Performance Appraisal,* Conference Board Research Bulletin 155 (New York: The Conference Board, Inc., 1984).

---

[34]  See Carla O'Dell and Jerry McAdams, "The Revolution in Employee Rewards," p. 31.

[35]  Indeed, as we will see in Chapter 18, compensation in the union sector is becoming more flexible, as union workers seem more willing to give up fixed pay to save union jobs.

# PART 5

## American Union Development

# CHAPTER 10

## The Development of Unions and Collective Bargaining

Our analysis of the workings of the employment relationship has, for the most part, omitted any mention of the role of labor unions and collective bargaining. In doing so, the analysis has stressed labor-market processes through which workers improve their work situations through *individual* actions—particularly by changing or threatening to change employers. Workers can also seek to improve their working conditions through *collective* action; historically this has been an important mechanism of change. Indeed, the development of labor unions and collective bargaining has been part of the process of economic growth in virtually every country in the world.

Because many people have strong and conflicting opinions about the role of unions in our society, it is often difficult to remain objective when discussing them. Some individuals view labor unions as forms of monopolies that, while benefiting their members, impose substantial costs on other members of society. In contrast, other individuals view unions as *the* major means by which working persons have improved their economic status and as important forces behind much social legislation. In fact, we shall see that there are important economic and legal constraints on collective actions by employees. While unions play an important role in our society, their influence is probably not as pervasive as either their supporters or opponents would have us believe.

To analyze the process and outcomes of collective bargaining, one must first understand the objectives of employers and unions who participate in the process. The objective of employers is assumed to be the maximization of profits, at least in the long run (see Chapters 3 and 4). The goals of unions are far more varied and complex. In contrast to business firms, unions may form for ideological as well as economic reasons, although historically, unions in the United States have placed more emphasis on economic objectives than their European counterparts. Even when restricted to economic considerations, the specification of union goals is complicated by the fact that unions are inherently political organizations whose members often have very different and even conflicting views of the benefits that they should receive from union representation and have methods of changing unions or union leadership if they feel they are not being represented adequately. Moreover, the security of the union as an institution is influenced by the general economic and legal environment.

In this chapter, we begin our study of collective bargaining by examining unions as organizations at both the macro and micro level. At the macro level, we examine the growth and recent decline of unions in the United States and the major historical events that shaped the present structure and attitudes of unions in the private and public sectors. We then turn to the micro level and examine decision-making by individual unions and the implications for a union's internal operations and collective-bargaining objectives.

Having established the nature of unions and discussed their objectives, we explore other aspects of the collective-bargaining relationship in subsequent chapters. In Chapter 11, we examine the legal regulation of union organizing and collective bargaining. In Chapters 12 through 14, we discuss the collective-bargaining process, examining the relationship between the structure and tactics of collective bargaining and bargaining power, the negotiating process, and labor disputes and dispute settlement. In Chapter 15, we examine the nature of collective-bargaining agreements, and in Chapter 16, we consider the apparent effect of collective bargaining on the workplace and on the economy.

# The Development of the American
# Labor Movement

## Distinctive Features

One of the most striking features of the American labor movement is its slow growth and relatively modest representation of American workers. In recent years, less than 20 percent of all employees on nonagricultural payrolls were union members. This percentage is considerably lower than that found in most Western countries (see Table 10.1). While the extent of unionization was small in most countries at the turn of the century, the subsequent growth of unions was much more rapid abroad than in North America. In contrast to most other countries, union penetration in the United States began to decline in the mid-1950s, first slowly but then quite rapidly since 1978. Some of the reasons for the recent decline are discussed later in the chapter.

In addition, the United states is one of the few Western countries in which labor unions are not intimately and uniformly associated with one political party (such as the Labor Party in England, which is dominated by trade unionists). While most of the leaders of the American union movement are generally more supportive of the goals of the Democratic Party than those of

**Table 10.1**  Union Membership as a Percent of Potential Union Membership by Country, Selected Years, 1900–1984

| Country | 1900 | 1930 | 1950 | 1975 | 1984 |
|---|---|---|---|---|---|
| Australia | 9[a] | 44 | 56 | 54 | 57 |
| Canada | — | 14[b] | 33 | 35 | 38 |
| Denmark | — | 32 | 52 | 67 | 98 |
| Germany | 6 | 34 | 33 | 37 | 43 |
| Great Britain | 13 | 26 | 44 | 49[c] | 53 |
| Norway | 3 | 18 | n.a. | 61 | — |
| Sweden | 5 | 36 | 68 | 87 | 95 |
| United States | 6 | 9 | 28 | 25 | 19 |

[a]  1901

[b]  1931

[c]  1974

Note:  Data for 1984 express union membership as a percent of nonagricultural employment. The definition of potential union membership used in data for 1900 through 1975 differs slightly from the concepts of labor force and nonagricultural employment against which union membership is compared in 1984, in Table 10.2, and elsewhere in this chapter.

SOURCE:  1900–1975: George Sayers Bain and Robert Price, *Profiles of Union Growth: A Comparative Statistical Portrait of Eight Countries* (Oxford: Basil Blackwell, 1980): 170. 1984: Michael Goldfield, *The Decline of Organized Labor in the United States* (Chicago: University of Chicago Press, 1987): 16.

the Republican Party, their influence on the selection of candidates and party programs has been variable. Moreover, some union leaders regularly support the Republican Party. For years, both the teamsters' union and the carpenters' union have supported Republican candidates for president. In the 1980 presidential election, the Professional Air Traffic Controllers' Association (PATCO) broke with most of the labor movement and supported Ronald Reagan, the successful Republican candidate, hoping that their support would gain sympathy for their bargaining demands. When the union later struck illegally after negotiations reached an impasse, however, the government held firm and fired most of the union's members, eventually driving the union into bankruptcy. (In 1987, air controllers voted to be represented by a new union.)

The absence of a permanent affiliation with a major political party is a symptom of another distinctive characteristic of American unions—an absence of ideological objectives. Again, in contrast to the experience of some other Western countries, the growth of unions in the United States was motivated more from efforts at economic advancement than from a general belief that workers had to band together to restructure society. American unions generally accept the capitalist form of economic organization and focus instead on increasing workers' share of national income.

Labor unions have two general methods for attaining their goals—*collective bargaining* and *legislative enactment*. Given the emphasis on economic objectives and the informality of political associations, American unions historically have placed more emphasis on the method of collective bargaining than their European counterparts. Fewer fringe benefits are provided by legislation in the United States and more by collective bargaining agreements, for example. While unions seek legislative support for improvements in the environment of collective bargaining and in the work environment (for example, through their support for laws regulating health and safety conditions at the workplace), they prefer to minimize government involvement in the bargaining process itself.

Finally, the process of collective bargaining is highly decentralized in the United States. While a few large negotiations in major companies and industries receive significant attention in the media, there are, in fact, about 180,000 collective bargaining agreements in force in the United States. Most collective-bargaining activity occurs unheralded in thousands of negotiations in individual plants and companies. This structure of collective bargaining contrasts sharply with negotiations in Europe, which are frequently conducted at the industrywide or nationwide level. It bears more similarity to the structure of collective bargaining in Japan, where negotiations occur most frequently at the plant or company level. (Detailed discussions of collective bargaining and dispute resolution in Europe, Japan, and Australia appear in examples in Chapters 12 and 14.)

## Union Growth in the Private Sector

Table 10.2 presents data on a century of union membership, from 1897 through 1984. While data on union membership are notoriously poor, the table nevertheless yields some striking patterns. First, union membership, in both absolute terms and as a percentage of the labor force (and of nonagricultural employment), grew slowly and somewhat erratically prior to the mid-1930s. Second, membership growth accelerated dramatically during the late 1930s and through World War II. The former result was somewhat surprising to analysts, since prior to the 1930s, periods of high unemployment were typically associated with declining union strength.[1] After a slight dip in the immediate postwar period, union strength reached a peak of 25 percent of the labor force in the mid-1950s. Since that time, however, the share of union members in both total nonagricultural employment and the labor force has declined steadily. Indeed, by 1984, union membership stood at about 16 percent of the labor force—a 43-year low.

To interpret the historical circumstances behind these developments and their relevance for the shape of the present-day labor movement in the United States, it is important to appreciate certain characteristics of unions. *Labor unions* are collective organizations whose primary objectives are to improve the pecuniary and nonpecuniary employment conditions of their members. Unions can be organized along two different lines: (1) an *industrial* union represents most or all of the workers in an industry or firm regardless of their occupations; and (2) a *craft* union represents workers in a single occupational group. Examples of industrial unions are the unions representing automobile

---

[1] For evidence and a discussion of the pre-1930s view, *see* John R. Commons, *The History of Labor in the United States,* vol. III (New York: Macmillan, 1918).

**Table 10.2**  Union Membership in the United States, 1897–1984

| Year | Total (in thousands) | Percentage of Labor Force | Percentage of Nonagricultural Employment |
|------|---------------------|---------------------------|------------------------------------------|
| 1897 | 455 | n.a. | 3.6 |
| 1900 | 932 | 3.3 | 6.5 |
| 1910 | 2169 | 5.9 | 10.3 |
| 1920 | 4823 | 11.7 | 17.6 |
| 1930 | 3750 | 7.5 | 12.7 |
| 1934 | 4003 | 7.7 | 15.4 |
| 1938 | 5962 | 10.9 | 20.4 |
| 1940 | 7297 | 13.1 | 22.5 |
| 1942 | 10,187 | 18.1 | 25.4 |
| 1944 | 12,130 | 22.2 | 29.0 |
| 1946 | 12,936 | 22.5 | 31.1 |
| 1948 | 14,272 | 23.5 | 31.8 |
| 1950 | 14,294 | 23.0 | 31.6 |
| 1952 | 15,632 | 25.2 | 32.0 |
| 1954 | 15,809 | 24.8 | 32.3 |
| 1956 | 16,446 | 24.7 | 31.4 |
| 1958 | 15,570 | 23.0 | 36.3 |
| 1960 | 15,516 | 22.3 | 28.6 |
| 1962 | 16,894 | 23.9 | 30.4 |
| 1964 | 17,597 | 24.1 | 30.2 |
| 1966 | 18,922 | 25.0 | 29.6 |
| 1968 | 20,017 | 25.4 | 29.5 |
| 1970 | 20,990 | 25.4 | 29.6 |
| 1972 | 21,206 | 24.4 | 28.8 |
| 1974 | 22,165 | 24.1 | 28.3 |
| 1976 | 22,153 | 23.0 | 27.9 |
| 1978 | 21,756 | 21.3 | 25.1 |
| 1980 | 20,958 | 19.6 | 23.2 |
| 1982 | 19,571 | 17.8 | 21.9 |
| 1984 | 18,306 | 16.1 | 19.4 |

n.a.  not available

SOURCE:  Leo Troy and Neil Sheflin, *Union Sourcebook* 1st ed. (West Orange, NJ: Industrial Relations Data and Information Services, 1985): Table 3.41.

workers, steel workers, bituminous coal miners, and rubber workers; while examples of craft unions are those representing printers, dock workers, and the various building trades (for example, carpenters and plumbers).[2]

To an important degree, the extent and form of union organization is influenced by the underlying economics of the labor markets in which unions operate. In this respect, some of the tools developed in previous chapters enable us to interpret the pattern of union growth observed in the United

[2] For reasons that will become apparent later in the chapter, many unions that originally organized on a "craft" basis now represent workers on an "industrial" basis. For example, the International Brotherhood of Electrical Workers often represents all employees of unionized electrical machinery firms. Likewise, many industrial unions have expanded their organizing efforts beyond their original industry. Both the United Autoworkers and the Teamsters, for example, now organize university employees.

States. Union growth can also be significantly influenced by another factor that has not been discussed yet—the legal environment in which unions operate. An analysis of the economic and legal environment facing unions helps to explain why prior to the mid-1930s the American labor movement was relatively small and consisted almost exclusively of craft unions.

**The early economic environment.**   With respect to the general economic environment, the major influences on labor-market conditions prior to the 1930s were the general scarcity of labor in the United States, large immigration flows, and periodic recessions. During most of this period, land and capital were in abundant supply relative to labor. As a result of the labor scarcity, real wages and the general standard of living of even unskilled workers were high relative to the European countries from which most U.S. workers emigrated. This aspect of the economic climate may have reduced the interest of some workers in unions as a vehicle of economic change.

More importantly, the prospects of relatively high wages and living standards helped induce large immigration flows into the United States. Immigration provided a flood of largely unskilled, manual labor until 1920, when the immigration laws became more restrictive. During the years of peak immigration in the late nineteenth and early twentieth centuries, the supply of unskilled labor effectively became infinitely elastic at the prevailing real wage (that is, the labor-supply curve was essentially horizontal; additional labor could be recruited without raising wages). Under these conditions, efforts by unions to organize and raise the wage of any group of low-skilled workers above the market level were likely to be undercut by the flow of new, unorganized workers willing to take jobs at the market wage. The challenge to early unions presented by immigration is an example of the broader problem of organizational security that all unions face. As a labor-market monopoly, a union's security as an institution depends importantly on the same factor that determines the durability of monopolies in product markers—barriers to entry. When a union is unable to prevent the entry of unorganized workers to perform the work being done by its members, the union's efforts to raise wages and improve working conditions above market levels will be undercut. Unions thus must seek to organize and police their entire jurisdiction. This objective is difficult to achieve with unrestricted immigration, which explains the handicap that early unions faced in trying to organize the unskilled and why unions generally oppose open immigration policies.

Even with the substantial flow of immigrant labor, the increases in labor demand that accompanied the geographic expansion of markets and the growth of large industry exceeded the expansion of the labor supply. Demand grew more rapidly than supply, labor remained relatively scarce, and real wages continued to rise.

How did unions adapt to an environment that was both relatively prosperous and also discouraged the organization of low-skilled workers? It is clear from our earlier labor-market analysis that only craft unions were likely to survive under these conditions. First, the security of craft unions was less likely to be threatened by the flood of unskilled immigrants because significant training was required to acquire skill in a particular craft. The union's strategy was then to acquire control of the training process, usually by setting up apprenticeship programs under which unskilled workers spent a period of years learning the skills of a trade, and to limit entry into the program. The simply analytics of apprenticeship-restriction are illustrated in Figure 10.1. Under normal labor market conditions, the supply of skilled workers ($SS$) would rise as the skilled wage increased, and the equilibrium wage and employment of skilled workers would be $W_S$ and $E_S$ respectively. When training is provided only through an apprenticeship program, and the union limits entry to $E_u$ individuals, labor supply becomes inelastic at $E_u$ and the wage for skilled workers becomes $W_u$. When a craft union is able to control the training programs, it can raise the wages of workers in the craft without even bargaining *if* employers make no defensive response! The union simply increases the scarcity of skilled workers (by limiting entry into apprenticeship) and lets market forces do the rest. Thus, craft unions had a tool (apprenticeship) not available to industrial unions, and during the nineteenth century, groups of skilled workers formed exclusive organizations to protect their own bargaining power.

The actual advantage derived from this tool by craft unions depends on the response of employers. The analysis traced in Figure 10.1 applies if a union is able to deal with each employer separately. However, the union's tactics provide an incentive for employers to band together to resist union pressures for higher wages. The formation of such multiemployer bargaining arrangements creates a situation of *bilateral monopoly* in the labor market, because both the sale of labor and the purchase of labor are regulated by single decision-making units (the union and the multiemployer bargaining association, respectively). A complete discussion of the outcome of bargaining under bilateral monopoly, which is less predictable than the outcome described in Figure 10.1, is postponed until our discussion of bargaining

**Figure 10.1**    Restriction of Labor Supply by Craft Unions

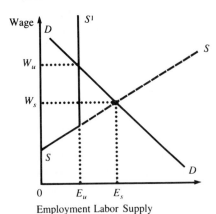

Employment Labor Supply

structures in Chapter 12. For the moment, the important point is that in analyzing labor-relations situations, one should consider *both* the strategic move by a party *and* the likely strategic response to the move by the party's opponent.

The second advantage that craft unions had over industrial unions can be appreciated by recalling the conditions governing the wage elasticity of the derived demand for labor. The laws of derived demand discussed in Chapter 3 imply that the derived demand for union labor will be relatively inelastic if it is difficult to substitute other inputs for union labor; if price elasticities of demand for the final product are relatively low; if the supply schedules of substitute inputs are unresponsive to their prices; and, under certain conditions, if union labor is a relatively small proportion of total cost. There are obviously fewer substitutes for skilled labor than for unskilled labor, and in many instances, the work performed by members of a single craft union may constitute a relatively small proportion of the total cost of a product. It may be, then, that the trade-off between employment and wages faced by the members of skilled craft unions is much smaller than the trade-off faced by the members of industrial unions. Therefore, even if craft unions bargained for wages in excess of $W_u$ in Figure 10.1, the negative employment consequences were likely to be modest.

These inherent economic advantages to craft unions drove skilled workers in the direction of forming rather exclusive organizations, in order to protect their bargaining power. These advantages were not unappreciated by many unskilled workers, and there were sporadic and ultimately unsuccessful attempts to develop more broadly based unions combining both skilled and unskilled workers, on the theory that the inherent bargaining power of the skilled could be used to improve the wages of the unskilled. Skilled workers recognized that such collaborations in industrial unions would result in a dilution of their power and generally remained aloof from such efforts. The net result was that prior to the 1930s, organized labor in the United States was to a large extent a movement of the skilled elite in the labor force.

**The development of national unions.**   There were several forces, however, that led local craft unions to coordinate their efforts across the country. First, even a craft union that effectively organized and controlled entry into one local labor market could be threatened by the spread of markets as the country expanded, and by the emergence of large multiplant companies. If new markets remained unorganized, or were organized by local unions that negotiated markedly lower terms and conditions of employment, the security of unions in other markets would be threatened. Similarly, the rise of multiplant companies gave management a "whipsaw" advantage over local unions. Efforts to raise wages in one plant could be thwarted by shifting production to other plants (usually in other locations). The threat to unions is easily seen by again recalling the determinants of the wage elasticity of the demand for labor. The elasticity is high when it is easy for consumers to substitute for the product that the members of a local union are producing.

Since the best substitute for any one group's product is the identical product being produced at lower cost in another location, there was a powerful incentive for unions to develop an institutional response that would effectively take labor costs out of competition by coordinating the bargaining of local unions in different areas. Second, in some areas, union standards were threatened by the in-migration of skilled labor, and some local unions sought a mechanism to regulate the conditions under which craftsmen from other locals could work in their area. Finally, some locals needed support from other unions simply to muster the resources necessary to counter successfully a large employer.

Following the Civil War, the institutional response that evolved in an effort to standardize the terms and conditions of employment across locations was the national union (often referred to as an ''international'' union when there are Canadian members), an umbrella organization of all the locals of a particular union. National unions acquired considerable power over the activities of local unions to coordinate bargaining activities in a way that tended to standardize the terms and conditions of employment across locations. In particular, the national unions used economic leverage in the form of large strike funds (accumulated from per capita dues paid by the local unions) to coordinate the activities of the locals. Funds were allocated to those local unions whose strikes were sanctioned by the national union and were withheld from locals engaging in unauthorized strikes. The authorization process frequently led national union officials to provide assistance in the negotiations between locals and employers and to direct efforts to organize nonunion workers in the union's jurisdiction.[3]

**Early legal environment.** The economic impediments to widespread union organization during the nineteenth and early twentieth centuries were reinforced by a legal environment that was unfavorably disposed toward unions and collective bargaining. Generally speaking, the legal environment for institutional behavior is conditioned by the common law and statutory law as interpreted by the judiciary. *Common law* consists of general principles and the accumulation of decisions over time, developed by the judiciary without the aid of explicit legislation. *Statutory law,* on the other hand, is established by legislation and can modify the common law. Prior to the 1930s, the legal environment of unions in collective bargaining was mainly set by the common law, and the frequent use of judicial discretion in interpreting the common law to thwart the activities of unions left the American labor movement with a deeply rooted opposition to substantial reliance on the courts in the institutional arrangements surrounding collective bargaining.

In considering the status of unions and union activity, the judiciary applied a number of doctrines from the common law.[4] The earliest unions

---

[3] Lloyd Ulman, *The Rise of the National Labor Union* (Cambridge, MA: Harvard University Press, 1954).

[4] For an extensive review of the early legal treatment of unions in the United States, see Charles O. Gregory, *Labor and the Law,* 2d revised edition with 1961 supplement (New York: Norton, 1961), Chapters I–VI.

encountered the high water mark of judicial emphasis on the freedom of contract, and were treated as criminal conspiracies. Under the *criminal conspiracy* doctrine, individual actions to raise wages or otherwise alter the terms and conditions of employment were permissible (on the grounds that they had no general impact on the economy), but group actions to achieve identical ends were unlawful, because of the purported economic power accruing from combinations of workers. What was legal for an individual was illegal for a group. (Some judges developed a curious double standard in applying the criminal conspiracy doctrine by permitting combinations of employers—which raised the possibility of monopsony power as discussed in Chapter 3—on the grounds that such combinations constituted defensive efforts to force wages down to their competitive level.)

The conspiracy doctrine was supplanted by the *illegal purpose doctrine*, which held that while the formation of unions by workers was lawful, the ends of such an organization might be illegal. While this doctrine established the legality of some of the more traditional union activities, such as strikes for improved wages and working conditions, it left the legitimacy of many other union objectives in doubt and a matter of judicial discretion. By the late nineteenth century, however, employers began to rely increasingly on the *labor injunction*. An injunction is a court order directing an individual or group to take, or to refrain from taking, a particular course of action. As a technique for restricting union activities, it is direct and to the point: failure to obey an injunction constitutes contempt of court and can be punished summarily with a jail sentence or fine. The issuance of labor injunctions was a matter of judicial discretion, but employers usually were able to locate a willing judge. While the general purpose of injunctions is to protect property from irreparable damage, U.S. courts had extended the concept of "property" to include intangible items (such as the right to run a profitable business) as well as tangible property. As a result, virtually any prospective union effort to organize and enforce demands for better wages and working conditions could be construed as a threat to "property."[5]

The final legal restraint on unions came from a statutory law that was not obviously directed at unions and collective bargaining. The Sherman Antitrust Act, enacted by Congress in 1890, provided that "every contract, combination, . . . or conspiracy, in restraint of trade or commerce among the several States, . . . is . . . illegal," but made no mention of unions. Nevertheless, the act was used for many years to curb certain union practices. The treatment of unions under antitrust law is discussed more extensively in Chapter 11.

**Structure of authority within the American labor movement.**  The remaining threat to those craft unions that managed to develop a toehold in the precarious economic and legal environment of the nineteenth and early twentieth centuries was from rival union organizations. The rivals undertook

[5] One study estimated that by 1931 employers had obtained 1845 injunctions against unions while unions had obtained only 43 against employers. Edwin D. Witte, *The Government in Labor Disputes* (New York: McGraw-Hill Book Company, 1932) pp. 231–34.

more broadly based efforts to establish industrial unions by mixing craft workers, with their superior bargaining power, with unskilled and semiskilled workers. Some of the rival organizations also had a distinctly different ideological position regarding the place of labor in society. Inevitably, the rival unions attempted to organize workers who the established craft unions viewed as working in their jurisdiction. While none of the alternative movements that arose during the nineteenth century survived for any appreciable period of time, the interorganizational rivalry challenged the institutional security of established craft unions and eroded their ability to present a united front to employers.

The challenges arose because the nature of industrial development left the craft form of union organization increasingly inappropriate for large groups of workers. With the growth of large-scale manufacturing enterprises came the widespread introduction of machines, which eliminated or diluted many skills, created a few others (for example, machinists), but on balance increased the ratio of semiskilled and unskilled jobs to skilled jobs in industry. With the westward economic expansion, skills also broke down on the frontier, where it became more important for a worker to be a jack-of-all-trades than a master of one. Despite the growth of employment outside of the traditional craft occupations, however, early attempts to form industrial unions proved unable to survive periodic recessions, when unions were generally unable to defend their members against wage cuts by employers.

Some of the tensions between the craft and industrial philosophies of union organization are illustrated by the experience of the Knights of Labor, which represented the first large-scale attempt to adopt the industrial-union principle of organization. Originally founded in 1869 as a secret society in the Philadelphia area, the Knights abandoned secrecy in the early 1880s to openly pursue political and social objectives. They shared with organizations of farmers and small shopkeepers an opposition to what was perceived at the time as the growing monopoly power of banks and railroads. In addition, the leadership of the Knights saw the established craft unions as labor market monopolists with, from their perspective, rather limited objectives. By uniting workers at all skill levels in one union, the Knights hoped to break down the divisions that they believed were associated with the craft approach to union organization and to use the bargaining power of the skilled workers to secure economic gains for all workers.[6] To this end, they organized workers of all skill levels into "assemblies." Unlike most unions, the Knights of Labor initially favored arbitration and consumer boycotts over strikes as a method of settling bargaining impasses. However, the inability to enforce arbitration decisions increasingly led the Knights to use the strike weapon.

---

[6] The Knights of Labor also pursued a number of political objectives, including the establishment of a federal bureau of labor statistics, a prohibition of child labor, an end to sex discrimination, and the establishment of an eight-hour day.

The Knights of Labor were bitterly opposed by the established craft unions with whom they competed for the allegiance of skilled workers. Several craft unions had established the Federation of Organized Trades and Labor Unions in 1881, and the Federation regarded skilled workers as being exclusively in their "jurisdiction" for the purpose of organizing. The Federation proposed a treaty under which the Knights would abandon the assemblies in trades organized by established craft unions, and would agree not to organize skilled workers without the permission of the Federation. Since this would have involved a total capitulation to the craft unions, the Knights refused. Following a surprisingly successful railroad strike in 1885 their membership grew from around 100,000 to almost a million. However, the Knights had developed only loose control over their assemblies, and a year later, another railroad strike, initiated by a local assembly without the approval of the leadership, was lost, and the Knights went into decline as an organization.

In an effort to resolve issues of union rivalry and to coordinate action on issues of interest to the labor movement as a whole, the members of the Federation of Organized Trades and Labor Unions formed a loose umbrella organization for the national craft unions, the American Federation of Labor (AFL). The principles on which this federation was established a century ago are important in understanding the behavior of its successor organization (the AFL-CIO) today. Although the Federation is on the top of the hierarchy of union organization, it is not the center of power within the American labor movement and has rather circumscribed authority compared to labor federations in many western European countries. The national unions that established the Federation insisted that it be founded on two broad principles— *exclusive jurisdiction* and *national union autonomy*.

The first principle, exclusive jurisdiction, addressed the problem of union rivalry by providing that only one union would be accorded the right to organize workers of a particular skill or performing a particular type of work. To implement this principle, the AFL was granted the authority to issue a charter to each national union, defining the jurisdiction or categories of workers within which the union was authorized to organize workers. New unions could not be given jurisdictions that overlapped with those of existing national unions. From the perspective of the national unions, the Federation therefore had an important role to play in awarding jurisdictions and in resolving jurisdictional conflicts between affiliated national unions. (In practice, conflicts appeared to be resolved in favor of the more powerful contestant. Since the Federation was financed by per capita payments from member unions, larger unions were more important to its economic well-being.) While subsequent developments have greatly modified the authority of the Federation with respect to jurisdiction, the notion of exclusive jurisdiction has been an important influence on the behavior of American unions.

The principle of national union autonomy also continues to have an important influence and constraint on behavior of the Federation. Under this doctrine (which is embedded in the Federation's constitution), the Federation has no authority over the internal affairs of its constituent national unions or their membership. In fact, workers are not permitted to belong to the Federation. Instead, they belong to a national union and the membership of the Federation consists of national union organizations that choose to affiliate. Thus, the AFL (and now the AFL-CIO) is constitutionally forbidden from interfering in national union practices regarding admissions to unions, apprenticeship programs, discipline of the membership, and internal government. In recent decades, this constitutional limitation on the Federation's authority has made it very difficult for it to respond actively to some of the more trenchant criticisms of unions with respect to discrimination and union corruption. As the organizational pinnacle of the labor movement, the Federation is a natural target for public criticism of union behavior. Yet, even when such charges were restricted to the activities of a few national unions, the national autonomy doctrine limited the extent to which the Federation was able to respond.

Furthermore, the Federation was given no real role in collective bargaining. The national unions were sufficiently determined to retain all decisions with respect to collective bargaining, so that the Federation was not given the authority to maintain a strike fund. To this day, the Federation has very little leverage over the bargaining policy or tactics of its constituent national unions. The net result of the relationship between the Federation and the national unions is that despite the organizational hierarchy, the real locus of economic power resides in the national unions. The Federation needs them more than they need the Federation. Indeed, when a national union chooses or is forced to disaffiliate, the Federation loses the dues payments (which can be substantial) that it received from the national union, while the union merely loses the Federation's protection from "raids" by other unions on its jurisdiction, something that has become a less consequential threat, particularly to large unions, in the twentieth century.

The other main function of the Federation is to represent the labor movement politically. In contrast to the situation abroad, the development of labor unions in the United States has been marked by a clear precedence of economic over political objectives. In fact, many European unions are formed with explicit political objectives, and many visitors to the United States are surprised by the lack of class consciousness in American unions. As noted earlier, American unions have emphasized the method of collective bargaining over the method of legislative enactment to a much greater extent than unions in most European nations. Rather than adopting any particular ideological stance or affiliating with any party, the AFL took the pragmatic stance of "rewarding one's friends and punishing one's enemies" in its quest to obtain legislation that improved the general climate of collective bargaining. For years, however, its legislative objectives were surprisingly limited. Until the 1930s, for example, the Federation opposed legislative proposals to establish minimum wages, Social Security, and other benefits on the grounds that these were tasks for collective bargaining. Since the 1930s, the Federation has been a major supporter of legislation in favor of these and other workplace benefits, such as regulations aimed at improving occupational health and safety.

**Challenges to the American Federation of Labor.**   The American Federation of Labor's emphasis on the interests of skilled workers, its limited demands on the political system, and its general acceptance of the capitalist economic system left it vulnerable to criticism from groups who believed that the economic position of workers could only be advanced through a more radical restructuring of society. The main radical challenge to the prevailing political and economic philosophy of the American Federation of Labor came from the Industrial Workers of the World (IWW), formed in 1905 by an alliance of western metal miners and socialist trade union leaders. Contrary to the AFL, the IWW rejected the idea that workers and employers had sufficient common interests to resolve their differences through collective bargaining. The stark philosophical difference between the two organizations is clear from the opening lines of the preamble to the IWW constitution, which state that "The working class and the employing class have nothing in common. . . . Between these two classes a struggle must go on until workers of the world unite as a class . . . and take possession of the machinery of production and abolish the wage system."

The IWW was equally opposed to the craft principle of organization that characterized unions in the AFL on the grounds that it led to competition rather than solidarity between different crafts in an industry. Interestingly, the IWW also saw a conflict between normal collective-bargaining arrangements and the goal of worker solidarity. If different groups of workers in an industry were represented by different unions or for other reasons worked under collective-bargaining agreements with different expiration dates, then some workers could be forced to continue working while others struck. In the view of the IWW, the sanctity of the contract took second place to worker solidarity. Few AFL unions shared this view. The difference in the authority granted the respective leadership of the AFL and the IWW reflected the difference in the philosophies of the organizations. In contrast to the limitations on the authority of the officers of the AFL, the leadership of the IWW could order all member unions to give financial or other assistance (including sympathetic work stoppages) to aid striking subordinates.

Nevertheless, this basic philosophical challenge to the trade-union organization under the AFL was accompanied by a footloose, anarchic style that rendered the IWW more colorful than effective. Despite a few successful strikes between 1905 and 1914, it proved unable to attract the durable allegiance of a large fraction of American workers. In general, American workers have shown little interest in radical political ideas. One reason for this may be the high standard of living of American workers relative to their European counterparts. Moreover, radical appeals could not be based on the political disenfranchisement of workers. Even in the nineteenth century, workers in the United States had the ballot. As with the Knights of Labor, the main aspect of the IWW philosophy that was to survive was the attack on the craft-union basis of early American organized labor.

**Union growth in the twentieth century.** In the face of the difficult economic and legal environment and the determined opposition of employers, unions established little more than a toehold in the United States until World War I, when at the behest of the government, a period of cooperation between labor and management was accompanied by a period of union growth (see Table 10.2). This was followed at the conclusion of the war by a sharp employer counter-offensive to restore a nonunion environment. In the absence of statutory support for collective bargaining, unions could be established by the voluntary consent of an employer or by striking an employer in an effort to compel recognition. Under prevailing employer attitudes toward unions, the first option was effectively ruled out. The second option was frequently countered by the use of the labor injunction, as noted previously. Where an injunction was not used, the techniques of employer opposition were often less delicate. Espionage, private detectives, and strikebreakers were employed to thwart union activities, and efforts to establish unions were frequently accompanied by violence.

In other situations, employers also required employees to sign "yellow dog" contracts—contracts in which potential employees had to agree *not* to join a union as a condition of employment. If a union then attempted to organize the employees, the union could be sued for inducing breach of contract. During the 1920s, employers also established "company unions" as a representational device for workers. While such organizations could discuss some terms and conditions of employment with employers, they were not independent employee organizations. Typically, the company union was financially supported by the employer, its officers were chosen by the company, and the agenda for its meetings was set by the company. Nevertheless, it provided a semblance of representation and was sometimes used to convince workers that they did not really need representation from an outside union. Employers also developed and introduced a number of innovative fringe-benefit plans as a way of maintaining the allegiance of employees during this period. The net result of these developments was that during the 1920s, unions lost most of the ground that they had gained during World War I.

However, some of the difficulties encountered by the American labor movement were traceable to its own internal structure. While most of the employment growth was occurring in large mass-production factories staffed by largely semiskilled, operative work forces, the American Federation of Labor remained, with a few exceptions such as the United Mine Workers, an organization of skilled craft unions. Since skilled workers constituted a small proportion of employment in the mass-production industries, no single craft union or group of unions had the resources to mount a successful organizing campaign. As a result, workers in the automobile, steel, rubber, and other large industries remained unorganized. Moreover, the craft unions within the AFL opposed attempts to charter industrial unions, which structurally would have been more suited to organizing in such industries, on the grounds that the minority of skilled workers found in the industries were within traditional craft-union jurisdictions and hence could not be organized by newly chartered industrial unions. Despite the efforts of John L. Lewis, the president of the United Mine Workers, and a few other leaders of AFL unions to get the Federation to charter new industrial unions to organize the mass-production industries, the internal stalemate in the AFL on the issue persisted into the mid-1930s.

These tensions within the labor movement and between employees and employers came to a head during the 1930s in the wake of the Great Depression. To many, the extraordinary losses in production and employment in the early 1930s signaled the failure of the *laissez-faire* theory of economic organization that formed the basis of the freedom-of-contract approach to public policy toward labor markets. This set the stage for the passage of two major pieces of legislation that established an explicit statutory policy toward unions and collective bargaining and significantly altered the legal environment of industrial relations. The first of these, the Norris-LaGuardia Act, passed in 1932, provided the first statutory statement that American public policy sanctioned unions and collective bargaining, and broadened the definition of a legally permissible labor conflict from a dispute between employers and employees (a standard developed in earlier court decisions) to a dispute between those having an economic interest at stake. This extension effectively freed strikes over union recognition from legal restraint. The act also went much further by forbidding the issuance of injunctions in most labor disputes and by declaring that ''yellow dog'' contracts were unenforceable in the federal courts. The basic effect of the statute was to remove the courts and judicial value judgments from labor disputes and to introduce a period of roughly equivalent legal rights and status for unions and management.

This brief period ended in 1935 with the passage of the National Labor Relations Act (NLRA), often referred to in its original form as the Wagner Act, which tipped the support of public policy toward unions. Support for this legislation within the Roosevelt Administration stemmed more from the view that the spread of collective bargaining would stimulate recovery from the Depression than from any inherent commitment to the idea of unionization. To the extent that unions were successful in raising the wages and purchasing power of workers, it was believed that the growth of collective bargaining would increase demand. A second objective of the Act was to reduce labor disputes and the associated disruptions of production.

The Wagner Act provided a fuller statutory guarantee than the Norris-LaGuardia Act of the basic rights of employees to organize, to bargain collectively, and to engage in strikes or other concerted activity in order to secure their objectives. It established two broad mechanisms to secure and enforce these rights. First, the law established a government-supervised election procedure to determine which union, if any, should represent employees in collective bargaining with their employers. By substituting an admin-istrative procedure for the use of force in determining bargaining status, the NLRA sought to reduce strikes over recognition. A union receiving the support of a majority of the employees in an election became the *exclusive bargaining representative* of all employees in the bargaining unit.

The concept of an exclusive bargaining representative is a unique feature of American labor law. It imposes on the union the duty to represent and bargain for all employees in the unit, including those who voted against it. At the same time, employers are required to deal with employees through the union rather than individually. On the one hand, the legal requirement is advantageous to unions because it reduces competition in the supply of labor to the bargaining unit in which the union wins an election. Rival unions are excluded, and the employer is prevented from hiring nonunion workers at lower wages in an effort to undermine the union's position. Exclusive repre-sentation effectively protects the monopoly position of a union within the bargaining unit. On the other hand, the legal requirement raises a *free rider* problem for the union—employees who do not support the union nevertheless receive the benefits of union activities. This has encouraged unions to develop *union security* arrangements, which are discussed more fully later in this chapter.

Second, while the Norris-LaGuardia Act had removed major judicial impediments to union organization, the Wagner Act sought to remove several employer techniques of union resistance by proscribing a number of employer unfair labor practices because they constituted interference with or restraint of employees seeking to exercise their rights under the act. (The specific unfair labor practices and their impact on modern American labor relations are discussed more extensively in Chapter 11.) To implement these provi-sions, an administrative agency of the federal government, the National Labor Relations Board (NLRB), was established to conduct elections for union representation and to investigate, prosecute, and adjudicate unfair labor-practice charges.

The passage of the NLRA, and its aftermath, had major consequences for the size and structure of the American labor movement. With union represen-tation decided by NLRB elections, the AFL lost the only major power that it had with respect to the national unions—the awarding of jurisdiction. Under the NLRA, the appropriate bargaining unit was to be decided by the NLRB (if the union and employer could not agree), and the choice of union depended on a vote of employees in the unit rather than an award by the AFL. More generally, the entire notion of exclusive jurisdiction, which was of such importance to the craft unions, was eroded under a system in which the majority of workers decided who would represent them.[7] Also, once majority

---

[7]   Recall that the concept of "exclusive jurisdiction" is different from the concept of "exclusive rep-resentation." The former refers to a founding principle of the AFL under which only one union was given the right to organize a particular group of workers; the second refers to the legal concept that the union winning a representation election under the NLRA is the sole representative of all workers in the bargain-ing unit.

rule rather than relative power became the criterion for establishing a bargaining relationship, unorganized employees rather than employers became the "targets" of union organizing efforts.[8] This change in the focus of organizing efforts raises a number of interesting questions concerning why workers join (vote for) unions that are discussed more fully in Chapter 11.

Most importantly, the passage of the NLRA brought the internal debate within the AFL over the structure of the labor movement to a head by providing procedures that effectively reduced the cost of organizing large industries. As the craft unions continued to oppose the principle of industrial unionization, John L. Lewis and a few other leaders of national unions affiliated with the AFL formed a Committee on Industrial Organization in 1935. Since this move was viewed by the craft unions as an attempt to set up rival union organizations (because there were a few craft workers in the mass-production industries), the unions involved were thrown out of the AFL. Subsequently, these unions formed a rival labor federation, the Congress of Industrial Organizations (CIO), with the avowed purpose of organizing workers in the mass-production industries into new industrial unions.

With the formation of the new federation and its assault on the mass-production industries, the American labor movement went through a period of extraordinary growth beginning in 1937 (see Table 10.2). Although the new statutory support for collective bargaining undoubtedly helped to persuade some workers to join unions, it must be said that this explosion of new union membership did not come about through the relatively civilized election procedures that had been established in the NLRA. Sitdown strikes, violence, and the use of force (mitigated only by an occasional secret negotiation over recognition) dominated efforts to gain union recognition during the period, but by 1940, the CIO had made major inroads into the automobile, rubber, steel, and electrical manufacturing industries.[9] Unionization was also extended during World War II, when most unions adhered to a no-strike pledge, and the War Labor Board, which was charged with regulating employment conditions to aid the war effort, encouraged resisting employers to establish collective-bargaining relationships with unions.

Following World War II, the public-policy pendulum shifted decidedly against union interests. The most immediate stimulus was a sharp increase in strike activity as unions attempted to press demands that had been muted during the wartime no-strike pledge. Although work time lost to strike activity amounted to only 1.4 percent of employee hours in 1946, it represented a record high, and inspired demands to protect neutral third parties—particularly the public at large—from the consequences of disputes between major unions and major employers. There was also concern over the potential use of coercive actions by unions against employees. The growing concern with the

---

[8]  Some of the coercion that unions had formerly practiced against employers in efforts to secure recognition were at times even exercised against employees.

[9]  For a detailed history of this period, see Walter Galenson, *The CIO Challenge to the AFL* (Cambridge, MA: Harvard University Press, 1959).

consequences of union power culminated with the passage in 1947 of the Taft-Hartley Act, which altered the National Labor Relations Act by amending it in significant ways.

While the new legislation maintained the basic rights to organization and collective bargaining that had been established in the Wagner Act, it sought to protect the individual's right to belong or *not* to belong to a union, to rehabilitate the employer's freedom of expression, and to protect neutral third parties from the consequences of major labor disputes. The legislation sought to achieve these objectives by adding a list of union unfair labor practices (discussed at greater length in Chapter 11) to the list of employer unfair labor practices in the Wagner Act, by providing for decertification elections in which employees could vote on whether a union should be removed as their bargaining agent, and by establishing a set of emergency dispute procedures that could be invoked under certain circumstances in major labor disputes. (The latter procedures are examined in Chapter 14 on disputes and dispute settlement.) It also includes the famous "Section 14B," which permits individual states to pass so-called *right-to-work laws*.[10] These laws prohibit contractual requirements that a person become, or promise to become, a union member as a condition of employment. By 1984, nineteen states, located primarily in the South, Southwest, and Plains areas, had passed such laws.

The increasing hostility of public policy toward unions and collective bargaining contributed to an interest on the part of the AFL and the CIO in exploring the possibility of an alliance. In addition to their common interest in improving the general public-policy climate for collective bargaining, some of the earlier philosophical differences between the two labor federations had dissipated by the early 1950s. In competing for membership, the AFL had overcome its initial craft orientation and established some industrial unions. For its part, the CIO had not been bashful about organizing new craft unions. That continued jurisdictional competition could be counterproductive seemed to be confirmed when a joint study by the federations showed that, when an AFL union competed with a CIO union in an NLRB representation election, the most frequent outcome was that workers voted for "no union." Following a period of negotiations, the two federations signed an agreement in which they agreed not to raid each other's memberships. Subsequently, in 1955, a merger of the two federations into the present American Federation of Labor-Congress of Industrial Organizations (AFL-CIO) was completed, with George Meany, the president of the AFL, as president of the merged federations, and Walter Reuther, the president of the CIO, as vice- president.

In addition, new public policy toward unions continued to diminish union power. Developments in the late 1950s, however, were not fundamentally directed at labor-management relations as were the Wagner and Taft-Hartley

---

[10] Federal labor legislation permits the negotiation of union security arrangements. Technically, when both federal and state legislation address the same issue, the provisions of the federal legislation take precedence. Section 14B of the Taft-Hartley Act creates an exception to this general convention for cases in which states have passed statutes forbidding the negotiation of union security clauses in collective bargaining agreements.

Acts. After a series of Congressional hearings that developed evidence of serious official corruption, mismanagement of financial resources, and undemocratic procedures in a few unions, Congress passed the Labor-Management Reporting and Disclosure Act (also known as the Landrum-Griffin Act after its chief sponsors) in 1959. This act marked a shift in legislative emphasis from union-management relations toward the regulation of internal affairs of unions to an extent not observed for corporations. The act provided a "bill of rights" for union members, required unions to file annual financial reports with the U.S. Department of Labor, limited the extent to which national unions could place local unions in trusteeship and take over their operations, imposed standards of fiduciary responsibility on union officials, and, perhaps most importantly, provided that the Department of Labor can set aside and rerun elections for union office when there is evidence of irregularities in the original election. These new procedures have increased the effective degree of democracy in unions by making it easier for union members to challenge union leaders through the internal election process.

## The Recent Decline of Private-Sector Unions

Union representation peaked at about the time of the merger of the AFL and the CIO in 1955. (Refer again to Table 10.2.) For the next two decades representation of nonagricultural employees declined gradually, but since the mid-1970s unions have lost ground rapidly. Membership fell by some 4 million members between 1974 and 1984, and some of the largest industrial unions, such as the United Automobile Workers and the United Steelworkers, experienced the most dramatic losses. Moreover, labor agreements often changed radically as many unions reluctantly accepted significant concessions in wages and work rules in an effort to retain their members' jobs. (Examples 10.1 and 10.2 later in the chapter describe specific concession negotiations.)

The decline in union membership is most dramatic in the United States. Some modest declines in union representation occurred in a few Western European countries in the 1980s, but these appear to be related to severe recessions in those countries, and in no case was there a decline in the absolute number of union members. Moreover, Canadian union representation has grown over the same period, so the causes are unlikely to be typical of North America in general. The decline of private-sector unions in the United States during the 1980s has been a social change as dramatic as the rise of unions in the 1930s. But what are its causes?

Part of the explanation is a decline in the availability of union jobs. During the postwar period, most of the employment growth occurred outside of the occupational and industrial sectors in which unions had been successful. The last 30 years have seen a substantial decline in the relative employment shares of manufacturing, mining, construction, transportation, and public utilities. Conversely, there has been a substantial increase in the share of employment in wholesale and retail trade, finance, insurance, real estate, and service industries. Indeed, the former group fell from 48.7 percent of nonagricultural payroll employment in 1955 to 31.6 percent by 1984. During the same period

**Table 10.3**   Union Membership by Industry in 1975 and 1984

| Industry | Percentage of Employees That are Union Members | |
|---|---|---|
| | 1975 | 1984 |
| Manufacturing | 36.0% | 26.0% |
| Mining | 32.0 | 17.7 |
| Construction | 35.4 | 23.5 |
| Transportation | 46.6 | 38.7 |
| Service | 13.9 | 7.3 |
| Government | 39.5 | 34.3* |
| Total | 28.9 | 19.4 |

* 1983 data

Note: "Services" includes wholesale and retail trade, finance, insurance, and real estate, as well as service industries.

SOURCE: Leo Troy and Neil Sheflin, *Union Sourcebook* First Edition (West Orange, NJ: Industrial Relations Data and Information Services, 1985), Table 3.63.

the latter group rose from 37.7 to 51.4 percent. As Table 10.3 indicates, the industries in the latter group are the ones that are least unionized. The shifting industrial composition of employment has led to a distribution that is weighted more heavily towards industries that are not extensively unionized.

Why does the latter set of industries tend not to be unionized? These industries are usually highly competitive, with high price elasticities of demand. As discussed in Chapter 3, other things being equal, industries with high price elasticities of product demand will also have high wage elasticities of demand for labor. High wage elasticities limit unions' abilities to increase their members' wages without substantial employment declines also occurring. As such, the net benefits individuals perceive from union membership may be lower in these industries, and an increase in their importance in the economy would shift the demand for union services to the left, thereby reducing the percentage of the workforce that is unionized.

**Table 10.4**   Private-Sector Union Membership by Region in 1975 and 1982

| Region | Percentage of Employees that are Union Members | |
|---|---|---|
| | 1975 | 1982 |
| New England | 18.6% | 13.1% |
| Middle Atlantic | 34.3 | 26.0 |
| North Central | 32.3 | 23.8 |
| South Atlantic | 13.8 | 10.1 |
| South Central | 15.6 | 11.4 |
| Mountain | 19.3 | 13.2 |
| Pacific | 35.1 | 25.1 |

SOURCE: Leo Troy and Neil Sheflin, *Union Sourcebook,* 1st ed., (West Orange, NJ: Industrial Relations Data and Information Services, 1985), Tables 7.11, 7.12.

Employment growth has also been more rapid in the South and Southwest, where union representation has traditionally been low, than in the East and Midwest, where representation has been high (see Table 10.4). This trend has even occurred in highly unionized industries such as manufacturing. Both American and Japanese automakers have opened nonunion auto assembly plants in southern states, eroding the virtually complete unionization of that industry.

Industrial and geographical shifts in jobs are not the whole story, however. Indeed, they appear to account for less than half of the decline of union membership between the early 1950s and the late 1970s and for almost none of the decline during the 1980s.[11] The broader problem facing private-sector unions is indicated by the data in Tables 10.3 and 10.4, which show that union representation has declined within all major industries and regions. General explanations are needed.

One important general factor influencing the supply of union jobs is the difference between union and nonunion labor costs. This difference (which is examined in detail in Chapter 16) grew throughout the 1970s, reaching a historical high in the early 1980s. We have seen in Chapter 3 that it will be easier for employers to pass on higher labor costs with little loss of sales and employment when consumers have few substitutes available (that is, when the elasticity of product demand is low). Several important developments have increased product market competition since 1970, giving consumers important alternatives to goods and services produced by union labor in the United States and making it more difficult for American producers to accommodate the higher costs often associated with union representation. One development is the growth of foreign competition. Market shares accounted for by imports have grown rapidly over the past 15 years; the share of imports in manufacturing sales rose from about 2.5 percent in 1958 to 11 percent in 1984. Changes in individual industries were even more dramatic. For example, the import share of new car registrations rose from 7.6 percent in 1960 to almost 30 percent in 1982. This had both direct and indirect effects on union jobs as unionized domestic producers sought ways to reduce costs and regain their market shares. A second development was the deregulation of such industries as air transport, surface transport, and communications. Deregulation removed important barriers to entry in these industries and was followed by significant increases in the number of nonunion competitors, typically with lower costs than the established unionized producers.

Employers intent on reducing labor costs to meet increased competition can follow a number of strategies. One method is to locate new production

---

[11] William T. Dickens and Jonathan S. Leonard, "Accounting for the Decline in Union Membership, 1950–80," *Industrial and Labor Relations Review* 38 (April 1985): pp. 323–34; Henry S. Farber, "The Extent of Unionization in the United States," *Challenges and Choices Facing American Labor*, ed. T. Kochan (Cambridge, MA: MIT Press, 1985); Henry S. Farber, "The Decline of Unionization in the United States: What Can Be Learned From Recent Experience?" National Bureau of Economic Research Working Paper No. 2267, (May 1987); and Michael Goldfield, *The Decline of Organized Labor in the United States* (Chicago: University of Chicago Press, 1987).

**Table 10.5**    Representation Elections, Decertification Votes
and Unfair-Labor-Practice-Charges Against Employers

| Fiscal Year | Union Elections | Percent Won By Union | Decertification Votes | Percent Lost By Union | Unfair Labor Practice Charges Against Employers |
|---|---|---|---|---|---|
| 1950 | 5731 | 73.7 | 112 | 67.0 | 4,472 |
| 1955 | 4372 | 66.4 | 157 | 65.0 | 4,362 |
| 1960 | 6617 | 57.6 | 237 | 68.8 | 7,723 |
| 1965 | 7776 | 60.2 | 200 | 64.0 | 10,931 |
| 1970 | 8074 | 55.2 | 301 | 69.8 | 13,601 |
| 1975 | 8577 | 48.2 | 516 | 73.4 | 20,311 |
| 1980 | 8198 | 45.7 | 902 | 72.7 | 31,281 |
| 1983 | 4405 | 43.0 | 922 | 74.8 | 27,749* |

\*  1982

SOURCE:  *Annual Report of the National Labor Relations Board,* Appendix Tables (various years).

facilities in areas in which unionization seems unlikely, based on historical experience.[12] As noted earlier, this may account for the establishment of many new plants in the South and in other (typically less-developed) countries. A second strategy was suggested by the analysis in Chapter 3. Employers may alter production methods to use more capital equipment and less union labor. A third strategy is to implement human resource management policies that effectively substitute for the services that a union can provide. Many of these policies have been discussed in earlier chapters and include employee-benefit plans and rules and procedures regarding promotion and dismissal.

A fourth strategy is union resistance—the adoption of tactics intended to oppose union organizing attempts or to encourage the decertification of a union. Examples of such tactics include hiring special consultants to run an antiunion campaign, using labor laws to tactically delay the holding of a representation election, and to delay certification of a bargaining agent.

Evidence of resistance to unions can be seen in the National Labor Relations Board data on union elections and charges of unfair labor practices, which are found in Table 10.5. These data indicate that while the number of elections in which unions have sought to win the right to represent unorganized workers grew moderately until the early 1980s, the share of the elections that unions actually won fell steadily from almost 75 percent in 1950 to 43 percent by 1983. Over the same period there has been a substantial increase in unfair-labor-practice charges against employers. The number of charges in 1980 was seven times the number 30 years earlier, while the number of representation elections was only 1.4 times higher. (With fewer elections in the early 1980s, the number of unfair-labor-practice charges declined.) Many of these charges allege unlawful employer behavior during

[12]  It is illegal to move an existing plant from one area to another solely to avoid union representation, however. A more extended treatment of this issue must await Chapter 11's discussion of the legal regulation of labor relations.

campaigns for union representation, and the willingness of employers to adopt such tactics is seen by many as a barrier to obtaining new union members. Furthermore, the annual number of decertification votes—votes in which union claims to represent a majority of workers in a firm were challenged—increased eight-fold over the period, with the share of these votes lost by unions increasing slightly to more than 70 percent in the 1980s.

A decline in the demand among workers for union representation also has contributed to the membership losses of private-sector unions. Surveys and polls indicate that while most union members are quite satisfied with their union's representation, the fraction of nonunion workers desiring union representation has decreased. This decrease appears to reflect both an increased satisfaction among nonunion workers with their jobs and a lessened belief that unions can improve wage and working conditions. This change in worker attitude is not fully understood, but it may reflect the dramatic concession bargaining of the 1980s in which unions often gave back prior gains in an effort to preserve employment opportunities for their members. Another hypothesis is that unions may in some respects be victims of their own success. Much of the social legislation that unions have supported in recent years—such as standards for pension plans and for occupational health and safety—affect all workers, irrespective of union membership. Many nonunion workers may adopt a ''free rider'' attitude toward unionization: Why pay union dues if one can get the impact of union legislative activity free? (Whether such legislation actually benefits workers was discussed in Chapter 6.) A counterargument is that unions may be valued for their role in monitoring the application of these regulations by government agencies. Evidence concerning the question of worker attitude is both sparse and conflicting.

How does the labor movement interpret the decline in union membership in the private sector in the United States? In February 1985, the AFL-CIO released a remarkable self-analysis prepared by its Committee on the Evolution of Work.[13] The report listed changes in the structure of employment and ''failures of labor law'' as causes of membership loss, but it also noted that many nonunion workers failed to perceive unions as responsive to the needs of their membership. The report also advanced several proposals. In order to increase the success rate in union representation elections, the report recommended choosing organizing targets more carefully, emphasizing new issues such as pay equity for women (see the discussion of comparable worth in Chapter 7), and making more use of ''corporate campaigns'' in which external pressures are brought to bear on companies that engage in extensive union resistance. (Example 11.4 in the next chapter describes the use of corporate campaign tactics against the J.P. Stevens Company.)

The report also urged the creation of a new category of membership—associate members—for workers who are sympathetic to unions but not employed in an organized bargaining unit. (For example, many workers lose

---

[13] AFL-CIO, Committee on the Evolution of Work, *The Changing Situation of Workers and Their Unions* (Washington, DC: AFL-CIO, 1985).

union status when they change employers. Polls indicate that about 28 percent of nonunion workers once belonged to a union.) It also urged the development of some membership benefits and services outside of collective bargaining structures. Credit cards with low interest rates are one example that has been implemented. Programs that would provide legal services, life insurance, and investment services are under study. These benefits would be available to both full and associate members; because they are developed unilaterally by unions outside of collective-bargaining negotiations they may be denied to workers who are currently covered by union contracts but refuse to join a union. This may provide an incentive for "free riders" to acquire union membership. It will be some years before the effectiveness of these recommendations can be judged.

## Union Growth in the Public Sector

The development of unions in the public sector has followed a much different course than in the private sector. Although a few unions of public employees were formed as early as the nineteenth century, for years public policy toward collective bargaining in the public sector rested on the view that the government's authority to act in the public interest was absolute. Collective bargaining by public employees, a process that implied a sharing of such authority with respect to the determination of the terms and conditions of employment, was held to be inconsistent with this "doctrine of sovereignty." Thus, in the mid-1930s, President Roosevelt could simultaneously support the rights of private employees to organize and bargain collectively (in the National Labor Relations Act) but invoke the doctrine of sovereignty to oppose the extension of similar rights to public employees, who to this day are not covered by the NLRA. In particular, most public employees still do not have the right to strike that was guaranteed private-sector employees by the labor relations legislation of the 1930s.

During the period of rapid union growth in the private sector, public-sector unions were virtually moribund. Since the 1960s, however, the expansion of unions in the public sector has been the main source of union-membership growth in the United States. While private-sector unionization declined, union membership in the public sector grew rapidly in both absolute and percentage terms from the mid-1960s until the late 1970s. For example, the proportion of federal employees represented by bargaining organizations rose from about 24 percent in 1960 to a peak of 41.5 percent in 1976 before dropping slightly (see Table 10.6). Similarly, the proportion of state-and-local-government (SLG) employees belonging to bargaining organizations—which include professional organizations such as the National Education Association—rose from 5.0 percent in 1960 to 40 percent in 1976 before declining somewhat. Although it was not their primary purpose, many professional associations have become increasingly and importantly involved in the collective-bargaining process in the public sector since the 1960s.

As in the private sector, union representation is unevenly distributed by occupation and geography. By the late 1970s, for example, the most rapid

**Table 10.6**  Membership in Public-Sector Bargaining Organizations

| Year | Federal Employees Belonging to Bargaining Organizations | | SLG Employees Belonging to Bargaining Organizations | |
|---|---|---|---|---|
| | Number (in thousands) | Percent | Number (in thousands) | Percent |
| 1945 | 390 | 13.9% | 159 | 5.1% |
| 1960 | 541 | 23.8 | 307 | 5.0 |
| 1970 | 1082 | 39.6 | 2958 | 30.1 |
| 1972 | 1163 | 43.3 | 3589 | 33.7 |
| 1974 | 1099 | 40.3 | 4244 | 37.1 |
| 1976 | 1133 | 41.5 | 4837 | 39.9 |
| 1978 | 1060 | 38.5 | 4610 | 35.7 |
| 1980 | 1049 | 36.6 | 4567 | 34.1 |
| 1982 | 1040 | 38.0 | 4382 | 33.5 |
| 1983 | 1020 | 37.1 | 4251 | 32.7 |

Notes:  Membership figures are the average annual, dues-paying, full-time equivalent membership of public sector bargaining organizations. Bargaining organizations include unions and professional associations that engage in collective bargaining. SLG data for 1945 and 1960 omit certain professional associations and are not directly comparable with later years.

SOURCE:  Leo Troy and Neil Sheflin, *Union Sourcebook* First Edition (West Orange, NJ: Industrial Relations Data and Information Services, 1985), Table 3.92.

growth of union membership among full-time public employees had occurred among teachers and fire-protection and police personnel (see Table 10.7). Unionism in the public sector also varied geographically, with the more rapid gains occurring in the larger and older cities. In 1979, 86 percent of state governments, but only 17 percent of local governments, had developed a labor-relations policy toward their employees. Local governments in southern

**Table 10.7**  Percent of Organized Full-Time Employees, by Function and Level of Government, 1979

| Function | State and local governments | State governments | Local governments |
|---|---|---|---|
| Total | 47.9 | 38.7 | 51.4 |
| For selected functions: | | | |
| Education | 55.2 | 29.0 | 61.1 |
| Teachers | 64.5 | 36.1 | 67.5 |
| Other | 38.2 | 25.4 | 44.9 |
| Highways | 43.6 | 50.7 | 37.0 |
| Public welfare | 40.8 | 40.3 | 41.3 |
| Hospitals | 39.5 | 48.4 | 29.6 |
| Police protection | 52.6 | 50.3 | 52.9 |
| Local fire protection | 70.5 | 0 | 70.5 |
| Sanitation other than sewerage | 43.8 | 0 | 43.8 |
| All other functions | 36.7 | 37.8 | 36.1 |

SOURCE:  U.S. Bureau of the Census, *Labor-Management Relations in State and Local Governments: 1979* State and Local Government Special Studies No. 100 (Washington, DC: U.S. Govt. Printing Office, Oct. 1980)

**Table 10.8** Number of States with Public-Sector Collective-Bargaining Regulations

| Type of Regulation | 1959 | 1969 | 1979 | 1984 |
|---|---|---|---|---|
| No Explicit Policy | 39 | 14 | 5 | 4 |
| Collective Bargaining Prohibited | 4 | 6 | 4 | 4 |
| Bargaining That Permits "Meet and Confer" | 6 | 15 | 8 | 8 |
| Bargaining Required | 1 | 18 | 33 | 34 |
| Arbitration or Other Final Dispute Resolution Mechanism | n.a. | 5 | 19 | 20 |

n.a.  not available
SOURCE:  Robert Valleta and Richard B. Freeman, National Bureau of Economic Research *Public Sector Collective Bargaining Law Data Set* (Cambridge, MA: NBER, 1985).

states, where private-sector unions are weakest, are least likely to have developed a labor-relations policy.[14]

One factor that continued to affect this growth in public-sector unionization was the change in public attitudes and legislation governing bargaining in the public sector. Given the early influence of the doctrine of sovereignty, laws governing collective bargaining in the public sector are of recent vintage. For example, Executive Order 10988, issued by President John F. Kennedy in 1962, legitimized collective bargaining in the federal sector for the first time, providing federal workers with the rights to join unions and bargain over working conditions—but *not* wages. While this executive order has been modified several times since then, in the early 1980s most federal employees' wages were still not determined by the collective-bargaining process, and the bargaining rights of federal employees did not include the right to strike.[15]

Instead of bargaining over wages, *comparability legislation* was passed at the federal level in 1962, tying the wages of federal white-collar workers to those of private workers found "comparable" in a survey, subject to possible presidential or congressional modification.[16] Federal blue-collar workers' wages are also determined, in the main, by the comparability process, with comparisons in this case being made at the local labor-market level. The influence of federal unions on wages operates, then, primarily through the

[14]  U.S. Bureau of the Census, *Labor-Management Relations in State and Local Government, 1979,* State and Local Government Special Studies No. 100 (Washington, DC: U.S. Government Printing Office, Oct. 1980): 2–3.

[15]  There were some major exceptions—namely, postal workers and employees of federal-government authorities, such as the Tennessee Valley Authority (TVA). In each of these cases the prices of the products or services produced (mail delivery, hydroelectric power) can be raised to cover the cost of the contract settlement, unlike other federal agencies where salaries are paid out of general revenues.

[16]  See Sharon Smith, *Equal Pay in the Public Sector: Fact or Fantasy* (Princeton, NJ: Princeton University, 1977) for a more complete description of the comparability process in the federal sector. For an interesting analysis of some of the anomalies and incentive problems presented by the current federal pay-comparability procedures, see Robert Hartman, *Pay and Pensions for Federal Workers* (Washington, DC: The Brookings Institution, 1983).

political pressure they can exert on the President and Congress to approve wage increases that the surveys suggest they deserve. The wage-determination process under collective bargaining in the federal sector clearly differs in many ways from wage determination under collective bargaining in the private sector.

Favorable state legislation for SLG employee collective bargaining appears to be a key factor in the growth of union membership in the SLG sector. Prior to the 1960s, few states had public-sector bargaining policies other than prohibitions of strikes by public employees. By the mid-1980s, most industrial states had adopted statutes that permitted SLG employees to participate in the determination of their wages and conditions of employment, although very few states permitted strikes by public employees (see Table 10.8).[17] Instead, many states and municipalities began to provide for the resolution of bargaining disputes by arbitration or related procedures. (The effect of such arbitration procedures on bargaining strategy will be discussed in Chapter 14.)

As employment and unionization were growing in the SLG sector, SLG employees' earnings started to rise relative to the earnings of private-sector employees; from the mid-1950s to 1970, for example, the relative-earnings position of SLG employees improved by some 15 to 20 percent. The growth in the relative-earnings position of SLG employees during the 1960s, coupled with the growing strength of public-employee unions, their increased militancy, and the trend towards allowing SLG employees to bargain over the wage issues, led to fears that inflationary wage settlements would continue in the sector and aggravate the financial problems faced by state and local governments. These fears were explicitly based upon the belief that many public services are both essential and produced under monopoly conditions, which implies that the wage elasticity of demand for public employees is very low and that unions in the public sector are therefore potentially very powerful. To many, the logical conclusion was that, in the absence of market constraints that would limit the wage demands of public employees, limitations should be placed on the collective-bargaining rights of these groups.[18]

Although, by the late 1970s, eight states did grant the right to strike in one form or another to selected public employee groups, most continued historic prohibitions against strikes. The states that prohibited strikes, however, often provided assistance to local governments and unions in settling contract disputes, with a number of states adopting forms of binding arbitration as the terminal stage in their impasse procedures. (The nature and implications of

---

[17] See discussion of public-sector labor-relations law in Chapter 11 and in B. V. H. Schneider, "Public-Sector Labor Legislation: An Evolutionary Analysis" in *Public-Sector Bargaining,* Second Edition, eds. Benjamin Aaron *et al.* (Washington DC: Bureau of National Affairs, 1988) for a more complete discussion of the evolution of legislation governing bargaining in the public sector. For some estimates of the effects of the legislation, see Richard B. Freeman and Robert G. Valletta, "The Effect of Public-Sector Labor Laws on Collective Bargaining, Wages, and Employment," National Bureau of Economic Research Working Paper No. 2284, June 1987.

[18] See for example, H. Wellington and R. Winter, "The Limits of Collective Bargaining in Public Employment," *Yale Law Journal,* 69 (June 1969): 1107–27.

modern techniques of dispute resolution are discussed more extensively in Chapter 14.) Some of the fears concerning public-sector unionism began to diminish in the late 1970s as the earnings of SLG workers rose less quickly than those of workers in the private sector.

## Union Structure

The present structure and operation of the American labor movement reflects the main historical developments reviewed above. Figure 10.2 describes the general organization of the AFL-CIO as of the mid-1980s. Among some 189 labor organizations counted by the U.S. Department of Labor, 104 were affiliated with the Federation in 1986. Those that were not affiliated included one of the largest unions in the United States—the Teamsters' union (1.6 million members), which had been expelled for corrupt activities in 1958. (The AFL-CIO later readmitted the Teamsters' union in late 1987.) While the supreme governing body of the AFL-CIO is the biennial convention, most of the Federation's business between conventions is guided by the Executive Council and the General Board. There are a number of staff departments that assist in developing the Federation's legislative positions and assist in general organizing activities. In addition to the central office, there are various state offices of the Federation as well as local labor councils of AFL-CIO affiliates.

The relationship of each of these bodies to the constituent national unions is much as it was when the Federation was founded in 1886. At all levels of the organization the real power over collective bargaining and the governing of union organizations remains lodged in the national unions and in their local units, while the Federation's activities remain more in the nature of advocacy of labor's political objectives and support for the movement in general. The Federation continues to have no direct bargaining role in the negotiations conducted by the national unions.

The limitations on the Federation's power with respect to the national unions is also evident from the nature of the financial relationships between the AFL-CIO and the unions, and from the distribution of financial resources through the union structure. Per capita payments from the constituent national unions form a major part of the Federation's annual revenues, whereas there is no comparable flow of revenues from the Federation to the unions. A similar picture emerges from a review of the assets of union organizations. When compared to national unions, the AFL-CIO ranked 20th in assets ($29.4 million) in 1982. Individual national unions with substantially larger assets in 1982 included the International Brotherhood of Electrical Workers (with assets of $408.2 million), the United Automobile Workers ($610.6 million), the United Steelworkers ($227.5 million), the International Brotherhood of Teamsters ($160.3 million), the International Ladies Garment Workers ($126.3 million), and the United Mineworkers ($55.1 million).[19] The Mineworkers were not affiliated with the AFL-CIO.

---

[19] Leo Troy and Neil Sheflin, *Union Sourcebook* 1st ed. (West Orange, NJ: Industrial Relations Data and Information Sources, 1985): Table 4.3.

**Figure 10.2**   Structure of the AFL-CIO

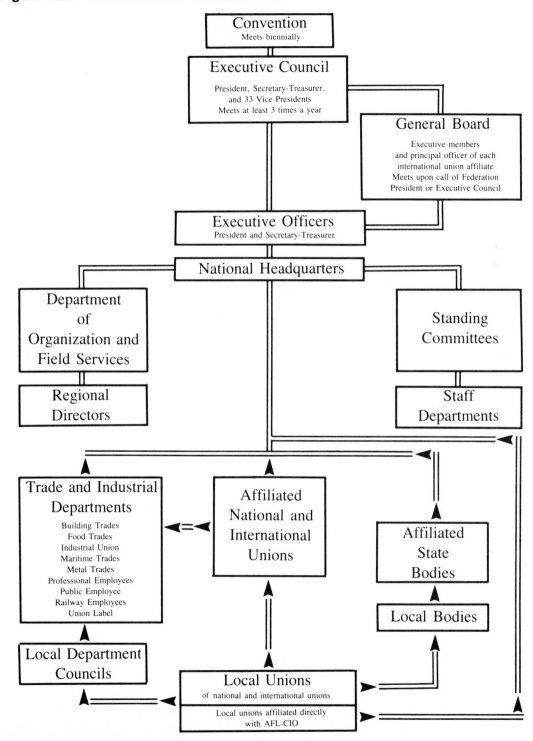

## Financial Resources of Unions

What are the aggregate financial resources of labor organizations in the United States, and how do these resources compare with those of other economic institutions? In 1976, the last year in which data were published in such detail, the consolidated assets of all levels of union organization were in the neighborhood of $4 billion, up from over $2.5 billion in 1970 (see Table 10.9). The liabilities were much lower than the assets, leaving unions in a strong net asset position. While the level of assets is larger than for unions in other countries, it is quite modest in comparison to the corporate world. If all the unions whose assets are represented in Table 10.9 belonged to a single, centrally-directed organization, that organization would have ranked 34th among the Fortune 500 corporations in 1976 and 31st in 1970. But our review of the historical development of organized labor in the United States has shown that unions are anything but a single, centrally directed organization. In addition to the constitutional limitations on the authority of the AFL-CIO, the data in Table 10.9 show that the financial resources at the Federation's command are small relative to those of the labor movement generally. By itself, the AFL-CIO accounts for about one percent of the assets of union organizations—not enough to place it in the Fortune 500.

The data in Table 10.9 also show that over half of organized labor's financial assets are held by local unions. In part, this reflects the needs of the relatively decentralized collective-bargaining structures that have emerged in the United States and that will be discussed more fully in Chapter 12. This significant concentration of wealth at the local union level, in many instances,

**Table 10.9**   Assets and Liabilities of Unions and Percent Distribution of Assets by Type of Union, 1970 and 1976 (dollars in millions)

|  | 1970 | | 1976 | |
| --- | --- | --- | --- | --- |
|  | *($)* | *(%)* | *($)* | *(%)* |
| Assets |  |  |  |  |
| All unions | 2,574 | 100 | 3,931 | 100 |
| AFL-CIO |  | 1 |  | 1 |
| National unions |  | 40 |  | 46 |
| Local unions |  | 59 |  | 53 |
| Liabilities |  |  |  |  |
| All unions | 254 |  | 609 |  |
| Net assets |  |  |  |  |
| All unions | 2,320 |  | 3,322 |  |

   Note:  Data are for unions required to file financial reports under the Labor-Management Reporting and Disclosure Act of 1959. This includes essentially all labor organizations except those whose members are not engaged in interstate commerce, most unions of state, county and municipal employees, and state and local units of the AFL-CIO. Unions of federal workers are only included in the 1976 data. Local unions include intermediate regional bodies.

   SOURCE:  U.S. Labor-Management Services Administration, *Union Financial Statistics 1976* (Washington, DC: U.S. Department of Labor, 1980), p. 6.

**Table 10.10**   Structure of Union Assets, 1976 (percent distribution)

| Asset | All Unions | National Unions | Local Unions |
|---|---|---|---|
| Total assets | 100% | 100% | 100% |
| Cash | 32 | 12 | 50 |
| Loans receivable | 3 | 4 | 3 |
| U.S. Treasury Securities | 13 | 19 | 7 |
| Other Investments[a] | 30 | 48 | 14 |
| Other Assets[b] | 22 | 17 | 26 |

See note to Table 10.9.

[a]  Marketable securities, mortgage investments, and investments in subsidiaries.

[b]  "Other Assets" include land, buildings, office furniture, office equipment, and automotive equipment.

SOURCE:  U.S. Labor-Management Services Administration, *Union Financial Statistics 1976* (Washington, DC: U.S. Department of Labor, 1980).

can place limitations on the authority of national union headquarters over their local units. Underlying these averages, however, there is substantial inequality in the distribution of assets across unions. For example, 99 percent of all national union assets were held by the 50 percent of national unions that reported total receipts of $1 million or more in 1976.

In what forms are these assets held by unions? A small number of unions—most notably the Teamsters—have been accused of using union funds to finance investments of very questionable quality. The impression obtained from data on the distribution of assets held by most labor organizations in the United States, however, is that unions are generally quite cautious in their financial policies. In particular, their assets tend to be held in highly liquid form. For example, fully half of the assets of *local* unions tend to be held as cash in standard bank accounts and hence earn relatively low interest (Table 10.10). Only about 14 percent of the assets of local unions go into higher yielding (and somewhat riskier) investments in marketable securities and mortgages. In contrast, almost half of the assets of *national* unions go into the "other investment" category that generally offers higher yields, with only about 30 percent of the assets kept as cash or in relatively liquid, low-risk, U.S. Treasury securities.

Why do so many local unions persist in following investment strategies that impose such a high opportunity cost on their organizations in terms of forgone opportunities to increase the growth of their financial resources? Unions frequently argue that an important potential use of their resources is to provide strike benefits to their members in the event of a work stoppage, and that they must keep their assets liquid to make the strike weapon a credible threat.[20] This argument, however, overlooks the fact that most

[20]  For a discussion of this point, see Leo Troy, "American Unions and Their Wealth," *Industrial Relations* 14 (May 1975): 134–44 and Neil Sheflin and Leo Troy, "Finances of American Unions in the 1970s," *Journal of Labor Research* IV (Spring 1983): 149–57.

collective-bargaining agreements have an explicit expiration date, so that the time at which strike benefits might be needed is known well in advance. In addition, there is an array of financial instruments available offering different maturity dates. It would not be difficult to place a larger percentage of union assets in investments (with higher yields than bank accounts) that matured at times when unions might need access to cash. One is left with the impression that the resources of labor unions could be significantly larger if unions were more imaginative in their use of the financial instruments now available in capital markets.

As a partial result of the high liquidity of their assets, most of the revenues of local unions come from dues (70 percent in 1976) and various fees, fines, assessments, and charges for work permits (8 percent). The main categories of expenditures are for affiliation payments (30 percent of expenditures), salaries for union officers and employees (25 percent), and administration (10 percent).[21] Because they follow different investment policies, national unions receive a larger proportion of their revenues (and disbursements) from the turnover of relatively short-term securities. Only about 30 percent of their receipts were from dues, per capita taxes, and fees in 1976.

## Union Decision Making at the Micro Level

Many theories of union behavior attempt to formalize the view that unions are organizations seeking to maximize some well-defined objective function.[22] A classic debate took place more than forty years ago over whether it was more meaningful to use standard maximization models or political models of union behavior.[23] In fact, the two approaches are not as far apart as past debates may have indicated. The relationship between a union and its members bears more resemblance to the relationship between a government and voters than to the relationship between a firm and its customers or workers. As a result, many aspects of union goals and behavior can best be understood from the

[21] The salaries of most major union leaders are considerably lower than the salaries of presidents of corporations of similar size. In 1983, for example, the president of the AFL-CIO and several national union presidents earned salaries in the range of $100,000 to $140,000, but the president of the United Automobile Workers received about $75,000. The exception at the high end of the scale was the president of the International Brotherhood of Teamsters, who received salaries and expenses totaling over $550,000; the exception at the low end was the president of the United Farm Workers, whose salary was just under $7500. Data are from the U.S. Department of Labor as reported in the *San Francisco Sunday Examiner and Chronicle,* July 3, 1983, p. A10.

[22] See Wallace Atherton, *Theory of Union Bargaining Goals* (Princeton, NJ: Princeton University Press, 1973) for an extensive discussion of the various theories. Several econometric studies have even attempted to estimate the parameters of such an objective function. *See* Henry Farber, "Individual Preferences and Union Wage Determination: The Case of the United Mine Workers," *Journal of Political Economy* 86 (October 1978): 923–42; and J. N. Dertouzos and J. H. Pencavel, "Wage and Employment Determination Under Trade Unionism: The International Typographical Union," *Journal of Political Economy* 89 (December 1981): 1162–81.

[23] The former approach is espoused in John Dunlop, *Wage Determination Under Trade Unions* (New York: Macmillan, 1944), while a political model of union behavior is articulated in Arthur Ross, *Trade Union Wage Policy* (Berkeley, Calif.: University of California Press, 1948).

perspective of government decision-making models. While these may reasonably be referred to as "political" models, they do not abandon the notion that unions may adopt maximizing behavior.

## A Political Interpretation of Internal Union Decision Making

Unions and governments differ from private firms in the importance of decisions made by voting and in the nature of the services provided. As with governments, many of the services provided by unions to their members are *public goods,* which differ importantly from the *private* goods and services produced by business firms. One distinctive characteristic of public goods is that they are "jointly consumed" and thus provide benefits to many people simultaneously; that is, one person's consumption does not reduce the amount available to another person.[24] (By way of contrast, an automobile purchased by one consumer is not available to benefit another consumer.)

Many of the benefits negotiated by unions in collective bargaining are in the nature of public goods at the workplace. Contractual rules governing the speed of a production line, safety conditions, and the amount of discretion accorded supervisors are examples of benefits that, once negotiated, are available more or less equally to all workers in the bargaining unit. The fact that one worker benefits from a contractual requirement that reduces the speed of a production line does not reduce the benefit that another worker can receive from the same rule. (Not all goods or services provided by unions have this characteristic inherently. In contrast to negotiated improvements in safety conditions, it is possible to vary the wage and fringe benefits received by workers of different seniority, for example.)

A second characteristic of public goods that influences union goals and behavior is that it is usually impossible (or at least very costly) to prevent individuals who refuse to pay their share of the cost of providing a public good from enjoying the benefits of it. When the speed of a production line is reduced, it benefits all workers on the line—not just those who pay union dues. This nonexclusion characteristic of public goods differs sharply from the situation for private goods, where possession of a good or service can be denied to those who do not pay. While unions could in principle attempt to prevent nonmembers from receiving those benefits of collective bargaining that are not jointly consumed (for example, increases in compensation or access to the grievance procedure), in practice, American labor legislation forbids this in the private sector. Once a union is certified by the National Labor Relations Board as the *exclusive* bargaining representative of workers in a bargaining unit, that union has the duty to represent *all* workers in the unit, and the benefits of collective bargaining accrue equally to members who pay dues to the union and to nonmembers who do not. Exclusive representa-

---

[24] For example, national defense is collectively consumed deterrence; person A's consumption of it does not reduce the deterrence available to person B.

tion therefore converts even those negotiated benefits that are not inherently jointly consumed into public goods.[25] This point is less generally applicable in the public sector, because the exclusive representation feature of the NLRA has not been adopted uniformly in the various state laws governing labor relations in state and local governments.

The nonexclusion characteristic of union-negotiated public goods can give rise to a *free rider* problem; workers who automatically benefit from any work-rule change may be inclined to hang back and wait for others to bear the costs of accomplishing the change. As we shall see, this has led unions to argue that they should be able to compel dues or service payments just as governments are able to compel tax payments to finance public goods produced for the population at large.

When public goods are an important aspect of the work environment, a collective institution, such as a union, has a comparative advantage over the actions of individuals in achieving change. The benefit to an *individual* worker of changing a particular working condition may be small relative to the total benefit received by a *group* of workers. If left to individual actions, the working condition may not be changed because the person who incurs the cost of lobbying for the change is unlikely to be compensated by others for the risk that he or she takes in confronting the employer. Since the benefit to the individual is small relative to the cost of seeking change, fighting for changes in the provision of workplace public goods is unlikely to occur if left to individual workers. Instead, dissatisfied workers will quit. Because a union is an organization that can represent the collective will of a group of workers, it has a comparative advantage in establishing or changing the levels of workplace public-goods without workers having to quit to express their preferences.[26]

**Making decisions about workplace public goods.**  What level of a public-goods working condition should a union bargain for? As we have seen, changes in working conditions often yield benefits to many workers simultaneously. At the same time a union incurs resource costs in negotiating, possibly striking over, and enforcing those changes. A union maximizing the welfare of the membership as a whole will seek improvements in a particular working condition until the total additional benefit to all members from further improvement equals the additional cost to the union of achieving the improvement.[27] If a union were to negotiate a smaller improvement in work-

---

[25] Even without the legal requirement, however, there would be nothing to prevent employers from providing the benefits negotiated by unions for their members to employees who were not union members. Indeed, many employers in the United States regularly extend the benefits negotiated in collective bargaining to workers (usually white-collar) who are not in the bargaining unit in an effort to remove the incentive for more widespread unionization of their work force.

[26] Mancur Olson, *The Logic of Collective Action* (Cambridge, MA: Harvard University Press 1965); Greg Duncan and Frank Stafford, "Do Union Members Receive Compensating Wage Differentials?" *American Economic Review* 70 (June 1980): 355–71; and Robert J. Flanagan, "Workplace Public Goods and Union Organizations," *Industrial Relations* 22 (Spring 1983): 224–37.

[27] An early exposition of this decision rule in a government setting is in Paul Samuelson, "The Pure Theory of Public Expenditure," *The Review of Economics and Statistics* 36 (November 1954): 386–89.

ing conditions, it would not be expending enough effort on the membership's behalf. If it were to negotiate a larger improvement, it would be wasting union funds in the sense that the cost of the additional negotiations would exceed the value received by the membership as a whole.

It is no easy task for a union leader to precisely determine the value that the membership places on various working conditions. If each union member could be charged dues according to the strength of his or her preferences for contract benefits, each would have an incentive to understate his or her interest in a benefit and hope that other members would bear the burden of paying. This tendency to "let the other members pay for it" is familiar free-rider behavior. In addition, the idea of differentiating dues payments among workers according to these criteria is contrary to the egalitarian principles of most labor unions.

Therefore, most unions adopt an approach that is easy to administer and consistent with their egalitarian philosophy—they charge each individual an equal amount (or an amount that depends on the member's wage) as union dues. This creates an internal political problem for a union when members differ in their preferences for specific benefits. (Younger workers are often less interested than older workers in improvements in pension plans, for example.) With a substantial dispersion of membership preferences regarding what a contract should contain, union leaders can be in the paradoxical situation of making many (and perhaps most) individual members unhappy in one respect or another even though they have negotiated a contract that is satisfactory as a whole to the majority of their members. Generally, the internal political stability of unions is probably directly related to the homogeneity of preferences among the union's members.

**Trade-offs faced by unions.**   One difficulty of meeting membership expectations is increased by the inherent trade-offs unions must face in collective bargaining. We have seen several examples of these trade-offs in earlier chapters in the book. The best-known is the one between wages and employment summarized in the demand curve for labor, which was first introduced in Chapter 2. Even seemingly powerful unions do not press for the highest wage rate possible because such a policy would greatly reduce the number of union jobs. Instead, as we shall see in Chapter 12, unions frequently try to secure legislation or bargaining structures that alter the terms of the trade-off. Even these activities, however, indicate that unions recognize that such trade-offs exist and that they form a constraint on their objectives.

Most unions face other important trade-offs as well. For example, we noted in Chapter 6 that demands for greater safety and other changes in nonwage working conditions often are costly to implement and therefore tend to be provided only at lower wages. A union may try to use its bargaining power to induce an employer to provide both higher pay and better working conditions, but if this raises the labor costs of the company relative to its competitors, the employment of union members will be jeopardized in the long run. Similarly, the trade-off between wages and fringe benefits that was discussed in Chapter 8 is present in union as well as nonunion employment relationships.

One of the difficulties facing a union leader is that different groups of members within the union may have different rates at which they may be willing to trade between wages and other benefits. For example, in companies in which the last person hired is the first to be fired, workers with relatively low seniority are likely to be more concerned about the employment consequences of high wages than workers with greater seniority. Younger members are also more likely than older workers to want the union to put more emphasis on cash wages and less emphasis on pensions or other fringe benefits that have a payoff in the distant future; that is, they will accept a smaller sacrifice of wages for additional pension benefits. Moreover, members who are less familiar than the union leadership with the basic economics of the industry may question whether trade-offs are necessary at all. Thus, one important task of union leaders is to ascertain, from among the diverse notions of different groups, what trade-offs are acceptable to a majority of the union membership.

## Political Pressures on Union Leaders

Probably the most difficult job facing union leaders is accommodating the heterogeneity of interests among the membership. Indeed, when the heterogeneity is great, the task of formulating bargaining demands within the union may be more difficult than actual collective-bargaining negotiations. Union leaders who fail to accommodate membership interests sufficiently face three possible consequences.

First, the membership may fail to ratify a collective-bargaining agreement on which management and the union negotiators have tentatively agreed. This is more than a theoretical possibility; some 10 percent of tentative labor agreements are rejected in the ratification process—usually in well-established bargaining relationships. In 1966, airline mechanics affiliated with the International Association of Machinists rejected a tentative agreement that had been negotiated in the White House with the personal intervention of President Johnson, who was interested in keeping wage increases within voluntary federal "wage guideposts" that existed at the time. In this instance, the willingness of the leadership to acquiesce in federal policy was out of step with the rank and file. More recently, efforts to negotiate wage concessions in the automobile and steel industries have received a mixed reception by the rank-and-file (see Examples 10.1 and 10.2). In these instances it has sometimes appeared that the rank-and-file and the union leadership had different views of acceptable trade-offs between wages and employment.

Ratification procedures can serve a number of useful purposes. In testing the acceptability of a proposed agreement to those who are to be governed by it, the process provides some indication of the willingness of the union membership to live by the terms of the agreement. A high degree of acceptability raises the likelihood that the contract will be self-enforcing—a factor that both the union and management are interested in.[28] The acceptability test also reduces the likelihood that union leaders will negotiate contracts that do not really benefit union members, but it may also limit their ability to negotiate provisions that are important to the long-term survival of the union when such provisions are contrary to the short-term interests of office.

Second, the membership may elect new leaders. At the present time the tenure of office for the principal officers of most national unions is less than ten years (although in 1979 the presidents of two such unions had taken office before 1950). The turnover of union presidents is relatively high in smaller unions where elections tend to be more frequent, so that the opportunity for change is higher; however, turnover is also relatively high in the largest unions despite longer terms of office and less frequent elections.[29] The lower probability of retaining office when an election occurs in larger unions is consistent with the hypothesis that larger unions are characterized by greater heterogeneity of interests among the membership and are therefore much more difficult to run successfully, although it may also be true that there are greater rewards to leading a large union, and, therefore, more competition for the positions. Also, as noted earlier in the chapter, the Landrum-Griffin Act, which was passed in 1959, included a procedure through which the results of an election for union office could be set aside and rerun under federal supervision in the event of election irregularities. In the ensuing years several major union elections were rerun with different outcomes under this procedure, so that incumbent officers are now more susceptible to challenges from the rank-and-file than previously.

Third, if a union is sufficiently unresponsive to membership needs, it may be decertified in a special election by the National Labor Relations Board. As the data in Table 10.5 indicated, such elections, while still small in comparison to representation elections, are increasing—as is the proportion of such elections that result in decertification of the union as bargaining agent.

Faced with the need to satisfy their members, union leaders develop *political* methods for deciding about issues of compensation and working conditions affecting their often heterogeneous membership. The adoption of a political approach to the formulation of bargaining objectives—which must be done when decisions about wages and other conditions of employment are made—can lead to employment contracts that are radically different from what would exist in the absence of unions. Prior to this chapter, virtually all of the analysis of the pricing and allocation of labor in this book has been concerned with nonunion labor markets, where workers who are dissatisfied

---

[28] The ratification process can also be used to a limited extent for tactical purposes during collective-bargaining negotiations. For an interesting discussion of this and other contract ratification issues, see Clyde W. Summers, "Ratification of Agreements," *Frontiers of Collective Bargaining,* eds. John T. Dunlop and W. Chamberlain (New York: Harper and Row, 1967): 75–102.

[29] U.S. Bureau of Labor Statistics, *Directory of National Unions and Employee Associations,* 1979 Bulletin 2079 (Washington, DC: U.S. Government Printing Office, September 1980): 51–52, 110–11.

**EXAMPLE    10.1**

# Wage Concessions in the Automobile Industry

In the early 1980s the U.S. automobile industry came under severe economic pressure from a combination of international competitive pressures and a deep domestic recession. The Ford Motor Company reported losses of $1.5 billion and $1.0 billion in 1980 and 1981, respectively, while General Motors (GM) reported a loss of $763 million in 1980 and a profit of $333 million in 1981. The Chrysler Corporation was near bankruptcy. By early 1982, each of the major companies had begun to close major assembly plants.

During the winter of 1981–82, Ford and GM approached the United Automobile Workers (UAW), the large industrial union that represents their workers in collective bargaining, to request contract concessions so that they could reduce their labor-cost differential with respect to foreign auto producers. (Chrysler, as a result of its "bailout" agreement with the federal government, had already secured concessions for its workers.) At that time, the collective-bargaining agreement between the UAW and the major automobile companies was not due to expire until September 1982, and there was a prohibition against major revisions during the term of the contract. Convinced of the seriousness of the economic problems facing the industry, the leadership of the UAW obtained permission to suspend this prohibition and to begin negotiations with the auto companies.

In fact, the membership of the UAW was seriously split over the issue of negotiating concessions in wages and other benefits. While members at Ford generally supported the move, members working for General Motors doubted the seriousness of the company's economic plight. At one point early in 1982, the UAW halted negotiations that had been initiated with GM because the margin of support for such negotiations among its members at GM was so narrow; however, negotiations were resumed again after several plant closings by GM appeared to convince some members of the seriousness of the company's economic situation.

Eventually, the UAW concluded separate negotiations with both Ford and GM in which union members agreed to forgo some annual pay increases, to defer some cost-of-living adjustments (COLAs) for 18 months, and to give up certain holidays. In exchange, they obtained participation in a profit-sharing plan, greater income security for workers with high seniority, and certain concessions on job security. The new contract was estimated to save about $2.00 per hour in labor costs, or $190.00 per car, over the life of the contract. One interesting feature of the concessions negotiated at Ford and GM (and those negotiated in other industries by other unions) is that they did *not* include wage *cuts*. Instead, the concessions involved the timing (for example, by deferring COLAs or other payments) and size of increases in compensation.

When the ratification vote was taken, however, it was clear that the membership remained sharply divided over the advisability of the concessions, even though the leadership was convinced that they were needed for the survival of the industry and hence the union as an organization. Normally, collective-bargaining contracts that are negotiated by the UAW receive the support of about 80 percent of the membership, and in fact 73 percent of the UAW members at Ford voted in favor of this new agreement. At General Motors, however, the agreement received the approval of only 52 percent of UAW members. The widely varying attitudes of union members on concessions was indicated when some union locals overwhelmingly endorsed the agreement while others soundly rejected it. Locals with many members on layoff tended to vote for concessions that they believed would restore jobs, while locals with many high-seniority workers tended to vote against concessions.

Why would a union leader support a proposition facing such opposition from the members who have the power to vote him or her out of office? One interesting aspect of the auto industry negotiations was that Douglas Fraser, the president of the UAW, was in his last term of office under rules set forth in the union's constitution. Freed from worries concerning the effects of an unpopular policy on his prospects for his survival in office, he had greater flexibility to consider concessions that improved the long-run viability of the union as an organization.

SOURCES:   John Holusha, "Ford's New Contract: Who May Win, Who May Lose," *The New York Times,* February 16, 1982; Robert L. Simison, "GM Workers' Narrow Vote for Concessions Might Hinder Further Cost Cuts at Plants," *Wall Street Journal,* April 12, 1982; John Holusha, "Union View: Auto Industry Sacrifices Should be Equal," *The New York Times,* April 29, 1982; Bruce E. Kaufman and Jorge Martinez-Vazquez, "Voting for Wage Concessions: The Case of the 1982 GM-UAW Negotiations," *Industrial and Labor Relations Review* 41(January 1988): 183–94; and Peter Cappelli and W. P. Sterling, "Union Bargaining, Decisions and Contract Ratifications: The 1982 and 1984 Auto Agreements."

with their employment can only "vote with their feet" by quitting. We have stressed that it is the choices made by the marginal workers—the workers most likely to change their place of employment or their employment status—that are crucial in the operation of most nonunion labor markets. Nonunion employers must offer favorable enough terms to attract a work force of optimal size; thus, the workers who have the greatest effect on the content of nonunion employment packages are those "at the margin"—those potentially mobile workers closest to the point of being attracted to or leaving employment at a given plant. Building on the applications of human capital analysis in Chapter 6, it is clear that younger workers who are still willing to invest in job search and mobility will tend to have the greatest influence on nonunion employment contracts.

Union leaders, who are of course involved in collective decision making, cannot afford to base their policies on the preferences of the marginal workers. If they wish to retain their jobs, they must formulate policies that command the support of at least half of the membership. The bargaining objectives of unions are therefore more likely to reflect the preferences of the average worker, who will in general be older and less mobile than the marginal worker. Thus, the structure of the compensation package and the nature of job allocation mechanisms are likely to differ substantially among nonunion and unionized firms.[30]

[30]   Richard B. Freeman and James L. Medoff, *What Do Unions Do?* (New York: Basic Books, 1984) and Henry S. Farber, "The Analysis of Union Behavior," *Handbook of Labor Economics,* O. Ashenfelter and R. Layard (eds.), (New York: North Holland, 1986).

**EXAMPLE    10.2**

## Wage Concessions in the Steel Industry: 1982–83

Efforts to negotiate wage concessions in the steel industry, where the union leaders were not free of concerns for their political futures, followed a somewhat different scenario from the auto industry. The basic steel agreement, covering around 286,000 steelworkers, was negotiated every three years between the United Steelworkers of America (USW) and the eight largest steel companies. Several other companies in steel adopted the terms of the basic steel agreement on a "me too" basis without further negotiations. Unlike the procedure in the automobile industry, the rank-and-file of the USW do not ratify proposed contracts directly. Instead, ratification is by the Basic Steel Industry Conference, which consisted in the early 1980s of the union's executive board, district directors, and the presidents of union locals at the eight major steel companies and the "me too" firms.

Under substantial economic pressure from foreign competition and a deep domestic recession, the steel industry sought in July 1982 to renegotiate the basic steel agreement that was scheduled to run until August 1983. At the time, the agreement provided the average steelworker a wage and fringe benefit package valued at $24.40 per hour. The industry proposed a virtual freeze on wages and fringe benefits for three years and a reduction of cost-of-living-adjustment (COLA) payments; the union proposed increased aid for unemployed steelworkers. The leadership of the USW recommended that the Basic Steel Industry Conference *reject* the employer proposals. The recommendation was promptly followed.

Subsequently, economic conditions in the industry deteriorated sharply, and by the autumn of 1982 the steel industry was operating at 40 percent of its capacity. At the biennial convention of the USW in September 1982, the leadership was authorized to reopen negotiations. In November, after several weeks of negotiations, the executive board of the union unanimously recommended approval of a tentative agreement providing for concessions, amounting to about an 11-percent cut in compensation and substantial changes in the COLA arrangement, in exchange for benefits for unemployed members. Despite the recommendation of the union's leadership, however, the Basic Steel Industry Conference again rejected the employer proposals.

Two months later, the executive board of the USW altered the ratification process by permitting only local union presidents from the eight major steel companies to vote on ratification (along with executive board members and district directors). Excluded were about 300 local union presidents representing workers at the "me too" companies. These officials and their members appeared to have less to lose (at least in the short run) by holding out for more favorable terms, since their companies would often continue to operate if a strike developed at the eight major companies. When yet another round of negotiations was held in late February, the revised ratification group approved an agreement providing for substantial pay concessions (including initial wage reductions that would be made up only near the end of the three-year agreement) and a commitment by the companies to invest in modernizing the industry. Given the political nature of union decision making, it was necessary to adopt a change that reduced the heterogeneity of interests among those voting in the ratification process to achieve changes that the leadership felt were in the long-run interest of the union. For later developments in bargaining in the steel industry, see Example 12.6

SOURCES: Carol Hymowitz and J. Ernest Beazley, "Steel's Recovery is Seen Set Back by Union's Vote," *Wall Street Journal* November 22, 1982, p. 2; Thomas F. O'Boyle and J. Ernest Beazley, "USW Chiefs, Backing Concessionary Pact, Slash Number Eligible to Ratify Contracts," *Wall Street Journal* January 13, 1983, p. 8; William Serrin, "Steel Union Leaders Ratify Concessions," *The New York Times* March 2, 1983.

## Union Security Arrangements

The public-goods aspects of union activities contribute to the intense union interest in the negotiation of *union security* arrangements. Despite the protection afforded a union by its status as exclusive representative of workers in a bargaining unit, the fact that workers in the unit who receive the benefits of union representation are not required by law to support the union financially has left unions extremely sensitive to the problem of free riders and concerned about protecting their institutional security. As a result, one of the first issues usually addressed in a new collective-bargaining relationship is the nature of the union security arrangement that will apply in the bargaining unit.

Over the years, a variety of union security arrangements have been devised in negotiations (see Table 10.11). By far the most common arrangement in labor agreements in the private sector is the *union shop,* which requires employees to become union members after a specified period of time (usually 30 to 60 days) of being hired and to remain members as a condition of employment in the firm. In contrast to a *closed shop* arrangement (now illegal in most industries), which requires the employer to hire only from among

**Table 10.11** Union Security Provisions in Major Collective-Bargaining Agreements, 1980[a] (Percent Distribution)

| | All Agreements | Union Shop | Modified Union Shop | Agency Shop | Maintenance of Membership | Other | Sole Bargaining[b] |
|---|---|---|---|---|---|---|---|
| All Industries | 100 | 60 | 6 | 8 | 3 | 6 | 17 |
| Manufacturing | 100 | 55 | 7 | 7 | 5 | 7 | 20 |
| Nonmanufacturing | 100 | 64 | 5 | 9 | 2 | 6 | 14 |
| Public Sector[c] | 100 | 7 | 3 | 12 | 10 | 2 | 66 |

[a] Labor Agreements covering 1,000 workers or more in the private sector.

[b] Union recognized as bargaining agent for all employees in bargaining unit, but union membership is not required as a condition of employment. Other types of union security are discussed in the text.

[c] Data are for 1974.

SOURCE: U.S. Bureau of Labor Statistics, *Characteristics of Major Collective Bargaining Agreements, January, 1980* Bulletin 2095 (Washington: U.S. Government Printing Office, May 1981): 23–24; U.S. Bureau of Labor Statistics, *Characteristics of Agreements in State and Local Governments, January 1, 1974.* Bulletin 1861 (Washington, D.C.: U.S. Government Printing Office, 1975): 10.

current union members, a union shop affords employers considerable freedom in hiring employees of their choice. Yet all union security arrangements contain an element of compulsion for individual employees and they have inspired opposition from some employers and politicians.

Although less popular with unions, alternative forms of union security arrangements have been devised in an effort to compromise between the interests of unions in obtaining financial support and the interests of some employers in protecting the rights of individual employees who may be philosophically or otherwise opposed to union membership. For example, a *modified union shop* exempts long-term employees who are opposed to joining a newly established union, but requires all other employees and all new hires to join the union. The *agency shop,* an arrangement that is used far more extensively in the public sector than the private sector, requires employees in the bargaining unit who do not join the union to pay a monthly "service charge" (usually the equivalent of the dues paid to the union by its members) as a condition of employment. *Maintenance of membership* provisions, which require employees who are members of a union when a labor agreement is negotiated (or who join subsequently) to remain members until the expiration of the agreement, have been used infrequently since World War II.

The union security issue—the question of whether unions should be able to compel membership and/or dues payments when they have a legal duty to represent all workers—has constituted one of the major controversies associated with the growth of unions in the United States. On the face of it, union security arrangements—particularly union-shop arrangements—appear to be popular with both unions and union members. Over 80 percent of the major collective-bargaining agreements in the private sector and about a third of the agreements in the public sector contain some form of security agreement (Table 10.11). There also appear to be few genuine conscientious objectors to unions among organized workers. At the urging of employers, Congress incorporated in the Taft-Hartley Act a provision that required a secret ballot of union members before a union-shop clause could be approved. Between 1947 and 1951, when the provision was repealed at the request of employers, well over 90 percent of the workers who cast ballots supported the union shop. Contrary to the expectations of employers and Congress, union-shop provisions do not appear to be negotiated by union leaders against the will of the rank-and-file.

As noted earlier, Section 14B of the Taft-Hartley Act also permits state laws addressing the union security issue to take precedence over federal law, which permits union security arrangements. Currently, 19 states passed so-called *right-to-work* laws, which prohibit union-shop provisions, and there are periodic attempts to pass similar legislation in other states or to repeal existing legislation. The contests over right-to-work legislation inspire considerable emotion on both sides which, like the term "right-to-work," does little to clarify the underlying issues. Underlying the philosophical debates, both unions and their opponents appear to believe that they are engaged in a power struggle that will influence the future of unions in the United States.

Just what is the evidence on the influence of right-to-work legislation on the support for labor unions? Most of the laws have been passed in southern and western states. Since there has been a general movement in population and employment since 1955 from the industrial Northeast and Midwest—the "snow belt"—to the "sun belt" of the South, where right-to-work legislation is more common, the effect of such laws on union membership could be of considerable consequence to the future of unions.

Table 10.12 presents data on the extent of unionization that existed in 1982 in right-to-work and other states. The data indicate quite clearly that union strength is lowest in states that have right-to-work laws. In 17 of the 19 right-to-work states, the proportion of nonagricultural employees that were

**Table 10.12**   Percent of Nonagricultural Employees That Are Union Members, 1982

| Right-to-Work States | Union or Association Members (percent) | Other States | Union or Association Members (percent) |
|---|---|---|---|
| Alabama | 18.2 | Alaska | 30.4 |
| Arizona | 12.8 | California | 25.4 |
| Arkansas | 13.2 | Colorado | 18.0 |
| Florida | 9.6 | Connecticut | 18.9 |
| Georgia | 12.7 | Delaware | 20.3 |
| Iowa | 20.4 | Hawaii | 31.4 |
| Louisiana | 13.8 | Idaho | 16.1 |
| Mississippi | 9.3 | Illinois | 27.5 |
| Nebraska | 16.3 | Indiana | 25.1 |
| Nevada | 22.1 | Kansas | 12.0 |
| North Carolina | 8.9 | Kentucky | 20.4 |
| North Dakota | 14.2 | Maine | 18.5 |
| South Carolina | 5.8 | Maryland | 18.6 |
| South Dakota | 10.3 | Massachusetts | 19.7 |
| Tennessee | 17.3 | Michigan | 33.7 |
| Texas | 12.5 | Minnesota | 24.5 |
| Utah | 16.8 | Missouri | 26.6 |
| Virginia | 10.9 | Montana | 21.7 |
| Wyoming | 15.9 | New Hampshire | 12.3 |
| | | New Jersey | 19.9 |
| | | New Mexico | 12.8 |
| | | New York | 35.8 |
| | | Ohio | 27.4 |
| | | Oklahoma | 12.9 |
| | | Oregon | 27.5 |
| | | Pennsylvania | 27.0 |
| | | Rhode Island | 19.4 |
| | | Vermont | 11.9 |
| | | Washington | 32.9 |
| | | West Virginia | 28.9 |
| | | Wisconsin | 24.5 |

SOURCE:   Leo Troy and Neil Sheflin, *Union Sourcebook* 1st ed. (West Orange, NJ: Industrial Relations and Information Services, 1985).

union or employee-association members was less than 20 percent. In contrast, in 18 of the other 31 states, the proportion exceeded 20 percent. While right-to-work states are not uniformly identical to those in the sun belt, there is considerable overlap. As a result, between 1955 and 1982, the proportion of employees working in right-to-work states increased from 24.1 to 31.8 percent. This shifting geographic distribution of the work force undoubtedly had a depressing effect on union membership.

It is not obvious, however, that the decline in unionization occasioned by the move to the sunbelt can be attributed to right-to-work laws *per se*. The extent of unionization in right-to-work states tended to be lower than that in other states even prior to the passage of the laws. In fact, there is growing evidence that these laws may only reflect attitudes towards unions that already exist in these communities.[31]

## Implications of Decision Making

There are a number of lessons for interpreting union behavior that may be drawn from the analysis of union decision making. First, there are likely to be inherent tensions between the leadership and the membership of a union. These tensions are tied to the fact that the leadership must consider the welfare of the organization as a whole and the membership as a group, while union members are more likely to act on the basis of their individual self-interest. The tensions are also related to the fact that a major role of unions is to provide for working conditions that are public goods for which different people will have different preferences. Second, while these tensions could, in principle, be resolved through an appropriate pricing mechanism for union services, there are practical barriers to implementing such a system. As a result, the internal political stability of unions is likely to be greatest when the preferences of members are similar.

Third, the absence of a pricing system that resolves these tensions forces the leadership of unions to develop political allocation mechanisms within the union, for where the preferences of individual members are diverse, there is likely to be considerable contention within the membership over specific union negotiating goals. Bargaining within a union over what its demands should be may be more difficult than the actual collective bargaining between the employer and the union. When preferences are widely dispersed, it may also be more difficult to achieve ratification of an agreement by the mem-

---

[31] Numerous econometric studies have sought to estimate the effect of right-to-work laws on union strength, wages, and industrial conflict. Studies concluding that these laws have little or no effect on union-membership levels include Keith Lumsden and Craig Peterson, "The Effect of Right-to-Work Laws on Unionization in the United States," *Journal of Political Economy* 83 (December 1975): 1237–48; William J. Moore and Robert Newman, "On the Prospects for American Trade Union Growth: A Cross-Section Analysis," *The Review of Economics and Statistics* 57 (November 1975): 435–45; Barry T. Hirsch, "The Determinants of Unionization: An Analysis of Interarea Differences," *Industrial and Labor Relations Review* 33 (January 1980): 147–61; William J. Moore, "Membership and Wage Impact of Right-to-Work Laws," *Journal of Labor Research* 1 (Fall 1980): 349–68; and Henry S. Farber, "Right-to-Work Laws and the Extent of Unionization," *Journal of Labor Economics* 2 (July 1984): 319–52.

bership. Indeed, unions with particularly heterogeneous memberships have devised special ratification procedures to mediate sharp differences in objectives among different segments of their membership.[32]

# Review Questions

1. It has been said that the American Federation of Labor (AFL) was founded on two broad principles: national autonomy and exclusive jurisdiction. (a) What was the effect of these principles on the structure of authority within the U.S. labor movement? (b) Give at least three instances in which these principles have been modified since the formation of the AFL.
2. How would you analyze the prospects for union growth in the next decade? Based on your analysis, what are the prospects for union growth? (Consider these questions again after you have read Chapter 11 and see if there are any aspects of your answer that you would like to change.) How would you have answered this question in 1930?
3. "It is hardly surprising that craft unions have been the earliest and most durable labor organizations in most countries, for craft unions are inherently more powerful than industrial unions." Evaluate this statement, being careful to delineate conditions under which it might hold and conditions under which it might not.
4. In recent years, there have been an increasing number of union mergers. Analyze the incentives and disincentives for two unions to merge. Under what circumstances would you expect a merger to increase the effectiveness of a union? Under what circumstances might effectiveness decrease?

# Selected Readings

Wallace Atherton, *Theory of Union Bargaining Goals* (Princeton, NJ: Princeton University Press, 1973).

Henry S. Farber, "The Analysis of Union Behavior," *Handbook of Labor Economics,* O. Ashenfelter and R. Layard (eds.), (New York: North Holland, 1986).

Richard B. Freeman and James L. Medoff, *What Do Unions Do?* (New York: Basic Books, 1984).

Mancur Olson, *The Logic of Collective Action* (Cambridge, MA: Harvard University Press, 1965).

Lloyd Ulman, "The Development of Trades and Labor Unions," Chapter 13, *American Economic History,* Seymour E. Harris (ed.), (New York: McGraw-Hill, 1961).

---

[32] For example, skilled workers in the United Automobile Workers can veto a national contract covering the entire membership of the union if they do not approve of its provisions. This provision was an outgrowth of attempts by the skilled membership, which constitutes a minority of the union's members, to secede from the UAW and join a separate union.

# CHAPTER 11

## Regulation of Union-Management Relations

The legal environment of the employment relationship has several elements: the general common law of contracts, wage and hours legislation (discussed in Chapters 3 and 4), equal-employment-opportunity legislation (discussed in Chapter 7), laws governing health and safety at the workplace (discussed in Chapter 6), regulations pertaining to aspects of the pay package (see, for example, the discussion of pension legislation in Chapter 8), and statutes governing the relationship between unions and employers. All but the last aspect of the legal environment largely address *substantive* aspects of the employment relationship, and as noted in Chapter 10, legislation has historically played a larger role in these areas in Europe than in the United States. On the other hand, the law has been more pervasive in its impact on the *procedural* aspects of the relationship between labor and management in the United States than in any other country in the world. We now examine the effect of legal regulation on the formation of unions and the collective-bargaining process.

With the growth of unions, nations inevitably face significant questions of public policy toward unions and collective bargaining. Unions raise fundamental conflicts between the right to combination and freedom of contract, between the right to group action and an employer's right to manage his or her business, between private collective bargaining and the public interest, and between majority rule and individual rights. All of these are issues over which there may be a significant conflict of values between different segments of the community. In making a choice or striking a compromise between the conflicting values, public policy must confront a number of specific issues in industrial relations. What should the stance of government be toward the process of union organizing? Should the government mandate collective bargaining? What legal status should be accorded collective-bargaining agreements? What limits should be placed on the use of force? Does the public have an interest in the relationship between a union and its members?

Different countries have taken sometimes radically different approaches to these issues, but all must choose between two broad principles of labor-relations policy. The first principle is that of *consensus,* under which the parties to collective bargaining (unions and employers) mutually develop and assent to a set of rules that is to govern their conduct for the duration of their collective-bargaining relationship. This approach is taken in some European countries, particularly in Scandinavia, often with the hope of keeping the government out of direct involvement in collective bargaining. It has the advantage that, when the parties to collective bargaining develop the rules governing their conduct themselves, they are more likely to bear responsibility for adhering to those rules than when the rules are imposed by third parties.

The second principle is *majority rule,* under which the conduct of some individuals or groups is governed without regard to their desires (that is, by the passage of legislation rather than by the negotiation of a set of rules by the parties to collective bargaining). As the broad outline of the National Labor Relations Act in the previous chapter indicates, the majority rule principle underlies public policy toward labor relations in the United States. While the adoption of a majority-rule approach is understandable given the determined resistance of American employers to unions, it is not without its costs. If the minorities under a majority-rule system strongly dissent, they will try to circumvent the objectives of the policy by taking advantage of loopholes or engaging in activities that do not seem to be covered by the existing law. The response to these efforts at evading the law's objectives is normally additional, more-detailed rule making by legislative and/or administrative bodies in an effort to close the loopholes. This effort in turn encourages a search for still other loopholes and subsequent rule making to close them. Experience with the NLRA provides a fascinating study of the evolution of regulatory activity over time from a limited amount of statutory language to a very detailed web of rules surrounding the conduct of labor relations. The result has been an extremely litigious system, which is one of several characteristics of the American approach to public policy toward labor relations that is unusual in comparison to other countries.

In this chapter, we examine some of the major consequences for unions, employers, and collective bargaining of the approach to public policy toward labor relations adopted in the United States. We begin with a review of the main objectives of the NLRA and of the employer and union unfair labor practices established by the Act. Since much of the policy is initiated in the interpretations of the NLRA by an unusual regulatory agency, the National Labor Relations Board, this review is followed by a discussion of the environment in which the agency's rulings are made. Subsequently, the requirements placed by the Board on unions and management during organizing campaigns and collective-bargaining negotiations are reviewed, along with a consideration of the apparent impact of the regulations on the behavior of the various parties and the efficacy of remedies for violations of the NLRA. This discussion is followed by an analysis of the effect of a very different type of legislation—antitrust law—on union power and collective bargaining. We conclude with a review of the main features of the legal regulations of labor relations in the public sector.

# Basic Provisions of the National Labor Relations Act

The present-day *National Labor Relations Act (NLRA)* consists of the Wagner Act (passed in 1935) as amended by the Taft-Hartley Act (1947) and by certain provisions in the Landrum-Griffin Act (1959). Coverage is limited to workers in the private, nonagricultural sector engaged in interstate commerce. Workers in federal, state, and local government have never been covered by the Act. Moreover, the agricultural sector was excluded to secure votes of southern members of Congress for passage. Thus the requirements of the NLRA have not applied to unions attempting to organize farm workers or to management in its efforts to block unions. The statute also does not cover supervisors. As we noted in our review of the historical development of union-management relations in the United States in Chapter 10, the Wagner Act guaranteed workers the right to engage in ''concerted activities'' such as collective bargaining and was passed with the explicit intention of facilitating the organization of unions and reducing the level of strife (mainly from strikes and related violence) associated with the efforts of unions to organize industry. The Norris-LaGuardia Act (1932) had already removed most judicial impediments to union activity, and the NLRA was structured to remove many of the employer impediments.

The Act set out to accomplish this in two ways. First, it provided for an election procedure to determine whether a group of employees wished to be represented by a union, and it established a government agency, the *National Labor Relations Board (NLRB)* to conduct the elections and certify the results. (Previously, workers had to use strikes or other forceful means in an effort to organize a resisting employer.) Second, it limited the opposition that employers could legally mount against workers' efforts to form unions and to engage in collective bargaining, by establishing a list of employer unfair labor-practices. These are listed in the left-hand column of Table 11.1 by the section of the NLRA in which they occur. Moreover, the NLRB was given authority to investigate, prosecute, and adjudicate allegations that unfair labor practices had occurred.

The limitations placed on employers by the unfair labor practices were substantial. The first (Section 8(a)(1)) was a broad proscription against any attempts to thwart employee efforts to form unions and to negotiate an agreement. Indeed, violations of any of the other employer unfair practices normally constitute a violation of this section as well. The second employer unfair labor-practice guideline was intended to eliminate the ''company

**Table 11.1**   Unfair Labor Practices Under the National Labor
Relations Act

| *Unfair Labor Practice for Employers* | *Unfair Labor Practice for Unions* |
|---|---|
| *Section:* | *Section:* |
| 8(a)(1): To interfere with, restrain or coerce employees in the exercise of their rights to join labor organizations and to bargain collectively. | 8(b)(1): To restrain or coerce employees in the exercise of their rights to join or to refrain from joining a labor organization. |
| 8(a)(2): To dominate or interfere with the formation or administration of any labor organization or contribute financial or other support to it. | 8(b)(2): To force an employer to discriminate against an employee (unless the employee refuses to pay union dues). |
| 8(a)(3): To discriminate against individuals supporting a labor organization with respect to any term or condition of employment. | 8(b)(3): To refuse to bargain collectively with an employer. |
| 8(a)(4): To discharge or otherwise discriminate against an employee because he has filed charges or given testimony under the NLRA. | 8(b)(4): To engage in a secondary boycott. |
| 8(a)(5): To refuse to bargain collectively with the union representing the employees. | 8(b)(5): To charge exorbitant initiation fees. |
| | 8(b)(6): To force an employer to pay for services that are not performed. |
| | 8(b)(7): To engage in ''organizational'' picketing to pressure an employer to recognize a union without a representation election. |

unions,'' which, as noted in Chapter 10, were often established and controlled by employers during the 1920s to thwart efforts by employees to form independent unions. An employee organization established for collective bargaining must be independent of the employer with which it bargains. The third employer unfair labor-practice statute forbids discrimination based on a worker's attitude toward, or support of, unions. Employers may not fire union supporters while retaining employees who oppose unionization. Once a union is established, employers may not treat employees in the bargaining unit who do not belong to the union differently from those who do. The application of this unfair labor-practice statute also raises more subtle issues that are discussed at greater length in the section on regulation of the union-organizing process. The fourth employer unfair labor-practice statute was included to assist in the enforcement of the act. For example, one employer violated this section of the act when he reduced the paycheck of employees who testified against him by the amount of time spent in an NLRB hearing but did not similarly reduce the paycheck of those who testified on his behalf. The final employer unfair-practice statute imposes an affirmative duty to bargain in an effort to ensure that meaningful collective bargaining would begin once a union won a representation election. The issues that have arisen in applying this requirement are discussed extensively in the section on the regulation of collective bargaining.

The NLRA also places certain obligations on both labor and management. If a union wins a representation election, it is certified as the *exclusive* bargaining representative of the group of employees who were eligible to vote. This requires the union to represent *all* employees in the bargaining unit equally—even though some may not support the union. Over the years, the exclusive representative status has been interpreted by the courts to impose on the union a "duty of fair representation." That is, the union may not discriminate in the way that it treats different union members. For example, a union may not refuse to process a reasonable grievance of a member because of the member's race or because the member may be associated with a dissident political faction within the union. The concept of exclusive bargaining representative also requires the employer to deal with employees through the union in matters affecting the terms and conditions of their employment.

Experience with the Wagner Act indicated that unions could be coercive in their efforts to organize workers, just as employers historically had been coercive in their efforts to resist unionization. The unfair labor practices established in the Wagner Act limited the coercive actions of employers, but left open the possibility for union coercion. By 1947, as noted in Chapter 10, there appeared to be considerable public sentiment for achieving a more-even balance of power between labor and management, for protecting the freedom of choice of individual workers (particularly if they chose *not* to have union representation), and for protecting neutral third parties (particularly the general public) from the consequences of major labor disputes. The Taft-Hartley Act addressed the first two concerns by permitting *decertification elections* and by adding a list of union unfair labor practices to the employer unfair labor practices established in the Wagner Act. (The union unfair practices are listed in the right-hand column of Table 11.1.)

The union unfair labor practices under Sections 8(b)(1) and 8(b)(3) simply parallel the employer unfair practices under Sections 8(a)(1) and 8(a)(5). They were intended to prevent unions from pressuring individuals from making a free and reasoned choice of whether or not to vote for union representation and to place a duty of bargaining on unions. There was also an effort to protect individual workers against unreasonable pressures by forbidding excessive dues requirements (Section 8(b)(5)), picketing pressures that might short-circuit the election procedure through which individual workers can express their preferences (Section 8(b)(7)), and closed shop or other preferential hiring arrangements. The latter was achieved in Section 8(b)(2), which effectively precludes an employer from giving preference to individuals who already are union members (as a closed shop arrangement requires). This requirement was relaxed somewhat for the construction industry in amendments to the NLRA passed with the Landrum-Griffin Act in 1959.

The prohibition against secondary boycotts (Section 8(b)(4)) was part of the effort to protect neutral third parties. A *secondary boycott* occurs when a union tries to bring pressure against an employer with whom it is negotiating by striking a third party (for example, a supplier or customer) that is not involved in the negotiations. It is not always clear who is "neutral" in a labor dispute, however, and efforts to enforce this unfair practice have raised difficult issues that are discussed more extensively in Chapter 14. The sixth union unfair practice listed in Table 11.1, forcing an employer to pay for services that are not performed, was included to prevent what many regarded as wasteful practices. For example, at one time, locals of the American Federation of Musicians required employers who used out-of-town musical groups to pay for an equal number of local musicians even though no local musicians were used. (The rationale was that the out-of-town groups were taking the employment opportunities of local musicians.) Section 8(b)(6) makes these types of activities illegal. It does not, however, prohibit payments for services that are performed although not really wanted, and the response of many locals of the Musicians' Union to this law was to require local bands to precede out-of-town musical groups! Among other things, this illustrates the difficulty of addressing problems involving job security through statutory language.

The preceding paragraphs provide an overview of the general objectives and approach to regulation taken in the NLRA. However, the role and impact of the law are understood best when the law is examined in the context of the industrial relations activity that it seeks to regulate. For this reason, detailed discussions of the requirements imposed by the unfair labor practices are integrated with specific discussions of union organizing and collective bargaining activities in the remainder of this chapter and in Chapters 12 through 15. The role of the law in union-organizing campaigns and the nature of the duty to bargain are discussed later in this chapter. The role of the National Labor Relations Board in determining election units and the effect on bargaining structure are discussed in Chapter 12. The legal status of strikes, lockouts, and secondary boycotts is examined in the discussion of labor disputes in Chapter 14, and the relationship between NLRB regulation and the private institution of arbitration is discussed in Chapter 15.

## The National Labor Relations Board

Under the National Labor Relations Act (that is, the Wagner Act of 1935 as amended by the Taft-Hartley Act in 1947 and by portions of the Landrum-Griffin Act in 1959), an independent regulatory agency, the National Labor Relations Board, was established for two broad purposes: (1) to conduct elections to determine whether groups of employees would be represented by a union in dealing with their employer over the terms and conditions of their employment, and (2) to investigate *and* adjudicate charges that one or another of the parties to collective bargaining had committed one or more of the unfair labor practices that are proscribed in the legislation.

Housing both the prosecutorial and the judicial functions within the same agency is somewhat unusual and presents a potential conflict of interest. The NLRB responded to this problem organizationally by establishing within the agency a separate Office of the General Counsel, which specializes in the administrative side of the Board's work: handling representation cases, conducting representation elections, investigating unfair labor-practice charges, issuing complaints, and prosecuting charges that are found to be meritorious. Much of this work is performed by the NLRB's regional offices, which are largely under the direction of the General Counsel. Most unfair-labor-practice charges—85 percent in 1980—are dismissed, withdrawn, or otherwise closed before formal prosecution is initiated. After a complaint is issued, the forum shifts to the judicial side of the NLRB. A hearing is held at a regional office by an administrative law judge who issues a decision. In a minority of cases— about 5 percent of the unfair-labor-practice cases closed in recent years—one of the parties will appeal the decision to the national Board in Washington, D.C. The five Board members, any three of which can constitute a panel to hear most cases, are appointed by the President of the United States to overlapping five-year terms, so that under normal circumstances, a president would not be able to appoint the entire Board during one term of office.

If a majority of the Board sustains the unfair-labor-practice charge, the Board issues an order that the employer or union ''cease and desist'' from the activity that gave rise to the charge. The Board may also impose a remedy for the damage to labor relations done by the commission of the practice. However, the NLRB has no direct enforcement power under the law. If a cease-and-desist order is not obeyed (that is, the unfair practice is continued), the NLRB must seek enforcement of its order in the U.S. Court of Appeals. In general, the court accepts the facts developed by the Board and reviews the case to determine whether the law has been applied properly. While the Appeals Court may choose not to enforce the Board's order, if it does agree to enforce the Board's cease-and-desist order, failure to end the unfair labor practice constitutes contempt of court. Either the Board or an employer or union can appeal a decision of the Appeals Court to the Supreme Court, and many of the most far-reaching decisions concerning unfair labor practices have been made by the Supreme Court.

What rules are established by these regulatory institutions, and what are their effects on labor relations? We will examine the Board's rule-making procedures in two central areas of labor relations: union organizing and collective-bargaining negotiations.

## Public Policy Toward the Formation of Unions

There are two methods by which a union becomes established in the United States. The first method—organizing from the top down—occurs when the union and the employer mutually agree that the union will be the recognized bargaining agent of the employees. As one might surmise from the historical resistance of American employers to unions, this consensus approach to union representation is rare in the United States. Prior to the passage of the Wagner Act in 1935, organizing from the top down was the only method available to unions, and conflicts over union representation were the source of considerable strike activity. This approach to union organization remains legal under the provisions of the NLRA, but its use is largely limited to situations in which the union has enormous economic power relative to the employer. The second method—the union-representation election procedure established in the Wagner Act—has no counterpart in most other countries, but was incorporated in the American labor-relations statute as an institutional mechanism to reduce the historical conflict surrounding efforts at union organizing. In fulfilling its responsibility to administer representation elections, the National Labor Relations Board seeks to ensure that employees have free choice in their legally guaranteed right to self-organization by regulating certain aspects of the organizing campaign that precedes an election.

## The Union Organization Process: An Overview

In this section, we will review the process of union organization under the second method, which is by far the more common, and then consider the apparent impact of NLRB activity on the outcome of representation elections. While it may appear unusual to study union organizing in the midst of a discussion of the legal environment of labor relations, union organizing is largely a legal process under the administration of the NLRA, far removed from the violent confrontations that often accompanied efforts to establish unions early in the century. It is a process, moreover, that is of the utmost importance to unions and management, for the proportion of representation elections won by unions has declined from almost 75 percent in 1950 to under 45 percent by 1983.

The union-organizing process begins when a union solicits, often surreptitiously, employee signatures on cards authorizing the union to represent the employee in collective bargaining with the employer. At some point, the union will send the employer a letter claiming to represent a majority of the employees and requesting an appointment to begin negotiating a binding contract that will establish the terms and conditions of employment for covered employees. When the employer invariably rejects the union's request, the union petitions the NLRB for an election and submits the signed authorization cards to satisfy the Board's requirement that at least 30 percent of the employees support the petition.

Before ordering a secret-ballot election, the Board must determine the scope of the election unit, that is, which employees will be eligible to vote in the representation election. While the unit question is often resolved by agreement between the employer and the union, there are issues that may prevent such agreement from occurring. For example, the size of the unit may influence the likelihood that the union will win the election and may also influence the relative bargaining power of a union once it is established. If the employer and union are unable to agree, the NLRB will determine the appropriate election unit and set a date for the election that is usually 15–30 days away.[1] During this period, the union and the employer typically engage in a campaign for the employees' votes. Unlike earlier periods of American labor history, these campaigns are generally quite bloodless, although often deeply felt. The use of detectives, physical violence, and sit-in strikes to settle union

---

[1] Because of the often close relationship between unit determination and bargaining structure, discussion of the NLRB's policy toward election units is postponed until Chapter 12.

representation issues has been supplanted by the use of lawyers, labor-relations consultants, campaign speeches, and unfair-labor-practice charges.

Essentially, the same procedures apply to decertification elections, but the process is initiated by a petition claiming that a majority of the employees in the bargaining unit do not want to be represented by the currently certified bargaining representative. Decertification and representation elections are governed by the same rules concerning election conduct and unfair labor practices.

## Regulation of the Union Organizing Process

Over the years, the NLRB has developed an elaborate set of rules governing the conduct of unions and employers during representation campaigns. The touchstone for these rules is the general statutory language defining unfair labor practices and the general purposes of the National Labor Relations Act. Given the objectives of the NLRA, the Board's task is to regulate elections in a manner that guarantees that employees have a free choice of bargaining representative. This is not a simple goal to achieve, however. In the first place, the Board's task calls for regulations that prevent the kinds of election campaign activity that distort employee voting behavior. But what sorts of campaign activity are likely to distort employee voting behavior? Throughout most of the Board's history, there has been very little information available on this fundamental issue, raising questions about the validity of the behavioral assumptions on which the Board's administrative rule-making rests. We shall return to this interesting question after reviewing the regulatory scheme that has developed for over fifty years as the NLRB has ruled, on a case-by-case basis, on the merits of unfair-labor-practice charges arising during the course of union-representation campaigns.

The second difficulty that the NLRB faces in regulating the election campaign is that, while the NLRA guarantees workers the right of self-organization, the first amendment to the Constitution guarantees all parties, including employers, freedom of expression. The Board must somehow find a balance that prevents employer interference with the workers' right to organize while protecting the employer's freedom of expression. The only guidance provided by the NLRA is a statement that the expression and dissemination of views on the desirability of unionization by employers is not evidence of an unfair labor practice as long as there is no threat of reprisal (if a union wins an election) or promise of benefit (if the workers vote against the union). This "threat-promise" test has been central to a number of determinations made by the Board and the federal courts. For example, employers cannot threaten to relocate their plant if a union wins and cannot promise wage or benefit increases to workers if the union loses. In fact, unexpected improvements in wages, benefits, or working conditions during a representation campaign would be viewed with suspicion by the NLRB.

On the other hand, the Board has developed a general standard for union election campaign tactics that is not required by the statute. In its own words, the Board seeks ". . . to provide a laboratory in which an experiment may be conducted under conditions as nearly ideal as possible, to determine the uninhibited desires of the employees."[2] Many observers have noted that this objective deviates substantially from the standards set for behavior in American political campaigns and have questioned whether it is either desirable or attainable given the uncertainty concerning the determinants of individual voting behavior.[3] Nevertheless, the Board maintains this standard in applying two levels of regulation to representation campaigns. Firstly, the parties can file objections to campaign conduct that deviates from "laboratory conditions" but nevertheless does not constitute an unfair labor practice. If the Board sustains the objection, it will set aside the results on the grounds that they were polluted by the objectionable conduct and rerun the election. Secondly, the losing party may file unfair-labor-practice charges alleging some form of interference with free choice. If the charge has merit, the Board will issue a cease-and-desist order and set aside the election's results. Moreover, when the Board believes that the results of a new election would be contaminated by the effects of past unfair labor practices, it may certify the union that lost the election as bargaining agent and order the offending employer to bargain. (The NLRB will take this unusual measure of reversing the outcome of a representation election only if over half of the employees in the unit had originally signed cards authorizing the union to bargain on their behalf.)

Union organizing campaigns most frequently give rise to charges under the first and third employer-unfair-labor practices. (See Table 11.1.) Any activity that can be construed as interfering with the employee's right to join or refrain from joining the union of his or her choice is a violation of the first unfair labor practice. Thus, violation of any other employer-unfair-labor practice automatically becomes a violation of Section 8(a)(1). The third section simply requires that workers who support unions be treated the same as workers who do not. Charges of employer-unfair-labor practices during an organizing campaign can also arise under Section 8(a)(2), which originally was included to prohibit company unions, which were prevalent in the 1920s and early 1930s. Under this provision an employer cannot solicit members, provide financial support, or otherwise express preference or support for a particular labor organization.

Broadly speaking, the NLRB has developed rules concerning union access to employees, campaign speech and literature, discrimination against union supporters, and the totality of conduct of an employer or union. Rulings on several specific issues are discussed below.

**Access.**    The basic idea behind the access rules is that a union or employer should win a representation election on the merits of the case rather than because the other side lacks the opportunity to express its views on unionization to the voters. At the same time, the Board has had to be sensitive to an

---

[2] *General Shoe Corp.*, 77 NLRB 124, 127 (1948).
[3] Derek Bok, "Regulation of Campaign Tactics in Representation Elections Under the NLRA," *Harvard Law Review*, 78 (November 1964): 38–141.

employer's right to operate a business in an orderly fashion. Under Board rulings, companies can keep nonemployee organizers off the premises, so long as the access policy is applied in a nondiscriminatory manner. Management can also prevent employee solicitation of union support during working hours, but cannot prevent employees from soliciting union memberships from fellow workers on company property during nonwork time (for example, lunch periods). More recently, the Board has required employers to place the names and addresses of eligible voters on file with the NLRB to facilitate union access to voters.

**The form of campaign speech.**   The NLRB also regulates both the form and content of campaign speeches by unions and employers. Employers can address their employees on the subject of unionization during company meetings (so-called *captive audience* speeches) up to twenty-four hours before the election without providing a similar opportunity to union supporters, as long as employees will have a reasonable opportunity to hear both sides during the course of the campaign. On the other hand, the interrogation of employees regarding their support for the union, surveillance of union activities, and the use of company spies, may be a basis for setting aside the results of an election on the grounds that the ultimate purpose of such activities is to threaten employees or discriminate against union supporters.[4]

**The substance of campaign speech.**   A more controversial area of Board rule making concerns its regulations governing the substance of campaign speech (including written forms of "speech" such as letters and printed literature). Given the purpose of the National Labor Relations Act, the Board's objective is to develop standards to determine when employer speech goes beyond permissible limits to constitute illegal interference with the employees' freedom of choice. In regulating the substance of campaign speeches, however, the Board faces a basic difficulty of distinguishing what the speaker says or intends from what the listener hears or understands. What is understood from a particular speech is likely to depend on the time and place of the speech, the relative power of union and management, and the personal values and beliefs of the individual listener. Words that will intimidate a southern textile worker may only antagonize a Detroit truck driver. Since the meaning that listeners may place on a given speech is likely to vary from situation to situation, it is hardly surprising that the Board's regulation of campaign communications is a relatively controversial aspect of its activities.

Campaign speeches or other communications that promise benefits to employees if the union is defeated, or threaten reprisals if the union is elected, constitute unfair labor practices. However, the boundary between an employer threat to close down the business if the union wins an election and an employer prediction that under collective bargaining, economic circumstances may force the closure of the firm, can be very thin. In practice, the

---

[4]  Case examples include *Isaacson-Carrico Mfg. Co.*, 200 NLRB 788 (1972); *Flight Safety, Inc.*, 197 NLRB 223 (1972); and *Cannon Electric Co.*, 151 NLRB 1465 (1965).

Board forbids outright threats of economic reprisal against workers taken at the employer's discretion, but permits predictions that are carefully phrased on the basis of objective fact, to convey an employer's belief concerning the probable consequences of unionism that are beyond the employer's control. If the predictions are based on economic necessity rather than antiunion animus, there is no violation of the Act.

**Appeals to prejudice.**   The Board has also taken the position that appeals to racial and religious prejudice can be coercive and grounds for setting aside the results of an election. While the Board will tolerate election propaganda that truthfully describes the employer or union position on matters of race, it will not accept inflammatory arguments or appeals that overstress and exacerbate racial feelings.[5] This area of regulation illustrates many of the basic conflicts between interference with free choice, on the one hand, and free speech on the other. Is it clear that inflammatory appeals, which are common in political campaigns, are unprotected by the First Amendment of the Constitution? Why do emotional appeals raise the question of employer *power* over employees when such appeals are not forbidden in political campaigns? Moreover, attempts to draw a line between temperate and intemperate speech imply that the Board (or anyone) can determine the point at which such speech begins to distort voting behavior.

**Factual Misrepresentations.**   The Board's policy toward factual misrepresentations by either the employer or the union has changed direction several times. Initially, such misrepresentations were grounds for ordering a new election. While the general principle that voting decisions should be made on the factual merits of the case is unassailable, this aspect of the Board's implementation of the principle resulted in the setting aside of some elections because of rather small factual errors in the claims of one side or the other. (For example, election results have been voided when a union made a modest misstatement of the wage rate that it had negotiated elsewhere, and when an employer misstated the union dues that employees would be required to pay if they voted for a union.) Subsequently, the NLRB abandoned this policy, later readopted it, and, in 1982, abandoned it again.[6]

**Discriminatory Treatment of Union Supporters.**   Organizing campaigns also regularly give rise to charges of discriminatory treatment of employees who support a union. A common example is when a worker is allegedly discharged by an employer in retaliation for union activities. (See Example 11.1.) A second form of discrimination is closing a plant to avoid dealing with a union that has won the right to represent employees at the plant. (See Example 11.2.) In most such cases, the Board must judge the relative merit of employer claims that a particular action was taken for sound business reasons and union claims that the action was motivated by a desire to thwart union objectives.

[5] *Sewell Mfg. Co.,* 138 NLRB 66 (1962).

[6] See NLRB decisions in *Hollywood Ceramics,* 140 NLRB 221 (1962); *Shopping Kart Food Market,* 228 NLRB 190 (1977); and *Midland Life Insurance Co.,* 263 NLRB 24 (1982).

EXAMPLE     11.1

## When Is a Discharge of a Union Member Discriminatory?

Section 8(a)(3) of the National Labor Relations Act prohibits employers from discriminating against workers because of their union activities. But what constitutes a discriminatory discharge? When a union supporter is discharged, the union alleges a violation of the Act, while the employer claims that the discharge was a result of poor job performance. Who is right? How does the NLRB or a court decide? The distinction between a discharge for cause and a violation of Section 8(a)(3) is illustrated in this amusing federal Appeals Court decision from 1943:

> The case of Walter Weigand is extraordinary. If ever a workman deserved summary discharge it was he. He was under the influence of liquor while on duty. He came to work when he chose and he left the plant and his shift as he pleased. In fact, when a foreman on one occasion was agreeably surprised to find Weigand at work and commented upon it, Weigand amiably stated that he was enjoying it.* He brought a woman (apparently generally known as the "Duchess") to the rear of the plant yard and introduced some of the employees to her. He took another employee to visit her and when this man got too drunk to be able to go home, punched his time-card for him and put him on the table in the representatives' meeting room in the plant in order to sleep off his intoxication. Weigand's immediate superiors demanded again and again that he be discharged, but each time higher officials intervened on Weigand's behalf because, as was naively stated, he was "a representative" [that is in the company union]. In return for not working at the job for which he was hired, the petitioner gave him full pay and on five separate occasions raised his wages. . . . [F]our raises were given Weigand at times when other employees in the plant did not receive wage increases.

Shortly after Weigand disclosed his membership in a CIO union, he was discharged on grounds of poor performance. In response to the CIO's subsequent unfair-labor-practice charge, the Appeals Court ruled:

> It is, of course, a violation to discharge an employee because he has engaged in activities on behalf of a union. . . . [I]t is certainly too great a strain on our credulity to assert, as does the petitioner, that Weigand was discharged for an accumulation of offenses. We think that he was discharged because his work on behalf of the CIO had become known to the plant manager. That ended his sinecure at the Budd plant.

The fact that the plaintiff's relentless incompetence was tolerated by the company only until he began to support an outside union indicated to the court that the discharge was a violation of Section 8(a)(3).

___

* Weigand stated that he was carried on the payroll as a "rigger." He was asked what was a rigger. He replied: "I don't know; I am not a rigger."

SOURCE: *Edward G. Budd Mfg. Co. v. NLRB,* United States Court of Appeals, Third Circuit, 1943, 138 F.2d 86, 13 LRRM 512.

## Application: Impact of NLRB Regulation of Organizing

The elaborate set of rules developed by the NLRB for its regulation of campaigns for union representation is unmatched elsewhere in the world and has been a source of controversy and uncertainty: controversy, because the Board's regulation undoubtedly dissuades both unions and employers from using some campaign tactics that they believe to be legitimate; uncertainty, because the Board has from time to time reversed its position on certain issues. Some of the volume of unfair-labor-practice charges may be related to this latter factor, since unions and employers may be more inclined to adopt campaign tactics whose legality remains ambiguous. Both the controversy and the uncertainty may be the result of a more basic underlying difficulty: an inadequate understanding by all parties of what types of campaign behavior really exert a coercive influence on the voting behavior of employees. Without a basic understanding of the determinants of voting behavior, unions, employers, and members of the NLRB, who are far removed from the campaign activities, may develop different beliefs about how much regulatory protection employees need in voting on union representation. But how valid are these beliefs? What effects do various union or management campaign tactics have on voting behavior? And what can the law hope to accomplish in this voting environment?

Until recently, there was very little information bearing on either the empirical validity of the assumptions about employee behavior underlying NLRB regulation or, more broadly, what factors, legal and otherwise, lead workers to join unions. Workers face a definite choice in a union-representation election, and the history of unions in the United States indicates that the choice is more likely to be made on the basis of economic rather than ideological considerations.

To the extent that the union-representation choice is governed by rational, economic decision making, workers will vote for a union only if the expected utility of their job is higher when they are represented by a union than when they are not. The expected impact of a union on wages and benefits is only one aspect of this calculation, since one consequence of negotiating higher wages and benefits through collective bargaining may be to reduce the probability of retaining one's job (as employers are forced up along their demand-for-labor curve). As a result, the availability of alternative jobs in the labor market and the utility attached to those jobs is also relevant to a worker's choice. Moreover, not all employees are likely to reach the same conclusions regarding the relative merits of union representation. To the extent that unions attempt to standardize rates and reduce wage differentials within a firm, the advantages of unionization will be inversely related to an employee's position in the firm's earnings distribution. Similarly, the substitution of a "web of rules" and a system of "industrial jurisprudence" to govern working relationships that were formerly governed by the individual discretion of supervisors will benefit those who had good relationships with supervisors less than those who did not. More generally, individuals are likely to have different subjective evaluations about their working conditions and how they expect unions to be able to change the work environment.

There is some empirical support for the view that voting decisions in union elections are made on the basis of an economic calculus. For example, one recent study found that the probability of voting for a union was inversely related to both the position of an individual in the wage distribution of a firm and concerns over job security when alternative jobs were not easily available; that is, workers with relatively high wages in their place of employment were less likely to vote for a union, as were those highly concerned about job security in markets with few opportunities. Voting behavior was also influenced by individual expectations of the effect of unions on the probability of promotion, fairness of treatment, and other nonmonetary issues of employment. In terms of personal characteristics, blacks and younger workers were more likely to vote union.[7] Studies in the organizational-behavior literature find uniformly that the probability a worker will vote for union representation is inversely related to his or her job satisfaction.[8] One implication of these studies is that workers may enter a union-representation campaign with a fairly strong predisposition to vote for a union or the employer based on their knowledge of employment conditions and their expectations about how unions are likely to influence them.

What, then, is the role of the union-representation campaign that the NLRB regulates? Both employers and unions use the campaign to try to change workers' predispositions (and persuade undecided employees) by altering expectations about what the union will achieve. Candidates for political office have a similar objective, but political scientists find that voters are often inattentive to a campaign, are unaware of issues (or even candidates), and in general, do not acquire the information necessary for rational choice among candidates. If there are also limitations on the inherent rationality of voters in union-representation elections, how important is the regulatory objective of "laboratory conditions" likely to be to the voting outcome?[9] The NLRB has rejected the political campaign analogy because of the employer's economic leverage over employees—a factor that is not present (or not as obvious) in political campaigns.[10] Like other Board positions, this rests on some untested assumptions concerning employee behavior when faced with the choice to unionize.

One study of voting choices in 31 union-representation elections reached provocative conclusions concerning the effectiveness of the NLRB regulation of campaign conduct.[11] The basic method of the study was to compare the

[7] Henry S. Farber and Daniel H. Saks, "Why Workers Want Unions: The Role of Relative Wages and Job Characteristics," *Journal of Political Economy* 88 (April 1980): 349–369.

[8] Herbert G. Heneman III and Marcus Sandver, "Predicting the Outcome of Union Certification Elections: A Review of the Literature," *Industrial and Labor Relations Review* 36 (July 1983): 539–44.

[9] This question is raised in Derek C. Bok, "The Regulation of Campaign Tactics."

[10] Actually, the fiscal policies pursued by elected federal officials may sometimes have more influence on an individual's employment prospects than the decisions of an individual employer.

[11] Julius Getman, Stephen B. Goldberg, Jeanne B. Herman, *Union Representation Elections: Law and Reality* (New York: Russell Sage Foundation, 1976).

voting intentions of employees—after the petition for a representation election had been filed with the Board but before the campaign had begun—with their actual voting behavior in the representation election at the conclusion of the campaign. The basic finding of the study was that employees vote in accord with intentions formed well in advance of the union-representation campaign, and little that occurs during the campaign itself has a significant effect on those intentions. Initial voting intentions were related to satisfaction with current job and employee attitudes toward unionism in general (rather than attitudes concerning the particular union(s) involved in the campaign). With this information alone, the authors were able to predict the outcome of 29 out of 31 elections. Moreover, the predictions were not improved by adding information on tactics used during the subsequent representation campaign to the information on voting intentions before the campaign began. Taken at face value, the conclusions of the study provide a powerful challenge to the assumptions that underlie the NLRB's current policy toward union-representation campaigns.[12]

Why is it that the campaign activities fail to influence the initial voting intentions of workers significantly? Largely, according to the study, because the basic behavioral foundations underlying the Board regulation are not valid. While the Board attempts to replicate laboratory-campaign conditions, the majority of employees are inattentive to the campaign. When surveyed, most either could not remember many of the issues raised by either side in the campaign or remembered a few issues imperfectly. Many were already knowledgeable about unions and industrial relations from their general work experience or prior employment at unionized firms. Campaign information that is received is subject to perceptual distortion; that is, the way that workers perceive the campaign is a function of their prior beliefs. Employees who are predisposed toward the union before the campaign begins are likely to interpret an employer's speech as more threatening than would workers who support the employer, and they may tend to interpret it as further evidence of the need for union representation. The general picture that emerges from the study is that misinformation, threatening behavior, and promises of benefit do not affect workers in ways that are likely to have a coercive influence on the choice of a union, and, by implication, much of the NLRB's current regulation of campaign conduct could be abandoned.

While there is very little difference between employees' original voting intentions and their final vote, the vote switching that does occur tends to be from union to employer rather than in the opposite direction. The study finds that union and company supporters among the employees are equally familiar with the company campaign (probably as a result of "captive audience" meetings on company premises), but company supporters are much less familiar with the union campaign than are union supporters. This finding may suggest that as a matter of public policy, unions should get greater access to

---

[12] Since all 31 elections took place under NLRB rulings, the study cannot tell us exactly what would happen if "no-holds-barred" campaigns were permitted; rather, it suggests that workers' decisions may not be as sensitive to many campaign tactics as the Board assumes.

employees during a representation campaign, but it conflicts somewhat with the more general finding of inattentiveness already noted.

Judging by the level of resources allocated to union-representation campaigns, the provocative results of this study contrast sharply with the prevailing beliefs of both unions and management concerning employee voting behavior. In fact, the conclusions of the study have not gone unchallenged, and there have been subsequent reanalyses of the underlying data using more extensive controls for noncampaign influences on voting behavior. These analyses generally confirm the importance of voting predispositions held by workers on the likelihood of voting for a union, but they only partially confirm the earlier findings concerning the impact of campaign tactics. While many aspects of employer campaign speeches and tactics that the NLRB finds illegal do not have a statistically significant relationship to the probability of voting for a union, one study found that employer threats had a substantial and statistically significant tendency to reduce the probability that an employee would vote for a union. This finding is more supportive of the Board's prohibition of overtly threatening behavior by employers.[13]

The commission of unfair labor practices is only one of the methods of union avoidance sometimes adopted by employers opposed to the unionization of their employees. Many employers hire consultants to plan and implement the strategy and tactics of the management side of a union-represenation campaign. Such consultants often manage the flow of information to workers during the campaign and advise employers on tactics that purportedly will undermine the success of the union campaign. The increasing use of such consultants during the 1970s has been opposed by the labor movement and led to proposals that their activities be subject to legal restrictions.

As with the use of unfair labor practices for union avoidance, however, recent research indicates that the use of consultants is not the major reason for the declining success of private sector unions in representation elections.[14] Why, then, has the use of consultants in representation campaigns become an important issue for both unions and management? It is possible that neither side realizes that among the confluence of factors influencing a worker's decision to vote for a union, the impact of consultant activities is small. It is also notable, however, that most union-representation elections nowadays involve relatively small employee units and are often decided by very few votes.[15]

---

[13] William T. Dickens, "The Effect of Company Campaigns on Certification Elections: Law and Reality Once Again," *Industrial and Labor Relations Review* 36 (July 1983): 560–75.

[14] One study of 130 representation elections in a sample of retail grocery stores in seven states in the 1970s found that the use of consultants had a weak tendency to reduce the probability of a union victory, but this result was only marginally significant in a statistical sense. John J. Lawler, "The Influence of Management Consultants on the Outcome of Union Certification Elections," *Industrial and Labor Relations Review* 38 (October 1984): 38–51.

[15] For example, one study found that a change of voting intention by as few as eight workers is sufficient to change the outcome of the average union-representation election. As is often the case, the behavior of the *marginal* workers, that is, those most prone to change their behavior, is more crucial to the outcome than the average behavior of all employees. Myron Roomkin and Richard Block, "A Preliminary Analysis of the Participation Rate and the Margin of Victory in NLRB Elections," *Proceedings of the Industrial Relations Research Association* (1982):220–26.

EXAMPLE    11.2

## Does a Plant Closure Discriminate Against Unions?

Example 11.1 indicated how an employer might illegally discriminate against an individual worker by discharging the worker for union activities. It has also been claimed that an employer can discriminate against an entire group of employees who support a union by closing a plant in which a union has won representation rights. Most charges of this nature arise in "runaway shop" situations, when an employer closes a unionized plant and subsequently opens a nonunion plant in a new location—usually in the South. In these cases, the NLRB seeks to distinguish closures that are motivated by "antiunion animus"—and hence illegal under the NLRA—and those that are motivated by economic pressures, which are legal. But what happens if a plant goes out of business permanently after being organized by a union?

In 1956, the Textile Workers' Union initiated an organizing campaign at the Darlington Manufacturing Company in South Carolina, one of several textile mills operated by Deering-Milliken & Co. During the strongly contested campaign for union representation, the company threatened to close the mill in the event of a union victory. When the union did win the election, the head of Deering-Milliken called together the directors of Darlington, and they promptly voted to liquidate the corporation. The union filed unfair-labor-practice charges.

The NLRB attributed the closure of the Darlington Company to antiunion animus, found a violation of Section 8(a)(3) of the NLRA, and ordered back-pay for all terminated employees until they obtained similar work or were put on preferential hiring lists at other Deering-Milliken mills. The Board's startling proposition that under certain circumstances an employer could not go completely out of business without violating the NLRA was rejected by both a Circuit Court of Appeals and the Supreme Court. Motivation is irrelevant in the case of a complete liquidation of a business.

In its 1965 decision, however, the Supreme Court went on to make a further distinction:

> On the other hand, a discriminatory partial closing may have repercussions on what remains of business, affording employer leverage for discouraging the free exercise of Section 7 rights among remaining employees of much the same kind as that found to exist in the "runaway shop" and "temporary closing" cases . . . . By analogy to those cases involving a continuing enterprise we are constrained to hold, in disagreement with the Court of Appeals, that a partial closing is an unfair labor practice under Section 8(a)(3) if motivated by a purpose to chill unionism in any of the remaining plants of the single employer and if the employer may reasonably have foreseen that such closing will likely have that effect.

Upon remand to determine the motivation for the closing, the NLRB found (and an Appeals Court agreed) that the Darlington plant had been closed by Deering-Milliken to deter union organization at its other plants.

In other words, a firm can go completely out of business, irrespective of the owner's motivation, but if one unit of an organization shuts down, the legitimacy of the action under American labor law depends on whether the motivation for the shutdown is to chill unionism.

SOURCE: *Textile Workers' Union v. Darlington Mfg. Co.* 380 U.S. 263 (1965); *Darlington Mfg. Co. v. NLRB,* 397 F. 2d 760 (4th Circuit, 1968).

Many studies have found that as the time between requesting a union-representation election and holding the election increases, the likelihood of a union victory declines.[16] Employers can achieve procedural delays and increase the odds of remaining nonunion by filing many charges against unions. Given the limited resources of the NLRB, each additional charge imposes a "congestion" cost on the entire regulatory system by lengthening the time that is required to decide each charge. Unions can attempt to shorten the adjudication period by limiting the number of unfair-labor-practice charges that they file against employers. This may be why only a fraction of the apparent violations of the NLRA by employers result in the filing of an unfair-labor-practice charge.

# Regulation of the Collective-Bargaining Process

In addition to establishing procedures for the selection of unions, Congress wished to assure, in drafting the NLRA, that workers would actually receive some of the benefits of a collective-bargaining relationship and sought to implement this intention by imposing a duty to bargain on employers and unions. At the same time, it appears that the legislation was not intended to give the government a substantive role in the collective-bargaining process. (One Senator stated that the government would lead the parties to the door of the bargaining room but "would not go one step beyond.") The tension between these two objectives can be seen from the way in which the legal environment of collective bargaining has developed under the NLRA.

Once a union has won a representation election, the National Labor Relations Act imposes certain obligations on both the union and the employer with whom it will bargain. These obligations are tied to the concept of *exclusive representation,* which is a unique feature of American labor law, and the duty to bargain established by the unfair labor practices in Section 8(a)(5) and 8(b)(3) of the Act (see Table 11.1). A union that wins a representation election is certified by the National Labor Relations Board as the exclusive bargaining agent for all employees in the bargaining unit. This status imposes on the union the duty to represent *all* employees in the unit—even those who may have opposed representation by the union. At the same time, an employer may not work out contractual relations with individual employees once a union has been certified. Nor may an employer deal with other organizations (for example, those of employees who voted against the union) on matters of employment conditions. In each instance, the employer must deal with the employees through their union. The principle of exclusive representation also prohibits an employer from taking unilateral action with

---

[16] Myron Roomkin and Richard N. Block, "Case Processing Time and the Outcome of Representation Elections: Some Empirical Evidence," *University of Illinois Law Review,* 98 (1981): pp. 75–97; Paula E. Stephan and Bruce E. Kaufman, "Factors Leading to a Decline in Union Win Rates, 1973–81," *Proceedings of the Thirty-Ninth Annual Meeting of Industrial Relations Research Association,* Barbara D. Dennis (ed.), (1986): 296–305.

respect to employment conditions until after the employer has bargained with the certified union to a point of impasse.

Exactly what constitutes collective bargaining and how does one know when a bargaining impasse has been reached? The legislative guidance on bargaining and impasse is provided by Section 8(d) of the National Labor Relations Act, which elaborates the meaning of the duty to bargain:

> . . . to bargain collectively is . . . [the] mutual obligation to meet at reasonable times and confer in good faith with respect to wages, hours, and other terms and conditions of employment, or the negotiation of an agreement . . . and the execution of a written contract incorporating any agreement reached if requested by either party, but such obligation does not compel either party to agree to a proposal or require the making of a concession.

In determining when a legal bargaining impasse has occurred, the NLRB as a matter of policy must determine what constitutes "good faith" and what constitutes "other terms and conditions of employment." To resolve these issues, the NLRB and the courts have had to review the reasonableness of the positions of the negotiating parties in an effort to assess the "state of mind" of the negotiating parties.

Over the years the NLRB and the courts have developed a set of standards or rules for what constitutes good faith bargaining that has some impact on the tactics and behavior used by unions and management in collective bargaining. First, there are a set of *per se* violations of the duty to bargain that pertain to behavior at the bargaining table. A violation of the duty to bargain in good faith will generally be found if either party simply listens to and rejects the other party's proposals, if counterproposals are not made (although, as Section 8(d) specifies, neither party is required to make concessions), if stalling tactics are used, or if either party suddenly shifts position when agreement is near. The Supreme Court has also held that good-faith bargaining requires that the parties provide data in support of their bargaining claims. For example, if a company claims it is unable to pay the costs that would be imposed by union demands, it must provide the financial data to support that claim if the union requests it.[17]

In addition to the tactical issues raised by the legal duty to bargain, the Board and the courts have been confronted with issues involving the substance of collective bargaining. The NLRA requires labor and management to bargain over "wages, hours, and other terms and conditions of employment." Is the NLRA violated when one party refuses to bargain with the other over a proposal that would violate other laws (for example, equal-employment-opportunity legislation)? Just what are "other terms and conditions of employment"? Is the NLRA violated when one party refuses to bargain with the other over an issue that it does not believe to be a "term and condition of employment" under the meaning of the law? In one important case, for

---

[17]  *NLRB v. Truitt Mfg. Co.* 351 U.S. 149 (1956).

example, an employer refused to bargain with a union over subcontracting decisions, on the grounds that such decisions were in the scope of management prerogatives.[18] These questions must ultimately be answered by the NLRB and the courts, but in the process, these institutions end up "defining" many of the issues that *must* be bargained under the law.

The NLRB has addressed these issues by developing a three-way classification of substantive bargaining issues: *illegal* issues, which should not be a topic of negotiations because they violate some other law; *mandatory* issues, which fall within the definition of "other terms and conditions of employment" and therefore must be bargained; and *voluntary* issues, which, although legal, do not fall within the definition of "terms and conditions of employment." Refusal to bargain over voluntary conditions does not constitute a violation of the legal duty to bargain.

The implications of this classification scheme for bargaining issues were expanded with the Supreme Court decision in the Borg-Warner case in 1958.[19] This case grew out of collective-bargaining negotiations in which the company insisted that two clauses be incorporated in a new labor agreement: recognition of the local (rather than the national) union and a "last offer ballot," that is, a requirement that employees be polled on whether or not they supported the employer's last bargaining offer before a strike was called. The union refused to bargain over these demands on the grounds that they were internal union matters and not subject to collective-bargaining negotiations. When the company continued to insist on the two clauses a strike was called, but the union eventually lost the strike and filed unfair-labor-practice charges, alleging that Borg-Warner had violated the duty-to-bargain provision of the NLRA. At the same time, Borg-Warner alleged that the union had violated the same provision by refusing to bargain over the issues. The Board and the courts found that the two proposed clauses were voluntary subjects of bargaining and, consistent with past policy, the union's refusal to bargain was therefore not an unfair labor practice. However, the duty-to-bargain concept was then extended by the further ruling that the company's insistence on bargaining a voluntary issue to the point where a bargaining impasse and strike occurred constituted bargaining in bad faith.

At first glance, this ruling may appear unusual. Although the company's bargaining conduct may be perfectly legal, its insistence on a voluntary topic of collective bargaining to the point of impasse is a violation of the duty to bargain. On the other hand, insistence on bargaining over a mandatory topic to the point where a strike or lockout occurs is not a violation of this duty. What is behind this distinction? Recall that Section 8(d) of the NLRA does not require that agreement be reached in bargaining over "wages, hours, and other terms and conditions of employment" so that work stoppages over these issues are consistent with the Act. On the other hand, a general objective of the NLRA was to reduce the general level of industrial conflict, and

---

[18] In this case, the Board and the courts agreed with the union that the employer was required to bargain over this issue. *See Fibreboard Paper Products Corp. v. NLRB*, 379 U.S. 203 (1964).

[19] *NLRB v. Wooster Division of Borg Warner Corp.*, 356 U.S. 342 (1958).

**EXAMPLE   11.3**

## How Well Are Workers Protected by the Duty to Bargain?

The original case for including the duty to bargain in the National Labor Relations Act was to ensure that meaningful collective bargaining commenced once a union won a representation election. Yet, as we have seen, Section 8(d) of the Act qualifies the duty by not requiring either side to concede. One outcome of collective bargaining under these legal provisions is illustrated by the following case. The language is that of the U.S. Court of Appeals, after considering an employer's appeal of an NLRB decision:

> Refusal to bargain in good faith [may] be sustained solely by reference to the terms of the employment contract which management finally says it is willing to sign if such proposed contract could fairly be found to be one which would leave the employees in no better state than they were without it. . . . [W]e may assume that the Board could find that [by] the terms of the contract insisted on by the company the union is in no better position than if it had no contract. It is perfectly apparent that the company representatives approached the bargaining table with a full understanding of their obligations to meet with, and discuss with, representatives of the employees any terms and conditions of employment that either put forward; that they must at least expose themselves to such argument and persuasion as could be put forward, and that they must try to seek an area of agreement at least as to some of the terms of employment; that if they were able to arrive at such agreement they must be willing to reduce it to writing and sign it. . . . The question is: Can the company's insistence on terms overall favorable to it in net result be taken as proof that it did not approach the bargaining table in good faith? . . . [T]he Board is saying that although the statute says no concession need be made and no item need be agreed upon, if a company fails to concede anything substantial, then this is too much, and such failure amounts to bad faith. The language of the Courts is not . . . entirely clear, but we find no case which precisely supports the proposition here asserted by the Board. . . . A careful study of the record before us . . . leaves us with the clear impression that the Board erred in finding adequate proof of a failure to bargain in good faith.

Note that a similar situation could arise if a powerful union simply presented a contract proposal to a weak employer on a take-it-or-leave-it basis. Indeed, instances of such behavior led Congress to extend the duty to bargain to unions in the 1947 Taft-Hartley amendments. But, in either case, what difference does this legal duty make to the outcome of collective bargaining? What factor(s) ultimately determine the content of the labor agreement signed by the union and management?

SOURCE:   *White v. NLRB*, United States Court of Appeals, 5th Circuit, (1958). 255 F.2d 564.

rulings that prohibit work stoppages resulting from refusals to bargain over issues that seem peripheral to the key issues in union-management relations are consistent with this.

But which issues are central to collective bargaining and which issues are peripheral? How do employers and unions know whether a proposal is mandatory or voluntary? If the Board has not ruled on a similar issue in a previous case, they do not know. Therefore, one result of the ruling is that as new issues are introduced into collective bargaining, the party opposing change can adopt the strategy of refusing to bargain over the new proposal in the hope that when the NLRB considers the unfair labor-practice charge normally following such a stance, it will rule that the proposal is voluntary and need not be bargained. Increases in the number of issues introduced into collective bargaining can therefore contribute to the increase in duty-to-bargain, unfair-labor-practice charges noted earlier in the chapter.

More fundamentally, rulings by the NLRB and the courts on the classification of bargaining issues can alter the relative bargaining power of unions and management in collective bargaining. Consider the Borg-Warner case. The union lost a strike and had to accept the company's proposals. The ruling by the NLRB and the Supreme Court (on appeal) effectively restored to the union a contractual position that it was unable to achieve by standard collective-bargaining methods. On this issue, the ruling effectively increased the bargaining power of the union relative to management and through legal intervention altered the outcome of the collective-bargaining process. At the same time, application of the Borg-Warner rule tends to influence the scope of collective bargaining. Topics that the NLRB labels "mandatory" are more likely to end up in collective-bargaining agreements than topics that are labeled "voluntary," simply because the ability to use NLRB rulings to back up the former demands raises the probability that they will be accepted.

When a single issue is being negotiated, NLRB rulings can alter the substance of a collective-bargaining agreement, despite the original intention of the NLRA to keep the government out of the substance of collective bargaining. If several issues are under negotiation, however, either party may behave strategically and use NLRB influence in support of a "voluntary" issue. A union or an employer may simply refuse to agree on a mandatory issue until a voluntary issue is resolved.

## Application: Good Faith and General Electric's Labor Relations

The labor-relations policy practiced by the General Electric Company for almost twenty years provides an interesting review of the issues raised by the duty-to-bargain requirement in the National Labor Relations Act. Following a serious strike in 1946, GE's Vice-President of Labor Relations, Lemuel R. Boulware, devised a new labor-relations policy for the firm that became known as "Boulwareism." Under the new plan, GE solicited considerable information on the benefits and working conditions desired by its employees, formulated specific proposals on the basis of this information, and then tried to sell the package of proposals to the employees and the general public through a massive marketing campaign that included bulletins to GE employees and newspaper advertising.

GE had a collective-bargaining relationship with the International Union of Electrical, Radio, and Machine Workers (IUE), and the new approach to labor relations became part of the company's overall bargaining strategy. Most companies enter collective-bargaining negotiations offering less than they can afford (or less than they believe they will have to settle for), to have something to trade during the negotiations process. GE objected to this approach on the grounds that the union typically received credit from the workers for any concessions that were received from the employer during negotiations, and the company's credibility with its employees was diminished. Instead, under Boulwareism, GE announced that its initial offer was proper and final and would not be altered unless it were faced with information that had not been considered in the research underlying the company's offer. This aspect of the strategy was an effort to deny the union a political victory in collective-bargaining negotiations, for the company was unwilling to alter its proposal solely because the union disagreed with it. It was the company's position that its extensive research left it at least as well apprised of what workers wanted out of a labor agreement as the union was, and it generally adopted a patronizing attitude toward union counterproposals.

Following negotiations in 1960, the IUE filed unfair-labor-practice charges alleging that GE had violated the duty-to-bargain provision of the NLRA. During those negotiations, GE had attempted to institute unilaterally a personal accident insurance benefit for employees, refused to release certain details (including the cost of the package of company proposals), and generally adopted the take-it-or-leave-it bargaining stance that was a feature of Boulwareism. After protracted legal proceedings, the Board and the courts sustained the unfair-labor-practice charge. The difficulty with the effort to institute the insurance proposal is that once a collective-bargaining relationship is established, under the NLRA, neither party to the relationship can terminate or modify the contract without giving 60 days' notice and offering to renegotiate. Even unilateral modifications that may *increase* the value of the contract (as GE's insurance proposal would have) cannot be instituted without bargaining, since the union may have other priorities and prefer that the cost of the modification be allocated to a different purpose. Generally, the courts took the position that the union's ability to serve as an effective bargaining agent is impaired by unilateral offers by an employer. Likewise, the NLRB and the courts had long held that employers and unions have a duty to provide information in support of their bargaining claims, and GE's failure to do so constituted a violation of the duty to bargain.

Fundamentally, the federal courts also ruled that the entire pattern of collective-bargaining conduct developed by GE under its policy of Boulwareism was inconsistent with good-faith bargaining. Part of the courts' rulings were based on GE's conduct at the bargaining table and included the company's refusal to furnish information, its patronizing attitude, its refusal to comment specifically on union proposals, and its reluctance to offer counterproposals different from its initial offer. The courts also took exception to the company's emphasis on selling its proposal through marketing techniques rather than collective bargaining. In the words of the Circuit Court of Appeals: ". . . The aim, in a word, was to deal with the Union through the employees, rather than with the employees through the Union" as is required by the NLRA.[20]

# Job Security and Labor-Relations Policy

Workers encounter many threats to their job security. There were roughly 35,000 business failures in an average year during the first half of the 1980s, and there were 57,000 failures in 1985 alone. Plant closings—the partial shutdown of a company's operations—are also a frequent threat to job security, as is the subcontracting of work to outside businesses. Further, a wave of mergers and corporate takeovers during the late 1970s and early 1980s changed the ownership of many companies, many of which had collective-bargaining agreements with their employees.

What requirements does the NLRA place on employers when issues threatening the job security of unionized workers arise? The key question is whether there is a duty to bargain over job-security issues. Subcontracting is a mandatory subject of bargaining, for example; employers have a duty to bargain with unions over proposed subcontracting arrangements. In contrast, even though closing a business usually has more substantial effects on job security than contracting out work, an employer need not bargain about the decision to go out of business for *economic* reasons (see Example 11.2). However, unionized employers *do* have a duty to bargain with the union about the *effects* of going out of business on their employees.

In the early 1980s the Supreme Court ruled that the partial closure of a business was a management prerogative, not a mandatory subject for collective bargaining.[21] In its reasoning, the Court noted that the law does not assume ". . . that the elected union representative would become an equal partner in the running of the business enterprise. . . ." An alternative to allowing complete managerial prerogatives regarding plant closings is the establishment of legislation requiring procedures, such as advance notice of layoffs, that must be followed in the event of shutdowns. Four states have such legislation, and a federal statute requiring 60 days' advance notice of a plant closing or a mass layoff was passed in 1988.

To what extent is a union able to protect the interests of its members when mergers and acquisitions change the ownership of a company? In the mid-1960s, the Supreme Court held that "the disappearance by merger of a corporate employer which has entered into a collective bargaining agreement with a union does not automatically terminate all rights of the employees covered by the agreement. . . ."[22] In a later ruling the Court held that the new employer (usually referred to as the "successor" employer) has a duty to

---

[20]   *NLRB v. General Electric Co.* 418 F.2d 736 (2d Circuit, 1969).

[21]   *First National Maintenance Corp.* v. *NLRB*, 452 U.S. 66 (1981).

[22]   *Wiley* v. *Livingston*, 376 U.S. 543 (1964).

recognize the union as the bargaining agent of the company's employees, but it does not have to honor the labor contract that was in effect before the merger; that is, the previous contract terms cannot be imposed on a new owner and future employment conditions must be determined by negotiations with the new employer.[23] A new employer is subject to this ruling when the company continues with similar production, organization, and job functions, and its obligation to bargain with the union rests on the extent to which the prior owner's work force is retained. When a new employer retains most of the seller's employees, there is an obligation to bargain over future working conditions, even though the owner is permitted to set the initial terms of employment unilaterally.[24] The new employer is not obliged to hire the previous owner's employees, however. Although no employer can discriminate in hiring on the basis of union membership, the rulings on successorship provide incentives for employers to avoid prior union contracts by hiring a new work force.

# Remedies for Unfair Labor Practices

Since its inception, the National Labor Relations Board has faced the problem of developing corrective measures for violations of the unfair labor-practice provisions of the NLRA. The array of sanctions that the Board has adopted has been limited by decisions of the U.S. Supreme Court that hold that the purpose of the NLRA is remedial rather than punitive. Under this concept, whatever sanctions the Board designs are supposed to restore the *status quo* in labor relations at the time of a violation, but they are not supposed to impose any additional penalty on the employer or union responsible for the violation.

### Remedies for Election Violations

Current remedies applied by the NLRB attempt to meet this standard. In response to modest violations of "laboratory campaign conditions," the Board may set aside election results that it views as tainted by illegal campaign conduct and rerun the election. For serious violations of unfair labor practices, the Board may order an employer to bargain with a union that lost an election, if a majority of the employees in the bargaining unit had originally signed cards authorizing the union to bargain for them. (Here the Board assumes that the *status quo* that existed at the time the authorization cards were signed was later distorted by unfair labor practices.)[25] The use of

---

[23] *NLRB* v. *Burns International Detective Agency*, 406 U.S. 272 (1972).

[24] *Howard Johnson Company*, 417 U.S. 249 (1974).

[25] In *NLRB* v. *Gissel Packing Co.* 395 U.S. 575 (1969), the Supreme Court ruled that while the results of a representation election were the preferred indication of employee preferences for union representation, authorization cards could be accepted as reliable indicators of employee voting intentions when extensive unfair labor practices by an employer were believed to have polluted the results of a representation election. A union with authorization cards signed by a majority of the employees could be certified as a bargaining agent. Absent unfair labor practices, however, an employer has a right to an election even when the union has authorization cards from a majority of the employees in a unit.

authorization cards for this purpose has been controversial, on the grounds that what workers do in the privacy of a voting booth is likely to be a more reliable guide to their preferences than what they may say (or sign) to get a union organizer to leave them alone. One study, though, found that authorization cards did reflect worker voting intentions accurately.[26] In instances where illegal forms of employer resistance to unionization occur before a union has obtained enough signed authorization cards to file an election petition with the NLRB, the Board may certify the union as the bargaining representative and issue an order to bargain *even though an election has not been held,* on the belief that, but for the employer's unfair labor practices, the union would have acquired the signed cards and won the election.

In the case of a discrimination discharge, the Board tries to compensate the employee for wage losses incurred as a result of the unfair labor practice; however, if the employee receives more than was lost, the corrective measure would be punitive. Therefore, the typical remedy is reinstatement with back pay (or back pay alone if the worker does not wish reinstatement).[27] Back pay due the employee by the employer responsible for the discharge is reduced by any interim earnings or unemployment compensation received by the worker, so that the total amount received since discharge from all sources does not exceed what the employee would have earned from the employer if the discharge had not occurred. Clearly, the back pay for which the employer is liable can be very small when a discharged worker immediately finds another job.

How well do these remedies restore the *status quo* in labor relations at the time of an unfair labor practice? One factor bearing on this question is the long delay in reaching decisions. More than a year typically passes between the filing of a charge and a Board decision. If that decision is appealed, another 1–2 years will be required before a U.S. Circuit Court of Appeals reaches a decision. With such delays, workers who have been discharged because of their union activities frequently have taken other jobs long before their case is resolved. While they may accept the back pay, few return to resume a career with the former employer.[28] It is by no means clear that this procedure restores the *status quo.* From the perspective of the employees who remain with the employer, an individual who supported unions was discharged and never reappeared. The loss of leaders and supporters will directly reduce union support and it may have indirect effects as well. The jeopardy in which

---

[26] Getman, Goldberg, and Herman, *Union Representation Elections,* Chapter 6.

[27] Back pay awards include fringe benefits, forgone interest, and wages including adjustments for expected promotions (based on the employment history of similarly situated workers within the firm). It does not include compensation for losses—such as repossession of car or eviction—that a worker might incur as a result of being unable to meet financial obligations while illegally discharged.

[28] A study of 217 reinstatement orders issued by one NLRB regional office in 1971 and 1972 found that 129 of the individuals refused reinstatement, largely because of fear of further mistreatment by the company. Only 5 percent of those offered reinstatement 6 months or more after they were discharged accepted the remedy. Of those who did accept, only a third remained with the company for more than six months. Elvis C. Stephens and Warren Chaney, "A Study of the Reinstatement Remedy Under the NLRA," *Labor Law Journal* 25 (January 1974): pp. 31–41.

**EXAMPLE    11.4**

# Union Avoidance and Labor Law

In 1963, the Textile Workers' Union of America (TWUA) began a drive to organize J.P. Stevens & Company, the second largest textile company in the United States, with some 39,000 hourly workers and 80 plants located primarily in southern states. Over the next 12 years the union lost 11 of 12 representation elections held at Stevens' factories and was certified as the bargaining agent for some 3,000 textile workers in the single election that it won. However, the election campaigns were accompanied by massive unfair labor practices on the part of the company. The NRLB ruled against the company in 22 out of 23 unfair-labor-practice cases, finding that Stevens had fired or otherwise discriminated against 289 workers for their union activities. In some cases, where the union lost an election, the Board concluded that Stevens' unfair labor practices had distorted workers' freedom of choice and ordered the company to bargain with the TWUA. The company ignored the orders and also refused to bargain with the TWUA at the plant where the union won the representation election. The federal courts upheld the Board in 13 of the 16 cases that were appealed when cease-and-desist or bargaining orders were ignored. In the 17 years following the beginning of the TWUA organizing campaign, J.P. Stevens violated more labor laws than any other company in the history of the National Labor Relations Act and had become a symbol of the use of union avoidance tactics by employers.

Given the company's resistance to legal remedies, and the failure of an attempted nationwide boycott of J.P. Stevens' products initiated by the labor movement, the TWUA devised an unusual strategy to induce the company to sign an agreement: it began to bring pressure on companies that had business or financial dealings with the J.P. Stevens Company or that had officials of Stevens on their boards of directors. By generating unfavorable publicity and suggesting that unions should shift their pension funds and other financial assets from financial institutions that had dealings with J.P. Stevens, the TWUA appeared to force the chairman of Stevens to resign from the board of two companies. Its most successful tactic, however, was to threaten to run two dissident candidates to oppose the official nominees for the board of directors of the major life-insurance company that held over 40 percent of J.P. Stevens' long-term debt. Faced with the unappealing and unusual prospect of a contested board-of-directors election that could cost between $5–7 million to conduct, the insurance company met with Stevens' officials and, after seventeen years of union avoidance, Stevens recognized the union and signed an agreement with the TWUA. (As part of the agreement the union agreed not to restrict "the availability of financial or credit accommodations to Stevens.")

The J.P. Stevens case is interesting in part because it illustrates the limitations of legal procedures and remedies in guaranteeing workers their statutory rights to union representation and collective bargaining in the face of determined employer resistance. Ultimately, the struggle between J.P. Stevens and the TWUA was determined by economic power. For plants where the union was not able to win a representation election, the case also raises several of the policy issues considered earlier in this chapter and in the discussion of "right-to-work" legislation in Chapter 10. Did workers vote against the union because of the employer's unfair

labor practices or because of personal preferences to remain nonunion? Do employer unfair labor practices dissuade workers from voting for a union or convince them of the need for a union to protect them from arbitrary exercise of employer power? Some of the research cited in this chapter indicates that the answers to these questions are not as obvious as is sometimes supposed.

SOURCES: Terry W. Mullins and Paul Luebke, "Symbolic Victory and Political Reality in the Southern Textile Industry: The Meaning of the J.P. Stevens Settlement for Southern Labor Relations," *Journal of Labor Research* III (Winter 1982): 81–88; and Gail Bronson and Jeffrey H. Birnbaum, "How the Textile Union Finally Wins Contracts at J.P. Stevens Plants," *Wall Street Journal,* October 20, 1980.

other union supporters may find themselves seems clear. From the perspective of the employer, the back-pay liability can be very small when the discharged worker takes a job soon after being dismissed—possibly much less than the costs of additional compensation that might be negotiated in a collective-bargaining contract after a successful organizing campaign. Some employers behave as if they believe that the expected costs of compliance with unfair labor-practice provisions of the NLRA exceed the expected costs of violations, a situation that raises doubts about how well the remedial objective of the NLRA is being attained in union-representation campaigns.

Several of the above issues concerning procedures and remedies were addressed in the Labor Law Reform bill that was sent to Congress in 1978. The bill provided for alterations in some NLRB procedures to cut down time delays and encouraged the use of temporary injunctive relief for employees (for example, the immediate reinstatement of a discharged worker) pending the resolution of unfair labor-practice charges. It also sought to raise the expected cost of violating the NLRA by providing for awards of up to double back pay for workers who had been discharged illegally and by barring companies that willfully violate NLRB orders from participating in federal contracts for a period of three years.[29] Nevertheless, after an intensive lobbying campaign, the legislation failed to secure passage in Congress.

Alert readers may have noticed a tension between this discussion of remedies for unfair labor practices and the discussion of the impact of NLRB regulation on the outcome of union election campaigns in the preceding section. If many of the activities that the Board regulates have no important effect on the outcome of the campaign, as indicated by some of the evidence that was reviewed in the previous section, then the *status quo* may be preserved even in the absence of remedies; that is, particular election results may have occurred independently of the behavior that the Board regulates and hence would not have been affected by the nature of the remedies available. Obviously, the intensity of the lobbying surrounding the relatively modest reforms proposed in the Labor Law Reform Bill of 1978 indicates that

---

[29] Experience with a similar provision regarding federal contracts in American equal-employment-opportunity policy suggests that the government is reluctant to enforce remedies of this nature.

this is not a view that is widely held among representatives of union and management.

Even if NLRB regulations have no effect on the vote, there may still be a case for remedies. For example, firing union leaders may not affect the vote, but it allows the employer to get rid of those employees he or she finds to be the most onerous and who might be the most militant if the employees gained collective-bargaining rights. In this case, the remedy of back pay and reinstatement serves to protect the "right" of nonunion employees not to be arbitrarily discharged *and* if a union wins the election, it protects the workers in place *prior* to the election (subject to normal turnover).

The NLRB also has the authority to remedy unfair labor practices by unions, although these constitute a relatively small proportion of its work load. The main remedy for a union unfair labor practice is the injunction. One section of the NLRA permits the Board to seek an injunction against mass picketing accompanied by violence, efforts to induce an employer to discriminate against individuals who are not union members, and other unfair practices. (The NLRA also permits the Board to enjoin employer unfair labor practices, but this occurs rarely.) Another section of the Act requires the NLRB to seek a temporary injunction if the union is charged with secondary boycott activity (a violation of Section 8(b)(4)), strikes in support of work assignment demands, or engages in unusually long picketing for the purpose of obtaining union recognition.

## Remedies for Refusal to Bargain

Violations of the duty-to-bargain are inherently difficult to remedy. When an employer simply refuses to negotiate with a union that has been certified by the NLRB, the union can only file an unfair-labor-practice charge and wait out the several years until the various appeals are exhausted. At that point, the remedy is an order to bargain, but from the perspective of the employees and the union this hardly restores the *status quo,* since several years of possible increases in benefits through collective bargaining have been forgone while the employer's refusal to bargain was being litigated. As an indication of the scope of this problem, during the 1970s about one quarter of union election victories did not result in the negotiation of a collective-bargaining agreement.[30]

Unions have urged that under the concept of adopting remedies that restore the *status quo* of labor relations, workers should be "made whole" for the benefits that were lost during the period of litigation. But what were those benefits? To determine what workers were owed would prejudge the outcome of the collective-bargaining process, for the Board would have to effectively decide what benefits would have been negotiated if collective bargaining had occurred over the period of litigation. This would constitute an even more intrusive impact on the substance of collective bargaining than the indirect

---

[30] William N. Cooke, *Union Organizing and Failure to Secure First Contracts* (Kalamazoo, MI: W. E. Upjohn Institute, 1985).

influence that the Board now has in its determinations of whether certain issues are mandatory or voluntary topics of bargaining. As a result, the Board has refused to adopt "make-whole" remedies for violations of the duty-to-bargain requirement.[31] The Labor Law Reform Bill of 1978, which was defeated in Congress, provided that when an employer refused to bargain for a first contract, employees would be "made whole" for their losses over the period on the basis of the average wages received by workers in companies where bargaining had occurred. Although the implication that newly established unions typically negotiate wages equal to the average union scale in their area is not well established, the passage of the proposed remedy would have substantially altered the bargaining power of new unions relative to employers. By raising the expected gains from union membership, the remedy presumably would have influenced the outcomes of union-representation elections.

## Labor-Relations Policy Issues in the Private Sector

The NLRB's unfair labor-practice rulings are inherently controversial, for as with many regulatory agencies, it is working in an area in which there is often intense disagreement over appropriate public policy. The evidence of steadily rising unfair labor-practice charges alone seems to indicate that there has been no general acceptance of the basic principle on which the National Labor Relations Act rests—that employees have the free right to join unions and engage in collective bargaining. It seems equally clear that there is no strong agreement between unions and management on their relative spheres of influence in industrial relations.

In this environment, the Board, like other regulatory agencies, is at times accused of bias in its decision making and of "making law" through the administrative process. In response to such charges, it is not uncommon for Board members to claim that their objectives are to make impartial decisions and to promote the public interest. Upon reflection, however, it is clear that impartiality is not a realistic goal for, or description of, the Board's rulings on unfair labor-practice charges. One reason for this is that the Board must often work with sketchy legislative guidance. Legislators frequently are unable to agree on the exact results that they want from a particular law and may choose statutory language that is deliberately imprecise in order to secure enough votes for passage of the legislation. As a result, a regulatory agency such as the Board can rarely implement legislation as written, because the language itself may not be clear. The breadth of the statutory language that defines unfair labor practices does not always provide a clear guide to interpreting specific factual situations. For example, under the NLRA it is an unfair labor practice for either management or labor to refuse to bargain collectively—but the statute provides little guidance on what constitutes a refusal to bargain.

[31] *Ex-Cell-O Corp.* 185 NLRB 107 (1970).

With only vague legislative guidance, the Board must spell out through administrative rule making the implications of the legislative language for specific factual situations that arise in the course of union organizing and collective bargaining. Under these circumstances, the best that a regulatory agency such as the Board can do is to attempt to promulgate rules that are consistent with the underlying purposes of the enabling legislation. Thus, in fashioning its decisions and rules, it is not unusual for the Board to emphasize congressional intent as much as particular legislative language.

A second difficulty of the impartiality standard is that the Board is administering public policy, which itself is not impartial. There are sharply conflicting values within any community concerning unions and collective bargaining. The presence of such conflicts creates a demand for some mechanism of choice or compromise between the values of different groups. The role of public policy is to specify this choice and, in the process, define the dominant values of the community at large. Therefore, some groups' values will always be compromised when a policy is chosen. The same may be said of the NLRB in administering labor-relations policy. Impartiality is basically impossible because any decision helps one party obtain its objectives over the other. This may explain why, after several decades of experience under the National Labor Relations Act, there is still considerable contention over public policy toward labor relations. With respect to the bias question, the key issue is really whether the NLRB "chooses the partiality imposed by the statute."[32]

## Compliance with the NLRA

Even when the NLRB chooses a course that is consistent with the statute, however, there remains the question of how the Board's regulatory strategy influences the behavior of unions, management, and employees. In the view of Congress, "[T]he ultimate purpose of the unfair labor-practice provisions of the National Labor Relations Act is to create a climate which will encourage voluntary compliance with the prohibitions stated in the Act."[33] Judging by the general trend in unfair-labor-practice charges, the Act has not yet achieved this purpose. The annual numbers of union-representation elections and unfair-labor-practice cases filed with the NLRB are graphed in Figure 11.1. The figure reveals a striking fact: The number of unfair-labor-practice charges filed by unions, employers, and workers grew very rapidly from the mid-1950s until the early 1980s, while the volume of labor relations activities subject to regulation remained relatively stable. Over fifty years of experience under the NLRA has not produced a consensus between labor and management in the United States on the country's labor relations policy.

The numbers of alleged unfair labor practices appear in Tables 11.2 and 11.3 on page 379. These data reveal two interesting features of regulatory activity under the NLRA. First, about 70 percent of the charges filed with the

[32] This point is made in Clyde W. Summers, "Politics, Policy-Making, and the NLRB," *Syracuse Law Review,* Second Annual Labor Law Conference, pp. 93–108.
[33] Senate Repo5[33]   Senate Report No. 95–628, 95th Cong. 2d Sess. (1978).

**Figure 11.1**    Representation Cases and Unfair-Labor-Practice Charges Filed with the National Labor Relations Board

SOURCE:  *Annual Report of the National Labor Relations Board,* Appendix Tables (various years)

Board allege violations of labor-relations laws by employers. Second, charges have increased in virtually all unfair-labor-practice categories and therefore cannot be traced to the effects of one or two key decisions on legal doctrine by the NLRB or the courts. Studies have also shown that very little of the growth can be explained by changes in the distribution of labor-relations activity from regions and industries where resistance to unions is low to sectors where resistance is high.[34]

Instead, during the 1970s there appears to have been a significant decline in compliance by employers with the nation's labor-relations laws and an increased tendency to file unfair-labor-practice charges by unions and workers. While some employers comply with the NLRA as a matter of principle, others appear to adopt a *strategic* approach to compliance. Strategic employers comply only if compliance maximizes expected profits; otherwise they do not. That is, the decisions of strategic employers are guided by the incentives to comply with the law. This begins to explain a puzzle raised by Figure 11.1: If employers found it in their self-interest to comply with the NLRA in the 1950s, why was it not in their self-interest to comply in the 1970s and 1980s? The answer may well be that the incentives to comply with the labor-relations laws have changed.

What are the benefits and costs of compliance with the NLRA? On the one hand, employers who comply avoid the remedies imposed for proven violations of the statute and the costs of litigating unfair-labor-practice charges. On the other hand, compliance may raise the odds of being unionized or increase the scope of a union contract, and the costs it avoids may seem

[34]  Myron Roomkin, "A Quantitative Study of Unfair Labor Practice Cases," *Industrial and Labor Relations Review* 34 (January 1981): 245–56; and Robert J. Flanagan, *Labor Relations and the Litigation Explosion* (Washington: The Brookings Institution, 1987), Chapter 3.

**Table 11.2**   Unfair Labor Practice Charges Against Employers, 1950–80 (numbers in parentheses are index numbers with 1950 = 100)

|      | 8(a)(1) | | 8(a)(2) | | 8(a)(3) | | 8(a)(4) | | 8(a)(5) | |
|------|---------|--------|--------|-------|--------|-------|------|--------|------|-------|
| 1980 | 31,281 | (699) | 979 | (172) | 18,315 | (570) | 1321 | (1347) | 9866 | (754) |
| 1970 | 13,601 | (304) | 592 | (103) | 9290 | (289) | 331 | (338) | 4489 | (343) |
| 1960 | 7723 | (173) | 820 | (144) | 6044 | (188) | 184 | (188) | 1753 | (134) |
| 1950 | 4472 | (100) | 570 | (100) | 3213 | (100) | 98 | (100) | 1309 | (100) |

Note:   Since any employer unfair labor practice is also automatically a violation of Section 8(a)(1) of the National Labor Relations Act, the 8(a)(1) column is also the total column.
SOURCE:   *Annual Report of the National Labor Relations Board,* Appendix Tables (various years).

**Table 11.3**   Unfair Labor Practice Charges Against Unions, 1950–80 (numbers in parentheses are index numbers with 1950 = 100)

|      | 8(b)(1) | | 8(b)(2) | | 8(b)(3) | | 8(b)(4) | | 8(b)(5) | | 8(b)(6) | | 8(b)(7) | |
|------|---------|--------|---------|-------|--------|-------|--------|-------|------|-------|------|-------|------|-------|
| 1980 | 8206 | (1137) | 1690 | (217) | 913 | (537) | 2987 | (876) | 46 | (418) | 42 | (124) | 600 | (220) |
| 1970 | 4055 | (562) | 1782 | (229) | 620 | (365) | 2290 | (672) | 22 | (200) | 25 | (74) | 409 | (150) |
| 1960 | 2196 | (304) | 1953 | (251) | 282 | (166) | 830 | (243) | 16 | (145) | 20 | (59) | 273 | (100) |
| 1950 | 722 | (100) | 778 | (100) | 170 | (100) | 341 | (100) | 11 | (100) | 34 | (100) | — | |

Note:   Definitions of unfair labor practices are in Table 13.1.
SOURCE:   *Annual Report of the National Labor Relations Board,* Appendix Tables (various years).

slight for two reasons. First, the remedies under the NLRA are weak and punitive remedies are forbidden. Second, remedial costs will only be incurred if a union or worker files a charge challenging the employer's actions *and* the NLRB finds that a violation has occurred. Neither action is certain. Moreover, the costs of compliance increased during the 1970s, when there was a substantial growth in the difference between the cost of union and nonunion labor. Employers thus had a growing incentive to avoid the costs of unionization.

Enforcement under the NLRA is initiated by the "victims." If an employer takes an action that is believed to violate the Act, an unfair-labor-practice charge must be initiated by a union or a worker. The filing of a charge is not automatic, however. A union must balance the gains from successfully challenging the employer's action against the likelihood that the challenge will receive a favorable ruling from the NLRB and the costs of litigating the charge. The incentives to file charges are muted by the absence of strong remedies under the act. During the 1970s, however, the growth of the union-nonunion labor-cost differential increased the benefits to union members of registering charges of unfair practices with the NLRB.

Empirical research indicates that much of the growth in unfair-labor-practice charges reported in Figure 11.1 is associated with the growing difference between union and nonunion wages, which lasted from about 1969 into the early 1980s. As employers had more to lose from compliance, they were more likely to violate the labor laws. As unions had more to gain from employer compliance, they were more likely to challenge employer behavior by filing unfair-labor-practice charges.[35]

The decline in the union-nonunion wage differential in the early 1980s undoubtedly contributed to the lower number of unfair-labor-practice charges in that period. The analysis of unfair-labor-practice charges suggests some difficulties of regulating labor relations. First, both compliance and the volume of unfair-labor-practice charges are often driven by incentives, such as the union-nonunion cost differential, that are beyond the direct influence of the NLRB. In evaluating trends in employee or employer behavior, it is difficult to distinguish what is motivated by ideology from what is rooted in economic incentive. Second, the NLRB could achieve more compliance if it had broader remedial authority. Third, the consistency of the Board's decisions may influence behavior. As membership on the NLRB changes, the Board's decisions on some issues change. Ambiguity about what the law requires can contribute to the level of charges and compliance.

There is an interesting international perspective on compliance with labor-relations laws. Managers in most European countries appear more accepting of the presence and role of unions, and the resistance of employers in the United States may in part result from the economic pressures associated with a more decentralized bargaining structure. Under the NLRB's representation election procedures, collective-bargaining relationships tend to be established on a company-by-company (and often plant-by-plant) basis, in contrast to Europe, where bargaining is frequently conducted on an industrywide or nationwide basis. Under decentralized bargaining agreements, employers cannot be assured that the costs they incur will be matched elsewhere, and the incentive to resist what is perceived as a threat to their competitive position may be strong. Moreover, the threat is real. American unions bargain hard, in part because American workers, in contrast to their European counterparts, are attracted to unions more on economic than ideological grounds.

## Deregulation and Other Policy Alternatives

In 1984 Lane Kirkland, the president of the AFL-CIO, and a few other union leaders suggested that unions would fare better if the National Labor Relations Act were repealed. In their view, the Act currently places more restrictions on the tactical freedom of unions than employers, and deregulation would permit unions to use secondary boycotts and other tactics currently prohibited by the NLRA. This view has not been adopted as official policy by the AFL-CIO, however. Interestingly, repeal of the NLRA has also been proposed by groups who want to weaken unions and, contrary to the labor leaders, believe that the Act is an important *source* of union power. A third

---

[35] See Flanagan, *Labor Relations and the Litigation Explosion*, Chapter 5.

group, composed mainly of academics, has proposed *selective deregulation,* the repeal of specific NLRB rules that have no important effect on the outcomes of labor-relations activities. Even irrelevant rules may encourage litigation, thereby adding to the workload of the NLRB and contributing to the delays in adjudicating charges. Some of the research on the impact of NLRB rules discussed earlier in this chapter indicates that there is considerable scope for selective deregulation.

**Complete deregulation.** The probable effects of completely deregulating labor relations depend in part on the possible development of legislative substitutes for the NLRA. For example, with deregulation of labor relations at the federal level there would be a larger regulatory role for state labor-relations statutes, which are often modeled on the NLRA. Regulation would not disappear, but the specific rules governing union organizing and collective bargaining in the private sector could vary substantially from state to state, just as the regulation of public-sector employers now does. Moreover, antitrust laws might constrain the tactics that unions could use if the NLRA were repealed. As we shall see shortly, the most common application of antitrust law to unions historically has been in controlling secondary boycotts. Union efforts to make greater use of secondary boycotts in a deregulated world might lead to an increase in the use of antitrust laws against labor.

Less drastic reforms of the NLRA have also been advanced. Several proposals for selective changes are reviewed below.

**Penalties.** We have already described the scope of the NLRB's remedial authority. It may construct remedies that are designed to *compensate* for damage resulting from unfair labor practices, but it may not construct remedies that go beyond compensation to *punish* the guilty party. One difficulty is that the Board has not used its authority to develop fully compensatory remedies. Its remedies typically try to compensate for damage suffered by individuals; for example, the Board awards back pay to workers who have been illegally discharged. The difficulty with the focus on the harm suffered by individual workers is that it ignores the external effects of the violations on the general effort to pursue union activities.[36] The firing of a union organizer may make everyone less willing to unionize.

Given the inability or unwillingness of the NLRB to construct fully compensatory remedies, many observers have proposed expanding the NLRB's remedial authority to permit it to assess punitive damages for serious violations. Under a punitive approach, the NLRB might be permitted to assess damages equal to two or three times the back pay of an illegally discharged worker, for example. As noted in the previous section, this would provide stronger incentives for compliance with the NLRA. (The previous section also showed that remedies are only one element of the package of

---

[36] Robert J. Flanagan, "Remedial Policy and Compliance with the NLRA," in *Proceedings of the Thirty-Ninth Annual Meeting of the Industrial Relations Research Association,* Barbara D. Dennis (ed.), (December 1986): 21–28.

incentives influencing compliance and litigation choices under the NLRA. The effects of the remedial policies of the NLRB may be swamped by the effects of factors that cannot be shaped by regulatory policy, such as differences between union and nonunion labor costs. Although a change in remedial policy might alter compliance choices, it would not guarantee a major change in the general level of compliance or of regulatory litigation.)

**Instant elections.** One recent proposal would require the NLRB to hold *instant elections* for union representation, as is now the practice in the Canadian province of British Columbia.[37] Most representation elections in the United States are now held two or more months after an election petition is filed. This campaign period produces about one third of all unfair-labor-practice charges in the United States, and as we noted earlier, the odds that employees will vote for union representation drop as the campaign period lengthens. Proponents of instant elections argue that if elections were held a few days after an election petition is filed, there would be little opportunity to violate the NLRA during representation elections. Others argue that the effect of instituting an instant election procedure may be to move up the timing and intensity of the campaign period. Employers often learn of union organizing attempts before a formal petition is filed with the NLRA and thus have the option of adopting resistance tactics sooner.

**Injunctions Against Employers.** The Taft-Hartley Act requires regional directors of the NLRB to obtain injunctions against secondary boycotts and certain other illegal union activities as soon as an unfair-labor-practice charge is filed with the Board. The injunction immediately halts the union's action pending resolution of the charge by the NLRB. When a union files a charge alleging an unfair-labor-practice by an employer, however, the employer's action is not halted until the Board resolves the charge, which can be a matter of months or even years. Many observers have proposed that in the interest of equitable treatment of both parties in labor relations, the NLRB should be required to seek injunctions when unfair labor-practice charges are filed against employers.

# Labor-Relations Policy Issues in the Public Sector

Public policy toward union-management relations is more varied and unsettled in the public sector than in the private sector. As noted in Chapter 10, a "doctrine of sovereignty" pervaded thinking about the rights of public employees to negotiate the terms and conditions of their employment. Public employees were therefore excluded from coverage under the NLRA, and even as recently as the late 1980s, some states and major cities did not have legislation specifying labor-relations policy beyond a general prohibition on strikes by public employees. At the other extreme, a few states had laws that

[37] Paul Weiler, "Promises to Keep: Securing Workers' Rights to Self-Organization Under the NLRA," *Harvard Law Review* 96 (June 1983): 1769–1827.

accorded some public employees the right to strike. Our purpose in this section is to summarize the main features of labor policy in the public sector and note important differences from policy in the private sector. A discussion of one of the most important issues, the question of the right-to-strike by public employees, is postponed until the discussion of labor disputes in Chapter 14.

Public employees along with private employees have a constitutional right to join unions. The difference between policy in the public and private sectors is in the scope of activities that unions can engage in. In developing policy, however, the same general issues are presented in each sector: procedures for recognition, the scope of the collective-bargaining rights that a union receives with recognition, permissible forms of labor-management conflict, and other dispute-settlement mechanisms.

In the federal government sector, labor-relations policy was initially specified in Executive Order 10988 issued by President Kennedy in 1962. The federal policy toward recognition bears some resemblance to private-sector policy under the NLRA in that a union that receives *majority* support from employees in a bargaining unit is granted *exclusive recognition,* which carries with it a right to negotiate agreements. Unlike the NLRA, however, the executive order also provides other levels of recognition. Unions representing up to 10 percent of the members of a bargaining unit receive *informal recognition,* which entitles them to be heard on employment issues by the management of a federal agency. Unions representing 10 to 50 percent of employees in a unit receive *formal recognition,* which entitles them to be consulted by management on changes in employment policy.

While the executive order seeks to guarantee the rights granted to employees and managers by proscribing certain unfair labor practices, it does not establish an independent agency to judge the merit of charges arising under the policy. Instead, charges are appealed to higher levels of federal management. However, the most substantial limitation of federal policy, both in comparison to policy in the private sector and in most states and localities, is the limitations on the topics appropriate for collective bargaining. Not only wages (which are set through the legislative process with reference to pay comparability studies, as described in Chapter 10), but also the methods of work, technology, mission of an agency, and many other issues affecting employment are excluded from bargaining.

Strikes are forbidden and strikes by federal employees have carried severe penalties. In 1981, for example, a strike by the Professional Air Traffic Controllers resulted in the dismissal of all striking workers, fines and jail sentences for several leaders of the strike, decertification of its status as bargaining representative by the Federal Labor Relations Authority, and ultimately, the bankruptcy of the union. While the courts recognize the right to belong to unions as a *constitutional* right, they have held that the right to strike is not a constitutional right and must be provided by statute. While such rights are now provided by the NLRA to private workers and, in a few instances, by state legislation to certain categories of public workers, federal workers do not have the right to strike.

While there is considerable variation in the policies pertaining to state and local government (SLG) employees, certain central tendencies have emerged. Recognition is normally established on the basis of representation elections similar to those that occur in the private sector and many of the rules followed by the NLRB are adopted. SLGs vary, however, in the rights accorded to recognized unions. In some jurisdictions, the public employer is authorized only to *meet and confer* with representatives of public employees. Under "meet-and-confer" legislation, the parties may sign a memorandum of understanding if some agreement is reached, but the public employer is not legally obligated to follow it. In other jurisdictions, the law permits collective negotiations in which labor and management are equal legal parties, and the outcome of negotiations can be a mutually binding labor agreement, as in the private sector. Moreover, the scope of permissible bargaining issues is typically not as constrained as in the federal sector.

With the difference in collective-bargaining rights between the public and private sectors, unions in the public sector generally prefer legislation imposing a legal duty to bargain in good faith. In the absence of a right to strike, the legal duty may be important to compel bargaining by recalcitrant public employers.

## Unions and the Antitrust Laws

When Congress passed the Sherman Antitrust Act—the nation's basic antitrust statute—in 1890, it established a national policy in favor of competition and its effects, including productive efficiency and a decentralization of economic decision making. The statute provided that "every contract, combination, . . . or conspiracy in restraint of trade or commerce among the several states . . . is illegal. . . . . Every person who shall monopolize, or attempt to monopolize, or combine or conspire with any other person or persons, to monopolize any part of the trade or commerce among the several states . . . shall be guilty of a misdemeanor''; treble damages were provided in the event of a violation. In the years since the passage of the Act, firms that have acquired a dominant position in an industry or have engaged in price-fixing or other anticompetitive practices have often been found to be in violation of the statute.

Over the same period, antitrust law has been applied infrequently to unions, despite the fact that unions in general advance the welfare of their members by monopolizing the sale of labor in a bargaining unit and otherwise reducing wage competition among workers. Some members of the public are often puzzled as to why certain union practices that appear to have an anticompetitive impact—for example, restrictive work practices and industry-wide collective-bargaining negotiations—and even unions themselves are not the target of antitrust enforcement. The Sherman Act itself contains no specific reference to unions and the intent of Congress concerning the application to unions is unclear from the legislative history. It is hardly surprising that unions stressed that they were not included in the statute while employers stressed that unions were not excluded.

Matters were not clarified with the passage of the Norris-LaGuardia Act in 1932 and the National Labor Relations Act in 1935. In providing statutory support for unions and collective bargaining, Congress established a policy that sanctioned large-scale labor organizations, despite the capacity of such organizations to interfere with the competitive objectives of the antitrust laws. This presented the federal courts with a significant policy dilemma: how are the national policies favoring competition, on the one hand, and unionization and collective bargaining, on the other, to be reconciled? Since the policy on unions and collective bargaining was established more recently, it is unlikely that Congress intended that it should be completely subordinated to antitrust policy. Yet neither the Norris-LaGuardia Act nor the NLRA contains language addressing the relationship between the newer labor legislation and the older antitrust legislation. Over the years, the federal courts have had considerable difficulty in accommodating the two policy objectives. Since almost any variety of union activity constitutes some sort of restraint on competitive market behavior, the problem faced by the courts has been to determine which types of market restraints resulting from union behavior are illegal under the antitrust statutes and which restraints are protected under the labor-relations statutes.

Even prior to the passage of the labor-relations statutes in the 1930s, the Sherman Act was not used against the more obvious signs of union monopoly power, such as efforts to organize all of the firms in an industry under the terms of a single collective-bargaining agreement. Instead, the Act was used to thwart "bad practices" such as the use of secondary boycotts.[38] In one early Sherman Act case, an action that became popularly known as the *Danbury Hatters'* case, the United Hatters of North America instituted a nationwide consumer boycott against an employer's products *and against individuals who purchased the employer's products,* after the failure of an organizing strike.[39] Because the union's action was not limited to the employer, it constituted a secondary boycott, and the Supreme Court ruled that this was a violation of the Sherman Act. Subsequent efforts by the labor movement to reverse this application of antitrust legislation culminated with the passage of the Clayton Act in 1914. Section 6 of the act provided that, "Nothing contained in the antitrust laws shall be construed to forbid the existence and operation of labor organizations from lawfully carrying out the legitimate objects thereof; nor shall such organizations, or the members thereof, be held or construed to be illegal combinations or conspiracies in restraint of trade, under the antitrust laws."[40] Although unions hailed Section 6 as an exemption from antitrust, the language of the statute was clear only on the point that the existence of union organizations was not by itself an antitrust violation. Section 6 said very little about the basic issue raised by the Danbury Hatters' decision—the tactical freedom permitted unions under the

[38] For an extensive discussion of this point, *see* Bernard D. Meltzer, "Labor Unions, Collective Bargaining, and the Antitrust Laws," *Journal of Law and Economics* 6 (October 1963): 152–223.

[39] *Loewe v. Lawlor,* 208 U.S. 274 (1908).

[40] *Clayton Antitrust Act* 6, 38 Stat. 730 (1914).

antitrust laws—and left it to the federal courts to interpret the key words *lawfully* and *legitimate*.

The limitations of Section 6 became clear with a 1921 Supreme Court decision in the Duplex Printing Press case.[41] The facts of the case were similar to those in the Danbury Hatters' case. A union of machinists that had organized all but one of the producers of a certain type of printing press instituted a secondary boycott of the lone holdout after a strike for recognition failed. The employer, Duplex Printing Press, alleged an antitrust violation, and the Supreme Court agreed. To the consternation of the unions, the Court held that the secondary boycott was not a "lawful" and "legitimate" activity, in large measure because it did not involve the direct relationship between an employer and his employees. From a legal perspective, the decision clearly indicated that the exemption of unions from antitrust was limited. From an economic perspective, the decision is of interest because of what it did *not* say. In the Duplex Printing Press decision, as in earlier decisions, the courts raised no objections to the scope of union organization or to the specific objective of extending union control over an entire industry. Even prior to the labor-relations legislation of the 1930s, applications of antitrust law were limited to questionable practices and the courts raised no antitrust barriers to union objectives of developing monopolistic market structures.

With the labor-relations legislation of the 1930s, the courts had to adopt a new approach to the relationship between unions and the antitrust laws. The Norris-LaGuardia Act broadened the definition of a legal labor dispute beyond the position taken in the Duplex case and freed most union tactics, including the secondary boycott, from judicial regulation. Nevertheless, the courts still faced a difficult issue in trying to decide when union activity violated antitrust law. It was not enough to restrict the application of antitrust to those union activities that have a product-market impact, since virtually all union labor-market activity with respect to wages, hours, fringe benefits, and so forth, is naturally linked to the product market so long as production costs influence prices. But these activities are basic to the existence of unions and are at the core of protected activity under the NLRA. The problem facing the courts is to determine the limits of labor's antitrust exemption when union activities have a serious noncompetitive impact on product markets.

The Court's struggle to resolve these conflicting national policies is still evolving, but certain tests that the Court applies in its efforts to balance conflicting interests are gradually becoming clear. With its power to inquire into the legitimacy of union activities apparently circumscribed by the Norris-LaGuardia Act and the NLRA, the Supreme Court in the early 1940s adopted the position that unions were exempted from the antitrust statutes so long as they acted in their self-interest and did not combine with nonlabor groups (usually businesses) to obtain their objectives. Combination with nonlabor groups was to be the main exception to labor's general exemption from the antitrust statutes. The application of this test seemed clear enough in situa-

---

[41]   *Duplex Printing Press v. Deering,* 254 U.S. 443 (1921).

tions like a case in which a local of the International Brotherhood of Electrical Workers formed an alliance with an electrical contractors' association to preclude the purchase of equipment that was not made by members of the local, and the Supreme Court found an antitrust violation.[42] However, if the union had achieved the same result alone, rather than in combination with a business group, there would not have been an antitrust violation. Generally, almost any interaction between a union and an employer in normal collective bargaining will have an impact on the product market. Contractual provisions influencing wages, fringe benefits, and the efficiency of production will all influence a firm's marginal costs and perhaps its market price. Since the bargaining that results in these effects involves a union in "combination with nonlabor interests," this test did not provide the clearest guide to the range of union behavior that was exempted from antitrust regulation.

In 1965, the Supreme Court modified this test in the *Jewel Tea* decision.[43] This case grew out of a collective-bargaining proposal by the butchers' union in Chicago that no meat sales occur in grocery stores after 6:00 P.M., despite the fact that most of the stores in the multiemployer bargaining unit remained open until 9:00 P.M. The owners of the Jewel Tea stores were opposed to the proposal, but when the other stores in the bargaining unit agreed to accept the rule, Jewel Tea realized that if it held out for its position in collective bargaining after the other stores signed the labor agreement, it alone would face a strike by the union while its competitors would continue to operate. Instead, Jewel Tea signed the new collective-bargaining agreement and then filed an antitrust action against the union.

There are two aspects of the Jewel Tea case that are particularly interesting. First, the "combination with nonlabor interests" standard is not relevant. Instead, the case involves an attempt by the butchers' union to impose, unilaterally, a practice that would reduce competition. Second, the case illustrates how the treatment of unions under the antitrust statutes may affect strategic behavior in collective bargaining. In this instance, Jewel Tea gave ground in collective bargaining that it hoped to regain later through an antitrust action. Therefore, the stance taken by the courts toward the union's antitrust vulnerability inevitably will feed back into behavior at the collective-bargaining table.

Recognizing that the "combination with nonlabor interests" standard was not relevant to the case, the Supreme Court ruled that the key question was whether the union's hours restriction was "intimately related" to the issues of "wages, hours, and other terms and conditions of employment" that are protected by the National Labor Relations Act, and, hence, are exempt from antitrust action. Although the court found that in this instance the union's demand did meet the "intimately related" test and did not constitute a Sherman Act violation, it clearly indicated that under the new standard, a union could lose its antitrust exemption by pursuing actions that did not meet

---

[42] *Allen-Bradley v. IBEW, Local 3*, 325 U.S. 797 (1945).
[43] *Local 189, Amalgamated Meatcutters v. Jewel Tea Company*, 381 U.S. 676 (1965).

the test. In the future, the Supreme Court would evaluate alleged union violations of the Sherman Act by balancing the relative impact of a union practice on the product market against the interests of union members in the practice on a case-by-case basis. At the present time, however, the Supreme Court is not very specific on the criteria that should be applied in establishing this balance.[44]

## Review Questions

1. Evaluate the advantages and disadvantages of removing the duty-to-bargain from the National Labor Relations Act. Would a duty-to-bargain obligation play a different role in the public sector? Explain.
2. "History here and abroad demonstrates the futility of trying to legislate good labor relations. There is much to be gained and little to be lost if we repeal all federal and state labor-relations statutes." Agree or disagree, and support your position.
3. As a member of a special commission, you are given authority to design a labor-relations statute to cover state and local employees in a state which has had only a public-sector strike prohibition in the past. You are instructed to develop a law that specifies the basic collective-bargaining rights that public employees are to have, prevents abuses of those rights, minimizes industrial strife, and is not too complex to administer well. What elements of labor-relations legislation governing the private sector (that is, the NLRA) would you include in your bill? What elements would you exclude? Why?
4. What aspects of public policy toward labor relations in the United States contribute to the large number of unfair-labor-practice charges?

## Selected Readings

Derek, Bok, "Regulation of Campaign Tactics in Representation Elections Under the NLRA," *Harvard Law Review,* 78 (November 1964): 38–141.

Robert J. Flanagan, *Labor Relations and the Litigation Explosion* (Washington: Brookings Institution, 1987).

Julius G. Getman, Stephen B. Goldberg, and Jeanne B. Herman, *Union Representation Elections: Law and Reality* (New York: Russell Sage Foundation, 1976).

William B. Gould, *A Primer on American Labor Law,* 2d ed. (Cambridge, MA: The MIT Press, 1986).

Bernard D. Meltzer, "Labor Unions, Collective Bargaining, and the Antitrust Laws," *Journal of Law and Economics* 6 (October 1963): 152–223.

Paul Weiler, "Promises to Keep: Securing Workers' Rights to Self-Organization Under the NLRA," *Harvard Law Review* 96 (June 1983): 1769–1827.

---

[44] In many respects, this involves making the same judgments that are made under the NLRA in evaluating whether unions and employers have a duty to bargain over novel collective bargaining proposals.

# CHAPTER 12

## Collective Bargaining:
## Structure and Tactics

In the past two chapters we reviewed the main features of labor unions and noted how the development and form of unions were constrained by, or related to, market forces and the legal environment. We now move into the study of the behavior and tactics of unions in their efforts to advance the economic position of union members. Later, in Chapter 16, we shall examine their actual impact.

Unions have always had two general methods for achieving their objectives—*legislative enactment and collective bargaining*. While unions in the United States use both methods, they rely less on legislative enactment than unions in other western countries, and their use of the political process is more frequently to influence the general environment of collective bargaining and union power than to secure specific benefits. We first examine some of the politically oriented methods through which unions pursue their objectives and then turn to the collective-bargaining process. The actual power that unions and management bring to the bargaining table is influenced by both the *structure* of bargaining and the specific bargaining *tactics* that each party can adopt. We begin the analysis, however, with a general discussion of market constraints faced by unions.

## Market Constraints Facing Unions

The variety of membership interests that a union is called upon to represent requires unions to play many roles in addition to negotiating wage rates for their members; hence, it is not surprising that there is no widespread agreement as to the specific objectives of unions. Nevertheless, it is generally agreed that in most cases unions value the wage and fringe benefits they can

**Figure 12.1**   Effects of Demand Growth and Wage Elasticity of Demand on Market Constraint Faced by Unions

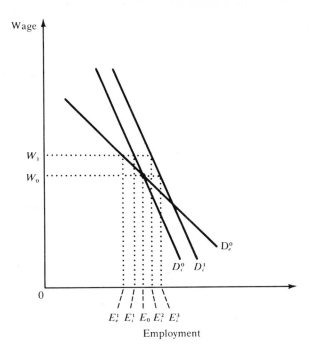

achieve for their members *and* their members' employment levels.[1] Therefore, the position and wage elasticity of the labor-demand curve are the fundamental market constraints that limit the ability of unions to accomplish their objectives.

Figure 12.1 shows two demand curves, $D_e^0$ and $D_i^0$, that intersect at an initial wage $W_0$ and employment level $E_0$. Suppose a union seeks to raise the wage rate of its members to $W_1$. To do so would require employment to fall to $E_e^1$ if the union faced the relatively elastic demand curve $D_e^0$, or to $E_i^1$ if it faced the relatively inelastic demand curve $D_i^0$. Other things equal, the more elastic the demand curve for labor, the greater the reduction in employment that will be associated with any given increase in wages.

Suppose now that the demand curve $D_i^0$ shifts out to $D_i^1$ while the negotiations are underway, due perhaps to growing demand for the final product. If the union succeeds in raising its members' wage to $W_1$, there will be no absolute decrease in employment in this case. Rather, the union will have only slowed the growth of employment to $E_i^2$ instead of $E_i^3$. Generally, the

---

[1]   As noted in Chapter 10, unions also negotiate important "workplace public goods" such as health, safety conditions, and limitations on managerial discretion. Since firms often incur costs in providing these "nonmonetary" benefits, they can produce the same trade-off with employment as wages and fringe benefits.

more rapidly the labor demand curve is shifting out (in), the smaller (larger) will be the reduction *in employment* or the reduction *in the rate of growth of employment* that will be associated with any given increase in wages. Hence, the unions' ability to raise their members' wages will be strongest in rapidly growing industries with inelastic labor-demand curves. Conversely, unions will be weakest in industries in which the demand for labor is highly wage-elastic and in which the demand curve for labor is shifting in.

Many actions that unions take are direct attempts to relax the market constraints that they face: either to increase the demand for union labor or to reduce the wage elasticity of demand for their members' services. The laws of derived demand discussed in Chapter 3 implied that four important determinants of the wage elasticities of demand were the price elasticity of demand for the final product, the ease of substituting other inputs for union members in the production process, the importance of labor compensation in total costs, and the responsiveness of the supply of other inputs to their prices. If price elasticities of demand for the final product are small, if it is difficult to substitute other inputs for union labor, if labor costs constitute a small percent of total costs, or if the prices of other inputs rise considerably if the demand for the inputs increases, a more inelastic demand for union labor will result.

As noted in Chapter 3, the wage elasticity of demand for labor is greater in the long run than in the short run. In the short run, for example, there may be only limited foreign competition in a given output market. As American automobile and steel manufacturers realized in the late 1970s and into the 1980s, however, in the long run foreign competition may increase, and the increased availability of foreign substitutes will raise the price elasticity of demand for domestic output. Likewise, production technologies may be fixed in the short run, while, in the long run, labor-saving technologies may be introduced. Finally, in the short run, the supplies of alternative inputs (for example, nonunion labor) may be fixed; in the longer run—due to immigration, or the training of other nonunion workers—supplies will tend to increase, providing more alternative inputs at lower cost to the employer. As a result, the market constraints unions face are more severe in the long run than in the short run; large wage gains won today may lead to substantial employment losses in the future. Such constraints often limit the economic gains that unions are able to win for their members.

# Legislative Enactment: Altering the Demand for Union Labor

Attempts by unions to shift the demand curve for union labor to the right and to reduce the wage elasticity of demand have taken many forms. Many of these attempts have *not* occurred through the collective-bargaining process *per se*. Rather, they have occurred through union support of legislation that, at least indirectly, achieved union goals and through direct public-relations campaigns to promote, or prevent decreases in, the demand for products made by union members.

## Policies to Shift the Product Demand Curve

Turning first to policies to *shift* out the demand curve for the final product, unions have lobbied for quotas or tariffs on foreign-produced goods that would limit the amount of these goods sold in the United States. Unions in the automobile, shoe, textile, and steel industries sought such forms of protection during the 1980s.

Other unions have opposed tax and deregulation policies that would reduce the demand for the services of their members (see Example 12.1). For example, with the deregulation of the airline industry in the United States in the late 1970s, competition between airlines increased substantially, stimulating mergers and other structural changes that threatened the employment of some union members in the industry. Rather than address the issues of job protection or compensation for displaced union members in collective-bargaining negotiations with individual airlines, the airline unions sought legislation requiring compensation for employees who lost their jobs as a result of economic adjustments in the industry. Officials in the industry argued that the cost of the proposal would retard the economic adjustments set off by deregulation.[2]

Union support of legislation is not the only way to shift product demand. Some unions have sought to directly influence people's tastes for the products they make. The International Ladies Garment Workers' Union (ILGWU) continually seeks to encourage people to "Buy American," featuring the song "Look For the Union Label" in some of its television ads. Unions in the printing trades encourage people to buy stationery and other printing products that carry a union "bug"—a small printed emblem signifying that the printing work was done in a union printing shop. When the deregulation of the telephone industry in 1983 ended AT&T's monopoly over long-distance telephone service, consumers were suddenly able to choose service from new nonunion companies, thus reducing the job security of union workers. The Communications Workers of America, the union representing workers at AT&T, initiated a "call union" drive, urging the public to buy long-distance services from unionized companies only.

## Policies to Limit Substitution of Other Inputs

Unions have also sought, by means of legislation, to pursue strategies that either directly restrict the use of other inputs that are potential substitutes for union members or increase the costs of using such inputs. (See Example 12.2.) For example, as noted in Chapter 3, labor unions have been among the

---

[2] Albert R. Karr, "Airlines, Unions Mount Lobbying Battle As Senate Nears Vote on Bill to Protect Jobs," *Wall Street Journal,* August 11, 1982, p. 42.

[3] For evidence that union support for minimum-wage legislation is often transformed into pro-minimum wage votes by members of Congress, *see* James Kau and Paul Rubin, "Voting on Minimum Wages: A Time-Series Analysis," *Journal of Political Economy* 86 (April 1978): 337–42; Jonathan Silberman and Garey Durden, "Determining Legislative Preferences on the Minimum Wage," *Journal of Political Economy* 84 (April 1976): 317–30; and James Cox and Ronald Oaxaca, "The Determinants of Minimum-Wage Levels and Coverage in State Minimum-Wage Laws" in *The Economics of Legal Minimum Wages* (Washington, DC: American Enterprise Institute for Public Policy, 1981).

**EXAMPLE   12.1**

## Legislative Enactment to Retain Union Jobs

Many of the factors influencing union jobs are not within the scope of normal bargaining structures or may involve factors that unions do not have the power to obtain through collective bargaining. In such situations, unions often turn to the legislative process to protect their interests. In addition to using legislation to shift demand for union services to the right or to reduce elasticity of demand for union labor, unions may also seek legislation that prevents a leftward shift in demand for union services.

For example, during the Congressional debate over proposed tax legislation in 1982, the Hotel Employees and Restaurant Employees International Union, which represented some 450,000 restaurant employees, lobbied extensively in the House of Representatives to block a provision passed in the Senate that would have eliminated half of the previous tax deduction for many business-related meals. By allowing only half of the price of such meals to be deducted from taxable income, the legislation would have increased the effective price of the meals, led to a reduction in the number of meals consumed, and led to a reduction in the derived demand for the services of the members of the union. The union estimated that between 55,000 and 150,000 jobs held by union members would be lost if the legislation passed. Yet it was an issue that could not be addressed through the normal collective-bargaining process in the industry. Indeed, in this instance, the union of restaurant employees, restaurant owners (who would suffer a loss of business if the proposal was passed), and many business groups (who stood to lose a valuable tax deduction) were of one mind in opposing the proposed change.* In other industries business and labor had a common interest in seeking legislative protection against imports.

* The 1986 tax reform limited deductibility of business-related meals to 80 percent of their cost.
SOURCE: Edward Cowan, "Meal Tax Bill Fought by Union," *New York Times*, July 27, 1982.

primary supporters of higher minimum wages.[3] While such support may be motivated by their concern for the welfare of low-wage workers, increases in the minimum wage *do* have the effect of increasing the relative costs to employers of low-skilled nonunion workers, thereby increasing the costs of the products they make and reducing employers' incentives to substitute (perhaps by moving their plants) nonunion workers for more skilled union workers.

Another example of a legislative strategy to discourage the substitution of cheaper inputs is union support for the Davis-Bacon Act. This act, a form of "prevailing wage" legislation, requires that wages paid to construction workers on projects that are federally financed, federally assisted through loans, or whose financing is insured by the federal government, be set at least equal to the prevailing wage in the area as determined by the Secretary of Labor. Since, typically, the prevailing wage has been set equal to the union wage

## EXAMPLE   12.2

# Domestic-Content Legislation

One approach to reducing the elasticity of demand for union services is to reduce the scope of substitution for union labor available to employers. In some instances, this is done by negotiating restrictive work practices in collective bargaining. In many instances, however, producers may seek to minimize costs by having some of the production done abroad at a lower labor cost. Some unions have sought a legislative defense against such practices in the form of *"domestic content" legislation* (that is, legislation requiring a certain proportion of a regulated product to be domestically produced).

Since 1890, for example, the Copyright Act has included a clause that books written in English by authors living in the United States must be printed in the United States or Canada in order to receive full copyright protection. This clause has been supported by unions in the printing trades to prevent the printing of such books abroad in countries with lower labor costs. In 1982, the U.S. Department of Labor estimated that in the absence of this provision, between 78,000 and 172,000 jobs in the printing trades would be lost to low-wage printing facilities in Asia.

Recently, the United Automobile Workers (UAW), historically a proponent of free international trade, has been concerned about the impact of foreign automobile production on the employment prospects for American autoworkers. A growing fraction of automobiles sold in the United States is produced in foreign countries and an increasing proportion of the components of automobiles sold by American manufacturers is made abroad. During 1982, the UAW supported legislative proposals to require both domestic and foreign automobile manufacturers with substantial sales in the United States to increase the share of their production in the United States. One proposal, for example, would have required firms with annual sales in the United States of 100,000 automobiles in 1986 to produce domestically or purchase auto components worth 10 percent of the value of sales. The "domestic-content" requirement would rise with the level of sales, reaching a maximum requirement of 90 percent of sales for producers with sales of 900,000 or more. If this proposal were to be enacted, what would you expect the impact to be on employment and auto sales in the United States?

SOURCES:  "Copyright Act Rule Cleared by Congress," *AFL-CIO News*, July 10, 1982, p. 5. "Auto Jobs Bill Pushed in House," *AFL-CIO News*, September 25, 1982, p. 1.

scale, the net effect is to eliminate any cost advantage that nonunion construction workers might have, thereby discouraging the substitution of nonunion for union labor.[4] Since the Davis-Bacon Act was passed in 1931, almost 100 similar "prevailing wage" statutes have been passed in fields such as education, health, housing, and transportation—and 35 states have passed "little Davis-Bacon statutes" covering state construction projects.

[4] John Gould, *Davis-Bacon Act: The Economics of Prevailing Wage Laws* (Washington, DC: American Enterprise Institute, 1971) and Armand Thieblot, Jr., *The Davis-Bacon Act* (Philadelphia, PA: Industrial Research Unit, Wharton School, 1975) contain more complete descriptions of the Act and its administration.

A third example of how unions can use legislative means to influence the demand for union labor (by reducing substitution possibilities) is the union position on immigration policy. The AFL-CIO has always been quite explicit about its concern that immigrants depress wages and provide competition for unionized American workers. Indeed, with respect to the problem of illegal immigration in the early 1980s, the AFL-CIO asserted that:

> while the nation should continue its compassionate and humane immigration policy, it is apparent that large numbers of illegal immigrants are being exploited by employers, thus threatening hard-won wages and working conditions. U.S. immigration policy should foster reunification of families and provide haven for refugees from persecution, while taking a realistic view of the job opportunities and the needs of U.S. workers.[5]

It is not surprising then, that unions have historically supported legislation restricting immigration, especially during recessionary periods.[6]

Finally, there are several ways in which unions or employee associations can seek legislatively to restrict entry into an occupation. One way is to control the accreditation of outside institutions that provide training; the American Medical Association's accreditation of medical schools is an example of this. Another way to restrict the entry of potentially cheaper substitutes into an occupation is to lobby for state occupational licensing laws, which limit the practicing of a given occupation to only those who meet certain standards.[7] Finally, some cities—usually reacting to the political influence of unions—have adopted codes that require union labor to be used in any construction or building-repair projects within their jurisdictions.

## The Structure of Collective Bargaining

Despite the importance of legislative influences on the environment in which unions operate, most union achievements are obtained through the process of *collective bargaining*. Indeed, unions often use collective-bargaining approaches to accomplish the very same goals of restricting the substitution of other inputs for union labor. Some unions, notably those in the airline, railroad, and printing industries, have sought and won guarantees of minimum crew sizes. (For example, at least three pilots have been required to fly certain jet aircraft.) Such *staffing requirements* prevent employers from substituting capital for labor.[8] Other unions have won contract provisions that

---

[5] *The AFL-CIO Platform Proposals: Presented to the Democratic and Republican National Conventions 1980* (Washington, DC: AFL-CIO, 1980): 14.

[6] F. Ray Marshall, Allan King, and Vernon Briggs, *Labor Economics: Wages, Employment, and Trade Unionism* 4th ed. (Homewood, IL: Richard D. Irwin, 1980): 196.

[7] *See,* for example, Alex Maurizi, "Occupational Licensing and the Public Interest," *Journal of Political Economy,* 82 (March/April 1974): 399–413.

[8] In cases in which these requirements call for the employment of workers whose functions are redundant—for example, fire stokers in diesel-operated railroad engines—*feather-bedding* is said to take place. For an economic analysis of this phenomenon, see Paul Weinstein, "The Featherbedding Problem," *American Economic Review* 54 (May 1964): 145–52.

prohibit employers from *subcontracting* for some or all of the services they provide. For example, a union representing a company's janitorial employees may win a contract provision preventing the firm from hiring external firms to provide it with janitorial services. Such provisions may limit the substitution of nonunion for union workers. Craft unions, especially those in the building and printing trades, often negotiate specific contract provisions that restrict the functions that members of each individual craft can perform, thereby limiting the substitution of one type of union labor for another. Finally, craft unions also limit the substitution of unskilled union labor for skilled union labor by establishing rules about the maximum number of *apprentice* workers—workers who are learning the skilled trades—that can be employed relative to the experienced *journeymen* workers.

Collective bargaining consists of negotiations between representatives of labor and management over the terms and conditions of employment to which both parties will be bound for the duration of the labor agreement that normally results from such negotiations. This process drastically alters the determination of the employment relationship. Under the market mechanisms that we have examined earlier in the book, the employment relationship emerges from the interaction of many buyers (firms) and sellers (workers), or through the interaction of a single employer and many workers (monopsony).[9] Under collective bargaining, the employment relationship is established through the interaction of a single representative of employee interests (the union) and a single representative of employer interests—a market structure known as *bilateral monopoly*.[10] Economic analysis cannot determine the exact wage and employment level that occurs under bilateral monopoly (see Appendix 12A). Where the final settlement ends up depends on the bargaining power and negotiating skills of *each* side; that is, the interests of *both* parties must be considered in determining the final outcome of bargaining. Some theoretical analyses using diverse assumptions that do not always correspond well to the realities of collective bargaining conclude that labor and management will "split the difference" and end up in the middle of the contract zone (the range of possible wage bargains), but the limited empirical evidence on this question reaches a different conclusion.[11] (See Example 12.3.)

Where the bargaining parties end up in the contract zone depends on each party's bargaining power, but a precise operational definition of this concept has proved elusive over the years. Bargaining power reflects the ability of either party to secure a labor agreement on one's own terms. One party's inducement to agree with another's proposal in negotiations depends on the cost of disagreeing with the proposal relative to the costs of agreeing with it.[12] The larger the costs of disagreeing relative to the costs of agreeing, the more

[9] See discussion in Chapter 3.

[10] As will become apparent, there may be several employers or unions participating in negotiations. The key feature of bilateral monopoly is that each side adheres to a single set of bargaining demands.

[11] Frederick Zeuthen, *Problems of Monopoly and Economic Warfare*, Reprints of Economic Classics Series (Fairfield, NJ: Augustus M. Kelley, 1968); John Nash, "The Bargaining Problem," *Econometrica* 18 (April 1950): 155–62.

[12] This is the approach developed in Neil W. Chamberlain and James W. Kuhn, *Collective Bargaining*, 2d ed. (New York: McGraw-Hill, 1965): 162–90.

**EXAMPLE    12.3**

## Do Labor and Management Split the Difference?

Where do negotiators end up in the contract zone? Does one party or the other tend to "dominate" in collective bargaining, or do the parties simply "split the difference" and settle halfway between their respective preferred positions? It is very difficult to obtain the data needed to answer these interesting questions, but two studies have made a start.

Each study compared data on the initial wage demands of labor and management in collective bargaining with the final wage increases agreed to. One study examined data from negotiations with the Tennessee Valley Authority (TVA), while the other used data from negotiations in the public sector involving unions of teachers, police, and firefighters. In each case, unions made larger concessions during negotiations than did management. In the TVA negotiations, unions demanded wage increases averaging 11 percent, employers offered increases averaging 3 percent, and the final settlements averaged 6 percent. The comparable figures for the public-sector negotiations were 23 percent, 8 percent, and 12 percent. Taken at face value, the data seem to suggest that collective-bargaining settlements tend to be closer to the employer's end of the contract zone.

Unfortunately, it is not clear that these data can be extrapolated "at face value" to collective-bargaining negotiations generally. In contrast to negotiations in the private sector, strikes were illegal in both the TVA and public-sector samples used in the studies. Unions may have bluffed—demanded more than their preferred amount—more than management in an effort to compensate for their reduced power.

SOURCES:  Roger Bowlby and William Shriver, "Bluffing and the 'Split the Difference' Theory of Wage Bargaining," *Industrial and Labor Relations Review* 31 (January 1978): 161–71; Daniel S. Hamermesh, "Who 'Wins' in Wage Bargaining?" *Industrial and Labor Relations Review* 26 (July 1973): 1146–49.

likely one party is to accept the other's proposal. These costs are influenced to a significant degree by the structure and tactics of collective bargaining. In the private sector, these costs are influenced to a large extent by the factors governing the elasticity of the derived demand for labor, which has an important influence on the ability to strike (in the case of unions) or to withstand a strike (in the case of employers). In the public sector, these considerations apply to a certain extent (since there have been many work stoppages despite the general illegality of the strike), but factors affecting the political influence of labor relative to management also have an important bearing on bargaining power. These factors are discussed in the following two sections.

## Bargaining Structure in the Private Sector

Bargaining structure refers to the scope of worker and employer interaction in an issue of labor relations. In any given industry, however, the bargaining structure consists of a spectrum of units defined by an often complicated set of economic, legal, and social relationships. Most bargaining structures have at their base *informal work groups*—groupings of the rank and file defined by technology and the organization of production—whose aspirations help to define a union's goals and the acceptability of a collective-bargaining agreement. An *election unit* (a group of jobs whose incumbents are eligible to vote in a union-representation election) typically consists of several informal work groups, and its scope is formally determined or endorsed by the National Labor Relations Board (NLRB) as part of the process of running a union-representation election. The unit for which collective-bargaining negotiations actually take place is called the *negotiation unit,* and, in many instances, this will be larger than the election unit, owing to industrywide or multiplant agreements. In some instances, emulation or pattern-following may result in a *unit of direct impact* that exceeds the scope of the negotiating unit.[13] We discuss the election and negotiation units below.

**Election unit.**   When a union petitions the NLRB for a representation election, the National Labor Relations Act (NLRA) requires the Board to conduct the election in "a unit appropriate for such purposes"—the election district. Often the district is jointly agreed to by the union and the employer involved, but when there is disagreement between them, the NLRB has the authority to determine a group of jobs that constitute an appropriate unit. Individuals employed in those jobs are entitled to vote in the representation election. In requiring the NLRB to choose *an* appropriate unit, the law recognizes that there may be several potentially appropriate units (for example, an occupational group within a plant, an entire plant, a group of plants within a company, an entire company). The board may therefore face considerable choice in its unit determination activities.

These determinations can have a significant influence on the ultimate power relationships in the industry for several reasons. First, the scope of the unit may determine whether or not an election is held (since unions must show evidence of support from at least 30 percent of the employees in the unit before an election can occur), and if it is, whether the union wins the representation election. The scope of the unit can therefore determine whether employment conditions in an industry will be subject to collective bargaining. When there is a disagreement between an employer and a union over the scope of an election unit, the employer typically argues for a larger unit, since unions tend to have more difficulty winning elections in relatively large units, where there is likely to be diversity of skills, interests, and objectives among employees.

Second, when more than one union is campaigning for representation rights, the unit that the NLRB determines to be appropriate for the purposes

---

[13]   These distinctions were suggested in Arnold R. Weber, "Stability and Change in the Structure of Collective Bargaining," *Challenges to Collective Bargaining,* Lloyd Ulman (ed.), (Englewood Cliffs, NJ: Prentice-Hall, Inc., 1967).

of the election may influence *which* union wins the election. A craft union that specializes in representing workers performing a particular occupation will find it easier to win an election if the unit is confined to the set of jobs in that occupation than if the unit is plantwide or companywide.

Third, the scope of the unit can also influence the effectiveness of a union's representation if it wins. We noted in Chapter 10 that the task of running a union organization effectively is easier if the preferences of the membership are relatively homogeneous. Larger units often include employees with rather diverse skills, interests, and objectives—raising the possibility that the union will encounter conflicts of interest among its members and internal opposition to its efforts to negotiate and administer a collective-bargaining agreement that is viewed as fair by a majority of the membership. Smaller, more homogeneous units are likely to increase the effectiveness of union representation and to accord individual members a greater opportunity to have their views on union policy heard.

Finally, to the extent that the election unit becomes the negotiating unit, the scope of the election unit will also influence the cost of labor relations to the employer. From the perspective of an employer, fragmented bargaining structures, in which employees are distributed among many small bargaining units and often represented by different unions, raise the costs of negotiating and administering labor agreements. More time goes into multiple negotiations, there are more opportunities for negotiations to break down and a strike to occur, and there is often the possibility that a strike in any one bargaining unit will influence operations in other units. Fragmented bargaining units represented by different unions also increase the likelihood of jurisdictional disputes between different unions over the right to represent employees performing new work or whose status may otherwise be uncertain. Employers must balance these considerations against the threat of a much larger work stoppage when bargaining is conducted in broader units.

For all of these reasons, the determination of an appropriate election unit can be a matter of substantial importance in labor relations. Yet the language of the NLRA provides the NLRB with little guidance concerning the criteria or standards for such determinations. Section 9(b) simply states that "... the unit appropriate for the purposes of collective bargaining shall be the employer unit, craft unit, plant unit, or subdivision thereof. . . ."[14] Over the years the NLRB has articulated a standard of *community of interest,* in which proposed units would be evaluated according to the extent to which they

---

[14]  The NLRA also does not permit the Board to include plant guards in a unit with other employees, forbids the inclusion of professional and nonprofessional employees in a single unit "unless a majority of the professional employees vote for inclusion," and permits craft employees to petition to establish a separate unit even if they were at one time included in a broader unit (for example, in an election establishing representation rights for an industrial union). However, the NLRB has often shown a preference for stability and thus has often denied craft employees' petitions to leave their industrial union bargaining units. In these cases, the NLRB must find a balance between the stability of large units and individual workers' rights to choose a bargaining representative. See D. Quinn Mills, *Labor-Management Relations,* 3d ed., (New York: McGraw-Hill, 1986): 125–26.

included workers sharing common interests and excluded groups of workers whose interests would conflict. But what determines the community of interest? The NLRB considers factors that include the similarity of work performed, similarity of compensation and working conditions, skill levels, geographic proximity, integration of production processes, common supervision or labor-relations policy, history of collective bargaining, desires of employees, and extent of union organization. But the variety of factors considered—as well as the fact that when considered separately they may not all give consistent guidance on the appropriate unit size—highlights the lack of precision in the determination of election units.

As already noted, negotiating units are often larger in scope than the election unit. Nevertheless, the NLRB's policies in determining election units have undoubtedly contributed to the fact that collective bargaining in the United States is generally decentralized, with over 150,000 labor agreements in force in the private and public sectors combined. When the interests of labor and management concerning unit size conflicted during the early years of the NLRA, the Board tended to give more weight to the preferences of unions for relatively small units to encourage the formation of unions and the spread of collective bargaining. In the Taft-Hartley Act amendments to the NLRA, Congress prohibited the NLRB from using the extent of employee support for unions as the sole criterion for determining an election unit. Subsequently, the Board (supported by the federal appeals courts) has held that extent of organization is nevertheless one of the factors that may be considered in determining which employees are eligible to vote in a representation election. After leaning toward the establishment of multiplant election units during the 1950s, the NLRB has increasingly permitted single-plant election units, even when the "plant" may be one of several stores operated with a common personnel policy by a single company in a single metropolitan area. In some cases a group of employees within a store may be found to be an appropriate election unit.

**Negotiation unit.** The outcome of collective bargaining can heavily depend on the structure of negotiating units—the size and scope of the units that conduct collective bargaining. The sheer number of agreements, already noted, is suggestive of the decentralization of the collective-bargaining structure in the United States. This decentralization is one of the more distinctive differences between the industrial relations system in the United States and in Europe, where collective bargaining is more frequently conducted at the industry, regional, and even national level. (See Example 12.4.) This difference, in part, reflects the public policy toward election units discussed in the previous section. Because so many election units are proposed and accepted at the plant and company level, collective bargaining tends to occur much closer to the workplace in the United States than in many European countries. For different reasons, negotiations also tend to occur at the plant or company level in Japan (see Example 12.5). However, a more complete analysis of collective bargaining in the United States requires that we look

**EXAMPLE    12.4**

## Centralized Collective-Bargaining Structures in Europe

European negotiating units are typically much broader than those in the United States, and, as a result, collective bargaining is more centralized. In most countries, collective bargaining occurs at the industry or regional level, and in some Scandinavian countries, bargaining normally occurs between the labor *federation* (that is, the equivalent of the AFL-CIO in the United States) and a management federation at the national level—with one agreement determining the employment conditions for all workers who belong to unions that are members of the federation. Centralized collective-bargaining agreements change the character of labor agreements and labor relations in interesting ways.

First, the scope of labor agreements resulting from relatively centralized collective-bargaining negotiations tends to be more limited than the scope of most agreements negotiated in the United States. It is very difficult for the language of a single collective-bargaining agreement to cope effectively with the wide variety of labor-relations problems faced by the many plants or industries covered by the agreement. On issues pertaining to work rules and safety, for example, a single contractual rule is unlikely to address the underlying heterogeneity of circumstances adequately. As a result, negotiators tend to focus on issues, such as wages and hours of work, that have a common meaning and method of application across companies. As a result, many topics that are of considerable concern to workers, but which vary in nature across firms, are not addressed by the official labor agreements.

Second, collective bargaining in Europe tends to produce contractual wage rates that are set sufficiently low to keep the least efficient firms covered by an agreement in business. (Historically, American unions have been willing to let some firms that are unable to meet their wage standards go out of business.) One result of this is *wage drift*—the tendency of the actual earnings received by workers to increase more rapidly than the contractual wage rates established in the collective-bargaining agreement. In many European countries, contractual wage rates are therefore not a reliable indicator of the true path of wage costs. Drift appears to result, in part, from decisions by employers in high-productivity firms to pay higher wages than the labor agreement requires, to attract or retain a high-quality work force. (With decentralized collective bargaining, as in the United States, the wage provisions of labor agreements are more likely to reflect the economic circumstances of individual companies.) Since drift commonly increases when the demand for labor is high and decreases in recessions, it appears to be a mechanism through which wages are brought into equilibrium irrespective of the contractual provisions of labor agreements.

The relationship between the wage provided for in a collective-bargaining agreement and the wage actually paid in Europe contrasts sharply with the situation in the United States where, under the National Labor Relations Act, unionized employers cannot unilaterally raise wages without first bargaining with the union. In some cases in the United States, unions that have been concerned with the internal political difficulties raised by altering traditional relative-wage relationships between different groups of members have refused to permit employers to voluntarily grant wage increases to selected groups of workers to increase the supply of workers with relatively scarce skills.

Third, workers tend to develop alternative institutional mechanisms to seek representation for issues that are not addressed by the labor agreements produced by centralized negotiating units. In the United Kingdom, a second and decidedly unofficial tier of bargaining developed at the plant level during the 1960s, when bargaining structures were more centralized than they are today. Shop stewards bargained with British plant management over issues (such as the pace of work, safety, and work assignments) that were addressed either inadequately or not at all in the official agreements (usually negotiated at the industry or regional level). Pressure at the second tier of bargaining can also be a source of wage drift. In Sweden, a country generally known for its record of labor peace, there was an outbreak of "wildcat" (unofficial) strikes in the late 1960s protesting the modest wage settlements resulting from centralized collective bargaining and demanding independent bargaining rights. More importantly, over the past twenty-five years, unions representing white-collar and professional employees have broken away from the main federation and formed separate federations that represent their own interests more effectively.

SOURCES:  Everett M. Kassalow, *Trade Unions and Industrial Relations: An International Comparison* (New York: Random House, 1969); T. L. Johnston, *Collective Bargaining in Sweden* (London: George Allen & Unwin, 1962).

---

beyond the election unit to the forces that influence the size and power of negotiating units.

With such a large number of separate collective-bargaining situations, one might wonder about the source of the monopoly power that is sometimes attributed to unions. In fact, union membership is not distributed evenly. Almost half of all unionized employees in the private sector work under the relatively small number of agreements (approximately 1500) that cover at least 1000 workers each and are henceforth referred to as major agreements. Moreover, the content of these major collective-bargaining agreements in the United States is determined in a wide array of bargaining structures (see Table 12.1). Thirty percent of the major contracts are determined in *single plant* negotiations between an employer or plant manager and a union at the plant level; another 30 percent are established through *multiplant* negotiations with an employer that will affect several plants of the same company; and some are conducted at the company level and will affect all of the operations. (The tens of thousands of agreements covering less than one thousand workers are largely the outcome of negotiations at the plant or company level.) The most prevalent bargaining structure among the "major" units, however, is *multi-employer* bargaining, in which a group of employers negotiate jointly with a union or group of unions to reach an agreement that will cover all workers in an industry. Over 40 percent of major collective-bargaining agreements (see Table 12.1), covering about half of the workers included in major contracts

**Table 12.1**   Structure of Major Bargaining Units, by Industry, 1980[a]
(percent distribution)

| | All Agreements | | Single Employer | | | Multiemployer |
|---|---|---|---|---|---|---|
| | Number | Percent[b] | Total | Single Plant | Multiplant | |
| All Industries | 1,550 | 100% | 60% | 30% | 30% | 40% |
| Manufacturing | 750 | 100 | 86 | 53 | 33 | 14 |
| Food | 79 | 100 | 63 | 37 | 27 | 37 |
| Apparel | 31 | 100 | 19 | 6 | 13 | 81 |
| Chemicals | 36 | 100 | 100 | 89 | 11 | 0 |
| Primary metals | 88 | 100 | 99 | 55 | 44 | 1 |
| Machinery (nonelectrical) | 81 | 100 | 98 | 68 | 30 | 2 |
| Electrical machinery | 83 | 100 | 97 | 66 | 31 | 3 |
| Transportation equipment | 112 | 100 | 96 | 40 | 56 | 4 |
| Nonmanufacturing | 800 | 100 | 35 | 8 | 27 | 65 |
| Communications | 80 | 100 | 100 | 5 | 95 | 0 |
| Construction | 327 | 100 | 1 | c | 1 | 99 |
| Hotels and restaurants | 31 | 100 | 10 | 3 | 6 | 90 |
| Retail trade | 123 | 100 | 53 | 11 | 41 | 47 |
| Services | 66 | 100 | 29 | 14 | 15 | 71 |
| Utilities | 81 | 100 | 96 | 26 | 70 | 4 |

[a] Labor Agreements covering 1000 workers or more, as of January 1, 1980.
[b] Rows may not add to 100 percent because of rounding error.
[c] Less than 0.5%.
SOURCE:   U.S. Bureau of Labor Statistics, *Characteristics of Major Collective Bargaining Agreements, January 1, 1980*, Bulletin 2095 (Washington, DC: U.S. Government Printing Office, May 1981): p. 19.

(and about a quarter of all union workers in the private sector), are negotiated in the context of multiemployer bargaining structures.

To evaluate alternative bargaining structures, it is useful to analyze the factors that tend to determine structure. In fact, bargaining structures are usually affected by a complex of legal determinations (discussed in the previous section), market forces, technological factors, representational factors, and even the nature of bargaining issues.[15] It is particularly important in collective bargaining that different bargaining structures imply different degrees of bargaining power. For this reason, changes in bargaining structures are among the most bitterly contested issues in labor relations.

To analyze what lies behind the preferences for different bargaining structures by unions and employers, one must appreciate the main economic considerations underlying bargaining power. For management in the private sector, the main consideration is to reduce the risk of losing business to competitors, both in the short run (during a strike) and in the long run (because other firms have lower labor costs). Therefore, in the short run, an employer's bargaining power (that is, the ability to take a strike) depends on

[15]   These factors are discussed extensively in Weber, "Stability and Change in the Structure of Collective Bargaining."

**EXAMPLE    12.5**

# Bargaining Structure and Labor Relations in Japan

On the surface, the structure of collective bargaining in Japan bears some resemblance to bargaining in the United States. The degree of unionization is about the same—around 22 percent of the labor force in the early 1980s—and bargaining is highly decentralized. Over 90 percent of the unions and union members in Japan are organized on an enterprise (company or plant) basis; bargaining on a craft or industrial basis is unusual.

Two factors appear to account for the enterprise-based bargaining structure. First, production support organizations, which were formed in each enterprise during World War II, served as a preliminary union structure and evolved into unions following the war. Second, an enterprise-based bargaining structure was consistent with a distinctive feature of Japanese personnel practice in larger companies—lifetime employment commitments. Contrary to practice in the United States and other Western countries, it is not unusual for the 20 to 30 percent of Japanese workers in large firms to spend their entire work life in a single company. The company effectively assumes much of the risk of employment uncertainty in exchange for the worker's heightened commitment to the goals of the organization. One consequence of this personnel system is that layoffs and quits are much lower in Japanese companies than in most Western companies; another is that there is much less mobility during the course of the average worker's work life. In forming unions, then, workers have been most concerned with negotiations that affect their company or plant, which is their effective labor market under this unusual personnel system. Indeed, there is a general resistance on the part of both employers and employees to the intervention of central or industrial unions whose members are not all part of a particular enterprise, and like the AFL-CIO in the United States, Japanese labor federations are not directly involved in collective bargaining.

All employees in an enterprise, irrespective of skill or occupational position, are members of the enterprise union. It is unusual to find, as one does in the United States and Europe, several unions in a company representing workers with different skills. In fact, the enterprise unions in Japan have worked to eliminate many of the distinctions between manual and nonmanual workers in terms of wages and social status, and have institutionalized seniority-based wage systems.

One apparent advantage of the enterprise-based bargaining structure is that Japanese unions are apparently better able to address issues relating to the operation of the enterprise and technical innovation than are their American and European counterparts. On the other hand, wages and other working conditions are less likely to be consistent throughout an industry or the economy. We have seen how the operation of a competitive labor market will tend to equalize the wages paid across firms and industries for a given skill, and how many unions in the United States and Europe form their bargaining objectives on the basis of what similar workers are paid in other industries. In Japan, however, bargaining objectives are formed on the basis of enterprise-specific criteria, such as ability to pay. As a result, there can be considerable dispersion *across* enterprises in the wage paid for a given skill (although the Japanese labor federations are trying to stimulate some coordination of wage demands within a given industry).

One other feature of the enterprise basis of unionization is that unions generally lack the power to mount a large-scale offense or defense against employers at the industrial or national level. This is illustrated by the unusual nature of strike activity in Japan. Most contracts expire annually, and each spring a "Shunto," or spring wage campaign, is organized by the federations. A target for wage demands is set and a timetable of warning strikes by different unions is scheduled to occur from mid-April to mid-May. Each union performs for about a day on schedule. Rather than being used as a weapon to counteract a bargaining deadlock, strikes in Japan therefore tend to be used to signal or symbolize the seriousness of the unions in their bargaining demands. In the end, however, the actual wage agreements are determined by each enterprise, so that the exercise does not necessarily succeed in coordinating conditions between enterprises.

SOURCES:  Japan Institute of Labor, *Labor Unions and Labor-Management Relations* (Tokyo: Japan Institute of Labor, 1979); Tadashi Mitsufuji and Kiyohiko Hagisawa, "Recent Trends in Collective Bargaining in Japan," *International Labour Review* 105 (1972): 135–53; Koji Taira, *Economic Development and the Labor Market in Japan* (New York: Columbia University Press, 1970).

the extent to which consumers are able to shift to substitute products or services. In the long run, when an employer must live with the consequences of a settlement, bargaining power will also depend on the ease with which nonunion competitors can enter the market and offer consumers lower-price substitutes.

The objectives of a union are more complex, as discussed in Chapter 10, but most unions seek to raise the wage of their members, to take the wage "out of competition" (that is, reduce the wage dispersion between employers for a given skill of worker, to minimize competition between employers on the basis of labor costs), and to prevent a substantial reduction in the employment of union members. As discussed earlier, these objectives are most easily attained when the demand for labor is relatively inelastic; that is, when it is relatively difficult to find technical substitutes in production for the skills of the union members, when substitutes exist but their supply can be increased only at increased cost, when labor is a relatively small proportion of total cost (in most situations), or when there are relatively few substitutes for the products that union members help to produce. (Note that reducing product-demand elasticity is desired by *both* unions and management.) In any particular set of negotiations, a union's bargaining power will also be influenced by its ability to finance a strike.

**Multiemployer bargaining.**   Many employers must choose between bargaining alone or joining a multiemployer bargaining association—a group of employers in the same industry who join together for the purpose of negotiating with a union or group of unions that represent employees in each company. On the one hand, negotiations between a single employer and one or more unions provide a company with considerable flexibility in devising a bargaining strategy best suited to its particular needs, rather than the average needs of a group of employers. On the other hand, many employers recognize that in industries in which competition in the product market is strong, a labor agreement establishing common labor costs insures them against some of the risks of competition.[16] In addition, the weakest management position may be to bargain as a single firm, since the best substitute for one company's product is the same product produced by another firm.

In the event of a bargaining impasse and strike, a firm bargaining alone would lose its market share to its competitors. At the same time, however, the union could be in a relatively strong position—for even if the struck firm lost a share of the market to its competitors, total employment in the industry would not necessarily fall by much. (Jobs would open up at the plants of competitors, but to obtain them those union members on strike might have to move and/or be willing to accept jobs with less seniority.) Moreover, by striking only one firm, the union would be able to finance a longer strike, since only a fraction of the total membership would qualify for strike benefits. When employers in a competitive product market have been organized by a single union, they are thus susceptible to *whipsaw* tactics, in which the union strikes or threatens to strike one employer (usually the weakest) and then extends the (relatively generous) agreement reached with that employer to others in the same industry. It is the threat of whipsaw tactics that provides a particularly strong incentive to employers in competitive product markets to form multiemployer bargaining structures.

Indeed, it is interesting to note from Table 12.1 that it is precisely in the most competitive industries that multiemployer bargaining occurs most frequently. Multiemployer bargaining structures are not a characteristic of most industries in which individual firms have substantial market power—for example, the oligopolistic market structures in durable goods manufacturing. They are most prevalent in nonmanufacturing industries characterized by substantial competition between small- to medium-sized firms in local or regional product markets (for example, construction, hotels and restaurants, supermarket chains, and so on).

The advantage of a multiemployer bargaining structure comes from reducing the potential for consumer substitution. Employers can offer a united front and at the same time be assured that the ultimate agreement will impose the same labor costs on all participants in the negotiations. Multiemployer negotiating units also permit both employers and unions to take advantage of economies of scale in negotiating labor agreements. Where there are many relatively small firms in an industry, a multiemployer negotiating unit also permits more expert representation in negotiations. In addition, if a strike occurs, it involves a much larger proportion of union membership, so that the financial resources of the union are depleted more rapidly and the union is unlikely to sustain as long a strike as it would if only one employer were struck.

One might think that by increasing the bargaining power of employers, multiemployer bargaining structures would reduce the size of settlements as compared to what would be agreed upon under a single-plant bargaining

---

[16] For a discussion of this point, *see* Wallace E. Hendricks and Lawrence M. Kahn, "The Demand for Labor Market Structure: An Economic Approach," *Journal of Labor Economics,* 2 (July 1984): 412–38.

structure. This is not necessarily the case, however, because reducing the elasticity of product demand is also favorable to workers, who can now attain wage increases with less loss of employment. (Remember that while total employment in an industry may change little if one plant is struck, job *locations* may change, so that the members of any one bargaining unit may be unwilling to demand too much.)

Put differently, if the union negotiated with a single firm, it would be equivalent to a labor-market monopolist negotiating with a product-market competitor, and the expectation might be that the ultimate wage would be higher than under competition. The formation of a multiemployer bargaining association effectively supplants this labor-market structure with bilateral monopoly, where, as we discuss in Appendix 12A, the ultimate outcome depends on the relative bargaining skills of labor and management. A multiemployer bargaining association may use its additional market power to resist the union's bargaining demands or it may accept the demands and try to pass the costs along to consumers.[17] As a result, *a priori* we cannot predict what the effect of having this bargaining structure on contract outcomes will be. The empirical evidence, however, indicates that after controlling for the characteristics of industries and workers, wages tend to be *higher* under multiemployer bargaining units in local product markets than in single employer units.[18]

In so-called casual labor markets, a worker typically works for more than one employer in the course of a year (for example, construction, longshoring, maritime, or music). In these industries both unions and management typically prefer a multiemployer bargaining unit. The assignment and payment of workers is then regulated through a "hiring hall" to which employers indicate their employment needs on a given day and from which the union assigns the requisite number and skill of workers.

Recent econometric analyses of the determinants of bargaining structures in the United States and in the United Kingdom confirm the importance of the degree of competition in the product market in determining the structure of negotiating units.[19] Although restricted to the manufacturing sector (thereby excluding many of the industries that are shown in Table 12.1 to be characterized by multiemployer bargaining), these studies also find that multiemployer bargaining units are more likely in industries with a relatively large number of firms and relatively small plant size, and in industries in which

---

[17]  Recall that the analysis in Chapter 3 shows that in most situations it is not possible to pass the entire increase in costs (here a result of a wage increase rather than the imposition of a payroll tax) on to consumers.

[18]  Hendricks and Kahn, "The Demand for Labor Market Structure"; Wallace Hendricks, "Labor Market Structure and Union Wage Levels," *Economic Inquiry* 13 (September 1975): 401–16; and Peter Feuille, Wallace E. Hendricks, and Lawrence M. Kahn, "Wage and Nonwage Outcomes in Collective Bargaining: Determinants and Tradeoffs," *Journal of Labor Research* 2 (Spring 1981): 39–53.

[19]  See Wallace E. Hendricks and Lawrence M. Kahn, "The Determinants of Bargaining Structure in U.S. Manufacturing Industries," *Industrial and Labor Relations Review* 35 (Janaury 1982): 181–95; D.R. Deaton and P.B. Beaumont, "The Determinants of Bargaining Structure: Some Large Scale Survey Evidence for Britain," *British Journal of Industrial Relations* 18 (July 1980): 101–16.

labor constitutes a large percentage of total costs. All of these features describe markets in which wage increases would lead to significant competitive pressures for a company bargaining alone. The tendency toward multiemployer bargaining is reduced to the extent that there are different unions at different companies in the industry.[20]

Multiemployer labor agreements infrequently extend beyond local or regional product markets. Among industries in which employers compete in much broader product markets, industrywide agreements were found only in the basic steel, bituminous coal, and trucking industries, and these agreements largely fell apart in the 1980s. The stability of national, industrywide bargaining associations of several employers is threatened by the greater potential for the emergence of nonunion firms and by the same general factors that were seen in Chapter 10 to threaten the stability of union organizations. As the number of members of an employer association grows, it becomes more difficult to formulate a bargaining position that is agreeable to all of the members of the association. Some members of an employer bargaining association may not be affected by an issue that most companies in the association are willing to take a strike over. (In a nationwide steel strike in 1959, brought about by employers' efforts to revise work rules in the industry, the Kaiser Steel Company, as a relatively new company that did not have the work-rule problems that troubled the other steel companies, pulled out of the joint negotiations and settled two months before the other companies reached agreement with the union.)

Generally, when there are wide variations in internal efficiency among members of the employer bargaining association, each member company may have a different "acceptable concession" that it is willing to make. The more efficient firms may be willing to make larger concessions (which they are better able to absorb) than less efficient firms to avoid the costs of a strike. In seasonal industries, such as construction, some contractors may be anxious to settle in periods of relatively high demand to avoid losses during the limited production season that would exceed the additional labor costs incurred from an early settlement. Not all members may be willing to hold out for the same period of time in support of their bargaining position. If they are unable to persuade other members of a multiemployer bargaining association to conclude an agreement, they may leave the association, leading to a weakening or breakdown of the association and possible restoration of whipsaw tactics by unions.

National industrywide agreements can raise serious problems for unions as well. It is usually more difficult for unions to maintain organization over all firms in a national market. The security of both the employer and union sides of a national, industrywide agreement is threatened by the emergence of new,

---

[20] See Thomas A. Kochan and Richard N. Block, "An Inter-industry Analysis of Bargaining Outcomes: Preliminary Evidence from Two-Digit Industries," *Quarterly Journal of Economics* 91 (August 1977): 431–52; Wallace E. Hendricks, "Labor Market Structure and Union Wage Levels."

**EXAMPLE    12.6**

# The End of Multiemployer Bargaining in the Steel Industry

In May 1985, the major steel companies in the United States announced that they were ending 30 years of multiemployer bargaining. They cited pressures from increased competition and from the different financial strengths of individual steel companies. What developments led to the demise of this previously durable bargaining arrangement?

In Example 10.2 we reviewed the growth of competitive pressures in the steel industry during the 1970s and 1980s and the negotiation of wage concessions in 1982. While the concession agreement helped domestic steel firms counter foreign competition, it could not, as a *multiemployer* agreement, address differences in profitability among individual domestic steel firms. Subsequently, the United Steelworkers (USW) granted additional concessions to try to forestall the bankruptcy of some steel companies. This action eliminated the uniformity of labor costs that is a major attraction of multiemployer bargaining arrangements, however.

Despite the concessions, the Wheeling-Pittsburgh Steel Company, the nation's seventh largest steel company, filed for protection from creditors under the bankruptcy laws in April 1985. Because National Steel, another major company, had left the bargaining association in 1984, other major steel producers were apprehensive about further disunity arising from special labor-cost concessions that Wheeling-Pittsburgh might obtain out of the bankruptcy proceedings. Facing different competitive pressures without the assurance that multiemployer bargaining would stabilize labor costs as it had in the past, the major steel companies decided to dissolve the arrangement and bargain with the union on a company-by-company basis. Steel industry labor contracts expired in August 1986.

The union's initial strategy was to develop pattern bargaining. One official said, "We'll pick out one company to bargain with first—obviously a company we have bargaining power over—and try to make that agreement the pattern." Later, the union appeared to develop a two-tier strategy, aiming for one pattern of settlement with struggling companies and a separate pattern with stronger producers. The USW adopted the following policy toward steel companies that claimed to be in the "struggling" category and in need of wage concessions: (1) concessions would be discussed only with companies that opened their books to the union's financial consultants; (2) negotiations would begin months in advance of the August contract expirations; (3) the union would only agree to wage and benefit concessions in exchange for profit sharing, stock options, and increased participation in company decisions; and (4) wage concessions would have to be accompanied by increased job security.

Most steel companies opened their books, and the USW's consultants informed it that the LTV corporation had the most serious financial problems, in part because their hourly labor costs were the highest in the industry. The USW chose LTV as the "target" company for 1986 and negotiated wage concessions in exchange for profit sharing and limitations both on overtime and on the use of nonunion subcontractors. The LTV agreement became a model for negotiations with other

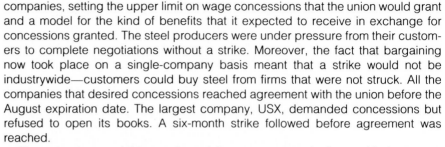

companies, setting the upper limit on wage concessions that the union would grant and a model for the kind of benefits that it expected to receive in exchange for concessions granted. The steel producers were under pressure from their customers to complete negotiations without a strike. Moreover, the fact that bargaining now took place on a single-company basis meant that a strike would not be industrywide—customers could buy steel from firms that were not struck. All the companies that desired concessions reached agreement with the union before the August expiration date. The largest company, USX, demanded concessions but refused to open its books. A six-month strike followed before agreement was reached.

The net outcome of this new bargaining arrangement in the steel industry was greater wage variation, but more similarity in job security provisions and a greater emphasis on profit sharing.

Similar pressures produced fragmentation of longstanding multiemployer or pattern bargaining arrangements in the aluminum, coal, copper, rubber, and cannery industries during the 1980s.

SOURCES:   J. Ernest Beazley, "Steel Firms End Coordinated Bargaining on Labor Pacts, Citing Industry Losses," *The Wall Street Journal,* May 3, 1985; Carol Hymowitz and Thomas F. O'Boyle, "Breakup of Big Steel Bargaining System for Labor Pacts Could Speed Cost War," *The Wall Street Journal,* May 6, 1985; J. Ernest Beazley, "Major Steelmakers Abandon Deadline for Labor Pacts After LTV Agreement," *The Wall Street Journal,* March 27, 1986.

nonunion firms paying lower wages and offering lower benefits.[21] Import competition is one such challenge. Another is the ability of competitors who enter bankruptcy proceedings to pay lower wages. Both of these factors contributed to the end of multiemployer bargaining in the steel industry in 1985 (see Example 12.6).[22] One of the most interesting illustrations of the possibilities and perils of a multiemployer bargaining association is provided by the development over a period of years of a national collective-bargaining agreement in the over-the-road trucking industry (see Example 12.7).

**Single-employer bargaining.**   In oligopolistic product markets in which most production is done by a few large companies (for example, the automobile, rubber, and meatpacking industries), single employer (companywide) bargaining predominates. Bargaining typically occurs between the union and a "target" company selected for each bargaining round. Until the late 1970s, the terms established at the target company became the "pattern" and were typically extended to other companies in the same industry. If a strike occurs, only a fraction of the union's membership (those employed at the target company) will draw strike benefits, and the union's financial resources will therefore support a longer strike than if the union faced a multiemployer

[21]   One empirical study of union wages concludes that in national product markets, union bargaining power (as indicated by the union wage level) is higher when the market is organized into company-level bargaining units than when it is organized into industrywide units. See Hendricks, "Labor Market Structure and Union Wage Levels." In other words, the value of multiemployer bargaining units to unions appears to be greater in *local* product markets than in *national* product markets.

[22]   See Example 14.2 for a discussion of corporate bankruptcy and its effects on collective bargaining.

**EXAMPLE   12.7**

## Multiemployer Collective Bargaining in the Trucking Industry

The trucking industry is a complicated array of local, regional, and national markets served by thousands of employers. Over the years the International Brotherhood of Teamsters, largely under the leadership of James Hoffa, developed a network of multiemployer bargaining arrangements in the various markets. By 1964, Hoffa succeeded in establishing a single, nationwide Master Freight Agreement covering all over-the-road truckers (those not operating solely in a local market) by combining the various regional employers' associations into a national association for the purposes of collective bargaining. The national agreement offered advantages to the union in terms of establishing uniform wages and working conditions on a nationwide basis, but there was considerable diversity among the hundreds of trucking firms that authorized Trucking Management Inc. (TMI) to bargain with the Teamsters on their behalf. In particular, the national trucking companies were typically in a stronger financial position than most of the smaller regional companies.

The Teamsters knew how to exploit such diversity in the multiemployer association to their advantage. During a strike that arose during the 1976 negotiations, for example, the union permitted employers who were willing to temporarily accept the union's last offer to operate during the strike with the understanding that when a new agreement was reached, the companies would only be subject to the terms of that agreement. This seemed like an attractive offer to financially pressed trucking companies. They could earn some money immediately and ultimately would suffer no competitive disadvantage, because they would be subject to the same terms and conditions of employment as their competitors. As fewer and fewer employers arrived at the bargaining table each day, the position of the employers became increasingly weak, and a settlement was rapidly reached. This was only the beginning of the troubles facing the multiemployer unit, however.

Although the structure of the trucking industry is essentially competitive, it had been subject to considerable regulation by the Interstate Commerce Commission (ICC) since 1935. The ICC effectively reduced price competition (by fixing freight rates), limited entry into the industry, and issued regulations that established excess capacity in the industry. By the late 1970s, however, there was increasing recognition that the regulation of industries with competitive market structures was detrimental to consumers, and the ICC began to deregulate the industry. Trucking companies came under intense competitive pressures, because as regulatory barriers to entry were dropped, new firms, many of them nonunion, entered the industry, and extensive rate cutting developed. These pressures were further increased by the deep recession of the early 1980s, when over 380 carriers left the industry.

In early 1982, the Teamsters and the TMI negotiated a new 37-month Master Freight Agreement, in which there were significant wage concessions in recognition of the economic pressures facing the industry. Nevertheless, intense product-market competition increased conflicts of interest among regional and national trucking companies. With nonunion firms taking over some of the full-truckload business from national firms, the latter successfully entered the market for less-than-truckload business that had been the main activity for regional trucking companies. Large national firms, with networks of terminals at which partial loads could be reassembled into full-truck loads for delivery to other terminals, were able to compete more effectively than the regionals in this market. As a result, when it came time to negotiate the new Master Freight Agreement, many regional trucking companies declined to authorize TMI to negotiate with the Teamsters on their behalf. The number of trucking companies authorizing TMI to represent them dropped from 487 in 1979 to 284 in 1982 to only 35 in 1985.

The trucking companies that abandoned the multiemployer bargaining arrangement argued that they needed more extensive concessions than were negotiated in the Master Freight Agreement to meet competitive pressures, which varied by region. The TMI was dominated, however, by the larger national companies whose interests were in conflict with the smaller regional companies. For example, it was in the interests of the larger companies to have a high labor-cost agreement imposed on the regional firms with whom they then competed for business. In the 1982 negotiation the TMI companies made it clear that they would abandon the Master Freight Agreement if any breakaway companies negotiated a more favorable contract with the Teamsters. Faced with the dissolution of the national multiemployer arrangement, the Teamsters initially insisted that the breakaway companies accept the terms of the Master Freight Agreement, and struck firms that insisted on negotiating an alternative arrangement. Several trucking firms went out of business. Eventually, however, the union negotiated further concessions in wages and work rules for workers whose jobs were most threatened by nonunion competition. A similar scenario occurred during the 1985 negotiations, but the TMI represented even fewer companies.

SOURCE: Agis Salpukas, "Regional Truckers Debate Labor Costs," *The New York Times,* February 24, 1982; Agis Salpukas, "Dilemma for Union Truckers," *The New York Times,* June 22, 1982; Robert S. Greenberger, "Teamsters Chief Offers Plan to Reduce Pay of Union Drivers Hauling Full Truckloads," *The Wall Street Journal,* June 27, 1983; Leonard M. Apcar, "Trucking Firms Are Divided on Strategy For Contract Bargaining With Teamsters," *The Wall Street Journal,* October 9, 1984.

bargaining unit. At the same time, the target company may be in a relatively vulnerable position. The target company's ability to take a long strike is normally undermined by the continued production and sale by unstruck competitors. By taking a strike the firm risks a permanent loss of market share, since whatever terms are agreed to at the first company will simply be extended to the others in the industry.

Other companies in the industry are never in a worse competitive position than the target company, and until the terms of the new agreement are actually extended to them, they may be in a better competitive position, either because the target company is not producing (if a strike occurs), or because there is a temporary period (after the target company signs a new agreement but before the terms of that agreement are extended to the other companies in the industry) when the target company is producing at higher cost. On the other hand, the sooner the target company signs, the sooner it will be in an equivalent competitive position with other firms in the industry and the lower and the lower the risk of a loss of market share. While market shares may be protected, the average product price is likely to be relatively high and the level of sales and production relatively low. The limited empirical evidence available indicates that unions achieve more generous contracts in company-wide bargaining units than industrywide bargaining units, at least in national product markets.[23]

There are long-run dangers with bargaining arrangements that result in relatively high labor costs. For the most part, such arrangements work to the union's advantage so long as the main substitutes available to consumers are produced under essentially the same union contract. Eventually, labor costs and product prices may become sufficiently high so that new producers entering the industry are not part of the bargaining arrangements and therefore can produce the product or service at lower cost, so that the exercise of union power implies a serious loss of employment to union members. The most dramatic recent example of this process occurred in the automobile industry in the United States in the late 1970s, as sales by foreign automobile producers captured an increasing share of the American market. The Chrysler Corporation was brought to the verge of bankruptcy, and the United Automobile Workers, the union that represents workers in the automobile industry, was forced to grant concessions to the company in order to protect its members' jobs. Unions in other industries in which product-market competition increased were also forced to abandon traditional patterns and negotiate concessions in order to protect the job opportunities of their members (see Example 12.6).

**Multiplant bargaining units.**   In multiplant companies, bargaining structures may be influenced by technological factors. When several plants of a company produce the same product, the union will normally prefer a bargaining unit that includes all of the plants, while the employer is likely to prefer a unit that is less broad—perhaps even plant-level negotiations. In each case, the reason is the same. If one plant is struck, it may be possible for the employer to reduce the costs of the strike substantially by shifting production to other plants that are not a part of the negotiating unit. The employer would balance this tactical advantage against the increased costs associated with negotiating separate contracts at each plant or at several groups of plants. On the other hand, if different plants carry out different stages of a vertically-integrated production process, a company will prefer companywide bargaining, since plant-level bargaining would create the potential for shutting down the company's entire production process, given the interdependence of the production conducted at different plants. Unions may also see an advantage in a multiplant bargaining unit in this situation, since a strike at any one plant would induce unemployment among union members at other plants that were forced to shut down.

---

[23]  See references in footnote 18.

**Influence of bargaining issues.**   The structure of negotiating units also can be influenced by the scope of the issues that are subject to collective bargaining. The product- and labor-market influences that have been stressed in the preceding discussion have a particularly important impact on collective bargaining over issues such as wages, hours of work, and employment conditions that have a marketwide impact. Some issues cannot be addressed sensibly in small units, however, even when the labor and product market served by union labor is relatively small. Pension and insurance plans, which for actuarial reasons often need large numbers of participants, are examples of issues that may not be handled effectively in plant-level or local labor-market negotiations.

On the other hand, there are many issues that arise in collective bargaining that may be unique to a plant, firm, or local labor market. Work rules, job safety, and job security are common examples. In most instances, the exact nature of the issues varies from plant to plant (for example, the nature of restrictive work practices or safety problems is likely to vary by place of employment), and efforts to settle these issues in a relatively large negotiating unit are rarely successful. For example, an epic strike in the steel industry during 1959 and 1960 was attributable in part to an effort to resolve work rules in industry-wide collective bargaining.

One solution to this problem is to develop a more flexible bargaining structure in which different categories of bargaining issues are negotiated at different levels. In the automobile industry, for example, negotiations at the national company level establish wages, fringe benefits, seniority policies, a grievance procedure, and many other provisions that have a market-wide impact or pertain to company-wide personnel policies. The national agreement is then supplemented by negotiations between local units of the United Automobile Workers and management representatives at individual plants of the company over "local issues" including work rules and safety. Much the same procedure was used in the telephone industry prior to deregulation.

Since the acceleration of union growth in the United States in the late 1930s, the trend has been toward larger negotiating units, as unions and management have adjusted to spreading markets, the emergence of potential substitute products, and the growing importance of fringe benefits in collective-bargaining agreements. Yet the expansion of negotiating-unit size, which may increase the bargaining power of unions, is not costless to unions or employers. In particular, as the scope of a negotiating unit expands, the diversity of interests of workers encompassed by the unit grows. Disputes may emerge between younger workers and older workers concerning whether collective bargaining should emphasize immediate wage gains or more generous pension provisions. Skilled workers may have a conflict of interest with unskilled workers concerning the form of wage increases: uniform cents-per-hour wage increases erode the relative wage differentials that uniform percentage increases protect. The analysis of the union as a provider of public goods developed in Chapter 10 is pertinent here. As the heterogeneity of the membership covered by a collective-bargaining agreement increases, it becomes more difficult for the union to represent the preferences of its membership. Any agreement that is negotiated will leave a larger proportion of the membership dissatisfied than if the union were negotiating for a smaller, more homogeneous membership.[24]

As a result, gains in bargaining power tend to be offset by loss in the ability to represent many of the interests embedded in the membership. Moreover, it may become increasingly difficult for individuals or even groups of members to influence union policy. With the increased heterogeneity of expanding negotiating units comes increased pressure on the union from membership groups who feel that their interests are not being adequately represented. Unions increasingly face a problem of how to reconcile pressures for market control and tactical striking power with membership demands for effective representation. As noted in Chapter 10, when union members are dissatisfied with the quality of representation, they have methods of expressing their dissatisfaction, including the election of new officers, refusal to ratify labor agreements that their leadership has negotiated, and wildcat strikes.

## Bargaining Structure in the Public Sector

Although labor unions in the public sector share most of the objectives of private-sector unions, collective bargaining in the public sector occurs in a very different legal and economic environment, and the structure and tactics of public-sector collective bargaining differ accordingly. One basic fact facing unions in the public sector is the inherent tendency for unit labor costs to increase more rapidly in the public sector than in the private sector, quite independently of the presence or absence of unions and collective bargaining. This tendency arises because the rate of growth of labor productivity in the public sector (and in service industries generally) is low relative to that experienced by goods-producing industries in the private sector. Yet most public-sector organizations must increase wages and benefits in line with the growth of compensation in the private sector in order to attract and retain their work force. To the extent that the growth of real compensation in the private sector is in line with the (higher) growth of labor productivity in private industry, wages in the public sector will tend to increase more rapidly than the productivity of public workers, and the labor costs of providing a given level of public services will rise steadily.[25] Since 50–75 percent of local government expenditures are for wages and benefits, the inherent upward pressure of labor costs on budgets in the public sector would occur even in the absence of collective bargaining.

---

[24] For a discussion of the consequences of expanding negotiating units for local unions and special groups within unions, *see* George Brooks, "Unions and the Structure of Collective Bargaining," *The Structure of Collective Bargaining*, Arnold R. Weber (ed.), (Chicago: Graduate School of Business, 1961): 123–40.

[25] See William Baumol and William Bowen, "Macroeconomics of Unbalanced Growth: The Anatomy of Urban Crisis," *American Economic Review* 57 (June 1967): 415–26.

**Table 12.2** Sources of Revenue of Federal, State, and Local Governments, 1984–85 (percent distribution)

| Source | Federal | State | Local |
|---|---|---|---|
| Intergovernmental revenue | | | |
| From federal govt. | 0 | 19.2 | 5.4 |
| From state govt. | 0.2 | 0 | 28.9 |
| From local govt. | 0 | 1.2 | 0 |
| Individual income tax | 41.0 | 14.5 | 1.6 |
| Corporation income tax | 7.6 | 4.0 | .4 |
| Property tax | 0 | 0.9 | 24.8 |
| General sales tax | 0 | 15.9 | 3.6 |
| Selective sales tax | 4.6 | 8.1 | 1.6 |
| Misc. taxes | 1.6 | 8.7 | 1.6 |
| Charges and misc. general revenue | 12.9 | 13.7 | 20.3 |
| Utility and liquor store revenue | 0 | 1.3 | 9.7 |
| Insurance trust revenue | 30.5 | 15.5 | 2.3 |

SOURCE: U.S. Department of Commerce, Bureau of the Census, *Government Finances in 1984–85* (Washington, DC: U.S. Government Printing Office 1987), Table 6, p. 7.

Federal, state, and local governments are differentiated from most (but not all) private-sector employers in that profit maximization is unlikely to be an objective of governmental units.[26] In addition, governments generally operate in a nonmarket environment. Many of the services provided by the governments are *public goods,* consumed jointly by all members of the community, and most government activities are not conducted under the normal exchange relationships that characterize the private sector. Most governments are effectively monopolists in the production of public services for a particular political jurisdiction and are not subject to the direct competitive pressures raised by the possibility of new entrants. Individual government services are not generally sold at explicit prices, as are private goods and services.

From the perspective of collective-bargaining strategies in the public sector, it is also notable that the flow of revenues to a public employer is not closely tied to the flow of service as it is in the private sector. As indicated in Table 12.2, most government revenues are from taxes levied on individuals, businesses, and property, and from intergovernmental transfers (mainly transfers from higher to lower levels of government. Only a minute portion of government revenues are tied to fees in which payment depends on delivery of service (for example, charging admission to a municipal zoo). While collective bargaining in the public sector may not be subject to the kinds of market pressures that are present in the private sector, there are clearly political forces that can influence the revenue sources reported in Table 12.2. During

---

[26] For interesting analyses of the *private* not-for-profit or voluntary sector, see Burton Weisbrod, *The Voluntary Non-profit Sector: An Economic Analysis* (Lexington, MA: Lexington Books, 1977) and Henry Hansmann, "The Role of Nonprofit Enterprise," *Yale Law Journal* 89 (April 1980): 835–901.

the late 1970s and early 1980s, voters in several states placed limits on the extent of property taxation, an important element of local government revenues, and changes in federal policies reduced the scale of transfers of revenues collected by the federal government to the states and the cities. Both of these developments reduced the growth in demand for public employees and served to increase the resistance of public employers in collective bargaining.

The fact that governments operate in a nonmarket environment does not mean that they are completely shielded from market forces and need not be concerned with market-like pressures when negotiating with public-sector unions. While individual public services do not carry a price, the package of services provided by a government carries a price in the form of the taxes noted in Table 12.2. When this tax/price becomes too high, a city or state may be faced with a market-like response as individuals or businesses exercise their option to "exit" and move to other cities or states where the packages of taxes and government services are more appealing.[27] (This is the public-sector analogy to a loss of market share in the private sector.) Alternatively, disaffected taxpayers can exercise their "voice" by voting political leaders out of office. A second market-like response to generous wage settlements can come through the capital markets, as Cleveland, New York, and other major cities discovered during the 1970s. When investors become concerned about the financial soundness of a city or state, the quality rating of that government's debt is likely to be downgraded so that it becomes more expensive, or in very extreme cases (such as New York City in the mid-1970s), impossible to borrow in private capital markets. Thus, the fact that governments generally operate in a nonmarket environment does not eliminate the economic pressures that public-sector managers and unions must consider in collective bargaining; however, these pressures may operate less directly and with greater time lags than market pressures on private producers.

There are also important differences in the structure of authority in private and public organizations that influence the structure and tactics of collective bargaining. In most private-sector organizations, management authority usually flows down from the top of the organization. This flow tends to facilitate the formulation of an organization's labor-relations policy, for when the policy is determined at the top, the interests of only a limited number of parties need be considered. In the public sector, authority flows from the bottom up through the electoral process. Political leaders are ultimately responsible to the voters that elect them. As a result, a more heterogeneous set of interests must be considered in determining labor-relations policy.

Some of this heterogeneity is reflected in the greater extent to which management power is shared in the public sector. The executive branch obviously shares power with the legislative branch at all levels of government, but power is also shared within the executive branch. Moreover, the goals of

---

[27] Charles M. Tiebout, "A Pure Theory of Local Expenditures," *Journal of Political Economy* 64 (October 1956): 416–24.

managers in different parts of the executive branch may be in conflict. For example, since few agencies have the ability or authority to raise the money to finance their activities directly, the revenue and expenditure functions of government are usually managed centrally in a budget agency. The head of an operating agency may be more willing to conclude a collective-bargaining agreement providing for large increases in compensation than the head of the budget agency for the city or state. What the head of the budget agency is willing to approve may in turn be determined by the size of the budget that the city council or state legislature is willing to approve. The limits on what management negotiators can agree to may be further constrained by Civil Service requirements, which are established on a citywide or statewide basis.

Collective bargaining by public employees is a part of the political process that determines the activities of government. Unlike the situation in the private sector, the ultimate public employers are the citizens who purchase and use public services and who elect public officials. Therefore, officials in the public sector are likely to be as sensitive to the effects of labor-relations policies on their share of the votes as private-sector managers are to the effects on their share of the market. Voters who are not employees share an interest in obtaining their public services at the lowest possible price, much like consumers in the private sector. But unlike the situation of workers in the private sector, voters who are also public employees are able to vote on decisions that may affect their conditions of employment. While public employees typically constitute a minority of the voters in any public-sector jurisdiction, they may find it easier than nonemployee voters to organize and direct pressure at political leaders. This becomes true when public employees organize into unions.[28] Interestingly, political efforts to require public employees to live in the cities in which they work (motivated by a desire that employees be more sensitive to the concerns of the community) can have the effect of increasing the amount of pressure that public employees are able to mount against public employers through the voting process.[29]

The political context of public-sector activities as well as the historical and legal opposition to collective bargaining have influenced the structure of collective bargaining. As in the private sector, bargaining structures in the public sector tend to be highly decentralized; in fact, there is an even greater tendency for single-employer collective bargaining in the public sector than in the private sector. The tendency toward single-employer bargaining reflects a reluctance among different governmental jurisdictions to give up some decision-making discretion for the purpose of maintaining a multiemployer bargaining arrangement. It also reflects the problem that confronts efforts to

---

[28] Clyde W. Summers, "Public Employee Bargaining: A Political Perspective," *Yale Law Journal* 83 (1974): 1156–1200; Paul Courant, Edward Gramlich, and Daniel Rubinfeld, "Public Employee Market Power and the Level of Government Spending," *American Economic Review* 69 (December 1979): 806–17.

[29] The use of political leverage through the voting process is sufficiently important to public employees that there have been reports from several cities of groups of public employees maintaining their voting registration at addresses in the cities in which they work, although they live in other communities.

**Table 12.3**    Public Sector Bargaining Units, by Level of Government, October 1979

| | Number of Governments | Percent with Bargaining Units | Percent of Employees Represented by a Bargaining Unit | Number of Units | | |
|---|---|---|---|---|---|---|
| | | | | 1–2 | 3–9 | 10+ |
| State and Local Governments | 79,928 | 16.3 | 38.0 | 9081 | 3743 | 220 |
| State | 50 | 68.0 | 25.8 | 3 | 8 | 23 |
| Local | 79,878 | 16.3 | 42.8 | 9078 | 3735 | 197 |
| Counties | 3040 | 22.6 | 30.9 | 350 | 291 | 45 |
| Municipalities | 18,878 | 13.0 | 45.6 | 1270 | 1099 | 82 |
| Townships | 16,827 | 6.0 | 35.6 | 618 | 353 | 41 |
| Special Districts | 26,010 | 3.1 | 28.9 | 695 | 108 | 7 |
| School Districts | 15,123 | 53.2 | 48.5 | 6145 | 1884 | 22 |

SOURCE:  U.S. Bureau of the Census, *Labor-Management Relations in State and Local Governments: 1979*, State and Local Government Special Studies No. 100 (Washington, DC: U.S. Government Printing Office, 1980): p. 148.

establish multiemployer arrangements in the private sector—the financial condition and the political pressures on elected officials differ considerably across states and cities, and as a result it can be difficult for different jurisdictions to agree on the degree of resistance or extent of concessions to be offered in collective bargaining.[30] As a result, collective bargaining in the public sector generally occurs between a single public employer and an individual union.

But it is also true that in many states and municipalities, there has been a proliferation of bargaining units so that a single public employer faces more unions than a typical employer in the private sector. For example, by the early 1970s, the state of Massachusetts had some 200 bargaining units in which employees were represented by more than 40 labor organizations. In the early 1970s, the city of New York had over 200 bargaining relationships with about 90 labor organizations; some bargaining units had as few as 2 employees. In the mid-1970s, Detroit had 78 separate bargaining units. While many governmental jurisdictions had succeeded in reducing or limiting the number of negotiating units by the late 1970s, public employers in 23 states and 82 municipalities, including some of the largest cities in the country, each faced over 10 bargaining units (Table 12.3). Almost 40 percent of the bargaining units at the state level and 50 percent of the units in municipalities contained fewer than 25 employees.

The proliferation of bargaining units in many sections of government is traceable to a combination of political and legal factors and to historical accidents. Many of the units were permitted to form as rewards for political support during periods in which there was little cost of another collective-

---

[30]  Thomas A. Kochan and Harry Katz, *Collective Bargaining and Industrial Relations*, 2d ed., (Homewood, IL: Richard D. Irwin, Inc., 1988): 435–36.

bargaining unit, since strikes were forbidden and unions appeared unwilling to strike in violation of the law. In this climate new bargaining units could effectively be ignored. Moreover, the public sector is not covered by the National Labor Relations Act, and under the prevailing legal climate in most public-sector jurisdictions, there were no formal unit-determination procedures during the 1960s and the early 1970s; further, the range of issues over which unions were legally permitted to negotiate was quite circumscribed prior to legislative changes during the 1970s. In short, neither party had much incentive to give a great deal of attention to the appropriateness of a particular bargaining unit. With the growing professionalism of labor relations in the public sector during the 1970s and 1980s, collective-bargaining agencies established by law at the city or state level of government increasingly moved to consolidate and reduce the number of units into more manageable numbers.

The fragmented bargaining structures just mentioned present severe problems for the management of labor relations. Public employers must allocate considerable resources simply to the negotiation and administration of a plethora of labor agreements. Collective bargaining itself may be uncoordinated if the expiration dates of different labor agreements are staggered. Multiple units can also give rise to unstable compensation structures as a result of "coercive comparisons" of wages and benefits between different groups. At one time, for example, the separately negotiated labor agreements covering police officers and firefighters in New York City provided (1) that the ratio of the wage of a police patrolman to a police sergeant be 3:3.5, (2) that the ratio of wages of a firefighter to a fire lieutenant be 3:3.9, and (3) that the wages of police sergeants and fire lieutenants be equal. This unstable formula, a product of uncoordinated collective-bargaining negotiations, yielded no equilibrium! Once either service received a wage increase, the contract of the other provided it with a case for an increase, which in turn would trigger a claim for an increase from the first service, and so on.

# The Tactics of Collective Bargaining

In the previous section we discussed how bargaining structure, the level at which negotiations are conducted, could be related to bargaining power. Within a given bargaining structure, however, the outcome of collective bargaining can also be influenced by the general environment of collective bargaining and the tactics adopted by the parties. In this section we discuss environmental and tactical factors influencing collective bargaining in the private and public sectors.

## Bargaining Tactics in the Private Sector

**Business fluctuations.**  One important determinant of the relative bargaining power of labor and management is largely beyond their influence. Business fluctuations, which in part reflect the monetary and fiscal policies of the federal government, influence the costs incurred by both parties in the event of a work stoppage. In general, the relative bargaining power of unions varies cyclically, increasing in business expansions with growth of demand in product markets and decreasing in recessions. When product demand is relatively weak, for example, an employer may have little to lose by offering stiff resistance to a union's demands. In the event that the resistance results in a bargaining impasse and strike, the employer may be able to meet orders from inventories, which are often relatively large anyway as a result of the slack demand. Alternatively, if the employer wants to continue to operate by hiring replacements for striking workers, there are likely to be many individuals willing to accept work, even as strikebreakers, when unemployment is high. Conversely, when demand expands and inventories are low, the employer risks a loss of orders and potentially a permanent loss of market share in the event of a work stoppage. The cost of a strike will also be relatively high to management because it is likely to be difficult or relatively expensive to hire replacements for strikers during periods when unemployment is low.

**Contract expiration date.** Unions have developed a number of tactics aimed at increasing the cost of a strike to management. One of the more common tactics is to try to time the expiration date of a labor agreement to a period when labor services are particularly crucial. In the automobile industry, for example, the major union contracts expire in early autumn at about the time that the auto companies expect their production and sales to build in response to the introduction of new models. Newspapers are particularly vulnerable to strikes called in the periods preceding the Christmas and Easter holidays when advertising revenues are particularly large. Strikes by farmworkers at harvest time would be very damaging to farmers. As these examples indicate, unions have an incentive to try to establish contract expiration dates during periods in which a work stoppage would impose relatively large costs on management. Employers, of course, have an incentive to resist such efforts.

Since an expiration date is itself established in collective bargaining, it is likely to reflect more basic underlying determinants of the relative bargaining power of the two parties. In situations in which a union is unable to negotiate an expiration date that places the employer under considerable pressure to settle, the union may achieve the same result by working without a new contract after the expiration date and continuing to negotiate until a time when the costs of a strike to an employer are relatively high. However, union control over the timing of work stoppages has been weakened in recent decades by the increasing latitude of the courts and the National Labor Relations Board toward the use of lockouts by employers. As discussed in Chapter 14, employers are free to use a lockout once a bargaining impasse has occurred and therefore have some control over the timing of a work stoppage.

**Inventory build-ups.** A common management tactic in manufacturing industries is to build up inventories in advance of a contract expiration to anticipate a possible strike. In some cases, the company itself holds the inventories if it is able to ship during a strike. In other cases, the company's customers may stockpile goods in advance of a potential strike date. During a long strike in the rubber industry in 1979, for example, automobile manufacturers were able to supply cars, initially by using tires that they had stockpiled in advance of the strike, and later by omitting the spare tire from new cars until the strike concluded. As a result, there was much less pressure from customers on tire manufacturers to settle the strike than the union had anticipated.

**Bargaining with multinational corporations.**   During the 1960s and 1970s, there was an unprecedented expansion into other countries of the operations of corporations based in the United States, Western Europe, and Japan. While earlier examples of multinational enterprise had primarily involved the vertical integration of a corporation with foreign sources of raw materials, the recent growth of multinational corporations (MNCs) has largely consisted of a horizontal extension of companies into new product markets.

Since many MNCs make the same product in several countries, unions bargaining in any one country face the possibility that production will be shifted across national borders during a labor dispute. "Production switching" of this nature increases the corporation's bargaining power by increasing its ability to take a strike. The risk of a serious loss of market share during a strike is reduced when production can be increased in other countries. (This is similar to the problem faced by a union bargaining at one plant of a multiplant firm.) Unions also complain that it is frequently difficult to pin down the locus of decision-making authority for industrial relations issues in many MNCs.

European and American unions have developed different strategies for addressing the collective-bargaining issues raised by the growth of MNCs.[31] Some European labor organizations have attempted to develop *transnational collective bargaining*—the coordination of collective-bargaining demands among workers of different nations in the same industry. As with the development of national unions discussed in Chapter 10, this particular institutional response represents an effort to develop a bargaining structure that reduces the elasticity of demand for the services of the workers of an MNC involved in negotiations in a particular country by limiting the scope for substitution of production activities to other countries. In particular, it represents an effort to prevent the bargaining objectives of unions in one country from being undermined by the activities of unions in other countries. As a result of these efforts, a few groups of workers have refused overtime or additional work resulting from attempts by an MNC to shift production from a struck plant in another country.

However, this tactical coordination has not been widespread to date, and efforts to counter MNCs through transnational collective-bargaining arrangements face more imposing barriers than the development of a national union structure within a particular country. Labor organizations in different countries frequently have very different mixes of economic and political objec-

---

[31] The strategies are discussed at greater length in *Bargaining Without Boundaries: The Multinational Corporation and International Industrial Relations*, Robert J. Flanagan and Arnold R. Weber (eds.), (Chicago: The University of Chicago Press, 1974) and B.C. Roberts, "Multinational Collective Bargaining: A European Prospect?" *British Journal of Industrial Relations* 11 (March 1973): 1–19.

tives, and the timing of strikes or other job actions to secure political objectives may not correspond well with the timing that is best for securing economic objectives. Moreover, the bargaining structures differ between countries, and labor federations are often fractured along political or religious lines (see discussion in Example 12.4), with the result that a particular plant or industry may employ workers represented by different federations and having diverse objectives.

Impressed by these barriers, unions in the United States have taken the position that the transnational collective-bargaining strategy is too slow to accommodate the immediate problems that they associate with the growth of MNCs. Viewing the MNC as the modern equivalent of the runaway shop, they have instead pressed for protectionist legislation to reduce the incentives for American corporations to establish subsidiaries in other countries. American unions may also view protectionist legislation as a bargaining position from which to achieve reductions in trade barriers erected by foreign countries. To the extent that MNCs establish foreign subsidiaries to get around such barriers, the ultimate effect of reducing such barriers could be to increase the extent to which foreign markets are supplied by exports from the source country rather than by production by subsidiaries—a development that would increase jobs in the source country. On the other hand, there is an inherent conflict between the approaches espoused by American and European unions: to the extent that the American unions are successful in obtaining protectionist legislation, the job opportunities of European union members are reduced.

**The ratification procedure.**   As noted in Chapter 10, most union constitutions call for some form of ratification of a tentative collective-bargaining agreement by the union membership or by a representative body elected by the membership. Effectively, the ratification procedure means that union negotiators do not have the final authority to bind the union to a proposed agreement. The authority of management negotiators may similarly be limited to the extent that an agreement must be approved by an executive or board that is not participating directly in the negotiations. There is sometimes a temptation to use the ratification procedure tactically. Either side may try to obtain more from the other by returning to the bargaining table claiming that their principals refused to approve the agreement without further concessions. Negotiators may even influence whether ratification occurs by the manner in which they portray a proposed agreement to their principals.

While the preceding use of the ratification procedure may appear to be a clever method of extracting further concessions, it rarely works more than once. In subsequent bargaining rounds, the party that was a victim of the tactic may simply hold back the best offer initially, anticipating the rejection of tentative agreements. To the extent that both parties adopt the strategy, the tactical use of a ratification procedure may ultimately reduce the concession that either side is willing to make initially and therefore raise the possibility of a strike. Yet the tactical use of the ratification procedure may be tempting because a failure to ratify need not be costly initially (see Example 12.8).

**EXAMPLE   12.8**

## Contract Ratification in the Automobile Industry

Although collective bargaining in the automobile industry is conducted at the company level, the industry historically has provided an example of "pattern bargaining," wherein the terms of the contract that are established in negotiations with a "target" company in each bargaining round are extended to other companies. In 1980 and 1981, however, the Chrysler Corporation came close to insolvency, and the United Automobile Workers (UAW), the union representing most Chrysler employees, agreed in 1980 to a contract that included significant wage concessions by union workers at Chrysler. By the summer of 1982, when a new round of collective-bargaining negotiations began, autoworkers at Chrysler had not received a wage increase for almost two years and were earning an average of $2.50 an hour less than workers represented by the UAW at the General Motors Corporation and at the Ford Motor Company.

After several weeks of negotiations, the UAW and Chrysler reached a tentative agreement in September restoring cost-of-living adjustments that had been dropped as part of the earlier concessions and providing for wage increases later if Chrysler attained certain levels of profitability. Although the union leadership urged ratification, workers at Chrysler wanted a labor agreement that included an immediate raise and voted 70 percent to 30 percent to reject the tentative agreement. Negotiators for Chrysler maintained that the company did not have the economic resources to improve its offer. One month later, Chrysler workers voted, also by a 70-percent-to-30-percent margin, *not* to strike, but to work under the terms of the old contract that had expired in September 1982 until new negotiations over immediate wage increases could be resumed in early 1983.

To many outsiders, the scenario seemed bizarre: a union rejects a tentative contract and then agrees to continue working under an old contract rather than striking the company to obtain an improvement over the rejected agreement! In many respects, however, the outcome reflects the fact that contract-ratification procedures in the automobile industry, as in many other industries, do not impose any costs on union members who reject a contract. In most unions, a failure to ratify a contract is not simultaneously a pledge by the union membership to strike in support of demands for a better contract. Strike votes are usually taken separately. Moreover, some unions require two-thirds of the membership to approve a strike but only one-half of the membership to reject a contract. As a result, union members often do not have to balance the consequences of taking action to obtain better contract terms against the contents of the proposed contract. A failure to ratify is no more than a statement that the membership would like more to come out of the negotiations, and as such, can be used, as in the Chrysler case, as an expression of frustration over the workers' economic position.

SOURCES:   Dale D. Buss, "UAW to Ask Chrysler Workers Tuesday: Strike or Work Under Old Pact Until '83," *The Wall Street Journal* October 22, 1982; Dale D. Buss, "Chrysler Corp. Workers Vote to Stay on Job," *The Wall Street Journal* October 27, 1982; and John Holusha, "Auto Workers Overwhelmingly Reject Strike Against Chrysler," *The New York Times* October 27, 1982.

**Strike insurance.**  Many industries provide products or services that have time value and cannot feasibly be placed in inventory for use during a strike. In several of these industries—notably newspapers, railroads, and the airlines—*strike-insurance* arrangements have been used at various times to reduce the cost of strikes to management. In the event of a strike, an employer participating in a strike-insurance plan is entitled to receive payments from other employers in the plan according to an established formula. Although the details of various plans differ, their objectives are similar—to reduce the costs of a strike to an employer by restoring some of the revenues that would otherwise be lost, as customers shift to nonstruck firms in the industry. To the extent that they are successful, strike-insurance plans will increase the ability of employers to take a strike.

Strike-insurance arrangements are not free of problems for employers, however. Although strike insurance will maintain some of the revenues of a firm during a strike, it does not guarantee that customers will return when the strike is over. Employers can still suffer permanent losses of market share to their competitors. In this sense, strike insurance provides less protection to individual employers than a multiemployer bargaining arrangement. Secondly, since strike insurance rests on the ability of firms that are operating to subsidize a struck firm, the development of a strike-insurance plan provides a strong incentive for unions in the industry to press for industry-wide strikes or bargaining structures, which would remove the value of the insurance arrangement.[32]

A broader difficulty presented by strike-insurance arrangements stems from the incentives set up by the mere existence of the insurance. Insurance generally works best when the events that are insured against are random events. But not all contingencies for which insurance is desired are random. Many such events (for example, fires and automobile accidents) are to some extent influenced by the behavior of the individuals who are insured. The mere existence of insurance may create a problem known as *moral hazard,* whereby the behavior of the insured is altered in ways that raise the likelihood that the event that is insured against occurs. (For example, fire insurance may lead insured individuals to be less careful about fire prevention.) The main defenses against moral hazard that have been devised by insurance companies are varieties of *coinsurance* which require the insured party to pay either a fixed amount (a ''deductible'') or a fixed proportion of the loss. While this reduces the moral hazard incentive, it does not completely eliminate it.

Strikes are not random events; they are influenced by the behavior of the parties to collective bargaining. As such, a strike-insurance arrangement that reduces the net cost of a strike may increase the probability that a strike occurs, since the employer will have a smaller incentive to take costly actions that might avoid a strike than if there were no insurance payments to cushion

---

[32]  Unions also argued (unsuccessfully) that strike-insurance arrangements violated federal antitrust laws.

the losses from a strike. Even in a coinsurance arrangement, which imposes some of the costs on the company that takes the strike, there is still a smaller incentive to reach agreement than would exist without strike insurance. Strike insurance therefore presents a moral hazard problem. Its existence may increase employer resistance in collective bargaining, but it may also provide a subsidy for inept labor relations.

In the case of strike insurance, the presence of moral hazard can give rise to a problem of *adverse selection,* which can undermine the risk-sharing function of the insurance. Adverse selection occurs when only those parties with a relatively high risk of suffering a loss purchase insurance. The cost of participating in an insurance arrangement tends to be based on the average loss experience for the group that is insured. Yet, individual participants are likely to differ in their risk of loss. Participants who know their risk of loss is high will see the insurance cost as a bargain, while participants who know that their risk of loss is relatively low will find that the insurance cost exceeds their expected loss and will decide not to purchase insurance. Over time, those with low risk will drop out of the insurance market and only individuals with a high risk of loss will want to purchase insurance.

Adverse selection is a real possibility in the case of strike insurance, because most strike-insurance arrangements have no screening procedure that can be used to identify poor risks and deny them insurance. Payments made by participants in a strike-insurance arrangement are not varied on the basis of participants' strike experiences. In fact, in some arrangements, the size of the payment may depend on the size of the losses suffered by other members of the insurance pact. Yet the individual members of a strike-insurance arrangement may differ in the quality of their labor relations, and hence, the likelihood that they will experience a strike. If firms that developed relatively good labor relations found themselves regularly making payments to firms that experienced many strikes as a result of poor labor relations, the former set of firms would rationally lose interest in participating in a strike-insurance arrangement. By remaining in the arrangement, they might be subsidizing the inept labor-relations practices of their competitors.

**Application: airline strike insurance.**   For 20 years, the airline industry in the United States maintained a Mutual Aid Agreement, which provided a form of strike insurance for participants in the arrangement. The agreement was established in 1958 by six of the largest airlines and initially provided that each member airline would make "windfall" payments to the struck member. Each member's windfall payment was "an amount equal to its increased revenue attributable to the strike during the term thereof, less applicable direct expenses."[33] In effect, if all of the business lost by a struck airline

[33] S. Herbert Unterberger and Edward C. Koziara, "Airline Strike Insurance: A Study in Escalation," *Industrial and Labor Relations Review* 29 (October 1975): 27. The discussion here draws on this study and its sequel by the same authors, "The Demise of Airline Strike Insurance," *Industrial and Labor Relations Review* 34 (October 1980): 82–89.

shifted to other airlines, the windfall payments would have fully indemnified the struck airline for any losses suffered as a result of the strike.

In fact, airlines faced considerable uncertainty concerning the level of compensation that they would receive in the event of a strike. During periods when nonstruck airlines normally operated at full capacity, such as major holidays, there would be no increase in revenues attributable to the strike. A similar problem confronted airlines flying routes on which there was no competition from other members of the Mutual Aid Agreement. In the event of a strike, consumers would either shift to nonmember airlines or to other means of transportation, neither of which would provide compensation for the struck airline. Also, if a union broadened a strike to include all members of the agreement flying on parallel routes, none of the members would receive strike benefits. As a result, some airlines chose not to join in the arrangement, since they saw little prospect of benefiting from it (given their route structures), and the windfall-payments approach meant that airlines that did become members of the agreement would benefit by different amounts in the event of a strike.

In an effort to solve these problems, the Mutual Aid Agreement was later amended twice, and by late 1969 payments were made irrespective of the windfall gains to other airlines during a strike. The revised Mutual Aid Agreement substantially reduced the net costs of a strike to the point where some member airlines actually earned operating profits during long strikes. For example, when National Airlines was struck for 114 days by the Airline Employees' Association in 1970, it earned an operating *profit* of $1,590,000. Without the benefits from the Mutual Aid Agreement it would have experienced an operating *loss* of $26,396,000. (Under the earlier windfall payments approach, it would have experienced a loss of $7,673,000.) At the same time, the revised agreement was in effect a coinsurance arrangement—the operating profits of National Airlines, while positive, were lower than they would have been in the absence of a strike. National incurred some of the costs of the strike in the form of forgone profits. With the reduction in the net costs of a strike, strikes in the airline industry lengthened significantly under the Mutual Aid Agreement.

Over time, there was evidence that the pact was running into the moral hazard, and ultimately, the adverse selection problems discussed in the previous section. Some airlines, such as Northwest, had a pattern of repeated and often lengthy strikes while participating in the Mutual Aid Agreement, while others experienced few, if any, work stoppages. As a result, some companies were regularly required to pay benefits and others regularly collected benefits. The pattern of payments and receipts by major airlines is summarized in Table 12.4. By the 1970s, some of the airlines that were the largest net contributors to the plan began to lose interest in regularly subsidizing the operations of a few strike-prone rivals. Pan American, which had paid in about $64 million under the agreement but received only about $5 million, gave notice in 1975 that it was withdrawing from the Mutual Aid Agreement. The announcement came at a time when Pan American was financially pressed and negotiating for wage concessions with the Airline Pilots' Associa-

**Table 12.4** Net Receipts by Major Airlines Under the Mutual Aid Agreement: October 1958–October 1978 (in thousands)

| Airline | Net Receipts[a] |
|---|---|
| American | −$83,181 |
| Braniff | −18,711 |
| Continental | −11,171 |
| Eastern | −63,021 |
| National | 120,124 |
| Northwest | 187,906 |
| Pan American | −58,782 |
| Trans World | 37,134 |
| United | −88,912 |
| Western | −26,310 |
| Total Major Airlines | −$ 4924[b] |

[a] Negative figures indicate the amount by which an airline's payments under the Mutual Aid Agreement exceeded its receipts.

[b] There was a net transfer over the period from major airlines to local service airlines.

SOURCE: S. Herbert Unterberger and Edward C. Koziara, "The Demise of Airline Strike Insurance," *Industrial and Labor Relations Review* 34 (October 1980): 84.

tion, but the management of Pan Am noted that the plan had not been advantageous financially to the company. Subsequently, Eastern Airlines, which had paid almost $90 million but received only around $26 million, announced that it would leave the Mutual Aid Agreement.

Unions in the airline industry were understandably opposed to the Mutual Aid Agreement, since by reducing the cost of a strike to the airlines it increased the bargaining power of employers in the industry. They were unsuccessful in their efforts to get the agreement overturned by the Civil Aeronautics Board (CAB), the federal regulatory agency whose approval was necessary before the arrangement could be implemented, or by the federal courts, which rejected claims that the agreement violated antitrust law.

The demise of the agreement came in late 1978 with the passage of federal legislation to deregulate the airline industry. In an effort to reduce the opposition of the labor movement to the legislation, Congress included a provision in the Airline Deregulation Act of 1978 that permits the CAB to approve only those strike-insurance plans that meet conditions that greatly limit the attractiveness of such plans to employers.[34]

## Bargaining Tactics in the Public Sector

As discussed earlier in this chapter, collective bargaining in the public sector occurs in an environment in which power is dispersed between appointed public managers and elected officials, economic pressures are often less immediate than in the private sector, and the law restricts the use of traditional union weapons. Some of the tactics of collective bargaining in the

---

[34] U.S. Congress, "Airline Deregulation Act of 1978," Public Law 95–504 Sec. 29(e)(2) (1978).

public sector resemble those in the private sector. For example, some of the ratification tactics discussed above may surface when professional negotiators have to bring a proposed agreement back to a mayor, commission, or school board for final approval. But it is hardly surprising that in the decidedly political atmosphere of the public sector, unions and management have frequently developed tactics that are quite different from those commonly observed in negotiations in the private sector. If unions in the private sector adopt tactics that threaten resistant employers with a loss of market share, unions in the public sector are attracted to tactics that threaten resistant public employers with a loss of vote share.

The most direct influence that public-sector unions have on their employers is through the votes of members who live or maintain a voting residence in the city or state in which they work. While it is often illegal for public employees to take political positions as individuals, unions or other *organizations* of public employees are free to lobby for improved working conditions. Through their unions and through their votes, public employees are likely to support ballot issues, political leaders and, where they are elected, judges who are likely to advance their cause. The contrast with the activities of private-sector unions is perhaps greatest with respect to the election of judges. Given the restrictive legal environment facing public-sector unions, judicial interpretations of the law and legal doctrine can have a substantial influence on the scope of activities open to public-sector unions. Unions representing public employees are therefore likely to be as concerned about certain state and municipal judgeships as the AFL-CIO and private-sector unions are about appointments to the National Labor Relations Board.

Some efforts by public employees at the ballot box have been strikingly effective. In some cities unions have succeeded in establishing their notions of equity through the political process. In San Francisco, for example, the city charter specified that the pay of certain groups of public employees had to equal the highest pay for similar jobs elsewhere in the state or in the country. Such criteria for wage setting generally have little connection with conditions in the labor market for such employees, and are achieved through the exercise of political power rather than bargaining power or negotiating skill. As in collective bargaining, however, political power is subject to alteration, and the voters can retract what they once provided (as they did in San Francisco in late 1975). Generally, the objectives of public employees often imply higher taxes, which are unlikely to appeal to the majority of voters.

With the professionalization of labor relations in the public sector, bargaining for state and local governments has increasingly been conducted by professional negotiators rather than elected officials. When confronted with a management negotiator who is taking a tough stance, unions in the public sector have frequently adopted the tactic of the "end run" around the negotiator to an elected official or legislative body in an effort to obtain their objectives. To the extent that elected officials or representatives offer concessions, the authority of the official negotiators is obviously undermined.

That the tactic pays off at all reflects the fact that power over employment conditions is widely shared in the public sector. In fact, some union representatives claim that while a successful "end run" may undermine the authority of the official management negotiators, the "end run" usually occurs because little authority is vested in the official negotiators in the first place. A tentative agreement may have to be approved by a school board, a mayor, a budget director, or a legislative body before it is binding. As with any ratification process, this extra step of approval can be used tactically to send a negotiator back for further concessions. Unions prefer to deal directly with the management body that has the authority to commit to a contract, and this can stimulate "end runs" when the political leadership is reluctant to grant full authority to its negotiators. The result is a greater tendency toward *multilateral bargaining*—in which three or more groups may be involved in negotiations—in the public sector than in the private sector. Demands for a different type of multilateral bargaining may also arise if a community interest group seeks to be involved in collective-bargaining negotiations over an issue that concerns them (for example, with teachers over the quality of schooling).

One difficulty that managers in the public sector have with collective bargaining is that its timing may not correspond well with the timing of the budget cycle. In most political jurisdictions there are statutory requirements for the submission and approval of budgets for future government expenditures. While the expiration dates of collective-bargaining agreements covering public employees ideally ought to precede the budget submission, this is not always the case, and even when it is, a settlement may occur some time after the formal expiration of the contract. The conflict between bargaining and budgeting is potentially serious, given that labor comprises a large percentage of costs in the public sector.

In the short run, the above budgetary conflict has not seemed very great in many bargaining relationships. In some cases, managers have "padded" their budgets by including amounts that they anticipate will have to be paid as a result of the outcome of collective bargaining. Union negotiators in the public sector have a strong incentive to develop expertise in the budgeting practices of states and cities, however, and efforts to hide anticipated future wage increases can usually be detected by skilled union negotiators. Once the wage concessions that employers are willing to make have been revealed (in the budget), there is then the danger that the anticipated amounts will become the floor rather than the ceiling on union wage demands. Generally, there is considerable flexibility in both the budgeting process (for example, unanticipated wage increases can be offset by reductions in other budget categories such as capital expenditures) and in the way in which public funds are raised (for example, new bond issues or grants from a higher level of government may cover some of the unanticipated expense).

By the mid-1970s, however, it was becoming clear that many of the short-run expedients used to reconcile bargaining and budgeting had extremely serious long-run consequences for the financial viability of cities and states. One illustration of the short-run measures sometimes used to balance public budgets is provided by the extent to which many public-employee retirement systems are underfunded (that is, these systems lack the assets to meet their

**EXAMPLE  12.9**

## Labor Relations and Fiscal Crisis in New York City

Developments in collective bargaining in New York City since 1965 illustrate many observations in this chapter about factors influencing bargaining structure and tactics in the public sector. Collective bargaining was formally introduced in the late 1950s during the administration of Mayor Robert Wagner, who limited its scope to salaries and a few fringe benefits and who, by his regular personal involvement in bargaining, made it a highly political process. With the limited scope of collective bargaining and seemingly few economic constraints (given a substantial flow of tax revenues and intergovernmental transfers from the federal government), wage increases for city workers ran ahead of increases in the private sector. Moreover, bargaining units were approved readily, and at one point, 85 different unions had established a total of 405 bargaining units to represent the city's 250,000 employees. By the mid-1960s, municipal unions formed a major political interest group in the city.

Beginning with the administration of Mayor Lindsay in the late 1960s, there was an effort to reduce the political element by delegating collective bargaining and other aspects of the city's labor relations to professionals. In 1967, the City of New York passed a collective-bargaining law establishing an Office of Collective Bargaining to bring the city's labor relations under central administration. Among other achievements, this office reduced the number of bargaining units to approximately 100 by 1975, and it established a citywide bargaining unit for the negotiation of certain benefits that had to be uniform for employees covered by the city's career and salary plan. Nevertheless, the political element in the city's labor negotiations was never entirely removed, and despite the city's claims of increasing financial difficulties brought about by the recession of the early 1970s, and a reduction in federal grants-in-aid, unions continued to negotiate as if there were no serious economic constraints on the city. They obtained substantial increases in compensation throughout the first half of the 1970s.

Suddenly, in March 1975, with an operating deficit of $2 billion and a need to refinance $6 billion of outstanding short-term debt, the city was unable to market its securities and faced the prospect of imminent default. When it became clear that the city would not be able to manage the crisis itself, the State of New York took two actions. In an effort to address the immediate financial problems of the city, the state legislature created the Municipal Assistance Corporation (MAC) in June of 1975, and it authorized the agency (1) to sell securities to finance the short-term debt and operating expenses of New York City and (2) to impose certain limits on the city's budgeting and accounting practices. In September, in an effort to address more basic management problems in the city government, the legislature established a state Emergency Financial Control Board (EFCB) with authorization to intervene in city management in an effort to develop long-term solvency. The net impact of these extraordinary measures was to increase the influence of the state and of private investment interests in running New York City at the expense of the city's political leaders and groups, such as the unions representing public employees (who previously had considerable influence with the local leaders).

The public-employee unions adopted several equally unusual strategies in an effort to maintain their influence despite the shift in power. Faced with hostile public opinion and the possibility that a freeze might be imposed by the mayor (at the request of the MAC) on a scheduled wage increase, virtually all of the public unions altered their former bargaining structure to form a coalition that negotiated a more favorable wage deferral agreement with the city and MAC officials than would have been imposed on them. In particular, they were able to preserve their cost-of-living increases and to obtain a promise from the city to pay their previously negotiated (but frozen) wage increases after the fiscal crisis was over if productivity increases allowed for it. In the autumn of 1975, when the city again seemed on the brink of default, the unions extended their influence in the discussions of the city's rescue by committing their pension funds, whose assets exceeded $7 billion, to the purchase of MAC securities. (This played an important role in helping the city qualify for federal loans.) Given the shift of power to the state and federal government, and to private investors, brought about by the financial plight of New York, the only way for the unions to be major players in the negotiations over the fiscal rescue of the city was by altering traditional tactics and becoming major financiers of the city.

In subsequent negotiations, the public-employee unions further altered their traditional bargaining arrangements in order to adjust to the new economic environment of collective bargaining. Under a two-tier bargaining arrangement adopted in 1976, a coalition of the unions first established the general guidelines for a two-year agreement. Subsequently, individual unions in the coalition negotiated separate agreements which could differ in detail, but stayed within the basic economic limits of the framework established by the coalition.

SOURCES: Raymond D. Horton, "Economics, Politics, and Collective Bargaining: The Case of New York City, *Public Sector Labor Relations: Analysis and Reading,* David Lewin, Peter Feuille, and Thomas A. Kochan (eds.), (Glen Ridge, NJ: Thomas Horton & Daughters, 1977): 205–17; David Lewin and Mary McCormick, "Coalition Bargaining in Municipal Government: The New York City Experience," *Industrial and Labor Relations Review* 34 (January 1981): 175–90.

accrued liabilities). Although most public-sector pension systems nominally require advance funding, the typical public-employee pension fund had only *half* of the assets it should have had to be fully funded in 1975. While some of the short fall was attributable to inappropriate actuarial assumptions and a failure to take account of the fact that pension benefits will increase as salaries increase, the simple refusal of employers to contribute sufficient funds to the pension systems also constitutes a major source of underfunding. Underfunding is clearly used as a means of balancing current operating budgets, suggesting that short-term considerations take priority over long-run consequences when government employers put together compensation packages.[35] Another illustration of this same general point is provided in Example 12.9.

[35] U.S. House of Representatives, *Pension Task Force Report on Public Employee Retirement Systems* (Washington, DC: U.S. Government Printing Office, March 15, 1978) and the *Report of the Permanent Commission on Public Employee Pension and Retirement Systems—Financing the Public Pension Systems, Part I: Actuarial Assumptions and Funding Policies* (New York, 1975).

# Review Questions

1. Critics of centralized bargaining units have argued that the best way to reduce the power of unions is to require that all contracts be negotiated at the plant level. Explain why you agree or disagree with this proposal.

2. A few American industries have adopted strike-insurance plans to reduce strike pressures. Why only a few? What may be the barriers to more widespread adoption of such plans?

3. Unionized plumbers are in unions that control the size of their membership. Wages are kept high by keeping membership highly qualified and therefore small. Employers needing or wanting to employ union labor must hire from the ranks of union membership. Suppose there is a plumbers' union in each of two cities. City A has an ordinance that states that all plumbing installations and repairs must be performed by union members. City B has no such ordinance. Analyze as completely as you can the effects of City A's ordinance on workers, consumers, and the general well-being of society. (*Hint:* you can gain insight into this question by comparing Cities A and B.)

4. The Jones Act mandates that at least 50 percent of all U.S. government-financed cargo must be transported in American-owned ships and that any American ship leaving an American port must have at least 90 percent of its crew composed of American citizens. What would you expect the impact of this act to be on the demand for labor in the shipping industry and the ability of unions to push up the wages of their members?

5. Suppose that a proposal for tax reductions associated with the purchase of capital equipment is up for debate. Suppose, too, that union leaders are called upon to comment on the proposal from the perspective of how it will affect the welfare of their members as workers (not consumers). Will they all agree on the effects of the proposal? Explain your answer.

# Selected Readings

Wallace E. Hendricks and Lawrence M. Kahn, "The Demand for Labor Market Structure: An Economic Approach," *Journal of Labor Economics,* 2 (July 1984): 412–38.

David Lewin and Mary McCormick, "Coalition Bargaining in Municipal Government: The New York City Experience," *Industrial and Labor Relations Review,* 34 (January 1981): 175–90.

S. Herbert Unterberger and Edward C. Koziara, "Airline Strike Insurance: A Study in Escalation," *Industrial and Labor Relations Review,* 29 (October 1975): 26–45.

Arnold R. Weber, "Stability and Change in the Structure of Collective Bargaining," in Lloyd Ulman, ed., *Challenges to Collective Bargaining* (Englewood Cliffs, NJ: Prentice-Hall, Inc., 1967).

# APPENDIX 12A

## Analysis of Bilateral Monopoly in the Labor Market

How are wages and employment determined under bilateral monopoly? Consider the interests on each side of the bargaining table. We have seen in Chapter 3 that when there is only one employer or employer organization in a labor market, profit maximization will lead that employer to behave as a monopsonist, tending to reduce both the level of wages and the level of employment below their competitive levels. In Figure 12A.1, employer profits will be maximized when the marginal labor cost equals the marginal revenue product of labor. Therefore, the employer will want a wage of $W_m$ at which $E_m$ workers will be hired. (These are lower than the competitive wage ($W_c$) and employment ($E_c$) levels that would be determined by the intersection of the marginal revenue product and labor supply schedules.) The union, which now monopolizes the sale of labor, will wish to use its power to raise wages

**Figure 12A.1**   Bilateral Monopoly

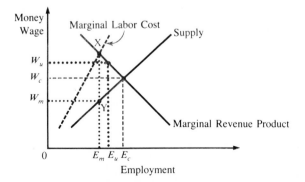

above the competitive level, say to $W_u$. This would result in employment of $E_u$, which is also less than the competitive employment level. Wages higher than $W_u$ would imply a greater employment loss than the union is willing to accept.[1]

Presumably labor will not want more than $W_u$, and management will not want a wage less than $W_m$. Therefore, $W_u$ and $W_m$ denote the upper and lower limits of a *contract zone,* or range in which the final collective-bargaining agreement must lie.[2] Where, exactly, will the final solution lie? Unfortunately, the analysis of bilateral monopoly cannot tell us. Instead, it describes how the respective interests of labor and management determine the location of the contract zone. Note, however, that if the union succeeds in negotiating wage $W_c$, employment will be $E_c$.

---

[1]  As discussed in Chapter 10, union objectives are difficult to formulate as precisely as those of employers because unions must adopt political methods of accommodating the often diverse goals of their individual members. Nevertheless, the final result will reflect the wage-employment trade-off that the union is willing to make.

[2]  The range may in fact be narrower, since a union is unlikely to insist on $W_u$ if it will bankrupt an employer, and an employer is unlikely to insist on $W_m$ if a union is willing to strike indefinitely rather than accept that wage. These issues are explored in Chapter 14.

# CHAPTER 13

## Negotiating Labor Agreements

At the heart of any collective-bargaining relationship is the negotiation of a collective-bargaining agreement that defines the terms and conditions of employment and the respective responsibilities of management and the union. Because there is so much at stake, these negotiations often produce a sharp conflict of wills between labor and management. To outsiders, major negotiations often appear as freewheeling drama; yet the outcome of collective bargaining is more likely to be shaped by the negotiating skills that the parties bring to the bargaining table than by the bombastic statements that either side may offer in public.

This chapter provides an introduction to the bargaining process. In it we discuss basic concepts of negotiations, strategic issues in the negotiating process, social and psychological barriers to the successful completion of negotiations, and techniques for determining the cost of collective-bargaining proposals. Since unsuccessful negotiations usually result in a strike or (in much of the public sector) resolution of the issues by an arbitrator, many of the issues discussed here also pertain to the material in Chapter 14.

## Negotiating a Single Issue

Suppose that an employer and a union sit down to negotiate a single issue—the wage that will be paid to employees represented by the union. This is an example of what is sometimes called *distributive* or *zero-sum* negotiations, because what one party gains, the other party loses. Labor and management are negotiating over the division of the "wage pie," and there is no way to make the pie larger.

If each party prepares carefully, it will enter negotiations with a clear notion of its *reservation wage*. The union's reservation wage is the lowest wage that the union membership will accept without striking. It will normally reflect the members' judgment about the wage they should receive, given considerations such as the profitability of the firm, the wages paid at other firms, past and present inflation, and so on. The employer's reservation wage is the maximum wage that the employer will agree to pay without taking a strike. It will normally reflect management's concern with the effect of higher labor costs on the company's profitability and its ability to compete in product markets.

A *contract zone* exists if the employer's reservation wage exceeds the union's reservation wage. When the maximum wage that the employer is willing to pay exceeds the minimum wage that a union will accept, there is room for an agreement. The contract zone extends from the union's reservation wage to the employer's reservation wage, and this zone may be a matter of pennies or of dollars. If the bargaining structure and prenegotiation tactics have established a balanced bargaining environment, the final agreement will tend to be in the middle of the contract zone, or about halfway between the two reservation wages (see Example 12.3). Inequalities in bargaining power, of course, can lead to outcomes closer to the reservation wage of the more powerful party. If the employer's reservation wage is below the union's reservation wage, there is no contract zone. When the maximum wage that the employer will pay is less than the minimum wage that the union will accept, a bargaining impasse results and a strike or lockout is likely.

Determination of one's reservation wage is thus an important starting point in preparing for collective-bargaining negotiations. It forces each party to work out its "bottom line" for the negotiations. Therefore, management and labor negotiators often spend months preparing for negotiations by reviewing problems under the old contract, gathering data on the company's performance and financial condition, and comparing employment conditions in the company to conditions in other firms or industries. The resulting reservation wage can serve two important purposes. First, during the course of negotiations, it may prevent negotiators from drifting into positions that their organization cannot tolerate. Second, the reservation-wage concept clarifies the fact that some agreements are just not possible. When negotiators understand the factors behind their reservation wage, they can be more comfortable with the idea of an impasse developing if the two parties' reservation wages are simply inconsistent with an agreement.[1]

## Tactics of Distributive Bargaining

One should not confuse reservation wages with bargaining demands. Both labor and management want to do better than their reservation wages, and hence should not reveal these positions to each other. Indeed, much of the

---

[1] As will become apparent later in this chapter, however, negotiations can fail even when a contract zone exists.

bluffing and deception that is a part of negotiations is an effort to disguise each party's reservation wage. What they do reveal are their bargaining demands. Labor opens negotiations by asking for a wage that exceeds its reservation wage, and management responds with a counteroffer that is lower than its reservation wage. (Negotiations over wage concessions during the 1980s often began the other way around. Management opened by demanding wage cuts that were greater than what it needed to survive.)

Initial demands are almost always incompatible in the sense that the union asks for more than the company offers. This does not mean that a contract zone does not exist, however. Initial wage demands and offers are normally intended to camouflage the reservation wages of each side. One interesting question is whether this camouflage confuses the bargaining situation to the point that labor and management fail to reach agreement even when a contract zone exists. If this occurred, bargaining would be *inefficient* in the sense that it imposes costs on both parties that could have been avoided, and both labor and management are worse off.

Fortunately, experimental evidence indicates that inefficient distributive bargaining is rare. Negotiators have a remarkable ability to identify even small contract zones when they exist.[2] There are a few factors that can raise the likelihood of inefficient bargaining, however. Rigid "take-it-or-leave-it" tactics, such as the Boulwareism strategy discussed in Chapter 11, appear to reduce the likelihood of agreement in situations where a contract zone exists. The problem seems to be that the addition of the objective of "being as tough as my opponent" to the original objective of establishing a wage interferes with forming an agreement. Inefficient bargaining may also occur when labor and management have different attitudes toward risk or different perceptions of the future. In Chapter 15 we discuss how the latter problem can be reduced by making future wage payments *contingent* on future events, such as inflation or profitability.

Besides deciding upon its reservation wage and initial demands, each party is guided in negotiations by its beliefs about what the other party will accept. How are such beliefs formed? How can one party influence the other's beliefs about its (the first party's) reservation wage? This is a key element of distributive bargaining, because when one side makes a concession, it is usually because it has become convinced that the other side will not concede.

How does one side convince the other that it will not concede? A widely used tactic is to accept constraints on its actions that effectively preclude concessions, and then to make sure that its adversary is aware of these constraints. Paradoxically, then, reducing one's freedom to maneuver through some sort of pre-commitment may increase negotiating power. In the words of one student of bargaining,

[2]  Howard Raiffa, *The Art and Science of Negotiations* (Cambridge, MA: Harvard University Press, 1983), Chapter 4.

. . . the power to constrain an adversary may depend on the power to bind oneself; . . . weakness is often strength, freedom may be freedom to capitulate, and to burn bridges behind one may suffice to undo an opponent.[3]

This pre-commitment tactic is open to both sides in collective bargaining. If unions convince their membership that no wage increase under X percent is worth considering, they may be able to claim credibly in negotiations that the membership will not ratify anything less. Public statements to the media are another way of developing such commitments. The same effect may be achieved if political challengers within a union convince the membership that the current leadership is incompetent if it negotiates less than X percent. Likewise, the management of a multiplant company may claim that it cannot deviate from company policy, which establishes the same terms and conditions of employment at each plant. Both labor and management may claim that they have a reputation to protect for other negotiating situations.

## Negotiations Over Many Issues

In most collective bargaining negotiations, there is more than the issue of wages on the bargaining table. Collective-bargaining contracts can be complex documents with dozens of provisions about, for example, fringe benefits, promotions, overtime work, layoffs, and procedures for handling disputes with management. (The exact nature of these rules is discussed in Chapter 15.) In this setting, while the concept of a "reservation price" remains an important guide to bargaining, the direct and indirect costs of these other provisions expands the concept somewhat. The appropriate concept of a reservation price becomes the entire *value of the contract* to the union membership or employer. If the minimum contract value that a union will accept is lower than the maximum value that the employer will provide, an agreement can occur; otherwise no agreement is possible.

The keys to negotiating contracts with several issues are the *tradeoffs between issues* that each party is willing to make. For example, a union may want to raise each member's pay by $10 per day, while an employer is only willing to agree to an increase of $8 per day. If wages were the only element of pay, they would be at an impasse, but when negotiations include fringe benefits or work rules the bargaining possibilities are enlarged. For example, the employer may be indifferent between higher wages and a dental plan of equal cost, while the union may strongly prefer the dental plan, because employer contributions to such a plan are not counted as taxable income for the union members. When labor and management face *different tradeoff rates* between wages and fringes, a mutually acceptable agreement may be possible. To continue the example, the dental plan may be valued by workers at $10 yet only cost employers $8 per day in the end.

---

[3] Thomas C. Schelling, "An Essay on Bargaining," *The Strategy of Conflict*, T. C. Schelling (ed.), (New York: Oxford University Press, 1960): 22.

In the example above, labor and management succeeded in finding a mutually beneficial trade-off between two elements of the contract, wages and a dental plan, because their relative preferences for the elements differed. Other differences that may facilitate agreements are differences in present versus future needs and different perceptions or expectations of future economic events.

For example, workers negotiating a multiyear contract may be willing to forgo future wage increases for a larger current increase, the parties may be able to agree to relatively large pension payments in return for lower current wage increases, or they may agree to a lower basic increase in pay and a generous cost-of-living adjustment (in this latter case the employer is betting against relatively large general price increases and the employees are betting on them).

When negotiations involve several issues, collective bargaining need not be a zero-sum game. As we have just seen, one party does not necessarily lose what the other gains. Bargaining can thus be *integrative* rather than just distributive. With integrative bargaining, the parties may be able to enlarge the "pie" (by identifying possibilities for joint gains) before facing the distributive issue of dividing it. Hence, a package of working conditions and various forms of pay may be easier to negotiate than a single issue.

When many issues are under negotiation, inefficient bargaining occurs when negotiators leave unexploited mutual gains on the bargaining table; that is, the parties settle for a smaller pie (sum of worker's pay and employer profits) than is necessary. How can parties identify the possibilities for mutually beneficial gains when renegotiating a large collective-bargaining agreement? While negotiations typically begin with labor and management each indicating the range of contractual changes that they wish to discuss, it seems to be a mistake to immediately begin serious bargaining over the entire package (experimental studies indicate that few parties reach agreement in this situation). The trade-offs that labor and management are willing to make among various issues are apparently just too difficult to discover if everything is on the table at once. A better approach is to choose a few issues to start with and build the contract from the bottom up. For example, the parties might start negotiating over two or three issues, trying to identify possibilities for joint gains. Gradually, other issues might be added. When a tentative labor contract has been constructed, it is good practice to review the entire package in an effort to identify further possibilities for joint gains.

Some negotiators make progress toward agreement by recognizing the limits of their expertise. When dealing with a somewhat technical subject, such as safety conditions, changes in work rules on the shop floor, or the design of a profit sharing system, the negotiators may agree on a general objective and appoint a joint labor-management committee of lower-level officials to work out the details of the arrangement.

How much should be revealed to the other party in the course of negotiations? We have already noted why it is bad practice to reveal one's reservation price in our discussion of distributive bargaining. When many issues are on the table, however, it generally makes sense for each party to reveal acceptable tradeoffs because this is the only way to discover mutually beneficial gains. Failure to disclose acceptable trade-offs raises the likelihood of negotiating an inefficient contract (that is, a labor agreement in which both parties are less well off than they might have been). The general rule seems to be to bargain cooperatively over integrative issues and to bargain hard over distributive issues!

# Social-Psychological Barriers to Resolving Negotiations

Even integrative bargaining, in which both labor and management can gain from successful negotiations, may be difficult to conclude. Not every aspect of collective bargaining negotiations is a cool, rational process. Some of the major sources of bargaining inefficiency—failure to make trades that produce mutual gains—can be traced to social and psychological processes that limit rational behavior by negotiators. A few of the more important factors are discussed in the following section.

## The Framing of Issues

One key to understanding why negotiations sometimes fail is to understand that the way in which bargaining proposals are "framed" or presented by one side can influence perceptions of their acceptability by the other. Some general issues of "framing" are discussed below.

**Loss aversion.** Which of the following two events do people generally consider less harmful from a worker's viewpoint?

1. During a period with no inflation, an unprofitable firm decides to cut wages by 5 percent.
2. During a period of 12-percent inflation, an unprofitable firm decides to raise money wages by 7 percent.

In both cases, workers' real wages have fallen by 5 percent, yet most people surveyed will claim that the second wage adjustment is preferred. The second adjustment is apparently more acceptable than the first because a nominal wage gain is part of the overall real wage loss.

Which of the following two events is considered more advantageous from a company's viewpoint?

1. A collective-bargaining agreement leaves a company with a net profits of $100,000 each year.
2. A collective-bargaining agreement leaves a company with $300,000 of sales revenues and $200,000 of expenses each year.

Most survey respondents perceive the first event as more advantageous to the company, even though net profits are identical in each situation. In the second event, the expense "loss" is explicit.

These two sets of studies illustrate a phenomenon that psychologists have labeled *loss aversion:* Individuals tend to treat the prospect of a gain differently from the prospect of a loss. As a result, proposals that are framed as gains are more likely to be favorably received.[4] This finding is immensely important to negotiators, for it suggests that changing the description of bargaining proposals from losses to gains can influence their acceptability. Agreement is more likely when proposals are framed as gains or in ways that avoid the appearance of losses.

**The reference point.** Whether a change is perceived as a gain or loss depends crucially on the reference point from which any given change is evaluated. In the first set of choices, for example, the perception of gain or loss rested on whether the reference point was money or real wages. Clearly, most people's point of reference for judging wage increases seems to be money wages.

Consider another example from wage negotiations. If a union establishes a position that anything less than its opening demand for an hourly wage of $12 is a loss, while management takes the position that any wage above its opening offer of $10 is a loss to the company, then the concessions that can lead to settlement will be hard to achieve. However, if the union can be made to view any wage above management's initial offer of $10 as a *gain,* and management can be made to view any wage below the union's initial demand of $12 as a gain, then concessions and agreement may be forthcoming.[5]

Clearly, the choice or manipulation of reference points can be crucial to the outcome of collective-bargaining negotiations, for the reference point is effectively the benchmark by which gains and losses are determined. Establishing a reference point that frames an issue as a gain greatly increases the prospects for a negotiated settlement. This suggests an important role for a mediator (discussed more fully in Chapter 14) in collective-bargaining disputes.

**Considerations of equity.** "Equity," or "fairness," is a key objective of most labor unions. A contract proposal that is viewed as fair is likely to be accepted over a proposal that is not. Yet equity is not a well-defined concept, and perceptions of it in particular cases can sometimes be influenced by the ways in which bargaining proposals are framed.

For example, recent research has found that events in which individuals incur losses are viewed as less fair—and hence less acceptable—than events

---

[4] Daniel Kahneman and Amos Tversky, "Prospect Theory: An Analysis of Decision Under Risk," *Econometrica* 47 (1979): 263–91.

[5] This example is from Max H. Bazerman and Margaret A. Neale, "Heuristics in Negotiation: Limitations to Effective Dispute Resolution," *Negotiating in Organizations,* M. H. Bazerman and R. J. Lewicki (eds.), (Beverly Hills, CA: Sage Publications, 1983). This article provides an excellent treatment of issues discussed in this section. See also, Max H. Bazerman and John S. Carroll, "Negotiator Cognition," *Research in Organizational Behavior,* 9, L. Cummings and B. Staw (eds.), (Greenwich, CT: JAI Press, 1987).

in which the same individuals forgo potential *gains*.[6] This finding has direct application to negotiations over reducing labor costs during periods of economic distress. Workers paid an hourly wage plus a profit-sharing bonus would resist as unfair a cut in their basic wage yet might not strongly object to a pay cut of similar size if it took the form of a reduced profit-sharing bonus. In general, the "loss" of one's normal wage rate is viewed as less equitable than receiving a smaller bonus (that is, forgoing potential income), even though the amounts may be the same.

Equity considerations may impede negotiations in other ways as well. The fact that both parties can gain from successful negotiations may not be enough to produce agreement. Labor and management may each be more interested in *relative* outcomes than in some absolute change in income. Even when a proposal benefits both parties, agreement may not be possible if one party feels that the other gains more from the proposal.[7] In negotiations over wage concessions during the 1980s, for example, "equality of sacrifice" was a frequent theme.

## Evaluating the Opposition

The most successful negotiators develop a clear understanding of the relative strength of their opponent, but there are psychological barriers to developing this important skill. It appears paradoxical to many people that one can achieve greater success in negotiations by taking the perspective of the *other* side when developing a negotiating strategy. Moreover, most of us tend to be overconfident about our skills in uncertain situations.[8] In negotiations, this can produce mutually inconsistent expectations between union and management negotiators that lead to bargaining impasses. In the private sector such impasses can result in strikes (see Example 13.1). In the public sector they can result in frequent recourse to arbitration, with each party's having an unrealistic view of what an arbitrator will award.

One of the more common barriers to an objective evaluation of a bargaining situation is the tendency to overestimate the value of one's own bargaining concessions and underestimate the value of concessions made by the other side. Yet most people have difficulty in receiving new information with an open mind. We tend to interpret facts in terms of our prior beliefs, and to fit new or ambiguous information into our own pre-existing theories of behavior.

Does an evaluation of a proposal depend on who makes the proposal? Suppose that three randomly chosen groups of people are each shown the text of a collective-bargaining proposal and asked to comment on whether it is more advantageous for labor or management. Suppose also that one group is

---

[6] Daniel Kahneman, Jack L. Knetsch, and Richard Thaler, "Fairness as a Constraint on Profit Seeking: Entitlements in the Market," *American Economic Review,* 76 (September 1986): 728–41.

[7] For an economic analysis of status (that is, relative standing), see Robert Frank, *Choosing the Right Pond: Human Behavior and the Quest for Status* (New York: Oxford University Press, 1985).

[8] For reviews of the research findings on this point, see Bazerman and Neale, "Heuristics in Negotiation," and Bazerman and Carroll, "Negotiator Cognition."

---

**EXAMPLE    13.1**

## The 1987 National Football League Negotiations

A strike by the players' association in the National Football League in the fall of 1987 illustrates the problems that can arise from overconfidence and failure to take the perspective of a bargaining adversary. The objective of the football players in their 1987 negotiations with team owners was to eliminate rules that restricted their ability to switch teams; in essence, they wanted to eliminate the monopsony power of the employers so they could play for the teams offering the most for their services. (See the discussion of a parallel situation of free agency in baseball in Chapter 3.) Since one result of increasing mobility between football teams would probably have been a large increase in the pay of many players, the owners were strongly opposed to the proposal.

Faced with the owners' resistance, the players' association called a strike at the beginning of the 1987 professional football season. On the surface, it appeared that the owners were in a tough spot. They immediately hired replacements for striking players on a week-by-week basis, but the quality of the replacements was so low that the games were very poorly attended. It turned out, though, that the owners were making money off the strike! Their labor costs were down because they did not have to pay the high salaries received by their striking star players. Moreover, their revenues were much higher than attendance figures implied because of contractual payments by television networks for broadcasting rights.

Because costs fell by more than revenues fell, profits increased during the strike, and the owners made no move to grant concessions. The strike ended after a few weeks, with no gains accruing to the players. It seems unlikely that the football players would have suffered such a costly defeat had their negotiators made a careful evaluation of the strengths of their adversary.

---

told that the proposal was made by the union, one that it was made by management, and one that it was made by an outside mediator. Would you expect the evaluations of who would benefit from the proposal to vary among the three groups? In general they will, with the group that has been told that it is a union proposal concluding that it is less advantageous for management than the group told it was a proposal made by management. This example illustrates "reactive perceptions," a psychological trait that can be an important source of bias in the evaluations of concessions by negotiating adversaries.

Not all reactive perceptions are irrational, however. When one side to a negotiation has information not available to the other, and when the party with such private information makes a proposal that on its face looks attractive to the second party, the latter may quite sensibly discount the proposal on the theory that the first party is trying to take advantage of the private information. In an environment of private information and reactive evaluation, unilateral concessions by one party to negotiations may not be successful, because they will not be interpreted at face value.

## Escalation of Commitment

A particularly serious barrier to negotiated settlements occurs when negotiators responsible for an unrealistic course of action continue or even escalate that action as a way of *justifying* their position to their constituency. A graphic example is provided by the "Dollar Game" that has been played in many classrooms. The rules of the game are simple: A professor offers to auction off a one-dollar bill to the highest bidder, but the second-highest bidder must also pay the professor their highest bid. Remarkably, bids typically escalate over the $1.00 mark as each tries to avoid being second highest and having to give their money away for nothing. But the expected monetary loss rises with each bid over $1.00. The escalation of bids therefore becomes an effort to justify an irrational course of action.[9]

Examples could also arise in collective bargaining. For example, a union president who promises the membership a huge wage gain only to find that management is solidly opposed to the proposal might call a strike or otherwise commit union resources to an impossible course of action as a way of justifying his or her decision. Alternatively, a company president out to "teach the union a lesson" may incur irrationally large costs for the company as a way of justifying the original decision.[10] (Of course, a strike that appears irrational for the union in terms of current costs and benefits may make sense if management's bargaining stance in the future is affected; conversely, a company may appear to gain little during a strike but may make the union more "reasonable" in the future.)

The escalation of commitment can occur in several ways. Once an initial position is staked out, inconsistent information may be discounted. Escalation becomes an exercise in saving face, despite being counter to the constituents' best interests. Negotiators often get into these situations because of their failure to consider the likely responses of their negotiating opponents.

## Overcoming the Barriers

Many of the potential barriers to negotiating an agreement can be reduced or overcome by certain structural or behavioral features of the negotiations. Definite *deadlines* for the completion of negotiations can play a simple but positive role. A deadline is a time past which both parties may lose a lot (through a strike or lockout) because they have failed to agree. Some proposals may appear more attractive when compared to the imminent costs of a work stoppage. More importantly, concessions offered near an impending deadline may be explained as a desire to avoid the costs of a work stoppage.

⁹ See Raiffa, *The Art and Science of Negotiation*, pp. 85–90.

¹⁰ The gradual escalation of the U.S. commitment in Vietnam has been mentioned as another example of this situation.

They are likely to be greeted with less suspicion and interpreted with less bias by the other side than concessions offered in the absence of a deadline. Finally, it is easier for each side to justify its flexibility to its own constituents when faced with a deadline and costly impasse.

The introduction of third parties, such as mediators, into the collective bargaining process can also overcome barriers to agreement. Third party dispute resolution procedures are discussed in the next chapter, but we can already see their potential role. In particular, third parties can make proposals that labor or management cannot without "losing face" in the bargaining process. Also, proposals made by a neutral third party will not receive the biased appraisal accorded proposals by one's adversary.

Even in the absence of third parties, a negotiator may get around the problems of biased evaluation by inviting an adversary to choose from a menu of small concessions (rather than offering only one) or inviting initial concessions from the other side.

## Evaluating the Cost of Labor Agreements

Both parties to negotiations are interested in evaluating the dollar value of proposed labor agreements. The union wants to know the value that its membership will receive from the contract; management wants to know what costs will be imposed by the contract. In this section we show how the cost of a collective bargaining agreement can be determined and discuss some of the issues surrounding costing procedures.

### Costs of a One-Year Labor Contract

Costing is most easily discussed with a specific example. Consider a bargaining unit with 100 employees who are paid for 2080 hours per year (40 hours a week for 52 weeks). Twenty-five of the employees work the night shift. The old contract provided a base hourly wage of $10.00, time and one-half for overtime, a premium of $1.00 per hour for working on the night shift, six paid holidays, two weeks of vacation for those who had worked for the company one to five years, and three weeks of vacation for those who had worked over five years. The new one-year agreement (1) increases the wage by one dollar per hour, (2) raises the night shift premium by 25 cents, (3) provides two more holidays, (4) provides a fourth week of vacation for employees with at least 15 years of service with the company, and (5) allows the four union stewards to take an additional hour per week during work time to handle union business. What is the increased cost of the new agreement?

Table 13.1 illustrates how an estimate of the annual cost of this contract (or contract proposal) can be developed. The first section of the table develops direct wage cost increases. All workers receive the general $1.00 per hour increase for each hour that they work, for a total of $208,000. Line 1b records the fact that the 25 employees on the night shift receive an additional increase of 25 cents per hour, raising total costs by $13,000. It may seem peculiar to have a line for overtime (line 1c), since the new contract makes no change in

**Table 13.1** Estimates Cost Increase of a One-Year Labor Contract

| *Contract Provisions* | | *Annual Cost Increase* |
|---|---|---|
| 1. Wages | | |
| (a) $1.00 general increase | | |
| (100 employees) (2080 hours/employee) ($1.00) = | | $208,000 |
| (b) Night-shift premium | | |
| (25 employees) (2080 hours/emp.) ($.25) = | | 13,000 |
| (c) Overtime | | |
| ($1.00) (1.5 overtime rate) (11,000 overtime hours) = | | 16,500 |
| | | |
| 2. *Other Payroll Costs\** | | |
| (a) Social Security (F.I.C.A.) | | |
| Day: (7.51%) ($1.00) (75 employees) (2080 hrs.) = | $11,716 | |
| Night: (7.51%) ($1.25) (25 employees) (2080 hrs.) = | 4,881 | |
| Total | 16,597 | 16,597 |
| (b) Federal and State Unemployment Insurance (U.I.) tax | | |
| (3.5% U.I. tax rate) (Change in earnings under $5200) | | No change |
| | | |
| 3. *Payments for nonwork time* | | |
| (a) Two new holidays | | |
| Day: (16 hours) (75 emp.) ($11.00) = | $13,200 | |
| Night: (16 hours) (25 emp.) (12.25) = | 4,900 | |
| Total | $18,100 | |
| Social Security taxes (7.51% of 9050) | 1,359 | $ 19,459 |
| (b) Fourth week of vacation for workers with at least 15 years of service | | |
| Day: (30 qualified employees) (40 hours) ($11.00) | $13,200 | |
| Night: (No qualified employees) | 0 | |
| Total | $13,200 | |
| Social Security taxes (7.51% of $13,200) | 991 | 14,191 |
| (c) Stewards' Time for Union Business | | |
| Day: (3 stewards) (1 hour) (52 weeks) ($11.00) = | $ 1,716 | |
| Night: (1 steward) (1 hour) (52 weeks) ($12.25) = | 637 | |
| Total | $ 2,353 | |
| Social Security taxes (7.51% of $2353) | 177 | 2,530 |
| TOTAL COST OF AGREEMENT | | $290,277 |

\* This example ignores changes in workers' compensation costs, private pension contributions, or other benefits whose costs to the employer are based on payroll costs.

the overtime provisions. Nevertheless, because the base rate has increased by $1.00, the cost of all overtime hours (we assume there are 11,000) will automatically increase.

Part 2 of Table 13.1 contains payroll costs that do not appear anywhere in the collective-bargaining agreement. These are federal and state payroll taxes that are required by law. As of 1988, most employers are required to pay a social security tax of 7.51 percent of the first $45,000 of each employee's earnings each year. With wages of $11 per hour it is unlikely that the earnings of employees at the company will exceed $45,000; therefore, the employer will have to pay additional social security taxes totalling $16,597 on the increased earnings from the new labor agreement. (Note that the tax must be computed separately for day and night workers, since they receive different increases.)

Federal and state unemployment insurance taxes are assessed the same way, but both the tax rates and the maximum earnings subject to the tax are lower than in the case of social security. In line 2b we assume that a rate of 3.5 percent is applied to earnings up to $5200. Since all workers earned more than this under the old contract, there is no increase in taxable earnings under the new contract, and unemployment tax payments do not change. Payments for workers' compensation insurance, state disability plans, pension contributions, and other benefits are often also influenced by changes in wages (these factors were not mentioned in Table 13.1 for the sake of brevity). Management negotiators must be aware that collective bargaining agreements can produce significant cost increases for items that are not (and often cannot be) a topic of negotiations.

Part 3 of Table 13.1 estimates the costs of new payments for time not worked (new holidays and vacations). New holidays or vacations result either in lost production or in the hiring of other workers to "cover" for those off duty. In either case, the cost to the employer is best approximated by the compensation paid to workers. (Remember that a profit-maximizing firm will set employment so that the value of labor's marginal product equals the costs of hiring labor.) Costs must, of course, include payroll taxes as well as wages. Under the assumption that 30 day-shift workers qualify and receive their normal wage for vacation pay (and that no night-shift workers qualify), we estimate the cost of the two new holidays at $19,459 and the cost of the new vacation policy at $14,191. Line 3c costs out the additional hour per week allotted shop stewards to conduct union business under similar assumptions.

The methods shown in Table 13.1 are commonly applied and may provide an acceptable first cut at estimating the costs of a collective bargaining agreement. There are significant limitations to the resulting cost estimates, however. Notice that the contract terms are evaluated on the basis of labor utilization in the past (under the old agreement) rather than utilization in the future (under the new agreement). Much of the analysis found earlier in this book cautions us against assuming that past and future labor utilization will be the same, however. If negotiations increase the cost of labor relative to capital and other inputs, the firm is likely to substitute other inputs for labor. Moreover, since the new contract raises labor costs the company is likely to raise prices in an effort to pass at least some of these costs on to consumers. At higher prices, however, consumers will buy less of the product and the company will need fewer workers. (For details, review our analysis of elasticity of labor demand in Chapter 3.) Finally, when a company produces several products, the importance of labor costs often differs by product. An increase in labor costs provides an incentive for the company to change its product mix, producing less of labor-intensive products and more of capital-intensive products. All of these adjustments tend to reduce future labor utilization below what it was in the past, thereby reducing the actual cost increases below those shown in Table 13.1.

## Costing a Multiyear Agreement

Most labor negotiations in the United States establish contracts that run for two or three years rather than the one year examined in Table 13.1. When estimating the cost of multiyear contracts, it is crucial to take account of the time value of money. For example, suppose that a three-year contract provides for wage increases of one dollar per hour in each year of the agreement. How is the cost of this agreement to be estimated? The concept of *present value,* first introduced in Chapter 4, is crucial.

Recall that a dollar today is worth more than a dollar tomorrow, because the dollar that you have today can be invested at market interest rates to give you more than a dollar tomorrow. If the interest rate is 10 percent, a dollar that you invest today will be worth $1.10 in one year, $1.21 in two years, and $1.33 in three years. Conversely, the present value of a one-dollar increase in wages next year is only $.91, because if this amount is invested now, it will grow to one dollar in a year's time. Similarly, the present values of one-dollar wage increases that must be paid two and three years from now are $.83 and $.75, respectively. In general, when the interest rate is $i$, the present value ($PV$) of a wage payment ($W$) made in $t$ years is:

$$PV = W_t / (1 + i)^t$$

The key implication of the present value concept is that the cost of a labor agreement can be influenced by the time at which a provision takes effect. *Backloaded* agreements, in which increases in wages and fringe benefits occur toward the end of the contract term, cost less than *frontloaded* contracts, in which the provisions take effect toward the beginning of the contract. On average, employers prefer backloaded contracts, while unions prefer frontloaded contracts. Nonetheless, concessions over the timing of contractual provisions can be an important source of flexibility in collective-bargaining negotiations.

Many multiyear agreements provide for payments that are contingent on the occurrence of some uncertain future event. Cost-of-living adjustments (COLAs), which require that wages be adjusted to some general measure of inflation, are the most common example of a contingent payment.[11] For example, a COLA might require that the hourly wage increase by one cent per hour for each .3 point increase in the Consumer Price Index published by the U.S. Bureau of Labor Statistics. COLA payments are an addition or supplement to the base wage, and they are usually negotiated to resolve disagreements between labor and management about how large future wage increases must be to compensate workers for (unknown) future inflation. The disagreements often rest on different forecasts of future inflation by the two parties. The fact that the amount of future inflation is unknown means that the eventual cost of a COLA is uncertain. Probably the most useful approach to costing a COLA provision is to determine the cost of the provision under a realistic *range* of assumptions about future inflation.

---

[11] See Chapter 15 for a more detailed explanation and discussion of COLAs.

Estimating the costs of the many proposals that arise as part of the give and take of collective bargaining is a crucial part of negotiations. Fortunately, in a world of personal or laptop computers and "spreadsheet" programs, the procedures outlined above can be performed quickly and repetitively as bargaining proceeds.

## Review Questions

1.  Is a negotiated settlement more likely to occur when labor and management are negotiating one issue or several issues? Why?
2.  Is a contract zone likely to exist in most collective-bargaining negotiations? Why? What factors might lead to the absence of a contract zone?
3.  Labor and management sometimes fail to agree on a contract even though a contract zone exists. What are the main impediments to concluding an agreement in this situation? How can they be overcome?
4.  In what ways might a mediator or other neutral third party increase the likelihood of a negotiated settlement between labor and management?
5.  How would you estimate the cost (or cost savings) of a proposal to reduce the number of job classifications in a company?

## Selected Readings

Max H. Bazerman and John S. Carroll, "Negotiator Cognition," *Research in Organizational Behavior*, 9, L. Cummings and B. Staw (eds.), (Greenwich, CT: JAI Press, 1987).

Max H. Bazerman and Margaret A. Neale, "Heuristics in Negotiation: Limitations to Effective Dispute Resolution," *Negotiating in Organizations*, M. H. Bazerman and R. J. Lewicki (eds.), (Beverly Hills, CA: Sage Publications, 1983).

Michael H. Granof, *How to Cost Your Labor Contract* (Washington, DC: Bureau of National Affairs, 1973).

Howard Raiffa, *The Art and Science of Negotiation* (Cambridge, MA: Harvard University Press, 1982).

Thomas C. Schelling, "An Essay on Bargaining," *The Strategy of Conflict*, T. C. Schelling (ed.), (New York: Oxford University Press, 1960): 21–52.

Richard E. Walton and Robert B. McKersie, *A Behavioral Theory of Negotiations* (New York: McGraw-Hill, 1965).

# CHAPTER 14

## Labor Disputes and Dispute Resolution

Work stoppages and dispute resolution procedures are at the heart of the collective-bargaining process. Collective bargaining only works as a method of fixing the terms and conditions of employment because a failure to agree can result in significant losses of income for both sides. The mere threat of a costly work stoppage or of an uncertain resolution of a labor dispute by a third party provides unions and management with a range of potential settlements—sometimes referred to as a *contract zone*—that are preferable to the losses associated with a work stoppage. It is the incentive to avoid such losses that induces labor and management to reach agreement without a work stoppage in the vast majority of collective-bargaining negotiations.

Unions are able to win management concessions at the bargaining table because of their ability to impose costs on management. These costs typically take the form of work slowdowns and strikes, but they may also come from having "outsiders" make decisions about the terms of a labor agreement (a point that we will fully discuss later in this chapter). A *strike* is a concerted refusal by union members to work. Termination of a strike is usually contingent on the granting of certain union demands by management, and without the strike weapon or the threat of binding arbitration, there would be little need for employers to take union demands very seriously. As noted in Chapter 12, however, employers are also able to impose costs on unions to the extent that employers have the capacity to endure or "take" a strike. Under certain circumstances, employers may also lock out their employees in the course of a labor dispute. A *lockout* is a refusal by an employer to let union members work. Conceptually, there may seem to be little practical difference between a lockout and taking a strike, but, as will be discussed, there are occasions when a lockout may have certain strategic advantages.

This chapter begins with a review of the basic trends in work stoppages in the United States and a discussion of how these trends relate to strike activity in other countries. One of the most notable features in the data is the different level of work-stoppage activity in the private and public sectors. We consider the public policy influences on this difference and then use elementary tools of labor-market analysis to evaluate the rationale for maintaining different public policies toward strikes in the private and public sectors.

Work stoppages do not occur randomly; in the aggregate, the level of strike activity varies systematically with economic events. Later in this chapter, we build on the political nature of union behavior discussed in Chapter 10 and aspects of the negotiating process discussed in Chapter 13 to consider some theories that link strike activity with economic developments. Because work stoppages can impose significant costs on society, most countries have, as a matter of public policy, considered other methods of resolving impasses. This has been particularly true in the United States with the rapid expansion of collective bargaining in the public sector. The final part of this chapter introduces several dispute-settlement procedures and considers the effect of these procedures on collective-bargaining behavior.

## Profile of Strike Activity

### Strike Frequency and Duration

While only a few major work stoppages are reported in the media, strikes are in fact a fairly common experience in industrial life. Table 14.1, for example, shows that during the 1970s, between 1 and 3 million workers were involved in the 4000 to 6000 strikes occurring each year.[1] On the other hand, there are thousands of labor agreements in the United States, and strikes occur in only 10–15 percent of contract negotiations. Although recent data cover only stoppages involving at least one thousand workers, strikes appear to have declined substantially in the first half of the 1980s.

In comparison to other countries, the United States has a relatively high *strike frequency* (usually measured as the number of strikes per thousand workers) and *strike duration* (usually measured as the number of working days lost per thousand workers), despite the fact that union membership in the United States is less extensive and less politically motivated than in most other countries.[2] One of the main reasons for this is that under the decentralized system of collective bargaining there are more negotiating situations in the United States and, hence, more opportunities for negotiations to break down. Therefore, the relatively high level of strike activity is related, in part, to the tendency for union-representation elections to be held at the plant

---

[1] The data in Table 14.1 enumerate work stoppages, which include lockouts of employees by employers. However, employer lockouts occur infrequently, so the figures in the table mainly reflect strike activity.

[2] Royal Commission on Trade Unions and Employer Associations, *Written Evidence of the Ministry of Labour* (London: HMSO, 1965): 69; Hugh Clegg, *Trade Unionism Under Collective Bargaining: A Theory Based on a Comparison of Six Countries* (Oxford: Basil Blackwell, 1976): 69.

**Table 14.1**   Work Stoppages in the United States, 1953–85

| Year | Unemployment Rate | Number of Stoppages | | Estimated Percentage of Working Time Lost | | Workers Involved (thousands) | |
|------|------|------|------|------|------|------|------|
| | | All | Major Stoppages | All | Major Stoppages | All | Major Disputes |
| 1953 | 2.9 | 5091 | | 0.22 | | 2400 | |
| 1955 | 4.4 | 4320 | | 0.22 | | 2650 | |
| 1957 | 4.3 | 3673 | | 0.12 | | 1390 | |
| 1959 | 5.5 | 3708 | | 0.50 | | 1880 | |
| 1961 | 6.7 | 3367 | | 0.11 | | 1450 | |
| 1963 | 5.7 | 3362 | | 0.11 | | 941 | |
| 1965 | 4.5 | 3963 | | 0.15 | | 1550 | |
| 1967 | 3.8 | 4595 | | 0.25 | | 2870 | |
| 1969 | 3.5 | 5700 | | 0.24 | | 2481 | |
| 1971 | 5.9 | 5138 | | 0.26 | | 3280 | |
| 1973 | 4.9 | 5353 | | 0.14 | | 2251 | 1400 |
| 1975 | 8.5 | 5031 | | 0.16 | | 1746 | 965 |
| 1977 | 7.0 | 5600 | | 0.17 | | 2040 | 1212 |
| 1979 | 5.8 | 4800 | 235 | 0.15 | 0.09 | 1700 | 1021 |
| 1981 | 7.6 | | 145 | | 0.07 | | 729 |
| 1983 | 9.6 | | 81 | | 0.08 | | 909 |
| 1985 | 7.2 | | 54 | | 0.03 | | 324 |

Note:   Major work stoppages involve at least 1000 workers.
SOURCE:   U.S. Bureau of Labor Statistics, *Handbook of Labor Statistics 1980,* Bulletin 2070 (Washington, DC: U.S. Government Printing Office, 1980), Table 167, *Handbook of Labor Statistics 1985,* Bulletin 2217 (Washington, DC: U.S. Government Printing Office, 1985), Table 123, and *Current Wage Developments* (April 1987), Table 1.

level, under the unit-determination policies of the National Labor Relations Board (NLRB). In contrast, we noted in Chapter 12 that formal collective bargaining often occurs at the industry, regional, or even economywide level in Europe. The number of negotiations, or opportunities for a work stoppage to occur, is therefore much lower in countries with relatively centralized bargaining structures, although when a stoppage occurs it is likely to idle a large number of workers. What one would like to know from a careful comparison of the propensity to strike is how the probability that a negotiation will lead to a strike (that is, the number of strikes resulting from a given number of negotiations) varies across countries. Unfortunately, precise data on the total number of negotiating situations are not available.

There is, however, a second structural aspect of collective bargaining in the United States that may contribute to comparatively high strike levels. As a general rule, collective-bargaining agreements cover a wider range of issues in decentralized bargaining systems (for reasons discussed in Chapter 12), so that there is often more to resolve in American collective-bargaining negotiations and more potential for negotiations to reach an impasse. Issues of safety, production standards, and grievance procedures, for example, arise more frequently in plant-level collective bargaining in the United States than in more centralized negotiations abroad.

**Table 14.2**    Strikes by Contract Status and Issue, 1961–72 (in percent)

|  | Strikes with Given Issue | | | | Workers Involved in Strikes with Given Issue | | | |
| --- | --- | --- | --- | --- | --- | --- | --- | --- |
|  | First Agreement | Renegotiation | During Term | Other | First Agreement | Renegotiation | During Term | Other |
| Wages, hours, and other contractual matters | 31.1 | 89.6 | 10.8 | 60.6 | 39.1 | 81.2 | 13.7 | 61.1 |
| Union organization and security | 61.7 | 3.6 | 3.9 | 6.3 | 51.5 | 5.3 | 2.4 | 3.7 |
| Job security, plant administration | 5.1 | 5.1 | 49.9 | 24.6 | 4.5 | 12.4 | 63.5 | 26.6 |
| Inter and intra union | 1.5 | 0.2 | 27.7 | 4.4 | 4.3 | 0.3 | 13.5 | 4.1 |
| Other work conditions | 0.6 | 1.5 | 7.8 | 4.2 | 0.6 | 0.8 | 6.9 | 4.5 |
| All | 100 | 100 | 100 | 100 | 100 | 100 | 100 | 100 |

Note:   Some columns may not add to 100 because of rounding error.
SOURCE:   P. K. Edwards, *Strikes in the United States 1881–1974* (New York: St. Martin's Press, 1981): 183.

Besides being affected by the level of centralization in collective bargaining, the scope of bargaining may also be influenced by the presence of a labor or socialist party. Where such parties are in power, some have argued that many union goals may be achieved through legislation, and the burden placed on collective bargaining will be relatively light—causing the likelihood of strikes to be correspondingly low. It has also been argued that union-controlled labor parties discourage strikes in order to maintain a reasonably broad base of political support. Analyses of the relationship between strikes and the characteristics of political systems tend to show the opposite, however. Strikes tend to be higher when left-of-center governments are in power, perhaps because workers tend to have higher expectations concerning what they should be able to achieve.[3]

## Wildcat Strikes

In addition to their frequency, a second important characteristic of strikes in the United States is that they are usually associated with officially sanctioned collective-bargaining negotiations. Unofficial, or *wildcat,* strikes that occur while a labor agreement is in effect account for less than 10 percent of American work stoppages and tend to be concentrated in a few industries, such as coal. As can be seen from Table 14.2, strikes associated with attempts to negotiate an initial agreement with an employer are most frequently over issues of institutional security, while official strikes within the context of an

[3]  See Douglas A. Hibbs, Jr., "Industrial Conflict in Advanced Industrialized Societies," *American Political Science Review* 70 (December 1976): 1033–58; Martin Paldam and Peder J. Pedersen, "The Macroeconomic Strike Model: A Study of Seventeen Countries, 1948–1975," *Industrial and Labor Relations Review* 35 (July 1982): 504–21.

established collective-bargaining relationship occur mainly during periods of renegotiation and are related to substantive issues of wages, hours, and employment conditions. Wildcat strikes, however, usually occur *during* the term of the contract and they often represent (1) attempts by groups within the union to secure gains that were not or could not be obtained in official negotiations or (2) protests against the manner in which certain provisions of the agreement are being administered (see Table 14.2). Most collective-bargaining agreements include provisions that are designed to channel conflict into a grievance procedure (see Chapter 15) to avoid work stoppages during the term of the agreement, but in some cases workers seek a more rapid resolution of a complaint.[4]

One important reason for the relatively low level of wildcat-strike activity is that the labor agreement is a legally binding contract between a union and an employer, so that if a strike occurs during the term of the agreement, the union as an organization may be liable for damages along with the individuals responsible for the strike. (For example, the United Mine Workers union has been fined several times for unofficial strikes that occurred in the coal fields.) For this reason, it is not unusual to see both the employer and the officers of a national union attempting to end an unofficial strike. By way of contrast, in the United Kingdom where the labor agreement is not a binding legal document, unofficial strikes are common.

### Public-Sector Strikes

A third feature of American work stoppages is that the level of strike activity is distinctly lower in the public sector than in the private sector. Strikes in the public sector were almost nonexistent until the mid-1960s, but have increased substantially since then as union organization has spread, particularly at the state and local level. Despite the significant increase in public-sector strike activity, however, the general level (adjusted for numbers employed) remains considerably lower. One reason for this is the distinctly different legal status of strikes in the private and public sectors, an issue to which we now turn.

## Legal Status of Strikes

The difference in the legal treatment of strikes in the private and public sectors is easily explained: there is no constitutional right to strike in the United States, so that whatever rights exist must be provided by statute. Federal labor-relations statutes guarantee the right to strike in the private sector, but most state and federal government legislation actually prohibits strikes by public employees. This legal stance raises three general issues concerning the collective withholding of labor services to support collective-bargaining demands:

---

[4] Some labor agreements stipulate that certain issues are not subject to the normal dispute-resolution procedures, such as arbitration, that apply during the term of an agreement. Strikes over these issues while an agreement is in effect do not violate the contract.

1.  what is meant by the right to strike;
2.  what limitations, if any, are placed on the right to strike in the private sector; and
3.  should public policy toward strikes differ in the private and public sectors?

We will address each of these issues as we examine the legal status of strikes in the private and public sectors separately.

## Legal Status of Strikes in the Private Sector

**Employee rights.**    The first statutory source of public policy toward strikes in the private sector was the Norris-LaGuardia Act of 1932, which basically immunized peacefully conducted strikes from injunction. One consequence of the statute was that federal judges lost the power to decide if the purposes of a particular strike were lawful. This general right-to-strike was extended by Section 7 of the National Labor Relations Act (NLRA), which provided that "employees have the right . . . to engage in other concerted activities for the purpose of collective bargaining or other mutual aid or protection. . . ."

Taken literally, the language of the NLRA seems to provide a broad protection to almost any action taken by a group of workers; it might also be viewed as drastically circumscribing employer antistrike actions, since almost any action that an employer might take could be interpreted as interfering with the rights provided by Section 7. In fact, the courts have not provided such broad protection to strikers or applied such broad restrictions to employers. While the legal right-to-strike in the private sector prohibits employers from discharging or disciplining employees who strike, the key to a statutory right-to-strike is the replacement rights accorded to striking employees. Employees *always* have a constitutional right to quit their jobs—individually or in groups—to protest disagreeable working conditions. A strike occurs when a group of workers temporarily leave their jobs in an effort to change the terms of employment. The difference lies in the expectation that striking employees will be reinstated at the end of the strike. Yet, even in the private sector, the reinstatement right is not absolute.

Shortly after the passage of the NLRA, the Supreme Court held that in a normal economic strike, the employer has a right to hire permanent replacements for striking employees.[5] Once the strike is over, however, strikers who have been replaced must be given preference for employment as vacancies occur. Moreover, strikers who have been replaced retain a right to vote in an NLRB election to determine the union's status at the plant for a year after their replacement. Without such a right, an employer might simply replace striking employees with workers who were not sympathetic to unions to reduce support for the union in the plant.

---

[5]  *Mackay Radio and Telegraph Co.*, 304 U.S. 333 (1938). Employers may also replace workers who exercise their legal right to refuse to cross a picket line during a strike.

Not all employers in the private sector take advantage of their legal right to replace striking employees, however, since it may be difficult to find replacements with the specific skills needed. Moreover, attempts to bring in replacements during the course of a strike often create considerable tension and even violence. For similar reasons, employers in the public sector often do not exercise their legal right to discharge or discipline public employees who strike. Overall, when viewed in terms of the implications for job security, the difference between the right-to-strike in the private and public sectors is not as great as is frequently thought.

In contrast to reinstatement rights pertaining to normal economic strikes, if a strike occurs as a result of an employer unfair-labor practice, the employees who went out on strike have an absolute right to reinstatement, even if it means displacing replacements who the employer hired during the course of the strike. If the law did not make a distinction between economic and unfair-labor-practice strikes, an employer could eliminate a union from the plant by violating the law—that is, by provoking a union into a strike by committing unfair labor practices—and then replacing the union strikers with new non-union employees.

The fact that the reinstatement rights of striking workers rest on whether the employer has committed an unfair labor practice creates an incentive for the union to file unfair labor-practice charges during negotiations, and even to try inducing the employer into committing an unfair labor practice in order to protect the reinstatement rights of its members. If an employer does not commit an unfair labor practice, he or she can replace all strikers. If an employer violates the Act, however, employees who have struck must be reinstated. This obviously introduces an important element of gamesmanship into bargaining.

**Limits on employees' right to strike.**  The seemingly broad rights accorded concerted pressure activities by employees by the language of Section 7 of the NLRA may also be limited because of (1) the method used, (2) the purpose of the activity, or (3) the activity being taken separately from a certified union. With respect to methods, violent strikes are illegal, as are nonviolent harassment tactics such as intermittent strikes or disparagement of the employer's product. With respect to illegal purposes, we noted above the proscription against wildcat strikes (that is, strikes in violation of a no-strike clause in a labor agreement). Strikes intended to force an employer to violate a law are also illegal, as are strikes in support of union-organizing activities, which could threaten the NLRA principle of employee free-choice by coercing employees to join (or employers to recognize) a union.

As we noted in our discussion of union unfair labor practices in Chapter 11, "secondary" strikes or boycotts—that is, strikes against neutral firms that are not a party to the collective-bargaining agreement—are also forbidden. This has been a difficult area for public policy. A moment's reflection reveals one reason—virtually all strikes have harmful effects on firms that are not a party to the collective-bargaining agreement! If a strike curtails or shuts down production at a company (the "primary" employer), that company's suppliers ("secondary" employers) lose orders and often have to lay off workers. Similarly, the company's customers (who also are secondary employers) suffer harm unless substitutes for the struck good are readily available. If the struck good is used in the production processes of other industries (for example, steel), the secondary effects of the strike may be quite substantial as the struck company's customers curtail production and employment.

Nevertheless, these secondary effects of a union's strike do not constitute an illegal secondary boycott because the union's action is not aimed directly at neutrals. A secondary boycott arises when, in addition to (or instead of) striking the primary employer, a union also strikes or otherwise brings direct pressure against a neutral employer. For example, an illegal secondary boycott normally occurs if a union strikes a supplier of the primary employer in order to induce the latter to settle on its terms.

In certain important situations, however, direct action against a secondary firm does not constitute illegal activity. One exception occurs if secondary employers take actions that effectively make them a party to the primary dispute. For example, if employers are found to be *allies* of a struck employer, they lose their neutrality; unions are permitted to strike an ally even though the ally is not directly involved in the labor dispute. Allies include firms with common ownership or management, as well as independent companies who knowingly accept work that otherwise would have been performed by the struck employer.[6] An example of this situation arose when a typewriter company, Royal, which normally maintained machines that it leased to outside companies, was struck by a union representing some of its employees. During the strike, the company gave the maintenance work normally performed by its employees to another company. When the union proceeded to picket the second company, it was charged with conducting a secondary boycott. The Supreme Court rejected the charge, however, ruling that the second firm had injected itself into the dispute as an ally when it accepted the work from Royal.

A second exception to the proscription against secondary boycotts has been "common situs" picketing, which has been one of the more prominent labor-policy disputes involving secondary boycott issues over the past few years. Common situs picketing problems arise when both primary and secondary employers perform duties at the same location—for example, a general contractor and several subcontractors at a construction site. In this situation, one or more unions might picket the unionized general contractor at a construction site in an effort to induce the firm to cease doing business with a nonunion subcontractor. If there is no direct dispute between the general contractor and the union, the Supreme Court has ruled that this constitutes illegal secondary activity, since the object of picketing is to use an "innocent" third party to bring pressure to bear on the party with which the union has a dispute.[7] An entire worksite cannot be shut down legally because of a dispute

---

[6] *AFL-CIO Brewery Workers' Union (Adolph Coors Co.).* 121 NLRB 35 (1958).
[7] *NLRB* v. *Denver Building Trades,* 341 U.S. 675 (1951).

between a union and one subcontractor. On the other hand, legal picketing can occur at a common situs if a reserve gate is established for workers who are not involved in the dispute and there is no picketing or interference with that gate. Construction unions have been deeply opposed to this interpretation of the law, particularly since the substantial growth of nonunion construction work during the 1970s and 1980s. To date, however, they have not been successful in obtaining legislation that would permit broader common situs picketing.

A third exception occurs if unions picket peacefully at a secondary establishment in an effort to persuade consumers not to buy *a particular product* sold by that establishment. The Supreme Court has ruled that this is legal activity.[8] However, if the picket signs, handbills, or any other aspect of the union's communications urge consumers not to patronize the establishment, the activity becomes an illegal secondary boycott. This issue arises most frequently in the picketing of retail stores. In the campaign to organize the J. P. Stevens Company (discussed previously in Example 11.4) the labor movement launched a nationwide consumer boycott of the *products* of the company. Interestingly, when the United Farm Workers were organizing in the California grape fields during the late 1960s, they were legally able to urge consumers to boycott *stores* selling nonunion grapes—because agriculture is not covered by the NLRA!

Actions by other than certified unions, taken at unionized locations, are also not protected by the NLRA. Such actions include strikes by unions that do not represent a majority of the workers in a bargaining unit (that is, unions that have lost an NLRB union-representation election) and actions taken by groups of employees independently of their union. (For an example of the latter, see Example 14.1.) These actions are unprotected because they are inconsistent with the principle of exclusive representation that forms the core of a union's rights and duties under American labor law. Efforts by other unions or groups of employees to determine employment conditions in the bargaining unit independently of the certified bargaining representative would undermine the legal effort to establish a single voice for employees with respect to employment conditions.

**Employers' rights.**    What actions can employers take during a labor dispute in defense of their interests? This question has raised difficult issues for the NLRB and the courts, for while an employer has a right to operate a business effectively, almost any action taken by an employer in the course of a labor dispute technically involves discriminating against employees on the basis of their union membership. For many years the use of the employer *lockout*—closing a plant in the course of a labor dispute—was restricted by the courts to situations where (1) the timing of a strike by a union could create unusual hardship for the employer because of the perishable nature of the product or the seasonal nature of production, and (2) a multiemployer bargaining unit existed and the union struck only one member of the unit. In this

[8]  *NLRB* v. *Fruit and Vegetable Packers, Local 760* ("Tree Fruits"), 377 U.S. 58 (1964).

---

**EXAMPLE    14.1**

## The Emporium Case: Can Workers Bring Action Independently of Their Union?

To what extent can a group of union members take action independently of the union to secure rights that they believe are guaranteed to them by public policy? The following case provides an interesting review of the issues raised by such activity. The language describing the situation is that of the U.S. Supreme Court:

> This case presents the question whether, in light of the national policy against racial discrimination in employment, the National Labor Relations Act protects concerted activity by a group of minority employees to bargain with their employer over issues of employment discrimination. . . .
>
> The Emporium Capwell Company (the Company) operates a department store in San Francisco . . . [and] was a party to the collective-bargaining agreement negotiated by . . . the Department Store Employees' Union (the Union). The agreement, in which the Union was recognized as the sole collective-bargaining agency for all covered employees, prohibited employment discrimination by reason of race, color, creed, national origin, age, or sex, as well as union activity. It had a no-strike-or-lockout clause, and it established grievance and arbitration machinery for processing any claimed violation of the contract, including a violation of the antidiscrimination clause.
>
> On April 3, 1968, a group of Company employees covered by the agreement met with the Secretary-Treasury of the Union, Walter Johnson, to present a list of grievances including a claim that the Company was discriminating on the basis of race in making assignments and promotions. . . . [The union investigated the charges of discrimination,] concluded that the Company was discriminating, and [announced] that it would process every such grievance through to arbitration if necessary. . . .
>
> [Later some employees] expressed their view that the contract procedures were inadequate to handle a systemic grievance of this sort; they suggested that the Union instead begin picketing the store in protest. Johnson explained that the collective agreement bound the Union to its processes. . . .
>
> [Subsequently,] several . . . dissident employees held a press conference . . . at which they denounced the store's employment policy as racist, reiterated their desire to deal directly with "the top management" of the Company over minority employment conditions, and announced their intention to picket and institute a boycott of the store. . . . [Later,] employees picketed the store throughout the day and urged consumers not to patronize the store. Johnson encountered the picketing employees, again urged them to rely on the grievance process, and warned that they might be fired for their activities. The picketers, however, were not dissuaded, and they continued to press their demand to deal directly with the Company president. . . . When the conduct was repeated . . . the two employees were fired.

When the case reached the Supreme Court, the Court ruled against the employees on the grounds that their activity undermined the union's status as the exclusive representative of employees within the bargaining unit. If the union had refused to represent the interests of minorities within the bargaining unit, legal remedies were available, but this was obviously not the case in this situation. An employer facing demands from each of several groups is unlikely to be able to satisfy each simultaneously and still fulfill the contractual obligations. Similarly, a union, as an organization for collective action, has a legitimate interest in presenting a united front and "in not seeing its strength dissipated and its stature denigrated by subgroups within the unit separately pursuing what they see as separate interests. . . . The policy of industrial self-determination as expressed in Section 7 does not require fragmentation of the bargaining unit along racial or other lines in order to consist with the national labor policy against discrimination."

SOURCE: *Emporium Capwell Co.* v. *Western Addition Community Organization,* 420 U.S. 50 (1975).

case, a lockout might be required to defend and preserve the multiemployer nature of the contract.

With a ruling in 1965, however, the Supreme Court permitted employers to use the lockout offensively in situations where a labor agreement with a union had expired and a bargaining impasse had developed over mandatory bargaining issues.[9] The Court held that the right to strike in the private sector provided by the NLRA did not carry with it the presumption that the unions have the exclusive right to determine the timing and duration of work stoppages. At the same time, the Court ruled that the use of lockouts must be in defense of a legitimate bargaining position rather than an effort to discourage unionization. One important difference between a strike and a lockout is that workers who are locked out by an employer have a right to be reinstated at the end of the dispute, whereas workers who strike do not. Since the hiring of permanent replacements is legal if the union initiates a work stoppage but is not legal if the employer does, some employers may try to enhance their long-term bargaining position by waiting for the union to strike rather than using their legal right to lock out employees once an impasse has been reached.

During the early 1980s, several employers tried to avoid union contracts by declaring bankruptcy. This legal tactic is discussed in Example 14.2.

## Legal Status of Strikes in the Public Sector

Perhaps the most critical issue concerning public policy toward labor disputes in the past 25 years has been raised by the rapid growth of unions and strike activity in the public sector. The recent growth of public-sector unions was analyzed in Chapter 10, and the broad outlines of the increased militancy among public employees is described by the data in Table 14.3. In particular, it can be seen that, after years of relatively placid labor relations in the public sector, 1966 marked a transition to a higher level of strike activity.

While the growth of work stoppages has increased more rapidly among public employees than private employees since the mid-1960s, the level of

[9] *American Ship Building* v. *NLRB,* 380 U.S. 300 (1965).

**EXAMPLE 14.2**

## Can Employers Evade a Labor Agreement by Declaring Bankruptcy?

We have seen how the National Labor Relations Act prohibits unions and management from unilaterally changing a labor agreement during its term. The Bankruptcy Code does, however, permit the judges of bankruptcy courts to set aside many contracts in an effort to rehabilitate and reorganize insolvent companies. Indeed, under the Bankruptcy Reform Act of 1978, business firms no longer have to demonstrate insolvency—they may file for bankruptcy protection on the basis of uncertain or "contingent" liabilities, such as potential claims from litigation.

In the early 1980s, some major corporations appeared to use bankruptcy proceedings to abandon their labor agreements without negotiating with unions representing their workers. In 1983, for example, Continental Airlines cut wages by more than half and resumed operations on a nonunion basis three days after filing for bankruptcy and months before a bankruptcy court would rule on the petition. The Wilson Foods Corporation cited excessive labor costs in its petition for bankruptcy and cut wages by about 40 percent before the bankruptcy court ruled on the petition. Unions and many members of Congress were outraged by the apparent effort of some employers to use the bankruptcy laws to circumvent the National Labor Relations Act.

After a split Supreme Court ruled in 1984 that companies filing for bankruptcy could unilaterally abrogate their labor agreements before the bankruptcy court approved their petition, Congress revised the bankruptcy legislation to limit the right of a bankruptcy court to set aside labor contracts. This put an end to the tactical use of the bankruptcy laws in labor disputes.

Suppose Congress had not revised the law in 1984. How would tactics such as those adopted by Continental and Wilson Foods have affected the relative bargaining power of unions? The key fact to remember in considering this question has been developed in this chapter: Under the NLRA, employers always have the right to hire permanent replacements for strikers in normal contract disputes. Now consider Continental's tactic in 1983. Once the company unilaterally changed the contract after filing for bankruptcy, the union could either accept the modification or initiate negotiations demanding its previous benefits. Moreover, the union can strike in support of its position (as the unions at Continental did). The final outcome—including the possibility that strikers might be replaced (as they were at Continental)—will be determined by the relative bargaining power of the parties. Now suppose that rather than use the bankruptcy tactic, Continental had waited until the end of its contract and requested the same concessions from the union in the normal course of renegotiating a new contract. The union may agree to a modification of the contract or it may resist the company's request to the point of impasse and strike to back up its demands. Eventually, the strike will end on terms that are determined by the relative bargaining power of the parties, and this includes the possibility that the employer will hire permanent replacements for the strikers.

The use of the bankruptcy tactic can alter the timing of a change (from the normal contract expiration date) but not the factors that determine the ultimate outcome.

**Table 14.3**   Work Stoppages by Level of Government, 1958–80
(workers in thousands)

|  | All Levels of Government | | Federal Government | | State Government | | Local Government | |
|---|---|---|---|---|---|---|---|---|
|  | Number of Stoppages | Workers Involved | Number of Stoppages | Workers Involved | Number of Stoppages | Workers Involved | Number of Stoppages | Workers Involved |
| 1958 | 15 | 1.7 | — | — | 1 | * | 14 | 1.7 |
| 1959 | 25 | 2.0 | — | — | 4 | 0.4 | 21 | 1.6 |
| 1960 | 36 | 28.6 | — | — | 3 | 1.0 | 33 | 27.6 |
| 1961 | 28 | 6.6 | — | — | — | — | 28 | 6.6 |
| 1962 | 28 | 31.1 | 5 | 4.2 | 2 | 1.7 | 21 | 25.3 |
| 1963 | 29 | 4.8 | — | — | 2 | 0.3 | 27 | 4.6 |
| 1964 | 41 | 22.7 | — | — | 4 | 0.3 | 37 | 22.5 |
| 1965 | 42 | 11.9 | — | — | — | — | 42 | 11.9 |
| 1966 | 142 | 105.0 | — | — | 9 | 3.1 | 133 | 102.0 |
| 1967 | 181 | 132.0 | — | — | 12 | 4.7 | 169 | 127.0 |
| 1968 | 254 | 201.8 | 3 | 1.7 | 16 | 9.3 | 235 | 190.9 |
| 1969 | 411 | 160.0 | 2 | 0.6 | 37 | 20.5 | 372 | 139.0 |
| 1970 | 412 | 333.5 | 3 | 155.8 | 23 | 8.8 | 386 | 168.9 |
| 1971 | 329 | 152.6 | 2 | 1.0 | 23 | 14.5 | 304 | 137.1 |
| 1972 | 375 | 142.1 | — | — | 40 | 27.4 | 335 | 114.7 |
| 1973 | 387 | 196.4 | 1 | 0.5 | 29 | 12.3 | 357 | 183.7 |
| 1974 | 384 | 160.7 | 2 | 0.5 | 34 | 24.7 | 348 | 135.4 |
| 1975 | 478 | 318.5 | — | — | 32 | 66.6 | 446 | 252.0 |
| 1976 | 378 | 180.7 | 1 | * | 25 | 33.8 | 352 | 146.8 |
| 1977 | 413 | 170.2 | 2 | 0.4 | 44 | 33.7 | 367 | 136.2 |
| 1978 | 481 | 193.7 | 1 | 4.8 | 45 | 17.9 | 435 | 171.0 |
| 1979 | 593 | 254.1 | — | — | 57 | 48.6 | 536 | 205.5 |
| 1980 | 536 | 223.6 | 1 | .9 | 45 | 10.0 | 493 | 212.7 |

* Fewer than 100.
SOURCE:  U.S. Bureau of Labor Statistics, *Work Stoppages in Government, 1980* Bulletin 2110 (Washington, DC: U.S. Government Printing Office, October 1981): 4.

strike activity among government employees remains low relative to the private sector. In 1978, for example, 0.04 percent of working time at all levels of government was lost as a result of work stoppages, as against 0.17 percent of working time in all industries. Public-sector strikes tend on average to be shorter but to involve larger bargaining units than private-sector strikes. While there are many small bargaining units, there are also many that are huge. In 1979, 12,000 Chicago transit workers left their jobs for 4 days. In 1970, there was a nationwide strike by postal workers. In Detroit, 19,300 teachers struck for 13 days in 1979, and three years later, 11,000 teachers struck for three weeks. Also in 1981, a nationwide strike by some 12,000 air-traffic controllers resulted in the dismissal of the union's membership—an unusual event in the public sector. (By 1987, the air-traffic controllers had formed a new union.) However, the average number of days that a worker is on strike in the public sector is about half as long as in the private sector.

Eighty to ninety percent of all government strike activity involves employees of local-government units (cities, counties, or special districts), and virtually all of the remainder is at the state level. Over half of the strikes by government employees are in the education sector. While strikes by police and firefighters are usually highly publicized, they accounted for less than 10 percent of strike activity in the public sector in the late 1970s.

The remarkable fact about the surge of strike activity in the public sector since the mid-1960s is that it is virtually all illegal. Although unions representing public-sector employees have long claimed a constitutional right to strike, the federal courts have not supported this claim. Any right to strike must be provided by statutes, such as the Norris-LaGuardia Act and the National Labor Relations Act in the private sector. In general, no comparable legislation exists in the public sector. While most states have passed legislation permitting collective bargaining by public employees, only a few states have also accorded public employees the right to strike. Those that have passed such legislation have not extended the right to strike to police officers or firefighters.

Why should public policy toward unions in the public sector differ from policy toward private-sector unions? If the strike weapon is necessary to compel collective bargaining in the private sector, why is it not equally necessary in the public sector? These questions, which have been under debate for decades, came under intense reexamination during the 1970s. One argument advanced for not extending the right to strike to the public sector is that collective bargaining in the public sector is less necessary to eliminate inequalities of bargaining power between labor and management.[10] It is argued that if inequalities of bargaining power are unlikely in the first place, providing labor groups with the right to strike will *create* inequalities that will place public employers at a disadvantage. The case against allowing public employees to strike is usually based on two assertions: (a) the demand for labor is less elastic in the public than in the private sector, and (b) the political power of unionized public employees, when buttressed by the economic power inherent in the right to strike, would distort the overall influence of public employees beyond their numbers in a community.

**Wage elasticity of demand for public employees.**  It is often argued that the costs to society of collective bargaining are greater in the public sector than in the private sector, because the economic restraints on collective bargaining are much weaker in the nonmarket environment of government. We have seen how the demand for labor in the private sector is derived, in part, from the demand for a product or service, which itself is closely related to the product's price. Therefore, unions in the private sector face a difficult trade-off between the wages they negotiate (which influence product prices) and the employment of union members. In contrast, the argument

---

[10]  This view has been developed most forcefully by Harry H. Wellington and Ralph K. Winter, Jr., in *The Unions and the Cities* (Washington, DC: The Brookings Institution, 1971).

runs, government typically does not sell a product for which there are close substitutes, or for which demand is very responsive to price. In short, the "conventional wisdom" has been that, because many forms of public services are both monopolized and "essential," the demand for public employees is wage inelastic (relative to the demand for labor in the private sector), so that the wage demands of unions representing public employees are less likely to be tempered by concern over potential loss of employment by union members.

Generally speaking, this argument is not strongly supported by the evidence. At the conceptual level, government services do carry a price—taxes. When consumers of government services feel that the tax-price has become too high, they have several options. Individuals and businesses can and do move to other cities or states where the taxes they pay for comparable services are lower. In so doing, they reduce the tax base of the jurisdiction that they leave, thereby reducing the ability of that jurisdiction to provide the same level of government services and government employment. Taxpayers may also adopt tax-limitation legislation or constitutional amendments that roll back taxes and drastically limit the ability of all levels of government in a state to increase future tax revenues, and they may vote out of office political leaders who do not keep taxes down. Also, as unions in New York and in several other major cities faced with fiscal crises discovered during the 1970s, the unseen parties at the bargaining table are often the investors in a city's bonds. When there are difficulties in floating a bond issue, cities have financial incentives similar to those faced by private employers to keep wage costs down and seek greater efficiency in the utilization of labor. Moreover, public sector jurisdictions can go bankrupt. In June 1983, for example, the San Jose, California, Unified School District declared itself insolvent and filed for bankruptcy when it ran out of funds to pay teachers and other employees of the District.

It is also important to keep in mind that the elasticity of demand for labor is affected by more than the characteristics of product demand. First, labor costs in the public sector form a very large proportion of total costs, which tends to make the demand for labor more elastic than it would otherwise be. Second, public employers who are faced with financial pressures have more opportunities for factor and product substitution than is commonly recognized. One can easily think of substituting capital for labor in the provision of public services. For example, police patrol cars could be substituted for officers on the beat, thus making it possible for the same area to be patrolled by fewer officers. Snowblowers could be substituted for snow-removal workers with shovels, and school buildings can be redesigned to hold larger classes. Further, private firms can provide the same services now provided publicly: garbage pick-up, towing of parking violators, and street repair work could be subcontracted to private employers, or private companies could be hired to handle janitorial services in public buildings. Further, given the limited resources that state and local governments can command, an increase in the relative price of one service should lead a government to substitute

**Table 14.4**   Estimates of Wage Elasticities of Demand for Labor in the State and Local Sector

| Category | (1) | (2) | (3) |
|---|---|---|---|
| Education | −1.06 | −0.08 to −0.57 | −0.57 to −0.82 |
| Noneducation | −0.38 | | |
| Streets and highways | −0.09 | −0.44 to −0.64 | |
| Public welfare | −0.32 | −0.33 to −1.13 | |
| Hospitals | −0.30 | −0.30 to −0.51 | |
| Public health | −0.12 | −0.26 to −0.32 | |
| Police | −0.29 | −0.01 to −0.35 | |
| Fire | −0.53 | −0.23 to −0.31 | |
| Sanitation and sewage | −0.23 | −0.40 to −0.56 | |
| Natural resources | −0.39 | −0.39 to −0.60 | |
| General control and financial administration | −0.28 | −0.09 to −0.34 | |

SOURCES: (1) Orley Ashenfelter and Ronald Ehrenberg, "The Demand for Labor in the Public Sector" in *Labor in the Public and Nonprofit Sectors,* ed. Daniel Hamermesh (Princeton, N.J.: Princeton University Press, 1975), Table 6. (2) Ronald G. Ehrenberg, "The Demand for State and Local Government Employees," *American Economic Review* 63 (June 1973): 366–79. (3) Robert J. Thornton, "The Elasticity of Demand for Public School Teachers," *Industrial Relations* 18 (Winter 1979): 86–91.

other services that would be relatively cheaper (for example, minimally supervised playground programs could be substituted for summertime instructional programs in sports or crafts). In other words, while a local government does not have the option of moving its plant to a nonunion area, it can substitute capital for labor, change its services, or subcontract with private firms if it feels its labor costs are too high. Hence, it is *not* obvious *a priori* that the economic constraints on collective bargaining are weaker in the public sector than in the private sector.

The operational question raised by these observations is whether the demand for state- and local-government employees is inelastic. Three studies have presented estimates of the wage elasticities of demand for eleven functional categories of state- and local-government employees, and these studies are summarized in Table 14.4.[11] In the main, these estimates suggest that demand curves for labor in state and local government *are* generally inelastic. The estimates also indicate that the scope for substitution for labor varies among the government functions. As expected, the services of police, fire, and public health workers appear to be most essential (that is, the wage elasticity of these groups of workers is lowest), while there appears to be greater scope for substitution for employees in education, streets and high-

[11] Orley Ashenfelter and Ronald G. Ehrenberg, "The Demand for Labor in the Public Sector," in *Labor in the Public and Nonprofit Sectors,* ed. Daniel Hamermesh (Princeton, NJ.: Princeton University Press, 1975); Ronald G. Ehrenberg, "The Demand for State and Local Government Employees," *American Economic Review,* 63 (June 1973): 366–79; and Robert Thornton, "The Elasticity of Demand for Public School Teachers," *Industrial Relations* 18 (Winter 1979): 86–91.

ways, and public welfare. Nevertheless, the estimated elasticities do not appear substantially lower in absolute value than the private-sector wage-elasticities of demand that were summarized in Table 3.3. Regardless of these estimates, one should recall, as stressed in Chapter 12, that public employees are also voters and, through the political process, seek to increase (shift) the demand for their own services.[12] To the extent that they are successful, the employment loss that would be associated with any wage increase would be smaller than if the demand curve had not been shifted out.

**Distortions of influence.**  A second line of argument advanced in opposition to extending the right to strike to public employees concerns potential distortions of the political process. This view begins with the observation that what a mayor, governor, or other chief executive gives unions must be taken away from some other group, and that political chief executives are inclined to allocate resources among different groups on the basis of their relative power. It is then argued that with the economic power that comes with the right to strike, public-sector unions would have an advantage over other groups that could rely only on political power. The result would be that the public would pressure government officials to settle labor disputes quickly and that the pressure would lower employer resistance in the public sector.

The main difficulty with this view is that it exaggerates the distinction between economic and political power in the context of public-sector collective bargaining. While elected officials are often attentive to the number of votes a group may be able to deliver (a type of political power), the political leverage of groups other than unions frequently appears to rest on economic considerations. For example, lobbying activities are frequently tied to the economic support of political figures via campaign contributions. As noted earlier, businesses can threaten to reduce the tax and employment base by moving to another political jurisdiction if a city does not keep down taxes (a large fraction of which are used to cover labor costs). Investors may be unwilling to acquire a city's debt if the city government appears to have weak control over its labor costs and productivity.[13] It is difficult to draw a clear distinction between these methods of bringing political pressure against a public-sector employer and the use of a strike by unions. In recent years, the popularity of tax-limitation movements in several states suggests that far from bringing pressure on a public employer to settle a labor dispute rapidly, the voting public may be more supportive of political leaders who offer considerable resistance to union bargaining demands.

[12]  For an analysis of this point *see* Paul Courant, Edward Gramlich, and Daniel Rubinfeld, "Public Employee Market Power and the Level of Government Spending," *American Economic Review* 69 (December 1979): 806–17.

[13]  For a discussion of these considerations and a generally skeptical view of the argument that the political process would be distorted if public employees had the right to strike, *see* John F. Burton, Jr., and Charles Krider, "The Role and Consequences of Strikes by Public Employees," *Yale Law Journal* 79 (January 1970): 418–40.

# Theories of Strike Activity

It is obvious that strikes can impose serious losses of income on both workers and firms. If strikes involve costs to both union members and employers, why do they ever occur? It would seem that if both parties were aware of these costs, they would have an incentive to reach a settlement before a strike results. In fact, as we have seen earlier in the chapter, only a small fraction of collective-bargaining negotiations result in strikes in any one year. Nevertheless, strikes do occur even in experienced collective-bargaining relationships, and students of labor relations have long been interested in the reasons for the significant variations in strike activity over time and across industries. Despite the apparent irrationality of strikes when negotiators are well-informed, the variations in observed strike behavior appear to be too strong to be attributed to accidents or miscalculations.

The first, and also simplest, model of strikes in the bargaining process was developed by Sir John Hicks.[14] While this model captures many features of the bargaining environment, and hence is a useful starting point, it also leads to the difficulties mentioned above. His analysis examines how the wage increases demanded by the union and offered by the employer vary with the length of a strike.

The strike begins because the wage increase that the employer offers, $W_e$ in Figure 14.1, is less than the raise that the union demands, $W_u$. Once the strike has started, what causes the two parties to eventually reach agreement? For the employer, the longer a strike lasts, the more costly it becomes in terms of lost customers. Struck firms may suffer a permanent loss of market share to the extent that former customers are able to find other suppliers or substitutes for their work. Faced with increasing costs, an employer should be willing to increase the wage offer as the strike progresses. This willingness is denoted by the upward-sloping *employer concession schedule, EC,* in Figure 14.1. The position of the concession schedule will reflect features of the bargaining environment. For example, if the employer joins a strike-insurance arrangement, the *EC* schedule will be shifted down. With the costs of a strike defrayed by the insurance, the employer would be willing to hold out longer before agreeing to a union wage proposal.

A strike also imposes costs on union members. As the loss in income that they are individually suffering increases with the length of the strike, they should begin to reduce their wage demands. This reduction is indicated by the *union-resistance curve, UR,* in Figure 14.1. The position of the union-resistance curve will also be influenced by the bargaining environment. For example, if strikers are permitted to collect unemployment insurance benefits, the *UR* curve will shift up. Increasing the financial support of union members raises union resistance.

As the strike proceeds, the union's demands decrease and the employer's offer increases until at strike duration $S_o$ the two coincide. At this point, a

---

[14]  John R. Hicks, *The Theory of Wages,* 2d ed. (New York: St. Martin's Press, 1966): 136–57.

**Figure 14.1**  Hicks's Bargaining Model and Expected Strike Length

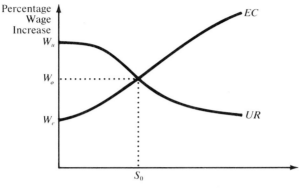

Expected Strike Length

settlement is reached, the parties agree upon a wage increase of $W_o$, and the strike ends.

Descriptively, this simple model captures important features of bargaining and strikes. Fundamentally, any strike reflects a conflict of interest between the *two* parties to collective bargaining. A growth in union militancy, for example, will not lead to more strikes *unless* employers resist union demands. Conversely, employer demands for wage concessions—a widespread phenomenon during the 1980s—will only produce strikes if unions resist. Indeed, the fact that work stoppages *declined* during the first half of the 1980s despite the demands for concessions indicates a decline in union resistance. The model also examines how institutional features, such as strike insurance and the availability of unemployment insurance to strikers, might affect the length of strikes through their effects on employer concessions or union resistance.

The model also poses a difficult question. *If* each party were aware of the position and shape of the other party's curve, each would know in advance both the strike length and the size of the final settlement. Thus, it would make sense for each party to agree to a settlement of $W_o$ *prior* to the strike so that each could avoid the costs associated with the strike. Why would strikes ever occur? One reason is that information is imperfect; one or both sides in the negotiation could fail to convey the true shape and position of its schedule to the other party.[15] A second possibility is that to enhance their bargaining positions and retain the credibility of the threat of a strike, unions may have to periodically use the weapon; a strike may be designed to influence *future* negotiations.[16] Finally, strikes may be useful devices by which the internal

---

[15] In the words of Hicks, "The majority of strikes are doubtless the results of faulty negotiations," (Hicks, *The Theory of Wages*, p. 146).

[16] Lest one carry this "rusty weapon" argument too far, the reader should consider its implications for the build-up of nuclear weapons.

solidarity of a union can be enhanced against a commonly perceived adversary—the employer.[17]

The major problem with these explanations of when a strike will occur is that they do not enable one to predict whether a strike will occur in a particular contract negotiation and, more importantly, they do not offer any insights about why the aggregate level of strike activity should vary over time. Many research studies indicate that strike activity is cyclical, increasing when unemployment rates are low and decreasing when unemployment rates are high. There are also important interindustry variations in strikes. Although there is no universally accepted explanation of strike activity, three approaches capture important features of bargaining impasses—the role of political conflicts within labor unions, the desire of the parties to avoid strike costs, and the role of differences in information.[18] We now discuss these.

## A Political Model of Strike Activity

The first approach is a political model of strike activity.[19] The political model is based upon the premise that it is inappropriate to view the collective-bargaining process as involving only two parties, an employer and a union. Rather, different members of the union will have different and sometimes conflicting objectives (as noted in Chapter 10). While union members are concerned primarily with their pecuniary and nonpecuniary conditions of employment, union leaders are also concerned about the survival and growth of the union and their own personal political survival. This divergence in objectives between union members and union leaders can lead to strikes.

Union leaders, who have been actively involved with management in the bargaining process, may have much better information than rank-and-file union members about the employer's true financial position and the maximum wage settlement the union will be able to extract. If this settlement is smaller than the membership wants, the union leaders face two options.

On the one hand, union leaders can return to their members, try to convince them of the employer's true financial picture, and recommend that management's last offer (the maximum that they know they can achieve) be accepted. The danger they face with this option is that the members may vote down the recommendation, accuse the leaders of selling out to management, and ultimately vote them out of office.

---

[17]  Richard Walton and Robert McKersie, *A Behavioral Theory of Labor Negotiations* (New York: McGraw-Hill, 1965): 32.

[18]  For an extensive consideration of these theories and related empirical evidence, see John Kennan, "The Economics of Strikes," in O. Ashenfelter and R. Layard (eds.), *Handbook of Labor Economics* Vol. II (Amsterdam, North Holland: 1986), Chapter 19.

[19]  Arthur Ross, *Trade Union Wage Policy* (Berkeley, Calif: University of California Press, 1948, and Orley Ashenfelter and George Johnson, "Bargaining Theory, Trade Unions, and Industrial Strike Activity," *American Economic Review* 59 (March 1969): 35–49. A more recent test of the model is found in Henry Farber, "Bargaining Theory, Wage Outcomes, and the Occurrence of Strikes," *American Economic Review* 68 (June 1978): 262–71.

On the other hand, union leaders can return to their members and recommend that the members go out on strike. This recommendation will allow them to appear to be strong, militant leaders, even though the leaders themselves know that the strike will not lead to a larger settlement. However, after a strike of some duration, in accordance with the notion of the union-resistance curve in Figure 14.1, union members will begin to moderate their wage demands, and ultimately, a settlement—for which the union leaders will receive credit—will be reached. Since the latter strategy is the one that is more likely to maintain the union's strength *and* keep the leaders in office, it is the strategy leaders may opt for, even though it is clearly not in their members' best interests in the short run (the members have to bear the costs of the strike).

The preceding model can provide insights about the forces that affect the frequency and duration of strike activity. In panel (a) of Figure 14.2, curve *UR* represents union members' minimum acceptable percentage wage increase as a function of the length of a strike; this curve is nothing more than the Hicks union-resistance curve. In this diagram, $\dot{W}$ is the union members' initial wage demand (the amount they would settle for without a strike), and $\dot{W}_m$ is the minimum amount they would ever settle for. Depending upon economic conditions and the members' hostility to management, $\dot{W}_m$ may be positive, zero, or even negative—the last possibility would occur if union members felt that they had to take a pay cut to preserve their jobs.

Panel (b) of Figure 14.2 plots the employer's present value of profits (*PVP*) as a function of the length of a strike. An increase in strike duration has two offsetting effects. In the immediate period, the employer loses profits because the firm loses some sales. However, in the future, the firm's profits may be higher because the longer strike means that the employees will be willing to settle for smaller wage increases [from panel (a) of Figure 14.2]. In panel (b), initially the second effect dominates and then, ultimately—since the union demands fall less rapidly (in absolute terms) and lost sales begin to mount up—the first effect dominates; that is, the employer's present value of profits first increases and then decreases with strike duration.

Suppose the employer's goal is to maximize the firm's present value of profits, and suppose the employer knows the position and shape of the curves in Figure 14.2. The employer can maximize the firm's present value of profits by offering the union a wage increase of $\dot{W}^*$ after a strike of length $S^*$. At that point, the union members will accept the offer and the strike will end. If the *PVP* curve in Figure 14.2 were always negatively sloped, the employer would either settle prior to a strike or go out of business if paying $\dot{W}$ would cause the firm to suffer losses.

If factors underlying the curves in Figure 14.2 change, the probability of occurrence and expected duration of a strike will be affected. For example, an increase in the rate at which the union's wage demands decline over time, other things equal, will increase the employer's payoff from prolonging the strike. In contrast, an increase in the union members' minimum acceptable

**Figure 14.2**   Graphic Representation of Ashenfelter-Johnson Model of Strike Activity

**(a) Union Members' Acceptable Wage Increase**

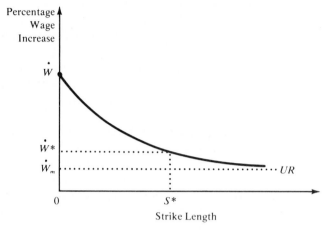

**(b) Employer Present Value of Profit Function**

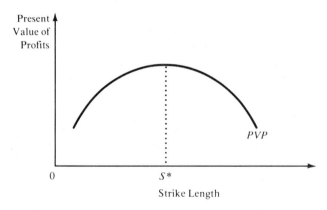

wage demand $\dot{W}_m$ (sometimes called the union's *resistance point*) will reduce the employer's gain from incurring a strike, and will reduce the probability of a strike occurring.

The Ashenfelter and Johnson study—which assumed that $\dot{W}$, $\dot{W}_m$, and the slope of the $UR$ curve in Figure 14.2 are influenced by the unemployment rate in the economy (as well as by past changes in wage rates and prices, and by the profit rates of corporations)—explains why strike activity tends to be reduced when the unemployment rate is high.[20] In the context of their model, an increase in the unemployment rate reduces the initial wage demands of unions ($\dot{W}$), since the wages of other groups are rising more slowly and

[20] Ashenfelter and Johnson, "Bargaining Theory . . ." pp. 42–46.

because there are fewer alternative job opportunities. Thus it is less likely that either side will see much to be gained by a strike.

Ashenfelter and Johnson also found that after statistically controlling for the unemployment rate, profits, and past wage and price changes, the level of strike activity (as measured by the number of work stoppages per year) tended to decline during the period they studied (1952–67). However, the decline took a particular form: while the pattern was downward from 1952 to 1959, the number jumped up in 1959 before resuming its downward trend.[21]

The general decline in strike activity in the American economy has been attributed by many observers to the maturation of industrial relations in the United States; fewer strikes are now caused by the parties' misunderstanding of other's intentions or by the need to use a strike today to enhance bargaining power tomorrow.[22] The increase in 1959 coincided with the passage of the Landrum-Griffin Act. By increasing union democracy, this act increased the chances that union leaders would be voted out of office if they failed to satisfy union members' expectations at contract-negotiation time. In the context of the model presented here, making union leaders more accountable to membership would increase the probability that leaders would recommend going on strike, rather than trying to sell an unacceptable contract to the rank-and-file. To return to a previous theme, social programs and legislation often have unintended side effects; the Landrum-Griffin Act may well have unintentionally led to an increase in the level of strike activity in the economy.

The model presented in this section focuses only on strikes that result from disagreements over economic issues and ignores strikes that may result from conflict over recognition procedures, grievance procedures, unsafe working conditions, and the like. It also makes certain assumptions that, while sometimes plausible, are unlikely to be true always. For example, in essence, this model suggests that union leaders and management implicitly collude to the detriment of union members. Union leaders are assumed to be willing to recommend a strike that will impose costs (in the form of lost income) on members, even though they may know that the strike will not increase management's ultimate wage offer. Management is assumed to know fully union members' resistance curves. Finally, union members are assumed to be ignorant, in the sense that they never learn how the bargaining process is actually working. Nonetheless, the model provides useful insights into the bargaining process and an explanation of why the Landrum-Griffin Act and the unemployment rate should be expected to influence the level of strike activity.

---

[21] Ashenfelter and Johnson, ''Bargaining Theory . . .'' p. 47.

[22] It is hard to discern a trend in any of the measures of strike activity over the 1953–79 period in the *raw* data presented in Table 14.1. One must remember, however, that during the period, all of the other variables (unemployment, wage and price changes, and profits) were changing. The trends Ashenfelter and Johnson observed are found after one statistically controls for these other factors. Further, the downward trend in strike activity appears to have resumed in the 1980s, perhaps as a result of union members' increasing concerns about job security.

## Interindustry Strike Activity: Other Explanations of Strikes

Persistent differences in the level of strike activity also exist across industries. In 1979, for example, the Bureau of Labor Statistics reported that two industries (tobacco and ordnance) each had only two work stoppages while two other industries (trade and government) each had over 500 stoppages.[23] While some of the wide interindustry variation in the number of strikes can be explained by interindustry differences in the number of bargaining units, substantial differences in the extent of strike activity between industries remain even after adjustment for this factor.

What explains this phenomenon? It has been suggested that variations in worker militancy and/or employer resistance by industry are the explanation, but these assertions simply raise the question of why militancy and/or resistance varies by industry.

Explanations of strike activity based on efforts to avoid strike costs and on imperfect information provide insights into these patterns. These explanations abstract from the union leader/union member dichotomy of the political model. They also reject that model's assumption that union members are passive participants in the strike-determination process; rather, they assume that unions are trying to optimize some well-defined set of objective.

**Reducing Strike Costs.** Other things equal, the more costly a strike is, the smaller is the "size of the pie" that will be left for the employer and the union to divide in any settlement. In situations in which the costs of strikes are high, this model predicts that the parties will strive to establish *bargaining protocols* that will help to avert future strikes; that is, they will seek to structure the bargaining process in ways that reduce the chances that strikes will occur.[24] For example, the parties might agree to start bargaining well in advance of a contract expiration, to limit the number of contract items they will discuss, or to submit the dispute to binding arbitration if they fail to reach agreement on their own. (For a discussion of a prominent bargaining protocol, see Example 14.3.)

What determines how costly a strike will be to the parties? In part, it depends upon whether inventories of the product can be built up prior to the strike to substitute for lost output during the strike; strikes will be particularly costly to producers of perishable products, for whom such substitution is impossible. In part, it also depends on the willingness of consumers to postpone their purchases of the product from a firm that is on strike: strikes will be particularly costly if there are domestic or foreign competitors who produce the same, or easily substitutable products, or if consumers cannot delay their purchases of the product. In part, finally, it depends upon subsidies that the firm or the union might receive from third-party sources during a strike: strikes will be less costly if such subsidies are present.

---

[23] U.S. Bureau of Labor Statistics, *Analysis of Work Stoppages,* 1979 Bulletin 2092 (Washington, DC: U.S. Government Printing Office, April 1981).

[24] Melvin Reder and George Neumann, "Conflict and Contract: The Case of Strikes," *Journal of Political Economy* 88 (October 1980): 867–86, and Kennan, "The Economics of Strikes."

**EXAMPLE 14.3**

## The Steel Industry's Experimental Negotiating Agreement

Uncertainty concerning the outcome of major collective-bargaining negotiations can influence industrial patterns of output and employment. In the steel industry, negotiations between the United Steelworkers of America and major steel producers occur every three years, and establish terms and conditions of employment for the industry. While there has not been an industrywide strike in steel since the 1959 negotiations, the *possibility* that a strike might occur led most substantial purchasers of steel to build up inventories in advance of the contract expiration date in the steel industry, so that they could continue to operate in the event of a strike. When negotiations were completed without a strike, the steel industry would fall into a slump with plant shutdowns and layoffs as the industry's major customers worked off their inventories. The cycle also produced permanent losses for the steel industry: foreign steel producers who assisted American firms in building up inventories of steel often signed long-term contracts with former customers of American steel producers.

In April 1973, the major steel companies and the United Steelworkers union signed a pact known as the Experimental Negotiating Agreement (ENA) that subsequently applied to negotiations in 1974, 1977, and 1980. The Agreement effectively provided insurance against the uncertainties formerly faced by the steel union, the steel industry, and steel consumers. Under the ENA, the union agreed not to strike over national bargaining issues, thus guaranteeing uninterrupted steel production. Issues that were not resolved in negotiations were referred to an arbitration board consisting of one union-appointed member, one company-appointed member, and three members appointed with the approval of both sides; only the three impartial members could vote. In return for forgoing the right to strike over national bargaining issues, union members were given a one-time bonus of $150, a guaranteed wage increase of 3 percent per year, and cost-of-living adjustments (COLAs). The union retained a limited right to strike over local issues.

This innovative agreement was retained for three rounds of national negotiations but was dropped in the early 1980s as a result of employer opposition. The opposition stemmed from two factors. First, while the ENA succeeded in eliminating national strikes, steel companies continued to face local strikes. Moreover, employers argued that some national issues were being redefined as local issues so that the union could bring the strike weapon to bear. In 1977, for example, several thousand steelworkers in the Minnesota iron-ore range struck over incentive pay on the grounds, disputed by employers, that it was a local issue. To the extent that national issues were "transformed" into local issues, some of the uncertainty that the ENA was designed to remove remained. Second, the pact proved to be expensive, particularly as the inflation of the late 1970s and early 1980s resulted in large COLA payments. By the early 1980s, imported steel still accounted for a large share of the American market, and the strategy of the steel industry shifted from buying a reduction in conflict to seeking wage concessions (see Example 10.2).

SOURCES:  National Academy of Arbitrators, *Arbitration of Interest Disputes: Proceedings of the 26th Annual Meeting*, pp. 79–80, 88. Michael Drapkin, "Steel Union Backs Arbitration Plan to Avoid Strike," *Wall Street Journal*, March 29, 1973; and Douglas R. Sease, "Fate of Steel Industry's No-Strike Accord in 1983 Depends on Three Major Factors," *Wall Street Journal*, April 28, 1980.

Empirical evidence also provides support for this "total cost" model. One study showed that in situations in which it was easy to vary inventory levels over time, strikes were more likely to occur.[25] A second study focused on strikes of schoolteachers in Pennsylvania, where such strikes are legal. Teachers lose pay for each day they are on strike in Pennsylvania *unless* the school district reschedules the lost school days; in the latter case the cost of the strike to the workers involved is minimal. Not surprisingly, the study showed that the more likely a district was to reschedule lost school days if a strike occurred, the more likely it was that a strike would be observed.[26] Finally, within the manufacturing sector, the incidence of strike activity is much higher in durable manufacturing (for example, automobiles), where the possibility of consumer postponement of purchase of goods is possible, than it is in nondurable manufacturing (for example, food), for which postponement of purchase is much less feasible.[27]

**Asymmetric Information.**  We have already stressed that strikes can occur because the parties are poorly informed or have not yet developed negotiating skills, such as those discussed in the previous chapter. Misinformation and miscalculation are most likely in new bargaining relationships, and there tend to be more strikes in industries with a relatively large number of new bargaining relationships.[28] Asymmetric information occurs when at least one of the parties in the negotiation does not have perfect information about the shape and position of the other's resistance or concession schedule (see Figure 14.1). In such situations, the process of bargaining per se can increase the accuracy of the information each party has about the other party's schedule and ultimately lead to a solution. However, the greater the initial level of uncertainty, the longer the bargaining process will take. By raising the cost to the parties of extending bargaining, a strike increases the incentive each has to reveal its true position more rapidly, and leads to a quicker solution.[29]

An implication of this model is that increased uncertainty about an employer's willingness to grant wage increases should increase both the probability that a strike will occur and the duration of the strike if it does occur.[30] Other things equal, therefore, more highly variable profits within a firm over the years might reasonably be expected to increase uncertainty about its willingness to grant wage increases, thus increasing the incidence and duration of strike activity. Empirical evidence does in fact suggest that both the

[25]  Reder and Neumann, "Conflict and Contract: The Case of Strikes."

[26]  See Craig Olson, "The Role of Rescheduled School Days in Teacher Strikes," *Industrial and Labor Relations Review* 37(July 1984): 515–28. We discuss dispute resolution in the public sector later in this chapter for, unlike Pennsylvania, in most states public sector strikes are illegal.

[27]  See, for example, U.S. Bureau of Labor Statistics, *Handbook of Labor Statistics 1973*, Bulletin 1790 (Washington, DC: U.S. Government Printing Office, 1973), Table 158, for industry strike frequency data between 1956 and 1971.

[28]  Reder and Neumann, "Conflict and Contract."

[29]  See, for example, Beth Hayes, "Unions and Strikes with Asymmetric Information," *Journal of Labor Economics* 2 (January 1984): 57–83.

[30]  Joseph Tracy, "An Empirical Test of an Asymmetric Information Model of Strikes," *Journal of Labor Economics* 5 (April 1987): 149–73.

incidence and duration of strike activity are higher in firms whose profitability varies widely over time.[31]

# Methods of Dispute Settlement

Bargaining impasses typically develop into strikes or lockouts that can impose significant costs on individuals who are not involved in a particular labor dispute. As a result, most societies have, as a matter of policy, attempted to devise methods of dispute settlement in an effort to reduce the likelihood that a bargaining impasse will occur. The development of such procedures is a delicate matter, since the objective is to reduce the probability of an impasse while maintaining collective bargaining as the main route to a settlement. Moreover, the nature of the procedure may itself influence the probability that an impasse will develop.

The most widely adopted approach to dispute settlement is to introduce *third-party procedures* into the collective-bargaining process. Third-party procedures inject one or more individuals who are not directly involved in the labor dispute into the bargaining process. Some procedures are available as a matter of course in virtually all collective-bargaining situations, while others are reserved for special situations, such as national emergency disputes or disputes in the public sector where strikes are forbidden. Paradoxically, the most effective third-party procedures in collective bargaining are those that are not used frequently; their function is to provide incentives for labor and management to reach agreement without resorting to the procedure. Such procedures are able to reduce the likelihood of a bargaining impasse by improving the information between the parties on settlement possibilities or by potentially imposing costs that labor and management seek to avoid. The potential effectiveness of alternative dispute-settlement procedures can be assessed in terms of their ability to improve information or impose such costs.

There are three third-party procedures that are commonly used, and these will be discussed in the order of increasing intrusiveness into the collective-bargaining process. *Mediation* involves the use of a third party in the negotiations to facilitate the fashioning of an agreement by labor and management. Mediators have no authority to impose a solution to a dispute, however. *Fact-finding* is simply a search for the basic facts and issues in a labor dispute by a neutral individual or panel of individuals. *Artibration* involves the use of a third party to actually determine the terms and conditions of a labor agreement.

---

[31] Joseph Tracy, "An Empirical Test . . ." and Tracy, "An Investigation into the Determinants of U.S. Strike Activity," *American Economic Review* 76 (June 1986): 423–36. While Tracy emphasizes differences in firm-specific information as a cause of strikes, general uncertainty can also lead to strikes. This is the case because the more uncertain the economic environment, the more contingencies the parties must plan for and the greater is the likelihood there will be differences in expectations about the economy between the bargainers. Recent evidence has shown that uncertainty about inflation has contributed to strikes in the 1970s. See Cynthia Gramm, Wallace E. Hendricks, and Lawrence M. Kahn, "Inflation Uncertainty and Strike Activity," *Industrial Relations*, 27 (January 1988): 114–29.

## Mediation

Perhaps the most common form of third-party intervention in labor disputes is *mediation,* in which an experienced neutral joins union and management negotiators in an effort to resolve the differences that remain between them. Unlike an arbitrator, however, a mediator has no authority to impose a settlement on the parties. His or her role is to facilitate the search for an agreeable compromise between the two parties. Most mediation in the private sector is conducted by members of the Federal Mediation and Conciliation Service (FMCS), who see more collective bargaining in the course of a year than many union and management negotiators see in a lifetime.[32] Many states also have mediation agencies or public employment relations agencies that, among other functions, provide mediation services to help resolve labor disputes in the public sector.

Why might mediation work to achieve a settlement? Unlike a strike, mediation does not directly impose costs on the parties or otherwise provide any particular incentive to avoid the procedure by settling their dispute. Instead, the main role of mediation is to facilitate a settlement by increasing the flow of information between labor and management. One of the limitations of mediation as a technique of dispute settlement is that it is unlikely to succeed in situations where a contract zone—a range of potential agreement between labor and management—does not exist because the parties to collective bargaining hold mutually inconsistent expectations. Only in situations where a mediator is able to suggest alternatives that the parties had not thought of themselves is mediation likely to facilitate agreement by creating a contract zone where none existed before.

More frequently, where a contract zone does exist, the role of mediation is to guide the parties to a settlement by facilitating the flow of information and concessions. Many professionals feel that mediation is a complement to, rather than a substitute for, strike activity; that is, labor and management may be more responsive to mediation efforts when faced with the threat of a strike if mediation fails. From this perspective, mediation may be more successful in the private sector than in the public sector, where there generally is no legal right to strike. Even in collective-bargaining situations in which a strike is possible, mediation can fail because of poor timing. Unless negotiations are sufficiently far advanced that the parties can feel the pressure of a failure to agree, they may be relatively unresponsive to efforts to mediate the dispute.

The mediator's task is generally to cut through the formally stated bargaining positions of union and management negotiators to discover what the essential goals of each side are and where the resistance points that could

---

[32] By the mid-1980s, the FMCS was involved in 20,000 labor disputes annually. About half of the disputes required only informal mediation while the other half involved joint mediation activities with labor and management. About 10 percent of the disputes requiring joint mediation were in the public sector. The FMCS also provides training and other technical assistance to negotiators and neutrals in dispute settlement. See Federal Mediation and Conciliation Service, *Thirty-sixth Annual Report, Fiscal Year 1983* (Washington, DC: U.S. Government Printing Office, 1982): 10.

trigger a strike lie. Sophisticated mediators also have to recognize that negotiators for both sides may be constrained by a need to satisfy different political
factions within their own organizations. There is no set format for handling
this task, and different mediators develop different styles and procedures.
Most mediators listen, at least briefly, to an initial statement of the issues by
each side in a joint meeting of the negotiating teams. Even though such
sessions are likely to be marked by considerable posturing and are unlikely to
reveal the real resistance points of either side, they clarify the nature of the
conflict and can reveal internal political tensions that may have an important
influence on the bargaining.

Real progress in mediation is usually achieved only after the parties are
separated and the mediator begins to shuttle between them in a series of
private discussions. During this more private part of the process, the mediator
attempts to get the parties to reveal their fundamental goals and to determine
possible trades that might form the basis for an agreement. This part of the
process is particularly delicate, since the parties are well aware of the mediator's objectives and may wish to release information selectively in order to
advance their own causes. Yet a relentlessly self-serving use of a mediator by
each side would probably result in a breakdown of mediation and create
consequences that might be quite costly. It is easily seen that when those
consequences are severe, as when strikes are permitted, the parties have
more inclination to treat the mediation process seriously. As noted above, an
able mediator may be able to suggest alternatives or compromises that the
parties had not thought of themselves.

A mediator may also propose to both parties an alternative that they had
thought of but were unwilling to propose, for fear of losing ground (if the other
side rejected it) or face (if it involved withdrawing from an earlier position).
Proposals advanced by a mediator may also relieve the negotiators of some
political pressures—they can always claim that an unpalatable result was the
mediator's idea. In smaller bargaining units in the public sector, for example,
it is not unusual for the parties to use "outside negotiators" (that is, teachers
may bring in a regional representative of their national union or professional
association, and the board of education may hire an attorney from a major law
firm). Often these experienced professionals may agree on a settlement but
need a way to "sell it" to their respective sides. The mediator becomes a
"seller" of the settlement to the negotiators' principals, overcoming unrealistic expectations about what is possible from the negotiations.[33]

It is not easy to evaluate the performance of mediation as a technique of
dispute resolution. While the basic objective of all professional mediators is to
obtain a collective-bargaining settlement, a determination of the number of
strikes avoided as a result of mediation would understate the effectiveness of
the process. Even when mediation is followed by a bargaining impasse and

---

[33]  For an extensive examination of the methods of federal and state mediators, see Deborah M.
Kolb, *The Mediators* (Cambridge, MA: The MIT Press, 1983).

strike, the mediator may have narrowed the range of issues under contention and, as a result, shortened the duration of the strike.

Professional mediators are single-minded in their efforts to secure an agreement between the parties to collective bargaining. To do this, they must remain acceptable to both labor and management; their usefulness is over when either party lacks confidence in them. Most mediators feel that the acceptability that is fundamental to their success would be jeopardized if they were to pursue goals other than achieving a settlement. As a result, they avoid becoming involved in some of the key issues that are raised by the presence of collective bargaining in society. Contrary to arbitrators, for example, mediators are generally unconcerned with the fairness or equity of a collective-bargaining settlement. Their task is to prevent breakdowns of negotiations, not to rectify inequalities in bargaining power. Similarly, mediators are unwilling to enforce laws or public policy, on the grounds that it would undermine their acceptability to labor and management. Therefore, if the parties were to negotiate a clause in a collective-bargaining agreement that violated a federal law—for example, a clause that discriminated against women or racial minorities—a mediator might inform the parties of the conflict with federal law, but not take further action. During the periodic experiments with incomes policy in the United States since the early 1960s, there has been an interest among some federal policy makers in having the FMCS enforce the guidelines for wage increases in such policies during their mediation efforts. The FMCS has successfully resisted such suggestions on the grounds that the effectiveness of mediators would be undermined if their primary responsibility was perceived to be the enforcement of an administration's wage policy.

## Fact-Finding

Under fact-finding the individual or panel that is chosen to determine and report on the issues at stake in a dispute does not intervene in the bargaining process directly. Instead, the publication of a fact-finding report, it is argued, may cut through the bluff and exaggerated claims of a bargaining situation. Supporters of fact-finding procedures hope that informing the public of the objective issues in a labor dispute will help muster public opinion in favor of an appropriate settlement and bring its weight to bear against the recalcitrant party. Particularly in public-sector negotiations, however, fact-finders may attempt to devise an acceptable compromise settlement; to that end, the fact-finding report may have the flavor of "advisory arbitration."

While fact-finding procedures have been available for many years for use in "national-emergency disputes" in the private sector (discussed more extensively below) and have more recently been adopted in the public sector, they have generally fallen short of expectations in promoting the resolution of bargaining impasses. In part, the fact-finding reports fail to muster public opinion. The ambivalence of many fact-finding reports is not well suited for focusing public opinion in a way that a recalcitrant negotiator might find costly. This is because in many disputes the fact-finder also acts as a mediator and is torn between (1) trying to help arrange a solution and (2) trying to state "objectively" what the solution should be. These two objectives are not always consistent. Even in the absence of such ambivalence, it appears that the public does not accord much attention to such reports. Finally, even if public opinion were more focused as a result of a fact-finding report, there is little cost imposed on the negotiators. Thus, fact-finding appears to offer weak inducements for ending a bargaining impasse, because it is a technique that is unlikely to introduce new information into the bargaining process or to threaten significant costs for labor and management that they could avoid by reaching agreement among themselves.

Evidence from the public sector indicates that the effectiveness of fact-finding procedures has declined over time. Their availability has generally not been effective in preventing strikes in the event of a bargaining impasse and, over time, labor and management in public-sector jurisdictions with fact-finding procedures have become less willing to accept the recommendations of fact-finders. In some states, arbitration procedures covering public employees have been adopted to provide another stage in dispute-settlement in case a fact-finding report is not accepted.[34]

## Interest Arbitration

The final third-party procedure that is often invoked to settle labor disputes is *arbitration,* in which an individual or a panel selected by the parties to collective bargaining (or appointed by a governmental body) actually determines the outcome of the labor dispute.[35] Arbitration procedures tend to take on the characteristics of a trial with the arbitrator serving as judge. Only those cases in which the parties are unable to develop "out-of-court" (negotiated) settlements "go to trial" (an arbitration hearing). Labor and management may present their cases to the arbitrator through their respective attorneys, and witnesses may be called to give testimony. Some time after the hearing, the arbitrator will hand down a written decision. Unlike most court hearings, however, there is generally no formal appeals mechanism.

Arbitration is therefore the most intrusive of the third-party procedures because it imposes the judgment of an outside individual or board on the union and management parties who must live with and implement the decision. Since even an experienced outsider is less likely to understand an industry and a particular collective-bargaining relationship as well as the parties themselves, it is often argued that arbitrated settlements are less likely to be self-enforcing than settlements achieved through normal collective-bargaining procedures. When negotiating parties do not shape the standards that are to govern their conduct during the period of the contract, they may be less apt to accept the responsibility for enforcing those standards.

---

[34]  For an extensive review of evidence on the performance of fact-finding and other third-party procedures in the public sector, see Thomas A. Kochan, "Dynamics of Dispute Resolution in the Public Sector," in *Public-Sector Bargaining,* eds. Benjamin Aaron, Joseph R. Grodin, and James L. Stern (Washington, DC: Bureau of National Affairs, 1979): 150–90.

[35]  Arbitration is also used extensively outside the field of labor relations—for example, to resolve disputes over obligations under commercial contracts and in developing divorce settlements.

There are two other ways in which arbitration may be incompatible with collective bargaining. First, arbitration may have a *chilling* effect on collective bargaining if labor and/or management believe that concessions made during a collective-bargaining period preceding arbitration may result in an arbitration award that is less favorable to their positions. Second, arbitration may have a *narcotic* effect if the parties forgo the rigors of bargaining in favor of an arbitrator's award.

For these reasons, *interest arbitration,* the use of arbitration to determine the terms and conditions of a collective-bargaining agreement, is used very rarely and only in rather special circumstances in the private sector, where the parties have the right to strike or lockout in support of their bargaining positions. In addition, the parties find it difficult to agree on the selection of the arbitrator empowered to determine the terms and conditions of employment in the industry. Regular use of interest arbitration might also lead workers to question the value of union representation. In recent years, the main private-sector examples of interest arbitration have been the use of arbitration in national-emergency disputes (discussed later in the chapter) and the resolution of salary disputes between professional baseball players and the owners of baseball clubs.

On the other hand, *grievance arbitration,* or the use of arbitration to resolve disputes over the interpretation and application of a collective-bargaining agreement is very common in the private sector. One important distinction between interest arbitration and grievance arbitration is that in the latter case, the parties to collective bargaining have the opportunity to limit the scope of the arbitrator's authority in advance through the language that they incorporate in the collective-bargaining agreement. (This and other aspects of grievance arbitration are discussed in the following chapter.)

The situation is much different in the public sector, as we have seen. Most states permit collective bargaining but prohibit strikes by state- and local-government employees, so that the traditional method of exerting leverage in support of bargaining demands is not available to unions. In the absence of a right to strike, most state and local governments have adopted alternative forms of impasse resolution, and some states have adopted binding interest arbitration as a final stage in their procedures, to be used after mediation and/or fact-finding have failed.[36] Between 15 and 30 percent of public-sector negotiations go to arbitration in states with compulsory interest-arbitration laws.

The growing use of interest arbitration in the public sector and, to a limited extent, in the private sector raises two broad questions about the effects of arbitration procedures. First, to what extent do the decision-rules that arbitrators use influence the likelihood of a negotiated settlement? Second, to what extent does arbitration influence the size of the final agreement?

---

[36] Arbitration is now used to settle labor disputes for some categories of public employees in Alaska, Connecticut, Iowa, Maine, Massachusetts, Michigan, Minnesota, New Jersey, New York, Oregon, Pennsylvania, Rhode Island, Washington, Wisconsin, and Wyoming.

**Interest arbitration and the likelihood of settlement.** As we noted earlier, the most effective dispute-settlement procedures may be those that are least likely to be used; that is, given the advantages of a mutual agreement between management and labor over the terms and conditions of employment, the most desirable arbitration procedures are those that provide the greatest incentive for the parties to collective bargaining to avoid arbitration by concluding a negotiated agreement.

Does the presence of an arbitration procedure provide the incentives to conclude such an agreement? At the beginning of the chapter we noted that the threat of a strike provides such incentives in the private sector to the extent that the cost of making concessions in collective bargaining is less than the costs of incurring a strike. The possibility of a strike, in effect, creates a "contract zone," or range of potential settlements, that both parties consider preferable to a strike.

While the parties using arbitration incur some direct costs (for example, the arbitrator's fee, fees for attorneys who may represent labor and management at an arbitration hearing, the costs of preparing for a hearing, and so on), these are not likely to be equivalent to the costs associated with a strike, except in the smallest bargaining units. Therefore, if arbitration provides an incentive for labor and management to settle, it must be mainly through different mechanisms. The characteristic of arbitration most often thought of as an inducement to settle is *uncertainty* concerning the arbitrator's award. Faced with this, risk-averse negotiators will be willing to forgo some of the expected gains from an arbitrated settlement to avoid uncertainty.

Consider a situation in which there is no uncertainty concerning the behavior of the arbitrator; that is, both labor and management can forecast exactly what the arbitration award in a particular dispute will be. It is easy to see that there is little incentive to bargain in this situation, because the party faced with an outcome more adverse than it could obtain through arbitration would hold out to the point of impasse. Suppose that one party, labor, attempted to obtain more through collective bargaining than it would receive in the arbitration award. Then the sensible strategy for management would be to refuse to agree so that a bargaining impasse developed and the dispute moved into arbitration, where the award was known to be more favorable. When each party knows with certainty what the arbitrator will award, neither party can obtain more than the arbitrator's award in collective bargaining. Collective bargaining may flourish in a mechanical sense (if only so that labor and management can avoid the costs of arbitration), but it cannot flourish in any substantive sense, because the outcome will be predetermined by the parties' advance knowledge of the arbitrator's award.[37] Arbitration procedures that are structured in ways that make the arbitrator's award highly predictable—for example, requiring that an arbitrator use only the criterion of

---

[37] This situation is analyzed in Vincent P. Crawford, "On Compulsory-Arbitration Schemes," *Journal of Political Economy* 87 (February 1979): 131–60.

recent cost-of-living increases in determining the appropriate wage increase—will therefore tend to be destructive of meaningful collective bargaining.

In fact, the behavior of arbitrators in the real world is rarely so predictable. Arbitrators may use a variety of criteria as well as their own judgments concerning what is "fair" in fashioning an award, and different arbitrators may use different criteria or accord different weights to alternative criteria. As a result, both labor and management may be uncertain that an arbitrator will make an award more or less favorable than what they could obtain by negotiating a settlement themselves. If the parties are risk-averse, on balance, they will prefer the certainty of a negotiated settlement, even though it may result in a contract that is somewhat lower in value than the expected value of an uncertain arbitration award. It is the existence of uncertainty that creates a contract zone (in which risk-averse labor and management may prefer to negotiate a solution), analogous to the contract zone created in the private sector by the threat of incurring costs from a strike or lockout. Therefore, any procedure that increases the amount of uncertainty concerning the outcome of an arbitration award should widen the contract zone and provide a stronger incentive for the parties to negotiate a solution. Because this incentive rests on the interplay of uncertainty and risk aversion, however, negotiated settlements will tend to be less favorable to the more risk-averse party than will settlements reached through the arbitration process.

One might wonder why arbitration would ever be used to establish the terms of a collective-bargaining agreement if labor and management would be willing to avoid the uncertainty by reaching a negotiated agreement. One reason is that the parties may simply have different information and expectations concerning the outcome of the arbitration process. Whether an arbitration procedure is used initially depends on how labor and management expect an arbitrator to rule relative to what they expect to achieve in negotiations without arbitration. If at least one party believes the arbitrator will award more than it will get out of negotiations, then the dispute may well go to arbitration. A second reason, reminiscent of one of the incentives to use mediation, is that either party may wish to place the blame for an unpalatable but inevitable outcome on a third party. (It would be easier, for example, for a labor leader to report that a wage concession had been imposed by an arbitrator than to defend the acquiescence of union negotiators in such a proposal.) In this case, the parties may prefer an arbitration award even when they know what the award is likely to be.[38]

A third possibility is that the uncertainty associated with arbitration may decline. Over time, labor and management learn more about the behavior of

[38] A study of dispute-resolution procedures in the public sector in New York State found that almost all decisions by a tripartite arbitration board were *unanimous,* suggesting that the arbitration procedure may have been a "cover" for bargaining. See Thomas A. Kochan, Mordechai Mironi, Ronald G. Ehrenberg, Jean Baderschneider, and Todd Jick, *Dispute Resolution Under Factfinding and Arbitration: An Empirical Analysis* (New York: American Arbitration Association, 1979).

arbitrators as they acquire more experience with arbitration proceedings. Most of the information that they receive tends to reduce their uncertainty concerning an arbitrator's award. They have their direct experience in arbitration proceedings to rely on. Moreover, because many arbitration decisions are published in reporting services, the previous track record of experienced arbitrators can be checked out. The standards that arbitrators rely on in fashioning their decisions become clearer, and there is less uncertainty concerning an arbitrator's ruling on a particular situation in the future.

One interesting question posed by the increased presence of interest-arbitration procedures in the public sector is whether the reduction in uncertainty that accompanies greater use is likely to reduce the incentives to bargain over time. In answering this question, one must remember that it is unlikely that uncertainty concerning the results of arbitration can ever be eliminated completely. Different rounds of arbitration may be held before different arbitrators, who weigh various criteria differently. Moreover, as economic and social conditions change, different criteria may become important. Compensation for increases in the cost of living is only introduced as an argument for wage increases during periods of inflation. The financial condition of a city may receive more weight from an arbitrator during a period of fiscal crisis than in more normal times. In general, then, it appears that uncertainty concerning the likely results of arbitration will be reduced, but not completely eliminated, as interest arbitration is more widely used. Because the major incentive to bargain is uncertainty concerning the arbitrator's award, there may be a tendency for arbitration procedures to be invoked more frequently over time, although not to the point where meaningful collective bargaining collapses. (Example 14.4 examines the effects of compulsory interest arbitration on strikes and collective bargaining.)[39]

**The decision-rules of arbitrators.** One approach to reducing the probability of a chilling effect is to develop institutional arrangements that increase the uncertainty associated with arbitration and, conversely, avoid arrangements that reduce the uncertainty associated with the procedure. For example, in some public-sector labor disputes, arbitrators have based their settlements on the reports of fact-finding that often precedes arbitration. Once labor and management come to recognize this as the arbitrator's approach, the results of arbitration become more predictable and the parties pattern

---

[39] There have been a number of studies that have attempted to test for the existence of a so-called narcotic effect from arbitration procedures in the public sector. Efforts to estimate whether the probability of going to an impasse requiring arbitration in one negotiation is positively related to the extent to which arbitration procedures were used by the parties in previous negotiations, raise relatively advanced issues of statistical methodology, and not all studies have been sufficiently attentive to the statistical issues. As a result, the tests for a narcotic effect of arbitration to date are inconclusive. For a discussion of the methodological issues and sample of the results, see the exchange between Richard J. Butler and Ronald G. Ehrenberg, "Estimating the Narcotic Effect of Public Sector Impasse Procedures," *Industrial and Labor Relations Review* 35 (Ocotber 1981): 3–20; and Thomas A. Kochan and Jean Baderschneider, "Estimating the Narcotic Effect: Choosing Techniques That Fit the Problem," *Industrial and labor Relations Review* 35 (October 1981): 21–28.

**EXAMPLE    14.4**

## Compulsory Arbitration in Australia

Australia provides the leading example of the use of compulsory arbitration as a means of preventing strikes. Since 1904, Australia has encouraged the use of arbitration tribunals rather than work stoppages as means of resolving disputes over contract terms and over the interpretation of labor agreements. Tribunals at the federal and state level set minimum standards for pay rates, hours of work, and paid leave, usually by industry or craft, for over 90 percent of Australian workers.

In principle, the system is voluntary; unions and employers must register if they wish to participate. In practice, the substantial benefits that are tied to registration have introduced a strong compulsory element to union participation in the arbitration system. Registered unions are accorded recognition as representatives of employees in an industry, and with recognition, unions can bring issues that employers refuse to negotiate over to arbitration. In addition, the members of registered unions receive employment preferences and benefit from minimum-pay standards set by an arbitration commission. Registered unions also give up the right to strike; with registration comes an obligation to submit unsettled disputes to arbitration and forgo the use of strikes or lockouts. Many employers were initially unwilling to participate in a system that extended such institutional security to labor unions, but the possibility of resolving disputes without work stopages and the fact that the awards of arbitration tribunals did not generally encroach on management's authority to control the operations of the firm eventually led employers to register as well.

What has been the impact of the Australian arbitration system on strikes and collective bargaining? First, the system has not eliminated work stoppages or prevented major upsurges in strike activity such as occurred in the late 1960s and early 1970s. There are several reasons for this. Not all parties to collective bargaining register with the tribunals. Moreover, the sanctions that can be effectively applied against unions that strike are modest. The major sanction is deregistration, but a well-established union may no longer need the institutional protection accorded by registration, and once deregistered, the union is outside of the influence of the arbitration system. The government can also fine unions that strike illegally, but even when imposed, such fines have rarely been collected. Another factor is that many strikes in Australia appear to have an element of symbolic protest. Most strikes end without the use of arbitration—indeed, about half end without any negotiations whatsoever!

If the arbitration system has not eliminated strikes, has it reduced the incidence of work stoppages? It is difficult to answer even this question definitively, because data on work stoppages prior to the introduction of the arbitration system are sparse. However, it does appear that while the annual number of strikes has increased since 1904 (as has the extent of unionism in Australia), the length of strikes and the time lost as a result of strikes have declined. Moreover, strikes appear to be concentrated in a few industries over issues concerning physical working conditions and grievances about the application of the agreement. Relative to other countries, there are few strikes over the issues of wages and hours that are most frequently addressed by the arbitration tribunals. The arbitration system may therefore have influenced the duration and nature of strikes in Australia.

The effect on collective bargaining is more difficult to pinpoint. Many observers feel that the possibility of an arbitrated settlement has reduced the willingness of negotiators to offer concessions at the bargaining table. On the other hand, considerable collective bargaining occurs, and when the parties reach an agreement, they can have it endorsed by a tribunal to give it the status of an arbitration award, setting industry standards. The parties may also voluntarily decide to negotiate "supplements" to an arbitration award, but these have no legal status in the arbitration system. There is some evidence that wage determination is dominated by the arbitration system when labor-market conditions are weak, but that under strong market conditions, unions may feel that they can obtain more from collective bargaining than arbitration. With the tight labor markets of the late 1960s and early 1970s, for example, there was an increase in collective bargaining and strikes that reduced the influence of the arbitration system in wage determination. It was not until a system of indexing wages to prices was introduced through the arbitration tribunals in the mid-1970s that the primacy of the arbitration system was restored.

SOURCES:  Kenneth E. Walker, *Australian Industrial Relations Systems* (Cambridge, MA: Harvard University Press, 1970); and Russell D. Lansbury, "The Return to Arbitration: Recent Trends in Dispute Settlement and Wages Policy in Australia," *International Labour Review,* 117 (1978): 611–24.

---

their offers accordingly. The range of potential settlements becomes narrower and more gauged to the arbitrator's standards than the original objectives of labor and management. A similar flow of information between an arbitrator and the parties is generated when an arbitrator is permitted to engage in mediation as well. The presence of information concerning the arbitrator's views of a desirable settlement will tend to reduce the uncertainty costs associated with arbitration and to move the final settlement away from the range in which a negotiated solution would have fallen.

The decision-rules applied by an arbitrator can also influence the amount of uncertainty associated with the arbitration process. Under *conventional arbitration* the arbitrator is free to fashion an award. The award may reflect the incentives faced by the arbitrator, however. Many arbitrators derive considerable income from their practices. At the same time, the parties to collective bargaining often have a direct input into which arbitrator is hired. Labor and management may choose an arbitrator themselves (for example, by crossing the names of arbitrators off a list with an odd number of names until only one remains), or may indicate their preferences to the state or municipal agency that appoints an arbitrator. Moreover, arbitration decisions cannot, in general, be overturned by a higher review body. As a result, arbitrators have an obvious incentive to be rehired, and to be rehired an arbitrator must be viewed as reliable by both the union and management sides of a dispute. This may require fashioning decisions that include elements that appeal to each side. It has been argued that, to be rehired, arbitrators will develop some form of compromise between the union and management positions, and that, at times, the compromise might take the form of splitting the difference between the union and management positions. The evidence on whether arbitrators simply split the difference under conventional arbitration is preliminary and mixed. Two studies found that arbitrators considered the facts surrounding a dispute as well as the final offers.[40] A later study by one of the authors found, however, that conventional arbitrators tend to split the difference between the final offers of labor and management.[41]

The central flaw of a split-the-difference approach to arbitration is that it discourages the settlement of a dispute by the parties themselves. It is hard to imagine a decision-rule that penalizes concession more. Any effort by one party to concede in the hope of encouraging settlement simply moves an award based on splitting the difference closer to the opponent's position. Compromise is penalized rather than rewarded, and the rational strategy for parties who know that an arbitrator is likely to split the difference is to take extreme bargaining positions.[42]

Is there a decision-rule that an arbitrator could follow that would reverse the incentives and encourage a convergence in bargaining positions? One proposal that has been advanced is the antithesis of splitting the difference. Under the *final-offer-selection* approach, an arbitrator would be instructed (under the terms of a labor-relations statute or collective-bargaining agreement) to select either management's final proposal or the union's final proposal—whichever was more reasonable in the arbitrator's judgment. This approach to interest arbitration has been adopted to resolve salary disputes in professional baseball and in several cities and states.

Since each party would face the possibility of losing everything under this decision-rule, the procedure appears to provide an incentive to offer concessions at the bargaining table by increasing the uncertainty concerning the outcome of arbitration and, therefore, raising the probability of a negotiated settlement.[43] It is also true, however, that the parties to collective bargaining

---

[40] Max H. Bazerman and Henry S. Farber, "Arbitrator Decision Making: When Are Final Offers Important?" *Industrial and Labor Relations Review* 40 (October 1985): 76–89, and David E. Bloom, "Empirical Models of Arbitrator Behavior Under Conventional Arbitration," *The Review of Economics and Statistics,* 68 (December 1986): 578–85.

[41] David E. Bloom, "Arbitrator Behavior in Public Sector Wage Disputes," NBER Working Paper No. 2351, (August 1987).

[42] It seems doubtful that arbitrators literally split the difference regularly. For example, we do not normally see labor and management taking the very extreme positions that would be encouraged if arbitrators mechanically split the difference between final offers. Moreover, evidence on the question of the behavior of arbitrators is difficult to interpret. Data indicating that arbitration awards tend to be at the midpoint of the final positions of labor and management are not necessarily evidence of splitting the difference. As long as an arbitrator gives any weight to some personal or external criteria for what constitutes a fair settlement (in addition to the actual final offers of the parties), labor and management will have incentives to position their final offers around the expected award of the arbitrator. The result may appear to be the outcome of splitting the difference, whereas, in fact, the opposite is occurring. That is, the offers of each party may be influenced by their perception of the arbitrator's notion of a fair settlement rather than vice versa. See Henry S. Farber, "Splitting-the-Difference in Interest Arbitration," *Industrial and Labor Relations Review* 35 (October 1981): 70–77.

[43] This proposal was originally advanced by Carl M. Stevens, "Is Compulsory Arbitration Compatible with Bargaining?" *Industrial Relations* 5 (February 1966): 38–52.

can influence the probability that their position will be accepted by the arbitrator by the very offers that they submit. For example, a risk-averse bargainer can reduce the probability that an adversary's package is accepted by submitting a more moderate package. The other party can respond in kind. In the end, this direct influence may reduce the uncertainty associated with final-offer selection below that inherent in conventional arbitration.

Uncertainty is also reduced if the arbitrator is permitted to choose between final offers on an issue-by-issue basis rather than selecting the entire package offered by the union or employer. When there are several issues at stake, the arbitrator has more latitude to make trade-offs between the union and employer positions in fashioning an award. As a result, the final package may be more of a compromise than if selection were not permitted on an issue-by-issue basis.

Final-offer arbitration does appear to encourage bargaining concessions. Several studies show that negotiated settlement rates are higher under final offer than conventional arbitration.[44] Even when the parties fail to agree on a contract, the final offers of labor and management tend to be closer together if disputes are resolved by final offer rather than conventional arbitration.[45]

## Effects of Arbitration Statutes on Wages of State- and Local-Government Employees

Binding-arbitration legislation is typically opposed by municipal-government officials who argue that arbitration takes the final decision over public employees' wages out of the hands of elected officials and leads to inflated wage settlements. Several studies have analyzed the consequences of arbitration statutes and have concluded that (1) the use of arbitration may compress differentials across cities (since arbitrators tend to award larger increases in cities where public employees are paid relatively low wages than they do in cities where public employees' wages are relatively high), but that (2) given initially comparable pay scales, on average, the wage settlements that go to the arbitration stage are no higher than the wage settlements in otherwise comparable cities that do not go to arbitration.[46] In other words, if the average percentage wage settlement in cities that went to arbitration, $\dot{W}_A$, is compared to the average percentage wage settlement in otherwise comparable cities that did not go to arbitration, $\dot{W}_N$, the difference (D) is roughly zero:

$$D = \dot{W}_A - \dot{W}_N = 0.$$

One might be tempted to conclude from such evidence that the arbitration process *per se* has had no effect on the size of the average wage settlement in

[44] Peter Feuille, "Final-Offer Arbitration and the Chilling Effect," *Industrial Relations* 14 (October 1975): 302–10, and Margaret A. Neale and Max H. Bazerman, "The Role of Perspective Taking Ability in Negotiating Under Different Forms of Arbitration," *Industrial and Labor Relations Review* 36 (April 1983): 378–88.

[45] David E. Bloom and Christopher L. Cavanagh, "Negotiator Behavior Under Arbitration," *American Economic Review,* 77 (May 1987): 357–58.

[46] *See,* for example, Thomas Kochan, et al., *Dispute Resolution Under Factfinding and Arbitration;* and James Stern, et al., *Final Offer Arbitration* (Lexington, MA: Lexington Books, 1975).

the public sector. However, this conclusion assumes that the rates of wage increase in cities in which negotiations did not go to arbitration ($\dot{W}_N$) are the same as they would have been in the absence of the arbitration statute—which is not necessarily correct. The existence of the arbitration statute *per se* may well alter the size of wage settlements even in cities that do not go to arbitration, as we will soon discuss.

For example, if municipal-government negotiators fear that there is some chance that arbitrators will award settlements that are substantially more generous than would otherwise occur, they may try to induce a settlement prior to the arbitration stage by voluntarily offering their employees a wage package in excess of what they would have offered in the absence of the statute.[47] Such an action would cause the estimated differential D to *understate* the effect of the arbitration statute on wages. Conversely, if public employers believed, and public-employee unions concurred, that arbitrators were likely to award low settlements, management might offer—and unions might accept—an offer less than what management would have offered in the absence of the statute. While we can not ascertain *a priori* whether the existence of the arbitration statute *per se* increases or decreases the size of wage settlements in cities that do not go to arbitration, it is very likely that the presence of an arbitration statute *does* affect the negotiations in cases where the settlement is made prior to arbitration.[48]

An assessment of the impact of arbitration on wages must be clear about the wage standard against which arbitration is being compared. For example, one might be interested in the difference between wage increases under arbitration and wage increases under collective bargaining in an environment without arbitration. (Comparisons of arbitration awards with nonunion wage increases may also be of interest in determining the standards that arbitrators appear to apply to wage disputes.) Alternatively, given the presence of an arbitration statute, one might be interested in the difference between wage increases in disputes that go to arbitration and wage increases in disputes that are resolved by a negotiated settlement. These will not be the same, in general, because, as noted before, a legal requirement that bargaining impasses must be resolved by arbitration is likely to influence the size of negotiated settlements. Unfortunately, there has been relatively little reliable research on these questions.

How does the *form* of arbitration influence the effect of arbitration? Does it make any difference whether conventional arbitration or final-offer arbitration is used in dispute resolution? This raises questions about the influence of final-offer selection on the bargaining proposals advanced by labor and management, as well as the comparison of the standards that arbitrators apply in

---

[47]   The union might agree to such a settlement even if it expected that, on average, an arbitrated settlement would be higher, because of uncertainty about how the arbitrator would rule (that is, there was some chance that his or her settlement would be lower). Put another way, "a bird in the hand may well be worth two in the bush."

[48]   For a more complete discussion of this point in the context of a simple bargaining model, see Henry S. Farber and Harry C. Katz, "Interest Arbitration, Outcomes, and the Incentive to Bargain," *Industrial and Labor Relations Review* 33 (October 1979): 55–63.

**EXAMPLE    14.5**

## Final-Offer Selection and the Wages of Police Officers

Studies of the salary determination of municipal police officers in New Jersey, where there is a statute providing for arbitration using final-offer selection in the event of impasse, indicated that, on the average, the wage increases obtained under final-offer arbitration did not differ significantly from either negotiated increases or increases determined under conventional arbitration (which the parties had the option of selecting). Yet, the pattern of the arbitration awards revealed some interesting aspects of the behavior of the parties under the final-offer-selection procedure.

Employer proposals were chosen by an arbitrator only a third of the time, but the wage increases provided for in these proposals were significantly *lower* than the average wage increases received by police officers in disputes that did not go to arbitration. Since an arbitrator is instructed to choose the most reasonable final offer, one may infer that employer offers were even further below the general wage increases for police officers in situations in which the arbitrator chose the union offer. The presence of a final-offer-selection procedure therefore was not driving employer wage offers to the center of the wage-offer distribution in New Jersey.

Union proposals, on the other hand, were selected by an arbitrator in two-thirds of the disputes that went to arbitration under final-offer selection, but the wage increases provided by the proposals were no larger than the increases received by similarly situated police officers elsewhere in the state. Unions, in effect, were winning more arbitrations because they submitted relatively conservative final offers, while employers were winning less frequently but gaining more from the arbitrations in which they did win. Judged by this evidence, the police unions were more risk-averse than public-sector employers. There is, no doubt, some real political appeal to the employer strategy, since public employers can argue that they submit proposals that are intended to keep the wage budget down, and if they lose the arbitration and a higher wage increase is awarded, they can blame it on the arbitrator.

SOURCE:   Orley Ashenfelter and David Bloom, "Models of Arbitrator Behavior: Theory and Evidence," *American Economic Review* 74 (March 1984): 111–124.

selecting one or the other to the standards they would apply in a conventional arbitration situation. Some evidence on the impact of a final-offer-selection procedure is offered in Example 14.5.

# National-Emergency-Disputes Policy:
# An Application

While the right to strike has long been accepted as a necessary component of collective bargaining in the private sector, there has been persistent concern about the social disruption caused by strikes having widespread consequences for neutral third parties—particularly the general public—either because of the crucial nature of the product or service for consumers (for example, coal or transportation), or because of the extreme importance of the struck product as an input to crucial products and services (for example, steel and transportation). The demand for a public-policy response resulted in the inclusion of *national-emergency-disputes* procedures in the Railway Labor Act, which was originally passed in 1926 and now covers the railroad and airline industries, and the Taft-Hartley Act, passed in 1947 following a brief postwar surge in strike activity, covering most other industries involved in interstate commerce. The structure of these procedures, as well as subsequent experience with them, provides a useful introduction to the first principles of dispute settlement.

## National-Emergency Procedures and Their Goals

The effort to devise national-emergency-disputes procedures presented a classic conflict of objectives for labor policy in the United States. On the one hand, there was the desire for a private system of collective bargaining, in which employers and unions would resolve their differences with a minimum of governmental intervention. On the other, there was a desire for industrial stability, which seemed to imply a need for some form of intervention. In an effort to strike a balance between these objectives, Congress wished to minimize the probability of strikes in key sectors of the economy (because of the cost of such strikes to the public at-large) while maintaining collective bargaining as the main mechanism through which a settlement was to be achieved. The basic policy objective was, therefore, to exert some pressure but allow and encourage an essentially voluntary settlement.

To maintain its commitment to collective bargaining, Congress did not actually outlaw strikes in key sectors of the economy. Instead, Congress left collective bargaining as the route to a settlement, but added a set of third-party procedures which were intended to reduce the probability of a bargaining impasse. If an impasse developed, the procedures were available to delay (but not prohibit) a strike.

**Taft-Hartley procedures.** The national-emergency-disputes procedures established in the Taft-Hartley Act are deceptively simple. If a labor dispute that concerns the President approaches an impasse, the President can appoint an emergency fact-finding board of inquiry to study the dispute and report back on its findings. Although the board is, in principle, the set of neutrals with the fullest command over the facts of a dispute, it is prohibited from making recommendations for a settlement in its report. A set of public recommendations, which might have a flavor of arbitration, was viewed as too intrusive into the bargaining process. (This contrasts with the use of fact-finding in labor disputes in the public sector, where, as we have seen, public policy places more emphasis on the goal of industrial stability and less on the goal of unrestrained collective bargaining than in the private sector. In the public sector, fact-finding reports are often made public in the hope of setting a standard for a negotiated settlement.) Congress apparently hoped that the determinations of the fact-finding board would muster public opinion against an obstinate union or employer, but in three dozen applications of the emergency-disputes procedures since 1947, there have been only four occasions when the board has placed the blame for a labor dispute solely on one party to the negotiations.[49]

Having received the board's report, the President may direct the Attorney General to petition a District Court for an injunction, which under the law is limited to 80 days. Although the court is supposed to judge whether an emergency actually exists, in practice, the President's assertion of an emergency is accepted without substantial judicial examination. The parties to the collective-bargaining dispute then have a duty to bargain during this 80-day "cooling-off" period.

If no settlement has been reached after the first 60 days of the injunction, the emergency fact-finding board makes a public report on the positions of the employer and union, and within the last 15 days of the injunction, the National Labor Relations Board must poll the union members to determine whether they favor the employer's last offer, irrespective of what their elected representatives are saying at the bargaining table. If the union members do not vote in favor of the employer's last offer—and they never have—the union is free to strike when the 80 days elapse. The President can then send a report and recommendations, if any, to Congress. Disputes have been settled during the injunction period in about half of the instances in which the procedures have been invoked.

**Railway Labor Act procedures.**    Under the Railway Labor Act, the first step is mediation of the dispute by the railroad industry's National Mediation Board. If mediation fails, and the parties do not mutually agree to accept arbitration, the Mediation Board decides whether the dispute is of sufficient magnitude to deprive the country of essential transportation service. It informs the President, who then appoints an emergency board (which is permitted to make recommendations) to investigate. Conditions in the industry are then frozen for 30 days, after which the parties are free to strike, unless there is some form of *ad hoc* government intervention.

While it was originally hoped that the mere existence of these procedures would reduce the likelihood of a major collective-bargaining impasse, the procedures were used quite frequently into the early 1970s, and most major disputes in the railroad industry still end up in the Railway Labor Act procedures. Increases in industrial conflict can reflect increased union militancy and/or increased employer resistance. Is there also something in the nature of

---

[49]  In the late 1940s and 1950s, the Taft-Hartley procedures were invoked for disputes in the atomic energy, bituminous coal, meatpacking, longshore, and metals industries. More recently, the procedures have been initiated for a coal strike in 1977 and considered, but not applied, for a national trucking strike in 1979.

dispute-settlement procedures themselves or in the way in which they are administered that encourages their use and discourages collective bargaining?

## Problems with National-Emergency Procedures

The first problem one encounters in trying to analyze the emergency-disputes procedures is deciding when they will be used. What constitutes a national emergency in labor negotiations? The *economic* approach to defining a potential national-emergency situation would stress the availability of substitutes. A *national* strike in the telephone industry might have created an emergency when only AT&T provided long-distance services, but since the deregulation of the industry several other long-distance companies have emerged providing similar services. The costs associated with strikes in some industries may thus change over time.

When the economic criteria are applied, one finds that relatively few of the disputes in which the national-emergency procedures were invoked actually qualified as true economic emergencies; the procedures have been used more frequently than would seem warranted if only potential economic costs are considered. The difficulty with the economic approach to defining national-emergency disputes is that it fails to satisfy the political pressures generated by a major work stoppage. When political criteria are admissible in defining a national emergency, either of the parties to collective bargaining can use this to its advantage, and recourse to the procedures will be more frequent. This appears to have occurred over the years in the railroad industry, where the government has only infrequently permitted disputes to result in work stoppages.

There is also a basic paradox built into the design of the national-emergency-disputes procedures. Although collective bargaining is the only method provided for settling a dispute, the procedures themselves impede collective bargaining. In particular, management and labor know in advance the timing and consequences of government intervention in national-emergency situations. This knowledge can be relied upon by either party and, therefore, forestall settlement. In particular, too-easy recourse to government intervention leads the parties to try to use the government to secure gains that they cannot achieve through collective-bargaining.

Thus, a first principle in designing dispute-settlement procedures is to avoid devices that have a built-in bias that alters the relative bargaining power of the union and the employer. When such a bias occurs, one party will have a stronger incentive to use the procedures than to engage in collective bargaining. Paradoxically, if collective bargaining is to be the main route to a settlement, then the best set of dispute-resolution procedures contains those that are least likely to be used. To minimize the use of dispute-resolution procedures, however, one must find procedures that do not alter the relative bargaining strength of labor or management.

From this perspective, the current national-emergency-disputes procedures have drawbacks. The fact that the parties know, in advance, that an injunction is likely to be imposed reduces the pressure to reach agreement in advance of the contract expiration. Moreover, in preserving the status quo, the injunction tends to work to the disadvantage of labor, which (except during periods such as the early 1980s, when collective bargaining in some industries was directed at wage concessions) is usually pushing to extend the terms of the current agreement. The employer, who generally desires less change, has little incentive to bargain. Most importantly, however, the presence of the injunction and cooling-off period does little to resolve the underlying dispute. While collective bargaining is left as the main route to a settlement, the injunction has the effect of weakening collective bargaining by removing the private sanctions (the strike and lockout) available to unions and management to force an agreement.

The requirement that the NLRB poll workers toward the end of the 80-day injunction on the acceptability of the employer's last offer also does not appear to contribute to the collective-bargaining process. In the period preceding the last-offer ballot, the union leadership must follow an essentially political strategy of lining up votes rather than focusing energies on the settlement of the dispute. Union members, recognizing that the employer is no doubt withholding the best offer until the end of the injunction period, have always rejected, by large majorities, the last offer—a result that serves only to reduce the union's negotiating flexibility in subsequent negotiations. Employers presume their last offers will be rejected by the membership and, therefore, withhold concessions. The net result is that, paradoxically, the last-offer ballot requirement tends to prolong a collective-bargaining impasse.

In practice, experience under the Taft-Hartley Act appears to have been less destructive of collective bargaining than experience under the Railway Labor Act. This is probably because, under the former legislation, the government normally allowed strikes to occur if no settlement was reached when the 80-day injunction expired. Under the Railway Labor Act procedures, however, the final step has been some form of governmental intervention into the bargaining process—usually in the form of arbitration by a specially appointed outside committee or by Congress itself. Indeed, experience under the Act indicates that the government is unlikely to tolerate major work stoppages in the railroad industry. As indicated in the previous section, knowledge that a dispute may be settled by split-the-difference arbitration if collective bargaining fails to produce a labor agreement is likely to *reduce* the probability of a collective bargaining agreement.

## Alternative Procedures

A number of alternatives to the national-emergency-disputes procedures in the Taft-Hartley and Railway Labor Acts have been advanced.[50] One is to require *partial operation* of an industry to maintain a level of production that would meet crucial national defense, health, and safety needs. This requires

---

[50] For further discussion of these alternatives see Donald E. Cullen, *Natinal Emergency Disputes,* ILR Paperback No. 7 (Ithaca, N.Y.: New York School of Industrial and Labor Relations, Cornell University, 1968).

some agreement on how much production is necessary to fulfill essential needs, and some mechanism for determining which union members shall work at full pay and which shall be on strike. However, some unions have voluntarily adopted a partial-operation strategy in an effort to forestall a court finding that their strike would constitute a national emergency. When a nationwide trucking strike occurred during the renegotiation of the national Master Freight Agreement in early 1979, for example, the Teamsters' union agreed to transport materials critical to the operation of hospitals and defense activities.

A second, and characteristically academic, proposal is the *non-stoppage strike* (sometimes called the *statutory strike*), under which there would not be a walkout by workers when an impasse is reached in collective bargaining. Instead, while full production continued, the economic pressures of a strike would be *simulated* by taxing management's profits and the workers' wages by the amounts that would be lost during a strike. Both parties would be left to settle the dispute themselves, and the collected taxes would go into the public treasury.[51]

The main difficulty with this proposal is the practical one of devising an appropriate tax structure to be applied against management and labor. The tax formula would be written into a statute or set by an administrative body, and centralized determinations always breed pressures for uniform rules to economize on the substantial information cost of devising a large set of tax rates. However, the relative cost of a strike to management and labor is anything but uniform across major collective-bargaining situations. With centralized determination of the tax on each party, the relative costs and the result of a strike might well differ from what would be observed without the law. One party or the other may gain from such legislation; that is, for one of the parties, the cost of the non-stoppage strike may be less than the cost of a real strike. This will then have the defect that we have noted in some other proposals: one party will have an incentive to avoid serious bargaining until an impasse develops and the simulated economic pressure begins.[52]

A third possibility would be for the government to take over the operation of an industry when a strike was judged to create a national emergency. This approach has been used on occasion—most notably by President Truman in the bituminous coal industry in the early post-World War II period. Government seizure is largely a change in legal status. The operation of the industry normally remains in the hands of its managers rather than government person-

---

[51] Stephen H. Sosnick, "Non-Stoppage Strikes: A New Approach," *Industrial and Labor Relations Review* 18 (October 1964): 73–80.

[52] The only method for devising a tax structure that is likely to reflect the relative bargaining power of management and labor is collective bargaining itself! If the parties set up the tax formula in collective negotiations, the result should reflect their relative bargaining strength at the time of negotiations. To date, labor and management in major industries have shown little inclination to negotiate such agreements. However, an example of a somewhat different arrangement, providing for an arbitrated settlement rather than a strike in the event of a bargaining impasse, is discussed in Example 14.3.

nel. Nevertheless, the procedure is intrusive, and actions that the government takes as owner may impose long-run obligations on industry management.[53]

If there are theoretical or practical difficulties with each of the main mechanisms of dispute settlement considered individually, is there any advantage to combining them into a single procedure? This is the essence of the *choice-of-procedures* or *arsenal-of-weapons* approach, which gives the Chief Executive several alternatives from which to choose when a dispute with national-emergency potential threatens. In considering this proposal, it is important to recall that, given the primacy accorded collective bargaining, the essence of any dispute-settlement procedure is to minimize its own use (that is, to maximize the incentive for private bargaining). The key to the choice-of-procedures approach is *uncertainty*. Neither management nor labor would know which procedure would be chosen; in fact, they would not know if *any procedure would be chosen,* for one of the most important alternatives is the choice of doing nothing about the dispute.

The effect of uncertainty on private bargaining behavior is intensified by including at least one alternative in the arsenal of weapons which is distasteful to each party. When bargaining, each party must then consider the probability that the Chief Executive will choose a procedure that is distasteful to that party if an impasse develops and government intervention is required. The possibility of gaining more from government-intervention procedures than from bargaining is minimized, and the incentive to actively engage in collective bargaining therefore increases.

# Review Questions

1. How does the general absence of the right-to-strike influence the nature of industrial relations in the public sector? To what extent are differences between the private and public sectors in bargaining behavior and pressure tactics ultimately related to the right-to-strike? What differences would you expect to remain if the right-to-strike existed in both sectors?

2. What are the advantages and/or disadvantages of substituting binding arbitration for the strike or lockout as a means of resolving impasses in collective bargaining?

3. When a national trucking strike appeared imminent in 1979, the federal government indicated that it might seek an injunction under the Taft-Hartley Act emergency-disputes procedures. The Teamsters' union responded by indicating that it would permit its members to carry materials needed for health care and defense activities. Was this response in the self-interest of the union? Why?

4. "It is often argued that the availability of interest arbitration can induce negotiators to settle without using arbitration in order to avoid the uncertain results of an arbitrator's award. One way to increase the uncertainty concerning the outcome of arbitration is to instruct arbitrators to select randomly between union and management proposals." Discuss the viability of this approach to interest arbitration.

---

[53] For a discussion of historical instances of the government seizure approach, *see* John L. Blackman, Jr., *Presidential Seizure in Labor Disputes* (Cambridge, MA: Harvard University Press, 1967).

## Selected Readings

Orley Ashenfelter and George Johnson, "Bargaining Theory, Trade Unions, and Industrial Strike Activity," *American Economic Review* 59 (March 1969): 35–49.

Ronald G. Ehrenberg, "The Demand for State and Local Government Employees," *American Economic Review* 63 (June 1973): 366–79.

Henry S. Farber and Harry C. Katz, "Interest Arbitration, Outcomes, and the Incentive to Bargain," *Industrial and Labor Relations Review* 33 (October 1979): 55–63.

John Kennan, "The Economics of Strikes," *Handbook of Labor Economics,* Vol. II, O. Ashenfelter and R. Layard (eds.) (Amsterdam, North Holland: 1986), Chapter 19.

Thomas A. Kochan, "Dynamics of Dispute Resolution in the Public Sector," in *Public-Sector Bargaining,* eds. Benjamin Aaron, Joseph R. Grodin, and James L. Stern (Washington, DC: The Bureau of National Affairs, 1979).

Carl M. Stevens, "Is Compulsory Arbitration Compatible with Bargaining?" *Industrial Relations* 5 (February 1966): 38–52.

# CHAPTER 15

## The Collective-Bargaining Agreement

The outcome of collective bargaining is a labor agreement that governs the relationship between labor and management in the bargaining unit until its expiration. Such agreements cover many aspects of the employment relationship and frequently are more than a hundred pages long. These formal labor agreements are not common in firms without unions, but the relationship between nonunion employers and their employees is often like an *implicit contract* in which each party has mutual expectations concerning the behavior of the other.[1] In such cases, employers implicitly offer the prospect of long-term employment security in exchange for reliable performance.

The task of explicit labor agreements is to establish the rights of labor and management in the employment relationship. Collective-bargaining agreements effectively establish a private system of law between employees and their employer. Specification of the benefits and conditions of employment that will apply at the time that the contract is signed is only part of this task. Most labor agreements now last for more than one year. Over 75 percent of all major agreements in the private sector last for at least three years. In the public sector, 25 percent of the agreements were at least three years in duration and 64 percent were in effect for two or more years by the

---

[1] As we have noted in earlier chapters, several state courts have recently recognized *de facto* implicit employment contracts between nonunion employers and employees in ruling that employers cannot necessarily terminate long-service employees "at will"—the original common-law standard for employment contracts. See William B. Gould IV, "The Idea of the Job as Property in Contemporary America," *Brigham Young University Law Review* (1986): 885–918.

mid-1970s.[2] As a result, negotiators of multi-year labor agreements must also frequently provide mechanisms for altering benefits and employment conditions during the term of the agreement in response to unforeseen future economic developments. Finally, most collective-bargaining agreements also establish procedures pertaining to the administration of the contract (specifying rules for promotions, layoffs, and disputes over contract interpretation, for example).

In the first section of this chapter we provide an overview of a typical collective-bargaining agreement and discuss the key issues that must be addressed in each section of the agreement. In the next section we consider the contractual arrangements that labor and management can develop to adjust future compensation payments to unforeseen changes in economic circumstances during the term of the agreement. In the final part of the chapter, we examine the administration of the collective-bargaining agreement, with particular attention to the role of the grievance procedure and grievance arbitration.

# The Collective-Bargaining Agreement

A *collective-bargaining agreement* is the joint outcome of negotiation between labor and management. As noted in the analyses in Chapters 13 and 14 each party begins bargaining with distinct objectives that are inevitably compromised during negotiations. Some provisions of the final labor agreement may be closer to the objectives of labor and others closer to the objectives of management, so that the overall document will normally reflect a compromise rather than the dominance of one party. The final agreement will also reflect the relative bargaining power of the parties, so there is considerable variation in the size, scope, and specific contents of individual labor agreements. Nevertheless, the general issues that are addressed in collective-bargaining negotiations are similar and it is possible to discuss the types of provisions that might appear in a typical collective-bargaining agreement (see Table 15.1). The general structure of labor agreements in the private and public sectors is similar, although the details of some provisions vary substantially.

## Institutional Protection of Labor and Management

A collective-bargaining agreement typically opens by addressing the issues concerning the institutional security of the union. The union is recognized as the sole bargaining agent for employees in the bargaining unit (as required by

---

[2]   Throughout this chapter "major" collective-bargaining agreements will refer to agreements covering 1000 or more workers. Data on the provisions of labor agreements can be found in U.S. Bureau of Labor Statistics, *Characteristics of Major Collective Bargaining Agreements, January 1, 1980,* Bulletin 2095 (Washington, DC: U.S. Government Printing Office, May 1981); U.S. Bureau of Labor Statistics, *Characteristics of Agreements in State and Local Governments, January 1, 1974,* Bulletin 1861 (Washington, DC: U.S. Government Printing Office, 19975); and Bureau of National Affairs, *Basic Patterns in Union Contracts,* 11th ed. (Washington, DC: Bureau of National Affairs, 1986).

**Table 15.1**   Outline of a Typical Collective-Bargaining Agreement

Article I.   Recognition and Representation
  a.  Recognition; definition of bargaining unit
  b.  Union security
  c.  Dues checkoff
  d.  Rights of union stewards and other officials
Article II.   Management Rights
Article III.   No Strike or Lockout
Article IV.   Hours of Work and Overtime
  a.  Normal workday and work week
  b.  Overtime premium
  c.  Allocation of overtime opportunities
Article V.   Wages
  a.  Wage schedule by job
  b.  Immediate and deferred wage increases
  c.  Contingent wage increases
    • Cost-of-living increases
    • Incentive payment plans
  d.  Shift premium
Article VI.   Vacations
  a.  Amount of vacation time
  b.  Eligibility
  c.  Vacation pay
  d.  Scheduling
Article VII.   Holidays
  a.  List of recognized holidays
  b.  Eligibility
  c.  Holiday pay

Article VIII.   Sick Leave
  a.  Amount
  b.  Eligibility
Article IX.   Insurance
  a.  Types (e.g., life, accident, health)
  b.  Coverage
  c.  Eligibility
Article X.   Pension Plan
  a.  Eligibility
  b.  Benefits
Article XI.   Seniority
  a.  Definition
  b.  Probationary period
  c.  Layoff and recall procedure
  d.  Promotion and transfer procedure
  e.  Loss of seniority
Artical XII.   Discharge and Discipline
Article XIII.   Grievances and Arbitration
  a.  Definition of grievance
  b.  Steps in procedure
  c.  Provision for arbitration
    • Selection of arbitrator
    • Scope of arbitrator's authority
Article XIV.   Duration of Agreement

the exclusive representation feature of the National Labor Relations Act), the scope of the unit represented by the union is defined (usually the election unit established by the NLRB), and the nature of the union-security arrangements, if any, are spelled out. For example, many labor agreements in the private sector provide for a *union shop* under which new employees are required to join a union within a fixed period of time following their hire. *Agency-shop arrangements,* under which employees are permitted to pay a "service charge" to a union rather than joining formally, are more common in the public sector. (There is a more extensive discussion of alternative union-security provisions and their implications in Chapter 10.) Dues-checkoff provisions, in which the employer withholds dues from employee paychecks when authorized to do so, are found in over 80 percent of major collective-bargaining agreements in both the private and public sectors. They are found most requently in labor agreements that do not include a union-security arrangement, but unions also find them desirable because they permit union officials to devote more time to aspects of contract administration other than the collection of dues. For management, a dues checkoff may also eliminate potential conflicts between dues-collection activities and production.

Having addressed the organizational interests of unions, most labor agreements then turn to the institutional interests of management. Two of the most important provisions for management in a collective-bargaining agreement are a management-rights clause and a clause prohibiting strikes while the contract is in effect (see Articles II and III in Table 15.1). A *management-rights clause* describes the functions of running an organization that are reserved in whole or in part for the employer, and the wording of such clauses often reflects the inherent conflict of interests between labor and management that the labor agreement seeks to mediate. In the public sector, management-rights clauses often do little more than define the scope of issues that are legally subject to collective bargaining.

Management will want the broadest possible statement of its rights to run the firm, while unions will want language that makes it clear that the collective-bargaining agreement itself constrains some activities of management. Management may seek to establish language that states that its rights "include but are not limited to" a list of functions involved in managing the business and directing the work force, such as hiring, scheduling production, promoting and transferring employees, and so forth. Unions will seek language that states that management's rights "will not be applied in a manner that violates other provisions of the agreement." The inherent tension between the interests of labor and management is perhaps best illustrated by a statement—typical in management-rights clauses—that permits the employer to "discharge employees for just cause." The employer is granted the right to act, but the phrase "for just cause" provides grounds for unions to protest the action and constrain the right granted to the employer.

The scope of management rights clauses is often at the heart of bargaining over *job security*—an issue of increasing concern to unions during the 1980s. One approach to increasing job security in the short run is to limit the right of management to unilaterally take actions that reduce the employment opportunities of union members. Many union contracts now place restrictions on the right of management to have supervisory workers perform work normally done by those in the bargaining unit, subcontract work, close or relocate a plant, or institute new technology (see Table 15.2). The most common con-

**Table 15.2**   Restrictions on Management Rights in Labor Agreements (percent of Contracts)

|  | Manufacturing | Nonmanufacturing |
|---|---|---|
| Supervisory Performance of Work | 74% | 34% |
| Subcontracting | 52 | 57 |
| Plant Shutdown or Relocation | 34 | 14 |
| Technological Changes | 26 | 24 |

SOURCE:  Bureau of National Affairs, *Basic Patterns in Union Contracts,* 11th ed., (Washington, DC: Bureau of National Affairs, 1986)

**EXAMPLE   15.1**

# Job Security in the Automobile Industry

Over half a million autoworkers—about one-third of the membership of the United Automobile Workers (UAW)—lost their jobs in the first half of the 1980s as a result of plant closings, new technology, productivity improvements, subcontracting of work to other companies, and declines in sales of automobiles produced in the United States. As the UAW began negotiating a three-year contract with the Ford Motor Company in the summer of 1987, employment at the company was 104,000, down from 190,000 a decade earlier. Understandably, the union's primary objective was to improve job security. The resulting agreement addresses virtually every threat to the job security of domestic autoworkers.

The centerpiece of the job-security arrangement is a Guaranteed Employment Number (GEN)—the 1987 employment level—for each of the 89 facilities run by Ford in the United States. The agreement then limits the situations in which actual employment can fall below the GEN. First, the company agreed not to close any plants during the term of the agreement. Second, the company promised not to lay off workers for any reason except a downturn in sales. Even then, Ford must rehire workers to restore the GEN when sales rebound (rather than increasing overtime work, for example). Third, the company agreed not to lay off Ford workers in the United States if sales of domestically produced Ford models fall below those of Ford models produced abroad. Fourth, the contract slowed the loss of employment, and hence union membership, from the normal "attrition" of retirements and labor turnover by requiring Ford to replace one worker for every two lost through attrition.

How is job security provided for workers who might be removed from their jobs for reasons *other* than a decline in sales? Under the Ford agreement, the GEN cannot decline for this reason, so workers whose jobs are terminated are placed in a "GEN pool" and assigned to training, another job, or nontraditional work within or outside the bargaining unit. Workers in the pool are paid their normal wages and benefits from a special job-security fund of $500 million set up to cover these costs over the three-year life of the contract. Given the limit on the job-security fund and the fact that half of the jobs vacated by attrition must be filled by new hires, the number of workers who could be protected under this arrangement would be determined by the amount of labor turnover.

Finally, when the number of workers with at least one year of seniority increases at a Ford facility, the GEN for that facility increases. Given the restrictions on reducing GEN levels, the company presumably faces incentives to have existing employees work longer hours rather than enter into a higher guarantee level. However, the agreement also imposes stronger "penalty" wage rates for overtime in excess of 5 percent of straight-time hours.

In subsequent negotiations, virtually all aspects of this job-security agreement were adopted by General Motors.

SOURCE:   UAW, *UAW-FORD REPORT*, September 1987; Jacob M. Schlesinger, "Ford-UAW Job Security Clause Contains $500 Million Cap on Payouts to Workers," *Wall Street Journal*, September 21, 1987.

tractual restriction is a requirement that management give advance notice of, and discussions with the union about, impending subcontracting, technological changes, or plant closures. Few contracts actually prohibit these actions, although subcontracting may be prohibited if it results in layoffs. Almost half of current plant-closure clauses provide displaced employees with transfer rights to a new location within the same firm, and some contracts also require the firm to pay a portion of employees' moving costs. Labor agreements generally restrict work in the bargaining unit by supervisory personnel to emergencies or to training activities.[3] By the second half of the 1980s, job security arrangements were becoming much more elaborate (see Example 15.1).

A *no-strike provision* is simply a guarantee of labor peace during the term of the agreement that most employers seek as a *quid pro quo* for the commitments and constraints that they accept in the rest of the labor agreement. The intention is that the clause will channel disputes that arise during the term of the agreement into grievance and arbitration procedures (discussed later in the chapter) rather than work stoppages. One important consequence of including a no-strike clause in a labor agreement is that the union may be legally liable for breach of contract if some of its members initiate an unofficial, or "wildcat," strike during the term of the agreement. As a result, it is not unusual to observe both the union and management trying equally hard to get wildcat strikers to return to the job.

## Economic Benefits

Following provisions addressing the institutional interests of labor and management, the major part of a collective-bargaining agreement specifies economic benefits and working conditions for employees, particularly hours of work (see Article IV in Table 15.1), wages (Article V), and fringe benefits (Articles VI–X).

### Hours of Work

**The normal workweek.**  Labor agreements uniformly address issues pertaining to hours of work. One purpose of the "hours" section of a typical agreement is simply to spell out the normal work week and work schedule. The normal workweek is 40 hours, consisting of five 8-hour days, but about 7 percent of the agreements specify workweeks between 35 and 37.5 hours. Scheduling work is generally left as a management prerogative.[4]

**Overtime work.**  Contracts also typically spell out the conditions under which premium pay for overtime work is given. Usually labor agreements require payment of the premium on a daily basis for hours worked in excess of

---

[3]  Bureau of National Affairs, *Basic Patterns in Union Contracts*, pp. 81–83.

the normal daily work schedule (for example, more than eight hours). In a few contracts, however, overtime may only be paid on a *weekly* basis for hours worked in excess of the standard weekly schedule (for example, more than 40 hours per week). The latter arrangement provides management with more flexibility to keep costs down; employees who work, say, ten hours one day can work six hours on another day during the week without exceeding the 40-hour threshold at which overtime begins.

The assignment of overtime work has been one of the more controversial issues in some recent collective-bargaining negotiations. In some bargaining situations employees are eager to work overtime and deciding who will be selected to work overtime is a major concern. In others, workers' desire for nonwork time is greater and the concern is whether employees can be *required* to work overtime. Overtime assignment issues seem sharper in the manufacturing sector, where 80 percent of the collective-bargaining agreements address the distribution of overtime, than in nonmanufacturing industries (in which less than half of the agreements do so). Most of the contracts with sections on overtime contain the general requirement that overtime hours will be distributed among employees as evenly as possible. Some contracts are more specific, however, and limit overtime assignments to employees within particular job classifications or departments.

Only about one-quarter of a sample of four hundred agreements addressed the acceptance by workers of overtime work. Overtime was voluntary, except in emergencies, in about 14 percent of these agreements. The remaining contracts split evenly between those in which overtime was mandatory and those in which it was always voluntary.[5]

Faced with dwindling memberships, many unions have recently been concerned that employers use overtime to avoid hiring more workers. During the 1980s, unions have increasingly sought to limit the use of overtime in negotiations over job security.

## Wage Provisions

One of the most striking features of American collective-bargaining agreements is that they contain often elaborate provisions governing the compensation of union members but leave decisions concerning the level of employment up to the employer. A labor agreement will usually delineate whether compensation is to be on the basis of time worked (hourly, daily, or weekly rates), the amount produced (incentive-payment plans or payment-by-results), commission payments, or mileage payments (used chiefly in the transportation industries) for various occupational groups in the bargaining unit. Most major agreements in the private sector specify wage rates, rate ranges, or, less frequently, minimum-wage rates along with the nature of the wage-progression plan that will apply to members of the unit. Labor agreements also spell out the nature of wage differentials for working less-preferred

---

[5]  Bureau of National Affairs, *Basic Patterns in Union Contracts,* pp. 50–52.

**Table 15.3**   Employment Provisions in Major Collective-Bargaining Agreements, 1980

| | Total Agreements | Wage-Employment Guarantees | Crew-Size Limitations | Subcontracting Limitations |
|---|---|---|---|---|
| Total | 1550 | 173 (11%) | 337 (22%) | 900 (58%) |
| Manufacturing | 750 | 59 ( 8%) | 94 (13%) | 399 (53%) |
| Nonmanufacturing | 800 | 114 (14%) | 243 (32%) | 501 (67%) |

Note: Since the contract provisions are not mutually exclusive, percentages may add to more than 100%.

SOURCE: U.S. Bureau of Labor Statistics, *Characteristics of Major Collective Bargaining Agreements, January 1, 1980.* Bulletin 2095 (Washington DC: U.S. Government Printing Office, May 1981): 104, 106, 109.

shifts, for hazardous work, for abnormal working conditions, and for overtime and weekend work, as well as the nature of extra payments for tools, clothing, and travel that are required as part of the job. As noted earlier in the chapter, the same sort of detail is characteristic of provisions governing fringe benefits. Contract provisions typically specify the eligibility (usually a minimum service period with the company) and pay for vacations and holidays, as well as the amount of vacation time (usually related to years of service), and the specific holidays that will be recognized.[6]

In contrast, American labor agreements are usually mute on the question of the employment level. Explicit wage-employment guarantees are infrequent (see Table 15.3). In 1980, only 11 percent of major private-sector collective-bargaining agreements—mainly those in transportation, retail trade, and construction—had such guarantees. Limitations on crew size, found largely in construction, printing, utilities, and transportation, are also relatively rare. Limitations on subcontracting work that was previously done by members of the bargaining unit are more prevalent but do not dominate the employer's choice of employment level. Even these provisions are virtually nonexistent in the public sector.

By default, then, the decision over employment levels in most collective-bargaining agreements in the United States is left to the catchall management-rights clause. It is not unusual for such clauses to contain language to the effect that "the rights to schedule work hours, to hire, promote, demote, and transfer, discharge for just cause, or to reduce employment because of lack of work or for other legitimate reasons are vested exclusively in the company, provided that such rights are not applied in a manner that violates the provisions of the agreement." Interestingly, theoretical analyses of wage bargaining indicate that *efficient* results can only be achieved when collective

---

[6] Data on the distribution of contractual provisions governing wages and fringe benefits by industry and by level of government may be found in U.S. Bureau of Labor Statistics, *Characteristics of Major Collective Bargaining Agreements, January 1, 1980;* and U.S. Bureau of Labor Statistics, *Characteristics of Agreements in State and Local Governments, January 1, 1974.*

bargaining negotiations determine *both* the wage and employment levels (see Appendix 15A for details).

**Two-tier wage structures.** Two-tier wage agreements provide that employees hired in the future will be paid less than current employees. Historically, many labor agreements allowed employers to pay new employees less than experienced employees for a period of two to three years before bringing them up to the full union wage rate. During the late-1970s and through the early 1980s, however, employers in retail trade, the airlines, and several other industries succeeded in negotiating wage structures in which newly hired employees would *permanently* be paid from a lower wage schedule than current employees hired in the past. By the mid-1980s, about 8 percent of collective-bargaining settlements provided for two-tier wage structures of this type.

The motivation for two-tier structures is cost reduction for the employer without reducing the wages of current employees. In principle, as a company fills vacancies with employees who are paid at the lower rate, its labor costs should fall. Two-tier wage structures also provide employers with incentives to lay off workers on the high rate, if their jobs cannot be protected by the union. But why should unions, as organizations that historically have favored equal pay for equal work, agree to two-tier wage structures? Two-tier proposals have arisen largely in industries and firms that are under intense competitive pressure. If unions become convinced that survival of the employer requires reduced labor costs, they face two choices. One is an across-the-board reduction in wages, preserving the objective of "equal pay for equal work." The other is preserving the wage level of current union members, who must vote on the acceptability of the contract terms, but reducing the wages of employees hired in the future. It is easy to understand how the choice plays out politically within a union organization.

Yet, acceptance of such structures may be short-sighted from the perspective of both management and labor. On the one hand, morale problems may lead the lower-wage employees to work less productively. On the other hand, unions can expect internal political problems as low-wage members demand equality with high-wage members; these pressures should grow with the number of low-wage workers and if not met could result in demands for decertification of the union.

## Fringe Benefits

Since World War II, fringe benefits have become an increasingly important part of the compensation package in both union and nonunion establishments, as noted in Chapters 4 and 8. The analysis in Chapter 8 stressed that both employers and employees are likely to have distinct preferences concerning the mix of wages and fringe benefits in the compensation package, and that these preferences are likely to be expressed as trade-offs that each is willing to make between wages and fringes.

Because of their importance in the compensation package, fringe benefits have become a significant component of labor costs and, hence, a potential source of conflict between labor and management in collective bargaining. While few managers in unionized firms would sensibly want to eliminate fringe benefits (since even nonunion firms offer such benefits to attract qualified workers), unions may seek to raise the level and change the composition of fringe benefits beyond what managers feel that they need to pay for competitive purposes. As noted in Chapter 10, the political nature of union decision-making causes union leaders to favor benefits that appeal to the median member—that is, bargaining goals that will be supported by a majority of the membership—while employers are more likely to favor benefits that appeal to new applicants and to the workers who are most likely to leave the company for another firm if their preferences are not met. Since the median worker is likely to be older and less mobile than the marginal worker, unions generally have an incentive to negotiate for compensation items that have particular appeal to older workers; thus, collective-bargaining contracts generally call for mixes of fringe benefits and wages different from those found in nonunion companies.

A progressive income-tax system, under which higher incomes are taxed at higher rates, also may influence the composition of the union pay-package. Since union members on average receive higher rates of compensation than their nonunion counterparts (as discussed more extensively in Chapter 16), they are likely to be subject to higher income-tax rates. Union members therefore have a stronger incentive than nonunion workers to have a larger proportion of their compensation package as untaxed fringe benefits.

Collective bargaining typically focuses on several key features of fringe benefits that determine their ultimate cost to the firm and benefit to the workers. First, the parties must determine which workers will be eligible to receive the benefit. For most fringe benefits, eligibility is determined by the length of time that an employee has worked for the firm. For example, a contract may require a minimum amount of time worked to qualify for any vacation time. Next, the parties must determine the level of the benefit, that is, the number of weeks of vacation and which holidays will be observed. Frequently, these decisions are also related to tenure of employment. For example, the amount of vacation time is likely to increase with years of service to the firm. The exact formula relating job service to the level of a fringe benefit is established in negotiations. Finally, the contract must specify the rate of pay that will be applicable—usually straight time—for holidays and vacations. In the case of insurance plans, to take another example, there is often considerable bargaining over the level of contributions and the respective shares of labor and management.

## Bargaining Over an Uncertain Future

One of the most difficult problems facing union and management negotiators is how to structure an agreement that addresses their respective interests in efficiency and equity when facing an uncertain future. One approach to uncertainty is to negotiate short-term contracts, possibly no longer than a year in duration, so that contract terms can be adjusted to unexpected events through frequent renegotiations. The renegotiation of a labor agreement is a costly process, however, and over the years, management and labor have sought to reduce negotiating costs by lengthening the duration of collective-bargaining agreements. With long-term labor agreements and highly imperfect economic forecasts, how can the parties deal with uncertainty?

There are two general approaches to adapting long-term contracts to uncertainty. One is to *preset* the terms based on a forecast of what future economic conditions will be. The second is to make certain benefits *contingent* on future events that may or may not occur. Both devices are used in modern collective-bargaining agreements. The data in Table 15.4, for example, show that labor agreements in both the private and public sector make some provision for wage adjustments during the term of the agreement. (Such adjustments are generally more frequent in the private sector, where the average duration of a collective-bargaining agreement is longer than in the public sector.) The data also show, however, that in both sectors preset, deferred wage increases which are scheduled to be received at particular times irrespective of actual economic developments, are more common than contingent increases. Preset deferred wages are often granted in response to union requests for an "annual improvement factor" (to reflect an implicit forecast of general productivity increases over the life of the contract) and in response to the negotiators' general forecasts of future economic events, such as inflation and unemployment. Preset wage increases involve risk to both

**Table 15.4**  Wage Adjustments During the Term of a Collective-Bargaining Agreement

| | Percent of All Agreements in Sector[a] with Provisions for: | | | |
|---|---|---|---|---|
| | All Agreements | Escalator (cost-of-living) Adjustments | Deferred Wage Increases | Contract Reopening |
| Private industry[b] | 100 | 49 | 89 | 21 |
| Manufacturing | 100 | 64 | 90 | 16 |
| Nonmanufacturing | 100 | 34 | 88 | 25 |
| State and local government[c] | 100 | 15 | 52 | 24 |
| State | 100 | 8 | 35 | 32 |
| County | 100 | 10 | 44 | 31 |
| Municipal | 100 | 20 | 66 | 15 |
| Special district | 100 | 50 | 50 | 21 |

[a] Percentages may add to more than 100 because some agreements have more than one type of wage adjustment provision.

[b] Agreements covering 1000 workers or more, January 1, 1980.

[c] Agreements in effect on January 1, 1974.

SOURCE:  U.S. Bureau of Labor Statistics, *Characteristics of Major Collective Bargaining Agreements, January 1, 1980,* Bulletin 2095 (Washington, DC: U.S. Government Printing Office, May 1981); 55; and U.S. Bureau of Labor Statistics, *Characteristics of Agreements in State and Local Governments, January 1, 1974,* Bulletin 1861 (Washington, DC: U.S. Government Printing Office, 1975); 25.

parties, because economic events may turn out more or less favorable to either party than anticipated. Because wage increases are predetermined and do not respond to *actual* economic events during the lifetime of the contract, employment fluctuations are likely to be larger than they would be if wage increases were contingent on economic performance.

Two common methods for providing for contingencies are to permit a contract to specify circumstances under which the parties can reopen negotiations prior to the scheduled expiration date of the agreement, and to automatically adjust wages to changes in a general index of prices (usually referred to as "cost-of-living" adjustments). Of these, the latter is more common in the private sector and raises a number of issues that are discussed in the next section.

One interesting feature of the arrangements providing for contingent increases that have been established in collective bargaining prior to the 1980s is that wage adjustments were almost always keyed to movements in external economic indicators rather than indicators of the performance of the firms that are parties to the agreement. Methods of making wage increases contingent on the performance of the firm have received far more attention during the "concession bargaining" of the 1980s, and we examine some of these methods later in this chapter.

## Cost-of-Living Adjustment (COLA) Clauses

One of the major uncertainties facing both union and management negotiators is the path that prices will follow during the term of the collective-bargaining agreement. Management is interested in the likely future path of the prices for its products and services, for those prices will affect the profitability of the company. Union leaders are interested in the future path of prices in general, because the general rate of inflation will affect the real earnings that their members achieve from the collective-bargaining agreement. When the period between contract negotiations is relatively short—less than a year— each party may be able to forecast the behavior of prices with reasonable accuracy. If a forecast turns out to be inaccurate, a relatively brief period of time passes before the parties have the opportunity to try to adjust to the new information in another round of collective-bargaining negotiations. When the period between negotiations is relatively long, however, the forecasts of price behavior in the later years of a contract are likely to be less accurate and the consequences of inaccurate forecasts can be substantial. The future behavior of prices becomes an important contingency that most unions require protection against before they are willing to sign a long-term agreement. In some cases, labor agreements provide for reopening a contract during its term under specified circumstances. More frequently, however, unions have pressed for *cost-of-living adjustment (COLA)* provisions (sometimes referred to as "cost-of-living escalators") as a *quid pro quo* for signing a contract of long duration.

A COLA imposes a contractual obligation on an employer to adjust the wages of workers in a bargaining unit in response to changes in a general index of prices (usually the national Consumer Price Index for urban wage earners and clerical workers) according to a formula that is specified in the contract. There is considerable variation in the formulas adopted in different collective-bargaining situations. For example, COLAs requiring that wage rates of all workers increase by the same percent as the price index offer complete real-wage protection. Such formulas are the exception rather than the rule in collective-bargaining agreements, however, in part because they maintain existing relative wage differentials by skill, which many unions want to narrow to conform to their egalitarian objectives. Instead, COLA formulas take a variety of other forms that generally provide less-than-full compensation for inflation. In the mid-1980s, for example, the compensation provided by COLAs ranged from 50 to 100 percent of the inflation rate in major collective-bargaining agreements, with an average of 65–75 percent. Historically, the most generous COLAs—offering essentially full compensation for general price increases—were negotiated by the United Automobile Workers and the major automobile manufacturers, but these were modified significantly in bargaining over wage concessions in the early 1980s.

The most common COLA formula provides for a uniform cents-per-hour wage increase for a specified absolute change in the price index—for example, one cent an hour for every change of 0.3 or 0.4 of a point in the Consumer Price Index (CPI). In providing the same absolute wage adjustment for inflation to all workers irrespective of their wage level, this formula provides higher percentage wage increases to low-wage workers than to high-wage workers and therefore has the effect of narrowing percentage wage differentials by skill. For this reason, the formula is favored by unions that want to achieve a more equal distribution of earnings. As wage levels change over time, however, the average compensation for price increases provided workers by a COLA based on this formula decreases, leading unions to attempt to renegotiate the parameters of the formula periodically. Employers are sometimes successful in limiting their potential obligation under a COLA by negotiating a "cap" or maximum payment to be made during a given period. Unions typically want a "floor" to the COLA so that their wages do not fall if prices fall (a very rare event in the past 40 years).[7]

Once a formula has been accepted, the yield of a COLA is also influenced by the frequency with which changes in the CPI are reviewed, to determine if payments are due. The shorter the period between reviews, the more closely the change in money wages follows the path of prices. Moreover, COLA payments received throughout a year (that is, under a quarterly or semiannual review) can be spent or invested and, hence, have more value for a worker than payments received at the end of a year (that is, under an annual review).

---

[7] One of the few examples of pay cuts under a COLA during the postwar period was in the initial COLA between the General Motors Corporation and the United Automobile Workers. Shortly after the agreement was signed in September 1948, the CPI fell, requiring union members to accept money-wage cuts under the COLA in parts of 1949 and early 1950.

Reviews found in major collective-bargaining agreements are usually quarterly, but annual reviews are also common.[8]

Cost-of-living escalation coverage is by no means uniform over time or across industries in the United States. Although the use of ''cost-of-living'' as a criterion for wage increases dates back to the beginning of this century, the first major post-World War II American labor contract to contain a COLA provision was the 1948 contract between General Motors and the United Automobile Workers, which also marked a shift from one-year to two-year agreements.[9] The subsequent development of COLAs has been fitful, and even after the substantial inflation of the 1970s, many union workers were not covered by COLAs (see Table 15.5). Moreover, formal COLAs are rare in nonunion firms, so the percentage of the labor force whose wages are formally indexed to price movements is much smaller than indicated by the data in Table 15.5.[10] The uneven incidence of COLAs is also apparent in the data on the industrial distribution of COLA coverage in collective bargaining (reported in Table 15.6).

The historical evidence suggests that the prevalence of COLA provisions in collective-bargaining contracts has fluctuated over time; in particular, they appear more frequently after a period of inflation has started and less frequently after a period of price stability. There was an expansion in COLA coverage in response to the increase in inflation in 1957 and 1958, but it took several years to drop the clauses when prices leveled off at the end of the 1950s and into the early 1960s. In part, this reflected the spread of long-duration agreements, which reduced the speed with which contract terms could be adjusted to external events. This lack of contractual response to external events was prevalent during the late 1960s. By the time unions reestablished COLA protection during collective-bargaining negotiations in the early 1970s, the rate of inflation had dropped. With the persistence of high inflation rates during the late 1970s, the extent of COLA protection reached a historical high, only to decline in the mid-1980s as inflation subsided.

[8] Sixty-three percent of the COLAs in effect in major collective-bargaining agreements in 1983 provided for quarterly review, sixteen percent provided for annual review, and fifteen percent for semi-annual review. (The remaining contracts had other review procedures.) William M. Davis, ''Collective Bargaining in 1983: A Crowded Agenda,'' *Monthly Labor Review*, 106 (January 1983): 11.

[9] For a discussion of the development of COLAs and an analysis of their effects, see Wallace E. Hendricks and Lawrence M. Kahn, *Wage Indexation in the United States: Cola or Uncola?* (Cambridge, MA: Ballinger, 1985).

[10] Information on COLA coverage in the nonunion sector is sparse, but one study of wages in manufacturing firms found that a maximum of 4 percent of nonunion workers were covered by a COLA during the 1970s. In a typical year, 2 percent of the workers were covered. As a result, only about a third of all workers in manufacturing were covered by COLAs during the mid-1970s. [The study also found that COLA coverage was more extensive in major bargaining units (1000 or more workers) than in smaller bargaining units.] George Ruben, ''Observations of Wage Developments in Manufacturing During 1959–78.'' *Current Wage Developments* 33 (May 1981): 49. A 1975 survey of a random sample of 480 private firms (both union and nonunion) found that 39 percent of the firms paid COLA wage increases to union hourly employees. The comparable percentages for nonunion employees were: nonunion hourly, 10 percent; exempt salaried, 9 percent; officers, 4 percent. David A. Weeks, *Compensating Employees: Lessons of the 1970s* (New York: National Industrial Conference Board, 1976).

**Table 15.5** Coverage of Cost-of-Living Escalator Provisions in Major Union Contracts*

| Date | Number of Workers Covered by Major Union Contracts (millions) | Number Covered by Cost-of-Living Provisions (millions) | Percent Covered by Cost-of-Living Provisions | Annual Percent Change in the Consumer Price Index in the Previous Year |
|---|---|---|---|---|
| 1/50 | n.a. | 0.8 | n.a. | 5.8 |
| 1/57 | 7.8 | 3.5 | 45 | 2.9 |
| 1/60 | 8.1 | 4.0 | 49 | 1.5 |
| 1/65 | 7.9 | 2.0 | 25 | 1.2 |
| 1/67 | 10.6 | 2.2 | 21 | 3.4 |
| 1/69 | 10.8 | 2.7 | 25 | 4.7 |
| 1/70 | 10.8 | 2.8 | 26 | 6.1 |
| 1/71 | 10.6 | 3.0 | 28 | 5.5 |
| 1/72 | 10.4 | 4.3 | 41 | 3.4 |
| 1/73 | 10.5 | 4.1 | 39 | 3.4 |
| 1/74 | 10.3 | 4.0 | 39 | 8.8 |
| 1/75 | 10.2 | 5.1 | 50 | 12.2 |
| 11/76 | 10.0 | 6.0 | 61 | 4.8 |
| 11/77 | 9.7 | 5.8 | 60 | 6.8 |
| 11/78 | 9.6 | 5.6 | 58 | 9.0 |
| 11/79 | 9.4 | 5.5 | 59 | 13.3 |
| 11/80 | 9.3 | 5.3 | 57 | 12.4 |
| 10/81 | 9.0 | 5.1 | 56 | 8.9 |
| 1/83 | 8.5 | 4.9 | 58 | 3.9 |
| 10/84 | 7.5 | 4.2 | 56 | 4.0 |
| 10/85 | 7.0 | 3.5 | 50 | 3.8 |
| 10/86 | 6.5 | 2.6 | 40 | 1.1 |
| 11/87 | 6.3 | 2.4 | 38 | 4.4 |

n.a. not available

* Contracts covering 1000 or more workers in private industry. Prior to 1966 the construction, service, finance, and real estate industries were excluded.

SOURCES: H. M. Douty, *Cost-of-Living Escalator Clauses and Inflation*, Table 1 (Council on Wage and Price Stability, August 1975) (for data through January 1975); *Monthly Labor Review*, January issues for 1976–88 (for data from November 1975 on); *1982 Economic Report of the President*, Table B55 (consumer price index) (Washington, DC: U.S. Government Printing Office, 1982); and *1988 Economic Report of the President*, Table B61 (consumer price index) (Washington, DC: U.S. Government Printing Office, February 1988).

What accounts for the variation in COLA coverage and the compensation for cost-of-living increases provided by COLAs over time and across industries? Evidence suggests that, over time, uncertainty about inflation rather than the level of inflation *per se* is a major factor causing changes in the extent of COLA coverage in the economy. Some of the variance across industries is related to differences in contract duration. However, this itself is related to more basic underlying forces. Recent studies suggest that the extent of COLA protection is related more fundamentally to the nature of the risks firms face in different industries and to the risk preferences of employers and employees. If firms were completely risk neutral, that is, unconcerned about year-to-

**Table 15.6**  Prevalence of Cost-of-Living Adjustment (COLA) Clauses in Major Collective Bargaining Agreements, October 1986

| Industry | All agreements | | | Agreements with COLA clauses | |
|---|---|---|---|---|---|
| | Number | Workers covered | Percent of workers covered by COLA clauses | Number | Workers covered |
| Total | 1968 | 8793 | 30 | 369 | 2677 |
| Private nonagricultural industries | 1360 | 6539 | 40 | 355 | 2637 |
| Metal mining | 3 | 7 | 0 | 0 | 0 |
| Anthracite mining | 1 | 1 | 0 | 0 | 0 |
| Bituminous coal and lignite mining | 1 | 105 | 0 | 0 | 0 |
| Building construction general contractors | 129 | 455 | 5 | 4 | 22 |
| Construction other than building construction | 95 | 281 | 3 | 3 | 10 |
| Construction-special trade contractors | 146 | 294 | 7 | 9 | 21 |
| Food and kindred products | 63 | 162 | 10 | 9 | 16 |
| Tobacco manufacturing | 3 | 16 | 100 | 3 | 16 |
| Textile mill products | 7 | 27 | 15 | 1 | 4 |
| Apparel and other finished products | 32 | 300 | 41 | 21 | 125 |
| Lumber and wood products except furniture | 9 | 50 | 3 | 1 | 2 |
| Furniture and fixtures | 5 | 9 | 17 | 1 | 2 |
| Paper and allied products | 39 | 57 | 0 | 0 | 0 |
| Printing, publishing, and allied industries | 21 | 36 | 43 | 9 | 15 |
| Chemicals and allied products | 29 | 54 | 20 | 6 | 11 |
| Petroleum refining and related industries | 12 | 36 | 0 | 0 | 0 |
| Rubber and miscellaneous plastics | 12 | 53 | 84 | 8 | 45 |
| Leather and leather products | 7 | 20 | 0 | 0 | 0 |
| Stone, clay, glass, and concrete products | 22 | 59 | 96 | 20 | 57 |
| Primary metals industries | 53 | 308 | 59 | 33 | 183 |
| Fabricated metal products | 26 | 51 | 78 | 18 | 39 |
| Machinery, except electrical | 34 | 112 | 81 | 25 | 91 |
| Electrical machinery equipment and supplies | 51 | 273 | 68 | 31 | 184 |
| Transportation equipment | 75 | 863 | 93 | 59 | 801 |
| Instruments and related products | 5 | 15 | 23 | 1 | 3 |
| Miscellaneous manufacturing industries | 6 | 8 | 44 | 2 | 4 |
| Railroad transportation | 26 | 369 | 96 | 22 | 354 |
| Local and urban transit | 6 | 22 | 66 | 2 | 14 |
| Motor freight transportation | 14 | 273 | 37 | 5 | 100 |
| Water transportation | 16 | 69 | 27 | 4 | 19 |
| Transportation by air | 36 | 166 | 4 | 2 | 6 |
| Communications | 38 | 551 | 51 | 18 | 280 |
| Electric, gas, and sanitary services | 75 | 243 | 21 | 11 | 51 |
| Wholesale trade—durables | 3 | 6 | 0 | 0 | 0 |
| Wholesale trade—nondurables | 6 | 32 | 78 | 1 | 25 |
| Retail trade—general merchandise | 16 | 59 | 23 | 2 | 14 |
| Food stores | 99 | 500 | 4 | 7 | 19 |
| Automotive dealers and service stations | 5 | 8 | 0 | 0 | 0 |
| Apparel and accessory stores | 2 | 5 | 0 | 0 | 0 |
| Eating and drinking places | 14 | 42 | 0 | 0 | 0 |
| Miscellaneous retail stores | 5 | 13 | 34 | 1 | 5 |
| Finance, insurance, and real estate | 23 | 118 | 47 | 6 | 55 |
| Services | 90 | 413 | 12 | 10 | 49 |
| State and local government | 608 | 2253 | 2 | 14 | 39 |

Note:  Due to rounding, sums of individual items may not equal totals.

SOURCE:  Joan Borum, James Conley, and Edward Wasilewski, "Collective Bargaining in 1987," *Monthly Labor Review* 110 (January 1987): 33.

**Table 15.7**   Profit-sharing, Savings, and Stock-Purchase Plans
by Industry (percent of all agreements in sector)

|  | All Agreements | Profit-sharing Plans | Savings Plans | Stock-Purchase Plans |
|---|---|---|---|---|
| Private industry* | 100 | 2 | 5 | 2 |
| Manufacturing | 100 | 3 | 8 | 4 |
| Nonmanufacturing | 100 | 1 | 2 | 1 |

\* Agreements covering 1000 workers or more, January 1, 1980.

SOURCE:   U.S. Bureau of Labor Statistics, *Characteristics of Major Collective Bargaining Agreements, January 1, 1980.* Bulletin 2095 (Washington, DC: U.S. Government Printing Office, May 1981): 49.

year variations in profits around their long-run level, they would presumably be willing to grant complete indexation, and COLAs would yield full compensation for general price increases. In fact, the data show that both COLA coverage and the degree of wage adjustment for inflation are far from complete. Workers receive only partial insurance for uncertain future price changes. Employers, too, must be risk averse. Evidence increasingly indicates that the variety in COLAs reflects patterns of risk-sharing between employers and employees in which each is partially insured for the risks incurred during a long-term labor agreement.[11]

## Indexing Wages to Firm Performance

An alternative form of contingent contracting would index changes in compensation for union members to the general performance of the firm. Payment-by-results (piecework) systems, productivity bargaining, profit-sharing, and employee stock-ownership of firms are all methods by which the compensation of labor can be made to depend on the output or productive efficiency of a firm. Historically, most unions that have agreed to contingent wage increases have been willing to index wages to general economic indicators (such as prices) but not to the fortunes of the firms that employ their members (see Table 15.7).

In the early 1980s, this situation changed dramatically in several industries with the severe product-market pressures brought about by a deep recession, increased foreign competition, deregulation of pricing, and new firm entry. In an effort to survive, employers in these industries proposed a number of changes that altered the nature of collective-bargaining agreements so that compensation (labor cost) was more directly related to the performance of the firm or industry. The fact that unions responded is a dramatic example that far from being insulated from market forces, collective bargain-

[11]   See Ronald G. Ehrenberg, Leif Danziger, and Gee San, "Cost-of-Living Adjustment Clauses in Union Contracts," *Journal of Labor Economics* 1 (July 1983): 215–45; David Card, "An Empirical Model of Wage Indexation Provisions in Union Contracts," *Journal of Political Economy* 94 (June 1986, Part 2): S144–75; and Hendricks and Kahn, *Wage Indexation in the United States: Cola or Uncola?*

ing can be a remarkably flexible and even innovative institution when the involved parties are under great pressure. We shall examine several methods of indexing wages to employer-specific contingencies that have been adopted in collective bargaining.

**Indexing individual wages to output.** The most widely used method of indexing individual wages directly to output in collective-bargaining agreements is *piecework* or *payment-by-results*. About a quarter of the major private-sector agreements provide for incentive payments to some employees (typically certain production workers in the manufacturing sector). While such systems can result in higher productivity, they also can have a number of undesirable consequences on production (see Chapter 8) that effectively limit their application. In particular, payment-by-results and related incentive-payment systems may be inappropriate when it is difficult to monitor the quality of output or to discern the contribution of individual workers to output. This helps to explain why payment systems that directly link wages and output are not found more widely in industry.

Unions often view incentive-payment systems with suspicion on the grounds that, when misused, they can become methods to disguise production speedup. This is a particular concern when management seeks to change incentive-pay rates as changes in technology, materials, or the organization of production alter the average output expected from a worker in a given period of time. In most situations piece rates are adjusted downward (for example, to compensate for greater efficiency made possible by increased capital intensity). But if rates are adjusted downward too far, workers will have to expend more effort to maintain their incomes. Unions, therefore, seek collective-bargaining agreements that establish a union role in setting or protesting revisions in incentive-pay rates. Efforts to alter incentive-payment standards can be a major source of grievances in unionized firms, and the additional cost of these payment-by-results systems may be another factor that limits their use in industry.

**Productivity bargaining.** *Productivity bargaining* occurs when labor and management directly negotiate the terms under which specific changes in methods designed to increase production will occur. In contrast to the more or less continuous incentives for efficiency embedded in the payment-by-results systems just discussed, productivity bargaining is usually part of an effort by management to establish major once-and-for-all changes in the work environment. Productivity bargaining is most likely to arise when management wants to introduce a major technical change, to eliminate work rules that reduce productive efficiency, or both. Either of these objectives normally constitutes a threat to the job security of union members, and productivity bargaining explores methods of gaining the benefits of greater efficiency while minimizing concerns over job security.

There is an inherent conflict between labor and management over the question of contractual work rules that specify the number of workers required to do a job or the flexibility with which employees can be assigned to different jobs. Employers are likely to view such rules as leading to reductions in productive efficiency, and it is usually the case that labor productivity would be higher in their absence. Unions, however, often argue that the rules are required to maintain reasonable health and safety standards at the workplace for their members. Does it take three people on a modern, computerized flight deck to fly an airplane safely, or only two? In Chapter 6 we discussed how well-informed, mobile workers would consider on-the-job health and safety risks when choosing their place of employment, and how employers offering unsafe conditions would have to pay a wage premium to attract workers. Unions hold the view that when information is imperfect and workers are immobile, so that the theoretical market incentives for employers to reduce unsafe working conditions are not always present, the task of providing for worker health and safety falls to collective bargaining.

In fact, some union work rules only become "restrictive" or inefficient as technology changes. Rules concerning the number of employees needed to do a job may be quite reasonable under one state of technology but quite inefficient when there is technical advance. For example, painting many surfaces with a brush is efficient until someone invents a spraygun. To take another example, a rule, negotiated long ago by railroad unions, specified that railroad workers receive a day's pay for every one hundred miles traveled—a sensible requirement when it took an eight hour shift to travel one hundred miles. However, when technological changes in railroading made it possible to travel three times that distance in an eight-hour day, the rule resulted in substantial inefficiency. It is the effort to maintain past work rules as technology changes that gives rise to restrictive union work practices ("featherbedding") in some industries. The most serious restrictive practices appear to have been limited to a few industries, such as construction, printing, and railroads, which are organized primarily by craft unions. In some of these industries, union concerns over the health and safety of the work environment are supplemented by the threat of some technological changes to the existence of the union itself. When a craft union represents workers in a relatively narrowly defined skill, there is a danger that some innovations may eliminate the need for that skill entirely and, hence, the need for the union. Efforts to maintain past work rules are stronger when the survival of a union is at stake.

Even in industries organized by industrial unions, however, there are frequently restrictions on the flexibility with which workers can be assigned to different jobs.[12] When the work force of a plant is divided into many craft groups, and the labor agreement does not permit workers in one craft to do

---

[12] Restrictive work rules are commonly associated with the presence of unions. In fact, norms of work behavior that many employers would view as restrictive develop among, and are enforced by, workers in nonunion firms. For an early study of restrictive working norms among nonunion employees, with some interesting observations on management actions that encouraged the development of the norms, see Stanley B. Matthewson, *Restriction of Output Among Unorganized Workers* (New York: Viking Press, Inc., 1931). Similarly, John R. Commons, a distinguished student of unions, is said to have remarked that, "The nonunionist does not change his nature when he becomes a unionist, but merely has more power to do what he wanted to do before."

jobs in others, employers may have to pay workers who are idle because there is a temporary shortage of work in their craft jurisdiction. A contract that established fewer craft units and broader definitions of the jobs that each craft could perform would result in more efficient production.

How are labor agreements structured to deal with technological change or adjustment of work rules? In some situations, productivity bargaining may not be necessary. The impact of new technology on a rapidly growing firm may be to slow the rate of growth of employment rather than to reduce the number of jobs. In cases in which some job loss occurs, if the introduction of new technology can be spread over time, the employment adjustment may be handled through attrition—the loss of employees through the normal turnover that every organization experiences.

Some collective-bargaining agreements require employers to provide advance notice of layoffs or major technological change. The purpose of advance-notice requirements is to provide time for adjustment to the change. With sufficient advance notice, it is easier to take advantage of the attrition approach to easing employment adjustments. Contractual provisions for advance notice are more common for layoffs (resulting from poor economic conditions, plant shutdowns, or relocation) than they are for technological change, however.

Another approach to protecting workers from changes in technology or economic conditions is to provide for income security in the event of displacement. That is, contractual provisions are negotiated that require an employer to provide severance pay—either a fixed sum or a monthly allowance graduated by length of employment—to workers whose employment is terminated, or supplemental unemployment benefits to workers who are laid off. In 1980, about a third of the major agreements provided for severance pay, while less than 15 percent provided for supplemental unemployment benefits.

A third general approach to economic change is to spread the available work opportunities by broadening seniority units or by establishing rights for workers to transfer between plants. In practice, this approach often creates severe political difficulties for the union or unions involved, because it usually grants rights to one group of members (in the threatened department or plant) to supplant or "bump" other, less-senior members (in another department or plant). In effect, it simply shifts the problem of job—and income—insecurity from more-senior workers to less-senior workers.

When employers want to achieve major changes in work rules or production methods, however, these changes can often occur only through *productivity bargaining,* in which agreement by the union to specific changes is sought in return for commitments from the employer concerning the job or income security of union members. One interesting feature of productivity bargaining is that it is not a zero-sum game, in which gains to one side are offset by losses to the other. If the result is an increase in the productivity of the organization, the size of the pie available for division between labor and management will be larger. This has been the exact outcome in several important instances of productivity bargaining (see Example 15.2). Nevertheless, this outcome is not

EXAMPLE 15.2

# Productivity Bargaining in the Longshore Industry

Pacific Coast longshore workers, who load and unload cargo for ships in ports such as Seattle, San Francisco, and Los Angeles, were organized by the International Longshoremen's and Warehousemen's Union in 1934, following a coastwide strike. The labor market for longshore workers was "casual"—meaning that the timing of work and one's employer varied daily, depending on the irregular arrivals and departures of cargo ships. Because the work itself was basically unskilled and many jobs lasted only a few hours, entry into the labor market was easy. While some individuals had a full-time attachment to longshore work, others worked only part-time, often "moonlighting" while holding a primary job in some other industry. Hours and earnings were erratic and unemployment was frequent.

Following the establishment of collective bargaining in the industry, several steps toward a more formal approach to the labor market were made with the assistance of a special arbitration board. A hiring hall run jointly by the ILWU and the Pacific Maritime Association (PMA), the employers' association for the industry, was established to dispatch workers to jobs. Experienced longshore workers were registered to use the hiring hall, and gradually, each port began to make a distinction between workers with a more or less full-time attachment to the industry (who were put on an "A" list) and workers with a more intermittent attachment (who were put on a "B" list and worked only after workers on the A list were dispatched to jobs).

The union also succeeded in establishing a number of restrictive work practices in an effort to offset the irregularity of hours and the extensive unemployment. To reduce the pace of work, limits were placed on the amount of cargo that could be moved between ship and shore in a sling load. The agreement required a basic work group of eight longshore workers in the hold while loading a ship, and six in the hold while unloading a ship. Typically, however, only half of each group actually worked, and the remaining members came to be known as "witnesses" of the work performed by their colleagues. Multiple handling of cargo was also common. Cargo delivered to the docks in pallet loads prepared by workers outside the ILWU were frequently required to be unloaded from the pallet at dockside and then reloaded on pallets by ILWU members. As is frequently the case with restrictive work rules, many of these practices had some basis in worker safety—but the cumulative effect of the rules was essentially that there was no gain in the productivity of longshore workers for 25 years.

In the late 1950s, there was considerable pressure to give up the rules. Given the inefficiencies, the West Coast ports were losing business to the East and Gulf Coast ports, where similar rules were not in effect. Moreover, there were important technological changes, including the containerization of loads, that employers wanted to introduce to compete more effectively. Yet it was widely assumed that there would be a severe reduction in the employment of longshore workers if employers were given a free hand in their choices of technology. Longshore employment appeared threatened whether the restrictive practices were retained or given up. The challenge to collective bargaining was to find some mechanism that would permit the employers to modernize the docks while handling workers' fears for their job security.

In 1959 the ILWU and the PMA signed a seven-year Mechanization and Modernization Agreement in which the union gave up the restrictive work practices and dropped its objections to containerization, and the employers set up a $29 million fund that was to be used to guarantee job security. First, it offered incentives for early retirement in an effort to induce the substantial number of older longshore workers to withdraw from the industry. More importantly, the agreement guaranteed the earnings equivalent of 35 hours of work per week at the basic straight-time wage rate to all longshore workers on the industry's A list. If someone on the A list averaged less than 35 hours a week, the difference between the actual earnings and the guaranteed earnings would be made up from the fund.

The impact of the agreement on productivity was remarkable. After 25 years of stagnation, labor productivity increased by a third between 1960 and 1964. One careful study found that most of the productivity was attributable to the elimination of work rules, and that increased capital intensity associated with employer investments—particularly in containerization—played a significant, but secondary, role. At the same time, the expected decline in longshore employment did not materialize. With increased productivity of longshore operations, more shippers used West Coast ports, and it was found that workers on the A list never had to draw on the $29 million dollar fund to attain their guarantees! The fund was distributed through lump-sum payments to workers on the A list at the end of the seven-year period.

Efforts to buy out work rules that are viewed as obsolete and inefficient through productivity bargaining are not inherently successful, however. The ultimate outcome depends on the balance between the efficiency gains from eliminating work rules, on the one hand, and the size of payments to union members necessary to secure an agreement to give up the rules. That this balance may not always be favorable is illustrated by experience under an agreement negotiated in the New York City longshore industry.

In 1966, the International Longshoremen's Association (ILA) gave up practices similar to those that were eliminated in the West Coast ports in exchange for a guarantee that any longshoreman who had worked at least 700 hours in 1965 would be guaranteed 2080 hours of work (40 hours per week for 52 weeks) annually or the equivalent pay—*forever!* The relatively low number of hours of work required for eligibility, the relatively high number of hours for which pay was guaranteed, and the fact that the guarantee was lifetime produced much higher costs than were experienced under similar plans on the West Coast and in other ports. As a result, the cost of the program to the steamship lines that paid for it rose from $1.7 million in its initial year to $70 million in 1983, when the annual guarantee was $29,120. Several hundred longshoremen did not work at all under prevailing levels of demand in the port of New York; they were only required to check in briefly each morning to qualify for payment.

The result was a vicious circle. The higher labor costs led shippers to use other ports. (It is estimated that the port of New York's share of all container cargo dropped from 17 percent to 10 percent during the 1970s, for example.) As demand declined, however, the number of people receiving pay for no work rose, thereby increasing the unit costs of the work that was done, which encouraged more shipping to be diverted to other ports.

SOURCES: Paul T. Hartman, *Collective Bargaining and Productivity: The Longshore Mechanization Agreement* (Berkeley: University of California Press, 1969); Sam Roberts, "On the Waterfront: Cost of Labor Could Make City a Noncontender," *The New York Times,* June 22, 1983, and "Economics on the Piers: Wage Guarantee Is the Crux," *The New York Times,* June 23, 1983.

always obvious in advance, and agreement over the change often requires provisions for job or income security (as Example 15.2 also illustrates).

One characteristic of productivity-bargaining negotiations is that the union is typically concerned with the security of current members only. Therefore, when the prospective efficiency gains from technological change or an alteration of work rules are sufficiently large, employers may find that income guarantees to those workers who are most threatened by the changes are economically feasible. Even when guarantees are feasible, though, they do not usually provide job or income security indefinitely. (For a notable exception and its consequences, however, see the last two paragraphs of Example 15.2) In some instances—particularly where the work force is relatively old, so that retirement places an implicit limit on the guarantee—an employer may agree to provide ''lifetime'' security. An agreement reached between a local of the Typographical Union and newspaper publishers and printing establishments in New York City during the mid-1970s provides a dramatic example. The parties signed 10-year agreements in which the union dropped all ''manning requirements'' (contractual rules requiring the use of union printers even when automated printers could do a task more efficiently) and allowed virtually unlimited introduction of automated composing techniques, in exchange for *lifetime* job guarantees for *regular, full-time* printers. Interestingly, the average age of regular, full-time printers at the time was 56, and the contract provided for mandatory retirement from the industry at age 68!

**Profit-sharing and worker ownership.**   Another method of structuring labor agreements so that compensation is linked to the performance of the firm is through *profit-sharing arrangements* in which workers receive a share of the profits of a business in addition to their regular pay. *Employee stock-ownership plans* are a related method of linking at least some of a worker's compensation to the economic fortunes of the firm.

Historically, profit-sharing arrangements have been rare in collective-bargaining agreements in the United States (see Table 15.7). Although neither the AFL-CIO nor many national unions have officially opposed profit sharing, they are wary of such plans. In the 1920s and 1930s, profit sharing was often a feature of company-dominated unions, which were subsequently prohibited by the National Labor Relations Act.[13] More importantly, profit sharing usually conflicts with the income security of the most-senior union workers. Protected by seniority from layoffs during moderate cyclical fluctuations, these workers are likely to support the negotiation of fixed wages. A fixed wage (plus protection from layoffs) provides them with a steady income, but because inflexible labor costs force adjustments to demand reductions to fall solely on employment, they impose costs on the minority of less-senior union

---

[13]   John L. Zalusky, ''Labor's Collective Bargaining Experience with Gainsharing and Profit-Sharing,'' *Proceedings of the Thirty-Ninth Annual Meeting*, Barbara D. Dennis (ed.) (Madison, WI: Industrial Relations Research Association, 1987): 174–82.

members who are more subject to layoffs during economic fluctuations. Under profit sharing the wages of all union members would be more variable (because they depend on the economic health of the firm), but employment might be more stable. A majority of union members might support profit sharing, however, if a major collapse of sales threatened to result in plant closings or layoffs affecting the employment and earnings of large numbers of union members.[14]

By the mid-1980s, a few unions in economically distressed firms or industries in the United States began to accept limited profit-sharing or stock-purchase arrangements in exchange for forgoing normal noncontingent wage increases. While generally slow, the spread of such arrangements was occasionally highly visible. Ford and General Motors adopted profit-sharing plans that supplemented base wages with annual bonuses based on each company's profitability, for example. In 1983, members of the Airline Pilots' Association working for Eastern Airlines, which had suffered serious financial losses, agreed to accept company bonds (later convertible into shares of Eastern's common stock) in exchange for *deferring* some of their pay. The pilots were eventually expected to own as much as 21 percent of Eastern's common stock under the arrangement. In addition, the pilots were given the right to name one or two of their members to the sixteen-member board of directors of the airline. By the mid-1980s, an estimated 8–10 percent of union members were covered by profit sharing of some form.

Negotiations over profit-sharing plans focus on two key issues: (1) how the pool of profits available for sharing is determined, and (2) how the pool is distributed through bonus payments to eligible union members. Few of the plans negotiated during the 1980s provided profit sharing from the first dollar of profits. Under most negotiated plans, the firm had to earn some minimum annual return before some profits were set aside for distribution to workers. The more generous plans set aside an increasing fraction of profits as the profit rate increases. An employed union member typically received shares of the profit pool equal to his or her share in total hours worked or in total compensation. Because the company generally has better information about its financial situation than the workers, unions will want their accountants to audit the company's determination of profit and/or seek representation on the board of directors as a condition of agreeing to profit-sharing plans.[15]

To the extent that profit sharing or stock ownership is an element of the pay package, at least part of compensation is effectively contingent on *all* of the uncertainties faced by the firm, including many factors—such as shifts in product demand—that may not be controllable by union members. Even

---

[14]   Robert J. Flanagan, "Wage Concessions and Long-Term Union Wage Flexibility," *Brookings Papers on Economic Activity,* (1984–1): 201–9.

[15]   Daniel H. Kruger, "Profit-Sharing Arrangements and Collective Bargaining," *Proceedings of the Thirty-Ninth Annual Meeting,* Barbara D. Dennis (ed.), pp. 152–58; Flanagan, "Wage Concessions . . . ," pp. 203–5.

**EXAMPLE    15.3**

# An Employee-Owned Steel Mill

From the early 1900s, the National Steel Corporation, the fourth largest steel producer in the United States, operated a large plant in Weirton, West Virginia. Workers at the Weirton Works were represented by the Independent Steelworkers' Union and traditionally received higher wages than workers at companies organized by the larger United Steelworkers of America (USW). The higher wages were paid in part to reduce the likelihood of organization by the USW and to guarantee that the plant would operate in the event of a national steel strike.

In the early 1980s, the steel industry in the United States was under considerable pressure from foreign competitors, who produced at lower cost, and from the general reduction in demand resulting from the deep international recession. Faced with low profits, National Steel announced in early March 1982 that it no longer intended to make substantial investments in its Weirton plant, and that it would gradually cut back operations at Weirton unless the workers chose to purchase the plant. The announcement initiated a vigorous effort by officials of the union, company, and community to find a way for the employees to buy the plant. There were significant incentives on each side to strike a bargain. The workers and the community had a stake in the jobs. Employment, which had been as high as 12,000, had fallen to about 7000 workers by early 1983, and over 3000 workers were on layoff. But the company also faced substantial costs if the plant ceased operations, in the form of pension obligations to past and present workers.

A year later, the company and the union announced an agreement under which the workers would purchase the Weirton plant. Given the depressed conditions in the industry, the company was willing to sell the plant and equipment for $66 million—about 22 percent of book value. Workers agreed to pay another $300 million for raw materials and other inventory, and to assume about $185 million in liabilities. Most of the liabilities were not due for several years, however, and it was assumed that the new company would be in a better position to handle them by then. As part of the agreement, workers took pay cuts of at least 32 percent—an amount that an independent study indicated was necessary to make the plant competitive—in exchange for stock in the new company. Effectively, workers were trading current wages for the uncertain prospect of higher future income that would depend on the performance of their new company. National Steel also assumed some of the risk of failure by agreeing to assume pension and other shutdown costs if the new company failed during the first five years of operations. With $1 billion of sales per year, the Weirton steel works was then the largest employee-owned company, the eighth largest steel company, and one of the 300 largest corporations in the United States.

The development of employee stock-ownership plans, such as the purchase of the Weirton Works, can require unusual financial and management arrangements. In the case of Weirton, the National Steel Corporation agreed to hold notes for a large portion of the purchase price, and principal payments were not scheduled to begin until 1989, some six years after the employee-purchase agreement was completed. The principal would be paid out over the next 10 years, but interest

payments would not be made until the Weirton Works had a net worth of $100 million. A board of directors, including union representatives, former company officials, and outside experts, would be responsible for major policy decisions and the selection of top management for the new company.

During its first year of operation as an employee-owned company, the Weirton mill was quite profitable. At a time when many steel companies were losing money, Weirton employees received substantial profit-sharing payments.

SOURCE:  William Serrin, "Employees to Buy Huge Steel Works in $66 Million Pact," *The New York Times,* March 14, 1983, Steven Greenhouse, "The Employees Make a Go of Weirton," *The New York Times,* January 4, 1985.

---

efforts to enhance employee productivity through profit sharing or employee ownership may encounter some of the risks inherent in group incentive plans, discussed earlier in Chapter 8. Chief among these is the "free-rider" problem. The benefits of increased profits are a public good; that is, they accrue to each worker, irrespective of his or her role in raising profits. Therefore, while some workers strive to improve efficiency, others may decide to take a "free ride" and collect the benefits of someone else's hard work. This is particularly easy to rationalize in a large organization in which a worker may reason that increasing his or her own individual effort would have a relatively small effect on profits. If most workers reason this way, improvements in profits and pay are unlikely.

The most extreme form of profit-sharing is when workers own or control a company's stock. In 1972, for example, Northwest Industries, Inc., sold the Chicago & Northwestern Railway to the railroad's employees. However, a group of independent trustees was given the authority to run the railroad, and, for ten years, the voting rights of employee-stockholders were limited to questions involving mergers and new stock issues. While only 10 percent of the employees initially purchased the stock, the profitability of the railroad and the value of the stock increased substantially over the next decade. Worker ownership of a company raises most of the issues that workers and unions confront in more limited profit-sharing plans. In addition, there is an array of complicated financial and management issues; in particular, the entire question of the union's role as a representative of the employees, who are now the owners of the firm. Is the strike threat now credible? Will unions play an important role in advising employees how to vote their stock? Is the question of the distribution of the firm's earnings between labor and capital any longer an issue? Why should a worker-owned firm be inherently more profitable? A widespread movement toward worker ownership of firms would undoubtedly raise serious challenges to traditional forms of collective bargaining as we have known them. To date, examples of worker ownership have largely been limited to situations in which companies of substantial size are in economic distress (see Example 15.3).

# Seniority and Economic Opportunity

Once the general provisions for wages and fringe benefits have been established, the welfare of employees is determined by their access to favorable
economic opportunities within the firm and by the way in which the contract
provisions are applied. Economic opportunities include promotions, transfers, opportunities to work overtime, and protection from layoff. In most
collective-bargaining relationships in the United States, unions give employers considerable freedom to determine the level and composition of employment within a firm, but they seek to establish the criteria by which
employment opportunities will be granted.

Evidence gathered in campaigns for union representation (see Chapter 11)
indicates that one of the most effective appeals for support that unions make
to workers is their claim that they will reduce managerial discretion and
favoritism in personnel decisions. Therefore, unions seek to define the criteria
for promotions, transfers, layoffs, and overtime opportunities in the collective-bargaining agreement, and to choose criteria that reduce the scope for
supervisory discretion. *Seniority,* or length of service, is the criterion most
commonly favored by unions because it is objective and because the application of seniority rules by management is relatively easy to monitor and
enforce. In addition, unions argue that seniority is related to productivity and
family need. Management often argues that when promotions and other
personnel decisions are governed by seniority, there is little incentive to work
hard.

Some aspects of the seniority debate raise the question of whether productivity and job performance are positively correlated with length of company service. Human-capital theory (reviewed in Chapter 6) argues that such
a correlation exists because workers become more productive through the on-
the-job training that they receive as part of their experience with a company.
Further, it has been argued that seniority rules promote on-the-job training by
removing a deterrent for older workers to show younger workers the "tricks
of the trade" (younger workers are not competitors with more senior workers
for promotion). To the extent that performance in fact improves with seniority, there is an incentive for *both* union and nonunion firms to use
seniority as a criterion for promotions and other economic opportunities.
However, some evidence from studies of white-collar workers indicates that
while pay rises with seniority, productivity does not. These studies find that
the earnings of professional and managerial workers are positively related to
seniority *within a job grade,* but that performance ratings were uncorrelated
with seniority.[16]

We have already seen (in Chapter 8) reasons why profit-maximizing
companies might adopt compensation systems for career employees in which

[16] James L. Medoff and Katharine G. Abraham, "Experience, Performance, and Earnings," *Quarterly Journal of Economics* XCV (December 1980): 703–36.

earnings would rise with seniority even if productivity did not. Such "deferred-compensation systems" might provide workers with an incentive to work hard *throughout* their employment with a company to qualify for relatively high compensation in their later years. Despite the incentives for firms to adopt these deferred compensation schemes, most recent research (as discussed in Chapter 8) has suggested that the monetary returns to *general* labor-force experience are in fact much greater than the returns to seniority with a particular firm.[17]

Given evidence on productivity and the dominance of general experience over firm-specific seniority in rewarding workers, it seems clear that without union pressure, management would not be inclined to make extensive use of seniority as a major criterion for personnel decisions. In fact, studies do show that seniority is used more frequently in union than in nonunion firms. A survey of 400 companies revealed that seniority was the most important factor affecting promotions in 41 percent of the union firms but in only 3 percent of the nonunion firms. In unionized firms, greater weight is assigned to seniority than to ability in promotion decisions. The same survey found that seniority also affords much greater protection against layoff in union than nonunion firms.[18]

Although more common in unionized firms, seniority is rarely established as the *sole* criterion for allocating opportunity in collective-bargaining agreements. In one broad sample of agreements, for example, seniority was one factor to be considered in promotion in about 70 percent of the contracts but was the sole factor in only 5 percent. In the same sample, over half the contracts provided for some consideration of seniority in determining transfers, but it was the sole factor in only 8 percent. Overall, some reference to seniority as a factor in ranking employees for intrafirm economic opportunities appeared in 90 percent of the labor agreements in the sample.[19] The most common factor used in conjunction with seniority is ability. For example, many contracts permit an employer to choose the most able worker available for promotion but require that seniority be used to choose from a pool of workers of equal ability. Moreover, unions will normally reserve the right to protest an employer's ability-rankings of employees.

Several important issues regarding seniority are typically addressed in the section of the collective-bargaining agreement that covers seniority (Article XI in Table 15.1). The first is the actual definition of seniority. Is it from the date of hire or the end of a probationary period? Is it lost in the event of layoff, unexcused absence, or failure to respond to a recall? A second set of issues

[17]  Katharine G. Abraham and Henry S. Farber, "Job Duration, Seniority, and Earnings," *American Economic Review* 77 (June 1987): 278–97; Joseph G. Altonji and Robert A. Shakotko, "Do Wages Rise with Job Seniority?" *Review of Economic Studies* 54 (1987): 437–59.

[18]  Katharine G. Abraham and James L. Medoff, "Length of Service and Promotions in Union and Nonunion Work Groups," *Industrial and Labor Relations Review* 38 (April 1985): 408–20; Katharine G. Abraham and James L. Medoff, "Length of Service and Layoffs in Union and Nonunion Work Groups," *Industrial and Labor Relations Review* 38 (October 1984): 87–97.

[19]  Bureau of National Affairs, *Basic Patterns in Union Contracts*, pp. 87–90.

surrounds the question of how seniority is to be applied. In most agreements, seniority is applied on a "last-in, first-out" (LIFO) basis; those with the highest seniority are ranked first for positive opportunities (for example, promotions) and last for negative opportunities (for example, layoffs) to the extent that seniority is used as a criterion for selection. More important is whether seniority applies on a departmental, plant, or companywide basis, for this indicates the scope of a worker's seniority rights. In departmental seniority systems, workers who transfer to a new department generally lose all seniority previously accrued in their first department, which may seriously limit their opportunities for promotion or overtime in a new department and leave them vulnerable to layoff in an economic downturn. (This possibility has raised an important public-policy issue in the implementation of equal-employment-opportunity laws, as discussed in Chapter 7.)

# Discharges

Workers invariably look to their unions to curb abuses of management discretion. Nowhere is this more apparent than in the area of job security. Virtually all collective-bargaining agreements contain discharge and discipline provisions (see Article XII in Table 15.1). While these provisions do not literally protect jobs, they do systemetize the discharge process by spelling out the grounds for discharge, the procedures to be followed, and the procedures for appealing a discharge decision.

Labor contracts typically state that a worker may be discharged for "cause" (or "just cause") or for specific offenses listed in the contract that constitute cause. Among the specific offenses most frequently mentioned in a sample of four hundred collective-bargaining agreements were violation of leave provisions (36 percent of the agreements), participation in illegal "wildcat" strikes (35 percent), unauthorized absence (28 percent), dishonesty or theft (23 percent), intoxication (21 percent), and violation of company rules (21 percent). Incompetence, failure to obey safety rules, misconduct, and tardiness are also frequently regarded as cause for discharge.[20]

Many labor contracts also specify procedures to be followed in the event of a discharge. Frequently notice of the discharge must be provided to the union as well as to the employee, and in some cases a hearing over the discharge is required. Most contracts also provide for appeals of a discharge decision within a certain time period. The appeal usually takes the form of a grievance lodged against the company. The operation of grievance procedures is discussed later in this chapter. Most contracts also indicate whether employees who are found to have been improperly discharged are entitled to reinstatement with back pay or to an amount of back pay to be determined by the arbitrator.

---

[20]    Bureau of National Affairs, *Basic Patterns in Union Contracts*, pp. 7–9.

The requirement that there be cause or just cause for discharge is one of the major differences between employment arrangements in the union and nonunion sectors. In nonunion companies, employment could until recently be terminated at the will of the employer, and in most states nonunion employers face fewer restrictions on discharges than do union employers.

## Administration of the Contract

When representatives of labor and management reach agreement over the terms and conditions of employment that each side recognizes as preferable to the alternative of incurring or continuing a work stoppage, it is likely that each party to the negotiations will bear some responsibility for enforcing the terms of the agreement. Nevertheless, labor agreements are not inherently self-enforcing, and it is not unusual for disagreements to arise between union and management representatives over the application of various clauses while the contract is in effect. While strikes or lockouts could, in principle, be used in an effort to compel agreement over the interpretation of the contract, we have seen how management often insists on a no-strike pledge while a contract is in effect, as a *quid pro quo* for signing an agreement in the first place. Moreover, most union leaders are unwilling to precipitate a strike that will result in lost wages for large numbers of union members over an issue of contract inter-pretation—the application of a discharge clause, for example—that affects only one or, at most, a few workers.

Therefore, some alternative method for resolving *grievances,* disputes that arise during the term of an agreement, is necessary. Ninety-nine percent of major private-sector collective-bargaining agreements in the United States and almost ninety percent of the agreements in state and local governments include provisions for a *grievance procedure* for this purpose (see Table 15.8). Grievance procedures first provide an opportunity for labor and management representatives to work out a solution to their disagreement. If the parties fail to resolve the dispute, the vast majority of labor agreements provide for arbitration as the final stage of the grievance procedure. *Grievance arbitration* is different in important respects from interest arbitration, which was dis-cussed in the previous chapter, and in the remainder of this chapter we discuss the role of both the grievance procedure and grievance arbitration in the administration and evolution of collective-bargaining agreements.[21]

### Role of Grievance Procedures

Disagreements between unions and management during the term of a collec-tive-bargaining agreement can occur for several reasons. Frequently, a union and management may disagree over the actual meaning or interpretation of a

---

[21] Many nonunion firms also have written appeals procedures, but few use an outside arbitrator as the final step. For an interesting study of the appeals procedures in three large U.S. companies, see David Lewin, "Dispute Resolution in the Nonunion Firm," *Journal of Conflict Resolution* 31 (September 1987): 465–502.

**Table 15.8** Grievance and Arbitration Procedures
in Collective-Bargaining Agreements
(percent of all agreements in sector)

| | All Procedures | Grievance and Arbitration | Grievance Only | Arbitration Only | No Reference to a Procedure |
|---|---|---|---|---|---|
| Private industry[a] | 99 | 97 | 2 | c | 1 |
| Manufacturing | 99.7 | 98 | 2 | — | c |
| Nonmanufacturing | 97.9 | 95 | 2 | c | 2 |
| State and local government[b] | 87 | 76 | 11 | — | 13 |
| State | 94 | 82 | 12 | — | 6 |
| County | 83 | 72 | 11 | — | 17 |
| Municipal | 86 | 75 | 11 | — | 14 |
| Special district | 100 | 79 | 21 | — | — |

[a] Agreements covering 1000 workers or more, January 1, 1980.
[b] Agreements in effect on January 1, 1974.
[c] Less than 0.5 percent.
— Data not available.
SOURCES: U.S. Bureau of Labor Statistics, *Characteristics of Major Collective Bargaining Agreements, January 1, 1980,* Bulletin 2095 (Washington, DC: U.S. Government Printing Office, May 1981): 112–13, and U.S. Bureau of Labor Statistics, *Characteristics of Agreements in State and Local Governments, January 1, 1974,* Bulletin 1861 (Washington, DC: U.S. Government Printing Office, 1975): 41.

part of the agreement. The interpretive difficulties may, in turn, stem from vague or ambiguous contractual language. For example, labor agreements frequently permit management to discharge workers "for just cause," but what is "just cause"? Who is to decide? Often the ambiguity is deliberate. It represents the best that the negotiators could agree to in the formal collective-bargaining negotiations. When neither party is willing to permit language that endorses the other's position on an issue, and neither is willing to accept language that precludes its own position, the resulting contract language on the issue is likely to be ambiguous. As a result, the application of contract language to specific situations that arise in day-to-day employment relations often is unclear.

In other instances, there may be a disagreement between labor and management as to whether a violation of an agreement has occurred. In some cases, a dispute may reduce to a disagreement over the facts of a particular incident. Finally, there may be differences of opinion between labor and management over the fairness or reasonableness of a disciplinary action or some other aspect of the employment relationship. For example, if an employee initiates an altercation with a supervisor, can the firm fire the employee, or is a suspension the more appropriate discipline?

In most cases, these disagreements cannot wait to be resolved in formal collective-bargaining negotiations at some distant time. Instead, they are resolved through a grievance procedure. As a result, a labor agreement takes on much of its ultimate meaning through the interpretations of contract language that are developed during the administration of the agreement, and particularly through the resolution of grievances. In this sense, negotiations do not stop with the signing of a collective-bargaining agreement. Disputes over grievances can be seen as an extension of the collective-bargaining process. In particular, there is an obvious incentive for either party to try to achieve, through the grievance process, objectives that it failed to obtain at the bargaining table.

Because grievances represent disagreements, the flow of grievances in an organization can be an index of the quality of industrial relations in different plants. Relative to quits, absenteeism, and wildcat strikes, grievances are a relatively costless method for workers to signal discontent with working conditions. However, the filing of grievances can also be used as a political tool by unions even when worker discontent is not deep-seated. The rank-and-file of a union may file grievances to remind its leaders about offending clauses in the existing union contract. Unions themselves may encourage the filing of many grievances as a way of increasing the company's labor-relations costs at a time when the union is having difficulty getting the company to acquiesce on other issues.

While unions may use grievances for tactical reasons, they also have an interest in allocating their resources where they will do the most good for the membership. As a result, most unions try to screen grievances and apprise members of complaints that either cannot be handled as a grievance (because there is no applicable contract language), or are so lacking in merit that the union would prefer not to pursue the complaint as a grievance. In making these decisions, unions must be cognizant of their legal "duty of fair representation." The federal courts have held that with the right to *exclusive* representation of workers granted unions under American labor law comes the obligation to refrain from arbitrary or discriminatory treatment of union members.[22] Thus, if a union refuses to process a member's grievance, it must have good reason for its action. Moreover, if an employee proves that an employer violated the collective-bargaining agreement, and the union violated the duty of fair representation in refusing to process the employee's grievance, *both* the union and the employer may be held liable for damages awarded to the worker.[23]

## Grievance Arbitration

As noted above, virtually all collective-bargaining agreements contain language discussing how disagreements over the application of the contract are to be resolved. In general, it is the task of the parties to negotiate language about the nature of the grievance procedure and of the arbitration arrangements that may apply to grievances. Most agreements also include language

---

[22] *Steele* v. *Louisville and Nashville Railroad*, 323 U.S. 192 (1944) and *Miranda Fuel Co.*, 140 NLRB 181 (1962).

[23] *Vaca* v. *Sipes*, 386 U.S. 171 (1967) and *Bowen* v. *U.S. Postal Service*, Case 81–525 U.S. (1983).

specifying that the grievance and arbitration procedures are the sole means of resolving disputes during the term of the collective-bargaining agreement. This reinforces the no-strike clause discussed earlier.

Typically, a collective-bargaining agreement will describe the various steps in the grievance procedure, indicate who is entitled to participate in the discussions at each step, and possibly set time limits for appeals of a decision made at each step. Each step of the procedure consists of a discussion concerning the merits of a grievance between the aggrieved individuals (usually accompanied or represented by a union official) and management. Successive steps involve discussions at higher levels of the union and the company. If the parties fail to agree at any stage of the procedure, they move onto the next stage. Initially, there will be an attempt to resolve a grievance at the level at which it occurred, perhaps by discussions between the supervisor of a grievant and a shop steward or other union representative on the shop floor. Failing agreement, the dispute may then move up to a discussion between middle management and a higher-level union official, and if agreement is still not reached, the grievance may be considered by the company's top industrial-relations personnel and top union leadership. Most grievances are resolved at one of the stages that precede arbitration.

About 97 percent of major private-sector collective-bargaining agreements (98 percent of contracts with grievance procedures) and three-quarters of state and local agreements now provide for arbitration as the final step in the grievance procedure (see Table 15.8). The extensive use of arbitration rather than the courts as the final step in procedures to resolve disputes over the application of the collective-bargaining agreement is a feature of labor relations peculiar to the United States. (As Example 15.4 illustrates, many European countries use special courts for this purpose.) Its strength stems from the fact that, relative to litigation, arbitration is flexible (the parties can design a system that suits their particular circumstances), informal, and generally more expeditious (although we shall see how grievances that go to arbitration can be costly in terms of money and time). Moreover, as we shall see, the parties to the collective-bargaining agreement can specify the standards that an arbitrator is to apply in reaching a decision.

Nevertheless, arbitration proceedings do have some of the characteristics of a trial. Each side presents its case and claim for relief in a hearing before the arbitrator (or arbitration panel), who has the authority to make a final determination and issue an award. Some of the informality of the arbitration process arises from the fact that arbitrators generally use less stringent procedures and rules of evidence than judges. More importantly, arbitrators are not bound to past legal doctrines or the precedent of past decisions (by the courts or by other arbitrators) to the extent that judges are. Instead, arbitrators may invoke a less well-delineated "law of the shop" and interpret the contract in the light of past practice in the firm or industry and what they regard as generally accepted standards of equity. Arbitration also differs from most judicial proceedings in that there is typically no appeal of the arbitrator's decision.

**EXAMPLE    15.4**

## Labor Courts in Europe

In Western European countries, arbitration is rarely used as a method of settling disputes over the interpretation of labor agreements. Instead, such disputes are referred to *labor courts,* which are usually appointed by the government but remain outside of, or as autonomous divisions of, the regular court systems. This separateness was designed to encourage cheaper and more expeditious settlement of grievances than would be possible in ordinary litigation. The actual structure and jurisdiction of the courts varies among countries, but in most countries decisions of the labor court are rendered by a tripartite panel of judges, often after some initial efforts to mediate a solution to the dispute. Under some systems the decisions can be appealed to higher courts (unlike the situation with most arbitration awards in the United States).

What accounts for this difference between the United States and Europe in the nature of the institutions that are established to resolve disputes over the interpretation and enforcement of the labor agreement? First, as we have noted, many of the terms and conditions of employment established through collective bargaining in the United States are established by legislation in European countries. It is natural to take grievances over alleged violations of legislated benefits to the courts rather than to arbitration. Second, in many European countries, the law provides for the extension of the terms of collective-bargaining agreements to firms that are not a party to the agreement and may not be unionized. Because the obligations are again imposed by law, it is more natural to grieve to an institution that is not directly established in formal collective bargaining. Finally, for reasons connected with the role of the courts in retarding the growth of unions in the United States prior to the 1930s (see Chapter 10), American unions are reluctant to have the courts involved in the actual determination or interpretation of the collective-bargaining agreement.

SOURCES:   Eileen B. Hoffman, *Resolving Labor-Management Disputes: A Nine-Country Comparison,* Conference Board Report No. 600 (New York: The Conference Board, 1973); William H. McPherson and Frederic Meyers, *The French Labor Courts: Judgment by Peers* (Urbana, IL: University of Illinois, 1966).

In negotiating the arbitration clause of a collective-bargaining agreement, the parties typically seek to specify the nature of the arbitration panel, the means of selecting the panel, and the jurisdiction of the panel. There are a number of forms that an arbitration panel can take. Perhaps the most important is a single impartial arbitrator. In some instances, such as labor agreements between the United Automobile Workers and the major automobile manufacturers, the arbitrator may be a "permanent umpire"—a single individual who hears all of the grievances arising under a particular collective-bargaining agreement. In other instances, the parties may select an arbitrator each time a grievance goes to arbitration.[24] A potential advantage of the latter procedure is that the background of the arbitrators can be varied to suit the nature of the grievance.

A second approach to arbitration is to use a tripartite board, consisting of one representative of management, one representative of labor, and one neutral. Since the management and labor representatives are likely to vote for the positions of their sides, the outcome is basically determined by the neutral. Why, then, bother with the tripartite procedure? One appeal of the tripartite procedure to labor and management is that it reassures them that their arguments will be fully heard. It also offers some assurance that an arbitrator will not wander too far from the general standards of the contract in fashioning a decision. In some instances of tripartite grievance arbitration, the voting is anonymous; that is, the award is announced, but neither the votes of the members of the arbitration panel nor the final vote counts are revealed. Arbitrators who have operated in this system revealed to researchers that the most frequent result is unanimity! Representatives of management and labor in an organization often have fairly common views as to what constitutes appropriate workplace behavior, but unions are often under political pressure to press grievances that they may not view as meritorious. With anonymous voting, all representatives can vote their consciences and later act as if they were outvoted on an unpopular decision.[25]

As in the case of interest arbitration discussed in Chapter 14, the incentive to resolve a grievance prior to the final step of arbitration depends on the costs associated with going to arbitration. The costs associated with grievance arbitration are largely uncertainty regarding the arbitrator's award. Unlike the situation with interest arbitration, however, with grievance arbitration the parties are able to reduce the uncertainty to a certain extent by explicitly limiting the arbitrator's authority. Most collective-bargaining agreements contain language that explicitly circumscribes the authority of the arbitrator to the contents and language of the collective-bargaining agreement and forbids the arbitrator to use other standards. That is, unlike the situation with interest arbitration, the parties are able to establish, in the language of their collective-bargaining agreement, the general standards under which an arbitrator will operate. For example, an agreement between the International Brotherhood of Teamsters and a midwestern manufacturing company provided that:

---

[24] The typical procedure is to obtain an odd number of names (usually five) from either the Federal Mediation and Conciliation Service or the American Arbitration Association and for the parties to alternately strike names from the list until only one name is left. The survivor becomes the arbitrator!

[25] As noted in Chapter 14, a similar outcome has been noted in the use of interest arbitration to determine the terms and conditions of employment for police and firefighters in New York State. Thomas A. Kochan, Mordechai Mironi, Ronald G. Ehrenberg, Jean Baderschneider, and Todd Jick, *Dispute Resolution Under Factfinding and Arbitration: An Empirical Analysis* (New York: American Arbitration Association, 1979).

**Table 15.9**   Charges for Arbitrator's Service, 1971 and 1981[*]

| Days charged for by arbitrator: | 1971 | 1983 |
|---|---|---|
| Total | 3.0 | 3.4 |
| Travel | 0.4 | 0.3 |
| Arbitration hearing | 0.9 | 1.0 |
| Post-hearing study | 1.7 | 2.0 |
| Per diem rates | $163.88 | $ 340.47 |
| Total charged | $566.59 | $1315.21 |

[*]   Average for sample of arbitrators selected by the Federal Mediation and Conciliation Service.
SOURCE:   Federal Mediation and Conciliation Service, *Thirty-Fourth Annual Report, Fiscal Year 1981* (Washington, DC: U.S. Government Printing Office, 1982): 37, and *Thirty-Sixth Annual Report, Fiscal Year 1983* (Washington, DC: U.S. Government Printing Office, 1984): 13.

> The arbitrator shall have no right to amend, modify, nullify, ignore or add to the provisions of this Agreement. He shall consider and decide only the particular issue(s) presented to him in writing by the Company and the Union, and his decision and award shall be based solely upon his interpretation of the meaning or application of the terms of this Agreement to the facts of the grievance presented.[26]

In addition to costs associated with the uncertainty of outcome, there are those resulting from time delays in resolving an issue and those arising from a need to compensate the arbitrator. In recent years, there has been increasing concern with both the compensation costs and the time delays associated with arbitration. Between 1971 and 1983, the average amount charged by an arbitrator for a single arbitration more than doubled to over $1300 as the amount of time spent (mainly on post-hearing study) and the daily fees increased (see Table 15.9). As a guide to the time consumed and money spent on grievance arbitrations, the data in Table 15.9 are only the tip of an iceberg. In one sample of arbitrations studied by the Federal Mediation and Conciliation Service, the average time elapsed between the filing of a grievance to the date of an arbitrator's award was 242 days—about eight months. On average, cases took almost six months to get to an arbitration hearing. Of this time, discussions in the lower stages of the grievance procedure consumed two and a half months, another month and a half was spent in appointing an arbitrator, and two more months passed before the arbitrator was able to hear the case. Following the hearing, an average of 46 days—including the time it took union and management to prepare and submit final briefs—passed before the arbitrator issued an award.[27] In addition, both sides incurred attorneys' fees as well as the costs of their own personnel who were involved in preparing for and participating in the hearing. Small wonder that many representatives of both management and labor are interested in devising less costly methods of resolving disputes during the term of a collective-bargaining agreement!

[26]   Bernard D. Meltzer, *Labor Law: Cases, Materials, and Problems* (Boston: Little, Brown and Co., 1970), Appendix, pp. 134–35.
[27]   Data are from the Federal Mediation and Conciliation Service, *Thirty-Fourth Annual Report, Fiscal Year 1981* (Washington, DC: U.S. Government Printing Office, 1982): 39, and *Thirty-Sixth Annual Report, Fiscal Year 1983* (Washington, DC: U.S. Government Printing Office, 1984): 13.

In an effort to reduce the burden of arbitration, some unions and management have begun to experiment with amended forms of grievance resolution. Under "expedited" arbitration arrangements, which have been adopted in several industries, including steel, longshoring, and the U.S. Postal Service, the parties may agree to dispense with a transcript of the arbitration hearing, with their briefs, and even with attorneys on the understanding that the arbitrator will hear the case promptly and issue an award rapidly. In contrast to the delays under conventional grievance arbitration noted above, the elapsed time from the request for arbitration to the hearing is in the range of five to seven days under these arrangements, and the award is either issued from the bench or within two or three days of the hearing.[28] In the longshore industry, arbitrators are "on call" to report immediately to the site of a disagreement (for example, over the implementation of work rules) between labor and management. The arguments of each side are heard on the spot, and the arbitrator issues a verbal award immediately, so that work can resume. In other instances, mediation has been found useful in resolving certain types of grievances before they reach arbitration (see Example 15.5).[29]

## Public Policy Issues Raised by Grievance Arbitration

Despite the spread of grievance arbitration arrangements following World War II, the legal status of agreements to arbitrate was uncertain. If one party to a labor agreement refused to arbitrate an issue, could the federal courts compel arbitration? If a party refused to arbitrate on the grounds that the issue involved was not subject to arbitration, could the courts determine if the issue was subject to arbitration under the terms of the collective-bargaining agreement? Although Section 301 of the Taft-Hartley Act gives the federal courts jurisdiction over suits alleging violations of labor agreements, these questions were not decided until 1957, when the Supreme Court ruled that the federal courts could enforce provisions to arbitrate in collective-bargining agreements.[30] The court ruled further, in the famous *Steelworkers' Trilogy* cases, that " . . . [t]he courts, therefore, have no business weighing the merits of the grievance, considering whether there is equity in a particular claim, or determining whether there is particular language in the written instrument that will support the particular claim. . . . The processing of even frivolous claims may have therapeutic values of which those who are not a part of the plant environment may be quite unaware."[31] In short, the Supreme Court

---

[28]  John Zalusky, "Arbitration: Updating a Vital Process," *The American Federationist* 83 (November 1976): 1–4.

[29]  Grievance mediation has been used extensively by the Labour Board in British Columbia since 1976, achieving a 71-percent settlement rate, and by several state mediation services. See *Avoiding the Arbitrator: Some New Alternatives to the Grievance Procedure*, Proceedings, 30th Annual Meeting (Washington, DC: National Academy of Arbitrators 1977).

[30]  *Textile Workers' Union* v. *Lincoln Mills*, 353 U.S. 448 (1957).

[31]  *United Steelworkers of America* v. *American Mfg. Co.*, 363 U.S. 564 (1960). The other cases in the *Trilogy* were *United Steelworkers* v. *Warrior & Gulf Nav. Co.*, 363 U.S. 574 (1960) and *United Steelworkers of America* v. *Enterprise Wheel & Car Corp.* 363 U.S. 593 (1960).

**EXAMPLE 15.5**

# Grievance Mediation in the Coal Mining Industry

The bituminous coal mining industry in the United States has had a high level of grievances, wildcat strikes, and labor strife. While the three-year agreement beginning in 1974 was in effect, for example, it is estimated that there were an average of 2700 grievance arbitrations per year resulting in arbitration costs of almost $2 million annually. Five to six months often elapsed from the time a grievance was filed until an arbitrator's decision was announced.

In late 1980, a one-year experiment in which grievance *mediation* was offered as an alternative to arbitration (after the steps in the internal grievance procedures were exhausted) was begun in two areas of the Appalachian coal fields. Under the procedure, the mediator tried to assist the parties to reach a mutually satisfactory resolution of the grievance, using the normal techniques of mediation. The parties retained the option of taking the grievance to arbitration if the mediation effort failed, however. Therefore, in a departure from normal mediation practice, the mediators involved in the experiment (who all had previous arbitration experience in the coal industry) provided the parties with an oral advisory arbitration opinion— the mediator's best judgment of what an arbitrator would decide upon hearing the case—if it appeared that no resolution of the grievance would be possible through mediation.

In an effort to reduce the cost and delays associated with resolving grievances through arbitration, the mediators scheduled three mediations per day, charged $375 per day plus travel expenses (but not for travel *time,* since there was no written decision and hence no "reflection," "study," or "writing" time), and scheduled regular dates for mediation conferences.

During the one-year experiment, mediation succeeded in resolving 73 percent of the 153 grievances presented. Another 16 percent were settled between mediation and arbitration. Only 11 percent went to arbitration. An advisory arbitration decision by the mediator was only needed in 20 percent of the mediations; in over half of these cases the ruling became the basis for resolving the grievance—the parties did not proceed to arbitration. In 75 percent of the cases taken to arbitration, the decision of the arbitrator (who, by arrangement, could not be one of the mediators) coincided with the advisory opinion. The mediation procedure also offered considerable savings in time and money over grievance arbitration. The directors of the study reported that "[t]he average time between the request for mediation and the mediation conference was 13 days compared to an average of 49 days between a request for arbitration and the arbitrator's decision. . . . The average cost (mediator's fee and expenses) of mediation was $250 per grievance, compared to an average arbitration cost (arbitrator's fee and expenses) of $1025." These advantages led one of the two areas participating in the experiment to adopt grievance mediation on a more permanent basis and encouraged other areas in the coal mining industry to initiate similar experiments.

SOURCE: Stephen B. Goldberg and Jeanne M. Brett, "An Experiment in the Mediation of Grievances," *Monthly Labor Review* 106 (March 1983): 23–30, and "Grievance Mediation in the Coal Industry," *Industrial and Labor Relations Review* 37 (October 1983): 49–69.

restricted the role of the courts to deciding whether a particular employment issue could be arbitrated under the terms of the labor agreement and instructed the courts to defer to arbitration except in instances in which the contract explicitly excludes an issue from arbitration. Moreover, the Court held that federal courts should enforce an arbitrator's award without reviewing its merits as long as the award was generally consistent with the labor agreement on which it was based.

In taking this strong position in favor of arbitration, the Supreme Court noted that as a *quid pro quo* for a no-strike pledge, grievance arbitration is an institutional arrangement that advances the National Labor Relation Act's objective of increasing industrial peace. The Court further expressed particular confidence in the qualifications of arbitrators for resolving disputes over the interpretation of a labor agreement, noting at one point that:

> The labor arbitrator is usually chosen because of the parties' confidence in his knowledge of the common law of the shop and their trust in his personal judgment to bring to bear considerations which are not expressed in the contract as criteria for judgment. . . . [t]he ablest judge cannot be expected to bring the same experience and competence to bear upon the determination of a grievance, because he cannot be similarly informed.[32]

The net effect of these decisions was to increase greatly the prestige and authority of voluntary arbitration as an institution for resolving disputes over the interpretation of the collective-bargaining agreement and to insulate arbitration awards from judicial review. As noted above, this aspect of the resolution of grievance disputes differs markedly from Europe, where the judiciary plays a much more direct role in disputes arising from the application of a labor agreement.

Not all observers would agree with the Court's perception of the value of voluntary arbitration or the unique competence of arbitrators in interpreting a collective-bargaining agreement. Many arbitrators, for example, do not appear to have any special qualifications for understanding or interpreting "the common law of the shop."[33] In addition, labor and management often appear to want an arbitrator to interpret the language of the contract much the way judges are called upon to interpret contracts outside of the employment area. Nevertheless, much of the basic deference accorded arbitration by the Trilogy decisions remains.

---

[32] The quote is from the majority opinion prepared by Justice Douglas in *United Steelworkers of America* v. *Warrior and Gulf Navigation Co.* 363 U.S. 574 (1960), 80 U.S. 1347 (1960).

[33] While information is sparse, one study of presumably favorable biographical sketches prepared by a group of 652 arbitrators revealed that other than legal training, most arbitrators in the sample did not appear to have experience that was particularly relevant to the task. Only 29 were full-time arbitrators, another 43 had experience as judges, 205 were lawyers, and 78 were law professors. Outside of the law, professors of economics (63) or industrial relations (50) were the most frequent backgrounds cited by the arbitrators. One hundred fifty-nine arbitrators did not list any experience that had relevance for arbitration. Generally, these data cast doubt on the proposition that arbitrators are likely to have more expertise for their task than "the ablest judges." See Paul Hays, *The Practice of Labor Arbitration* (New Haven, CT: Yale University Press, 1966): 51–56.

More recently, the domain of arbitration has been challenged by the passage of social legislation that has important implications for the employment relationship. Examples include equal employment legislation (discussed more extensively in Chapter 7), the Occupational Health and Safety Act (OSHA) of 1970 (discussed in Chapter 6), pension reform legislation [for example, the Employee Retirement Income Security Act of 1974 (ERISA) discussed in Chapter 8], and even aspects of the Fair Labor Standards Act (FLSA), discussed in Chapters 3 and 4. These laws raise two general questions for the conduct of arbitration and the protection of the rights of workers at the workplace. First, should an arbitrator be bound by the language of a statute or by the language of the collective-bargaining agreement when the two are in conflict? Second, should the courts defer to arbitration—the proposition advanced by the Supreme Court in the Steelworkers' Trilogy—when both collective-bargaining agreements and statutory law address an issue that has arisen? These questions have been the source of considerable controversy within the arbitration profession, and each is discussed below.

The arbitration profession is deeply divided over the question of whether it should expand the criteria to be considered in fashioning arbitration awards to include the requirements of external law as well as the language of the labor agreement. The dominant view appears to be that arbitrators should restrict their activities to interpreting the language of the agreement. It has been argued that many arbitrators may not have either the knowledge of federal statutes or the expertise to interpret them in a manner that is consistent with decisions of the federal judiciary. Therefore, efforts by arbitrators to interpret federal legislation might simply invite the judicial intervention into the arbitration process that has been absent since the Steelworkers' Trilogy decisions. On the other hand, many arbitrators feel that the institutional expertise of arbitrators ought to reflect the current realities of the employment relationship and, that by incorporating the standards of external law, the arbitration process could expedite social progress in the areas addressed by federal legislation. As of the early 1980s, the former view of the role of the arbitrator in the grievance procedure appeared to be more widely adopted.

When a labor agreement and a statute address the same issue [for example, equal employment opportunity (EEO) or occupational health and safety], an employee who has a complaint faces a choice between filing a grievance alleging a violation of the labor agreement or initiating a complaint or suit alleging a violation of the statute. Is the employee free to choose either forum—the grievance procedure or the courts? The thrust of the Steelworkers' Trilogy decisions was that the courts should defer to arbitration, which implies that unionized employees facing this choice should use the grievance procedure. Suppose an employee processes a grievance alleging discrimination to arbitration, but receives an adverse ruling. Should the employee then be permitted to file suit under EEO legislation? The question is an important one for public policy, because unions and employers—the parties who are often accused of discrimination—control the arbitration process. As we have seen, they jointly select the arbitrator and establish through contractual language the scope of the arbitrator's authority. Since arbitrators serve at the behest of both labor and management, they may be reluctant to take positions that will jeopardize their future employment. Moreover, if discrimination is the direct result of contract language, the tendency of arbitrators to interpret the contract rather than statutory law may produce a result that is at variance with public policy.

The Supreme Court recognized this conflict in holding that an employee who receives an adverse arbitration award in a grievance concerning employment discrimination is not precluded from filing a court suit on the same issue.[34] Contrary to the implications of the Steelworkers' Trilogy cases, the courts need not defer to arbitration awards on employment-discrimination issues, although the Supreme Court noted in its decision that the courts could give some weight to prior arbitration on an issue before them. Subsequent decisions indicate that the courts also need not defer to arbitration awards when workers bring suits under statutes that guarantee minimum-employment standards to workers—for example, OSHA, ERISA, and the FLSA.

# Review Questions

1. In what specific respects would you expect the content of explicit employment contracts negotiated by unions and management in the private sector to differ from the content of "implicit" employment contracts governing the employment relationship in nonunion firms? On what grounds do you expect these differences?
2. What differences would you expect between negotiated labor agreements and nonunion employment arrangements in the public sector? What general differences would you also expect between private-sector and public-sector employment arrangements?
3. What is the relationship between the collective-bargaining process and the administration of the labor agreement?
4. Some employers oppose COLA clauses on the grounds that changes in the prices of their product(s) may move differently from changes in the CPI to which wages are generally indexed. How would you expect labor and management to react to a proposal to index wages to the price of the company's product(s)? Why?

# Selected Readings

Bureau of National Affairs, *Basic Patterns in Union Contracts,* 11th ed. (Washington, DC: Bureau of National Affairs, 1986)

David E. Feller, "A General Theory of the Collective Bargaining Agreement," *California Law Review* 61 (May 1973): 663–856.

Wallace E. Hendricks and Lawrence M. Kahn, *Wage Indexation in the United States: Cola or Uncola?* (Cambridge, MA: Ballinger, 1985).

Wassily Leontief, "The Pure Theory of the Guaranteed Annual Wage Contract," *Journal of Political Economy* 54 (February 1946): 76–79.

Albert E. Rees, *The Economics of Trade Unions,* 2nd. ed. (Chicago, University of Chicago Press, 1977).

Sumner H. Slichter, James J. Healy, and E. Robert Livernash, *The Impact of Collective Bargaining on Management* (Washington, DC: The Brookings Institution, 1960).

---

[34] *Alexander* v. *Gardner-Denver* 415 U.S. 36 (1974).

# APPENDIX 15A

## "Efficient" Wage Bargains

In bargaining over wages, unions and management seek to establish a level and structure of wages by job, and changes in wages over time. Each of these dimensions of the wage bargain raises issues relating to the efficiency with which labor resources are allocated—the primary touchstone of the analysis in the first nine chapters of this book—and to equity, a concept of "fairness" that is much more difficult to define. Employers are likely to be motivated primarily by market considerations, which leads them to stress the need to remain competitive and to provide desirable work incentives to different groups of workers. Employers would prefer that compensation be related to the productivity of their work force. Unions are not insensitive to competitive considerations and often propose that wages be increased because a firm has been profitable. However, they are more likely than employers to stress equity considerations and propose that wages be increased even when a firm's profits are low, because prices have increased more rapidly than expected or because the wages of workers at other firms have increased. Thus, the labor agreement can have equity effects as well—it can influence the distribution of earnings between labor and capital and between union and nonunion labor.

The distinction between the allocative and equity issues raised by employment and compensation relationships can be seen with the assistance of Figure 15A.1, which describes the preferences of unions [in part (a)] and employers [in part (b)] between the rate of compensation and the amount of employment. As noted in the discussion of union objectives in Chapter 10, most unions are concerned with *both* the rate of compensation and the level of

**Figure 15A.1**  Bargaining Preferences of Unions and Employers

**(a) Union Indifference Curves**

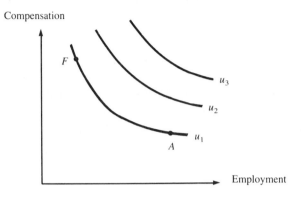

**(b) Employer Isoprofit Curves**

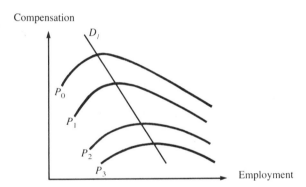

employment of their members.[1] That unions are willing to trade between higher wages and higher employment to maximize the welfare of their members was dramatically illustrated by the "concession bargaining" of the early 1980s, in which unions in several industries made wage and fringe-benefit concessions in exchange for greater job security for their members. The preferences of unions with respect to compensation and employment may therefore be represented by the curves $u_i$ in Figure 15A.1(a). Each union indifference curve describes the combinations of wages and employment that leave the union (and its average member) equally satisfied; each curve is

---

[1] Discussing a document as complex as a collective-bargaining agreement solely in terms of compensation (or wages) and employment is not as artificial as it may appear initially. The terms *compensation* and, in the subsequent discussion, *wages* are used in a broad sense to include not only wage and fringe-benefit payments but also the value or monetary costs of other provisions in the labor agreement which, while often referred to as nonmonetary, have obvious value to union members (since they want to negotiate such provisions) and costs for employers (who frequently oppose union proposals).

negatively sloped (falls downward to the right) to reflect the fact that unions are willing to trade-off between compensation and employment. For a given employment level, higher indifference curves represent higher wages and therefore index greater levels of satisfaction (that is, $u_2$ is preferred over $u_1$).

The particular curvature of the $u_i$ curves reflects the assumption that the rate at which unions are willing to trade between compensation and employment is not constant. At point $F$ in Figure 15A.1(a), the union is willing to sacrifice more compensation for an increase in employment than at point $A$. At $F$ the relatively high rate of compensation permits employed union members to enjoy a relatively high standard of living, but the relatively low employment level may threaten the bargaining power of the union and its viability as an organization. As a result, members may be willing to "pay" a relatively large amount in terms of forgone compensation to increase the employment of union members. At point $A$, however, the opposite is the case: employment is larger, but the standard of living is considerably lower. Under these circumstances, union members would have to receive much larger employment gains in order to give up more compensation.

Consider next the interest of employers. Assuming that the objective of the firm is to maximize profits, employers will be indifferent between various compensation and employment combinations that leave profits unchanged. These employer trade-offs between compensation and employment can be graphed through the use of *isoprofit curves*—curves that show the various combinations of compensation and employment levels that yield a given level of profits (*iso* means equal). Therefore, all the points along a given curve—such as $P_1$ in Figure 15A.1(b)—are pay and employment combinations that yield the *same* level of profits. In this sense, each isoprofit curve can be interpreted as an "indifference curve" for the firm (see Appendix 5A). At any given employment level, lower isoprofit curves are associated with lower wages and therefore index *higher* levels of profits; that is, profits are higher along $P_2$ than along $P_1$.

What accounts for the shape of the isoprofit curves? The slope of each curve describes the rate at which an employer can trade between wages and employment while keeping profits constant. Recall that profits are simply revenues minus costs. For simplicity, we assume that costs are the rate of compensation times the number of employed; that is, each additional employee adds the same amount to costs. Each additional employee does *not* add the same amount to revenue, however. This is because the marginal product of labor decreases at higher levels of employment as a result of the law of diminishing returns (first discussed in Chapter 3). Now, at relatively low employment levels the marginal revenue received by the firm as a result of employing more workers (the marginal revenue product) exceeds its marginal cost (the rate of compensation), and profits increase when employment is expanded. Equal (iso) profits can only be maintained if the rate of compensation increases to offset the relatively high marginal revenue product in this range, and this accounts for the positively sloped segment of the isoprofit curve. The argument is reversed when marginal revenue product falls below the wage rate.

To summarize, the shape of an isoprofit curve reflects a basic technological condition of production—the law of diminishing returns. Over the range of employment for which the marginal revenue product *(MRP)* exceeds the marginal cost of labor, the isoprofit curve is rising; when the *MRP* is less than marginal costs, the curve is falling. Therefore, the marginal revenue product equals marginal labor cost (the rate of compensation) at the peak of the isoprofit curve. But we learned in Chapter 3 that the demand-for-labor schedule is the locus of wage-employment combinations for which this equality holds. Therefore, the firm's demand-for-labor schedule cuts the peak of each isoprofit curve [see $D_l$ in Figure 15A.1(b)].

Given the preferences of unions and employers, we can now characterize an efficient solution to bargaining between the employer and the union. The value premise underlying the concept of an efficient solution is that of *mutual benefit,* which was first discussed in Chapter 1. In the context of collective bargaining, a mutually beneficial bargain is one in which neither labor nor management loses and at least one party gains. Alternatively, an efficient bargain has been reached when it is impossible to increase either the satisfaction of labor or the profits of management without reducing the welfare of the other party.

The application of this concept of efficiency is illustrated in Figure 15A.2 (on page 545), in which parts (a) and (b) of Figure 15A.1 have been combined. Suppose that when bargaining begins, the wage is $W_0$ and the employment level is $E_0$ so that the parties are at point A. Position A is inefficient in the sense that there are other positions that could be reached that would improve the position of at least one of the parties without making the other any worse off. For example, bargaining that raised the wage rate and lowered the employment level could place the parties at either points B or C. At point B, where a relatively large wage increase is accompanied by a relatively small loss of employment, the union's satisfaction is increased and employer profits are held constant. At point C, where the wage increase is smaller and employment losses are larger, the union's level of satisfaction is constant and employer profits are increased. These are just extremes of the array of efficient points that could be attained through collective bargaining.

Generally, when negotiations begin at position A, mutual gains by both labor and management are possible to the extent that negotiations lead to any point in the shaded area that represents higher levels of satisfaction and profits to the respective parties. The line running between B and C represents the locus of *efficient* preferred points in the sense that it is not possible to move from that line without reducing the well-being of at least one of the parties to collective bargaining. Each point on the line segment *BC* consists of a tangency between an employer-isoprofit curve and a union-satisfaction curve. Since the slopes of these curves must be equal for a tangency to occur, at each point on *BC*, the rate at which employers are willing to trade between wages and employment at a given profit level is identical to the rate at which the union is willing to trade between these two dimensions of the employment relationship. No further mutual gains from trade are possible. Recognizing that bargaining might start from points other than *A*, it becomes clear that the line segment *BC* is just one part of a much longer locus of efficient wage and employment combinations. This locus of efficient points is known as the *contract curve*.

Each point on the contract curve is therefore efficient in the sense described above, but each point represents a different distribution of income between the union and the firm. Unlike bargaining to reach an efficient position when the parties start away from one, collective bargaining over the distribution of income between unions and employers along the contract curve is a zero sum game—what one party wins, the other party loses. For this reason, collective bargaining over purely distributional issues is likely to be more contentious than bargaining that leads to a more efficient wage-employment combination (recall Chapter 13's discussion of this point).

Suppose now that a union specifies a rate of compensation, but allows the employer to choose the level of employment. To determine whether the result of this arrangement is efficient, one must consider the response of a profit-maximizing employer to a contractual wage or compensation requirement. When confronted with a contractual wage requirement, the employer will choose the level of employment that maximizes profits at that wage rate. In terms of Figure 15A.2, this is reflected in the (graphically) lowest isoprofit curve that touches a horizontal line from the chosen wage. This is another way of demonstrating that the demand for labor curve of the firm, $D_l$, is the locus of the maximum points of the isoprofit curves of the firm. To clarify the effects of collective bargaining on the market, we shall define the competitive rate of compensation—that is, the supply price of labor to the firm in the absence of unions—to be $W^*$. Faced with this market-determined wage, a profit-maximizing employer would choose employment level $E^*$.[2]

Since the employer is permitted to choose the level of employment, any wage-employment combination on the employer's demand-for-labor schedule is available to the union. Therefore, the union will choose the wage, $W_f$, which in combination with the employment level ($E_f$) chosen by the profit-maximizing employer at that wage will maximize the union's welfare. This wage-employment combination is indicated by point *F* in Figure 15A.2 where the union-indifference curve, $u_1$, is tangent to the employer's demand-for-labor schedule. Any other point on that schedule will leave the union at a lower level of satisfaction (that is, on a lower indifference curve). The interesting feature of this solution is that it is *not* efficient. When the union, acting as a monopolist, simply sets the wage and allows the employer to choose the level of employment, the outcome is not on the contract curve. At point *F*, further mutually beneficial gains from negotiation are possible. Specifically,

---

[2] Since workers can get $W^*$ from other employers, no contract establishing a lower rate would sensibly be negotiated in a competitive labor market, and, for this reason, the contract curve does not extend below this point in Figure 15A.2.

**Figure 15A.2**    Analysis of Bargaining

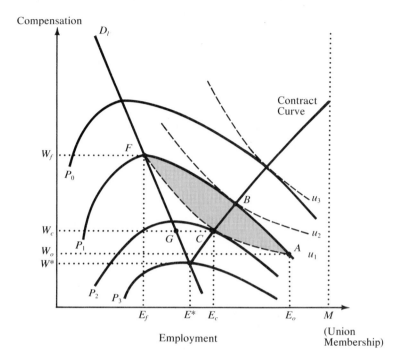

any point on the contract curve between points *B* and *C* would improve the welfare of at least one party while leaving the other party no worse off. To reach an efficient solution, the collective-bargaining agreement would have to specify the level of employment as well as the rate of compensation.[3] In specifying an efficient solution, however, the distribution of income between the union and the employer could be drastically altered from what it would be at *F*.

The divergence between the solution at a point such as *F* and an efficient solution is tied to the fact that while the union's satisfaction is determined by both employment and wages, the employer is interested only in maximizing profits. For example, while a union that negotiated $W_f$ would be equally happy at point *C* where the lower wage, $W_c$, was offset by a higher employment level, $E_c$, it would never agree to a wage as low as $W_c$ without an explicit employment guarantee written into the collective-bargaining contract. For while the firm receives higher profits at *C* than at *F*, its profits are higher still

[3] This was first pointed out by Wassily Leontief, "The Pure Theory of the Guaranteed Annual Wage Contract," *Journal of Political Economy* 54 (February 1946): 76–79; and William Fellner, "Prices and Wages Under Bilateral Monopoly," *Quarterly Journal of Economics* (August 1947): 503–32. More recent discussions and extensions include Ian M. McDonald and Robert M. Solow, "Wage Bargaining and Employment," *American Economic Review* 71 (December 1981): 896–908; and Robert E. Hall and David M. Lilien, "Efficient Wage Bargains Under Uncertain Supply and Demand," *American Economic Review* 69 (December 1979): 868–79.

at $G$. Therefore, in the absence of an employment guarantee, the firm would select point $G$, where the employment of union members, while higher than at point $F$, was not sufficiently high to offset the union's loss of satisfaction from the lower wage. The lower wage induces employers to hire more workers, but not enough more to fully compensate the union for the loss in satisfaction due to the reduced wage. (The union's satisfaction level is lower at $G$ than at $C$.)[4]

[4]   For reviews of the applications of wage bargaining models, see Andrew J. Oswald, "The Economic Theory of Trade Unions: An Introductory Survey," *Scandinavian Journal of Economics* 87 (1985): 160–93 and John Pencavel, "Wages and Employment Under Trade Unions: Microeconomic Models and Macroeconomic Applications," *Ibid*, pp. 197–225.

# CHAPTER 16

## The Effects of Unions

Our discussion of unions and collective bargaining has examined changes in the institutions and public policy influencing relations between employers and employees when workers are represented by unions. We have examined the nature and objectives of union organizations, the legal environment of union-management relations, the interaction of labor and management in collective bargaining, and the labor agreement, which is the outcome of the collective-bargaining process. For the most part, however, our discussion has not addressed the actual economic effects of unions. How do they change the patterns of compensation, employment, productivity, and profits that would be observed in a market economy without unions? This is an important question, for, as noted in Chapter 1, surface impressions of union economic effects can be misleading.

This chapter examines the effects unions have had on wage *and* nonwage outcomes. Economists have traditionally focused on estimating the amount by which unions have increased the wages of their members *relative* to the wages of comparable nonunion workers—and their conclusion that unions have a negative effect on the allocation of resources in society is based on these estimates, which will be discussed in the first part of this chapter. Recently, however, analytical labor economists have begun to rediscover the variety of roles that unions play and have concluded that unions may play many positive roles that leave society as a whole better off.[1] Therefore, in subsequent sections, we shall also consider the effects of unions on productivity, labor turnover, and profitability.

---

[1] This "new" view of unions is described by two of its exponents in a nontechnical fashion in Richard B. Freeman and James L. Medoff, *What Do Unions Do?* (New York: Basic Books, 1984).

# Union Effects on Pay

The most frequently stated economic objectives of unions are to raise the wages of union members and to take wages "out of competition." The former goal is the more commonly understood interest of unions in raising the compensation of their members relative to that of nonmembers. To the extent that unions succeed in this objective, they would seem to increase the inequality of wages among workers of comparable skill levels. Also important to unions, however, is the elimination of competition between employers on the basis of differential labor costs. This goal implies reducing the wage differences among employees performing the same job in different geographical areas and even among employees of different skills in the same area. In this section, we examine, first, union effects on *relative* compensation and, then, turn to the broader effects they have had on inequality and the distribution of income in the United States.

## The Theory of Union Wage Effects

Suppose one had data on the wage rates paid to two groups of workers who were identical in every respect except that one group was unionized and the other was not.[2] Let $W_u$ denote the wage paid to union members and $W_n$ the wage paid to nonunion workers. If the difference between the two could be attributed solely to the presence of unions, then the *relative-wage advantage* that unions would have achieved for their members would be given, in percentage terms, by

$$R = (W_u - W_n)/W_n \qquad (16.1)$$

Contrary to what one might expect, this relative-wage advantage does *not* represent the absolute amount, in percentage terms, by which unions would have increased the wages of their members because unions both directly and indirectly affect *nonunion* wage rates also. Moreover, one can not *a priori* state whether estimates of $R$ will overstate, or understate, the absolute effect of unions on their members' real wage levels. Figure 16.1 presents a simple two-sector model of the labor market. Except for the fact that the labor-supply curves slope upward in both sectors, this model is identical to the one used in Chapter 3 to analyze the effects of the minimum wage in the presence of incomplete coverage; the analysis here will proceed along similar lines.

Panel (a) is the union sector and panel (b) is the nonunion sector. Suppose initially, however, that both sectors are unorganized. If mobility is relatively costless, workers will move between the two sectors until wages are equalized between them. With demand curves $D_u$ and $D_n$, workers will move between sectors until the supply curves are $S_u^0$ and $S_n^0$, respectively. The

---

[2] Much of the discussion in this section is based upon the pioneering work by H. G. Lewis, *Unionism and Relative Wages in the United States* (Chicago: University of Chicago Press, 1963), and *Union Relative Wage Effects: A Survey* (Chicago: University of Chicago Press, 1986).

**Figure 16.1**  Spillover Effects of Unions on Wages and Employment

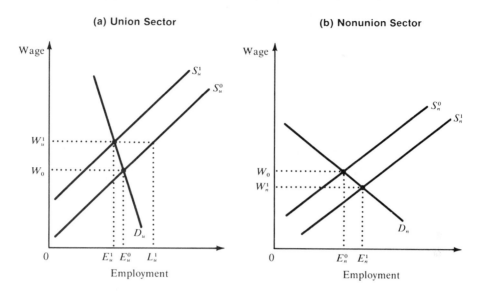

(a) Union Sector

(b) Nonunion Sector

common equilibrium wage will be $W_0$, and employment will be $E_u^0$ and $E_n^0$, respectively, in the two sectors.

Now suppose a union succeeds in organizing the workers in the first sector and also succeeds in raising their wage to $W_u^1$. This increased wage will cause employment to decline to $E_u^1$ workers in the union sector, resulting in $L_u^1 - E_u^1$ unemployed workers in that sector. These workers have several options; one is to seek employment in the nonunion sector. If all of the unemployed workers *spill over* into the nonunion sector, the supply curves in the two sectors will shift to $S_u^1$ and $S_n^1$ respectively. Unemployment will be eliminated in the union sector; however, in the nonunion sector an excess supply of labor would exist at the old market-clearing wage, $W_0$. As a result, downward pressure would be exerted on the wage rate in the nonunion sector until the labor market in that sector cleared at a *lower* wage ($W_n^1$) and a higher employment level $E_n^1$.

In the context of this model, the union has succeeded in raising the wages of its members who kept their jobs. However, it has done so at the expense of shifting some of its members to lower-wage jobs in the nonunion sector and, because of this spillover effect, at the expense of actually lowering the wage rate paid to individuals initially employed in the nonunion sector. As a result, the observed union *relative-wage* advantage ($R_1$), computed as

$$R_1 = (W_u^1 - W_n^1)/W_n^1, \qquad (16.2)$$

will tend to be greater than the true *absolute* effect of the union on its members' real wage. This true absolute effect ($A_1$), stated in percentage terms, is computed as

$$A_1 = (W_u^1 - W_0)/W_0. \qquad (16.3)$$

The relative effect will not necessarily be larger than the absolute effect, however, because there are several other responses that employees or employers can make. Employers in the nonunion sector may be concerned that unions will subsequently try to organize their employees—employers may view a union as undesirable if unionization both increases their wage costs and limits their managerial flexibility. Therefore, they may try to "buy off" their employees by offering them wage increases to reduce the probability that the employees will vote for a union.[3] Because of the costs associated with union membership, noted earlier, some wage less than $W_u^1$ but higher than $W_0$ would presumably be sufficient to assure employers that the majority of their employees would not vote for a union (assuming that the employees are happy with their nonwage conditions of employment).

The implications of such *threat effects*—nonunion wage increases resulting from the threat of union entry—are traced in Figure 16.2. The increase in wage in the union sector, and resulting decline in employment there, is again assumed to cause the supply of workers to the nonunion sector to shift to $S_n^1$. However, in response to the threat of union entry, nonunion employers are assumed to *increase* their employees' wages to $W_n^*$, which lies between $W_0$ and $W_u^1$. This wage increase causes employment to decline to $E_n^*$; at the higher

**Figure 16.2**   Threat Effects of Unions on Wages and Employment

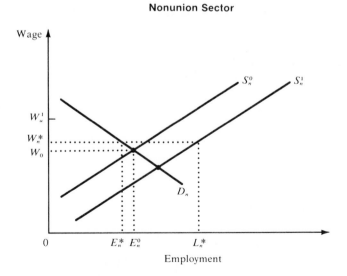

[3] For a more formal discussion of this possibility, see Sherwin Rosen, "Trade Union Power, Threat Effects, and the Extent of Organization," *Review of Economic Studies* 36 (April 1969): 185–96.

wage nonunion employers demand fewer workers. Moreover, since the non-union wage is now not free to be bid down, an excess supply of labor, $L_n^* - E_n^*$, exists, resulting in unemployment. Finally, because the nonunion wage is now higher than the original wage, the observed union relative-wage advantage,

$$R_2 = (W_u^1 - W_n^*)/W_n^*, \tag{16.4}$$

is smaller than the absolute effect of unions on their members' real wages.

One might question whether workers who lose their jobs in the union sector, as a result of unions' increasing the wage rate, will necessarily seek jobs in the nonunion sector. Even with a fixed employment level in the union sector, job vacancies occur due to retirements, deaths, and voluntary turn-over (including quits to take other jobs in the same area, geographic migra-tion, and individuals who are temporarily leaving the labor force). It may pay union members to remain attached to the union sector *and* temporarily unem-ployed if they believe that they will ultimately obtain a job in the union sector. Indeed, it may actually pay some employed nonunion workers to quit their jobs and move to the union sector in the hopes that they will obtain a relatively higher-paying union job in the future. Such decisions lead to *wait unemployment:* workers rejecting lower-paying nonunion jobs and waiting for higher-paying union jobs to open up.[4]

Because unions *are* present in the economy, at any point in time all one can observe are the union and nonunion wage rates ($W_u$ and $W_n$). One *cannot* observe the wage that would have existed in the absence of unions, $W_0$. Hence, direct estimates of a union's effects on the absolute level ($A_1$) of its members' real wages—refer back to equation (16.3)—cannot be obtained. Care must be taken not to mistake relative-wage effects for absolute-wage effects.[5]

## Evidence of Union Wage and Total Compensation Effects

In recent years, economists have expended considerable effort to estimate the extent to which unions have raised the wages of their members relative to the wages of comparable nonunion workers.[6] These studies have tended to use data on large samples of individuals and have attempted to separate wage

---

[4] See the appendix to this chapter for a detailed analysis of wait unemployment.

[5] This discussion has assumed a partial-equilibrium model. Once one considers a general-equilibrium framework and allows capital to move between sectors, even more possibilities may exist. On this point, see Harry Johnson and Peter Mieszkowski, "The Effects of Unionization on the Distribution of Income: A General Equilibrium Approach," *Quarterly Journal of Economics* 84 (November 1969): 539–61.

[6] For surveys of these estimates, see Lewis, *Union Relative Wage Effects: A Survey;* C. J. Parsley, "Labor Unions and Wages: A Survey," *Journal of Economic Literature* 18 (March 1980): 1–31; George E. Johnson, "Economic Analysis of Trade Unionism," *American Economic Review* 65 (May 1975): 23–28; Daniel J. B. Mitchell, "The Impact of Collective Bargaining on Compensation in the Public Sector," in *Public Sector Bargaining,* eds. B. Aaron et al. (Washington, DC: Bureau of National Affairs, 1979); Free-man and Medoff, *What Do Unions Do?*; and Barry T. Hirsch and John T. Addison, *The Economic Analysis of Unions: New Approaches and Evidence* (Boston: Allen and Unwin, 1986).

differentials due to unionization from wage differentials due to differences in personal characteristics and differences in industry and occupation of employment. That is, these economists have sought to ascertain how much more union members get paid than nonunion workers, after controlling for any differences between the two groups in other factors that might be expected to influence wages.[7]

**Private-sector wage studies.** The various studies use several different data bases that span various years, and they often employ different statistical methodologies. As such, they do not yield a single unambiguous estimate of the extent to which union members' wages exceed the wages of comparable nonunion workers in the private sector. After a careful review of over 200 studies, H. G. Lewis concluded that the union relative-wage advantage probably averaged 15 percent between the mid-1950s and late 1970s.[8] Union wage effects are neither constant over time nor constant across groups, however.

Lewis found that the estimated union relative-wage advantage rose from around 12 percent in the late sixties to about 20 percent in the mid-1970s. Unemployment was low in the late 1960s and much higher in the mid-1970s. Since unionized workers' wages tend to be less responsive to labor-market conditions than nonunion workers' wages, this result is not surprising; the union relative-wage advantage tends to be larger during recessionary periods.[9]

Table 16.1 summarizes Lewis' conclusions regarding union wage effects for different demographic groups, occupations, and industries. The numbers

**Table 16.1**  Comparisons of Union vs. Nonunion Relative-Wage Effects by Race, Sex, Occupation and Industry, 1970s.

| Group | Differential | Group | Differential |
|-------|-------------|-------|-------------|
| Black/White: | .05 to .10 | Female/Male: | 0 |
| Nonmanufacturing/ | | | |
| Manufacturing | .10 | Laborer/Operative | .05 |
| Construction/Other | | | |
| Nonmanufacturing | .10+ | Operative/Craft | .03 |
| Private/Public | .13 | Blue collar/White collar | .14 |

Note:  The numbers describe the extent to which the union relative wage effect for the first group exceeds the union relative-wage effect for the second group. For example, the union-relative wage effect is .05 to .10 percentage points higher for black workers than white workers.

SOURCE:  H. G. Lewis, *Union Relative Wage Effects: A Survey* (Chicago: University of Chicago Press, 1986): 118, 125, 131, 153.

---

[7]  Some of the more ambitious studies also attempt to control for the fact that unionization and wages may be simultaneously determined; as noted earlier, workers' decisions to join a union are partially based on the expected gains from union membership. See, for example, Lung-Fei Lee, "Unionism and Wage Rates: A Simultaneous-Equations Model with Qualitative and Limited Dependent Variables," *International Economic Review* 19 (June 1978): 415–33.

[8]  Lewis, *Union Relative Wage Effects.*

[9]  Lewis, *Unionism and Relative Wages,* provides evidence that this relationship appeared to hold during the 1930–60 period as well.

in the table describe the *difference* in the union wage effects for two groups. For example, the interpretation of the number in the upper left-hand corner of the table is that the union relative wage for black workers is 10 percentage points higher than the union relative wage for white workers. That is, if the unionized white workers on average receive a wage that is 15 percent higher than their nonunion counterparts, unionized black workers on average receive a wage that is 20 to 25 percent higher than the wage of nonunion black workers.

In spite of well-publicized conflicts between some unions and civil-rights organizations over union seniority rules and the use of racial quotas, the data indicate that unions appear to have improved the economic well-being of blacks relative to whites; being a union member enhances black males' earnings more than it does white males' earnings. Moreover, black workers are more likely to belong to unions than white workers.

In contrast, union membership does not appear to affect the difference between male and female wages, on average. Women and men gain an equivalent amount from union membership, although female workers are less likely to be union members than are male workers.

Unions do not explicitly negotiate wages for demographic groups, however; they negotiate wages by job and by industry. Therefore, the patterns of union-wage effects noted above are to a large extent the result of the interaction between (1) the effects of unions on relative wages within industries and occupations, and (2) the employment distribution of different demographic groups by industry and occupation. Evidence from early studies of union-nonunion wage differentials indicated that craft unions in the construction and transportation industries achieve the largest relative-wage effects, while industrial unions generally had a somewhat smaller relative-wage effect. This pattern is still evident in the data in Table 16.1. Union relative-wage effects are higher in nonmanufacturing than in manufacturing industries, and higher in construction than in other nonmanufacturing industries. There is substantial variation among industries within these broad sectors, of course. For example, in a few highly competitive industries, such as textiles and apparel, unions appear to have no effect on wages.[10]

The union relative-wage impact also varies by occupation, largely because most unions adopt the egalitarian strategy of negotiating equal absolute (that is cents-per-hour) wage increases for all workers. In relative (percentage) terms, workers in lower-wage occupations achieve larger gains than more highly skilled workers. As a result, among blue-collar workers, the union-wage impact is generally largest for laborers, next highest for operatives, and lowest for craft workers (in industrial unions). The union-wage impact is also much higher for blue-collar workers than for white-collar workers, and higher for workers with less than a high school education than for high school graduates. One reason for the larger union relative-wage

---

[10]   For a summary of the early studies, see Lewis, *Unionism and Relative Wages,* p. 280.

impact for blacks reported in Table 16.1 is that they are disproportionately employed in low-wage jobs, for which the union-wage impact is generally largest.

The findings from the studies cited (and many others) indicate that the wage impact of unions in the private sector is anything but monolithic. What accounts for the fact that the estimated wage effects associated with unions have varied from as little as zero to as much as 40 percent from industry to industry? One key determinant appears to be the ability of a union to maintain control of its jurisdiction—to extend its standards to all firms in a particular market. When there are few barriers to the entry or location of new firms (as, for example, when the capital requirements for an industry are low), it is often difficult for a union to keep its jurisdiction organized. Negotiating a relative-wage increase at unionized firms may simply lead to the emergence of non-union firms paying lower wages in other areas (for example, southern states). If a union is unable to organize these newly emerged firms, their (lower) wages will attract business (and jobs) from the union firms. Thus, when a union is unable to keep its jurisdiction organized, its power to raise relative wages is limited by the availability of cheaper nonunion substitutes. (Ultimately, most explanations of union power seem to lead back to the factors governing the elasticity of the demand for labor that we have discussed in Chapters 3 and 12.)

Difficulties in maintaining jurisdictional control tend to limit the ability of unions to obtain large relative-wage gains for their members in many highly competitive industries. The textile industry, where, as noted above, there is a negligible difference between union and nonunion wages, represents an example of an industry where unions (in the North, primarily) were unable to prevent the movement of jobs to nonunion areas. In an environment where wages cannot be raised much by unions, a union's appeal stems from its ability to regularize the allocation of economic opportunities, establish a grievance procedure, and reduce the extent of supervisory discretion in personnel matters.

Interestingly, however, relatively large union/nonunion wage differentials are found in some competitive product markets, such as trucking, longshoring, and construction. How are unions in these industries able to achieve a large relative-wage impact while unions in other competitive industries may have none? Again, the key factor appears to be the union's ability to maintain its jurisdictional control. One characteristic of each of these industries is that there are distinct geographical limitations on the area of product-market competition. Longshoring is restricted to key ports; the Teamsters could achieve considerable leverage by controlling terminal facilities in a few major cities where freight was delivered or transferred; construction sites are not particularly mobile. When the product market is confined to a particular area, it is less costly for unions to organize and police their jurisdictions.[11]

---

[11] *See* Harold M. Levinson, *Determining Forces in Collective Bargaining* (New York: John Wiley & Sons, Inc., 1966).

As noted in Chapter 12, there is also evidence that the wage impact of unions is related, in general, to bargaining structure, so that the patterns of union wage impact by industry will reflect, in part, differences in bargaining arrangements. Another factor that can influence labor relations and union wage impacts is the economic regulation of an industry by government agencies. For many years, the government regulation of industries such as air transportation and surface transportation tended to limit the entry of new firms and thereby made it easier for unions in these industries to maintain their degree of organization. With deregulation, the union wage impact in these industries may be reduced. In the case of public utilities, which are often "natural" monopolies that are not threatened by the entry of competing firms, the regulation of utility rates may have influenced the bargaining stance of employers and the wage impact of unions (see Example 16.1).

In our discussions of the elasticity of labor demand earlier in the book, we noted that demand is less elastic in the short run than in the long run. Application of this analysis suggests that even the more powerful unions might incur limitations on their ability to raise wages over time. Recent history provides many examples. The power of the United Mine Workers, for example, has been eroded in more recent times with the opening of nonunion mines as new coal deposits are discovered. A more dramatic change in fortunes occurred in the construction industry, in which negotiated wages increased relative to virtually every other group in the country in the late 1960s and early 1970s. One consequence of this increase was a significant increase in the amount of nonunion construction activity. By the mid- and late 1970s, employment opportunities for unionized construction workers had deteriorated so severely that negotiated wage increases in construction were among the smallest in the country.

The estimates cited above are of the relative-wage advantage (R) that unions in the private sector have achieved for their members in comparison to nonunion workers. These estimates do not indicate what effects unions have had on the absolute real-wage levels of their members. In other words, the estimates do not reveal how unions have influenced *nonunion* workers' wages. Though limited, evidence on how the presence of unions affects wages of nonunion workers is mixed. In the 1960s unions may have in some instances depressed nonunion wages, but in the 1970s and early 1980s they appear to have raised nonunion wages.[12] That is, in the 1960s, the spillover effect described in Figure 16.1 dominated the threat and wait-unemployment effects described in Figure 16.2 and in Appendix 16A; however, in the 1970s and early 1980s, the latter two effects dominated. It is possible that as the union-nonunion wage differential rose in the 1970s and early 1980s, nonunion firms had more to gain by staying nonunion than was the case earlier, and thus

---

[12] See Lawrence M. Kahn, "The Effect of Unions on the Earnings of Nonunion Workers," *Industrial and Labor Relations Review* 31 (January 1978): 205–16; and Barry T. Hirsch and John L. Neufeld, "Nominal and Real Union Wage Differentials and the Effects of Industry and SMSA Density: 1973–83," *Journal of Human Resources* 22 (Winter 1987): 138–48.

**EXAMPLE** 16.1

## Unions in Regulated Public Utilities

A union's effect on relative wages in an industry can be influenced by government policy. For example, state commissions that regulate public utilities (such as telephone, electric, and gas companies) must decide whether all the costs that the utilities incur should be legitimately charged to consumers. Deciding whether or not labor costs should be charged to consumers raises particular difficulties. On the one hand, it is often conjectured that employers in regulated industries have less of an incentive to "bargain tough" with the unions that represent their employees than do employers in nonregulated industries, because historically, regulatory commissions have allowed utilities to pass on all labor-cost increases to consumers (in the form of higher utility prices). If such an argument is valid, it would indicate the need for commissions to carefully scrutinize utilities' wage settlements. On the other hand, it is difficult to decide upon what wage rates a commission should consider "just and reasonable."

At the very least, it is important to take into account any qualitative differences among the work forces of the utility and of other employers in the same labor-market area. By statistically controlling for such factors as education and experience, it should be easier to see if employees in a regulated industry are paid more than employees in other firms. When such a comparison was made for telephone workers in New York State, it was found that the utility's employees were paid approximately 9–12 percent more than were other employees with comparable education and experience levels in the state, in 1970.

However, these estimates can be fraught with difficulties. Part of any estimated wage premium paid to unionized workers in regulated industries may be justified as a differential to compensate them for having relatively unfavorable working conditions or more difficult jobs than employees in other industries. Wage comparisons may not accurately reflect total compensation comparisons because they ignore fringe benefits. They also may neglect the potential positive effects that the union and a high-wage policy might have (for example, reduced employee turnover and reduced strike activity). In the particular case mentioned above, the commission decided not to limit the permissible wage increase but did reserve the right to limit future wage "pass-throughs" if similar comparative studies illustrated the need for such limits. By even considering the issue, however, a commission raises interesting issues for public policy.

A commission's decision to disallow part of any collectively bargained wage settlement from being passed on to consumers would not violate the National Labor Relations Act, since it would not affect the terms of the settlement. However, it would undoubtedly affect management's willingness to grant the union large wage increases in the future; if the commission refuses to grant price increases to cover cost increases, the firms' profits must fall. In other words, the commission's intervention would affect the environment in which bargaining takes place and the relative bargaining power of the union. Thus, implicitly, the commission's action would affect future wage settlements.

We should also note, however, that commissions that uncritically allow all labor-cost increases to be passed on to consumers will also affect the environment in

which bargaining takes place—by increasing the relative bargaining power of unions. This outcome, which corresponds closely to the status quo in most states, is not necessarily more desirable. In any case, it should be clear that it is difficult for government to remain neutral; its mere presence—whether or not it takes any action—affects labor markets.

SOURCE: Ronald G. Ehrenberg, *The Regulatory Process and Labor Earnings* (New York: Academic Press, 1979). See also Wallace Hendricks, "Regulation and Labor Earnings," *Bell Journal of Economics* 8 (Autumn 1977): 483–96.

had a greater incentive to pay high wages to keep unions out, as we argued in the Chapter 11 discussion of compliance with the labor laws. The implication of these research findings is that for the 1970s and early 1980s, estimates of relative wage effects of unions may well have been less than their effects on the absolute level of their members' wages.

**Private-sector total compensation effects.**  Estimates of the extent to which the wages of union workers exceed the wages of otherwise comparable nonunion workers may prove misleading for two reasons. First, such estimates ignore the fact that wages are only part of the compensation package. It has often been argued that fringe benefits, such as paid holidays, vacation pay, sick leave, and retirement benefits will be higher in firms that are unionized than in nonunion firms. The argument states that because tastes for the various fringe benefits differ across individuals, and because there is no easy way to communicate the preferences of the average employee to the employer in a nonunion firm, nonunion firms will tend to pay a higher fraction of total compensation in the form of money wages.[13] Recent empirical evidence tends to support this contention; fringe benefits and the share of compensation that goes to fringe benefits do appear to be higher in union than in nonunion firms.[14] Ignoring fringes may therefore understate the true union/nonunion total compensation differential.

In contrast, ignoring nonpecuniary conditions of employment may cause one to overstate the true effect of unions on their members' total compensation vis-a-vis nonunion workers. For example, some recent studies have shown that for blue-collar workers, unionized firms tend to have more structured work settings, more hazardous jobs, less flexible hours of work, faster work paces, and less employee control over the assignment of overtime hours than do nonunion firms.[15] This situation may arise because production set-

[13] This line of reasoning goes back at least as far as Richard Lester, "Benefits as a Preferred Form of Compensation," *Southern Economic Journal* 33 (April 1967): 488–95.

[14] Richard Freeman, "The Effect of Trade Unions on Fringe Benefits," *Industrial and Labor Relations Review* 34 (July 1981): 489–509; William T. Alpert, "Unions and Private Wage Supplements," *Journal of Labor Research* 3 (Spring 1982): 179–99.

[15] Greg Duncan and Frank Stafford, "Do Union Members Receive Compensating Wage Differentials?" *American Economic Review* 70 (June 1980): 355–71; Ronald G. Ehrenberg and Paul L. Schumann, *Longer Hours or More Jobs?* (Ithaca, N.Y.: ILR Press, 1982), Chap. 7; and J. Paul Leigh, "Are Unionized Blue Collar Jobs More Hazardous Than Nonunionized Blue Collar Jobs?" *Journal of Labor Research* 3 (Summer 1982): 349–57.

tings that give rise to interdependence among workers and the demand for specific work requirements by employers also give rise to unions. That is, the decision to vote for unions may be heavily influenced by these nonpecuniary conditions of employment. While unions often strive to affect these working conditions, they do not always succeed. Part of the estimated union/nonunion earning differential may be a premium paid to union workers to compensate them for these unfavorable working conditions. Indeed, one study estimates that two fifths of the estimated union/nonunion earnings differential reflects such compensation—suggesting that the observed union/nonunion earnings differential may overstate the true union/nonunion differential in total compensation.[16]

**Public-sector studies.**    Several studies have attempted to estimate what the effect of unions representing state- and local-government (SLG) employees has been on their members' wages relative to the wages of otherwise comparable nonunion public employees. As Table 16.1 indicates, unions in the SLG sector appear to have had more moderate effects on the relative wages of their members than unions in the private sector.

As emphasized, however, wages are not identical to total compensation. In addition to those reasons presented in the previous chapter, there are other reasons to believe that the effects of public-sector unions on nonwage benefits may well exceed their effects on wages. On the one hand, public employees' wages are much more visible to the public than are their fringe benefits. The public may be more aware of the cost of a $200 increase in annual starting salaries, which is well publicized, than they are of the cost of an improvement in health-insurance benefits that will also cost $200 per employee. As such, it may be politically easier for governmental negotiators to make concessions on fringe-benefit items than on wages.

On the other hand, while the costs of increased wages must be borne in the present, the costs of improved fringe benefits are often not known at the time of settlement or are borne in the future. For example, the true cost of agreeing to pay 100 percent of employees' health-insurance costs depends upon future increases in health-insurance rates. To take another example, if public-employee pension plans are not fully funded, the costs of agreeing to more generous retirement provisions today will become evident only in the future when employees begin to take advantage of these provisions.[17] Since

---

[16]  Duncan and Stafford, "Do Union Members Receive Compensating Wage Differentials?" The true effect of unions on wages may also be overstated because some quality differences between workers in union and nonunion firms cannot be measured for statistical analyses. Portions of the relative-wage effect reported above may therefore reflect greater ability among union workers rather than union power. See Wesley Mellow, "Unionism and Wages: A Longitudinal Analysis," *The Review of Economics and Statistics* 63 (February 1981): 43–52; and particularly Lewis, *Union Relative Wage Effects* . . . , Chapter 5.

[17]  That most public retirement systems are not fully funded (that is, they do not have assets sufficient to meet their accrued liabilities) is well known. For example, one study found that in 1975 state- and local-government pension funds had assets equal to only 38 percent of their accrued liabilities. *See* U.S. House of Representatives, *Pension Task Force Report on Public Employee Retirement Systems* (Washington, D.C.: U.S. Government Printing Office, 1978).

**EXAMPLE   16.2**

## Codetermination and Union Relative-Wage Gains in West Germany

Since the early 1950s, legislation has encouraged greater employee participation in management in West Germany. These *codetermination laws* give employees in the German iron-steel and mining industries one half of the seats on company Boards of Directors and give employees in all other industries (save for shipping and air transport) one third of the seats. The position of labor director has also been established on Management Boards in the steel and mining industries; this director cannot be approved or dismissed without a majority vote of the employee representatives to a company's Board of Directors.

German employee representatives on Boards of Directors participate in decisions about industrywide collective-bargaining agreements. One might expect that these laws have increased labor's bargaining power, especially in the iron-steel and mining industries, and have thus increased the size of observed wage differentials between unionized workers in these industries and other employees in the economy. A recent study concluded that codetermination has increased the earnings of the average unionized German iron-steel and mining employee by roughly 6.2 percent relative to the earnings of primarily nonunion employees in the textile industry. The effects of unions on relative wages clearly depend upon the prevailing institutional arrangements.

SOURCE:  Jan Svejnar, "Relative Wage Effects of Unions, Dictatorship, and Codetermination: Econometric Evidence from Germany," *The Review of Economics and Statistics* 63 (May 1981): 188–97.

government officials' tenure in office is often short, and since they typically will depart from office well before the true costs of such fringe benefits become known, it is in their *short-run* political interests to win favor with public-employee unions by agreeing to increased fringes; moreover, the short-run costs of such agreements to taxpayers may well be small.[18]

For both of these reasons then, one might expect that the effect of public-sector unions on fringe benefits would be larger than their effects on wages. Although the limited empirical evidence on this point is somewhat ambiguous, it does suggest that this has occurred.[19]

[18]  We say short run because in the long run facts become known. The best example of this occurred in New York City when Mayor Lindsay agreed to generous fringe-benefit packages for New York City employees during the late 1960s and early 1970s. Many people subsequently blamed him for all of the financial problems that the city experienced in the mid-1970s, and when he ran for U.S. Senator in the Democratic primary in 1980 he finished well behind the winner.

[19]  *See* Carey Ichniowski, "Economic Effects of the Firefighters' Union," *Industrial and Labor Relations Review* 33 (January 1980): 198–211; and David Rogers, "Municipal Government Structure, Unions, and Wage and Nonwage Compensation in the Public Sector" (unpublished Cornell University M.S. thesis, 1979).

**Effects on wage dispersion.** One might think that the above evidence suggests that, contrary to their expressed objectives, unions increase the dispersion of labor earnings by increasing the wages of high-paid union members relative to the wages of lower-paid nonunion members. In fact, however, several studies indicate that unions actually do tend, on balance, to *decrease* the dispersion of labor earnings. The major reason for this decrease is to be found in the effect of unions on the types of payment systems used in industry. In their efforts to "take the wage out of competition," unions prefer payment systems that establish a single "standard rate" for a particular job or occupation and permit upward adjustments or "progression" in the rate on the basis of seniority. Employers, on the other hand, generally favor systems that permit payment on the basis of merit reviews or some other method of making distinctions among different workers performing the same job. In the political setting within which much union decision-making occurs (see Chapter 10), it is easy to see that if the wage received by the median worker is less than the mean wage paid all workers, then a majority of union members will favor a payment system, such as the standard rate, which redistributes wages toward lower-paid workers. There is strong evidence that unions increase the proportion of workers paid by single (standard) rate plans (and reduce the percent paid by methods of individual wage determination) as compared to pay practices used in the nonunion sector.[20]

We have noted that one effect of the different wage-payment practices adopted in union and nonunion firms is to reduce the extent of wage dispersion among workers covered by union contracts. An interesting aspect of reduced wage dispersion is that the rates of return to education and job training are lower in the union than nonunion sector. These lower payoffs in the union sector are caused by the earnings there being more equal among workers with different human-capital investments than would otherwise be the case. Recent evidence indicates that some of the union wage-leveling effect is felt in the nonunion sector as well. That is, unions appear to indirectly reduce nonunion wage inequality. This outcome may occur because nonunion firms respond to the potential threat of unionism by giving the highest raises to those who would benefit most from a union (the lowest-paid workers).[21] Unions also influence wage inequalities by reducing the relative-wage advantage of white-collar workers vis-a-vis blue-collar workers.

Thus, unions have conflicting impacts on the distribution of wages. On the one hand, unions tend to create wage differences among union and nonunion workers at the same occupational level in industry. On the other,

[20] Richard B. Freeman, "Union Wage Practices and Wage Dispersion Within Establishments," *Industrial and Labor Relations Review* 36 (October 1982): 3–21.

[21] On the payoffs to human capital, see Farrell Bloch and Mark Kuskin, "Wage Determination in the Union and Nonunion Sectors," *Industrial and Labor Relations Review* 31 (January 1978): 183–92; and Gregory M. Duncan and Duane E. Leigh, "Wage Determination in the Union and Nonunion Sectors: A Sample Selectivity Approach," *Industrial and Labor Relations Review* 34 (October 1980): 24–35. On the union effect on nonunion wage inequality, see Lawrence M. Kahn and Michael Curme, "Unions and Nonunion Wage Dispersion," *The Review of Economics and Statistics* 69 (November 1987): 600–607.

unions tend to narrow the wage differences between different blue-collar occupations and between blue-collar and white-collar workers. Moreover, we have seen that unions also tend to standardize the wages paid union workers within an occupation, and this standardization occurs for some nonunion workers as well. One study suggests that the latter effects dominate the more widely known union effects on union/nonunion worker wage differentials in the sense that, on balance, unions appear to reduce wage dispersion in the United States.[22] Finally, another study suggests that, other things equal, inequality of earnings within metropolitan areas tends to be less widespread in areas in which the extent of unionization is high.[23]

# Union Effects on Productivity and Output

According to the traditional neoclassical view of unions, although they may improve the welfare of their members by improving their pecuniary and nonpecuniary conditions of employment, on balance their effects on the economy at large are negative. Three reasons support this view.

First, to the extent that unions do succeed in driving a wedge between the wage rates of comparable-quality workers who are employed in the union and nonunion sectors, there is a loss of output. Recall from Chapter 3 that the demand curves for labor reflect the marginal product of labor. If the "spillover" model in Figure 16.1 holds, the union wage, $W_u$, exceeds the nonunion wage, $W_n$, and the marginal product of labor is higher in the union sector than in the nonunion sector. Consequently, output could be increased if labor were reallocated from the nonunion sector to the union sector where its marginal product is higher. Put another way, unions cause a misallocation of workers: too many workers are employed in the nonunion sector and too few in the union sector. Of course, if the union wage gain also induces some unemployment (see Figure 16.2 and Appendix 16A), the loss of output due to these idled resources must also be considered.

Second, union-negotiated contract provisions that establish staffing requirements or other restrictive work practices limit firms from employing capital and labor in the most efficient ways and may cause output losses. Several examples of such provisions include minimum-crew sizes in jet aircraft, maximum apprentice/journeymen ratios in construction, provisions limiting subcontracting or mandatory assignment of overtime, and requirements that redundant employees be employed (fire stokers in diesel-operated railroad engines, typesetters in printing plants where type is set by computer). By limiting substitution possibilities or forcing firms to use redundant inputs, unions reduce output below its maximum achievable level.

---

[22] Richard B. Freeman, "Unionism and the Dispersion of Wages," *Industrial and Labor Relations Review* 34 (October 1980): 3–23.

[23] Thomas Hyclak, "The Effects of Unions on Earnings Inequality in Local Labor Markets," *Industrial and Labor Relations Review* 33 (October 1979): 77–84.

Third, unions are thought to reduce output because strikes called either at the time that collective bargaining is occurring (to influence the settlement) or during the term of a contract (to protest the way the contract is being administered) result in lost work days. In this view, if strikes were eliminated, output would increase.

Actual empirical estimates of the magnitudes of these alleged losses are few and far between. In an often cited study, Albert Rees estimated that society lost no more than 0.3 percent of gross national product because of the creation of wage differentials between comparable quality union and non-union workers.[24] Rees also estimated that the loss of output due to restrictive work practices was at least as large. Finally, Table 14.1 indicated that the estimated percentage of working time lost due to strikes over the 32-year period from 1953–85 averaged 0.2 percent. Summing these three figures yields an estimated loss in output of less than 0.8 percent due to these three factors. Of course, whether one considers this an acceptable or unacceptable cost depends upon the benefits that one believes society as a whole receives from unionization.

## New Evidence of Union Effects on Productivity and Output

To the extent that unions are successful in raising their relative wage, employers will have an incentive to raise the marginal product of labor by substituting capital for labor, by increasing the general quality of the work force, or by simply reducing employment. Although these employer adjustments to a higher wage will have the effect of raising observed labor productivity, the total cost of producing a given level of output will have increased. In this section we shall consider whether union effects on productivity go beyond these induced adjustments by employers.

Recently labor economists have begun to rediscover the possibility that unions may also have positive influences on productivity.[25] These new analyses are based heavily upon the assumption that unions function as institutions of *collective voice* operating within structured internal labor markets.[26] That is, because unions can communicate the preferences of workers on various issues directly to management and can help establish work rules and seniority

[24] Albert Rees, "The Effects of Unions on Resource Allocation," *Journal of Law and Economics* 6 (October 1963): 69–78. Rees's estimate also included consideration of output losses due to union effects on intra-industry wage differentials—for example, requiring all unionized firms in an industry to pay the same wage.

[25] For a discussion of the evidence supporting this view, see Freeman and Medoff, *What Do Unions Do?*

[26] Albert Hirschman, *Exit, Voice and Loyalty* (Cambridge, Mass.: Harvard University Press, 1973), and Richard Freeman, "Individual Mobility and Union Voice in the Labor Market," *American Economic Review* 66 (May 1976): 361–68 provide discussions of unions' role as institutions of collective voice. Oliver Williamson, Michael Wachter, and Jeffrey Harris, "Understanding the Employment Relation: Analysis of Idiosyncratic Exchange," *Bell Journal of Economics* 6 (Spring 1975): 250–80, emphasize the interrelationship between unions and internal labor markets.

provisions in the context of structured internal labor markets, they can contribute to increases in productivity in a number of ways.

First, by providing workers with a direct means to voice their discontent to management and by establishing job rights based upon seniority, unions may reduce worker discontent, thus reducing voluntary turnover (quit rates). As discussed in Chapter 4, reductions in job turnover increase employers' incentives to provide their employees with *firm-specific training*, which will lead to increased productivity. Considerable evidence suggests that unions do in fact reduce quit rates.[27] Moreover, seniority systems weaken the extent of rivalry between inexperienced and experienced employees and consequently increase the amount of informal on-the-job training that the latter are willing to give to the former.[28]

Second, by increasing the economic rewards to employment and providing grievance mechanisms, unions may directly enhance productivity by increasing worker morale, motivation, and effort. Third, unions provide an explicit mechanism by which labor can point out possible changes in work rules or production techniques that will benefit both labor and management.

Several studies have been undertaken in recent years that attempt to estimate the net effect of unions on productivity. These studies are summarized in Table 16.2. The method used in all but studies (4) and (8) is to estimate the extent to which value of output per worker (the *value added*) is associated with the level of unionization in an industry or establishment, after controlling for other factors that affect productivity.[29] (Studies (4) and (8) use data on the physical volume of output.)

The studies on manufacturing (Studies 1–4) show ambiguous results: unions are estimated to have an effect on productivity ranging from $-3$ to $+25$ percent, although three of the four studies cited in Table 16.2 show positive effects. In those instances in which the union productivity effect is positive and large, the unit labor cost (the cost of labor per unit of output) of unionized firms would not be much higher than that for nonunion companies. Under such conditions, it would be possible for high-wage union firms and lower-wage nonunion firms to coexist in the same competitive industry. However, the decline in the union sector in many industries (documented in Chapter 10) suggests that nonunion firms have—on average—a unit-labor-cost advantage over unionized companies.

In the bituminous coal industry, positive union productivity differentials are found in 1965, but substantial negative ones appear in 1975. Indeed, in

---

[27]   *See* Richard B. Freeman, "The Exit-Voice Trade-off in the Labor Market: Unionism, Job Tenure, Quits, and Separations," *Quarterly Journal of Economics* 94 (June 1980): 644–73; and James Medoff, "Layoffs and Alternatives Under Trade Unions in United States Manufacturing," *American Economic Review* 69 (June 1979): 380–95.

[28]   *See* Peter Doeringer and Michael Piore, *Internal Labor Markets and Manpower Analysis* (Lexington, MA: D. C. Heath, 1971).

[29]   Value added is the difference in dollar terms between the sales price of a product and the value of the materials that went into making it.

**Table 16.2** Estimates of the Impact of Unionism on Productivity in American Industries

| Industry and Year of Data | Estimated Impact of Unions on Produc- tivity (percent) |
|---|---|
| 1. All U.S. manufacturing, 1972 | 20 to 25 |
| 2. All U.S. manufacturing, 1970–80 | −2 to −3 |
| 3. Wooden household furniture, 1972 | 15 |
| 4. Cement, 1953–76 | 6 to 8 |
| 5. Underground bituminous coal, 1965 | 25 to 30 |
| 6. Underground bituminous coal, 1975 | −20 to −25 |
| 7. Construction, 1972 | 17 to 22 |
| 8. Construction of office buildings, 1973–74 | 30 |

SOURCES OF ESTIMATES: (1) Charles Brown and James Medoff, "Trade Unions in the Production Process," *Journal of Political Economy* 86 (June 1978): 355–78; (2) Kim Clark, "Unionization and Firm Performance," *American Economic Review* 74 (December 1984): 893–919; (3) John Frantz, "The Impact of Trade Unions on Productivity in the Wood Household Furniture Industry" (Honors Thesis, Harvard University, 1976); (4) Kim Clark, "The Impact of Unionization on Productivity: A Case Study," *Industrial and Labor Relations Review* 33 (July 1980): 451–69; (5)–(6) Richard Freeman, James Medoff, and Marie Connerton, "Industrial Relations and Productivity: A Case Study of the Bituminous Coal Industry," (mimeo, Harvard University, 1979); (7) Steven Allen, "Unionized Construction Workers Are More Productive," *Quarterly Journal of Economics* 99 (May 1984): 251–74; (8) Steven Allen, "Unionization and Productivity in Office Building and School Construction," *Industrial and Labor Relations Review* 39 (January 1986): 187–201.

1975 unionized workers were estimated to be 20 to 25 percent *less* productive than nonunion workers in the industry. This decline in relative productivity has been attributed to the well-known breakdown of the United Mine Workers' (UMW) national leadership that occurred in the late 1960s and early 1970s, which resulted in deteriorating industrial-relations practices, including increased occurrence of *wildcat* (unauthorized) strikes over local issues.[30] These results emphasize that the effects of unions on productivity are neither constant nor always positive; they vary across industries and time periods as industrial-relations practices vary.

Studies (7) and (8) cited in Table 16.2 find surprisingly large union productivity differentials in construction—surprising because in the construction industry unions were widely thought to have adverse effects on productivity owing to their restrictive work rules (limits on apprentice/journeymen ratios, limits on the jobs members of each craft can do, and so forth).[31] The author of the studies, however, attributes the differential to better training in union apprenticeship programs, changes in the occupational mix induced by unions (for example, fewer supervisors), reduced screening and recruitment costs for

[30] Richard Freeman, James Medoff, and Marie Connerton, "Industrial Relations and Productivity: A Case Study of the U.S. Bituminous Coal Industry" (Cambridge, MA: Harvard University mimeo, 1979).

[31] Steven Allen, "Unionized Construction Workers Are More Productive," *Quarterly Journal of Economics* 99 (May 1984): 251–74, and Allen, "Unionization and Productivity in Office Building and School Construction," *Industrial and Labor Relations Review* 39 (January 1986): 187–201.

contractors, and greater use of technologies and materials that reduce labor usage.

On balance, then, the studies summarized in Table 16.2 suggest that unions have *increased* productivity in certain industries, although this judgment is by no means unanimous.[32] There is also no consensus on whether these increases more than offset the loss of gross national product caused by union effects on wage structures and union strike activity. These studies suggest, however, that like most questions in economics, whether unions have had a net positive or negative effect on output is an empirical question. The answer is not as obvious as either the supporters or opponents of unions would have one believe.

## Effects of Unions on Profits

The evidence that we have reviewed in this chapter gives a conflicting impression of the economic effect of unions. On the one hand, there is evidence that, *on average,* wages are about 15–20 percent higher for union workers than for comparable nonunion workers. On the other hand, one study showed that, *on average,* labor productivity in manufacturing is at least 20-percent higher in union than in nonunion establishments. Taken together, these two findings raise the possibility that profitability is greater in firms that are organized by unions. This intriguing possibility does not accord well with the rather substantial efforts of most firms to oppose demands for recognition by unions and of employer organizations to oppose proposed labor law reforms that might facilitate the process of union organization. If unions improve the competitive position of firms, why are they not welcomed by managers?

One hypothesis is related to the fact that in the process of negotiating changes in the work environment that are associated with higher employee productivity, unions place substantial constraints on the prerogatives and discretion that managers value in a nonunion employment environment. Managers may therefore oppose unionization, despite its potentially beneficial effects, to protect their power and discretion. That is, managers may not be maximizing profits alone; instead they may be *utility-maximizers,* where their utility is a combination of profits and job discretion. Managers therefore may be willing to sacrifice some profits to maintain their discretion. It is argued that since it is difficult for shareholders to monitor managerial performance, it may be possible for managers to take actions (such as resisting unions and

---

[32] Some economists question the findings of these studies. See Barry T. Hirsch and John T. Addison, *The Economic Analysis of Unions,* pp. 192–208, for criticism of these findings and citations to other studies that fail to find positive effects. Moreover, even if unions increase productivity at a point in time, they may slow down the rate of productivity growth if they discourage employers from investing in research and development because of their unwillingness to adopt new production techniques. Evidence that unionization is often associated with slower rates of productivity growth is surveyed in Hirsch and Addison. Moreover, Steven Allen, "Productivity Levels and Productivity Change Under Unionism," *Industrial Relations* 27 (Winter 1988): 94–113, finds that even in construction, unionization appeared to be negatively associated with productivity growth during the 1972–82 period.

their beneficial effects) that may be in their best interests but not the interests of the shareholders.

A direct approach to this issue is to examine the evidence on the effects shareholders expect unions to have on the performance of a firm, and the actual effects of unions on profitability. With respect to shareholder behavior, the literature on finance offers considerable evidence that new, publicly available information on factors influencing the profitability of a corporation is quickly reflected in stock (equity) prices. Therefore, announcements of union-organizing drives and victories in representation elections could either increase the equity value of the firm (if the effect on profitability is believed to be positive) or decrease it (if the effect is believed to be negative). One study of 253 NLRB representation elections between 1962 and 1980 found that stock prices *fell* in respose to both the announcement that a petition for election had been filed with the NLRB and the certification of a union as bargaining agent.[33]

A second approach is to compare the profitability of union and nonunion firms directly. Here it is important to distinguish between different product market structures. If the effect of unions is to reduce the profitability of firms in a competitive industry, those firms will earn less than normal profits and will leave the industry until the product price increases sufficiently to restore a normal rate of return. In equilibrium, therefore, the profitability of the unionized firms that survive this process and nonunion firms should be the same. In concentrated industries, however, firms may earn excess profits in equilibrium and a union may be able to capture some of these profits. Several recent studies indicated that unions, in fact, do reduce profits (consistent with the shareholder expectations discussed above), but, in equilibrium, the reduction of profits is observed only in concentrated industries.[34] While some of the evidence is still preliminary, it appears that the general effect of unions is to reduce profits, and that stockholders are aware of this impact.

# Concluding Remarks: Noneconomic Effects of Unions

Unions play many roles in any society and can be assessed from different perspectives. In keeping with the basic perspective of this book, we have focused our attention on the main economic effects of unions in labor markets.

---

[33] Interestingly, the fall in the stock price when a petition was filed (before the campaign and election) was larger in cases in which the union ultimately won the election than in cases where the union lost, a result that the authors interpret as indicating that the market is able to anticipate the outcome of the election. See Richard S. Ruback and Martin B. Zimmerman, "Unionization and Profitability: Evidence from the Capital Market" *Journal of Political Economy* 92 (December 1984): 1134–57.

[34] Richard B. Freeman, "Unionism, Price-Cost Margins, and the Return to Capital," National Bureau of Economic Research (January 1983); Kim Clark, "Unionization and Firm Performance"; *American Economic Review* 74 (December 1984): 893–919; and Paula Voos and Lawrence Mishel, "The Union Impact on Profits: Evidence from Industry Price-Cost Margin Data," *Journal of Labor Economics* 4 (January 1986): 105–33.

The direct economic effects that have been discussed in this chapter are important and are among the most frequently studied effects of unions. In some respects, however, they provide a limited vision of the effects of unions as social institutions. Most notably, much of the analysis of the direct economic effects tends to slight the role of unions in securing workplace and political representation for workers. At the workplace, unions provide employees with an alternative to quitting to register dissatisfaction over working conditions. Moreover, the alternative is likely to provide employers with more information on specific plant labor-relations problems than an increase in the quit rate would. Grievances not only provide a mechanism for interpreting the labor agreement (as stressed in Chapter 15) but also provide a signal to managers about the quality of employer-employee relations. As several recent analyses of unions have stressed, the contractual rules that limit managerial discretion (for example, seniority systems and grievance procedures) may also provide a workplace environment that results in smoother production operations.

Unions also serve an important function in providing a voice for workers and for low-income individuals in a pluralistic political system in which one must be organized to be heard. Most of the important social legislation of the past two decades—for example, legislation pertaining to equal employment opportunity, occupational health and safety, and health care for the aged—has been passed with the active support of the labor movement. That economic analysis can often suggest ways in which such legislation might be structured differently to achieve greater efficiency does not alter the importance of the role of the labor movement in providing representation of the interests and rights of groups of citizens that might otherwise be ignored in the political process. Unions also seek legislation that enhances their power and supports their activities as collective-bargaining institutions. In recent years, however, labor has been able to claim more success in securing passage of legislation addressing the concerns of workers generally than in securing passage of legislation addressing the more parochial concerns of unions in their adversary relationship with employers. Ironically, the more successful unions are in securing benefits for workers generally through legislation, the more difficult it may become to convince workers that they need unions at the workplace to represent their interests.

Some observers have suggested that the function unions serve in representing the rights of workers at the workplace and in the political arena fosters a commitment of American workers to the basic economic system that is not observed in many other countries in which there is often a distinct ideological component to union activities.[35] In this sense, American unions may have a role in fostering political stability. These latter effects of unions are much more difficult to measure than the effects that we have discussed in this chapter. Perhaps because of this, they are easier to ignore. When one com-

[35] Albert Rees, *The Economics of Trade Unions* (Chicago: University of Chicago Press, 1962): 195, 202. See also Robert M. MacDonald, "An Evaluation of the Economic Effects of Unionism," *Industrial and Labor Relations Review* 19 (April 1966): 335–47.

pares the behavior of workers and their unions in different countries, however, one cannot help but be impressed by the general political stability of workers in the United States and their acceptance of the economic system. To the extent that this is related to the direct (through collective bargaining) and indirect (through legislative efforts) effects of unions on the welfare of workers, it should be balanced against the economic effects stressed earlier in this chapter in forming a general assessment of the role of unions.

## Review Questions

1. The head of a large national union is trying to decide where to concentrate efforts at organizing a union. There are three perceived options: Firm A, Firm B, or Firm C. The three firms are identical except that: (1) Firm A faces a perfectly elastic (horizontal) supply curve of labor and a rather inelastic demand curve for its output; (2) Firm B behaves as a monopsonist (faces an upward-sloping supply curve of labor) and faces a perfectly elastic (horizontal) demand curve for its output; (3) Firm C faces a perfectly elastic supply curve of labor and a perfectly elastic demand curve for its output. This union head would like to know where a new union will pay off in large wage gains and small reductions in numbers of workers. Rank the three options from best to worst giving reasons for your ranking.

2. Is the following statement true, false, or uncertain? "The host of empirical studies that indicate that unions raise the wages of their members by 10 to 15 percent relative to the wages of comparable nonunion workers imply that unions have a negative effect on national output." Explain your answer.

3. "Craft workers generally are highly skilled, difficult to replace, and constitute a small percentage of total cost. Straightforward application of the factors governing the elasticity of derived demand for labor indicates that craft workers will benefit the most from union representation." Explain why you do or do not concur with this analysis. Is empirical evidence on union relative-wage effects consistent with the conclusion of the analysis?

4. Are unions likely to raise, lower, or leave unchanged the wages of nonunion workers?

5. In the late 1970s, Congress passed legislation that deregulated much of the air transportation industry, making it easier for new carriers to begin service on many routes and to alter their fares. Would you expect unions representing airline employees to support or oppose such legislation? Why?

## Selected Readings

Charles Brown and James L. Medoff, "Trade Unions in the Production Process," *Journal of Political Economy* 86 (June 1978): 355–79.

Richard B. Freeman, "Unionism Comes to the Public Sector," *Journal of Economic Literature* 24 (March 1986): 41–86.

Richard B. Freeman and James L. Medoff, *What Do Unions Do?* (New York: Basic Books, 1984).

H. G. Lewis, *Union Relative Wage Effects: A Survey* (Chicago: University of Chicago Press, 1986).

Daniel J. B. Mitchell, "The Impact of Collective Bargaining on Compensation in the Public Sector," in *Public Sector Bargaining*, eds. B. Aaron, et al. (Washington, DC: Bureau of National Affairs, 1979).

# APPENDIX 16A

## Unions and "Wait" Unemployment

"Wait" unemployment occurs when workers reject lower-paying (often, nonunion) jobs and wait for higher-paying (frequently, union) jobs to open up.[1] The wait unemployment that can be caused by union-nonunion wage differentials can best be analyzed by assuming that workers will move between the union and nonunion sectors until their *expected earnings* in each are equal. If one ignores complications such as the costs of union membership, the presence of unemployment-insurance benefits for some unemployed workers, fringe benefits, and the like, expected earnings will be equal when the wage rate paid in each sector, multiplied by the fraction of each period ($F$) that individuals in the sector expect to be employed, are equal, or when

$$W_u F_u = W_n F_n. \qquad (16A.1)$$

Figure 16A.1 illustrates the process. If threat effects are ignored, the consequences of an increase in the union wage to $W_u^1$ would be a decline in employment in the union sector to $E_u^1$, a shift in the supply curves to $S_u^1$ and $S_n^1$, and a resulting decrease in nonunion wages to $W_n^1$ and increase in nonunion employment to $E_n^1$. Since there is no unemployment in this situation, $F_u$ and $F_n$ are both equal to unity. Hence, labor-market equilibrium, as indicated in equation (16A.1), would require that wages be equal in the two sectors. But

---

[1] *See* Jacob Mincer, "Unemployment Effects of Minimum Wages," *Journal of Political Economy* 84 (July/August 1976, Part 2): S87–S104. Although Mincer discusses minimum-wage effects, union-imposed "minimum wages" can be analyzed analogously, and his model has been adapted to the analysis of the union and nonunion sectors by Lawrence M. Kahn and Kimio Morimune, "Unions and Employment Stability: A Sequential Logit Approach," *International Economic Review* 20 (February 1979): 217–35.

**Figure 16A.1**   Wait Unemployment (nonunion wage falls)

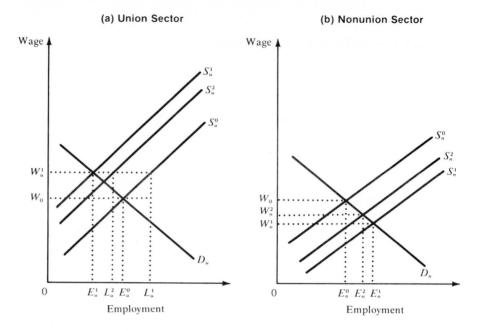

(a) Union Sector

(b) Nonunion Sector

they are *not;* $W_u^1$ is greater than $W_n^1$; hence, individuals' expected earnings are higher in the union sector.

This difference in expected earnings would induce some individuals to move from the nonunion sector to wait for jobs in the union sector. This movement leads to an increase in the expected earnings in the nonunion sector (as supply decreases there, wages are bid up) and a decrease in expected earnings in the union sector (as supply increases there, the probability of obtaining a job in that sector decreases). Eventually expected earnings are equalized between the two sectors by this process.

We have *assumed* that expected earnings are equalized in Figure 16A.1 at the points at which the supply curves in the two sectors are $S_u^2$ and $S_n^2$, respectively. The resulting wage in the nonunion sector is $W_n^2$, and the resulting employment level is $E_n^2$. *Wait unemployment* now exists in the union sector; its level is given by $L_u^2 - E_u^1$. Finally, although $W_n^2$ is greater than $W_n^1$, $W_n^2$ is less than $W_0$. Thus, if the union relative-wage advantage is measured as

$$R_3 = (W_u^1 - W_n^2)/W_n^2, \qquad (16A.2)$$

it will again be larger than the true absolute effect of the union on its members' real wage levels.

Of course, we have assumed that the expected earnings would be equalized as indicated in Figure 16A.1. Under certain assumptions, the equalization may not occur until after the supply of labor to the union sector has shifted to the *right* of its initial position and after the supply of labor in the nonunion sector has shifted to the *left* of its initial position. This situation is more likely to occur if the demand curve in the union sector is inelastic. An inelastic demand curve would cause *expected earnings* ($W_u^1 F_u$) in the union sector to increase immediately after the increase in the union *wage*, because employment losses are so small. This immediate rise in expected earnings induces employees to migrate from the nonunion to union sector.[2] As Figure 16A.2 indicates, supply in the union sector shifts right (to $S_u^3$) and supply in the nonunion sector shifts left (to $S_n^3$). In this situation wait unemployment would increase to $L_u^3 - E_u^1$, and the nonunion wage would increase to $W_n^3$, which is greater than $W_0$. The union relative-wage advantage in this case, which is computed as

$$R_4 = (W_u^1 - W_n^3)/W_n^3, \tag{16A.3}$$

would be less than the absolute effect of unions on their members' real wages.

One final case will complete our discussion. Suppose the union increases its members' wages by means of increasing the demand for union labor—using any of the methods discussed in Chapter 12. Figure 16A.3 illustrates an increase in the demand for labor in the union sector to $D_u^1$. If this increase comes at the expense of the demand for labor in the nonunion sector, the latter curve will fall—say, to $D_n^1$. Initially, the effect is to increase both wages

**Figure 16A.2**   Wait Unemployment (nonunion wage increases)

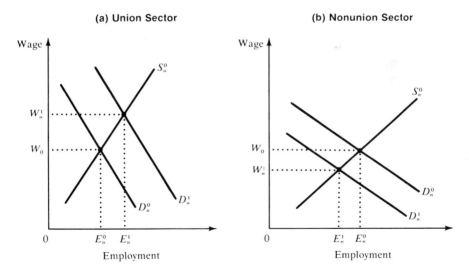

(a) Union Sector                    (b) Nonunion Sector

[2] *See* Mincer, "Unemployment Effects of Minimum Wages," Edward Gramlich, "The Impact of Minimum Wages on Other Wages, Employment, and Family Incomes," *Brookings Papers on Economic Activity*, 1976–2, pp. 409–51, and L. Kahn and K. Morimune, "Unions and Employment Stability: A Sequential Logit Approach," pp. 217–35, for a more complete discussion of when this is likely to occur.

**Figure 16A.3**   Union "Shifts" the Demand Curve

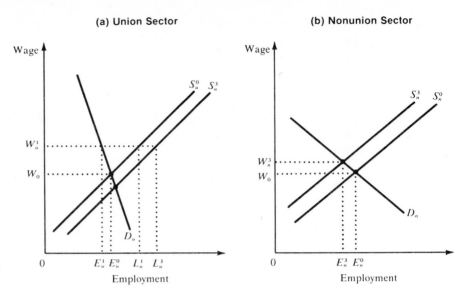

(a) Union Sector

(b) Nonunion Sector

($W_u^1$) and employment ($E_u^1$) in the union sector and decrease wages ($W_n^1$) and employment ($E_n^1$) in the nonunion sector. The ultimate change in the nonunion wage, however, will depend upon the extent to which threat effects or wait unemployment are important. So again, estimates of the union *relative*-wage effects alone tell us little about the *absolute* effects of unions on their members' real wage levels.

# PART 6

## The Future of the Employment Relationship

# CHAPTER 17

## Labor and the Macroeconomy

As noted in Chapter 2, the population can be divided into those people in the labor force ($L$) and those not in the labor force ($N$). The labor force consists of those people who are employed ($E$) and those who are unemployed but would like to be employed ($U$). The concept of unemployment is somewhat ambiguous, since in theory virtually anyone would be willing to be employed in return for a generous enough compensation package. Economists tend to resolve this dilemma by defining unemployment in terms of an individual's willingness to be employed at some prevailing market wage. Government statistics take a more pragmatic approach, defining the unemployed as those who are on temporary layoff waiting to be recalled by their previous employers or those who have actively searched for work in the previous month (of course, "actively" is not precisely defined).

Given these definitions, the unemployment rate (**u**) is further defined as the ratio of the number of the unemployed to the number in the labor force:

$$\mathbf{u} = \frac{U}{L}. \tag{17.1}$$

Much attention is focused on how the national unemployment rate varies over time and how unemployment rates vary across geographic areas and age/race/gender/ethnic groups.

It is important, however, to understand the limitations of unemployment-rate data. They *do* reflect the proportion of a group that actively wants to work but is not employed. For a number of reasons, however, they do *not* necessarily provide an accurate reflection of the economic hardship that members of a group are suffering.[1] First, individuals who are not actively searching for work, including those who searched unsuccessfully and then gave up, are not counted among the unemployed (see Chapter 5). Second, unemployment statistics tell us nothing about the earnings levels of those who are employed, including whether these exceed the poverty level. Third, a substantial fraction of the unemployed come from families in which other earners are present—for example, many unemployed are teenagers—and the unemployed often are not the primary source of their family's support. Fourth, a substantial fraction of the unemployed receive some income support while they are unemployed, either in the form of government unemployment-compensation payments or private supplementary unemployment benefits. Finally, unemployment-rate data give us information on the fraction of the labor force that is not working but tell us little about the fraction of the population that is employed.

To emphasize the last point, Table 17.1 contains data on the aggregate unemployment rate, the labor-force-participation rate, and the *employment rate*—the last being defined as employment divided by *population*—for 1948, 1958, 1968, 1978, 1985, 1986, and 1987. The unemployment rate rose from 3.8 percent in 1948 to 6.8 percent in 1958, but because the aggregate labor force participation rate rose by 0.7 percentage points during the period, the employment rate (the fraction of the population that is employed) fell by only 1.2 percentage points. In contrast, while between 1968 and 1978 the employ-

**Table 17.1**   Civilian Labor Force Participation, Employment, and Unemployment Rates

| Year | Unemployment Rate (U/L) | Labor Force Participation Rate (L/POP) | Employment Rate (E/POP) |
|------|-------------------------|-----------------------------------------|--------------------------|
| 1948 | 3.8 | 58.8 | 56.6 |
| 1958 | 6.8 | 59.5 | 55.4 |
| 1968 | 3.6 | 59.6 | 57.5 |
| 1978 | 6.1 | 63.2 | 59.3 |
| 1985 | 7.2 | 64.8 | 60.1 |
| 1986 | 7.0 | 65.3 | 60.7 |
| 1987 | 6.2 | 65.6 | 61.5 |

$U$ = number of people unemployed.
$L$ = number of people in the labor force.
$E$ = number of people employed.
$POP$ = total population.
SOURCE:   U.S. Bureau of Labor Statistics, *Employment and Earnings* 35 (January 1988), Table 1.

[1]   This discussion draws heavily on the final report of the National Commission on Employment and Unemployment Statistics, *Counting the Labor Force* (Washington, DC: U.S. Government Printing Office, 1979), and Glen G. Cain, "Labor-Force Concepts and Definitions in View of Their Purposes," in *Concepts and Data Needs* (Appendix Volume 1 to the Commission's final report).

ment rate once again rose (this time from 3.6 to 6.1 percent), the employment rate actually *rose* during the decade because of the relatively large increase in the labor-force-participation rate (over 3 percentage points) that occurred during 1968–78. A similar pattern existed between 1978 and 1987, with an increasing labor-force-participation rate again permitting a simultaneous increase in the unemployment rate and the employment/population ratio.

Nonetheless, the unemployment rate remains a useful indicator of labor market conditions. This chapter will be concerned with why *anyone* is unemployed; with why the unemployment rate varies over time, regions, or age/race/gender/ethnic groups; and with how various government policies affect, in either an intended or unintended manner, the level of unemployment.

In this chapter, we will discuss how unemployment arises. Economists conceptually categorize unemployment as being *frictional, structural, demand-deficient,* or *seasonal* in nature. After defining each type of unemployment and discussing its causes, we shall focus on issues that are raised by the discussion. Among the issues that will be considered are how the unemployment-insurance system and unemployment are interrelated, why unemployment rates vary across age/race/gender/ethnic groups, and why the "full employment" unemployment rate has risen since 1960.

Finally, we will analyze the relationship between unemployment and inflation, because policies designed to reduce unemployment may lead to higher prices later on. For most of the 1970s, the United States experienced both high rates of wage and price *inflation* (that is, relatively rapid and pervasive increases in wages and prices). Further, these increases were taking place in the context of rather high unemployment rates, so that the country seemed to suffer the consequences of both inflation *and* unemployment at the same time (a condition some call "stagflation"). Simultaneously high rates of inflation and unemployment challenged the long-held belief that inflation would diminish if unemployment rose—a belief that seemed to have held out hope that government fiscal or monetary policies could be skillfully used to maneuver the economy to tolerable levels of both inflation and unemployment.

The causes and consequences of inflation—and the fiscal and monetary policies to remedy it—are beyond the scope of labor economics. Our intent here is to analyze the relationship between inflation and unemployment so that the connections between what happens in the labor market and what happens to prices in general are more clearly understood. Moreover, because our focus is on the labor market, we will emphasize the price of labor—the wage rate—when discussing the issue of inflation.

# Types of Unemployment and Their Causes

## Frictional Unemployment

Suppose a competitive labor market is in equilibrium, in the sense that at the prevailing market wage the quantity of labor demanded just equals the quantity of labor supplied. Figure 17.1 shows such a labor market, in which the demand curve is $D_0$, the supply curve is $S_0$, employment is $E_0$, and the wage

**Figure 17.1**   A Simple Model of the Labor Market

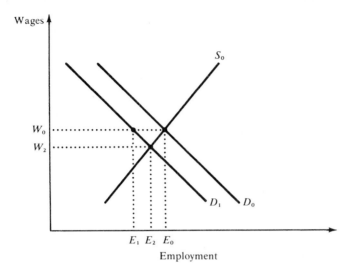

rate is $W_0$. Thus far the text has treated this equilibrium situation as one of full employment and has implied that there is no unemployment associated with it. This implication is not completely correct, however. Even in a market equilibrium or full-employment situation there will still be some *frictional unemployment,* because some people will be "between jobs."

Frictional unemployment arises because labor markets are inherently dynamic, because information flows are imperfect, and because it takes time for unemployed workers and employers with job vacancies to find each other. Even if the size of the labor force is constant, in each period there will be new entrants to the labor market searching for employment while other employed or unemployed individuals are leaving the labor force. Some people will quit their jobs to search for other employment. Moreover, random fluctuations in demand across firms will cause some firms to lay off workers at the same time that other firms will be seeking to hire new employees. Because information about the characteristics of those searching for work and the nature of the jobs opening up cannot instantly be known or evaluated, it takes time for job matches to be made between unemployed workers and potential employers. Hence, even when, in the aggregate, the demand for labor equals the supply, frictional unemployment will still exist.

The level of frictional unemployment in an economy is determined by the flows of individuals into and out of the labor market and the speed with which unemployed individuals find jobs. This speed is determined by the prevailing economic institutions, and institutional changes can influence the level of frictional unemployment. For example, instituting a computerized job-bank system, in which job applicants at the U.S. Employment Service are immediately informed of all listed jobs for which they are qualified, might reduce the time it takes them to find jobs. This system would increase the probability that an unemployed worker would become employed in any period and hence would *decrease* the unemployment rate. On the other hand, one should be aware that if the time it takes unemployed workers to find jobs decreases, more employed workers may consider quitting their jobs to search for better-paying employment, thereby *increasing* the unemployment rate. (This example should remind us again that social policies often have unintended adverse side effects.)

## Structural Unemployment

*Structural unemployment* arises when changes in the pattern of labor demand cause a mismatch between the skills demanded and supplied in a given area—or cause an imbalance between the supplies and demands for workers across areas. *If* wages were completely flexible *and* if costs of occupational or geographic mobility were low, market adjustments would quickly eliminate this type of unemployment. However, in practice these conditions may fail to hold, and structural unemployment may result.

Our by-now familiar two-sector labor-market model, represented by Figure 17.2, can illustrate this point. For the moment we shall assume the sectors refer to markets for skill classes of workers; later we shall assume that they are two geographically separate labor markets. Suppose that Market A is the market for semiskilled workers in the shoe industry and that Market B is the market for skilled computer programmers—and suppose that initially both markets are in equilibrium. Given the demand and supply curves in both

**Figure 17.2** Structural Unemployment Caused by Inflexible Wages and Costs of Adjustments

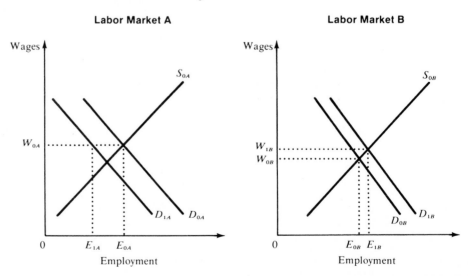

markets [$(D_{0A}, S_{0A})$ and $(D_{0B}, S_{0B})$], the equilibrium wage/employment combinations in the two sectors will be $(W_{0A}, E_{0A})$ and $(W_{0B}, E_{0B})$ respectively. Because of differences in training costs and nonpecuniary conditions of employment, the wages need not be equal in the two sectors.

Now suppose that the demand for semiskilled shoe workers falls to $D_{1A}$, due to foreign import competition, while the demand for computer programmers rises to $D_{1B}$ as a result of the increased use of computers. If real wages are inflexible downward in Market A because of union contract provisions, social norms, or government legislation, employment of semiskilled shoe employees will fall to $E_{1A}$. Employment and wages of computer programmers will rise to $E_{1B}$ and $W_{1B}$, respectively. Unemployment of $E_{0A} - E_{1A}$ workers would be created in the short run.

If shoe-industry employees could costlessly become computer programmers, these unemployed workers would "move" to Market B, and, since wages are assumed to be flexible there, eventually all of the unemployment would be eliminated.[2] Structural unemployment arises, however, when costs of adjustment are sufficiently high to preclude such movements. The cost to displaced individuals—many in their fifties and sixties—may prove to be prohibitively expensive, given the limited time horizons that they face. Moreover, it may be difficult for them to borrow funds to finance the necessary job training.

Geographic imbalances can be analyzed in the same framework. Suppose we now assume that Market A refers to a snowbelt city and Market B refers to a sunbelt city, both employing the same type of labor. When demand falls in the snowbelt and unemployment increases because wages are not completely flexible, these unemployed workers may continue to wait for jobs in their city for at least three reasons. First, information flows are imperfect, so that workers may be unaware of the availability of jobs thousands of miles away. Second, the direct money costs of such a move, including moving costs and the transaction costs involved in buying and selling a home, are high. Third, the psychological costs of moving long distances are substantial because friends and neighbors and community support systems must be given up. These costs are sufficiently high that many workers who become unemployed, due either to plant shutdowns or to permanent layoffs, express no interest in searching for jobs outside their immediate geographic area.[3]

Structural unemployment arises, then, because of changing patterns of labor demand that occur in the face of both rigid wages and high costs of

---

[2] Actually, this statement is not quite correct. As we noted in Chapter 16 when analyzing the effects of unions using a similar model, *wait unemployment* may arise. That is, as long as the wage rate in Market A exceeds the wage rate in Market B and unemployed workers in Market A expect that normal job turnover will eventually create job vacancies in A, it may be profitable for them to remain attached to Market A and wait for a job in that sector. Wait employment is another example of a type of frictional unemployment.

[3] See, for example, Robert Aronson and Robert McKersie, *Economic Consequences of Plant Shutdowns in New York State* (Ithaca, NY: New York State School of Industrial and Labor Relations, 1980).

occupational or geographic mobility.[4] Structurally unemployed workers have a low probability of moving from unemployed to employed status, and any social policies that increase this probability should reduce the level of structural unemployment (other things equal). Examples of such policies include the provision of subsidized training, the provision of information about job-market conditions in other areas, and the provision of relocation allowances to help defray the costs of migration.

Each of these policies is part of the *Trade Adjustment Assistance Program,* which was initiated under the Trade Expansion Act of 1962 and expanded under the Trade Act of 1974. This program was designed to aid individuals who became unemployed because of changes in product demand brought about by foreign competition, and it also provided for an expanded form of unemployment-compensation benefits (the effects of unemployment compensation on unemployment will be discussed later in the chapter). The available evidence indicates, however, that perhaps due to restrictive eligibility rules, this program has had little effect on increasing the probability that these structurally unemployed workers will find employment.[5]

On a more general level, since the early 1960s the federal government has been heavily involved in policies to reduce structural unemployment. These policies include the provision of relocation allowances to unemployed workers residing in depressed areas (under the *Area Redevelopment Act of 1959),* the provision of classroom and on-the-job training to both disadvantaged and unemployed workers (under the *Manpower Development and Training Act of 1962*), and, more recently, the provision of both training and public-sector employment opportunities (under the *Comprehensive Employment and Training Act of 1973*) and of training opportunities only (under the *Job Training Partnership Act of 1982*). Indeed, in fiscal year 1981 more than 3.3 million individuals were enrolled at some time during the year in federally funded employment and training programs.[6] Although the evidence on the effectiveness of these programs is mixed, several studies suggest that some of them have succeeded in increasing the earnings or employment probabilities of those individuals who were enrolled in the programs.[7]

---

[4] For recent evidence on the magnitude of structural unemployment in the U.S. economy, see Katharine Abraham, "Structural/Frictional vs. Deficient Demand Unemployment," *American Economic Review* 73(September 1983): 708–24; David Lilien, "Sectoral Shifts and Cyclical Unemployment," *Journal of Political Economy* 90(August 1982): 777–93; and Katharine Abraham and Lawrence Katz, "Cyclical Unemployment: Sectoral Shifts or Aggregate Disturbances?" *Journal of Political Economy* 94(June 1986): 507–22.

[5] See, for example, George R. Neumann, "The Labor Market Adjustment of Trade-Displaced Workers: The Evidence from the Trade Adjustment Assistance Program" in *Research in Labor Economics,* ed. Ronald Ehrenberg, vol. 2, 1978; and Walter Corson and Walter Nicholson, "Trade Adjustment Assistance for Workers: Results of a Survey of Recipients Under the Trade Act of 1974" in *Research in Labor Economics,* ed. Ronald Ehrenberg, vol. 4, 1981.

[6] *1982 Employment and Training Report of the President* (Washington, DC: U.S. Government Printing Office, 1982): Table F.1.

[7] See Lauri Bassi and Orley Ashenfelter, "The Effects of Direct Job Creation and Training Programs on Low-Skilled Workers," in *Fighting Poverty: What Works and What Does Not,* Sheldon Danziger and Daniel Weinberg (eds.), (Cambridge, MA: Harvard University Press, 1986).

To this point in our analysis of the structural causes of unemployment, we have implicitly attributed mismatched labor demands and supplies to the high costs of adjustments on the *supply* side of the labor market. However, it has recently been postulated that at least some unemployment may be attributed to profit-maximizing behavior of *employers*. Specifically, it has been argued that structural unemployment may also arise if some employers are paying above market-clearing (or *efficiency*) wages to reduce employee turnover and/ or shirking and to increase productivity.[8] Workers employed at other lower-paying firms could not obtain employment at a high-wage firm by offering to work at some wage between the low (market-clearing) and the high (efficiency) wage level because the high-wage employers would want to maintain their wage advantage to discourage turnover and shirking. Voluntary decisions by these employers, then, would prevent their wage rates from falling.

Employees in the low-wage firms would still prefer to work at a high-wage firm and, as long as there is some normal turnover at the latter (which implies that future job vacancies will exist), some employees from low-wage firms may quit their jobs, "attach" themselves to the high-wage sector, and "wait" for job vacancies to occur. That is, using reasoning similar to that used in Appendix 16A, one can show that if some firms pursue an efficiency wage policy, a form of wait unemployment will arise.

## Demand-Deficient Unemployment

Frictional and structural unemployment can arise even when, in the aggregate, the demand for labor equals the supply. Frictional unemployment arises because labor markets are dynamic and information flows are imperfect; structural unemployment arises because of geographic or occupational imbalances in demand and supply. *Demand-deficient* (or *cyclical*) *unemployment* occurs when the *aggregate* demand for labor declines in the face of downward inflexibility in real wages.

Returning to our simple demand and supply model of Figure 17.1, suppose that a temporary decline in aggregate demand leads to a shift in the labor demand curve to $D_1$. If real wages are inflexible downward, employment will fall to $E_1$ and $E_0 - E_1$ additional workers will become unemployed. This employment decline occurs when firms temporarily lay off workers and reduce the rate at which they replace those who quit or retire.

One appropriate government response is to pursue macroeconomic policies to increase aggregate demand; these policies include increasing the level of government spending, reducing taxes, and increasing the rate of growth of the money supply. Another policy is to use labor-market programs that focus

---

[8] The concept of efficiency wages was discussed in Chapter 8. Our argument here draws on, and abstracts from, many of the complications discussed in Carl Shapiro and Joseph Stiglitz, "Equilibrium Unemployment as a Worker Discipline Device," *American Economic Review* 74(June 1984): 433–45; Janet Yellen, "Efficiency Wage Models of Unemployment," *American Economic Review Papers and Proceedings* 74(May 1984): 200–205; and Jeremy Bulow and Lawrence Summers, "A Theory of Dual Labor Markets with Applications to Industrial Policy, Discrimination and Keynesian Unemployment," *Journal of Labor Economics* 4(July 1986): 376–414.

more directly on the unemployed. Examples here include temporary employment-tax credits that lower the cost to firms of employing labor.

Of course, it still remains for us to explain *why* employers respond to a cyclical decline in demand by temporarily laying off some of their work force rather than reducing their employees' real wages. If the latter occurred, employment would move to $E_2$ and real wages to $W_2$ in Figure 17.1. Although employment would be lower than its initial level, $E_0$, there would be no measured demand-deficient unemployment because $E_0 - E_2$ workers would have dropped out of the labor force in response to this lower wage.

According to one explanation for rigid money wages, employers are not free to unilaterally cut money wages because of the presence of unions. However, this cannot be a complete explanation because less than 20 percent of American workers are represented by unions (see Chapter 10), and unions could, in any case, agree to temporary wage cuts to save jobs instead of subjecting their members to layoffs. Why they fail to make such arrangements is instructive.[9] A temporary wage reduction would reduce the earnings of all workers, while layoffs would affect—in most cases—only those workers most recently hired. Since unions represent their entire membership, not just the newly hired, and since union leaders are not likely to be drawn from the ranks of new members, unions tend to favor a policy of layoffs rather than one that reduces wages for all members.

Although layoffs occur less frequently than in union firms, they occur in nonunion firms for three related reasons.[10] First, in the presence of investments in firm-specific human capital, which often lead to structured internal labor markets (see Chapter 4), employers have incentives both to minimize voluntary turnover and to maximize their employees' work effort and productivity. Across-the-board temporary wage reductions would increase all employees' incentives to quit and could lead to reduced work effort on their part. In contrast, layoffs affect only the least experienced workers—the workers in whom the firm has invested the smallest amount of resources. It is likely, then, that the firm will find choosing the layoff strategy a more profitable alternative.

Second, if potential job applicants and existing employees are aware that a firm is pursuing a temporary layoff rather than a temporary-wage-cut strategy, they may be willing to work for a lower *average* wage rate. Individuals are typically assumed to be *risk-averse*; that is, they are assumed to prefer a constant earnings stream to a fluctuating one.[11] In effect, a system of layoffs

---

[9]  *See* James L. Medoff, "Layoffs and Alternatives Under Trade Unions in United States Manufacturing," *American Economic Review* 69 (June 1979): 380–95, for the following argument and evidence.

[10]  *See* Medoff, "Layoffs and Alternatives Under Trade Unions," for evidence that layoff rates are higher in union than nonunion firms, *ceteris paribus* (other things equal).

[11]  This line of reasoning follows that found in Costas Azariadis, "Implicit Contracts and Underemployment Equilibria," *Journal of Political Economy* 83 (December 1975): 1183–1202; and Martin Baily, "Wages and Employment Under Uncertain Demand," *Review of Economic Studies* 41 (January 1974): 37–50.

EXAMPLE  17.1

# International Unemployment-Rate Differentials

International comparisons of unemployment rates are difficult because the exact definition of unemployment differs across nations. For example, in the United States "discouraged workers" who leave the labor force are not counted among the unemployed, while in Italy they are. Nevertheless, it is possible to adjust the unemployment data reported by various industrial countries so that the data correspond approximately to the U.S. definition of unemployment. These adjusted unemployment rates are reported in the table below for ten industrial nations and four years during the 1970s and 1980s.

| Nation | 1975 | 1978 | 1981 | 1984 |
|---|---|---|---|---|
| United States | 8.5 | 6.1 | 7.6 | 7.5 |
| Canada | 6.9 | 8.3 | 7.5 | 11.3 |
| Australia | 4.9 | 6.3 | 5.8 | 9.0 |
| Japan | 1.9 | 2.3 | 2.2 | 2.8 |
| France | 4.2 | 5.3 | 7.5 | 10.1 |
| Germany | 3.4 | 3.4 | 4.1 | 7.8 |
| Great Britain | 4.5 | 6.2 | 10.4 | 13.0 |
| Italy | 3.0 | 3.7 | 4.3 | 5.6 |
| Sweden | 1.6 | 2.2 | 2.5 | 3.1 |
| Netherlands | 5.2 | 5.2 | 9.3 | 15.0 |

Note: The definitions of unemployment have been adjusted to approximate the U.S. concept of unemployment.

SOURCE: Joyanna Moy, "Recent Trends in Unemployment and the Labor Force: 10 Countries," *Monthly Labor Review* 108(August 1985): 9–22, Table 2.

This table indicates that there are large differences in the adjusted unemployment rate across these nations in each year; in 1984 the adjusted unemployment rate varied from 2.8 percent in Japan to 15.0 percent in the Netherlands. Part of the difference results from differences in aggregate demand across nations; labor markets were tighter in Japan than they were in the Netherlands in 1984. Another part of the difference, however, reflects differences in social and institutional forces that affect the underlying labor market flows.

The adjusted unemployment rate in Japan, for example, is typically lower than that in the United States. As we first saw in Chapter 4, a large sector of the Japanese labor market is characterized by a system of long-term, often lifelong, employment relations between employers and employees. Employees in this sector rarely quit their jobs voluntarily, and their employers rarely lay off workers during economic downswings. As a result, the proportions of employed workers who voluntarily leave or involuntarily lose their jobs each period and enter unemployment status are low in Japan relative to the United States, as are the proportions who leave the labor force.

How are Japanese employers able to maintain almost all their employees on their payrolls during economic downswings? A *Monthly Labor Review* article suggests one way:

> A number of Japanese enterprises with underutilized skilled labor (such as steel mills, shipbuilders, or textile producers) have adopted a novel method of maintaining employment for their regular workers. Excess workers are "loaned" for a specified period of no longer than 6 months to enterprises experiencing current labor shortages (such as automobile manufacturers). The workers maintain their affiliation with and receive their full wages from the lending company. The borrowing company usually pays temporary-worker wages to the lending company, and the difference in wages plus benefits is made up by the lending employer. Thus, the borrowing company is able to temporarily increase its labor force with workers whose turnover rate is close to zero, while the lending company is able to maintain its regular work force at reduced cost.

SOURCES: Joyanna Moy, "Recent Labor Market Trends in Nine Industrial Nations," *Monthly Labor Review,* 102(May 1979): 14; Masanori Hashimoto, "Bonus Payments, On-the-Job Training, and Lifetime Employment in Japan," *Journal of Political Economy* 87(October 1979): 1086–1104; and Masanori Hashimoto and John Raisian, "Employment Tenure and Earnings Profiles in Japan and the United States," *American Economic Review* 75(September 1985): 721–35.

in which the newest employees are laid off first provides an *implicit contract* (a guarantee or form of insurance to experienced workers) that they will be immune to all but the severest declines in demand. Put another way, after an initial period when the risk of layoff is high, earnings are likely to be very stable over time.[12] To the extent that experienced employees value stable earnings streams, they should be willing to pay for this stability by accepting lower wages in such situations—thereby reducing employers' costs. Of course, during the initial period, workers will be subject to potential earnings variability and may demand higher wages then to compensate them for these risks. However, if the fraction of the work force subject to layoffs is small, on average employers' costs should be reduced.

Third, employers may have better information than employees have on the true state of demand conditions faced by the firm. If a firm requests its employees to take a wage cut in periods of low demand, the employees may believe that the employer is falsely stating that demand is low and, noting that the employer loses nothing by the wage cut, resist the request. In contrast, if a firm instead temporarily lays workers off, it loses the output these workers would have produced, and workers may therefore accept such an action more readily. Put another way, the *asymmetry of information* between employers and employees makes layoffs the preferred policy.[13]

---

[12]   We are ignoring here any real earnings growth over time.

[13]   See, for example, Sanford Grossman, Oliver Hart, and Eric Maskin, "Unemployment with Observable Aggregate Shocks," *Journal of Political Economy* 91 (December 1983): 907–28; Sanford Grossman and Oliver Hart, "Implicit Contracts, Moral Hazard and Unemployment," *American Economic Review* 71 (May 1981): 301–7; and Costas Azariadis, "Employment with Asymmetric Information," *Quarterly Journal of Economics* 98(Supplement, 1983): 157–72.

## Seasonal Unemployment

*Seasonal unemployment* is similar to demand-deficient unemployment in that it is induced by fluctuations in the demand for labor. Here, however, the fluctuations can be regularly anticipated and follow a systematic pattern over the course of a year. For example, the demand for agricultural employees declines after the planting season and remains low until the harvest season. Similarly, the demand for construction workers in Snowbelt states falls during the winter months. Finally, the demand for production workers falls in certain industries during the season of the year when plants are retooling to handle annual model changes; examples here include both the Detroit automotive industry (new car models) and the New York City apparel industry (new fashion designs).

The issue remains, why do employers respond to seasonal patterns of demand by laying off workers rather than reducing wage rates or hours of work? All the reasons cited for the existence of cyclical unemployment and temporary layoffs for cyclical reasons also pertain here. Indeed, one study has shown that the expansion (in the early 1970s) of the unemployment-insurance (UI) system that led to the coverage of most agricultural employees was associated with a substantial increase in seasonal unemployment in agriculture.[14]

One may question, however, why workers would accept jobs in industries in which they knew in advance they would be unemployed for a portion of the year. For some workers, the existence of UI benefits along with the knowledge that they will be rehired as a matter of course at the end of the slack demand season may allow them to treat such periods as paid vacations. However, since UI benefits typically replace less than half of an unemployed worker's previous gross earnings and even smaller fractions for high-wage workers, most workers will not find such a situation desirable. To attract workers to such seasonal industries, firms will have to pay workers higher wages to compensate them for being periodically unemployed. In fact, casual observation suggests that the hourly wages of construction workers are substantially higher than the hourly wages of comparably skilled manufacturing workers who work more hours each year. More formally, recent econometric studies confirm that, other things held constant (including workers' skill levels), wages are higher in industries in which workers' expected annual durations of unemployment are longer.[15]

The existence of wage differentials that compensate workers in high-unemployment industries for the risk of unemployment makes it difficult to evaluate whether this type of unemployment is voluntary or involuntary in

---

[14] Barry Chiswick, "The Effect of Unemployment Compensation on a Seasonal Industry: Agriculture," *Journal of Political Economy* 84(June 1976): 591–602.

[15] John Abowd and Orley Ashenfelter, "Anticipated Unemployment, Temporary Layoffs, and Compensating Wage Differentials," in *Studies in Labor Markets*, ed. Sherwin Rosen (Chicago: University of Chicago Press, 1981): 141–70, and Robert H. Topel, "Equilibrium Earnings, Turnover, and Unemployment: New Evidence," *Journal of Labor Economics* 2(October 1984): 500–522. Topel also shows that, other things equal, high UI benefits *reduce* the compensating wage differential paid for the risk of unemployment.

nature. On the one hand, in an *ex ante* ("before the fact") sense, workers have voluntarily agreed to be employed in industries that offer higher wages *and* higher probabilities of unemployment than offered elsewhere. On the other hand, once on the job (*ex post,* or "after the fact") employees prefer to remain employed rather than becoming unemployed. Such unemployment may be considered either voluntary or involuntary, then, depending upon the perspective one is taking.

## Policy Issue: The Unemployment Effects of Unemployment-Insurance Benefits

The characteristics of our system of unemployment-insurance (UI) benefits serve to increase unemployment rates in two ways: (1) the UI system contributes to the use of temporary layoffs rather than real-wage fluctuations as a means of adjusting to shifts in labor demand, and (2) the UI system provides incentives for laid-off workers to remain unemployed for longer periods of time than they would without UI benefits. While the unemployment insurance system is actually a collection of individual state systems, and while certain aspects of the individual systems differ, it is possible to sketch the broad outlines of how they operate in enough detail to gain an understanding of how the UI program affects the unemployment rate.[16]

Today virtually all private sector employees are covered by a state UI system. When such workers become unemployed, their eligibility for unemployment insurance benefits is based upon their previous labor market experience and reason for unemployment. With respect to their experience, each state requires unemployed individuals to demonstrate "permanent" attachment to the labor force, by meeting minimum earnings or weeks-worked tests during some base period, before they can be eligible for UI benefits. In all states, covered workers who are laid off *and* meet these labor market experience tests are eligible for UI benefits. In some states workers who voluntarily quit their jobs are eligible for benefits, while in only two states (New York and Rhode Island) are strikers eligible for benefits. Finally, new entrants or reentrants to the labor force and workers fired for cause are, in general, ineligible for benefits.

The ratio of an individual's UI benefits to his or her previous earnings varies according to his or her past earnings. This ratio is often called the

---

[16] A more complete description of the characteristics of the UI system is found in Daniel S. Hamermesh, *Jobless Pay and the Economy* (Baltimore: Johns Hopkins University Press, 1977). The connection between temporary layoffs and these characteristics of the UI system was pointed out in Martin Feldstein, "Temporary Layoffs in the Theory of Unemployment," *Journal of Political Economy* 84 (October 1976): 937–58; empirical evidence on the relationship was provided in Robert Topel, "On Layoffs and Unemployment Insurance," *American Economic Review* 73 (September 1983): 541–59. In most states employees working reduced hours are not eligible for UI benefits; this explains why layoffs rather than hours reductions are typically used to adjust employment to cyclical-demand changes. See Kenneth Burdett and Randall Wright, "The Effect of Unemployment Insurance on Layoffs, Hours per Worker and Wages" (mimeograph, Cornell University, February 1986), for a formal treatment of this.

replacement rate, the fraction of previous earnings that the UI benefits re-place. Most states aim to replace around 50 percent of an unemployed worker's previous earnings. It is important to stress that up until 1978 *UI benefits were not subject to federal income tax;* since then, however, UI benefits have been increasingly subject to taxation, and federal tax reform legislation passed in 1986 made all UI benefits taxable starting in 1987.

The benefits paid out by the UI system are financed by a payroll tax. Unlike the Social Security payroll tax, in all but four states the UI tax is paid solely by employers.[17]

The employer's UI tax rate is determined by general economic conditions in the state, the industry the employer is operating in, and the employer's *layoff experience*. The last term is defined differently in different states; the underlying notion is that since the UI system is an insurance system, employ-ers who lay off workers frequently and make heavy demands on the system's resources should be assigned a higher UI tax rate. This practice is referred to as *experience rating*.

Experience rating is typically *imperfect* in the sense that the marginal cost to an employer of laying off an additional worker (in terms of a higher UI tax rate) is often less than the added UI benefits the system must pay out to that worker.

The key characteristics of the UI system that influence the desirability of temporary layoffs are the *imperfect experience rating* of the UI payroll tax and the *federal tax treatment* of UI benefits that workers receive. To under-stand the influence of these characteristics, suppose first that the UI system were constructed in such a way that its tax rates were perfectly experience-rated and the benefits it paid out (for example, half of previous earnings) were completely taxable. A firm laying off a worker would have to pay added UI taxes equal to the full UI benefit received by the worker, so it saves just half of the worker's wages by the layoff; the *worker's* income would be cut in half if he or she were laid off.

Now suppose instead that the UI tax rate employers must pay is totally independent of their layoff experience (no experience rating) and that UI benefits are not subject to any personal income taxes. A *firm* saves a laid-off worker's *entire* wages because its UI taxes do not rise as a result of the layoff. The worker still gets a benefit equal to half of prior earnings, but since these benefits are not taxable, his or her spendable income drops by *less* than half. Thus, compared to a UI system with perfect experience rating and completely taxable benefits, it is easy to see that a system with incomplete experience rating and no taxation of benefits will tend to enhance the attractiveness of

---

[17] Recall from our discussion in Chapter 3 that this fact tells us nothing about who really bears the burden of the tax.

layoffs to both employer and employee.[18] While the taxation of all UI benefits beginning in 1987 increased the costs to workers of layoffs, the persistence of imperfect experience rating continues to increase the level of demand-deficient unemployment over what it would be with perfect experience rating.

In addition to its effects on layoffs, the UI system reduces the costs of being unemployed and may prolong unemployed workers' job search.[19] This effect would increase the measured unemployment rate, given the number of laid-off workers. Supporters of the UI system respond that an explicit purpose of the UI system when it was founded in the late 1930s was to provide unemployed workers with temporary resources to enable them to turn down low-wage jobs that were not commensurate with their skill levels and to keep searching for better jobs.[20] That is, many believe that while the existence of UI benefits might prolong spells of unemployment, such benefits also might lead to higher post-unemployment wages and better job matches—and better job matches might reduce subsequent job turnover, thus providing a further benefit to society.

In recent years, numerous studies have sought to estimate the effects of UI benefits on durations of unemployment and post-unemployment wages.[21] In the main, these studies use data on individuals and exploit the fact that the replacement rate (the fraction of previous earnings that UI benefits replace) varies (*within* states) with individuals' previous earnings levels and also varies *across* states. Evidence from these studies suggests quite strongly that higher UI replacement rates are associated with longer durations of unemployment; raising the replacement rate from 0.4 to 0.5 of previous weekly earnings may increase the average spell of unemployment by one half to one week. In contrast, the evidence on the effects on post-unemployment wages is much more mixed. For example, one study found that higher replacement rates were associated with higher post-unemployment wage rates for adults but not for teenagers.[22]

---

[18] This statement is not always true, since employed workers often lose fringe benefits and the ability to take advantage of on-the-job training options. Research by Robert H. Topel, "Equilibrium Earnings, Turnover and Unemployment: New Evidence," indicates that unemployment insurance increases the probability of layoff and reduces the probability of leaving unemployment—with the former effect being the stronger. He also finds that both effects are stronger for temporary than permanent layoffs.

[19] Martin Feldstein, "The Economics of the New Unemployment," *Public Interest* 33 (Fall 1973): 3–42.

[20] William Haber and Merrill Murray, *Unemployment Insurance in the American Economy* (Homewood, IL: Irwin, 1966): 26–35.

[21] *See*, for example, Ronald G. Ehrenberg and Ronald L. Oaxaca, "Unemployment Insurance, Duration of Unemployment and Subsequent Wage Gain," *American Economic Review* 66 (December 1976): 754–66. Many of the studies are summarized in Hamermesh, *Jobless Pay and the Economy* and are critiqued in Finis Welch, "What Have We Learned From Empirical Studies of Unemployment Insurance?" *Industrial and Labor Relations Review* 30 (July 1977): 451–61. See also Gary Solon, "Work Incentive Effects of Taxing Unemployment Benefits," *Econometrica* 53 (March 1985): 295–306.

[22] Ehrenberg and Oaxaca, "Unemployment Insurance. . . ." The results for teens may imply that (a) unemployed teens do not search actively for work, (b) unemployed teens' job search is not productive, perhaps because of the narrow range of job opportunities they face, or (c) unemployed teens may search for jobs that offer greater training options and possible higher future wages, although not higher current wages. The available data do not permit one to determine which of these alternatives is correct.

**Table 17.2**  Unemployment Rates in 1987 by Demographic Groups

| Age | White Male | White Female | Black Male | Black Female | Hispanic Male | Hispanic Female | All |
|-----|-----------|--------------|-----------|--------------|---------------|-----------------|-----|
| 16–17 | 17.9 | 15.5 | 39.0 | 40.5 | 28.2 | 27.1 | |
| 18–19 | 13.7 | 11.7 | 31.6 | 31.7 | 19.3 | 19.9 | |
| 20–24 | 8.4 | 7.4 | 20.3 | 23.3 | 10.2 | 11.4 | |
| 25–54 | 4.5 | 4.3 | 9.9 | 10.3 | 7.3 | 7.2 | |
| 55+ | 3.2 | 2.8 | 6.3 | 4.3 | 6.8 | 4.9 | |
| Total | 5.4 | 5.2 | 12.7 | 13.2 | 8.7 | 8.9 | 6.2 |

SOURCE:  U.S. Department of Labor, *Employment and Earnings* 35 (January 1988), Table 44. "Hispanic" refers to individuals of Hispanic origin; depending upon their races these individuals are included in both the white and black population group totals.

# The Demographic Structure
# of Unemployment Rates

Table 17.2 presents data on unemployment rates for various age/race/gender/ethnic groups in 1987. The patterns indicated in Table 17.2 for 1987 are similar to the patterns for other years: high unemployment rates for teens and young adults of each race/gender group relative to older adults in these groups; black unemployment rates roughly double white unemployment rates for most age/gender groups, with Hispanic-American unemployment rates falling between the white and black rates. The high unemployment rates of black teenagers, which ranged between 31.6 and 40.5 percent in 1987, have been of particular concern to policymakers and have led to numerous programs during the late 1970s and 1980s to reduce nonwhite teenage unemployment.

Over recent decades, the age/race/gender/ethnic composition of the labor force has changed dramatically with the growth in labor-force-participation rates of females and the increase in the relative size of the black and Hispanic population. Between 1960 and 1987, the proportion of the labor force that was female grew from 33.4 to 44.8 percent, and the proportion that was nonwhite grew from 11.1 to 13.8 percent.[23] Similarly, between 1973 (when statistics first were collected) and 1984, the Hispanic-American labor force almost doubled (three times the national average rate of growth) to 7.2 million.[24] The increase

[23]  U.S. Department of Labor, *1981 Employment and Training Report of the President* (Washington, DC: U.S. Government Printing Office, 1981): Table A4, and U.S. Department of Labor, *Employment and Earnings* 35 (January 1988): Tables 1, 2, and 3. The proportion that was teenage grew from 7.0 percent in 1960 to 9.5 percent in 1978 as the teenage population grew, but the decline in the teenage population share in recent years caused this teenage proportion of the labor force to fall to 6.7 percent in 1987. So in recent years, this demographic shift served to decrease the overall unemployment rate.

[24]  See Gregory DeFreitas, "A Time-Series Analysis of Hispanic Unemployment," *Journal of Human Resources* 21 (Winter 1986): 24–43.

in the relative labor force shares of those groups that have relatively higher unemployment rates has led to an increase in the overall unemployment rate associated with any given level of labor-market tightness. Indeed, one investigator has concluded that demographic shifts in the composition of the labor force alone probably are responsible for pushing the overall unemployment rate at least 1 percentage point higher in the late 1970s and early 1980s than it was in the mid-1960s for any given level of overall labor-market tightness.[25] These demographic changes have also led to an increase in the *full employment* (or *natural*) rate of unemployment—the unemployment rate that is consistent with a zero excess demand for labor. While an aggregate unemployment rate of 4 percent was considered a reasonable unemployment goal for policymakers in the mid-1960s, policymakers and academic economists rarely referred to targets below 5 percent by the late 1980s.

## Why Do Unemployment Rates Vary Across Groups?

Calculations such as those just referred to take the age/race/gender/ethnic structure of unemployment rates as fixed, and hence it is natural to ask why this structure exists.[26] A group's unemployment rate might be high because its members have difficulty finding jobs once unemployed, because they have difficulty (for voluntary or involuntary reasons) remaining employed once a job is found, or because they frequently enter and leave the labor force. The appropriate policy prescriptions will depend on the relative size of these monthly flows from one labor market status to another (for example, employed to unemployed) and on which of the flows is most responsible for the high rate.

The major cause of high nonwhite adult (25–59) male unemployment is the group's high probability of voluntarily or involuntarily leaving employment to become unemployed; on average, nonwhite adult males have difficulty holding jobs. In contrast, the relatively high nonwhite adult female unemployment rate is due primarily to the group's high probability of leaving the labor force from employment status and to the low probability that unemployed group members will find employment.

High teenage unemployment rates (relative to adult male unemployment rates) stem primarily from the high probability that teenagers will leave employment to drop out of the labor force or that they will move into

---

[25] James Tobin, "Stabilization Policy Ten Years After," *Brookings Papers on Economic Activity,* 1980–1, pp. 19–72. Table 17.2 shows that by 1987, women's unemployment rates were about the same as men's. However, in the 1960s and 1970s, women had higher unemployment rates than men. The growing share of the labor force consisting of women during this period thus tended to raise the unemployment rate. Other researchers have argued that increased generosity of social-insurance programs, such as unemployment insurance, welfare benefits, and food stamps, which are received only if the individual is unemployed or family income is below certain levels, have contributed to higher unemployment rates; that is, unemployed workers may now have smaller incentives to find employment quickly.

[26] This section draws heavily on Ronald G. Ehrenberg, "The Demographic Structure of Unemployment Rates and Labor Market Transition Probabilities," *Research in Labor Economics,* vol. 3, Ronald G. Ehrenberg (ed.), (Greenwich, CT: JAI Press, 1980): 241–93.

unemployment from either employment or out-of-the-labor-force status. Teens, then, move into and out of the labor force frequently, and frequently lose or voluntarily leave their jobs. Involuntary job loss occurs more frequently for teenagers than for adults, both because teenagers typically have low seniority and are vulnerable to layoffs and because they are much more likely to be discharged for cause, as they often have not yet learned the limits of acceptable behavior on the job.[27] Higher voluntary job leaving of teens reflects the low quality of jobs many teens have, the normal job-matching process, and the fact that some teens quit their jobs as soon as they have earned enough to buy a specific item they were working for (for example, a stereo).[28] For nonwhite teens, low probabilities of finding a job also play a role.

Nonwhite teenage unemployment rates tend to be double those of white teenagers. For both males and females, lower probabilities of finding employment have the largest influence on the relative teenage unemployment rates (in addition, non-white teens have a greater probability of being laid off by their employers).[29] A key question for policymakers to answer then is, "Why do nonwhite teens have greater difficulty finding employment than white teens?"

A number of potential explanations have been offered. Some revolve around the methods of job search used. For example, it has been argued that nonwhites rely on institutions such as the Employment Service to find jobs, while white teens tend to find jobs through friends and neighbors.[30] Others focus on the growing concentration of nonwhite youths in the central cities, while employment opportunities have been moving to the suburbs and nonmetropolitan areas. However, the data indicate that nonwhite teenage unemployment rates are higher than white teenage unemployment rates in all types of geographic areas (central city, suburban, and nonmetropolitan).[31] Moreover, even if nonwhite youths were reallocated across areas so that, in each, their proportionate representation relative to white youths was the same, the data suggest that the overall black/white teenage unemployment-rate differential would have fallen by less than 10 percent.

[27]  For example, Peter Jackson and Edward Montgomery, "Layoffs, Discharges and Youth Unemployment," in *The Black Youth Unemployment Crisis,* Richard Freeman and Harry Holzer (eds.) (Chicago: University of Chicago Press, 1986), offer evidence that frequent absenteeism was often the reason that black teens in Boston gave for their being discharged.

[28]  Paul Osterman, *Getting Started: The Youth Labor Market* (Cambridge, MA: MIT Press, 1980), presents evidence on the first jobs held for a sample of Boston youth. Very few required any skills or offered any opportunities to learn on the job.

[29]  See Francine D. Blau and Lawrence M. Kahn, "Causes and Consequences of Layoffs," *Economic Inquiry* 19 (April 1981): 270–96.

[30]  Paul Osterman, "Racial Differentials in Male Youth Unemployment," in U.S. Department of Labor, *Conference Report on Youth Unemployment: Its Measurement and Meaning* (Washington, DC: U.S. Government Printing Office, 1978), and Harry J. Holzer, "Search Method Used by Unemployed Youth," *Journal of Labor Economics* 6 (January 1988): 1–20.

[31]  U.S. Department of Labor, *1978 Employment and Training Report of the President* (Washington, DC: U.S. Government Printing Office, 1978): 73, and David Ellwood, "The Spatial Mismatch Hypothesis: Are There Teenage Jobs Missing in the Ghetto?" in *The Black Youth Unemployment Crisis,* Richard Freeman and Harry Holzer (eds.).

Focusing on the relative unemployment rates of black teenagers does not fully capture the magnitude of their *nonemployment* problem. For example, while the employment/population ratio for 18- and 19-year-old white males remained roughly constant during the 1955–84 period at about 0.60, the comparable ratio for minority 18- and 19-year-old males fell from 0.66 to only 0.33.[32] The reasons for this decline, unfortunately, are not well understood.

## Normative Issues in Unemployment

Is unemployment a serious problem? Certainly some level of frictional unemployment is unavoidable in a dynamic world fraught with imperfect information. Moreover, as we have seen, the parameters of the UI system encourage both additional-search unemployment and temporary-layoff (cyclical and seasonal) unemployment. More than 25 years ago, Arthur Okun pointed out that every one-percentage- point decline in the aggregate unemployment rate was associated with a three-percentage-point increase in the output our society produces. That relationship appears to have held up through 1975, although since 1975 it is more in the range of a two-percentage-point increase in output. Even this latter number, however, suggests the great costs our society bears from excessively high rates of unemployment.[33] Thus, while it is unlikely that zero unemployment would be an optimal rate, policies to reduce cyclical unemployment (in a noninflationary manner) are clearly desirable. Improving the functioning of labor markets would also reduce frictional and structural unemployment; however, the benefits of reduced unemployment must be weighed against the costs generated by the policies designed to accomplish this objective in each case.

In addition to concern over the cost of unemployment, society should also be concerned about the distribution of unemployment across age/race/sex groups. As Table 17.2 indicated, the incidence of unemployment is higher among nonwhites than whites, and among teens than nonteens. Since the major cause of high nonwhite adult male unemployment rates is the high probability of members of that group leaving or losing their jobs to become unemployed, the fact that they remain attached to the labor force suggests that their unemployment problem is serious and that the case for government intervention is strong. The high layoff rates of young black adults must also be of social concern.

What about the high teenage unemployment rates, especially those of nonwhite teens? Is the high unemployment rate for teens a serious problem

---

[32] Albert Rees, "An Essay on Youth Joblessness," *Journal of Economic Literature* 25 (June 1986): 613–28, Table 2.

[33] Arthur M. Okun, "Potential GNP: Its Measurement and Significance," reprinted in *The Political Economy of Prosperity,* ed. Arthur M. Okun (Washington, DC: Brookings Institution, 1970). More recent evidence suggests that the relationship is more in the range of 2.2 to 1. See Robert J. Gordon and Robert E. Hall, "Arthur M. Okun 1928–1980," *Brookings Papers on Economic Activity,* 1980-1, pp. 1–5.

that policymakers should address? Some doubt the seriousness of the problem, pointing out that unemployment rates decline rapidly as youths reach their early twenties (see Table 17.2). To these doubters, high teenage unemployment rates are symptomatic of the process of job turnover and search that occurs when new entrants to the labor force seek to acquire information about labor markets and their own productive ability. Moreover, proponents of this view could note that approximately 50 percent of the unemployed 16 to 19 year olds and 90 percent of the unemployed 16 to 17 year olds are enrolled in school.[34] Of these in-school unemployed youths, 50 percent were searching only for temporary jobs in 1976 and only 10 percent had become unemployed by losing their previous job.[35] Finally, they could cite evidence that teenage unemployment is not always associated with low family incomes. For example, data from the *1976 Survey of Income and Education,* a large national survey conducted by the Census Bureau, indicate that less than 26 percent of unemployed youths age 16 to 24 came from families whose family income fell below the poverty line.[36]

Of course, these arguments neglect a number of important points. First, a substantial body of evidence indicates that youth unemployment is highly correlated with youth criminal activity; thus there are costs to society, as well as to the youths, of youth unemployment. Second, much youth unemployment is concentrated among nonwhite youths—and the distributional implications of this fact may be unacceptable to society, especially given the higher correlation between youth unemployment and poverty that exists for nonwhites. Finally, it is possible that the effects of youth unemployment may be long-lasting and that unemployed teenagers may face reduced long-run earnings and employment prospects, as compared to teenagers who do not suffer unemployment. Although unemployment rates do decline rapidly with age for younger adults, individuals who suffer unemployment as teenagers might be "scarred" in the sense of having relatively higher probabilities of adult unemployment or commanding relatively lower wages as adults. While there have been several studies of this scarring effect, they have yielded ambiguous results. Our knowledge about whether teenage unemployment has long-run negative effects is still imprecise.[37]

---

[34] See Arvil Adams and Garth Mangum, *The Lingering Crisis of Youth Unemployment* (Kalamazoo, MI: W.E. Upjohn Institute, 1978), Chap. 3.

[35] Adams and Mangum, *The Lingering Crisis of Youth Unemployment.*

[36] U.S. Congressional Budget Office, *Youth Unemployment: The Outlook and Some Policy Strategies* (Washington, DC: U.S. Government Printing Office, April 1978). Appendix Table A–5. It is worth noting, however, that this table also indicates that youth unemployment rates decline with family income and that more than 45 percent of unemployed *nonwhite* youths come from families with family incomes below the poverty line. Put another way, youth employment is much more highly correlated with poverty for nonwhites than it is for whites.

[37] See David Ellwood, "Teenage Unemployment: Permanent Scars or Temporary Blemishes"; Mary Corcoran, "The Employment, Wage, and Fertility Consequences of Teenage Women's Nonemployment"; and Robert Meyer and David Wise, "High School Preparation and Early Labor Force Experience,"; all in *The Youth Labor Market Problem: Its Nature, Causes, and Consequences,* eds. Richard B. Freeman and David A. Wise (Chicago, University of Chicago Press, 1982).

# The Wage-Inflation/Unemployment Trade-Off

For many years economists believed that stable negative relationships, or *trade-off curves,* existed between the rates of wage (and price) inflation on the one hand, and the overall unemployment rate in the economy on the other. That is, higher levels of unemployment were thought to be associated with lower rates of wage and price inflation, and vice versa. The relationship between unemployment and wage inflation was dubbed the *Phillips Curve* after the noted economist who was an early observer of its existence.[38] The Phillips Curve was thought to provide a range of feasible options for policymakers—through the appropriate use of monetary or fiscal policy they could choose any unemployment/inflation combination along the curve. For example, a paper in 1959 by two well-known economists claimed that the country could choose among the following alternatives (illustrated in Figure 17.3): 8-percent unemployment and zero wage inflation, 5–6-percent unemployment and 2–3-percent wage inflation, and 3-percent unemployment and 7-percent wage inflation.[39]

Unfortunately, the well-defined, stable set of choices once thought to exist appears to have vanished. Table 17.3 contains data on both the unemployment and wage-inflation rate from 1960 through 1987. These data indicate that during the 1960s a negative association did appear to exist between the unemployment rate and the rate of wage inflation. Indeed, the steady tighten-

**Figure 17.3**   ''Phillips Curve'' Showing the Trade-off Between Wage Inflation and Unemployment for 1960

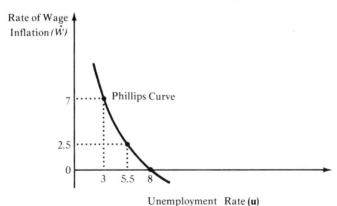

SOURCE:   Adapted from Paul A. Samuelson and Robert M. Solow, ''Our Menu of Policy Choices,'' *The Battle Against Inflation,* ed. Arthur M. Okun (New York: W. W. Norton, 1965): 74.

[38]  See A. W. Phillips, ''The Relation Between Unemployment and the Rate of Change of Money Wage Rates in the United Kingdom, 1862–1957,'' *Economica* 25 (November 1958): 283–99.

[39]  Paul A. Samuelson and Robert M. Solow, ''Our Menu of Policy Choices,'' in *The Battle Against Unemployment,* ed. Arthur M. Okun (New York: W. W. Norton, 1965): 71–76.

**Table 17.3** Unemployment Rate and Percentage Change in Earnings and Prices in the United States

| Year | Percent Change in Adjusted Hourly Earnings of Non-supervisory Workers in the Private Nonagricultural Sector | Civilian Unemployment Rate | Percent Change in the GNP Deflator |
|------|---------|---------|---------|
| 1960 | 3.4 | 5.5 | 1.6 |
| 1961 | 3.0 | 6.7 | 1.0 |
| 1962 | 3.4 | 5.5 | 2.2 |
| 1963 | 2.8 | 5.7 | 1.6 |
| 1964 | 2.8 | 5.2 | 1.5 |
| 1965 | 3.6 | 4.5 | 2.7 |
| 1966 | 4.3 | 3.8 | 3.6 |
| 1967 | 5.0 | 3.8 | 2.6 |
| 1968 | 6.1 | 3.6 | 5.0 |
| 1969 | 6.7 | 3.5 | 5.6 |
| 1970 | 6.6 | 4.9 | 5.5 |
| 1971 | 7.2 | 5.9 | 5.7 |
| 1972 | 6.2 | 5.6 | 4.7 |
| 1973 | 6.2 | 4.9 | 6.5 |
| 1974 | 8.0 | 5.6 | 9.1 |
| 1975 | 8.4 | 8.5 | 9.8 |
| 1976 | 7.2 | 7.7 | 6.4 |
| 1977 | 7.6 | 7.1 | 6.7 |
| 1978 | 8.2 | 6.1 | 7.3 |
| 1979 | 7.9 | 5.8 | 8.9 |
| 1980 | 9.0 | 7.1 | 9.0 |
| 1981 | 9.1 | 7.6 | 9.7 |
| 1982 | 6.9 | 9.7 | 6.4 |
| 1983 | 4.6 | 9.6 | 3.9 |
| 1984 | 3.2 | 7.5 | 3.7 |
| 1985 | 3.1 | 7.2 | 3.2 |
| 1986 | 2.4 | 7.0 | 2.6 |
| 1987 | 2.5 | 6.2 | 3.0 |

Note: Hourly earnings are adjusted for overtime (manufacturing only) and for shifts in employment across industries.

SOURCE: *1988 Economic Report of the President:* February 1988 (Washington, DC: U.S. Government Printing Office, 1988): Tables B3, B39, and B44.

ing of labor markets and decreasing unemployment rates of the late 1960s were associated with increasing rates of wage inflation. However, during the 1970s the relationship appears, at first glance, to have broken down; one often observes a simultaneous increase in the rate of unemployment and the rate of wage inflation during that decade. The result is that while an unemployment rate of 5.5 percent was associated with a wage-inflation rate of 3.4 percent in the 1960s, an almost identical unemployment rate of 5.6 percent was associated with wage-inflation rates of 6.2 to 8.0 percent in the 1970s. Moreover, the relationship changed again in the mid-1980s. In 1980 an unemployment rate of 7.1 percent was associated with wage inflation of 9.0 percent, but in 1985 an

**Figure 17.4**   The Changing Trade-off Between the Rate of Wage Inflation and the Level of the Unemployment Rate

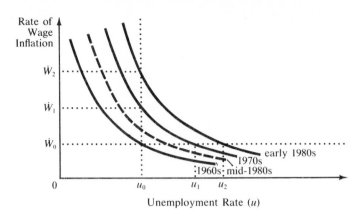

unemployment rate of 7.2 percent was accompanied by wage inflation of 3.1 percent. The data in Table 17.3 cast doubt on the existence of a stable negative trade-off between inflation and unemployment.

An alternative interpretation of these data, however, is that while a trade-off between the rates of inflation and unemployment exists at a *point in time*, the *position* of the trade-off curve is determined by a number of other factors that can change over time. The net effect of these other factors in recent years, it can be argued, has been to shift the trade-off curve shown in Figure 17.3 *upward and to the right*. Thus, the trade-off society faced in the early 1980s lay everywhere above the one that prevailed during the 1970s, which in turn was itself higher than the curve that prevailed during the 1960s (see Figure 17.4). Put another way, the argument underlying Figure 17.4 is that between 1960 and 1980, progressively higher rates of wage inflation became associated over time with any given level of unemployment. Conversely, progressively higher unemployment rates became associated with any given level of wage inflation. Indeed, some economists suggest that between 1960 and 1980, the trade-off may have shifted to the right by as much as 3 percentage points.[40] Since 1980, the curve appears to have shifted back to the left (see the dashed curve in Figure 17.4). It is also possible that the Phillips Curve has become much flatter over recent years, so that the decrease in wage inflation accompanying a one-percentage-point increase in the unemployment rate is now smaller than it once was. This growing downward rigidity of wages has caused a loss of effectiveness in the traditional macroeconomic policies to combat inflation—and has increased the importance of alternative labor-market policies.

---

[40]   See, for example, James Tobin, ''Stabilization Policy Ten Years After.''

**Figure 17.5**  The Relationship Between Wage Changes and the Excess Demand for Labor: Prices Held Constant

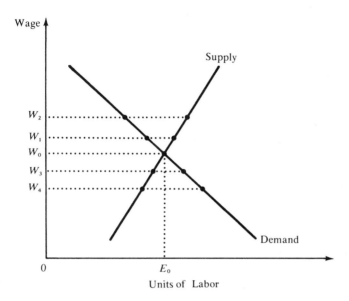

The next subsections explain why the trade-off between wage inflation and unemployment may exist and discuss the forces that may have caused the trade-off to shift out from 1960 to 1980 and in since 1980. This framework can be used to discuss the various labor-market policies that might enable policymakers to shift the trade-off curve in a more favorable direction. We also discuss the relationship between wage and price behavior and the effect of the rate of productivity growth on this relationship.

## The Basic Model

Figure 17.5 represents a competitive labor market.[41] For simplicity we will *initially* take product prices as fixed so that the demand and supply curves can be drawn in terms of the money wage ($W$) rather than the real wage. In this labor market, the equilibrium wage is $W_0$, and the equilibrium employment level is $E_0$. We know from earlier chapters that whenever the wage is above $W_0$ it will fall, and that whenever it is below $W_0$ it will rise, to restore equilibrium.

---

[41]  This section initially draws heavily on Richard Lipsey, "The Relation Between Unemployment and the Rate of Change in Money Wage Rates in the United Kingdom, 1862–1957: A Further Analysis," *Economica* 27 (February 1960), 1–31.

How rapidly will the wage rate change when it is away from its equilibrium value? It seems reasonable to assume that the speed at which the wage rate changes is related to the extent to which the labor market is in disequilibrium, as measured by the excess demand for labor. Thus, although the wage rate will be increasing whenever the wage rate is below $W_0$ and a positive excess demand for labor exists, it is likely to be increasing more rapidly when it is at $W_4$ in Figure 17.5 than when it is at $W_3$. Similarly, while the wage rate will be falling whenever the wage rate is above $W_0$ and an excess supply (or negative excess demand) for labor exists, it is likely to be falling more rapidly when the wage rate is at $W_2$ than when it is at $W_1$.

A simple way to formalize this idea is to assume that the percentage rate of change of wages ($\dot{W}$) is a positively sloped function of the excess demand for labor ($X$). Because a given *absolute* difference between demand and supply ($D - S = 1000$, say) would indicate a greater degree of disequilibrium if 10,000 people were seeking work than if 100,000 were in the market, we will measure excess demand as $(D - S)/S$, so that:

$$\dot{W} = f[X] = f[(D - S)/S].  \qquad (17.2)$$

In equation (17.2), "$f[-]$" stands for a function, so the equation postulates that wage changes are affected by the excess demand for labor. While we have not specified the precise mathematical relationship between $\dot{W}$ and $X$, it is clear that this relationship should be positive: the greater the excess demand for labor, the greater wage inflation will be. Unfortunately, because the excess demand for labor is usually not observable, it is necessary to replace $X$ with an observable variable—such as the unemployment rate—when empirically analyzing wage changes. What is the relationship between the excess demand for labor and the unemployment rate (**u**)?

We know that some unemployment exists even when labor markets are in balance with the overall demand for labor just equal to the overall supply ($X = 0$). This frictional unemployment occurs because normal job turnover and movements of people in and out of the labor market take place in circumstances where information is imperfect and job matching takes time. For this reason, the curves in Figure 17.4 do not show the unemployment rate reaching zero.

As the excess demand for labor increases and labor markets become tighter, the unemployment rate will fall. Although the time it takes to make job matches can be reduced, it will probably take some time to fill job vacancies. As a result, the unemployment rate is not likely to fall below some positive level, and as that level is approached, any increases in excess demand will call forth progressively smaller reductions in the unemployment rate. The resulting Phillips Curve will become very steep at low unemployment rates (see Figure 17.4). In contrast, at high unemployment rates, the curve flattens out, in large part because of the downward rigidity of the nominal wages.

In the context of this simple labor-market model, the trade-off between

the rate of wage inflation and the unemployment rate arises from the postulated responsiveness of wages to the excess demand for labor. However,
there are numerous forces that affect the *position* of the curve that traces out
the aggregate relationship between the unemployment rate and the rate of
wage inflation. Four of these forces are (1) the current and expected rates of
price inflation, (2) the age/sex distribution of the labor force, (3) the dispersion
of unemployment rates across markets, and (4) the growth rate of employment and the labor force.

## Forces Affecting the Wage-Inflation/ Unemployment Trade-Off

**Price inflation.**  So far we have assumed the price level to be fixed. However, current and expected future rates of price inflation clearly influence the
rate of *money*-wage inflation associated with any given level of excess demand for labor. Since both the demand and supply curves of labor are
functions of the *real*-wage rate, an increase in the *price* level requires a
proportional increase in the *money-wage* rate simply to keep the real wage
and the excess demand for labor constant. The relationship between wage
changes and the excess demand for labor described in equation (17.2) actually
refers to changes in the real wage (prices were assumed fixed while wages
changed). Hence, the effect of price inflation is to *increase* the rate of money-
wage inflation associated with any given level of the excess demand for labor.

Our discussion so far has assumed that labor markets are competitive and
that all real wages are renegotiated continuously as labor-market conditions
change. Later in the chapter we will introduce several institutional features of
the collective-bargaining process in the United States in our discussion. Here,
we will consider how the introduction of one such feature—contracts that are
negotiated only periodically—affects the analysis. From employees' perspective, past price changes may influence wage demands during contract negotiations, because they signify that real wages are below the level employees
expected *if* such price changes were not fully anticipated at the time of the
previous contract negotiations. Expected future price changes may also matter, because they translate money-wage changes into expected real-wage
changes. Similarly, from employers' perspectives, past and expected future
price changes may affect their willingness to increase wages, as increases in
output prices, *ceteris paribus,* reduce real wages and hence employers' real
costs of doing business.

Unambiguously then, higher expected price changes should lead to higher
wage changes in a world where wages are adjusted only periodically. It is
unclear, however, whether an extra 1-percent increase in expected price
inflation will lead to an extra 1-percent increase in money wages; this depends, among other things, on the relative bargaining power of employees and
employers. Let us assume that a 1-percent increase in the expected rate of
price inflation ($\dot{P}^e$) shifts the rate of money-wage inflation associated with a

given excess demand for labor up by γ percent, where γ may be less than one.[42] That is,

$$\dot{W} = f[x] + \gamma \dot{P}^e \qquad 0 \leq \gamma \leq 1. \qquad (17.3)$$

**Age composition of the labor force.** We noted earlier that teenagers tend to have higher unemployment rates than adults. The aggregate unemployment rate associated with any given degree of labor-market *tightness*—or excess demand for labor—is simply the weighted average of the unemployment rates for the various age groups, with the weights being the share of the group in the overall labor force. During the 1960s and 1970s, the share of teenagers in the labor force increased because of the growing share of teenagers in the population. Since this group tends to have higher-than-average unemployment rates, the overall unemployment rate associated with any level of excess demand for labor also increased.[43]

An increase in the level of unemployment associated with each level of the excess demand for labor implies, other things equal, that a higher unemployment rate will be associated with each rate of wage inflation. Put another way, the changing age composition of the labor force also caused the wage-inflation/unemployment trade-off curve to shift up between 1960 and 1980. At any level of the aggregate unemployment rate, the rate of wage inflation was higher in the early 1980s than in the 1960s. The falling teenage share of the labor force in the late 1980s has contributed to the leftward shift in the wage inflation-unemployment tradeoff.

**The dispersion of unemployment rates.** The model of the wage-inflation/unemployment trade-off that we have presented applies to a *single* labor market.[44] To obtain the wage-inflation/unemployment trade-off for the *economy,* one must aggregate all of the individual labor-market relationships. If the unemployment rate differs across labor markets, the aggregate rate of wage inflation associated with any given level of aggregate unemployment may be higher than it would be if the unemployment rate were the same in all markets.

To see why this is true, suppose the economy consisted of two labor markets of the same size with the same inflation/unemployment tradeoff. If both markets had, say, 6-percent unemployment, we could expect lower wage

---

[42] For simplicity, we have focused only on expected price inflation and ignored past price inflation *per se* here. We also have restricted γ to be no greater than one; this need not always be the case.

[43] An early exposition of the importance of this factor is found in George L. Perry, "Changing Labor Markets and Inflation," *Brookings Papers on Economic Activity,* 1970–3, pp. 411–41. Table 17.2 shows that in 1987, men and women had roughly equal unemployment rates. However, in the 1960s and 1970s, women had higher unemployment rates than men. During that period, the growing share of women in the labor force increased the aggregate unemployment rate corresponding to a given level of excess demand for labor.

[44] The role of geographic dispersion in unemployment rates was emphasized early by Lipsey and by G. C. Archibald, "The Phillips Curve and the Distribution of Unemployment," *American Economic Review* 59 (May 1969): 124–34. The importance of dispersion of unemployment across age and gender groups was emphasized in Perry, "Changing Labor Markets and Inflation."

inflation than if one market had 3-percent unemployment and the other had 9-percent unemployment (averaging to approximately 6-percent unemployment).[45] Recalling Figure 17.4, the increase in wage inflation caused by a fall from 6-percent to 3-percent unemployment is likely to be greater than the decrease in wage inflation caused by going from 6-percent to 9-percent unemployment. The Phillips Curve becomes steeper at lower unemployment and flatter at high unemployment. Over a wide range of values of the unemployment rate, increases in the dispersion of unemployment rates across labor markets will increase the aggregate rate of wage inflation associated with the *aggregate* unemployment rate. Put another way, increases in the dispersion of unemployment rates can cause the aggregate wage-inflation/unemployment trade-off curve to shift up.

**The Growth of Employment and the Labor Force.**  Another factor that might cause the excess demand for labor/unemployment rate relationship to shift up is the growth rate of employment and the labor force. Other things equal, the more rapidly aggregate employment is growing, the greater the number of job vacancies employers will have to fill. Even if the labor force is growing to keep pace with employment opportunities, rapid expansion may make it more difficult to match workers and jobs and, since voluntary and involuntary job turnover is highest among new employees, rapid expansion also increases the need to hire replacements, compounding employers' problems. Because of this, one might expect to observe a larger excess demand for labor associated with any given unemployment rate when employment is growing rapidly than when it is growing slowly.

In fact, both the civilian labor force and employment grew considerably faster during the 1970s than during the 1960s. There is evidence that the job-vacancy rates (measured only by indices of help-wanted advertisements) associated with any given unemployment rate were also higher in the 1970s.[46] Between 1980 and 1985, however, the growth rates of the labor force and employment fell back to roughly their levels during the 1960s.

## Reasons for Shifts in the Trade-Off Curve Over Time

Have the four major factors discussed above been responsible for the upward shift of the short-run wage-inflation/unemployment tradeoff between 1960 and 1980 and its downward shift since 1980? First, as Table 17.3 indicates, the percentage rate of change in the gross national product (GNP) *implicit price deflator*—a broad measure of the prices of all goods produced in the econ-

[45]  We say "approximately" because once the unemployment rate differs between the two markets, a slightly higher weight should be assigned to the low unemployment market because it will have relatively more *employed* workers.

[46]  James L. Medoff, "U.S. Labor Markets: Imbalance, Wage Growth, and Productivity in the 1970's," *Brookings Papers on Economic Activity,* 1983-1, pp. 87–120, and Katharine Abraham, "Structural/Frictional vs. Demand Deficient Unemployment."

omy—trended upwards over that period.[47] To the extent that past price changes affect expectations of *future* price changes, this trend should have shifted the trade-off curve out (as employees incorporated these expected price changes into their wage demands). Further, survey data indicate that people's expectations about future inflation rose in the 1970s and early 1980s, but they also suggest such expectations fell after 1981.[48] This pattern fits the inflation and unemployment data in Table 17.3 and pictured in Figure 17.4.

Second, as noted earlier in this chapter, during the 1960s, 1970s, and early 1980s, there was an increase in the fraction of the labor force subject to higher unemployment rates. Since 1980, however, the share of the labor force consisting of teenagers has fallen. This fall in the teenage share may have contributed to the apparent leftward shift of the Phillips Curve in the mid-1980s.

Third, as noted above, there is evidence that the rapid growth of employment and the labor force during the 1970s caused the job-vacancy rate associated with any given rate of unemployment to increase. One study suggested that these changes may have caused the wage-inflation/unemployment trade-off to shift up by as much as one-half to one percentage point.[49] As noted above, however, between 1980 and 1985 these growth rates slowed, which probably caused the trade-off to shift down.

Finally, while the unemployment rates of teenagers rose relative to those of adult white males, and those of nonwhite teenagers rose relative to those of white teenagers, this increase in dispersion apparently did not have a substantial impact on the aggregate wage-inflation/unemployment trade-off curve.[50] However, during the 1970s there was an increase in the dispersion of employment growth rates across *industrial sectors* that is thought to have contributed to the increase in the full-employment unemployment rate.[51]

## Improving the Trade-off: What Can Government Do?

The analyses above suggest ways government policies can reduce the rate of wage inflation associated with any given unemployment rate.

1. They can attempt to reduce the rate of wage inflation associated with any level of excess demand for labor.

---

[47] Another widely publicized price index is the Consumer Price Index (CPI), a measure of the cost of living for urban households that is published monthly by the Bureau of Labor Statistics. This index is in fact the one that is typically used to calculate cost-of-living increases due under union contracts with cost-of-living escalator clauses. Because the GNP deflator and CPI measure different things, year-to-year percentage changes in the two indices often differ. However, over longer periods of time they yield roughly the same picture about the upward trend in the inflation rate.

[48] These survey data are supplied by the Federal Reserve Bank of Philadelphia.

[49] James Medoff, "U.S. Labor Markets," pp. 110–11.

[50] For econometric evidence on this point, see Robert J. Gordon, "Can the Inflation of the 1970s Be Explained?" *Brookings Papers on Economic Activity*, 1977–1, pp. 353–74.

[51] See David Lilien, "Sectoral Shifts and Cyclical Unemployment."

2.   They can attempt to reduce the unemployment rate associated with any given level of the excess demand for labor.

3.   Finally, they can attempt to reduce the geographic or demographic dispersion of unemployment rates.

A number of policy tools are potentially available to achieve each goal.

Turning to the wage-inflation/excess-demand-for-labor relationship first, one obvious objective here is to reduce the expected rate of growth of prices. Over long periods of time this goal is accomplished primarily by restrictive monetary or fiscal policy. In the short run, *incomes policies*—policies by which the government tries directly to control or influence wage and price levels by the specification of standards governing when prices or wages can be changed—may also have an effect. Examples here include wage/price guidelines, temporary wage/price freezes, and tax-based income policies. (A later section of this chapter will discuss incomes policies.)

The wage-inflation/excess-demand-for-labor relationship may also be, and has been, shifted down through government policies that increase the competitiveness of labor markets and remove institutional barriers that reduce the downward flexibility of wages. Examples of such policies include eliminating or relaxing the Davis-Bacon Act (discussed in Chapter 12) and deregulating certain industries, such as airlines, telephone, and trucking, that historically had been regulated in ways that tended to reduce competition (see Chapters 12, 16, and 18 for discussions of deregulation).

With respect to reducing the rate of unemployment associated with any given level of excess demand for labor, the goal here would be to improve the efficiency of labor markets.[52] Many policies related to this goal were discussed earlier; they include improving job-market information, improving the "job-matching services" offered by the U.S. Employment Service and private employment agencies, and increasing government-sponsored training programs to help reduce skill bottlenecks. One caution here, however, is that policies designed to reduce the unemployment rate may actually serve to increase it. For example, if potential job-leavers—workers who feel some dissatisfaction with their jobs—knew that the government was actively pursuing a policy to reduce the length of time unemployed workers spent out of work, this knowledge might increase the probability that these workers would quit their jobs. One would have to balance the benefits from shorter durations of unemployment against the costs of a higher incidence of unemployment before deciding if such policies were worthwhile to implement.

The government can seek to reduce the geographic dispersion of unemployment rates by providing information about jobs in other areas to unemployed workers, by providing relocation allowances and subsidies for job

---

[52]   A long-time advocate of such policies is Charles Holt. See, for example, Charles Holt et al., "Manpower Proposals for Phase III," *Brookings Papers on Economic Activity*, 1971–3, pp. 703–22. For a more critical evaluation of these policies, see Robert Hall, "Prospects for Shifting the Phillips Curve Through Manpower Policy," *Brookings Papers on Economic Activity*, 1971–3, pp. 659–701.

search in different areas, and by administering public employment and training-program budgets in a way that increases allocations to areas with above-average unemployment rates.[53] The government can also seek to reduce the dispersion of unemployment rates across occupational, industrial, or demographic groups by targeting employment and training programs, wage subsidies, tax credits, and relocation allowances on the groups with high unemployment rates.

# Unions and Inflation

Less than 20 percent of the labor force is made up of union members (see Chapter 10). In spite of this fact, unions and the collective-bargaining process in the United States are thought to exert a considerable influence on the position and shape of the wage-inflation/unemployment trade-off curve for a number of reasons. In particular, we must explore why the spread of *multiyear agreements* with *cost-of-living escalator clauses* may have been responsible for some of the stagflation problems of the early 1980s.

## Wage Patterns and Norms

First, in several industries—such as steel, automobiles, mining, trucking, and telephone—collective-bargaining negotiations are conducted at the national level and are well publicized in the media. The resulting settlements are often thought to set a pattern for wage settlements in less heavily unionized industries and in the nonunion sector because of either imitative behavior in the former or attempts to compete for labor and keep unions out in the latter.[54] Our model suggests that if the economic conditions facing firms and unions in only a few key industries heavily influence the rate of wage inflation in other sectors, the effect of the *aggregate* unemployment rate on inflation will be reduced.

Evidence to support this view is mixed, however. On the one hand, during the 1970s wages in the above-mentioned highly unionized industries grew substantially relative to wages in the rest of the economy, suggesting that the settlements reached in these industries do not automatically spill over to other industries.[55] Wage patterns did appear to exist among firms *within* certain industries, such as automobiles, during much of the postwar period, but even these patterns broke down in the concession bargaining of the early 1980s, when firms in these industries faced different economic circumstances (see Example 10.1). More generally, attempts to formally test whether key

---

[53]   Employment and training program funds are often administered in this way.

[54]   For an early exposition of this view, see Otto Eckstein and Thomas Wilson, "The Determination of Money Wages in American Industry," *Quarterly Journal of Economics* 76(August 1962): 379–414.

[55]   See Daniel Mitchell, *Unions, Wages, and Inflation* (Washington, DC: Brookings Institution, 1980), and Marvin Kosters, "Wage and Price Behavior: Prospects and Policies," in *Contemporary Economic Problems, 1977*, ed. William Fellner (Washington, DC: American Enterprise Institute for Public Policy Research, 1977), pp. 159–203.

wage bargains, or union wage gains in general, set a pattern for the rest of the economy have not reached definitive conclusions.[56]

On the other hand, some economists have recently argued that the position of the wage-inflation/unemployment trade-off curve is determined not by expectations of price inflation (which may change continuously as economic conditions change) *per se*, but rather by a *wage norm*, or a generally accepted standard for rates of wage increases.[57] Such a norm is thought to be affected little by short-run cyclical conditions, such as small variations in actual inflation rates; rather, it is thought to be shifted only by extreme economic developments such as major recessions or prolonged expansions. In part, the norm may reflect the behavior of large unionized *and* nonunionized firms seeking to maintain their relative wage positions. Empirical evidence suggests that models using proxies for wage norms predict recent inflationary behavior better than models using past rates of price inflation as proxies for the expected rate of price inflation; however, the wage-norm relationship seems to hold primarily in the union sector.[58]

The existence of a *wage norm* that is relatively insensitive to small variations in economic conditions has important implications.[59] It suggests that fiscal and/or monetary policy can be used to stimulate the economy over some range without fear that it will lead the short-run trade-off curve to shift up rapidly and further exacerbate any inflation that exists. However, in extreme times (deep recessions or prolonged booms) that lead to changes in wage norms, the short-run trade-off curve may shift up or down quite rapidly. This notion of wage norms also suggests that the causes of price-level increases may affect how wages respond to price inflation. For example, price increases that accompany a prolonged boom are more likely to increase wage norms than are price increases caused by exogenous shocks, such as the oil-price shocks of the '70s.

## Multiyear Contracts

Second, union contracts have increasingly become multiyear in nature, calling for wage increases not only at the time the contract is signed but also in subsequent years. While these increases may well be sensitive to the unemployment rate at the time the contract is signed—or, more precisely, to unions' and employers' *expectations* of the unemployment rate over the term

---

[56]   See Daniel Mitchell, "Union Wage Determination: Policy Implications and Outlook," *Brookings Papers on Economic Activity*, 1978–3, pp. 537–82; Robert Flanagan, "Wage Interdependence in Unionized Labor Markets," *Brookings Papers on Economic Activity*, 1976–3, pp. 635–73; and Susan Vroman, "The Direction of Wage Spillovers in Manufacturing," *Industrial and Labor Relations Review* 36 (October 1982): 102–12.

[57]   See George Perry, "Shifting Wage Norms and Their Implications," *American Economic Review Papers and Proceedings* 76(May 1986): 245–48, and George Perry, "Inflation in Theory and Practice," *Brookings Papers on Economic Activity*, 1980–1, pp. 207–41.

[58]   See George Perry, "What Have We Learned About Disinflation?" *Brookings Papers on Economic Activity*, 1983–2, 587–602; Daniel Mitchell, "Union vs. Nonunion Wage Norm Shifts," *American Economic Review Papers and Proceedings* 76(May 1986): 249–52; and Daniel Mitchell, "Shifting Wage Norms in Wage Determination," *Brookings Papers on Economic Activity*, 1985–2, pp. 575–99.

[59]   George Perry, "Shifting Wage Norms and Their Implications."

of the contract—the contractual increases are not directly affected by the *actual* unemployment rate during the duration of the contract. Furthermore, these contracts tend to be staggered; only a fraction are negotiated each period.[60]

Formal econometric analyses indicate that wage increases specified in the *first year* of multiyear union contracts appear to be about as sensitive to the unemployment rate as wage increases in the nonunion sector. However, *deferred* wage increases specified in union contracts—those that occur in the second or third year of multiyear contracts—do not appear to be related to the actual unemployment rates during those years.[61] Hence, the increasing frequency of long-term union contracts in the economy *does* reduce the sensitivity of the overall rates of wage and price inflation to the unemployment rate, making the trade-off curves flatter.

## Cost-of-Living Adjustments

Third, accompanying the growth of multiyear contracts has been the growth of *cost-of-living adjustment (COLA) clauses* in union contracts—clauses that call for wages to be automatically adjusted periodically as the price level changes. Approximately 20 percent of workers covered by major collective-bargaining agreements (those that cover 1000 or more workers) had such provisions in their contracts in 1966. However, by the early 1980s this proportion had grown to about 60 percent.[62]

Escalator clauses typically give workers less than 100-percent protection against price inflation. Such contracts usually call for wages to increase by less than 1 percent for each 1-percent increase in prices, and sometimes *caps*—maximum allowable cost-of-living increases—are also specified. Nevertheless, their existence should increase the sensitivity of wage inflation to price inflation, and the evidence bears this out; union wage changes, especially those in contracts that call for cost-of-living escalators, appear to be more sensitive to price changes than do nonunion wage changes.[63] As noted earlier, larger values of $\gamma$ in equation (17.3) lead to a higher short-run price-inflation/unemployment trade-off curve. Hence, the growing prevalence of cost-of-living escalator clauses in union contracts may well have contributed

---

[60] For a formal analysis of how *staggered contracts* affect the inflationary process, see John Taylor, "Staggered Wage Setting in a Macro Model," *American Economic Review Papers and Proceedings* 69(May 1979): 108–13.

[61] Mitchell, "Union Wage Determination."

[62] See Ronald G. Ehrenberg, Leif Danziger, and Gee San, "Cost of Living Adjustment Clauses in Union Contracts: A Summary of Results," *Journal of Labor Economics* 1(July 1983): 215–45; Wallace Hendricks and Lawrence Kahn, "Cost-of-Living Clauses in Union Contracts: Determinants and Effects," *Industrial and Labor Relations Review* 36(April 1983): 447–60; and David Card, "An Empirical Model of Wage Indexation Provisions," *Journal of Political Economy* 94(June 1986, part 2): S144–S175, for discussions of the forces that caused this growth over time. As part of the concession bargaining that took place during the mid-1980s, many contracts (such as those in telecommunications) began to eliminate COLA provisions.

[63] Mitchell, "Union Wage Determination," and Wallace E. Hendricks and Lawrence M. Kahn, *Wage Indexation in the United States: Cola or Uncola?* (Cambridge, MA: Ballinger, 1985).

EXAMPLE   17.2

## Wage Inflation and Unemployment Around the World: The Role of Bargaining Structures

During the 1980s, in the face of rapid job growth, unemployment in the United States declined from over 10 percent of the labor force in 1982 to around 5.5 percent in the first half of 1988. In contrast, the four largest western European nations (West Germany, England, Italy, and France), whose combined labor force in 1970 exceeded the size of the American labor force, experienced no job growth and persistently high unemployment. In 1987 the internationally "standardized" unemployment rate was 6.2 percent in the United States, while its value in the four European countries was 7.9, 10.4, 10.6, and 11 percent, respectively. Yet, in smaller European countries such as Austria, Switzerland, and Sweden, the unemployment rate rarely exceeded 3 percent.

Much has been written about recent job-creation and unemployment-rate differentials between the United States and European countries, and a variety of explanations for these differentials have been proposed. These explanations include differential rates of labor-force growth, rates of decline in hours of work, rates of growth of social-insurance programs, differences in the level of real wages, and differences in the scope and coverage of protective labor legislation. One additional factor to emphasize in this example is the role of differences in collective-bargaining structures.

As we have noted, collective bargaining in the United States is very decentralized. Negotiations often occur at the company or plant level. In contrast, collective bargaining in many European countries occurs at the industrywide or economywide level. Some observers have argued that the relatively centralized European bargaining structures produce lower wage pressure and less unemployment. After all, centralized bargaining structures limit interunion rivalries that often produce wage pressure. Moreover, negotiators in centralized bargaining structures may temper their wage demands, since the resulting nominal wage increases will cause a comparatively large increase of consumer prices, thus limiting the real wage gains of union workers. On the other hand, wage drift (introduced in Example 12.4) is more likely in countries with centralized bargaining.

Others have argued that the demand for labor is less elastic in countries with more centralized collective bargaining, so that the cost of a given wage increase—in terms of less employment of union members—is lower. This argument associates *greater* wage pressure with centralized bargaining structures. Taken together, these arguments imply that relatively favorable wage and unemployment experience may be associated with the most centralized *and* the least centralized collective-bargaining structures. Intermediate bargaining structures might produce the greatest wage pressure and unemployment.

There is conflicting evidence on this important situation. For certain time periods, the most-centralized bargaining systems seem to be associated with superior macroeconomic performance, while for other periods, outcomes seem somewhat better in countries with either centralized or decentralized structures. The only

consistent pattern is that countries with centralized bargaining have lower unemployment. Yet these same countries do not have a superior inflation record, as one
might expect if bargaining restraint was the key mechanism.

SOURCES:  C. R. Bean, P. R. G. Layard, and S. J. Nickell, "The Rise in Unemployment: A Multi-
Country Study," *Economica* 53 (Supplement, 1986): S1–S22; M. Bruno and J. Sachs, *The Economics of
Worldwide Inflation* (Oxford: Basil Blackwell, 1986); L. Calmfors and J. Driffill, "Centralization of Wage
Bargaining and Macroeconomic Performance," *Economic Policy* (April 1988).

to the upward shift in the short-run trade-off curves that took place between
(roughly) 1960 and 1980. However, by 1987, the incidence of COLA clauses
had fallen to 38 percent among workers covered by major agreements (see
Table 15.5). This fall probably has helped the Phillips Curve shift downward.

## Wage Imitation

A final reason why unions are thought to influence the position and shape of
the trade-off curve is that union members are clearly concerned about maintaining their wage position relative to what they perceive are the wages of
their *peer groups*. At the national level, for example, automobile workers look
at the wage gains won in the steel industry and vice versa. Whichever union
settles first may set a pattern for the other union to follow in its negotiations,
regardless of economic conditions in the latter industry. If this occurs, the
responsiveness of wage and price inflation to unemployment would again be
reduced.

Wage gains in several large national industries, such as automobile, steel,
and rubber, clearly are highly correlated. However, it is difficult to disen-
tangle the above *wage-imitation* hypothesis from the hypothesis that wages in
these industries are affected by a common set of variables. After all, steel is a
major component of automobiles, as is rubber for the tires. It would, therefore, not be surprising to find that wage changes for workers in the three
industries are highly correlated. Attempts to formally test whether wage
imitation occurs among unions in these and other industries have not met with
success.[64]

Our discussion suggests, then, that the collective-bargaining process per
se may well have contributed to the flattening and shifting up of the short-run
inflation/unemployment trade-off curves from 1960 to 1980. The increased
prevalence of multiyear contracts is partially responsible for the flattening,
and the increase in cost-of-living escalator clauses for the upward shift.[65] The

---

[64]  See, for example, Robert Flanagan, "Wage Interdependence in Unionized Labor Markets," and
Y. P. Mehra, "Spillovers in Wage Determination in U.S. Manufacturing Industries," *The Review of Economics and Statistics* 58(August 1976): 300–312.

[65]  Another reason for the flattening of the trade-off curve in the nonunion sector relates to the
growth of structured internal labor markets in which fluctuations in demand are met by temporary layoffs
rather than money-wage reductions, as discussed earlier in this chapter. The "quantity adjustments"
(layoffs) rather than "wage adjustments" at the individual firm level contribute to the growing insensitivity
of wage changes to unemployment at the aggregate level. For an extensive discussion of this point, see
Arthur Okun, "Inflation: Its Mechanics and Welfare Costs," *Brookings Papers on Economic Activity*,
1975–2, pp. 351–90, and Arthur Okun, *Prices and Quantities* (Washington, DC: Brookings Institution,
1981).

effects of key settlements or other imitative behavior are uncertain, although there is some evidence that, in the aggregate, *wage norms* that change rather infrequently—not expectations of price inflation per se—may affect the wage-inflation rate. During the 1980s, however, the reduction of cost-of-living escalators (see Table 15.5) and the breakdown of industry patterns (see Chapter 12) may have helped reverse some of the changes occurring between 1960 and 1980.

# Structural Policies to Reduce Inflation

The inflation/unemployment trade-offs for both wages and prices that we face today are unfavorable and appear to indicate that persistent high rates of unemployment will be required to keep inflation at relatively low levels. How, then, can we hope to return the economy to a situation of both low unemployment and low inflation?

Clearly, the answer is to resort to structural policies that will improve the inflation/unemployment trade-off per se. Many of these policies were discussed earlier in the chapter. In the remainder of the chapter we shall focus in more detail on two of these—*incomes policies* and the use of *share wages*. Incomes policies are policies in which the government tries to directly influence wage and price behavior by specifying *desired behavior*. Sometimes the policies are completely voluntary, and sometimes enforcement mechanisms are built in to increase or guarantee compliance. Share wages are systems of compensation that involve a significant use of revenue or profit sharing among owners and workers.

## Incomes Policies in the United States

During the 1960–80 period, a period over which the inflation/unemployment trade-off curve steadily shifted out, the United States tried several different types of incomes policies. In the early Kennedy-Johnson years (1962–66), a system of voluntary wage guideposts was announced in which companies were encouraged to grant wage increases no higher than 3.2 percent. Since the estimated growth in output per work hour (productivity) was 3.2 percent, the wage guideline meant that companies on average could keep prices constant and not change their profit margins. Put differently, labor cost per unit of output can be expressed as:

$$\text{(Labor cost per hour) / (Output per hour)}.$$

If both the numerator and denominator increase by 3.2 percent, then unit labor costs are constant, and there is no need for any price increases.

The next experience with incomes policies occurred in the Nixon Administration. In August 1971, a 90-day freeze of wages and prices was announced. This was followed by a 13-month period of strict wage-and-price controls, with a wage-increase standard of 5.5 percent and a price standard of 2.5 percent (that is, a 3-percent productivity growth rate was assumed). Finally, in the Carter Administration, a voluntary system of guidelines was announced for the 1978–80 period, with a target compensation increase of 7 percent.

In attempting to determine whether these examples of incomes policies were effective, it is necessary to know how wages and prices would have behaved if there had been no controls. This knowledge is difficult to obtain, since other factors besides controls affect wages and prices. In statistical studies that attempted to correct for other influences on wages and prices, results have been ambiguous. We have no clear answers about the effect of incomes policies on wage and price inflation.[66]

## Why Are Incomes Policies Unpopular Among Economists?

Independent of the evidence on the effectiveness of incomes policies in moderating the rates of wage and price inflation, many economists are opposed to their use because the policies create inequities and efficiency losses in the economy.[67] The scope of this text does not permit our cataloguing the case against incomes policies, but a few arguments can be mentioned.

First, rigid guidelines or standards implicitly freeze the distribution of income and create inequities. For example, individuals who have recently received large increases gain relative to those whose increases will be constrained by the policies. Unless most individuals are happy with their relative income positions at the time the policy is imposed and there is a social consensus on the need for the policy, the policy will invariably break down.

Second, such policies may create efficiency losses, because rapidly expanding sectors of the economy that face personnel shortages are prevented from bidding up wages to attract labor. Once exceptions are systematically granted for the above reason, as was done in the latter phase of the Nixon economic policy, the process of controlling wage increases becomes highly politicized, and the exceptions may be used to justify wage increases that exceed the standard in cases when waiving the standard is not justified by economic conditions. More generally, incomes policies tend to be unevenly applied to different groups; those with political power gain relative to those without.

Finally, the administrative costs of incomes policies that contain enforcement procedures may be enormous. Simply costing out tens of thousands of labor contracts to ascertain compliance is no trivial task, especially when numerous fringe benefits are involved—many of those costs can only be actuarially estimated or guessed at, as is true with pensions. The resources

---

[66] See Robert Gordon, "Wage Price Controls and the Shifting Phillips Curve," *Brookings Papers on Economic Activity,* 1972-2, pp. 385–421, and his "Comment." See also Bradley Askin and John Kraft, *Econometric Wage and Price Models: Assessing the Impact of the Economic Stabilization Program* (Lexington, MA: D. C. Heath, 1974). More recently, John Hagens and R. Robert Russell, "Testing for the Effectiveness of Wage Price Controls: An Application to the Carter Program," *American Economic Review* 75(March 1985): 191–207, found relatively small effects during the Kennedy-Johnson guidepost period and that a "catch-up" occurred *after* the Nixon incomes policy. They could not, however, identify the effects of the Carter incomes policy.

[67] A now classic article that presents the case against incomes policies more completely is Milton Friedman, "What Price Guideposts?" in *Guidelines, Informal Controls, and the Market Place,* George Schultz and Robert Aliber (eds.), (Chicago: University of Chicago Press, 1966): 17–40.

**EXAMPLE   17.3**

# Incomes Policies in Western Europe

European countries have been drawn to experiment with incomes policies much more than the United States for two reasons. As we have seen in Chapter 10, there are substantial differences in the extent of unionization; unions represent about 20 percent of workers in the United States but over 50 percent of the workforce in most major countries of Western Europe. As a result, a larger proportion of the national wage bill is determined in collective bargaining in Western Europe than in the United States, and the potential impact of collective bargaining on inflation is larger. In addition, international trade accounts for a larger fraction of economic activity in Europe than in the United States. As a result, European governments are usually highly concerned about the ability of their industries to compete effectively in international markets, and are more likely to take policy actions in response to balance-of-payments deficits than is the United States.

For these reasons, Western European countries have experimented with a wide variety of policies. During the 1960s, the policies were adopted to prevent or retard the development of inflationary pressures as governments pursued full-employment growth policies. Most of the policies have included some form of guideline for the growth of wages and prices (and occasionally other incomes) accompanied by an enforcement mechanism and penalties for noncompliance. At different times and in different countries the guidelines have ranged from wage and/or price "freezes," to formulas based on aggregate productivity growth (such as the wage guide used in the U.S. wage-price guideposts, described above), to formulas basing wage adjustments on rates of productivity growth in particular industries. Enforcement mechanisms have included exhortation by government officials, the establishment of special review committees to evaluate wage and price decisions for compliance with policy guidelines, and even the inspection of companies' books to determine whether wage payments were in compliance with the policy. Penalties for noncompliance have generally been more severe than in the United States, and in some instances included the possibility of fines or jail sentences.

At the other extreme, in Sweden, a country with very centralized collective-bargaining institutions, there has been no "official" incomes policy run by the government. Instead, the main federations of labor and employers have run what amounts to a "privately operated incomes policy" by giving weight in their negotiations to government forecasts of what would constitute "responsible" wage behavior given expected economic conditions. Both labor and management understand that if they are not able to achieve settlements roughly consistent with the government's macroeconomic objectives, the government has the option of introducing an official incomes policy that they may find unpalatable. Such privately operated incomes policies appear to work best when the number of parties who must agree is small; and hence, these policies are more likely to be found in countries, such as Sweden, with highly centralized bargaining institutions.

For the most part, the European incomes policy experiments of the 1960s were not regarded as successful in their efforts to improve the trade-off between inflation and unemployment. While econometric evaluations (similar to those used to evaluate incomes policies in the United States) indicate that money wage growth was at times restrained by one to two percentage points for one to two years, these periods were often followed by outbreaks of wildcat strikes and wage "explosions" in which wages increased far more rapidly than would normally have been expected under prevailing economic conditions. The evaluations also indicated that even less price restraint was achieved, so that the net effect of the policies may have been to reduce real wages. Moreover, the inability of incomes policies to improve the inflation/unemployment trade-off seemed independent of such factors as the centralization of the collective-bargaining institutions, the degree of political support by the trade union movement, the particular policy guidelines, and the degree of compulsion adopted by a government to enforce the policy.

The reasons for the difficulties encountered by incomes policies in Europe are rooted in many of the aspects of market and institutional behavior that we have discussed in earlier chapters. For example, *wage drift*—the tendency of actual earnings to rise above negotiated wage rates—in countries with relatively centralized level (industrywide or nationwide) negotiations—may offset government efforts to enforce a wage guideline on negotiated wages. Wage drift may develop because incomes policy guidelines imply a wage that is less than the market equilibrium wage—a situation that appeared common in Europe in the 1960s, when many governments appeared to introduce incomes policies to control inflations that resulted from excess demand and therefore would have been more appropriately addressed through restrictive fiscal and monetary policies. In this situation, wage drift will tend to restore the market-equilibrium wage irrespective of the government guideline. Wage drift may also result from institutional pressures and unofficial local bargaining, as workers try to restore wage differentials that may have been disturbed by the incomes-policy rules.

The growth of wage drift also threatens the institutional security of union organizations, as workers notice that a smaller and smaller fraction of their compensation comes from wages negotiated by the union. Thus, even union leaders who are predisposed to cooperate with a government incomes policy (as can be the case, for example, if the trade-union movement is affiliated with the political party that is in power) may be sharply limited in their *ability* to both support the policy and maintain the political support of the union's rank and file. The political stature of union leaders who sought to cooperate in incomes policies also was not enhanced by the fact that even with the compensating tendencies of wage drift, workers experienced a net reduction in real wages as governments were less successful in restraining price increases than in restraining wage increases.

Even in relatively decentralized collective-bargaining structures in which wage drift is less likely to arise, the ability of union leaders to comply with an incomes policy may be limited by *compliance risk*. Compliance risk arises because workers complying with a pay guideline have no assurance that other workers will exercise similar restraint. The failure of other unions to comply will result in reductions in real and relative earnings for the members of unions that comply—a result that will not increase the political security of the leaders of the latter unions. In addition, the members of noncomplying unions will benefit (in terms of increased real earnings) from whatever reduction in inflation occurs from the wage restraint of complying unions. That is, the benefit of wage restraint (lower inflation) is what we referred to in Chapter 10 as a public good; the benefit cannot be restricted to those who comply with the incomes policy.

In summary, it appeared that if incomes policies were to improve their track records, they would have to be designed in a manner that compensated union members for some of the losses that they incurred under the policies and offered some form of institutional protection for union organizations in exchange for their cooperation. This challenge became all the more difficult during the 1970s, when the combined effects of OPEC oil-price increases and reduced profitability of industry in many European countries led governments to explicitly seek real-wage reductions through incomes policies. In an effort to address these issues, several governments explored the possibility of establishing a *social contract* through multilateral negotiations between labor, management, government officials, and possibly other economic interest groups. The most striking difference between the social contract idea and the incomes policies of the 1960s was the presence of the government as an explicit participant in the negotiations. This difference rested on the premise that the government had policy concessions to trade that would compensate labor for wage restraint.

One bargaining tool available to governments was tax policy. In countries with very high marginal tax rates on personal income and high rates of inflation, such as Sweden and Denmark, it was increasingly difficult to achieve significant advances in the real disposable earnings of union members through bargaining over money wages. This left open the possibility of a social contract involving tax reductions in exchange for wage restraint. Other policies that unions, at times, indicated might be the price of wage restraint included price controls (thereby limiting the risk of real-wage losses), greater wage indexation, and legislation supporting the institutional position of unions. The basic difficulty raised by the social-contract approach under the economic conditions of the 1970s was that the policies requested by unions as compensation for wage restraint conflicted with the general objectives of incomes policies. For example, tax reductions tend to stimulate the economy, and wage drift increases with labor demand. Therefore, the negotiated wage restraint achieved through a tax reduction would tend to be canceled by increasing drift. Policies such as price controls and wage indexation tended to conflict with the need for real wages in Europe to fall during the period. By the end of the decade it was clear that, under prevailing economic conditions, the social-contract approach had been no more successful than the incomes-policy approaches of the 1960s.

SOURCE:   Robert J. Flanagan, David Soskice, and Lloyd Ulman, *Unionism, Economic Stabilization, and Incomes Policy* (Washington, DC: Brookings Institution, 1983).

devoted both by government agencies to monitor the programs and by private employers to assure that they are in compliance may represent a substantial cost to society.

## Recent Proposals to Improve the Inflation-Unemployment Tradeoff: Taxed-Based Incomes Policies and Share Wages

In the 1970s and 1980s, two new kinds of proposal surfaced in an attempt to deal with inflation. First, some proposals suggested that the tax system be used to give firms and workers an incentive to moderate wage and price increases.[68] Such *tax-based incomes policies* (TIPs) include lower individual

---

[68]   See, for example, Henry Wallich and Sidney Weintraub, ''A Tax-Based Incomes Policy,'' *Journal of Economic Issues* 5 (June 1971): 1–19, and Robert J. Flanagan, ''Real Wage Insurance as a Compliance Incentive,'' *Eastern Economic Journal* 5 (October 1979): 367–78.

income tax rates (or give tax credits) for those who work in companies that give wage increases lower than some standard. An alternative approach is to lower corporate taxes on firms paying wage increases below the standard. Such policies would not prohibit high wage increases, they would only reward workers for accepting, or firms for giving, low wage increases.

TIPs have some advantages and disadvantages. They would encourage management to stiffen its resistance to union wage demands, but they might increase the frequency and duration of strikes if their workers did not directly benefit from tax relief.

TIPS could, however, help break an inflationary spiral caused, say, by an initial increase in oil prices. In the absence of a TIP, the rise in oil prices might get reflected in wage increases, which would then cause rising prices in a spiral-like fashion. The hope is that a decrease in wage inflation induced by a TIP would lead to a decrease in price inflation, leading to further moderation in both wages and prices.

Second, instead of paying workers conventional, time-based wages, it has recently been proposed that employers pay workers share wages—that is, wages based upon revenue or profit sharing. The critical characteristic of a share basis for paying workers is that a firm's labor costs become, at least in part, a function of its performance. Under such schemes, the firm agrees to set aside a certain fraction of its profits (or revenues) in a fund that will then be split among its employees. If its product demand falls, either from a general recession or a permanent shift away from its products, the firm's labor costs fall without its having to lay off workers. If its profits rise when demand is strong—because it can raise product prices—its workers receive an automatic wage increase. It is the sharing, among firms and workers alike, of profit reductions in the bad times and profit increases in the periods of "boom" that has the potential for bringing down wage and price inflation.

If share wages constitute a substantial portion of employee compensation, the wages paid to each worker will fall automatically when product demand slackens and firms' revenues are decreased. This fall in the unit cost of labor will permit (encourage) firms using markup pricing to reduce product prices in periods or sectors characterized by slack demand.

How will product-price increases of share firms compare with those of conventional firms when business is brisk? Suppose that a conventional firm selling items of equipment for $100 apiece realizes that it can now get $110 for them. If it altered its traditional markup and charged $110, its profits would rise by $10 per item; a firm contemplating such an increase would have to balance this $10 rise in profits per unit of output against the *costs* of the price increase (reprinting price lists and possible loss of customer "goodwill" when the traditional markup is raised). The share firm, however, must—by the very nature of its pay scheme—share the $10 rise in profits with its workers. If, for example, the share firm had agreed to put 40 percent of its profits into the compensation pool, then it could keep only $6 of the added $10 in revenues per unit of output. If there are costs to raising prices, the share firm is more likely than the conventional firm to find that these costs outweigh the benefits.

By making it more likely that firms would reduce prices in periods of slack demand and less likely that firms would raise them in periods of strong demand, share systems have been suggested by some economists as a structural change in the economy worth contemplating. Critics range from those who question the feasibility of implementing share systems to those who argue that the claims of share-wage supporters have been overstated. Advocates encouraging (usually through tax incentives) the widespread adoption of share wages contend that, at the very least, share systems would not make stagflation worse and would stand a good chance of improving the economy's performance vis-a-vis unemployment and inflation.[69]

As documented in Chapters 9 and 18, American compensation practices are moving in the direction advocated by those who favor the share-wage concept. Pay is becoming more tied to individual and company performance. To the extent that such a trend continues, we may expect an improved inflation-unemployment relationship.

# Review Questions

1. A presidential hopeful is campaigning to raise unemployment compensation benefits and lower the full-employment target from a 5-percent to a 4.5-percent unemployment rate. Comment on the compatibility of these goals.

2. Is the following assertion true, false, or uncertain? "Increasing the level of unemployment insurance benefits will prolong the average length of spells of unemployment. Hence, a policy of raising UI benefit levels is not socially desirable." Explain your answer.

3. In the 1970s, Sweden adopted several new labor market policies affecting layoffs. Three were notable: (1) plants that provided in-plant training instead of laying off workers in a recession received government subsidies; (2) all workers had to be given at least one month's notice before being laid off, and the required time in the average plant was two to three months; and (3) laid-off workers had to be given first option on new jobs with the former employer. What probable effects would these policies, taken as a whole, have on wages, employment, and unemployment in the long run?

4. Why are the size of wage increases and the unemployment rate thought to be negatively related? How (and why) is this negative relationship affected by price inflation and the rising labor-force participation of women? What can the government do to reduce the wage inflation associated with any level of unemployment?

5. Suppose the government were to adopt an incomes policy that allows workers to receive wage increases each January equal to the increase in the cost of living during the previous 12 months but *no* other increases. Would such a scheme help reduce the rate of inflation?

6. Some members of Congress have supported legislation requiring the federal government to undertake massive employment programs as long as the overall unemployment rate is above 4 percent. Evaluate such a program with respect to its effects on inflation.

---

[69] For a sense of the discussion, see Martin L. Weitzman, *The Share Economy* (Cambridge, MA: Harvard University Press, 1983), and a set of articles reviewing the Weitzman book that appeared in *Industrial and Labor Relations Review* 39 (January 1986): 285–90.

# Selected Readings

Martin Feldstein, "The Economics of the New Unemployment," *Public Interest* 33(Fall 1973): 3–42.

Robert Flanagan, "Wage Interdependence in Unionized Labor Markets," *Brookings Papers on Economic Activity,* 1976–3, pp. 635–73.

Richard Freeman and Harry Holzer (eds.), *The Black Youth Unemployment Crisis.* (Chicago: University of Chicago Press, 1986).

Richard Freeman and David Wise, *The Youth Labor Market Problem: Its Nature, Causes, and Consequences* (Chicago: University of Chicago Press, 1982).

James Medoff, "U.S. Labor Markets: Imbalance, Wage Growth, and Productivity in the 1970s," *Brookings Papers on Economic Activity,* 1983–1, pp. 87–120.

Daniel Mitchell, *Unions, Wages, and Inflation* (Washington, DC: Brookings Institution, 1980).

Arthur Okun and George Perry (eds.), "Innovative Policies to Slow Inflation," *Brookings Papers on Economic Activity,* 1978–2.

George Perry, "Shifting Wage Norms and Their Implications," *American Economic Review Papers and Proceedings* 76 (May 1986): 245–48.

# CHAPTER 18

## Labor-Management Relations in the 1980s and 1990s

The 1980s and 1990s are a challenging period for the employment relationship. In Chapter 9 we mentioned some recent trends in company compensation practices, and in Chapter 10 we discussed the reasons for the decline of the labor movement in the 1980s. In this concluding chapter, we examine the current economic and legal environment facing firms and workers, and we discuss responses in both the union and nonunion sectors. Our goal is to provide some idea of where the employment relationship is headed in the near future.

We begin by discussing competitive pressures in the labor market brought about by deregulation of key sectors and increased international competition. Next, we discuss management and union responses to these and other changes in the economic environment. Examples of these responses include union-avoidance strategies by firms, innovations in collective-bargaining agreements, and attempts by unions to increase their bargaining strength, broaden their appeal to workers, and lobby for governmental protection. Finally, we examine changes in the employment relationship for nonunion workers, some of which we have already mentioned in Chapter 9. We focus on the challenges that demographic changes in the labor force pose to the employment relationship. Key themes in our discussion are the increased use of flexible compensation and changes in what is expected of workers and firms in the employment relationship. Chapter 17 examined the macroeconomic consequences of this flexibility in the discussion of share wages. This chapter focuses on the implications of flexibility for individual workers and companies.

# Economic Pressures in the 1980s and 1990s

As we mentioned in Chapter 10, two important reasons for the decline of unions in the 1980s were increased international competition and deregulation of key sectors in the economy. Both of these changes increase the availability to consumers of substitutes for union-produced commodities or services. The elasticity of demand for labor in the affected industries has thus increased, reducing unions' ability to maintain high levels of wages and benefits.

## International Trade

Table 18.1 illustrates the increase in import penetration of the manufacturing sector from 1972 to 1984. This increase occurred in virtually all manufacturing industries, but it was most pronounced in the apparel, leather, steel ("primary metal"), machinery, electric and electronic equipment, auto, and instruments industries. With the exception of apparel, these industries tend to be highly unionized, and all but apparel and leather have relatively high wage and

**Table 18.1**   Domestic Imports of Manufactured Products, 1972–84

| Product | Import Penetration Ratio* (percent) | | | |
|---|---|---|---|---|
| | 1972 | 1977 | 1982 | 1984 |
| Manufacturing | 6.1 | 7.0 | 8.5 | 10.9 |
| Nondurable | 4.7 | 5.4 | 5.8 | 7.5 |
| Food and kindred products | 3.9 | 3.8 | 3.6 | 4.2 |
| Tobacco products | .6 | .7 | 1.8 | .6 |
| Textile mill products | 5.6 | 4.2 | 5.4 | 7.2 |
| Apparel, other mill products | 7.0 | 10.3 | 14.3 | 20.3 |
| Paper and allied products | 5.6 | 6.3 | 6.1 | 6.9 |
| Printing and publishing | 1.0 | .9 | .9 | 1.2 |
| Chemicals and allied products | 3.2 | 3.9 | 4.5 | 6.1 |
| Petroleum and coal products | 7.1 | 8.5 | 7.3 | 10.4 |
| Rubber and plastics products | 4.7 | 5.4 | 5.1 | 5.9 |
| Leather and leather products | 15.9 | 21.2 | 33.9 | 44.4 |
| Durable | 7.2 | 8.3 | 11.2 | 13.8 |
| Lumber and wood products | 9.4 | 9.3 | 8.2 | 10.0 |
| Furniture and fixtures | 2.6 | 3.6 | 5.3 | 7.4 |
| Stone, clay, glass products | 3.7 | 4.0 | 5.3 | 7.0 |
| Primary metal industries | 8.9 | 10.0 | 14.7 | 16.4 |
| Fabricated metal products | 2.5 | 3.2 | 4.3 | 4.9 |
| Machinery, exc. electrical | 5.4 | 6.3 | 8.4 | 12.6 |
| Electric and electronic equipment | 7.6 | 10.4 | 12.4 | 16.4 |
| Transportation equipment | 9.8 | 10.2 | 15.4 | 16.5 |
| Instruments and related products | 6.7 | 9.2 | 10.1 | 12.4 |
| Miscellaneous manufacturing industries | 13.3 | 17.2 | 24.0 | 30.5 |

\*   Ratio of imports to new supply (product shipments plus imports)

SOURCE:   U.S. Government of Commerce, *Statistical Abstract of the United States 1987* (Washington DC: U.S. Government Printing Office, 1986): Table 1320.

**Table 18.2**   Indexes of Unit Labor Cost in Manufacturing by Country in U.S. Dollars (Base year is 1977)

|  | *1977* | *1980* | *1985* | *1986* |
|---|---|---|---|---|
| United States | 100.0 | 130.6 | 145.1 | 144.3 |
| Japan | 100.0 | 116.8 | 104.3 | 148.7 |
| France | 100.0 | 154.1 | 103.9 | 138.0 |
| W. Germany | 100.0 | 147.9 | 99.6 | 139.2 |
| Italy | 100.0 | 141.4 | 114.8 | 151.4 |
| Sweden | 100.0 | 125.3 | 80.6 | 102.5 |
| Great Britain | 100.0 | 220.5 | 144.8 | 171.9 |

Note:  For each year, this table converts unit labor cost for each country into dollars using that year's prevailing exchange rate for the country's currency in terms of dollars. The result is then expressed as a percentage of the 1977 figure.

SOURCE:  U.S. Bureau of Labor Statistics, *Monthly Labor Review* 110 (August 1987), Table 47.

benefit levels. They are thus good targets for penetration by lower-cost imports.

To the extent that firms base their prices on costs, unit labor costs (total labor costs per unit of output) will be an important determinant of prices, since labor is by far the most important element of total cost. Table 18.2 compares the growth of unit labor costs (in dollars) from 1977 to 1986 for various countries with which the United States competes in international trade. For any country besides the United States, these dollar costs can increase either if compensation rises faster than productivity or if the dollar depreciates in value (that is, if a dollar buys less foreign currency). For example, a German wage of 20 marks per hour is equivalent to $10 per hour if the dollar is worth two marks, because each mark can be converted to 50 cents. However, this wage rises to $20 per hour if the dollar falls in value to one mark, because then each mark can be converted to one dollar. Because dollars are cheaper for foreigners to acquire, a falling dollar lowers the cost of American labor compared to that in other countries. In contrast, a rising dollar raises the relative cost of American labor and therefore of American-made products (dollars become more expensive for foreigners to buy).

According to Table 18.2, from 1977 to 1980, unit labor costs measured in dollars rose faster in the United States than in Japan or Sweden; however, in all of the other countries, unit labor costs rose faster than in the United States. For example, West German unit labor costs (expressed in dollars) rose 47.9 percent, while those in the United States rose only 30.6 percent. Thus with the exceptions of Japan and Sweden, American manufacturing labor was better able to compete with Western industralized countries in 1980 than in 1977. In contrast, during the 1980–85 period, one in which we saw accelerated decline of unions in America, international competition told a different story. Unit labor costs for *all* of the countries besides the United States fell in terms of dollars. For example, the labor cost of the average West German manufactured good fell by about 33 percent in dollars, while American unit labor costs were rising by 11 percent. This does not mean that German compensation fell by 33 percent relative to productivity; in German marks, unit labor costs actually rose by about 9 percent.[1] Rather, the decreases in dollar unit labor costs shown in Table 18.2 were due to the appreciation of the dollar from 1980 to 1985. For example, the dollar was worth 1.82 German marks in 1980 but had risen in value to 2.68 marks by 1985.[2]

While currency movements placed enormous competitive pressure on American manufacturing industries in the 1980–85 period, the situation has alleviated somewhat since 1985. Table 18.2 shows sharp increases in the dollar value of unit labor costs for 1986 in all countries except the United States. These rises have been due to the falling dollar; for example, in 1986 the dollar was worth 2.29 German marks, and by November 1987, the dollar was worth only 1.72 marks (recall the 1985 value of 2.68 marks per dollar).[3]

It can be seen from Table 18.2 that by 1986 unit labor costs, in dollars, for all countries except Sweden and Great Britain showed roughly equivalent increases from 1977 levels. The continued fall of the dollar during 1987 undoubtedly further improved the American manufacturing position relative to these countries. International trade will continue to be a force requiring a response from American manufacturers; however, as long as the dollar does not return to its 1985 levels, import pressures on American manufacturers in the next few years are likely to be less severe than in the 1980–85 period. (In Appendix 18A we discuss the ability of high-wage countries to compete in foreign trade.)[4]

## Deregulation

As we mentioned in Chapters 10 and 12, starting in the 1970s the Federal government began to deregulate several key sectors of the economy: airlines, trucking, and communications. In each of these industries, the government has made it easier for new companies to enter the industry—which, in turn, should lower prices and expand both output and employment.

The trucking industry is regulated by the Interstate Commerce Commission (ICC), a Federal agency.[5] Beginning in 1976, the ICC made more types of trucking services exempt from regulation and made it easier for new applicants to enter the trucking business. In 1980, Congress passed the Motor Carrier Act, which allowed deregulation to continue. A major change in the way trucking is regulated is that, unlike before, a new company does not now

---

[1]  See U.S. Bureau of Labor Statistics, *Monthly Labor Review* 110 (August 1987): 105.

[2]  See U.S. Department of Commerce, *Statistical Abstract of the United States 1987* (Washington, DC: U.S. Government Printing Office, 1986): 839.

[3]  See U.S. Department of Commerce, *Statistical Abstract of the United States 1987*, p. 839 and *Wall Street Journal*, November 4, 1987, p. 37.

[4]  This discussion has not mentioned the pressure of imports from the Far East (other than Japan) or Latin America. Continued import penetration from these regions will place added competitive pressures on some sectors of the American economy.

[5]  This discussion of trucking deregulation is based on Martha Derthick and Paul J. Quirk, *The Politics of Deregulation* (Washington, DC: The Brookings Institution, 1985): Chapter 1.

have to prove to the ICC that its services are needed; instead, the burden of proof is on the rest of the industry to show that current service is adequate. Further, price competition is much freer, as the ICC has virtually eliminated collective rate-setting by the industry. As a result of these deregulation policies, there were over 27,000 licensed trucking companies in 1983, compared to 16,600 in 1977.

Events in the airline industry since the 1970s have been similar to those in trucking.[6] Starting in 1976, the Civil Aeronautics Board (CAB), the regulatory agency for the airline industry, began to reduce the effects of regulation. For example, it permitted greater freedom to offer discount fares and shifted the burden of proof (of already-adequate service in the industry) to the existing carriers from new entrants. In 1978, Congress passed the Airline Deregulation Act, which codified what the CAB had been doing. Further, the Act provided that as long as a new entrant was fit and able to give service, then entry was not to be denied on the grounds that it would divert traffic from existing carriers. Again, as in the case of trucking, many new companies, some of which were nonunion, entered the industry. Example 18.3 discusses some of the responses of airline companies and unions to deregulation.

Finally, in 1981, the Justice Department brought an antitrust suit against American Telephone & Telegraph (AT&T), in which the company was charged with monopolizing the telecommunications industry. An agreement was reached in 1982 between the Justice Department and AT&T whereby the company agreed to divest its 22 local divisions but keep its long-distance business.[7] As a result, by 1983 more than two hundred companies were competing with AT&T in long-distance service, and hundreds of companies manufacturing communications equipment were now competing with AT&T.[8]

## Further Economic and Legal Pressures

Despite well-publicized concessions made by unions in the 1980s (some of which were discussed in Chapter 10), union labor in the 1980s remains on average considerably more expensive than comparable nonunion labor. For example, controlling for other factors that affect wages (such as education, occupation, industry, and the like), one study estimated that in 1984 there was a 25-percent wage premium for blue-collar workers covered by collective bargaining compared to those without union coverage. For 1979, the figure was 27 percent; thus, union firms in the 1980s still face a considerable hourly labor-cost disadvantage compared to nonunion firms, despite the concessions

  [6] See Martha Derthick and Paul J. Quirk, *The Politics of Deregulation*, Chapter 1; and *Airline Deregulation: The Early Experience*, John R. Meyer and Clinton V. Oster, Jr. (eds.), (Boston: Auburn House, 1981): Chapter 1.

  [7] See Wallace E. Hendricks, ''Telecommunications,'' *Collective Bargaining in American Industry* David Lipsky and Clifford Donn (eds.) (Lexington, MA: D.C. Heath, 1987): 103–33.

  [8] See Martha Derthick and Paul J. Quirk, *The Politics of Deregulation*, p. 3.

EXAMPLE   18.1

## The Paradox of Large Wage Increases in Declining Sectors

The fact that union members' wages relative grew in the 1970s and early 1980s, as mentioned in Chapter 11, appears paradoxical against the backdrop of a declining union employment share and the increased resistance to unions among nonunion employers. The ten manufacturing industries with the highest growth in wages between 1970 and 1980 had a higher rate of union membership and lower output growth rates than the manufacturing sector as a whole. Indeed, the increase in the pay of steelworkers was the highest of all, rising during the '70s just as the steel industry was experiencing a wrenching decline in output of 16 percent! What explains the ability of unions to negotiate large wage increases from industries that are in relative, if not absolute, decline?

One possibility is that when industries that are capital-intensive experience declining demand for output (or at least not a growing one), their ability to substitute capital for labor in response to wage increases is diminished. Capital can be most easily substituted for labor when output is expanding and new capital is being purchased; however, once machinery and production processes are "in place," the substitution possibilities are substantially diminished. It is true that even with constant production levels substitution could occur when capital needed to be replaced, but much of the capital in manufacturing is long-lived and highly industry-specific (so that selling it "used" is not attractive). The result is that the demand for labor may be less elastic in contracting industries than in growing ones!

Rapidly rising wages exacerbate the contraction of output, however, and it is clear that when firms cannot cover their variable costs, plant closings become imminent. At this point (or when a majority of union members face the threat of permanent layoff) unions have incentives to engage in an "end-game" strategy and to agree to wage concessions in an effort to preserve the firms for which their members work. For example, following their extraordinary wage gains in the 1970s, unionized steelworkers since 1982 have traded away wage gains for increased job security (see Example 10.2).

SOURCE:  Colin Lawrence and Robert Z. Lawrence, "Manufacturing Wage Dispersion: An End Game Interpretation," *Brookings Papers on Economic Activity*, 1985–1, pp. 47–106.

that many unions have made in the 1980s.[9] Example 18.1 gives one explanation for the persistence of high union wages in the face of adverse economic conditions.

[9] See Richard Freeman, "In Search of Union Wage Concessions in Standard Data Sets," *Industrial Relations* 25 (Spring 1986): 135. These figures are higher than the 15–20-percent range discussed in Chapter 16 for overall union relative wage effects, because unions raise *blue-collar* wages by more than white-collar wages (see Table 16.1).

An additional economic factor affecting American labor in the 1980s and 1990s is the nature of competition in the product market. It is likely that consumer demand and international currency movements have become more fluid in the 1970s and 1980s than in the 1950s and 1960s.[10] In addition, as we have shown previously, American manufacturers are more vulnerable to foreign competition than previously. This combination of events, according to some experts, has increased companies' incentives to frequently change product lines and to move production from one location to another. It is predicted that, to compete successfully, companies will need workers who can do several types of jobs and can be reassigned at relatively short notice. In the 1980s and 1990s, there will be an increasing advantage to those companies that have flexible systems of allocating their production labor.

At the same time that deregulation and international competition are introducing increased flexibility into labor markets, several other governmental policy decisions are serving to decrease that flexibility. For example, as we discussed in earlier chapters, many states, through their court systems, are acting to limit firms' ability to discharge workers—the employment-at-will doctrine in the United States is under attack. In addition, in Chapter 8 we noted that amendments to age-discrimination legislation have reduced companies' freedom to retire older workers. Further, compulsory employer-funded health insurance may be on the agenda in the near future, as discussed in Chapter 4.

Another factor affecting labor markets in the future is an apparent change in people's attitudes toward unions. For example, when a random sample of Americans was asked in 1985 to rate the moral and ethical practices of people in 25 occupations, only car salesmen were rated more negatively than union leaders.[11] Groups receiving higher public approval included politicians, the media, advertising executives, and lawyers. Perhaps as significant is that public approval of unions has deteriorated since the 1950s; according to Gallup polls, in 1957, 76 percent of the public approved of unions, while in 1985 the figure had fallen to 58 percent.[12] Whether justified or not, the deteriorating public image of the labor movement is an additional factor with which unions are struggling. In view of the concessions unions have made in recent years, there are indications that this decline in the public's view of unions may have stopped. A December 1986 Gallup Poll showed a slight increase in the public's confidence in unions over the previous year.[13]

---

[10] This discussion is based on Michael J. Piore and Charles F. Sabel, *The Second Industrial Divide* (New York: Basic Books, 1984).

[11] This discussion of public attitudes toward unions draws from Seymour Martin Lipset, "Labor Unions in the Public Mind," *Unions in Transition,* Seymour Martin Lipset (ed.), (San Francisco: Institute for Contemporary Studies Press, 1986): 287–321.

[12] Percentages of the public giving favorable ratings of unions vary according to the poll and the particular wording of the questions. The long-run downward trend in public approval is clear, however.

[13] See Alex Kotlowitz, "Unions May Be Poised To End Long Decline, Recover Some Clout," *Wall Street Journal,* August 28, 1987, pp. 1 and 8.

# Management and Labor Responses to the Environment of the 1980s and 1990s

We have presented a discussion of some of the new challenges faced by labor and management in the 1980s. We now examine some of the ways they are coping in this new environment.

## Government Aid: Protection from Imports

In the face of foreign competition, many industries have successfully won a measure of government protection against low-cost imports. While this kind of response may save some jobs in the affected industries, it raises consumer costs above what they would be under free trade (see Appendix 18A). In general, it is likely that import protection given to some industries will lower employment in both the export sector and in domestic firms that compete with unregulated imports. More particularly, government policies that reduce imports for specific industries reduce the demand for both foreign products and foreign currencies. In the absence of any other policies, the value of foreign currencies will fall relative to that of the dollar, making dollars more expensive for foreigners to acquire. As a result, American exports will become more expensive for foreigners, and American imports of products not protected by government policy will become less expensive. It is therefore likely that any increases in production and employment in the protected industries will be accompanied by decreases in production and employment in the export sector and in industries competing with unprotected imports.

In Chapter 12, we discussed the unsuccessful attempts of the auto industry and UAW to obtain domestic content legislation—a requirement that a minimum percentage of the value of cars sold in the United States be made in America. However, the auto and steel industries have been able to obtain other forms of protection against imports. It is useful to examine the effects such efforts have on these sectors.[14]

**Steel Import Restraints.**  The United States has experienced three periods of steel-import restraints since 1969. First, from 1969 to 1974, a system of import quotas was negotiated with Japanese and European producers. One study estimated that, by themselves, these restraints raised American steel prices by 1.2 to 3.5 percent by reducing competition.[15] Next, from 1979 to 1982, the United States imposed a system of trigger prices, an effective floor below which foreign steel companies were not allowed to sell to the American customers. The system of trigger prices, in its early days, may have raised domestic-steel prices by 1 percent above what their level would otherwise

---

[14]  This discussion of import protection in the auto and steel industries draws from Robert W. Crandall, "The Effects of U.S. Trade Protection for Autos and Steel," *Brookings Papers on Economic Activity* 1987-1, pp. 271–88.

[15]  See Robert W. Crandall, *The U.S. Steel Industry in Recurrent Crisis: Policy Options in a Competitive World* (Washington, DC: The Brookings Institution, 1981): Chapter 5.

**Table 18.3**   U.S. Steel Consumption, Imports, and Prices, 1970–86
(Dollars per metric ton unless otherwise indicated)

| Year | Apparent consumption[a] (millions of tons) | Imports (millions of tons) | Import share (percent) | U.S. producers' price[b] | Antwerp spot export price[c] | U.S. price minus Antwerp price |
|------|------|------|------|------|------|------|
| 1970 | 97.1 | 13.4 | 13.8 | 149 | n.a. | — |
| 1971 | 102.5 | 18.3 | 17.9 | 159 | n.a. | — |
| 1972 | 106.6 | 17.7 | 16.6 | 169 | n.a. | — |
| 1973 | 122.5 | 15.2 | 12.4 | 179 | 249 | −70 |
| 1974 | 119.6 | 16.0 | 13.4 | 238 | 354 | −116 |
| 1975 | 89.0 | 12.0 | 13.5 | 261 | 237 | 24 |
| 1976 | 101.1 | 14.3 | 14.1 | 276 | 283 | −7 |
| 1977 | 108.4 | 19.3 | 17.8 | 298 | 251 | 47 |
| 1978 | 116.6 | 21.1 | 18.1 | 330 | 315 | 15 |
| 1979 | 115.0 | 17.5 | 15.2 | 365 | 369 | −4 |
| 1980 | 95.2 | 15.5 | 16.3 | 376 | 382 | −6 |
| 1981 | 105.4 | 19.9 | 18.9 | 412 | 357 | 55 |
| 1982 | 76.4 | 16.7 | 21.8 | 399 | 332 | 67 |
| 1983 | 83.5 | 17.1 | 20.5 | 376 | 293 | 83 |
| 1984 | 98.9 | 26.2 | 26.4 | 389 | 296 | 93 |
| 1985 | 96.4 | 24.3 | 25.2 | 366 | 273 | 93 |
| 1986 | 89.7 | 20.7 | 23.1 | 361[d] | 302 | 59 |

n.a.  Not available.

[a] Apparent consumption excludes changes in inventories.

[b] Weighted average of the prices of six carbon steel categories, using 1979 shipment shares as weights.

[c] Weighted average Free on Board (FOB) spot export price of six carbon steel products from Antwerp.

[d] Estimate by the author of the study (Robert W. Crandall).

SOURCE:  From "The Effects of U.S. Trade Protection for Autos and Steel" by Robert Crandall from *Brookings Papers on Economic Activity 1987,* William C. Brainard and George L. Perry, editors. Copyright © 1987 The Brookings Institution. Reprinted by permission.

have been.[16] Finally, in 1984, President Reagan announced a system of voluntary steel-import restraints that were to be in place for the 1985–89 period.

Table 18.3 shows a continually increasing import share in the steel industry until 1984, when the import share began to decline. While the sharp reduction in 1986 may be related to the declining value of the dollar, the domestic price level of steel since 1981 has been much higher than world prices, perhaps indicating that import restraints have indeed restricted foreign competition and allowed domestic producers to raise their prices. However, the import share is still high by historical standards, and overall American production of steel is much lower in the 1980s than it was in the 1970s.[17] Despite these import-restraint programs, the membership of the United Steel-

[16]  Robert W. Crandall, *The U.S. Steel Industry in Recurrent Crisis,* Chapter 5.

[17]  According to Table 18.3, consumption minus imports (which is approximately equal to domestic production) was 69 million tons in 1986, as opposed to 97.5 million tons in 1979.

**Table 18.4**   U.S. Automobile Sales and Import Shares, 1975–86

| Year | Total U.S. new car sales (millions) | Import share (percent) Total | Import share (percent) From Japan |
|------|------|------|------|
| 1975 | 8.63 | 18.2 | 9.4 |
| 1976 | 10.10 | 14.8 | 9.3 |
| 1977 | 11.18 | 18.5 | 12.4 |
| 1978 | 11.31 | 17.7 | 12.0 |
| 1979 | 10.64 | 21.9 | 16.6 |
| 1980 | 8.98 | 26.7 | 21.2 |
| 1981 | 8.53 | 27.3 | 21.8 |
| 1982 | 7.98 | 27.9 | 22.6 |
| 1983 | 9.18 | 26.0 | 20.9 |
| 1984 | 10.39 | 23.5 | 18.3 |
| 1985 | 11.04 | 25.7 | 20.1 |
| 1986 | 11.45 | 28.3 | 20.7 |

SOURCE:   From ''The Effects of U.S. Trade Protection for Autos and Steel'' by Robert Crandall from *Brookings Papers on Economic Activity 1987,* William C. Brainard and George L. Perry, editors. Copyright © 1987 The Brookings Institution. Reprinted by permission.

workers fell from 1.07 million in 1973 to 497 thousand in 1983, and we have seen in Example 10.2 that steelworkers have had to make wage concessions in the 1980s.[18] Thus, in the steel industry, import restraints have not prevented a precipitous decline in union membership and employment.

While the United Steelworkers union is not nearly as strong as it used to be, the industry itself rebounded in 1986 and 1987 due to a falling dollar, union concessions, and the rapid growth of small producers known as ''minimills.'' In early 1988 it was estimated that the cost to American producers of making a ton of steel fell to $431 from a 1982 level of $607; in contrast, the dollar cost per ton of steel made in Japan rose from $410 in 1982 to a level of $508.[19] However, with growth in the industry confined to minimills and with continued overcapacity in the large integrated steel companies, it is very difficult for the Steelworkers union to regain its former strength.

**Auto Import Restraints.**   In 1981, the United States made an agreement with Japan in which the Japanese voluntarily restrained automobile exports to the United States through 1988. Table 18.4 indicates generally increasing total-import and Japanese-import shares of American car sales until 1982. We then observed a sharp rollback until 1984, despite an appreciating dollar. The import share rose through 1986 but is likely to have fallen after that due to the falling dollar. One study found that American prices of imported Japanese cars were, on average, $2400 higher per car due to the reduced supply caused by the import restraints. This reduced competition allowed American pro-

[18]  See Leo Troy, ''The Rise and Fall of American Trade Unions: the Labor Movement from FDR to RR,'' *Unions in Transition,* Seymour Martin Lipset (ed.), p. 92.

[19]  See Gregory L. Miles, ''A Second Year of Hard-Forged Gains,'' *Business Week,* January 11, 1988, p. 94.

ducers to raise prices on domestically produced autos by $750–1000 more than they would have been able to charge without the restraints.[20] Another study casts doubts on whether the import restraints caused higher domestic *output;* this study argues that the restraints may have made the demand for domestically produced cars less elastic (by reducing the availability of foreign-produced substitutes), thereby raising the profit-maximizing price and reducing the profit-maximizing level of production.[21] Thus, while the restraints raised firm profits and may have allowed the UAW to avoid steeper concessions than those mentioned in Chapter 10, it is doubtful that they generated (or saved) a large number of jobs for UAW members. In any case, the import restraints did not prevent the UAW's membership from falling from a peak of 1.43 million in 1969 to 904 thousand in 1983.[22]

## Union Avoidance Strategies

In Chapters 10 and 11 we examined the strategies, some legal and some illegal, that firms have used to resist union organizing drives. In addition to directly combating union organizing, many firms are increasingly operating new plants on a nonunion basis and reducing their investments in older, unionized plants. Table 18.5 illustrates this strategy for several large companies in a variety of industries. In virtually each case, a substantially unionized company opened new plants that were to be operated on a nonunion basis. A study of company expansion decisions in the 1970s found that union avoidance was an important consideration.[23] The study covered roughly 1700 on-site plant expansions and over 1600 new plants constructed. Those firms most likely to add onto existing plants were nonunion at the site, and labor costs were an important consideration in decisions about new plant locations. An additional study of new plants in the 1975–83 period found that only 15 percent of them became unionized.[24] This figure is considerably below the overall percentage of *employees* unionized in manufacturing for this period, which was 27.8 percent in 1983, and since many white-collar workers in unionized plants do not have union representation, it is likely that even less than 15 percent of employees in these new plants are in fact unionized.[25]

Table 18.6 (on page 629) illustrates some characteristic of the nonunion labor-relations systems found at partially unionized companies. The vast majority of such companies seem concerned about making sure that employees have a chance to communicate with management in running the workplace. Such involvement can take the form of a grievance system (72.9

---

[20]   See Robert W. Crandall, "The Effects of U.S. Trade Protection for Autos and Steel," p. 276.

[21]   See Kala Krishna, "Trade Restrictions as Facilitating Practices," National Bureau of Economic Research Working Paper 1546, Cambridge, MA, January 1985.

[22]   See Leo Troy, "The Rise and Fall of American Trade Unions," p. 92.

[23]   See Roger W. Schmenner, *Making Business Location Decisions* (Englewood Cliffs, NJ: Prentice-Hall, 1982).

[24]   See Thomas A. Kochan, Harry C. Katz, and Robert B. McKersie, *The Transformation of American Industrial Relations* (New York: Basic Books, 1986): 67.

[25]   See Leo Troy, "The Rise and Fall of American Trade Unions," p. 87.

**Table 18.5**   Development of the Nonunion Sector via New Plants

| Company | Strategy |
| --- | --- |
| General Mills | A new plant was opened in Iowa on a nonunion basis. The company continues to operate existing facilities (all unionized) in Chicago, Buffalo, and on the West Coast. |
| Pepsi Cola | Over the past decade, this company has opened a number of distribution centers and warehouses on a nonunion basis, with the bottling plants remaining unionized. |
| Paper companies such as Mead, Champion International, International Paper, Union Camp, and Weyerhauser | All of these companies have opened new paper mills and kept them nonunion. This is in addition to fabricating plants, which have traditionally been less unionized and are becoming increasingly less unionized. |
| Mobil Oil | In the early 1970s, the company opened a new refinery at Joliet, Illinois, which has remained nonunion. |
| Tire companies such as Goodyear, Firestone, General, and Uniroyal | All of these companies have opened major new tire plants, often in the Oklahoma/Tennessee region, and these plants have been kept unorganized. |
| Corning Glass | Despite the fact that all of the plants in Corning, New York, and the expansion plants opened during the 1950s and 60s were unionized—often by the company voluntarily recognizing the union—when a new medical-products plant was opened in Medfield, Massachusetts, the decision was made to keep it union-free. |
| Cummins Engine | New plants opened during the 1970s in Jamestown, New York, and Charleston, South Carolina, have remained nonunion. The core facilities in Columbus, Indiana, are unionized by an independent union. |
| Pratt & Whitney | Satellite nonunion plants (to the Hartford, Connecticut, base) have been opened in Maine and Georiga. |
| ACF Industries | In the early 1980s the company closed a key carburetor plant in St. Louis and opened a replacement facility on a joint-venture basis with a European automobile company. The latter plant, located in North Carolina, has operated on a nonunion basis. |
| Piper Aircraft | This company opened a new facility in Florida. This plant, which produces many of the same models of aircraft as those produced at the home plant in Lock Haven, Pennsylvania, has remained nonunion. |
| Electric Boat Division of General Dynamics | A new major facility opened in Providence, Rhode Island, employing over four thousand workers, has remained nonunion despite the state's supportive union atmosphere and a number of organizing drives by the Craft Council that represents the workers at the home base in Groton, Connecticut. |

SOURCE: From *The Transformation of American Industrial Relations* by Thomas A. Kochan, Harry C. Katz, and Robert B. McKersie. Copyright © 1986 by Basic Books, Inc. Reprinted by permission of Basic Books, Inc., Publishers.

percent of these companies have such a mechanism) or other participation programs, such as regular meetings with employees. In addition, about 20–30 percent of these nonunion plants have flexible labor-allocation systems, including work sharing, work teams, and flexible work schedules. Over 30 percent have profit sharing, a flexible form of compensation, while about 20

**Table 18.6**   Workplace Innovations in Nonunion Plants Owned by
Partially Unionized Companies

| Question: *Does Your Company Encourage Managers to Set Up Any of the Following for Nonunion Groups?* | *% Yes* |
|---|---|
| Formal Complaint or Grievance Systems | 72.9% |
| Employee Participation Programs | 71.9 |
| All-Salaried Compensation Systems | 34.2 |
| Profit-Sharing Plans | 33.3 |
| Work Sharing | 31.8 |
| Flexible Work Schedules | 29.3 |
| Payment for Knowledge | 19.8 |
| Autonomous Work Teams | 19.3 |

SOURCE: From *The Transformation of American Industrial Relations* by Thomas A. Kochan, Harry C. Katz, and Robert B. McKersie. Copyright © 1986 by Basic Books, Inc. Reprinted by permission of Basic Books, Inc., Publishers.

percent base pay at least partially on the knowledge of workers. Pay-for-knowledge systems usually have a hierarchy of pay grades that a worker moves up as he or she learns to do additional jobs or becomes more skilled in a particular job.[26] This pay-for-knowledge system typically allows firms to assign workers to a variety of jobs; since pay is not tied to the job, but is instead keyed to what the employee knows, workers are presumably less averse to being reassigned to various jobs than if pay were tied to each job.[27]

Table 18.6 indicates an interest by partially unionized companies both in flexible forms of labor allocation and compensation and in union-like grievance systems (without outside arbitration) for their nonunion employees. We noted in Chapter 9, however, that nonunion employment systems are in general becoming more flexible in some of these dimensions. There is some evidence that union avoidance has reinforced the trend toward greater communication and flexibility shown in Table 18.6. Indeed, the trend is apparently stronger among partially unionized firms than among completely nonunion companies.[28] This difference may well be due to a greater perceived threat of unionism among partially organized companies than for those with no union representation. Later in this chapter, we will report on evidence that these work-organization innovations actually do deter union organization. Example 18.2 discusses the strategy of one firm that has both union and nonunion plants.

## Changes in Collective-Bargaining Agreements

**Wage levels.**   While expanding or reorganizing operations on a nonunion basis is an option for many companies in responding to the recent changes in

---

[26]   See G. Douglas Jenkins, Jr. and Nina Gupta, "The Payoffs of Paying for Knowledge," *National Productivity Review* 4 (Spring 1985): 121–30.

[27]   See G. Douglas Jenkins, Jr. and Nina Gupta, "The Payoffs of Paying for Knowledge."

[28]   Thomas Kochan, Harry Katz and Robert McKersie, *The Transformation of American Industrial Relations*, p. 100.

## Corporate Strategy in a Partially Unionized Firm

In this chapter, we have presented data suggesting that union avoidance is an important objective of many firms when they expand their operations. This example describes the expansion strategy of one partially unionized company. The company in question (its identity was kept confidential) was started in 1901 and it resisted unions until 1947, espousing a philosophy that workers did not need them if management treated the workers well. From 1947 to 1957, 80 percent of the workers in the firm's eight plants organized into independent unions, which were more loyal to the company than national or international unions typically would have been. After a 1958 merger, the company acquired 42 plants, 60 percent of which

| Work practice | % of Plants | |
|---|---|---|
| | Nonunion | Union |
| 1. Salaried payment for workers: (% employees) | 63% | 0% |
| 2. Pay-for-knowledge schemes | 40% | 0% |
| 3. COLA | 40% | 100% |
| 4. Job and wage structure: | | |
| No. of job classifications | 30 | 96 |
| No. of wage grades | 9 | 14 |
| No. of job classifications in maintenance | 4.8 | 11.3 |
| % of employed classified as "General Maintenance" | 38% | 1% |
| 5. Subcontracting | | |
| Obligation to meet with the union/employees | 0% | 100% |
| Reduced to zero before layoffs occur | 40% | 0% |
| Reduced proportionately | 0% | 33% |
| Reduced to zero except for some work | 0% | 67% |
| 6. Employees eligible to request a transfer | 100% | 67% |
| % of employees requesting transfers | 5–10% | 10–25% |
| Eligibility criteria for transfers: | | |
| Minimum service in the company | 20% | 0% |
| Minimum service in the department | 0% | 0% |
| Performance on current job | 80% | 33% |
| Willingness of the department to release | 40% | 0% |
| Cost of training in the new job | 20% | 0% |
| Minimum time on the present job | 40% | 100% |
| 7. Temporary transfers: | | |
| Higher pay on a higher-level job | 40% | 100% |
| 8. Dominant role of seniority: | | |
| Promotion decisions | 80% | 100% |
| Transfer decisions | 80% | 100% |
| Layoff decisions | 80% | 100% |
| Seniority relaxation for temporary transfers | 80% | 67% |
| 9. Supervisor prohibited from doing subordinates' work | 0% | 100% |

SOURCE: Adapted from "The Growth and Nature of the Nonunion Sector within a Firm" by Anil Verma and Thomas Kochan from Challenges and Choices Facing American Labor edited by Thomas A. Kochan. Copyright © 1985 by The Massachusetts Institute of Technology. Reprinted by permission.

were unorganized. Most of the unionized acquisitions were represented by international unions, a significant departure from the experience of the original company.

Partly because of the merger, the company was spurred to develop a nonunion strategy for its newly opening plants. From 1970 to 1982, the firm opened 17 new plants, 16 of which remained unorganized. When opening a new plant, the firm implemented autonomous work teams, pay for knowledge, and productivity bonuses. By 1982, the company was only 50-percent unionized, as compared to the 80-percent figure in 1957. As of 1982, total hourly labor costs were about 31-percent higher in the company's union plants than in its nonunion plants. In addition, the following table illustrates considerably greater flexibility in allocating and rewarding labor in the company's nonunion than in its union plants.

In particular, the table shows that the company's nonunion plants were more likely to put their workers on salary, have pay-for-knowledge, and not index their wages to consumer prices. The compensation system was thus more flexible for the nonunion plants. Further, there were many fewer job classifications in the nonunion plants, allowing the company to assign workers to various tasks. The pay-for-knowledge scheme gave workers the incentive to acquire the skills that would permit the firm to assign them to do these tasks. The nonunion plants have fewer limits on subcontracting, place more emphasis on performance and less on seniority in approving transfers and promotions, and have no restrictions on supervisors doing the work of subordinates.

The net effect of the wage differential between union and nonunion workers at this company and the different systems of personnel administration was that the company placed its new investment in nonunion plants. Between 1979 and 1983 it cut production and maintenance employment in its older, unionized plants from 15,902 to 10,089, while increasing the number of workers in nonunion plants from 10,741 to 11,017. These decisions made by the company indicate that it perceived considerable advantages in the nonunion employment system.

SOURCES:   Anil Verma and Thomas A. Kochan, "The Growth and Nature of the Nonunion Sector within a Firm," *Challenges and Choices Facing American Labor*, Thomas A. Kochan (ed.), (Cambridge, MA: The MIT Press, 1985): 89–117; and Thomas A. Kochan, Harry C. Katz and Robert B. McKersie, *The Transformation of American Industrial Relations* (New York: Basic Books, 1986): 105.

the economic environment, many firms have sought changes in the type of collective-bargaining contracts to which they will agree. In Chapter 10, we discussed wage concessions made by the Auto Workers and the Steelworkers during the deep recessions affecting their industries. In addition, in Chapter 12 we examined the breakdown of traditional pattern bargaining in the steel- and trucking-industry negotiations. While overall data on the incidence of industry patterns are not available, a survey of executives in unionized companies revealed a reduced emphasis in the 1980s on industry patterns compared with the 1970s. In particular, in 1983 only 39 percent of unionized companies ranked industry patterns as among the most important influences on their wage and benefit targets; in 1978, 81 percent had placed primary

**Table 18.7**   Annual Average Increase in Hourly Compensation
by Union Status, Private, Nonfarm Sector (in percent)

|  | *Union* | *Nonunion* |
|---|---|---|
| 1980 | 11.2% | 8.9% |
| 1981 | 10.7 | 9.4 |
| 1982 | 7.2 | 6.0 |
| 1983 | 5.8 | 5.7 |
| 1984 | 4.3 | 5.2 |
| 1985 | 2.6 | 4.6 |
| 1986 | 2.1 | 3.6 |
| Cumulative increase | 52.3% | 52.0% |

Note:  Compensation includes wages, salaries, and fringe benefits. Changes are measured from December of the previous year to December of the indicated year.

SOURCE:  U.S. Bureau of Labor Statistics, *Current Wage Developments* 39 (March 1987), Table 9.

importance on patterns. Conversely, 37 percent of these executives placed primary importance on their own company's labor costs or productivity in forming wage and benefit targets in 1983, as compared to an 8-percent figure for 1978.[29]

In the aggregate, the changes in management philosophy already discussed have been associated with a decrease in the union-nonunion hourly labor cost differential, although the retrenchment is not dramatic. Table 18.7 reveals the annual increases in total hourly compensation in the union and nonunion sectors. From 1980 to 1982, union compensation rose faster than nonunion compensation, while since 1984, the opposite has occurred. Table 18.8 shows that union wage concessions, as measured by the incidence of wage cuts or the forgoing of wage increases, were concentrated in the recession years of 1982 and 1983. However, as of 1986, a substantially higher number of union workers were still making wage concessons than in the 1979–81 period (although inflation was also lower in 1986).

While union compensation has risen more slowly than that of nonunion workers since 1983, the differences in these rates of change are modest, and over the 1980–86 period, union and nonunion labor costs have risen by roughly equal percentages. Further, forces other than union wage concessions were at work. The years 1980 and 1981 were periods in which inflation outran workers' expectations, while in the 1982–86 period, inflation was lower than expected. Union workers are far more likely than nonunion workers to have automatic cost-of-living allowances (COLAs), while nonunion workers are much more likely to have expected inflation incorporated into their basic wages. Thus, when inflation is higher than expected, union wages tend to rise faster, and when inflation is lower than anticipated nonunion wages tend to

[29]  See Audrey Freedman, *The New Look in Wage Policy and Employee Relations,* Conference Board Report 865 (New York: The Conference Board, 1985): 9.

**Table 18.8**   Proportion of Union Workers with Increases, Decreases, or No Wage Change Under Settlements Covering 1000 Workers or More in Private Industry, 1979–86 (in percent)

| Year | First year | | | Over the life of contract | | |
|---|---|---|---|---|---|---|
| | *Increases* | *Decreases* | *No Change* | *Increases* | *Decreases* | *No Change* |
| 1979 | 96 | 0 | 4 | 100 | 0 | 0 |
| 1980 | 100 | 0 | 0 | 100 | 0 | 0 |
| 1981 | 92 | 5 | 3 | 94 | 5 | 1 |
| 1982 | 56 | 2 | 42 | 64 | 1 | 35 |
| 1983 | 63 | 15 | 22 | 73 | 13 | 14 |
| 1984 | 77 | 5 | 18 | 84 | 4 | 12 |
| 1985 | 63 | 3 | 33 | 85 | 3 | 12 |
| 1986 | 70 | 9 | 21 | 79 | 9 | 13 |

SOURCE:   John Lacombe and Joan Borum, "Major Labor Contracts in 1986 Provided Record Low Wage Adjustments," *Monthly Labor Review* 110 (May 1987): Table 2.

rise faster.[30] A further influence tending to compress the union-nonunion wage differential recently is the normal cyclical pattern: it falls as unemployment falls and rises as unemployment increases (see Chapter 16).

The slower growth of union compensation continued into 1987; from January to June 1987, union compensation rose at a 2.2-percent annual rate, while nonunion compensation rose at a 3.8-percent annual rate.[31] It would take several years of these levels of differences in compensation increases before the union-nonunion compensation differential would change substantially, however.

**Lump-sum payments and two-tiered payment systems.**   In addition to requesting and winning lower wage and benefit increases, management has been able to institute new forms of compensation: lump-sum payments and the two-tiered payment system. A lump-sum payment plan replaces some or all of scheduled wage increases with one lump payment. An advantage for companies of such plans is that many benefits, such as overtime pay and defined-benefit pensions, are tied to hourly wage rates, and lump-sum payments are not included in the calculation of wage rates. In addition, lump-sum payments do not become part of the wage base upon which future negotiations are centered. Thus, this form of compensation may help firms avoid being locked into high rates of pay if a recession comes along.

The incidence of lump-sum pay plans is on the increase; 40 percent of workers covered under newly negotiated major contracts (those covering at

[30]   Recall from the previous chapter that in the absence of a COLA, an increase in expected inflation will be reflected in wage increases, but an increase in inflation that was not foreseen would not immediately affect wages. See Wallace E. Hendricks and Lawrence M. Kahn, *Wage Indexation in the United States: Cola or Uncola?* (Cambridge, MA: Ballinger, 1985).

[31]   See U.S. Bureau of Labor Statistics, *Monthly Labor Review* 110 (October 1987), Table 24.

least 1000 workers) in 1986 were to receive lump-sum payments; this figure represented an increase over the 31-percent incidence for 1984 and 1985 negotiations. Further, among those covered by lump-sum plans negotiated in 1986, about 10 percent tied the payment to company profits.[32] Thus, for these workers, the lump-sum-payment system represents a variant of the idea of share wages discussed in the previous chapter.

As we discussed in Chapter 15, two-tiered pay systems put newly hired employees on a lower pay scale than current employees in an attempt to preserve the compensation levels of incumbent employees while giving the firm cost concessions on new hires. Table 18.9 (on page 636) illustrates the incidence of such plans, by industry, over the 1983-86 period. Two-tier systems are more common in nonmanufacturing industries than in manufacturing, and they are the rule in airlines due to the effects of deregulation (see Example 18.3).

There are two kinds of two-tier plans. First, some plans are temporary in the sense that after some time on the job, new employees eventually are placed on the same pay schedule as those hired earlier. Second, some plans are permanent in that new workers will never reach the same scale on which previously hired employees are paid. Roughly half of unionized companies with two-tier plans have the temporary variety, 30 percent have permanently separate scales, and the remainder use a combination of both types of plan.[33]

While two-tier plans are a short-term compromise between current union members and companies under cost pressure, they may cause problems for both parties. Such systems may lead to internal union problems if newer union members (who may not have voted on the initial contract calling for a two-tier system) feel underpaid compared to upper-tier employees doing the same work.[34] Unions may even be vulnerable to charges that they have violated their duty of fair representation of their junior members, particularly those unions that agree to permanent two-tier plans.[35] As for employers, one study of two-tier systems found that after their implementation, 25 percent of companies experienced declining productivity, 63 percent had no change, and 13 percent reported higher productivity.[36] Declining productivity was blamed

---

[32] See John Lacombe and Joan Borum, "Major Labor Contracts in 1986 Provided Record Low Wage Adjustments," *Monthly Labor Review* 110 (May 1987): 11; Joan Borum and James Conley, "Wage Restraints Continue in 1985 Major Contracts," *Monthly Labor Review* 109 (April 1986): 23; John Lacombe and James Conley, "Major Agreements in 1984 Provided Record Low Wage Increases," *Monthly Labor Review* 108 (April 1985): 40.

[33] See Sanford Jacoby and Daniel J. B. Mitchell, "Management Attitudes Toward Two-Tier Pay Plans," *Journal of Labor Research* 7 (Summer 1986): 229.

[34] For example, American Airlines estimated that its two-tier system lowered starting salaries by 32 percent, a substantial savings. In addition, reductions of entry-level wages of $4–5 an hour have been negotiated in two-tier plans in the copper, trucking, auto, and aerospace industries, cuts that are a similar percentage of starting pay as American Airlines' pay cuts. See Shane R. Premeaux, R. Wayne Mondy, and Art L. Bethke, "The Two-Tier Wage System," *Personnel Administrator* 31 (November 1986): 92–93.

[35] See Malcolm H. Liggett, "The Two-Tiered Labor-Management Agreement and the Duty of Fair Representation," *Labor Law Journal* 38 (April 1987): 236–242.

[36] The study was conducted by Daniel J. B. Mitchell and was summarized in Mollie H. Bowers and Roger D. Roderick, "Two-Tier Pay Systems: The Good, the Bad and the Debatable," *Personnel Administrator* 32 (June 1987): 106.

**EXAMPLE   18.3**

## Deregulation, Concession Bargaining, Two-Tier Wage Structures, and the Airlines

As we have noted in this chapter, the *Airline Deregulation Act of 1978* opened up the airline industry to competition. Price competition was permitted on routes with more than one carrier, and new airlines, which were often nonunion and had lower labor costs, began to compete with the existing carriers. As a result, profits of many of the established carriers dropped dramatically. Indeed, during the recession of the early 1980s, many carriers suffered substantial losses. Revenue and employment fell substantially at the established, unionized carriers; one study suggests that their employment of mechanics had fallen by 15 to 20 percent as of 1983 because of deregulation.

These forces led the established airlines to "request" that their unions make *concessions,* in the form of reduced wages and fringes and longer workweeks, in exchange for at least implicit promises that employment levels would be maintained. In some cases concessions were made voluntarily by the unions, in the sense that new contracts were written that agreed to temporary or permanent concessions. In at least one case, however, an airline (Continental) filed for bankruptcy and unilaterally reduced its employees' wages by almost 50 percent in an attempt to compel the unions to negotiate new contracts (see Example 14.2).

Often these concessions took the form of the adoption of *two-tier wage structures.* Over 60 percent of the settlements negotiated in 1985 that applied to the previously regulated airline carriers contained such provisions. These provisions have the effect, of course, of reducing the costs of newly hired employees relative to more senior employees, and they provide a financial incentive for the airline to try to substitute newer for more senior employees. At least one airline, Northwest, tried to take advantage of this potential savings by "encouraging" senior flight attendants to take early retirement through offers of cash and travel benefits.

SOURCES:  "Airlines in Turmoil," *Business Week,* October 10, 1983, pp. 98–102; David Card, "The Impact of Deregulation on the Employment and Wages of Airline Mechanics," *Industrial and Labor Relations Review* 39 (July 1986): 527–38; Sanford Jacoby and Daniel Mitchell, "Management Attitudes Toward Two-Tier Pay Plans," *Journal of Labor Research* 7 (Summer 1986): 221–37; Bureau of National Affairs, "Facts for Bargaining," no. 1062, February 13, 1986.

on reduced morale caused by the two-tier systems. Moreover, implementing a two-tier plan may leave a company open to charges of discrimination if women and minorities are disproportionately represented in the lower tier.[37] It is likely that some combination of these problems has led to the slight decline in two-tier systems in 1986 shown in Table 18.9.

---

[37] See Sanford Jacoby and Daniel J. B. Mitchell, "Management Attitudes Toward Two-Tier Pay Plans."

**Table 18.9** Percentage of Collective-Bargaining Contracts with Two-Tier Wage Settlements, by Industry

| Industry | 1983 | 1984 | 1985 | 1986 |
|---|---|---|---|---|
| All industries, excluding Construction | 5 | 8 | 11 | 10 |
| Manufacturing | 2 | 4 | 6 | 6 |
| Chemicals | 1 | 1 | 0 | 2 |
| Electrical machinery | 0 | 5 | 16 | 3 |
| Fabricated metals | 0 | 15 | 0 | 10 |
| Food | 5 | 4 | 17 | 4 |
| Instruments | 0 | 13 | 0 | 0 |
| Machinery, except electrical | 3 | 11 | 10 | 5 |
| Misc. manufacturing | 0 | 10 | 0 | 0 |
| Paper | 2 | 2 | 8 | 6 |
| Petroleum | 0 | 4 | 0 | 4 |
| Printing | 1 | 0 | 0 | 5 |
| Textiles | 0 | 5 | 0 | 0 |
| Transportation equipment | 13 | 16 | 20 | 24 |
| Nonmanufacturing | 9 | 17 | 18 | 16 |
| Airlines | 8 | 35 | 62 | 70 |
| Communications | 0 | 7 | 0 | 2 |
| Health services | 0 | 9 | 7 | 12 |
| Insurance and finance | 0 | 5 | 0 | 27 |
| Motor transportation | 5 | 17 | 16 | 20 |
| Services except health | 3 | 11 | 5 | 22 |
| Utilities | 4 | 14 | 0 | 2 |
| Wholesale and retail trade | 28 | 32 | 37 | 25 |

SOURCE: From "The 2-Tier Wage System Is Found To Be 2-Edged Sword by Industry" by Agis Salpukas, *The New York Times*, July 21, 1987. Copyright © 1987 by The New York Times Company. Reprinted by permission.

**Changes in the Organization of Work—New Work Rules, Quality of Worklife Programs, and Labor-Management Cooperation.** We have noted in several places that union work rules can reduce productivity by requiring more workers than necessary to be hired to achieve a given level of production. Both the increasing competitive pressures on companies and union demands for job security (as discussed in Chapter 15) have made workplace flexibility a more important concern for companies. In 1983, a survey of unionized companies showed that 63 percent of these firms had recently obtained work-rule concessions from their unions.[38] Such changes included fewer job titles, more managerial discretion in giving out overtime, and fewer restrictions on subcontracting. Further, this concern over work rules appears to have increased in the 1980s. A survey of unionized companies found that in 1978 about 50 percent placed a high priority on getting more flexibility in the assignment of employees, while by 1983 the figure had risen to about 70 percent.[39] Offering union workers more job security, a trend

---

[38] See Thomas Kochan, Harry Katz and Robert McKersie, *The Transformation of American Industrial Relations*, p. 118.

[39] See Audrey Freedman, *The New Look in Wage Policy and Employee Relations*, p. 15.

discussed in Chapter 15, may be a way of reducing union resistance to increased flexibility of assignment.

Several important unions have made work-rule concessions in the 1980's. For example, in 1982 the Teamsters permitted over-the-road drivers to make local pickups, thus reducing the number of drivers a company needs to hire.[40] In addition, in 1981 the pilots at United Airlines agreed to reduce the cockpit crew from three to two on Boeing 737 flights and to increase the flying time expected of each pilot. In return, the company agreed to a no-layoff provision.[41]

At the same time that companies have been pressing unions for less restrictive work rules, there has been an expansion since the 1970s in programs to increase the participation and involvement of individuals in the production process.[42] Such innovations, called Quality-of-Work-Life (QWL) programs, often involve work teams, regular meetings with management, and rewards for improved product quality. These QWL programs were first implemented in the 1970s, and by 1985 36 percent of workers said that there was a QWL program at their workplace. Union workers were as likely to have reported such a program as nonunion workers.

Quality-of-Work-Life programs are intended to increase productivity and product quality by increasing employee morale. In addition, it is hoped that regular communication with management will raise the degree to which workers identify with the goals of the firm. In a study of the effects of QWL programs at General Motors, it was found that a plant's product quality (as measured by the reduced incidence of faults and demerits in inspections of output) was positively related to the presence of a QWL program, other things equal.[43] Such a finding is at least suggestive that QWL programs can have their desired effect. Another study found that other things equal, nonunion firms using such QWL innovations as grievance systems, worker-participation plans, and communication with employees were better able than otherwise to win elections against union certification or to keep new plants from becoming organized.[44] It is possible that in both of these studies we are merely observing that workers producing better-quality output and having more pro-company attitudes are more receptive to the implementation of such plans. However, their spread suggests that many companies believe QWL programs are cost-effective (see Example 18.4 for an illustration of some of these trends in work rules and QWL innovations).

---

[40] Thomas Kochan, Harry Katz, and Robert McKersie, *The Transformation of American Industrial Relations*, p. 118.

[41] See Herbert Northrup, "The New Employee-Relations Climate in Airlines," *Industrial and Labor Relations Review* 36 (January 1983): 167–81.

[42] This discussion of worker participation is based on Thomas Kochan, Harry Katz, and Robert McKersie, *The Transformation of American Industrial Relations*, Chapter 6.

[43] Harry C. Katz, Thomas A. Kochan, and Kenneth R. Gobeille, "Industrial Relations Performance, Economic Performance, and QWL Programs: An Interplant Analysis," *Industrial and Labor Relations Review* 37 (October 1983): 3–17.

[44] See Jack Fiorito, Christopher Lowman, and Forrest D. Nelson, "The Impact of Human Resource Policies on Union Organizing," *Industrial Relations* 26 (Spring 1987): 113–126.

EXAMPLE    18.4

## Workplace Innovations in the Union Sector: GM's Saturn Plant

In 1985, GM and the UAW agreed on the design of an innovative labor-relations system at the firm's Saturn Corporation division. This branch was scheduled to begin production in 1989 of small cars that compete in price and quality with imports. Under the agreement, production takes place in autonomous work teams consisting of 6 to 15 employees, with each worker undertaking several tasks and assuming some planning and quality-control tasks traditionally handled by supervisors. Union representatives serve on a strategic advisory committee, which conducts long-range business planning. Thus, the work system embodies many aspects of the Quality-of-Worklife programs discussed in this chapter.

It was agreed that compensation would be more flexible at Saturn than at traditional auto plants. Each employee is paid on a salaried basis, eliminating the need for punching-in and watching the time clock. Base wages are 80 percent of what autoworkers at other plants make; however, there are bonuses based on both work-team performance and how well the Saturn Corporation does. These bonuses, which were to be determined in subsequent negotiations, could raise workers' total earnings above what other GM workers receive. Barring catastrophic events or severe economic conditions, 80 percent of the Saturn workers will be protected against layoffs, a seemingly stronger job-security provision than offered by the 1987 GM and Ford contracts covering other auto workers (see Example 15.1).

While the Saturn plant embodies many of the innovations discussed in this chapter, several labor leaders have expressed reservations about such a system. First, they fear that the committee system will usurp the traditional adversarial functions of a union. Second, some do not wish to see such a strong link between pay and performance, a link that might be subject to management manipulation. The choice facing the UAW in this case, however, was whether GM was going to build a plant at all; having some untraditional union jobs was deemed by the union to be better than none at all.

SOURCE:   Harry C. Katz, "Automobiles," *Collective Bargaining in American Industry*, David B. Lipsky and Clifford B. Donn (eds.), (Lexington, MA: D.C. Heath, 1987): 13–53.

While the increased use of QWL programs for unionized companies has obvious potential for increasing productivity and product quality, certain aspects of their implementation may be in violation of our Federal labor laws. For example, recall from Chapter 11 that it is an unfair labor practice for an employer to dominate or interfere with a labor union. When a company sets up a QWL plan and has ongoing meetings with unionized employees, does this plan constitute employer domination of a union? According to a recent Department of Labor study, the U.S. Federal Court system has in effect ruled that such a plan does not constitute an unfair labor practice as long as it is a sincere attempt to increase workers' participation in company decision-making and is not a deliberate attempt to infringe on workers' right to choose a union to represent them.[45]

A further legal issue raised by QWL programs concerns the duty of union leaders to represent their members. If a union's leader participates in a QWL program, its members may be able to compel him or her to divulge sensitive company information learned during the process. This possibility may deter union leaders from participating in such programs.[46] Additionally, joint labor-management committees may appear to usurp the union's right to negotiate over mandatory issues (see Chapter 11 for a discussion of the distinction between mandatory and voluntary issues) such as work scheduling, overtime, promotion, discipline, and so forth. However, a union can protect itself against charges of failure to adequately represent its members on such issues by making sure that under such labor-management committees, workers retain their due-process rights through the grievance procedure.[47]

**Employee Buyouts and Employee-Stock-Ownership Plans.** In Chapter 15, profit-sharing and employee-stock-ownership plans were mentioned as responses by unions and management to change or economic distress. An extreme example of such a response occurs when, faced with their employer's impending bankruptcy, workers have agreed to buy out a company to save their jobs (see Example 15.3). As of 1983, it was estimated that 60 companies had been bought by their workers to stop a shutdown, while approximately 50,000 jobs had been directly saved. Further, with minor exceptions, such reorganized companies, as of 1983, had invariably remained viable.[48]

Such buyouts usually involve large wage concessions in return for some amount of stock in the company. For example, in 1981–82, the employees of Hyatt Clark Industries, Inc., a 1700-employee division of GM that the parent company was considering closing down, acquired their division.[49] The workers, who were represented by the UAW, took a 25-percent cut in wages and a 50-percent cut in benefits; in return, a financing package was put together with GM and several banks to buy the division's assets. It was doubtful that, even though bonuses and profit sharing were part of this package, employee compensation would reach what it was under the standard UAW contract. However, the employees evidently preferred working for Hyatt at reduced wages to their next-best alternatives.

---

[45] See Stephen I. Schlossberg and Steven M. Fetter, *U.S. Labor Law and the Future of Labor-Management Cooperation* (Washington, DC: U.S. Department of Labor, 1986).

[46] Stephen I. Schlossberg and Steven M. Fetter, *U.S. Labor Law and the Future of Labor-Management Cooperation*, p. 25.

[47] Stephen I. Schlossberg and Steven M. Fetter, *U.S. Labor Law and the Future of Labor-Management Cooperation*, p. 25.

[48] See Linda Wintner, *Employee Buyouts: An Alternative to Plant Closings,* Conference Board Research Bulletin 140 (New York: The Conference Board, 1983): 4. Of course, this 50,000 estimate does not mean that 50,000 additional jobs were created in the economy. Had these plants closed, many of the laid-off workers would have found other jobs, although probably at less pay than they were making even after wage concessions.

[49] This discussion is taken from Linda Wintner, *Employee Buyouts: An Alternative to Plant Closings,* pp. 7–12.

While buying out a failing company is an extreme measure, there have been several instances in which unions have helped out their companies by acquiring some of the firms' stock. For example, in the 1983–85 period, there were 16 cases of employee-stock-ownership plans and worker representation on boards of directors in the trucking industry.[50] These conversions were spurred by the threat of bankruptcy induced by deregulation and the entry of nonunion competition into the over-the-road trucking industry. The Teamsters' Union members under such plans do not acquire a majority of stock, and they leave to management the task of running the business. While participation is voluntary, a minimum of 80–90-percent participation by the employees is required by creditors in bankruptcy situations.

There have also been several cases in which unions have been granted membership on boards of directors in return for wage and work-rule concessions. Examples include Chrysler, Pan Am, Eastern Airlines, Western Airlines, Wheeling-Pittsburgh Steel, Weirton Steel (see Example 15.3), and Rath Meatpacking. While being represented on the board of directors gives a union some say in the running of the business, in many of these cases control remains with management, as is true in the trucking industry and in the case of Hyatt Clark discussed earlier in this chapter.

## Union Strategies in the 1980s and 1990s

Much of this chapter and portions of Chapter 10 depict unions as being on the defensive. Membership is declining, competitive pressures are severe, many companies are aggressively resisting unions, and public opinion is considerably less positive toward the labor movement than in years past. In Chapters 10 and 11, we mentioned some strategies to reverse this trend suggested in 1985 by the AFL-CIO, including corporate campaigns and improving services offered to workers. As we noted in Chapter 11, the passage of labor laws more favorable to unions might help slow the decline of union coverage, although the labor movement has not been successful recently in obtaining Congressional approval of its legislative agenda. One partial legislative success for unions occurred in June 1987, when the U.S. House of Representatives passed a bill outlawing the practice of "double breasting" in the construction industry. This bill would prevent a unionized company from setting up a nonunion subsidiary, but it was not clear whether the more conservative Senate would go along with such a measure. In any case, such a bill is at best defensive from the standpoint of the union movement.[51]

While legislation can help unions, new organizing techniques are needed as well. For example, there is some evidence that union organizers are listening more to the workers they are trying to unionize—this often takes the form of employee surveys similar to the communication approaches taken by

---

[50] This example is based on Thomas Kochan, Harry Katz, and Robert McKersie, *The Transformation of American Industrial Relations*, pp. 193–4.

[51] Bureau of National Affairs, *Daily Labor Report*, No. 116, June 18, 1987.

successful companies.[52] In addition, unions are attempting to organize white-collar workers, a group with which they have not had much success. Unions may well also place more emphasis on organizing small companies, because a union would have more economic leverage there than at large firms.[53] Of course, to the extent that small companies are often in competitive industries, it may be difficult, as seen in Chapter 12, to keep them organized.

The era of cost cutting by both union and nonunion firms may have put unions in a better light than in previous years. A recent survey of 220,000 workers found concerns about job security and increased dissatisfaction with their supervisors, issues that could make workers more receptive to unions.[54] Further, as we have noted earlier in this chapter, the decline in the labor movement's public image may have halted.

# The Future of the Employment Relationship

The increased openness of the American economy to international competition and the spirit of deregulation are forcing union and nonunion firms to control their labor costs and improve product quality. We seem to be in an era of increasing flexibility of compensation, as workers are being asked to bear more of the risk of business fluctuations than in the past. On the other hand, increased government regulation in the form of exceptions to employment-at-will, and the possibility of plant-closing and health-insurance legislation, will put even more pressure on companies. To maintain even its relatively low levels of union coverage of the economy, the labor movement is likely to have to accept a lower union pay premium over nonunion workers and to allow unionized companies to use many of the employment practices of nonunion firms.

This chapter has emphasized economic and legal pressures that are constraining both union and nonunion companies. While it is risky to speculate about the future, demographic trends that we can forecast are likely to affect employment in the 1990s. A recent study commissioned by the Employment and Training Administration of the U.S. Department of Labor made the following forecasts for the year 2000.[55]

1.  The labor force will grow more slowly than in the past. For example, while the labor force grew 24.1 percent from 1970 to 1980, it is expected to grow by 18.0 percent from 1980 to 1990 and by only 15.6 percent for the decade ending in the year 2000.

---

[52] See Kenneth Gilberg and Nancy Abrams, "Union Organizing: New Tactics for New Times," *Personnel Administrator* 32 (July 1987): 53.

[53] See Kirkland Ropp, "State of the Unions," *Personnel Administrator* 32 (July 1987): 38–39.

[54] Alex Kotlowitz, "Unions May Be Poised to End Long Decline, Recover Some Clout," pp. 1 and 8.

[55] See William B. Johnston, *Workforce 2000: Work and Workers for the 21st Century* (Indianapolis: Hudson Institute, 1987). Except where otherwise indicated, the forecasts and data reported here are taken from Chapters 2 and 3 of this study.

2.   The labor force will age considerably by the year 2000. By that time, the share of the labor force 35 years and older is expected to reach 62 percent, compared with 51 percent in 1985.

3.   The share of women in the labor force is expected to grow from 42.5 percent in 1980 to 45.8 percent in 1990 and to 47.5 percent by 2000.

4.   New job creation will be heavily tilted toward occupations requiring high levels of skill and education. While in 1987 about 22 percent of existing jobs required at least four years of college, roughly 30 percent of the new jobs created by the year 2000 will require at least that amount of education.

5.   The economy is expected to continue to shift towards the production of services, with an increasing share of employment in that sector. For example, employment in service industries is expected to grow by 32.9 percent from 1985 to 2000, while that in goods-producing industries is predicted to shrink by 8.8 percent over that time period.

If these demographic and economic forecasts come to pass, the employment relationship is likely to be changed in several ways. First, the shrinking and aging of the labor force will mean a tightening of the labor market for entry-level employees. In combination with the expected increased demand for highly skilled workers, this tightening may raise companies' incentives to invest in the training of their new workers; the alternative is to pay escalating salaries to highly educated entry-level workers. Thus, we would expect more businesses to implement training programs (such as the one described in Example 4.6).

The aging of the labor force is also expected to increase the costs of company-sponsored health insurance and pension plans.[56] To the extent that these increased costs are associated with the number of workers rather than the hours of work, we expect demand-side incentives for longer work hours. (Of course, *actual* work hours in the future also depend on the extent to which increased wages and incomes affect workers' desires for shorter work hours.)

The aging of the labor force and the expected increased incidence of two-career families are likely to mean a geographically less-mobile work force. The compensating wage differentials firms must pay to get workers to relocate are likely to increase (see Example 6.2), but if workers are any less prone to quit their jobs, turnover will be reduced and company investments in firm-specific training may become more profitable.

Finally, the shift toward services is likely to mean that a larger share of the work force will be employed in small establishments (in the 1968–77 period, the average manufacturing workplace had 60 employees, while the figure in services was only 11). A larger share of workers would likely be working in small work teams rather than large bureaucracies. The influence of

---

[56]   See John B. O'Donnell, ''Employee Benefits in the Year 2000,'' *Compensation and Benefits Review* 19 (September–October 1987): 25–35.

work rules and rigid job-assignment patterns, already on the wane due to increased competition, will probably continue to decline as a result of this shift.

# Review Questions

1. What economic pressures are currently constraining the union movement? What responses can unions offer?
2. "Import restraints save high-wage jobs and thus contribute to the overall economic well-being of workers." Comment.
3. What advice would you offer AFL-CIO organizers in attempting to unionize white-collar workers?
4. Evaluate the following competing claims about employee buyouts of failing companies:
    a. "Employee buyouts should be discouraged, since they prevent the natural shrinkage of sectors in which there is overcapacity."
    b. "Employee buyouts should be encouraged, since they save many workers' jobs and pour money back into the communities where the affected plants are located."

# Selected Readings

Audrey Freedman, *The New Look in Wage Policy and Employee Relations,* Conference Board Report 865 (New York: The Conference Board, 1985.)

Thomas A. Kochan (ed.), *Challenges and Choices Facing American Labor* (Cambridge, MA: The MIT Press, 1985).

Thomas A. Kochan, Harry C. Katz, and Robert B. McKersie, *The Transformation of American Industrial Relations* (New York: Basic Books, 1986).

Seymour Martin Lipset (ed.), *Unions in Transition* (San Francisco: Institute for Contemporary Studies Press, 1986).

David B. Lipsky and Clifford B. Donn (eds.), *Collective Bargaining in American Industry* (Lexington, MA: D.C. Heath, 1987).

Michael J. Piore and Charles F. Sabel, *The Second Industrial Divide* (New York: Basic Books, 1984).

Linda Wintner, *Employee Buyouts: An Alternative to Plant Closings,* Conference Board Research Bulletin 140 (New York: The Conference Board, 1983).

# APPENDIX 18A

## International Trade and the Demand for Labor: Can High-Wage Countries Compete?

The question of how international trade affects labor demand in the long run has been highlighted recently by the increasing importance of exports and imports in the United States economy. The public is often inclined to support laws restricting free trade on the grounds that lower wages and living standards in other countries inevitably cause employment losses among American workers—losses that could only be mitigated by a large decline in American living standards. This appendix will show that international trade does not depend on relative living standards, and that two countries will generally find trade mutually beneficial regardless of their respective wage rates. To keep things simple, we assume that goods and services can be traded across countries but that capital and labor are immobile.

### Production Without International Trade

Consider two countries, which we shall call the United States and China, that can use two factors of production—labor and capital—to produce two goods, food and clothing.[1] Suppose that in the United States, if all inputs were devoted to food production, 200 million units of food could be produced; similarly, if all available resources were devoted to the production of clothing, 100 million units could be produced. If, say, 15 percent of the resources were devoted to food and 85 percent to clothing, 30 million units of food and 85 million units of clothing could be produced. Thus, we assume that if the United States wants to produce one more unit of clothing, it must give up two

---

[1] The assumptions of two countries, factors, and goods, are made in order to simplify the analysis. The results are applicable to more complex situations.

units of food; conversely, to produce one more unit of food, it must forgo one-half unit of clothing.[2]

The ultimate mix of food and clothing produced by the United States depends on consumer preferences. If the United States is assumed to have 100 million workers and chooses to allocate 15 percent to the production of food, incomes would average 0.30 units of food and 0.85 units of clothing per worker.

Let us turn now to China. Because the quality and quantity of its factors of production are likely to differ from those of the United States, the relative amounts of food and clothing it can produce are likely to differ as well. Suppose that China can produce either 300 million units of food and no clothing, or 500 million units of clothing and no food. As in the United States, food can be "transformed" into clothing at a constant ratio. For China, this ratio is assumed to be 3/5 (units of food per unit of clothing).

If 40 percent of its productive inputs were devoted to farming, China could produce 120 million units of food and 300 million units of clothing. With a population of, say, 500 million workers, China's average income per worker would be 0.24 units of food and 0.60 units of clothing. Clearly, then, living standards (real wage rates) are lower in China than in the United States (since *both* average food and clothing consumption per worker are lower in China).

It can be calculated that the real cost of a unit of food within China is 1.67 (500/300) units of clothing; to produce one more unit of food means that 1.67 fewer units of clothing can be produced. Conversely, the real price of a unit of clothing in China is 0.60 (300/500) units of food.

## The Mutual Benefits of International Trade

The price of food within the United States is 0.50 units of clothing and the price of clothing is 2 units of food. In contrast, the price of food in China is 1.67 units of clothing and the price of clothing is 0.60 units of food. Because the real internal cost of food is lower in the United States than in China, while the real internal cost of clothing is higher, economists therefore say that the United States has a *comparative advantage* in producing food and that China has a *comparative advantage* in the production of clothing.

It is important to note that the real costs of each good in the two countries depend *only* on the *internal trade-offs* between food and clothing output. Despite the assumed fact, for example, that real wages in China are lower than in the United States, food is much more costly in the former country than in the latter! Further, despite the generally more productive inputs in the United States, the real cost of clothing is lower in China.

Both countries could obviously benefit from trade. China would be willing to buy food from the United States as long as it had to give up something less than 1.67 units of clothing per unit of food (its internal real cost of produc-

---

[2]  We are assuming in effect that food can be "transformed" into clothing at a constant rate. This assumption is not necessary to the argument but does make it a bit easier to grasp.

tion). The United States would be willing to trade away food as long as it could obtain something more than 0.50 units of clothing in return (0.50 units represents what the United States can now obtain internally if it gives up one unit of food). The divergent internal values placed on food and clothing make it possible for mutually beneficial trades to take place.

With a lower-bound price of 0.50 units of clothing per unit of food, and an upper-bound price of 1.67, the ultimate price at which the two countries would trade is not predictable. Trade at any price in between these two bounds would benefit both countries and be preferable to each over no trade at all; however, the closer the price of food is to 0.50 units of clothing the less the United States gains and the more China benefits.

To obtain a sense of how trade could affect per capita consumption in our example, let us suppose that the United States specialized in food production and that China specialized in the production of clothing; let us also assume that the bargaining strengths of the two countries are such that a unit of food is traded by the United States to China in return for 0.90 units of clothing.[3] The United States would produce 200 million units of food, and if it consumed 40 million units the remaining 160 million units could be traded to China for 144 million units of clothing (0.9 × 160). China would produce 500 million units of clothing, exporting 144 million so that its total internal consumption of clothing would equal 356 million units. China, of course, would consume 160 million units of food under these assumptions. Thus, per capita real incomes rise in both countries as a result of trade.

## Labor Market Implications

International trade is driven by the relative internal (real) costs of producing various goods. Conclusions from our two-good analysis of trade between the United States and China are not at all affected by the assumptions about living standards (real wages) in the two countries. If the production possibilities curves remained the same but the assumed populations of the two countries had been reversed—and living standards were posited to be higher in China—trade would still have taken place and the United States would still have traded food for Chinese-made clothing.

The general conclusion one can reach from this simple model of trade is that the advent of free trade between two countries will tend to cause each to specialize in producing goods for which it has a comparative advantage and to reduce its production of goods for which its real internal costs are relatively high. Trade, just like an important technological improvement in a given industry, will tend to *shift* employment from one industry to another. However, there is no reason to believe that the advent of free trade will create a

---

[3] Complete specialization in production will occur in one or both countries if the internal rate of transformation between the two goods is unchanging. Specialization may not be total when the real costs of food production, say, rise with food output so that at some point the United States could lose its comparative advantage.

permanent loss of employment in the country with higher real wages. To repeat, it is the internal production trade-offs, not real-wage rates, that drive international trade.

If, within a country, individual *firms* paying very high wages are "punished" by the market and forced out of business, what prevents a high-wage *country* from being similarly punished by international trade? Put differently, if the average wages for production workers in, say, Haiti are 20 percent of the average wages in the United States, why cannot Haiti undersell American producers in every product line? How can American workers hope to remain employed at high wages when faced with such low-wage competitors?

It is important to realize that Haiti has labor and capital resources that are fixed at any moment. It cannot produce *everything!* If, for example, several thousand Haitian workers are employed sewing garments for export to the United States, they are thus not available for (say) the growing and harvesting of agricultural produce. Thus, while there may be a benefit to Haiti when jobs in the garment trades open up, there is also a cost in terms of forgone output that must now be purchased from the United States (the place where dollars received from the export of clothes must ultimately be spent). Haiti will benefit from increasing the labor it devotes to garment exports *only* if it can replace its forgone production of food more cheaply.

To make the preceding concepts more concrete, suppose that shirts costing $10 to sew in the United States can be produced in Haiti for $2. Will American garment workers lose their jobs to foreign exports? If the food production forgone in Haiti when one additional shirt is made cannot be purchased from the United States for $2 or less, neither Haitian workers nor their country as a whole will be better off by taking the new jobs. In this case, American workers—despite their higher wages—would not lose jobs to Haitians.

If, however, the food production forgone when a shirt is produced can be purchased from the United States for $2 or less, American jobs in the garment trades will tend to be lost to Haitians. However, it is equally true that Haitian agricultural jobs are thereby lost to the much higher-paying agricultural sector in the United States!

To repeat, international trade can cause employment to shift across industries, and these shifts may well be accompanied by unemployment if workers, employers, or market wages are slow in adapting to change. However, there is no reason to believe that the transitional unemployment associated with international trade will become permanent; trade does not condemn jobs in high-wage countries to extinction.

# APPENDIX

## Collective-Bargaining Exercise

Chapters 13, 14, 15, and 18 discuss many aspects of collective-bargaining negotiations and agreements. This appendix presents a collective-bargaining exercise in which students can develop and apply negotiating skills, drawing upon what they have learned in those chapters.

The materials consist of instructions; descriptive background on the company, the union, and industrial relations at the plant; tables of background data that may be helpful for some aspects of the negotiations; and a copy of the collective-bargaining agreement that is to be renegotiated.

## Instructions

1.  The instructor will assign each student to the union or management negotiating team and will designate a leader for each team.
2.  The instructor may also assign each student a specific position within his or her organization (such as company president, personnel director, union president, shop steward, and so on) and may provide the student with a description of the role that goes with that position. While the position assignments are known to all participants, students should not discuss the information that they are given regarding their role with anyone—not even other members of the same bargaining team.
3.  The instructor will establish a time for the beginning and end of negotiations. Each negotiating team should meet, possibly several times, before the beginning of negotiations to establish its objectives, its negotiating strategy, and how team members will

participate in the negotiations. Each team may be asked to provide the instructor with a list of its objectives, its demands, and minimum acceptable achievements for each bargaining issue. (Hint: In classroom settings, negotiations that focus on a relatively small number of issues are usually more successful.)

4. The form that negotiations take, including the number of joint negotiating sessions, the number of caucuses outside the negotiating room, and so forth, can be determined by the parties as negotiations proceed. The deadline for completion of negotiations should be remembered at all times, however, because the contract expiration date will not be extended.

5. During negotiations, all participants should remember that this is an ongoing collective-bargaining relationship, so behavior during this negotiation can influence the character of future negotiations and interactions between labor and management.

6. If agreement is reached by the deadline, the participants may be asked to determine the cost of the new agreement.

7. The instructor may supplement these instructions.

## Additional Sources of Information

National and regional data on wages, price, employment, and output data are available from the following U.S. Government publications: U.S. Department of Labor, Bureau of Labor Statistics, *Employment and Earnings, Handbook of Labor Statistics,* and *Area Wage Surveys;* and U.S. President, *Economic Report of the President* (statistical appendix).

National information on specific provisions in collective-bargaining agreements is available from the Bureau of National Affairs, *Collective Bargaining Negotiations and Contracts.*

## Background to the Negotiations

The Cardinal Company, a manufacturer of electrical power machinery and electrical household appliances, has operated a plant in Oakland, California since 1947. The company began with about three dozen employees, but expanded over the years to its present payroll of 155 employees, 122 of whom are in the production and maintenance departments. The company markets its products nationwide and is considering expanding sales into European markets, a move that would require some additional investment to alter current products for the different voltages used in these markets.

Most of the Cardinal Company's domestic competition is from companies located in the Midwest and industrial northeastern states. In the past, Cardinal has more than held its own against these companies. Indeed, its market share of domestically produced electric power machinery and household appliances has increased modestly over the years. The industry itself is highly volatile and subject to a "boom or bust" pattern of demand for its products; total industry hours of employment peaked in 1973 and in the early 1980s, employment was at roughly the same level as in the late 1960s.

Part of the reason for this decline in employment was the growth of foreign competition, notably from the Pacific Basin. Imports have accounted for an increasing share of the North American market since the 1970s and have proven to be a more serious challenge to the Cardinal Company than are the products of domestic companies. The management has even considered establishing a manufacturing plant in Asia.

In 1953, the Amalgamated Electrical Union (AEU) organized the production and maintenance employees of the Cardinal Company. The union won the representation election, and was certified as the bargaining representative for these employees by the NLRB. A collective-bargaining agreement was negotiated and has subsequently been renegotiated every three years. The bargaining unit consists of both skilled and unskilled workers. Within the union, the skilled workers have argued that the wage differential between skilled and unskilled work should increase. Since the late 1970s, many of the union's members have complained that wages are higher at other plants in the industry.

Labor relations were fairly placid until the past five years. As the management of the company became increasingly concerned about import penetration during the 1970s, it began to look for ways in which to moderate the growth of labor costs. The previous negotiations in early 1986 were very tense and almost resulted in a strike. Management sought and ultimately obtained two changes in the compensation structure: (1) profit sharing instead of a general wage increase, and (2) a lower wage for workers hired after January 1, 1986. By January 1989, 21 of the production and maintenance employees were in the lower-wage tier.

This background information, the following five tables, and the copy of the agreement to be renegotiated provide the general setting for the January 1989 negotiations.

**Table 1**  Average Hourly Earnings, Overtime Hours,
and Total Weekly Hours Worked, Electrical
and Electronic Equipment Industry

| Year | Average Hourly Earnings (dollars) | Weekly Overtime hours | Index of Total Weekly Hours Worked (1977 = 100) |
|------|-----------------------------------|-----------------------|--------------------------------------------------|
| 1975 | $ 4.54 | 1.9 | 86.5 |
| 1976 | 4.82 | 2.3 | 93.2 |
| 1977 | 5.22 | 2.6 | 100.0 |
| 1978 | 5.63 | 2.8 | 106.5 |
| 1979 | 6.11 | 2.7 | 112.1 |
| 1980 | 6.75 | 2.3 | 106.0 |
| 1981 | 7.42 | 2.2 | 105.0 |
| 1982 | 8.02 | 1.8 | 95.5 |
| 1983 | 8.38 | 2.6 | 99.8 |
| 1984 | 9.04 | 2.6 | 100.2 |
| 1985 | 9.46 | 2.7 | 100.5 |
| 1986 | 9.65 | 2.7 | 100.9 |
| 1987 | 9.91 | 2.5 | 101.9 |
| 1988 (est.) | 10.24 | 2.3 | 103.4 |

SOURCE:  U.S. Bureau of Labor Statistics, *Handbook of Labor Statistics,* Bulletin 2217 (Washington, DC: U.S. Government Printing Office, June 1985): Tables 74 and 77, and authors' estimates.

**Table 2**  Consumer and Producer Price Indexes (1967 = 100)

| Year | Consumer Price Index | Producer Price Index Electric Machinery | Household Appliances |
|------|----------------------|------------------------------------------|----------------------|
| 1975 | 161.2 | 140.7 | 132.3 |
| 1976 | 170.5 | 146.7 | 139.2 |
| 1977 | 181.5 | 154.1 | 145.1 |
| 1978 | 195.4 | 164.9 | 153.0 |
| 1979 | 217.4 | 178.9 | 160.9 |
| 1980 | 246.8 | 201.7 | 174.2 |
| 1981 | 272.4 | 220.2 | 187.3 |
| 1982 | 289.1 | 231.6 | 199.1 |
| 1983 | 298.4 | 240.1 | 206.9 |
| 1984 | 311.1 | 245.1 | 211.2 |
| 1985 | 322.2 | 250.3 | 215.7 |
| 1986 | 328.4 | 255.4 | 220.3 |
| 1987 | 340.4 | 261.2 | 225.4 |
| 1988 (est.) | 354.1 | 269.8 | 234.2 |

SOURCE:  U.S. Bureau of Labor Statistics, *Handbook of Labor Statistics,* Bulletin 2217 (Washington, DC: U.S. Government Printing Office, June 1985): Table 112; U.S. President, *Economic Report of the President, 1988* (Washington, DC: U.S. Government Printing Office, 1988), Table B–58; U.S. Bureau of Labor Statistics, *Producer Price Index,* December 1987; and authors' estimates.

**Table 3** Wage Rates in Manufacturing, by Region, 1987 (dollars)

| Job | West | North Central | South | Northeast |
|---|---|---|---|---|
| Shipping Packers | $5.72 | $8.70 | $6.02 | $7.31 |
| Material Handlers | 6.39 | 9.03 | 6.73 | 7.32 |

SOURCE: U.S. Bureau of Labor Statistics, *Handbook of Labor Statistics,* Bulletin 2217 (Washington, DC: U.S. Government Printing Office, June 1985): Table 96 and authors' estimates.

**Table 4** Hourly Compensation Costs of Production Workers in Manufacturing in Various Countries (Index Numbers: United States = 100)

| Country | 1975 | 1976 | 1977 | 1978 | 1979 | 1980 | 1981 | 1982 | 1983 | 1984 | 1985 | 1986 | 1987 |
|---|---|---|---|---|---|---|---|---|---|---|---|---|---|
| United States | 100 | 100 | 100 | 100 | 100 | 100 | 100 | 100 | 100 | 100 | 100 | 100 | 100 |
| Australia | 84 | 85 | 79 | 80 | 78 | 82 | 85 | 81 | 73 | 70 | 69 | 74 | 85 |
| Hong Kong | 12 | 13 | 14 | 14 | 15 | 15 | 14 | 14 | 13 | 13 | 12 | 14 | 15 |
| Japan | 48 | 48 | 53 | 67 | 61 | 57 | 57 | 49 | 51 | 49 | 45 | 53 | 61 |
| Korea | 5 | 6 | 8 | 10 | 12 | 10 | 10 | 10 | 10 | 10 | 9 | 11 | 12 |
| Singapore | 13 | 12 | 12 | 13 | 14 | 15 | 17 | 17 | 18 | 18 | 17 | 18 | 19 |
| Taiwan | 6 | 7 | 7 | 7 | 9 | 10 | 11 | 10 | 10 | 10 | 9 | 10 | 11 |

SOURCES: U.S. Bureau of Labor Statistics, "International Comparisons of Hourly Compensation Costs for Production Workers in Manufacturing, 1975–86," Report 745 (September 1987) and authors' estimates.

**Table 5** Income Statements, Cardinal Corporation

| Item | 1987 | 1988 |
|---|---|---|
| Net sales | 51,076,311 | 58,215,100 |
| Costs & Expenses: | | |
| Labor costs | 7,785,406 | 8,133,291 |
| Materials | 23,864,177 | 25,716,432 |
| Administrative | 2,900,014 | 3,190,333 |
| Marketing | 3,160,451 | 3,750,012 |
| Other | 867,602 | 981,255 |
| Total costs: | 38,577,650 | 41,771,323 |
| Income before taxes | 12,498,661 | 16,443,777 |
| Taxes | 3,778,422 | 4,211,444 |
| Net Income | 8,720,239 | 12,232,333 |

# Collective-Bargaining Agreement

entered into on

January 1, 1986

between

Cardinal Corporation

and

Amalgamated Electrical Union

## Article I: Recognition and Representation

### Section 1: Union Representation

The company recognizes the Union as the exclusive collective-bargaining representative for all production and maintenance employees with respect to wages, hours of employment, and other conditions of employment, excluding office and clerical employees, plant guards, and supervisors as defined in the Labor Management Relations Act of 1947.

### Section 2: Union Security

All present employees who are union members as of the date of this agreement shall remain members in good standing as a condition of employment. All other present employees and employees hired hereafter shall become union members on or after 31 days following the beginning of their employment, or on or after 31 days following the date of this agreement, whichever is later.

An employee shall not be required to become a member of or continue membership in the Union if employed in a state that prohibits union membership as a condition of employment.

### Section 3: Dues Checkoff

The Company agrees to deduct initiation fees and dues from the pay of each employee covered by this agreement. Deductions shall be made monthly beginning with the first pay period after this agreement becomes effective. The employer shall make a lump-sum payment to the Union before the end of each month during which a deduction is made. The payment shall equal 95 percent of dues and fees deducted, the other 5 percent being retained by the Company to cover administration costs.

The monthly dues deducted from an employee's pay will be equal to one and one half hours of straight-time pay and will be based upon the employee's hourly wage at the time of the deduction.

### Section 4: Rights of Union Stewards and Other Officials

The Union may appoint one employee as a steward to represent each 30 employees in each shop. A letter of appointment by the Union must be *received* by the Company before the appointment may become effective. Shop stewards may conduct union business during working hours for a maximum of four hours per week without loss of pay.

Shop stewards or local union officials shall not be subject to layoff in the case of long-term work-force reductions as long as they can do a job that is operating. This provision does not apply to temporary layoffs.

Each steward shall obtain permission from his or her supervisor before leaving work to investigate a complaint or grievance. So long as he or she obtains permission and the discussion is not unreasonably long, as judged by the supervisor, he or she shall not be required to clock out.

Other local union officials are authorized to conduct union business during working hours provided that their supervisors receive 24-hours' notice. Officers will not be paid by the Company for time spent conducting union business.

## Article II: Management Rights

The Union recognizes the right of the Company to manage the business and to determine the products to be manufactured, the methods and scheduling of production, the level of production, and the location of its plants, as long as the Company does not operate in a manner that violates other provisions of this Agreement. The Union also recognizes the right of the Company to direct the work force; to hire, promote, transfer, demote, and lay off employees; and to suspend, discharge, or otherwise discipline employees for just cause, subject to the right of any employee to lodge a grievance as provided for in this Agreement.

## Article III: Strikes and Lockouts

The Company agrees that, during the life of this Agreement, there will be no lockout of covered employees. The Union agrees that, during the life of this Agreement, there will be no strike, sit down, or walkout; and the Union will not authorize nor encourage its members to take part in nor shall any member take part in any curtailment of work or interference with production of the Company. Any member who violates this article shall be subject to discipline by the Company.

## Article IV: Wages

### Section 1: Wage Schedule by Job Classification

Employees who are already on the payroll on January 1, 1986, shall receive a base rate of pay equal to that given in the following table for their respective labor grade.

Employees who are hired after January 1, 1986, shall be hired at a base rate pay equal to 80 percent of the base-rate pay given in Table 1 for their respective labor grade. Such employees shall receive an automatic increase to 85 percent of the base rate for their labor grade at the expiration of two years of service with the Company.

| Labor Grade | Job Classification | Base-Rate Pay |
|:---:|:---|---:|
| 1 | Custodians, Janitors | $ 6.25 |
| 2 | Packers, Shippers | 6.90 |
| 3 | Material handlers | 7.70 |
| 4 | Assemblers | 8.50 |
| 5 | Fork-lift operators | 9.25 |
| 6 | Production inspectors | 10.05 |
| 7 | Machine operators | 11.00 |
| 8 | Machinists | 12.05 |

**Section 2: Cost-of-Living Allowance**

Each employee covered by this Agreement shall receive a Cost-of-Living Allowance that shall be added to his or her hourly wage rate and included in computing overtime premium, night-shift premium, vacation payments, holiday payments, call-in pay, bereavement pay, jury-duty pay, paid-absence allowance, and short-term military-duty pay.

The amount of the Cost-of-Living Allowance shall be $2.10 per hour, effective January 1, 1986. It shall then be adjusted one cent for each .3 change in the Consumer Price Index for Urban Wage Earners and Clerical Workers (All Items) published by the U.S. Bureau of Labor Statistics (1967 = 100). Adjustments in the Cost-of-Living Allowance shall be made every six months from the effective date of this Agreement.

**Section 3: Incentive Pay**

Full-time employees covered by this contract and with at least one year of service shall receive an annual bonus, payable each December 31 of this Agreement. Workers who quit or who are discharged prior to this date are not eligible for a bonus payment that year. The funds available for the bonus shall be determined by profits before income taxes and executive bonuses according to the following schedule:

| Profits as a Percent of Sales | Percent of Profits Available for Bonus |
|:---|:---:|
| 0.0–2.0% | 0.0% |
| 2.1–4.5 | 10.0 |
| 4.6–7.0 | 12.5 |
| Over 7.0 | 15.0 |

Each worker eligible for the profit-sharing bonus shall receive a share of available profits equal to the worker's share of total hours worked by eligible workers.

# Article V: Vacations and Sick Leave

**Section 1: Eligibility**

An employee shall become eligible for vacation and sick leave after one year of service with the Company.

### Section 2: Hours of Vacation and Sick Leave

Contingent upon eligibility, each employee of the Company shall receive a certain number of hours of credit for the purpose of vacation and sick leave. The hours of credit depend on the employee's seniority and shall be computed as follows:

| *Seniority* | *Annual Hours of Full-Paid Credit* |
|---|---|
| 1–4 years | 120 |
| 5–9 years | 140 |
| 10–14 years | 160 |
| 15–19 years | 180 |
| 20 or more years | 200 |

The first 40 hours credited each year shall be allocated to the employee's Sick Leave Credit. The hours in excess of forty shall be the employee's Vacation Credit.

### Section 3: Pay for Credit Hours

For each credit hour, the employee shall receive his or her hourly base-wage rate to which shall be added the current Cost-of-Living Allowance.

### Section 4: Scheduling

The employee shall apply to the Company, on Company forms, for use of Sick Leave Credit within five days of returning to work. The employee shall request dates for Vacation Credit hours on Company forms.

## Article VI: Holidays

The following holidays shall be observed by the Company:

New Year's Day

Memorial Day

Independence Day

Labor Day

Thanksgiving

Friday following Thanksgiving

Christmas Eve

Christmas Day.

Should a holiday fall on a Sunday, the following Monday shall be observed as a holiday. All employees covered by this Agreement who worked the last day before a holiday shall be eligible for Holiday Pay for that holiday. Holiday Pay for holidays not worked shall be equal to each employee's base-wage rate plus a Cost-of-Living Allowance. Employees who work on a paid

Holiday shall receive the Holiday Pay as just described, *plus* double their base-rate wage for each hour worked.

## Article VII: Insurance
### Section 1: Insurance Offered
The Company shall pay the entire cost of Life Insurance, Accidental Death and Dismemberment Insurance, and Survivor Income for all employees covered by this Agreement. The Company shall pay 80 percent of the cost of Medical, Dental, Prescription-Drug, and Vision-Care Benefits for covered employees and their dependents. The Company shall choose the Insurance Carriers and need not negotiate with the Union concerning that choice.
### Section 2: Coverage
The Group Life-Insurance Benefit shall be $50,000. The Company shall guarantee coverage of other health expenses listed above, up to $3000 per year.
### Section 3: Eligibility
An employee may enroll in the Company insurance programs after completing 60 days of employment. For each type of insurance, he or she may enroll on the monthly premium date that next follows the required sixty days of employment.

## Article VIII: Grievances and Arbitration
### Section 1: Scope of Grievances
Matters dealing with the interpretation or application of the provisions of this Agreement shall be settled using the grievance machinery described in this article.
### Section 2: Grievance Procedure
The following procedure applies to resolution of grievances on behalf of employees.

Step 1: Oral discussion between employee, steward, and supervisor.
Step 2: Written statement of grievance by steward, submitted to supervisor.
Step 3: Submittal of written statement to designated Company representative if Step 2 results in no solution after 15 days.
Step 4: Artibration if Step 3 results in no resolution after 15 days.

### Section 3: Arbitration

**Selection.** The arbitrator will be chosen in the following manner. The Company and the Union shall jointly request the Federal Mediation and Conciliation Service to provide a list of five qualified arbitrators. The parties shall alternately strike names from the list until only one name remains. This person shall be the arbitrator.

**Authority.** The power of the arbitrator is limited to the application and interpretation of this Agreement as written. The arbitrator shall not alter, add to, subtract from, or amend any part of this Agreement.

**Decision.**  The arbitrator shall submit a written decision to each party within 30 days of the date on which the case is submitted. The arbitrator's decision shall be final and binding.

## Article IX: Duration of Agreement

This Agreement shall remain in full force and effect until December 31, 1991.

# NAME INDEX

# SUBJECT INDEX